Terenure College, 1860–2010 *A History*

Eddie Thornton, champion hurdler, *c.* 1959.
© Irish Press.

TERENURE COLLEGE

1860 ∗ 2010

A History

FERGUS A. D'ARCY

Terenure College, 1860–2010: A History

First published 2009

by Terenure College
Templeogue Road
Dublin 6W
www.terenurecollege.ie

The majority of the archival items reproduced in this book
came from the Terenure College Archives and the Carmelite
archives in Gort Muire. Additional items were sourced from:
past pupils' personal papers; National Library of Ireland; the
National Archives of Ireland; Dublin Diocesan Archives; the
Irish Times; the *Irish Press*; and the *Irish Independent*.

ISBN 978-0-9564260-0-0

British Library Cataloguing in Publication Data.
A CIP catalogue record for this book is available
from the British Library.

Printed in Ireland by Turner Print Group.

10 9 8 7 6 5 4 3 2 1

To the Terenure family of times past, present and to come ...

C O N T

E   N   T   S

viii

XXVI

Advertisement in *Terenure College Annual*, 1950s.
Previous page: Sixth years, 1962. *Left to right*: N. Sparks, P. Smyth, J. Fitzgerald, R. O'Siochain, R. Murphy, J. O'Donnell.

PREFACE

Remembering our History, Celebrating our Life, Planning our Future

These three elements are central to the celebration of the one hundred and fiftieth anniversary of the foundation of Terenure College in 1860. An initial meeting held in October 2006 called for the setting up of different groups to plan and execute the 'remembering, celebrating and planning' for our jubilee year, 2010. And thus the working group behind this history of Terenure College was formed.

Mindful of Anthony Trollope's words; 'It is necessary to get a lot of men together, for the show of the thing, otherwise the world will not believe. That is the meaning of committees. But the real work must always be done by one or two men', our working group was always small in number, namely Colin McKeon, former president and active member of the Past Pupils' Union; Pauric Dempsey, past pupil; and the under named, past pupil, current teacher and parent of a recent past pupil.

Fr Micheál Ó Néill, O. Carm., the then Prior, was adamant at one of our first meetings that the college wanted a publication that would tell the story of the college, written with the rigours of academic discipline and present a history that would be received and used by scholars in the future. This was to be the first formal history of Terenure College. He was certain the college did not want a populist, anecdotal hagiography.

Our working group was soon joined by Professor Fergus A. D'Arcy. Professor D'Arcy was eminently qualified to research and write the history of the college. He has spent his professional career researching, writing and teaching on British and Irish history. Our group was joined later by our editor, Lucy Hogan.

What is presented here is the first formal history of the college. Professor D'Arcy has been meticulous in navigating, ordering and then trawling through the college archives. He has captured the corporate memory of those associated with the college since the 1930s through interviews and discussions. All of this research will provide a great treasury for future students.

Our work as a group proceeded smoothly until we had to decide on a name for Professor D'Arcy's history. We knew we wanted to have the spirit of friendship, learning, fun and faith that we feel sums up the ethos of the college. We toyed with *Learning, Playing and Praying* (too patronising), *The Best of Times* (too clichéd), *In Pursuit of Excellence* (arrogant and triumphalistic), all of these were the antithesis of what we feel Terenure is about. We ultimately agreed, to the relief of our designer, Fidelma Slattery to call it as it is — *Terenure College, 1860–2010: A History*.

To be associated with the publication has been a great privilege and a delight. We thank Professor D'Arcy for his ardour and dedication to this work, most certainly, but also for his charm and enthusiasm, which make the task of our working group so pleasant.

BRENDAN McCAULEY

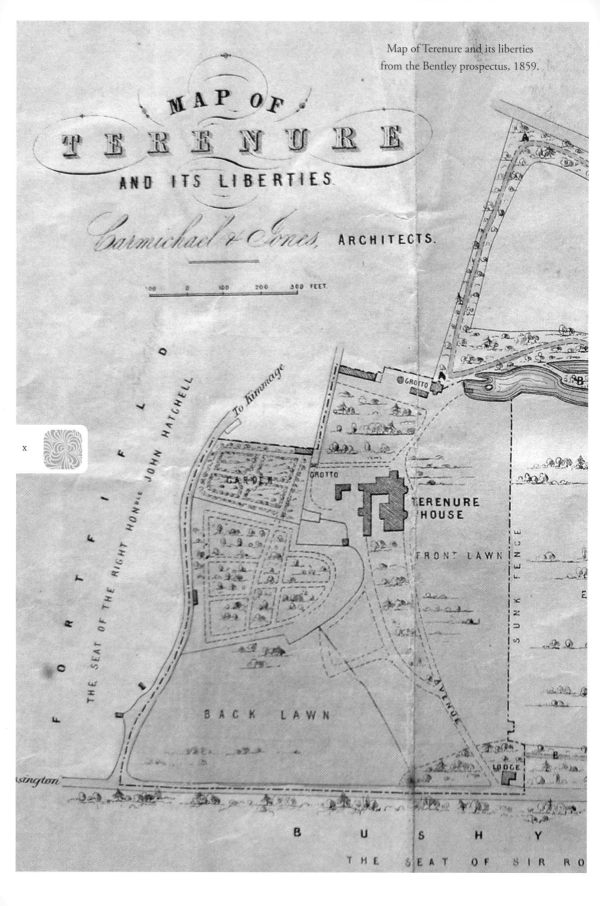

Map of Terenure and its liberties
from the Bentley prospectus, 1859.

INTRODUCTION

The construction of a college history can present some paradoxical challenges. Those who teach in or manage such institutions sometimes say that, ideally, schools should have no dramas, only peace, serenity and sound learning — safe havens, free of incident.

This ideal does not lend itself to any engaging narrative, but happily, in the present instance, while the ideal may be striven for, the real successfully intrudes.

Then there is the radical view that a true school history is an impossibility or a fiction since the people who matter most are silent or unresearched — the pupils. Fortunately, for this particular project, such has not been the case. The pupils, or at least the past pupils, have spoken and spoken richly their tales of reminiscence. More fortunately still, some of these one-time pupils, a good many of them indeed, spoke not only as past pupils but also as teachers or as Carmelites or indeed, as both. Without their evocative testimonies the silences may have been deafening in places, and the yawning serenities quite underwhelming. It is to these persons, therefore, who spoke willingly and frankly, that the primary debt is due. It should be added that none of the living who appear in these pages sought to be mentioned; some of the several thousand living alumni may feel aggrieved that they do not appear among them in name: the offence, if there be one, is the author's alone; the defence, if permissible, is that the work had to have some limit even as it sought to be balanced and representative of period and personal experience.

When recounting some of that history by way of marking the centenary of the college in 1960, the compilers of a commemorative review commented on the difficulties they encountered:

> This review bristled with problems. We had to wrestle with gaps in the records, defective records, pictures without names attached, feeble memories, oral traditions that could not be substantiated, and a hundred and one other enemies of authentic history. How easy it would be if we could publish the apocryphal with the authentic.[1]

So, to some extent, it has remained, but not completely: gaps certainly, but a richer record than any thought possible at the outset. The surviving records were many and diverse and the people who made access to them possible enthusiastic and affable. In the task of transforming that access into a narrative, in order to realise this history, many debts were incurred and many thanks are due.

The acknowledgement of this must begin with the Carmelite Fathers themselves; they invited a stranger into their midst to try to chronicle Terenure's tale and, in thanking them for that invitation two things need to be stated, and forcefully so: for one, the access they granted was total; for another, the freedom to tell it as the author found it has been total, too. There was the literal liberty to come and go to the college and the Community archives in Terenure and equally to the Province's archives at Gort Muire. Here, therefore, the first obligations are acknowledged: to the Priors of Terenure College, Fr Micheál Ó Néill and Fr Michael Troy, and to the Priors Provincial of the Carmelite Order in Ireland, Fr Fintan Burke and Fr Martin Kilmurray. Far from limiting access to archives or to individuals, they enthusiastically sought out sources, were unfailing in their interest and hopeful that I might speak to many more persons than the time allowed; for that, one is grateful. Their editorial committee, Brendan McCauley, former pupil, school captain and then long-time teacher; Colin McKeon, former pupil and for a time president of the Past Pupils' Union; and former pupil, now scholar, Pauric Dempsey; were a joy to work with: they too could not do enough to promote the cause. They were ever-assiduous in the suggestion of sources and contacts but punctilious to a point in not intruding in the substance of what came forth. They and editor, Lucy Hogan, were paragons of patience, displaying heroic faith when the author disappeared for seeming ages into a hermit's cave; for their faith, hope and works, sincerest thanks.

A special acknowledgement is due to Emer McElduff, college secretary in Terenure, who responded to many requests for advice and assistance with matchless speed and effectiveness, to Breda Moore, long-serving receptionist who was helpful to a fault, and to Eddie Geraghty, teacher, editor of the *Annual* and photographic archivist *par excellence* who provided access to a treasure trove of historic Terenure photographs. To Ruth Long, librarian at Gort Muire, a special vote of thanks is equally due for practical help on countless occasions, for fertile suggestions and for finding and fetching out long-buried booty. Apart from their kindness in agreeing to interviews, many of the past pupils were generous in offering the use of personal and institutional memorabilia.

Librarians and archivists from many external institutions went beyond the call of duty to assist in the construction of this history: Laura Magnier in the Carmelite Archives at Gort Muire; as also Carmelite legal advisor, Denis Barror; John Foley, Terenure alumnus and senior administrator in the National University of Ireland and its registrar, Dr Attracta Halpin; Professor David Kennedy of UCD; Greg Harkin of All Hallows College; Gregory O'Connor and Caitriona Crowe at the National Archives; Noelle Dowling at the Dublin Diocesan Archives; Teresa Whitington at the Central Catholic Library; Penny Woods in the NUIM Library, Maynooth; Ríonach Uí Ógáin of Roinn Béaloideas Éireann, UCD; Seamus Helferty at UCD Archives, School of History and Archives; Tony Eklof and colleagues at the James Joyce Library of University College Dublin; and Fr John Keating went out of his way to assist with Carmelite Archives in Rome.

The scope of the subject combined with the constraints of time meant that transferring a tangled manuscript into a readable typescript was a major one and in that urgent task a great debt of thanks is due to Ann and Caitriona D'Arcy for undertaking it with such despatch and success. Finally and most importantly, I wish to thank my wife, Ann, for her patience and always encouraging support in a very happy project but one that entailed long absences, even when present.

Fergus A. D'Arcy

Terenure College senior rugby team, 1927–8.

CHAPTER 1

The First Pupils

Terenure College, undated.

THE COLLEGE OF OUR LADY OF MOUNT CARMEL, TERENURE, OPENED ITS doors to receive its first students on Tuesday, 10 January 1860. Advance notice of this development was conveyed in an extremely modest and brief announcement in the *Freeman's Journal* of Friday, 6 January 1860:

> The Clergymen of the Carmelite Church Whitefriar Street beg to inform the public that they will open a seminary in the Mount Carmel House, Terenure, Roundtown, on Wednesday next, 10th January and also will reopen their seminary in Lower Dominick Street on the same day.[1]

The porter was hardly overcome by the rush of entrants on that day. Indeed, it is not clear that anybody entered as a student on that first day or the days immediately following. The surviving evidence records the first student as having been thirteen-year-old Patrick O'Brien from Rutland House, Rathgar. He had previously attended a local school, St Laurence's, and beyond the fact that he entered Terenure College on 6 February 1860 nothing else has emerged relating to him. If the records are to be believed he had a distinctive if solitary initial schoolboy experience there — as the next pupils did not enter until 1 March. There were four of them, two Moran boys from Garnavilla, Roundtown — fourteen-year-old John and thirteen-year-old William, and two Lyons boys, Patrick aged thirteen and John aged ten. They came from Landore, Rathgar. Almost a week later, these pioneers were joined on 6 March by fifteen-year-old Redmond Barrett from Lakelands — more local one could not be.

There followed a sizeable gap before these six were joined by three others — the Conroy brothers, Michael and Edward, fifteen and sixteen years old respectively, whose home was nearby Redan Lodge, Rathgar, and by Richard Read, fourteen, from Eagle Lodge, Rathgar Avenue. This trio appeared on 24 April. Young Richard came from a long-established firm of brewers. They were situated in the heartland of Dublin City brewing, their premises being in Ardee Street, at the intersection of Cork Street and Chamber Street. These first nine boys of Terenure College had something in common — apart from living locally, all of them had previously attended St Laurence's School, and all bar one were in their teenage years. They were followed on 21 May by the solitary Francis Cowling of Firhouse whose previous schooling had been in Tallaght and then three weeks later by another sole entrant — on 4 June — when thirteen-year-old Patrick Magee came from Rathmines Road. Then, presumably, the summer holidays intervened when, after the first six months of its existence, Terenure College had enrolled some eleven boys.

When the new school year began in August, the strong local connections or antecedents of the first new entrants were clearly in evidence. There came, on 20 August 1860, three young men from Rathfarnham, Pentonys all — a name that was to have a distinguished recurrence in the college's future when Mr V.S. Pentony joined the staff in the early 1940s. His responsibility was teaching instrumental music, which he did without a break until his retirement in 1968–9. All three had also been

St Laurence's men, eight-year-old Richard, nine-year-old John and thirteen-year-old Thomas. Their father was probably John Pentony of Rathfarnham, a victualler,[2] though there were also Henry Daniel Pentony and Richard Pentony, both of Rathgar Avenue — occupations unknown.

There were a further seven entrants between late August and mid-November of 1860. With one exception, all came from the surrounding suburbs or immediate countryside. Peter Carty, a fourteen year old from Charleville, Templeogue, was enrolled on 26 August; he was joined three days later by fifteen-year-old John Gahan of Whitechurch. They had both been schooled previously in Clondalkin. Then came two Marlowe boys from Butterfield Avenue, Reginald aged fifteen and Richard aged sixteen. Entering on 4 September 1860, they were the first whose schooling had been away from the general vicinity — both having been schooled previously by the Jesuits in Tullabeg, Co. Offaly.

This establishment, founded in 1819, was to have a flourishing academic, literary and sporting history for over 60 years but — in ecclesiastical as in secular politics — success was no guarantee of survival: despite its thriving condition, even in the 1880s, it was to be closed down to ensure the survival of Clongowes Wood.[3] Ironically, the Carmelites of the Irish Province were almost to anticipate this when their Provincial, Fr Thomas Albertus Bennett, ordered the closure of the equally flourishing and impressive Knocktopher College, Kilkenny, as will emerge in the next chapter. One cannot help but contrast the elaborate front page advertisement for Knocktopher that appeared in the *Freeman's Journal* of Friday, 29 December 1859 with the diminutive announcement of Terenure's opening as advertised in the same newspaper eight days later, as already noted.

The Marlowes were preceded the day before by two more Read brothers from Eagle Lodge, Rathgar, Thomas aged ten and Patrick aged fifteen, following in the footsteps of their older brother Richard. The last of the 21 pioneer entrants in this foundation year was the most marked exception. Enrolling on 12 March 1860, George O'Beirne from Athlone was 21 years of age: he had previously been educated at Summerhill College, Co. Sligo, and he entered Terenure as a university student, the first such in the college's history.[4] He would soon be followed, in January 1861 by Peter Conway of Galway who came to take university classes in the city.[5]

It would seem therefore that the college started modestly, drawing exclusively on local youth for its enrolments. Over the next twelve months, this situation changed. From November 1860 to October 1861, there appear to have been some 54 enrolments — a substantial increase. Of the first 50 enrolments in these two years, 32 came from the area and surrounding districts of Rathgar, Rathmines, Roundtown, Templeogue, Firhouse and Whitechurch. A further ten came from Dublin City or its suburbs such as Phibsboro; and the remaining eight from counties Galway, Donegal and Westmeath. From Dublin City itself, for example, there came in March 1861, the two Coghlan boys, John (thirteen) and James (twelve), whose father Thomas made his living at 56 Watling Street, in the business of parchment manufacturer and who lived in Whitecross, Ballyfermot.[6] On 14 May, they were followed by the two Douglas brothers from Crumlin, Christopher (sixteen) and Charles (fifteen).

As to the school backgrounds, apart from St Laurence's, which supplied the early majority of enrolments and excepting the two Marlowes from Tullabeg, a surprising eight entrants came from Dominick Street — presumably from the Carmelite Academy located at No. 41. The eight included the two Coghlan boys; John Fallon of Great Brunswick Street; Christopher Nixon of Amiens Street; Christopher King of Phibsboro; and Joseph O'Connor of Smithfield. The Academy of St Mary on Dominick Street had been opened through the initiative of Fr Bennett in 1854, transferring his original establishment from Jervis Street. Throughout the 1860s, it was faring well and was staffed by some twelve priests from the Whitefriar Street Community. The Academy of St Mary on Lower Dominick Street had its share of characters: most memorable among them was John F. Byrne, who attended there, as a pupil in the late 1880s. Byrne was a close school and university friend and confidante of James Joyce and was the Cranly of Joyce's *A Portrait of the Artist,* and *Stephen Hero.* Byrne recalled the remarkable chaos that prevailed in the class conducted by Carmelite novice, John Scanlan: when the pupil first entered Scanlan's class there, the place was in uproar:

> It was that way when I entered because it was never any other way. There were about fifteen pupils in the class and they were all doing just what they pleased, and what most of them pleased to do was to climb up on the teacher's back, on his lap, under his chair, knock his biretta off, scamper to get it, put it on again and knock it off again. It was all great 'gas' and the absolutely unbelievable part of this pandemonium was that Mr Scanlan showed every sign of enjoying himself more than anybody else … In my life I have met many easy-going, smiling, good-humoured, tolerant people, but not one of them fit to hold a candle to this young cleric Scanlan.[7]

Of course, at that time and for some decades afterwards there was a striking extent of students transferring between one college and institution to another. There became almost a small traffic for example, between Terenure and its coeval and rival, Blackrock College, and similar institutions. Thus, one young man who shall remain nameless and who came to Terenure College in September 1861 was 'removed for insubordination' and went to Castleknock College.[8] He was joined a few months later by John Nugent who, having enrolled at Terenure in March 1862, left for Castleknock College in March 1863. And in that first twelve months, boys came to Terenure from Newbridge College and Clongowes as well as from Tullabeg. Unfortunately, after the first entries in the early 1860s, the home addresses of the boys were recorded in the surviving registers only by exception. Following the 75 entrants of the first two years, enrolments seem to have slackened off a little, with some 15 over October 1861 to September 1862 but this then doubled in the following year: over October 1862 to December 1863 some 39 additional pupils appear to have entered the college. Had there been no leakage — and large leakage there must have been — the total enrolled by December 1863 would have stood at over 120 pupils, a sizeable cohort by the standards of any other Irish college of the day. Blackrock College, opening in the same year, counted 36 boarders and 21 day-pupils in 1861, rising to 112 and 20 in 1865, but increasing to 148 and 25 respectively by 1870; Catholic University School starting at its Leeson Street location in October 1867 did so with 80 pupils, none of them boarders of course.[9]

However, a figure in excess of 120 has to be greatly off the mark. The surviving Terenure registers of the 1860s sow confusion rather than shed light. There is a 'Day Book' of 1862–9 recording the boys by name and number. Starting on 18 January 1862, it lists 30 names, rising to 33 on 15 February, 35 on 1 March and then moving between 30 and 34 until the Easter vacation in April. On resuming in late May 1862, it fluctuated above and below 25 and apparently the summer vacation did not come until 2 August, lasting until 5 September 1862. From resumption on 6 September until late December 1862, the numbers fell from 30 to 26. Following the start back on 4 January 1863 until 4 July 1863, they recorded numbers varied from 24 minimum to 28 maximum. Over September to December 1863, they went from a minimum of 22 to a maximum of 35. The start of 1864 saw numbers rise to a maximum of 39 by June of that year. In the autumn term of 1864, the numbers averaged in the low 40s, peaking at 45 on 29 October and remained around 44 from then until well into 1865, peaking at 48 on 10 June. However, at the start of the new school year in September the numbers had fallen to 30 and averaged around 33 until December 1865. By January 1866, the numbers recorded had risen from 36 to a maximum of 44, averaging 43 until the summer. By December 1866, they had peaked at 48 and fell back to the low 40s and high 30s in the period of January to June 1867. The number of students fell from 38 in September to 33 in December 1867. These figures stayed in the low 30s over the first half of 1868, and then rose from 41 in September 1868 to 46 in 16 January 1869.[10] There is a clear discrepancy between the number of enrolments entered in the *Register, 1860–1940*, indicating in excess of 120 over 1860–3, and these figures as recorded in the *Day Book, 1862–69*. A separate *Daily Roll of the School, 1869–1885* gives a steady 50 boys enrolled throughout May 1869 and 51 over June 1869; this seems to suggest that the low figures in the *Day Book, 1862–69* are a more accurate total.[11] The discrepancy therefore seems only explicable by way of a fairly substantial leakage.

On another matter, it is by no means clear how many of any given number were boarders and how many were day-pupils. One hazards that a majority of the first year's intake may have been day-pupils since they were so local in their home addresses. Nevertheless, in June 1861 there were at least sixteen boarders: an account entry for that time refers to a hair-cutting bill for some sixteen boarders as costing 4s 8d.[12] By the end of the first decade the ratio had reversed — there were some 44 boarders and 9 day-boys when the new term, and year, began in September 1869.[13] At the commencement of the following year, there were 36 boarders and 8 day-boys on 1

September 1870, but by January 1871 this had risen to 52 boarders and 18 day-pupils. These figures dipped in the following two years and by January 1874 the complement stood at 43 boarders and 24 day-pupils. The figure for boarders remained in the low 40s until 1880 when it reached 56, rising to 59 by spring 1881. By January 1882, there were some 55 boarders and 11 day-pupils. By 1885, the boarders had fallen to *c.* 35 with a further 15 day-pupils.

The boarders at the time paid varying fees for board and tuition — with reductions for pairs or trios of brothers — but the annual bill was averaging £30 from the mid-1860s through the 1870s. By contrast, the tuition fee for day-pupils seems initially to have been set at £2 per quarter per boy, but again there were variations in this, perhaps relating to individuals' circumstances or to the likelihood that they took additional classes such as music, singing or dancing. Thus John Fallon, who entered in 1861 and left in March 1862, paid £25 per annum for board and £1 for laundry, also had paid 10s for singing, £2 for piano and £1 for drawing lessons, apart from stationery and medical bills. Similarly John Flynn who paid £30 per annum and £1 10s for laundry, paid an additional £1 for half a year's music lessons and 5s for half a year's singing lessons. Over the 6 months from September 1861 to March 1862, his haircutting cost him 4d and boot repairs 7s 5d: one gathers that while his boots were stout his hair was long. Certainly, neither boarding nor tuition fees were exorbitant by contemporary standards: Blackrock charged 30 guineas basic and 40 guineas for extras that included Italian and German, piano and dancing, drawing and gymnastics, washing and repairs, while Clongowes charged 35 guineas for most of the nineteenth century.[14] It can be added that Terenure's students were hardly harassed to take expensive additional subjects. The three Lyons boys, James, Patrick and John, for example, paying £90 per annum for boarding in 1864, received a refund for their singing classes 'as the children did not receive teaching — not having voices for singing'.[15] As for the boarding, the costs were doubtless supplemented by the development of the college farm. Precious little is known about this for the nineteenth century, but an account entry for 1861 sees the early emergence of farming activity with the purchase of a cow, bought for £19 on 5 October. Other provisions for keeping boarders had emerged some months earlier when, in April 1861 the college purchased eight hair mattresses at 30s each, seven straw palliasses for £1 6s 6d, eight pillows at 3s 6d each, eight bolsters for £2 8s, one chest of drawers for £1 10s and a single iron bedstead for 16s.

Within that first year, a drawing master, Mr Rogers, was being paid 31s a month for his efforts and special music tuition was also being provided within that first year — but perhaps without benefit of a piano since the college paid for the hire of one in December 1861 in order to cater for the music examinations before that Christmas.

By the late 1860s, the institution appears to have been holding its own financially. There is, in the Dublin Diocesan Archives, a surviving balance sheet for the college for the year 1867: its provenance is uncertain but its presence in this repository suggests the continuing interest of Cardinal Archbishop Paul Cullen in the college's welfare. Over fourteen months from October 1866 to 31 December 1867, student board and tuition brought in £1,831; Mass offerings £85; the sale of hay from the farm yielded close on £60; the sale of fruit produced over £31; and of pigs, cows and poultry over £34. After total outgoings on food, fuel and various services, medical, dental etc., there was a stated credit balance of £161. While most of the teaching was done by the priests — possibly assisted by novices — over £150 had been expended in payments to 'secular masters'.[16]

However tentative the college may have been in its beginning in terms of enrolments, its name was spreading somehow. It was not by virtue of any extensive or aggressive advertising. It took out simple modest notices in the *Irish Catholic Directory* but it certainly did not go in for the quite aggressive and ambitious self-promotion of other institutions who took out fulsome front page advertisements in the national daily press. If anything, Terenure College's approach was understated. For all that, however, its reputation spread by word of mouth. Within twenty years it was receiving pupils from, or sending former pupils to, the furthest corners of the country and of the earth. Consider a single page of enrolments running from November 1864 to June 1866 listing some 39 boys. There were the inevitable Dubliners, of course, such as the Spadaccinis, Charles and Christopher from Kenilworth Square; the Tench boys, Charles and Gerald from Dolphin's Barn; and the Coffey lads, Henry and Robert from Lower Bridgefoot Street. Then from Buttevant, Co. Cork, came Laurence and James McGrath and Cornelius Lynch; from Belturbet, Co. Cavan, William Winston; and from Cavan town James McCabe; from Cullenswood, Co. Wexford, Patrick Barden, Francis Corr and Mark Strong; from Roscommon came Henry Boyd; from Tralee, Co. Kerry, Thomas Crosbie and from Cahir, Co. Tipperary, the three Cusacks, Henry, Peter and Edward all on 21 June. From further afield came eighteen-year-old James Simpson from New Zealand and from Capetown in South Africa came five boys — the three Begleys, Joseph, Arthur and John; together with Edward Keating and Denis McAuliffe. There followed, in August 1867, James Carey from South America. How these came to find themselves in Terenure College within four years of its opening is at this point a matter of conjecture but clearly word of mouth was the key.

However imposing the new establishment may have been, the foundation scholars were hardly overawed. A censorious report on their high jinks was given by one J. Hynes in June 1869:

> The lavatory seems to be a rendezvous for two thirds of the students every Saturday evening where anything but moderation, not to say silence, is observed; talking as if they were in the yard, laughing, throwing water at each other is but a common thing. Henry Butler, Herbert Barry and Thomas Fagan pick and eat the little apples off the trees in the orchard.

Six months later the Butler boys, Henry and Percy, together with a James O'Brien were in trouble again: 'Three boys went over the orchard wall or out in the door next to the laundry to follow an ass which was out in the field'; so reported one L.W. Maddock in October 1869.[17] Of another pupil it was recorded: 'Wednesday, at Rec, William Maunsell made use of expressions not calculated to edify his hearers'.[18]

Nor indeed were the boarders from Capetown any better. Denis McAuliffe appears to have been larger than life: from his arrival in 1865 he was in trouble, on more than one occasion. Consider these reports from Fr Davis and his prefects:

> 30 SEPTEMBER 1865:
> Denis McAuliffe, James McKeon and A. O'Farrell crossed the gate leading into the garden during the walk on Sunday. The boys in general have contracted a habit of pulling and tossing each other during recreation. Denis McAuliffe, A. O'Farrell and James McKeon left the playground on Sunday (1 o'clock) for the purpose of pulling walnuts.

> 7 OCTOBER 1865:
> John Coghlan, Denis McAuliffe, James McKeon and A. O'Farrell went outside the green gate and having filled their pockets with horse chestnuts, commenced throwing them at the other students and the servant boy. (Thomas Cullen, Prefect).

> 14 OCTOBER 1865:
> Denis McAuliffe has been disobedient. (Fr. Moore).

> 28 OCTOBER 1865:
> Denis McAuliffe is in the habit of tipping the persons preceding him from the refectory to the Oratory.

> 18 NOVEMBER 1865:
> Denis McAuliffe and Joseph McCabe fought most brutally in the orchard immediately before going to walk on Sunday. (Prefect, Fr Davis).

> 3 JULY 1866:
> Joseph Begley and Denis McAuliffe went through the window in St Joseph's while the boys were on the walk on Sunday.

But Denis and these few characters were not alone in mischief: '10 July 1866: All the boys of St Teresa's Dormitory disturbed the House with shouting, singing and dancing between the hours of 5 and 7 o'clock in the morning', but perhaps Denis was one of its occupants.[19]

For all that, the Carmelite spirit moved Denis to more serious things. Born in Capetown in 1851, he became a priest in the 1870s, the first South African to be ordained in the Catholic Church. The ceremony took place in 1875 at the Basilica of St John Lateran in Rome. After his ordination, he went on to Holland to study Dutch in preparation for his pastoral life in the Cape; and before returning to South Africa he paid a return courtesy visit to the scene of his schoolboy misdemeanours — a visit warmly received by the college then, and fondly recalled later. Indeed, it was a tribute to the Carmelites that Fr McAuliffe delivered his first ever public sermon in Whitefriar Street Church during the visit. By the end of a long life he had the distinction of becoming Terenure College's oldest past pupil by the mid-1930s. In 1935, he was elected to honorary membership of the Past Pupils' Union. In May 1936, the now Very Reverend Dr McAuliffe of Capetown wrote to the college president, James Carmel O'Shea, recalling those wilder early days. He retired from his African ministry in 1937 and passed away in 1938 at 87 years of age — the oldest priest on the subcontinent.[20] As for the College of Our Lady of Mount Carmel, at the end of its first decade it had clearly established a reputation that attracted pupils from far and wide.

Date of Entrance.	Name.	Address.	Age.	~~Occupation of Parents or Guardian~~	Where last at School.	English			
						1st	2nd	3rd	4t
1860									
Feb. 6	Patrick O'Brien	Rutland House Rathgar	13		St. Laurence's				7/61
March 1	John Moran	Garnavilla Clonmston	14		" "	'61	3/60		
" "	William Moran	Do.	13		" "			3/60	
" "	Patrick Lyons	Landore Rathgar	13		" "			3/60	
" "	John Lyons	Do.	10		" "				
" 6	Redmond Barrett	Lakelands Terenure	15		" "	'61	3/60		
April 24	Edward Conroy	Redan Lodge Rathgar	16		" "	'61	4/60		
" "	Michael Conroy	Do.	15		" "		4/60		
" "	Richard Read	Eagle Lodge Rathga. ave.	14		" "		4/60		
May 21	Francis Cowling	Firhouse	15		Tallaght	'61	5/60		
June 4	Patrick Magee	Rathmines Road 94 [23]	13		Fitzpatrick		4/60		
August 20	Thomas Pentony	Rathfarnham	13		St. La...			3/61	
"	Richard Pentony	Do.	8		"				
"	John Pentony	Do.	9		"				
" 26	Peter Carty	Charleville Templeogue	14		Clondalkin			5/60	
									1/61

11

Top: Page from the first *Pupils' Register*, February–November 1860.
Detail from *Day Book, 1862–69*. 'Denis McAuliffe and [?] Begley went
through the window of St Joseph's [dormitory]'.

Engraving of Terenure House from the inside front
cover of the Bentley prospectus, 1859.

12

13

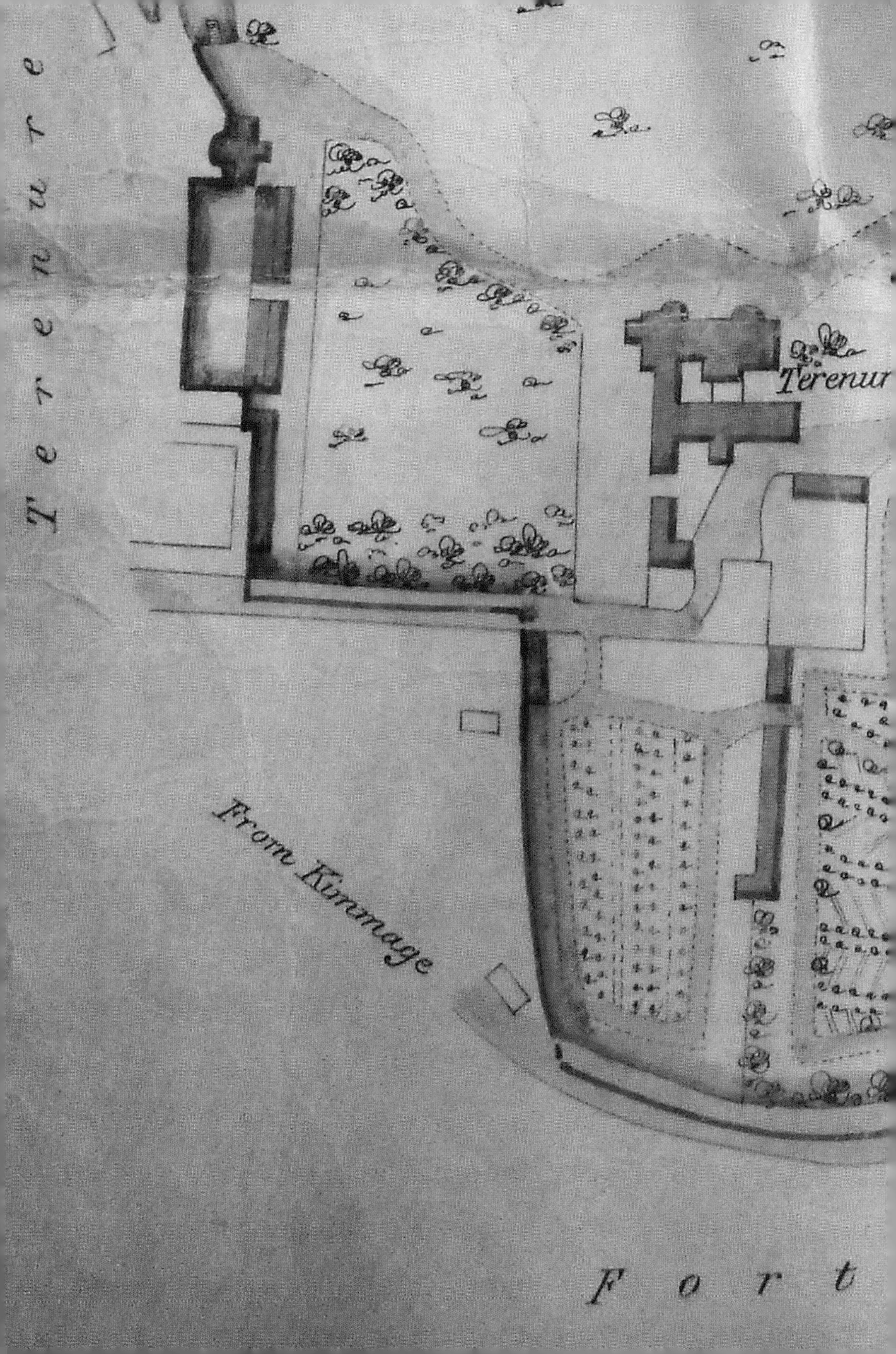

Terenure

Terenur

From Kimmage

Fort

CHAPTER 2

The Founding Fathers

Lease map referred to in the
title deed, 1854.

THE OPENING OF TERENURE COLLEGE IN JANUARY 1860 IS CLEAR ENOUGH but the process by which the Carmelites acquired the property is less transparent. Different sources offer varying accounts of when the Carmelites established themselves in Terenure. The centenary history, *Terenure College Centenary Record 1860–1960*, refers to the Carmelites coming into possession of Terenure House and Estate in 1858. So also does an editorial article in *Whitefriars* of May–June 1960.[1] Against this, an earlier *Whitefriars'* account, in August 1936, spoke of the Carmelites purchasing Terenure House in 1860.[2] In fact, however, it appears that the process came in at least two steps.

Firstly, in 1858 came the purchase of two houses in what was to become Terenure Terrace further down Templeogue Road at Roundtown Village, almost opposite what today is Terenure Public Library. There is an indenture dated 6 April 1850 whereby Robert Shaw granted to one Joseph Taylor, a Roundtown builder, one and a half acres of land at a yearly rent of £15 — for 999 years — on condition that Taylor build two 'substantial' houses thereon: he subsequently sold these to a Ms Mary Barrett of Great Charles Street, Dublin, for £500; in November 1853, she then sold these two houses and land to Thomas Emmanuel Fallon of Rathmines. On 17 December 1858, John Conroy acting on behalf of the Carmelite Fathers Eugene Cullen, Thomas Bennett and John Simon Carr purchased the lot for £1,450.[3]

Whether from the beginning, the purchase involved more than two and possibly four houses or not is unclear: however, as early as 1862 *Thom's Directory* listed Terenure Terrace as comprising four houses. By 1897, from the same source, No. 3 is named as 'Lockerbie' and No. 2 as 'Ruthville'. Quite separately from these, already by 1874 the Carmelites were advertising to let 'Two New Semi-Detached Houses, Having all modern improvements, at Lakelands Park': though semi-detached, these were substantial five-bedroom houses of great convenience since 'the tram station is only eight minutes' walk'.[4] By September 1877, the Carmelites were already letting No. 4 Terenure Villas to gunmaker, Charles Weekes, of Essex Street,[5] and by 1883 they were letting No. 3 Terenure Terrace, together with a field adjoining No. 4, to a Miss Kathleen Reade of 2 Cambridge Villas. By 1898, they were also letting No. 4 Terenure Terrace to a Mrs Jane Holmes of Rookwood, Rathfarnham.

In addition to these early Lakelands properties, whether the Carmelites owned all, or only part, of Terenure Terrace from the beginning is unclear — but they certainly were developing their portfolio of leased properties — by 1890, they were letting three houses of Lakelands Park between Terenure Terrace and the college, and by 1929, the number was four.[6] A story handed down to Fr Peter O'Dwyer, historian of the Irish Carmelites, is that one of the houses, called 'Lockerbie', was purchased to provide a suitable dwelling for a sick member of the Order, Fr Thomas Carton, who was suffering from tuberculosis and who died in 1860. O'Dwyer first recorded this tradition in 1948, in an article in the Carmelite journal, *Zelo.* He repeated and elaborated on it in his magisterial volume *The Irish Carmelites* in 1988.[7] This information was supplied to him by an old Terenure hand, Fr Stan Meganetty. Fr Meganetty, born in Belfast in 1872, entered the Carmelites in 1892; he was ordained in Rome in September 1898 and taught Classics at Terenure College in the 1890s. He was therefore well placed to have heard this account. 'Lockerbie' itself was certainly in Carmelite possession in the late nineteenth century, along with a neighbouring house, 'Parkfield': according to a manuscript volume in the Valuation Office,[8] 'Lockerbie' had been let by the Carmelites to a Florence Montgomery while 'Parkfield' was let by them to a Patrick Jennings. The Montgomerys remained Carmelite tenants into the 1920s at least. Fr James John Cogan who was Prior of the Terenure Community from 1909 to 1913 concluded a lease agreement for 'Lockerbie' with J.A.M. Montgomery in 1909 and as late as April 1929, the Carmelites renewed the lease of 'Lockerbie' to Mrs Florence Montgomery.[9]

As for Terenure House and Demesne, it was acquired by the Carmelites in 1859 but whether it was acquired in its totality in one lot or in two is not quite clear.

TERENURE HOUSE AND DEMESNE

The general history of Terenure House and Demesne down to the 1850s is well rehearsed. The land of the yew trees or *Tír an Iúir* was known as such from as far back at the thirteenth century. The lands of Terenure, Kimmage and Drimnagh were granted in 1215 by King John to Hugo de Barnewall. Almost four centuries later, a member of the family, Peter Barnewall, built a residential castle on the site of the present college in 1592. The Barnewalls were ejected in 1652, and their estate confiscated by the Cromwellians. With the restoration of Charles II, the estate and the adjoining lands of Bushy Park and Kimmage were granted to Richard Talbot, earl of Tyrconnell. In 1671, Talbot sold the estate to Major Joseph Deane of Crumlin, and, for close on a century the Deanes modernised the house and redeveloped the estate. From them, Terenure House passed into the ownership of Robert Shaw who had been leasing the property from the Deanes since 1785.

The Shaws were descendants of a Scot, William Shaw (1651–1738), who fought for the Williamites at the Battle of the Boyne. For his reward he was given lands in Kilkenny and Tipperary. His great-grandson, Robert (1749–1796), left Kilkenny for Dublin and became, among other things, a successful financier and accountant-general for the Post Office. From such success, he purchased Terenure House. He greatly extended and upgraded the dwelling, providing a large entrance hall with balustraded balcony and new rooms with bay windows, and finely rendered stucco ceilings.

A financially and socially successful entrepreneur, Robert Shaw died suddenly at the age of 47 but not before he acquired the means of firmly establishing his family. The eldest of his five sons, also Robert, became the 1st Baronet Shaw. He married the daughter of the neighbouring Abraham Wilkinson of Bushy Park whose splendid house was given as dowry in the marriage. By their own success and marriage the Shaws now became one of the largest shareholders in Dublin, possessing the three stately properties of Terenure House, Kimmage Manor and Bushy Park House.

The newly-weds lived in Bushy Park and let Terenure House to Henry Taaffe before selling the house and demesne to Frederick Bourne, proprietor of a successful stage-coach business. While some sources record this as occurring in 1806, the foundation legal document is an original lease of 26 November 1817 between Robert Shaw and Frederick Bourne. By its terms, Shaw effectively sold Terenure House and Demesne to Bourne to the extent of 39 acres, 3 roods and 26¾ perches — Irish plantation measure — subject to a yearly ground rent of £239 10s.

According to P. Kelly, 30.25 Irish or plantation acres equal 49 English or statute acres:[10] consequently, the effective extent of the estate, as sold by Shaw to Bourne, was 64.6 statute acres. For this, Bourne paid Shaw the sum of £4,000stg in addition to the yearly ground rent. Bourne then apparently spent 'a large fortune' in extending the house and enriching the demesne, sparing nothing in securing rare specimen flowering trees, stocking the lake with fish and erecting on its banks a rustic banqueting house and a fishing 'temple'. When Frederick died in 1843, the Bourne family fell on hard times and the house and estate then entered upon something of an odyssey: it went to an Elizabeth Hargreaves and Rev J.M.H. Thomas. In November 1854, they in turn appear to have sold to a wool merchant of South William Street, named Alexander Hall, the house and some twenty plus acres of the whole — that is to say, the portion of the present day property to the right of the main avenue through the property facing to Templeogue Road.

Alexander Hall, however, ended up in the bankruptcy courts in 1863.[11] Whether or not he was already falling into financial difficulties by the end of the 1850s — some five years after he took over the house — in the autumn of 1859, Terenure House and 22 acres immediately surrounding it were put up for auction by a property developer, Bentley of Grafton Street. It was W.W. Bentley who at this very time was developing the villas of Foxrock, where he had already built a hotel.

Bentley produced a detailed prospectus of the entire property, providing a summary history of the estate, an account of its various legal transmissions, a detailed description of the house and its surroundings and to cap it all, a series of developmental proposals for extensive house-building on the land. By one enticing scheme, he suggested the construction of some eleven Siamese villas between the house and the frontage along Templeogue Road; far from devaluing Terenure House, this scheme, Bentley argued, with ornamental pleasure gardens to the front of these villas, 'would be rather an improvement than otherwise, to the appearance of the grounds'.[12] In an alternative scheme No. 2, he suggested the total demolition of Terenure House, thus 'throwing the remainder of the land into building ground' and the paddock to the north-west of the house, fronting on to Kimmage Road could provide for a terrace for some twelve cottages.

However, he did not confine his persuasions to prospective builders, but also suggested that the house and demesne, as they were, could provide a delightful seat for a gentleman, or finally, for use as a religious or educational institution. Whether the auction successfully took place or not is unclear: however, on 14 October 1859, Alexander Hall sold his interest in Terenure House and 22 acres of the demesne to the

Carmelites for £2,300.[13] So it was that in 1859 they came to be occupying owners of what three months later became the College of Our Lady of Mount Carmel at Terenure. The Valuation Office records for 1864–75 show the Order holding two large adjoining tracts of land by 1868 at the latest — one large tract of 43 acres plus, and a second tract consisting of the house at 19 acres and 3 roods — almost 20 acres. In addition, they possessed two gate-lodges, let to occupiers Mary Byrne and John Deegan respectively, and a vacant house and garden on 1 rood 3 perches. Altogether this equates to the 66 statute acres that translated from Shaw's original sale to Bourne of 39 plantation acres, and the mystery that remains is whether they purchased the 43 acres and 19 acres at the same time or purchased the 19 acres first from Hall and the remaining 43 acres from the Hargreave holding later. They would have had to put up the full amount in cash for the 19 acres purchased from Hall in 1859 — yet it is interesting that the Order borrowed or raised a loan of some £1,500 from Fr Patrick Doyle and Mrs Catherine O'Brien a few months later on 9 February 1860. They paid Mrs O'Brien back £500 in 1871 and a further £500 by the early 1880s. It may be that this loan was used to help purchase the remaining 43 acres in the 1860s.

Whatever the correct account is, the names of three Carmelite confreres recur in the various property transactions from 1858 to the 1870s. These, in effect, were the college's 'Founding Fathers'.

THE FOUNDING FATHERS

Eugene Cullen

The principals acting on the Carmelite side in the various legal transactions around the purchase were three — Fr Eugene Cullen, Fr Thomas Albertus Bennett and Fr John Simon Carr. Of these three, Fr Cullen was the eldest, having been born in Wicklow in 1796. This is according to the *Catalogus Fratrum*, in the Carmelite Provincial Archives at Gort Muire, which gives his age at 83 when he died on 6 February 1879. O'Dwyer however, gives his birthday as 1 January 1799. Either way, he was the senior in age of the three. He entered the Order in 1829 and was professed on 31 August 1830. He had already a distinguished record of achievement behind him before the Terenure purchase.

In the early 1840s, he was sent to the friary at Knocktopher, Co. Kilkenny, as Vicar-Prior with a mandate for reform. Described in one source as a rough, uncultured man, he was nonetheless trusted and energetic. By 1842 he was Prior there, and the Provincial Chapter of 1843 reappointed him. He virtually resurrected the establishment from a pair of miserable hovels into a decent priory and a splendid church, solemnly consecrated in June 1843. Furthermore, in what was pre-Famine Ireland, he managed to raise the funds to acquire a substantial adjoining farm. He thereby laid the groundwork that enabled Prior Matthew Scally to establish Knocktopher College in 1852.[14] When the Carmelite Provincial made his formal visitation to Cullen's priory in August 1845, he found that although the establishment was in debt, its assets — including eighteen acres of wheat, four acres of barley and miscellaneous movable goods — well exceeded its liabilities: furthermore, there was perfect peace and harmony prevailing between Cullen and Fr Scally. He was reappointed Prior by the 1846 Provincial Chapter, and was chosen as vicar to the Prior Provincial in 1849. That was as far as his promotions to office proceeded — indeed the illustrious, redoubtable and self-confident Carmelite, Dr John Spratt, confided to John Simon Carr, when he voted for the latter's election as Prior of Whitefriar Street, that Cullen was incapable of holding any office. For all the acerbity of this observation, when Eugene Cullen passed away in 1879, after a short illness, it was more kindly said that he died 'full of days but even more full of works';[15] so commented his confrere, Michael Aloysius Moore, who at the time was simultaneously president of Terenure College and Provincial of the Order.[16]

John Simon Carr

The youngest of the three was Fr John Simon Carr. He was born in Gurteen, Co. Galway, in 1816, son of Thomas Carr and Maria Mitchell. He joined the Carmelites in 1834, studied at Louvain and was ordained in 1839. The following year found him as one of the two-member Carmelite Community in Ballinasmale, a medieval foundation, three miles from Knock, Co. Mayo, 'a miserable house … chapel like a stable … Prior (Fr. Lavin) … excellent but old': so complained Fr Richard Colgan — soon to be Provincial — to Prior General Joseph Cataldi in 1840, but consoled his correspondent by adding, 'recently a very fine young man has been sent there and he gives great hopes'.[17]

Neither Colgan nor his Carmelite confreres were to be disappointed, even if Carr was downcast at being consigned to the outback: the 27-year-old Carr was regarded as 'a learned young priest of excellent qualities', Vicar-Prior to the aged, innocent and childlike Fr Lavin. In May 1843, the Provincial Chapter appointed him Prior of Ballinasmale but he resigned the post in late September of the same year. This notwithstanding, the next Chapter of the Province in May 1846 unanimously elected him Prior of Tohergar, Co. Roscommon, and three years later he was elected Prior of Kildare: by 1860 he had become Prior of the premier Carmelite house, Whitefriar Street. No Provincial Chapters were held during the 1850s and when one was finally held in late April 1860, Carr was elected Prior with three votes to Cullen's two. Carr himself wanted Cullen to have the position but Cullen declined and matters were settled when that other Cullen, Paul, the Archbishop — and no relation — insisted on Carr's accepting the position.[18] Although undoubtedly learned and able, Carr was a humble individual who not only sought to decline the Priorship of Whitefriar Street but also the position of Vicar Provincial when the Prior General Savini appointed him to this post in 1871. The fates conspired however, and when the incumbent Provincial, John Spratt, died suddenly in 1871 the archbishop intervened to make Carr temporary superior. The ensuing Provincial Chapter of August 1871 made the then 55-year-old Provincial, a position he held until 1875, while simultaneously teaching in their Dominick Street Academy. As will be seen later, his was one of the most significant provincialships in the history of the Order. Even after he ceased to hold high office, Carr remained an important influence and an important channel of communication and advice between the Irish Province and the Prior General in Rome. He remained a member of Dublin's Whitefriar Street Community until his death on 24 July 1893.[19]

Thomas Albertus Bennett

The third of the Carmelites who negotiated the purchase of Terenure is the one who is generally regarded as *the* Founding Father, Thomas Albertus Bennett. Possibly the best known and most distinguished of Carmel's nineteenth-century sons in Ireland — with the possible exception of Spratt — Bennett was born in Arles, Co. Laois, on 30 January 1802. He was apprenticed in the jewellery trade under his uncle, who ran a gold- and silver-smith business on Dame Street in Dublin. In September 1834, he entered the Carmelites, was professed in 1835 and at the end of 1836 was ordained by Archbishop Daniel Murray. Thereafter, he was sent for further theological studies to Louvain where his academic ability and attainments impressed. He secured his degree in 1841 and returned to Ireland the following year when Fr Richard Colgan was Provincial, and was assigned to Whitefriar Street.

He proved to be a dynamic force in the revival of the Carmelites and in the Catholic revival generally. Through his initiative, in approximately 1851, they opened a classical and commercial school on Jervis Street which, on transfer in 1854, became the well-known and successful Carmelite Academy of 41 Dominick Street. He was instrumental in securing recruits to the Order and for enlarging its foundation house on Whitefriar Street. Through Richard Colgan, he became involved in All Hallows Missionary College founded by Fr John Hand in 1842. Colgan was joint secretary with Hand in the steering committee that established the college and probably introduced Bennett to the college. Uniquely and significantly, Bennett joined the staff and Community of All Hallows while remaining a very active member of the Whitefriar Street Carmelite fraternity.[20] From 1843, he taught theology and scripture there at the same time as running his Jervis Street–Dominick Street School.

The All Hallows commitment did not impede his progress in the Carmelite Order. In 1849, he was appointed Prior in Moate[21] and in the following year at the greatly significant Synod of Thurles, he was theologian adviser to Archbishop Cullen. He remained one of Cullen's closest confidantes — so 'confidante' indeed that not a single Bennett letter has survived in any of the major Irish archives. In 1851, he was effectively appointed Carmelite Provincial for Ireland by the Order's General, Joseph R. Lobina. It was a position he held for the unusually long period of twelve years until 1863. Remarkably, while holding this position he took up the post of vice-president of All Hallows from 1856 to 1861 and then succeeded Bartholomew Woodlock as president of the college on the latter's becoming Rector of the Catholic University of Ireland. Bennett's key role in the reorganisation of the Carmelites will be considered in more detail later: suffice it here to say that while immersed in all these concerns, he also became the dominant figure in the acquisition of Terenure College.

As if this were not enough, he simultaneously was responsible for assisting and accommodating the Holy Ghost Fathers in their arrival in Ireland from France in 1860 and, ironically, in finding them the land and premises that became the hugely successful rival establishment of Blackrock College. Although considered a kindly and compassionate character Bennett cannot have had an easy relationship with Eugene Cullen in one regard. Before he had set about acquiring Terenure College, this devoted educationalist was central in what — at this remove — can only be described as a bizarre proposal to close down the thriving Carmelite College of Knocktopher. According to Fr Stan Meganetty, Bennett in 1858 took Knocktopher's Prior, Fr Scally, aside at Whitefriar Street and told him to close down this Kilkenny college. As the place had been thriving — according to Scally — since its foundation in January 1852 the proposal seemed an extraordinary one, not least since it was, among other things, recruiting young men for the Carmelites and also for All Hallows. No account of Bennett has painted him as vindictive, although he could be stern as occasion demanded. Can it have been that this was in anticipation of the founding of Terenure College? Peter O'Dwyer in his *The Carmelite Order in Post-Reformation Ireland,* remarks that 'being anxious to concentrate the Order's educational activities in Dublin, he told Fr Scally, Prior of Knocktopher, to close the seminary there'. However, to have ordered the closure of Knocktopher before Terenure was opened, or before it had even come on the market, would appear rather odd. Given that Bennett was a strict reformer and that the otherwise excellent Fr Scally apparently had a serious drink problem perhaps had something to do with this.[22] On one recorded occasion, as Prior of Knocktopher, Scally had presented himself to John Simon Carr, on the eve of the Provincial Chapter of 1860, in a state of intoxication. For all that, his general reputation in other respects and Knocktopher's repute as understood by authorities in Rome was sufficient for Bennett to be instructed to reconsider his stance on Knocktopher. The college survived until the early part of the twentieth century. As for Fr Bennett, he continued his association with All Hallows until the Vincentian Order took over its management in 1891. He thereupon retired and returned to Terenure College to live out his last years until his death there on 2 November 1897.[23]

THE PRESIDENT

To these three Founding Fathers of Terenure College must be added the name of Fr Michael Joseph Gilligan, its first president and Prior. A Dubliner, born in October 1832, he joined the Carmelites in 1854, was professed in 1855 and ordained in

January 1857. He appears to have presided over a relatively benign regime in the course of his eleven-year tenure as Terenure's head. Nevertheless, it was not without its troubles as the 1860s progressed — as is often the case in large educational establishments the greater problems may have been posed more by staff than students. His health was deteriorating towards the end of the 1860s and his office became increasingly burdensome. By 1871, he was so debilitated as a result of these pressures that in April he wrote to his Provincial, Fr John Francis Spratt, from Lisdoonvarna whither Spratt had permitted him to go for a few days rest. Suffering from rheumatism and general debility, he had reached the end of his tether: 'Long-continued anxiety about the affairs of the College has affected me very much and I am not in strength or otherwise equal to the responsibilities of the place'. He politely reminded Fr Spratt that over the previous seven years he had on three or four occasions asked the Provincial to remove him from the office and now announced: 'I hereby resign my office of Superior of Terenure College which resignation I most respectfully urge you to accept — my having held the office for now over ten years affords, I trust, sufficient evidence that I am not urged to this resolve by impulse or in haste'. He added that 'the presence of 52 boarders and 15 day-boys during the session just terminated, testifies, I submit, to the comparatively flourishing condition of the College'. Concluding that the college accounts would be found in a satisfactory condition, he requested Spratt to allow him to remain in Lisdoonvarna for two or three weeks to seek improvement in his leg and joint pains.

Anticipating a refusal to accept his resignation, or that Spratt would ask the cardinal-archbishop to bring direct pressure on Gilligan to remain in office, Gilligan took the strategic step of writing to him on 26 April, enclosing a copy of the resignation letter he had posted to Spratt the previous day. He told Cardinal Cullen that his Provincial would almost certainly consult Cullen to get His Eminence to persuade Gilligan to retract the resignation: he requested the Cardinal to advise Spratt to accept the resignation. He then explained what constituted his breaking point: the affair of the boat. A member of the Carmelite Community of the college decided it would be a good thing if they would acquire a boat for the college lake. This unnamed priest came to Gilligan for permission to proceed with this project. Gilligan refused and refused without explanation, but, as he explained to the Cardinal, there was: 'the danger of accident to the boys and what I consider the impropriety of religious in their habits rowing about on a lake along the edge of which there is a walk much frequented by visitors, friends of the boys etc'. Gilligan heard no more of this matter till:

> in a few days after I saw a man coming home with it from Kingstown at an hour on a Saturday evening when I was supposed to be in the Dublin house — next morning, Sunday, on my return, I found three priests in their habits rowing about the lake … Fr Provincial, it appears, … had given the leave to get the boat without saying a word to me.[24]

So ended the first presidency of Terenure College; the lake was to figure again, often and significantly in the history of the college, but happily without precipitating a presidential crisis.

As for the principals in this drama, Fr Spratt died suddenly later that same year, thereby precipitating a change of Provincial — but not before he had secured the replacement of Fr Gilligan with the Priorship and presidency of Andrew Elias Farrington. This is a matter for another place. As for Fr Gilligan, still only 39 when this drama ran its course, he was appointed Master of Novices: always a significant appointment, it had a special importance in 1871 as it coincided with the re-establishment of a formal Carmelite novitiate system in Ireland, following explicit instructions from the great Carmelite Prior-General, Angelo Savini. Gilligan continued to experience ill health and had to abandon his Mastership in 1873 and on medical advice was advised to pursue his vocation in a drier, warmer climate. In April 1877, he was transferred to Malta to help in the reconstruction of the Carmelite presence there. It was not to last long — in May 1878, following the Irish Provincial Chapter, he was appointed Sub-Prior in Whitefriar Street.[25] By 1881, he was caught up in successful negotiations for the opening of the Irish Carmelite mission to South Australia. Three years later, he was elected Prior of Whitefriar Street. He continued to be plagued by his rheumatism and passed away on 12 April 1888 at the comparatively early Carmelite age of 56.

Private offers received by
Hodges Smith & Co

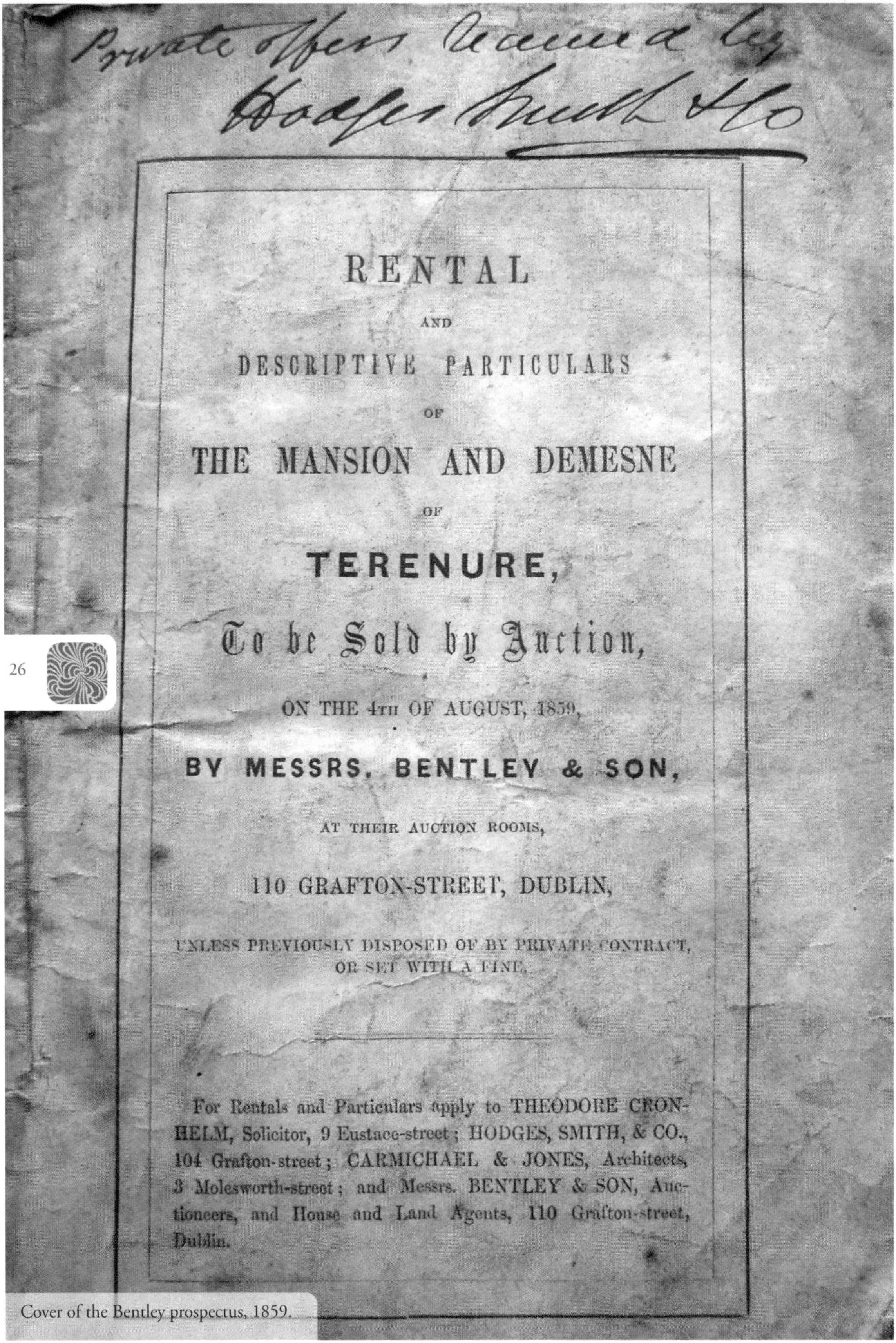

RENTAL

AND

DESCRIPTIVE PARTICULARS

OF

THE MANSION AND DEMESNE

OF

TERENURE,

To be Sold by Auction,

ON THE 4TH OF AUGUST, 1859,

BY MESSRS. BENTLEY & SON,

AT THEIR AUCTION ROOMS,

110 GRAFTON-STREET, DUBLIN,

UNLESS PREVIOUSLY DISPOSED OF BY PRIVATE CONTRACT, OR SET WITH A FINE.

For Rentals and Particulars apply to THEODORE CRONHELM, Solicitor, 9 Eustace-street; HODGES, SMITH, & CO., 104 Grafton-street; CARMICHAEL & JONES, Architects, 3 Molesworth-street; and Messrs. BENTLEY & SON, Auctioneers, and House and Land Agents, 110 Grafton-street, Dublin.

Cover of the Bentley prospectus, 1859.

Map of Terenure College referring to the eighteen-acre paddock, 1854.

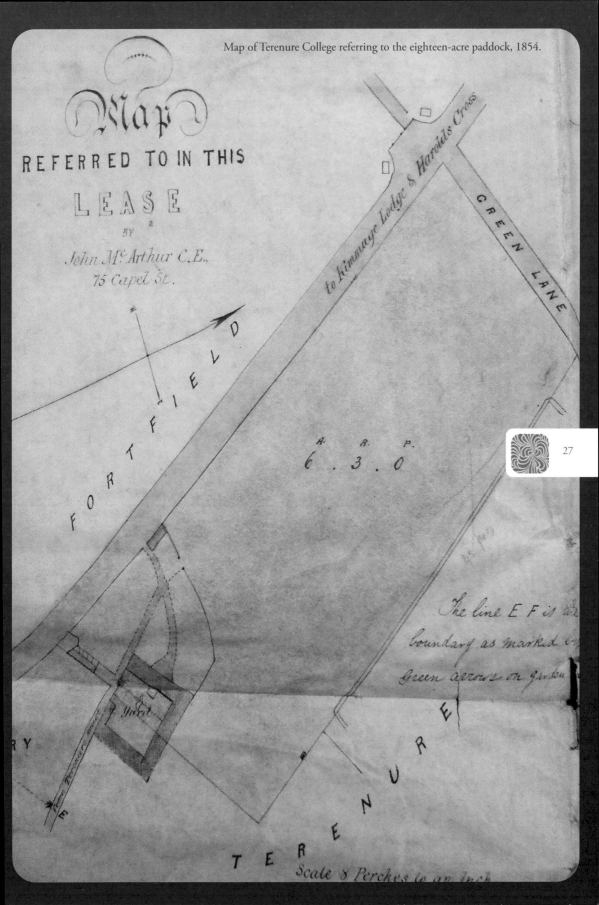

Map

REFERRED TO IN THIS

LEASE

BY

John Mc Arthur C.E.,
75 Capel St.

FORTFIELD

to Kinmage Lodge & Harolds Cross

GREEN LANE

A. R. P.
6 . 3 . 0

27

The line E F is the
boundary as marked by
Green arrows on garden

Yard

TERENURE

TERENURE

Scale 8 Perches to an Inch

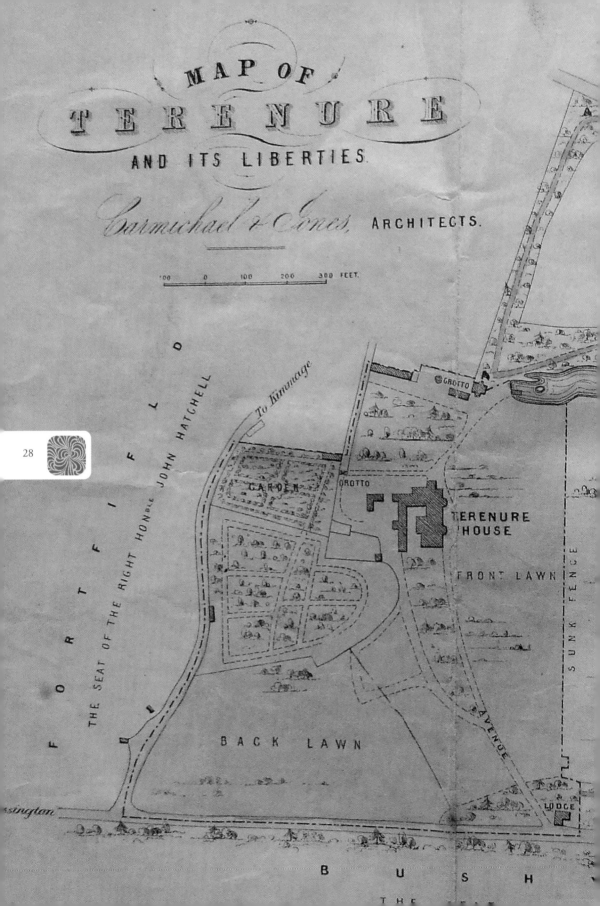

MAP OF TERENURE

AND ITS LIBERTIES.

Carmichael & Jones, ARCHITECTS.

100   0   100   200   300 FEET.

28

FORTFIELD

THE SEAT OF THE RIGHT HON.BLE JOHN HATCHELL

To Kimmage

GROTTO

GARDEN

GROTTO

TERENURE HOUSE

FRONT LAWN

SUNK FENCE

AVENUE

BACK LAWN

LODGE

ssington

B U S H

Map of Terenure and its liberties
from the Bentley prospectus, 1859.

LAKE

B   B   B

SWAN ISLAND   B A

EIGHTEEN ACRE
PADDOCK

B

B   LODGE

To Dublin

P   A   R   K

29

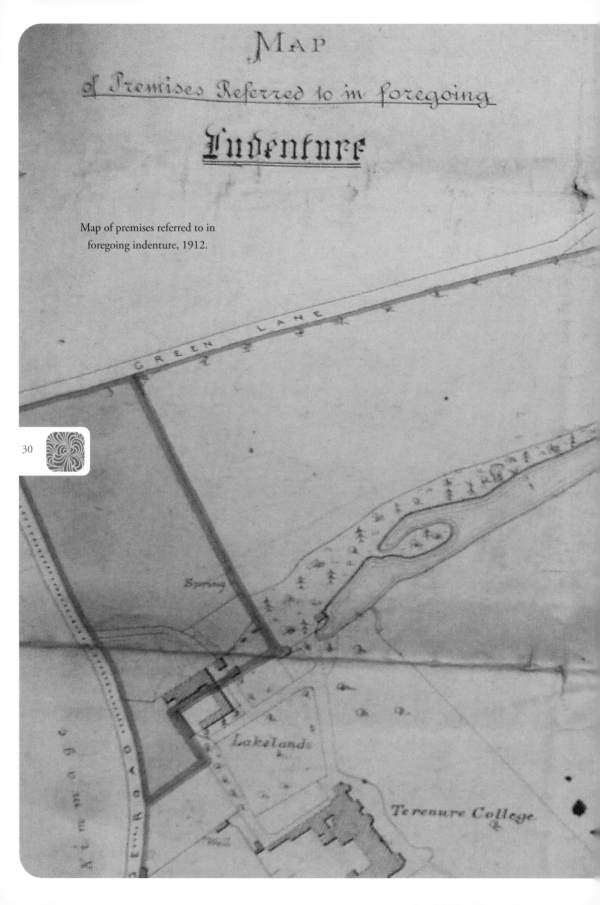

MAP
of Premises Referred to in foregoing
Indenture

Map of premises referred to in
foregoing indenture, 1912.

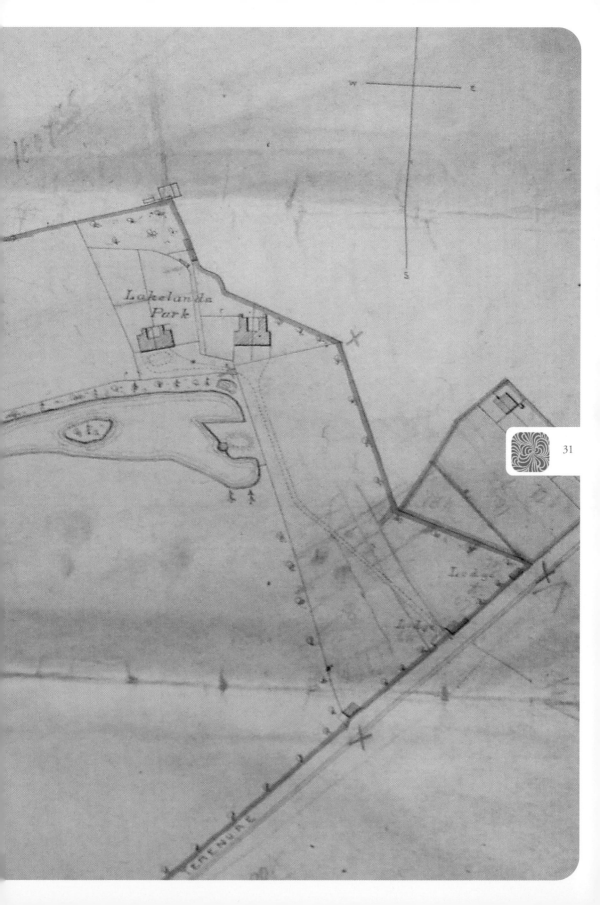

31

Felix Eugene Cullen, one of Terenure's founding fathers, 1880s.

Michael Joseph Gilligan, first president and Prior of Terenure College, 1880s.

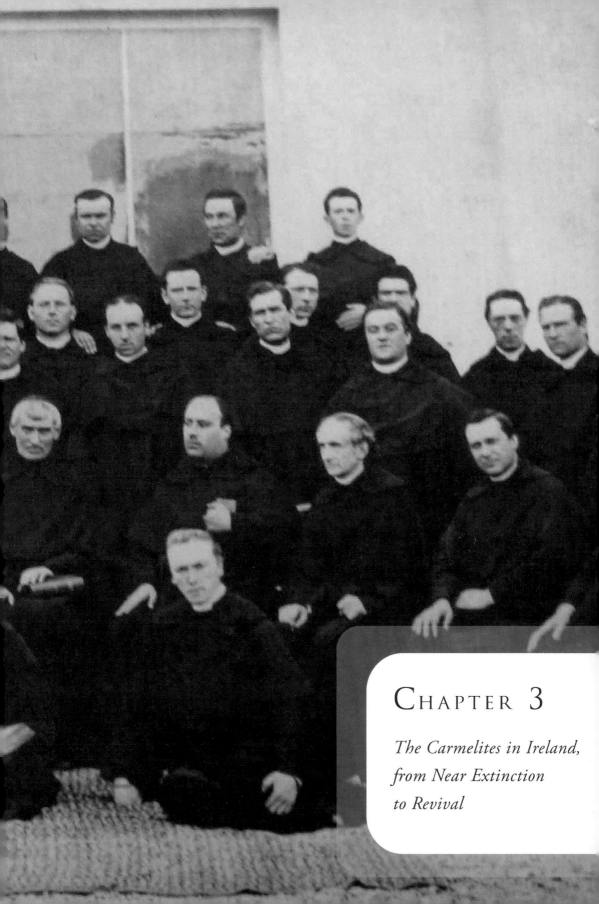

CHAPTER 3

*The Carmelites in Ireland,
from Near Extinction
to Revival*

Group photo of the Provincial
Council Meeting, 1871.

THE CARMELITES OF THE IRISH PROVINCE WHO FOUNDED TERENURE IN 1860 had come a long way over the previous century and more. For all that, they were still far from strong in numbers or resources and the Terenure venture was as much an expression of hope as of confidence. Around 1860 their numbers were quite modest for what they were attempting. Until the Carmelite Community established itself in Terenure the Order had five monasteries in the Province: Whitefriar Street, Kildare, Kinsale, Knocktopher and Moate. Alone among these, only Whitefriar Street, with sixteen priests in 1856, had the critical mass that made for a strong conventual Community: and even then, its members, apart from sacramental, social and charitable commitments and running a school on Longford Street, also ran and taught at the Dominick Street Academy as already noted. Their most eminent member, the Prior Provincial, Fr Bennett, was heavily involved in All Hallows Missionary College. The addition of Terenure as the sixth house of the Province further stretched the resources of the Whitefriar Street Community.

Still, matters were improving. Ten years before that, in 1850, Whitefriar Street as the premier foundation, had only eight priests. In that year, there were a total of seven houses, but some of these were conventual Communities or friaries in name only and certainly not in conditions and numbers. Of the others: Kildare, Kinsale, Knocktopher and Moate, each only had two priests while the houses at Tohergar in Co. Roscommon and Ballinasmale in Co. Mayo had only one each.

This was all a far cry from the happier and more prosperous Middle Ages. Having first established themselves in Ireland in the thirteenth century, the Carmelites, like other mendicant Orders, expanded steadily until, on the eve of the Reformation, they numbered 34 separate foundations. In the two centuries which followed, from Reformation to Restoration and 'Glorious Revolution', they were not just decimated but as good as annihilated. It is a sign of how desolate the situation was that, even before the Cromwellian invasion, when the Carmelite priest, William of St Patrick — who had been professed in Bordeaux — came to Ireland in the early 1640s, he failed to encounter a single Irish Carmelite: on a second visit he came upon two Carmelite priests in Waterford who turned out to be Flemish. On these visits he had learned that there had been 21 Carmelite friaries within memory but those which were not abandoned to ruins had been sequestered by other Orders — storing seeds of conflict for a later period.

Even in the wake of the Cromwellian *interregnum*, in 1665, the Franciscan, Fr Peter Walsh, knew of only one Irish Carmelite in Ireland. The situation remained so as late as 1683: when Fr William Shee (or Shea) — who had been born in Ireland in 1634 and who had gone to Spain in the 1650s — contacted the Carmelite Prior General, Angelus Monsignani, to seek permission to receive four young men into the Order, he claimed to be the only Carmelite on the island. Monsignani did not, or could not, contradict him in this and expressed delight at learning of even one Carmelite in the country.

Fr Shee's ministry may have been the point when the tide turned and the fortunes of Carmel changed from near extinction to gradual revival. One of his novice recruits, Peter Hughes, who was professed in France, returned to Ireland in 1702 — following the death of William III — and recovered for the Order the friary at Ballinasmale. In turn, he recruited young men there whom he sent to France and Spain for training, including his own nephew, Patrick Hughes. By the late 1720s, the Carmelites had re-established themselves in Dublin with a small Community at Ash Street. Apparently they managed a continuous presence there until 1806 when they moved to French Street.

By 1731, there was a sufficient number of Carmelites in the country to lead them to request the General Chapter of the Order to re-establish Ireland as a separate Province, and to provide for a Provincial and a Definitory (or Executive). A Carmelite document of that year, in the Roman archives, refers to some 38 members in a number of Irish houses, while a later Roman document, of 1766, places the number of Carmelites at around 50 in some 14 Irish locations. On 10 October 1737, Pope Clement XII formally restored the Irish Province, with Matthew Lyons as Provincial. Lyons had been appointed Commissary General for Ireland in 1729 with a mandate to recover former Carmelite properties, to recruit novices and to send them to Spain for training. There followed, in 1741, the first Irish Provincial Chapter since the Reformation, presided over by Patrick Hughes, then the most senior, in age, of the Irish Carmelites. This significant gathering elected Patrick O'Mahony as Provincial — a position he held for an unprecedented fifteen years — and appointed Priors to some fourteen houses.

It could well have been, however, that some of these appointments were nominal at best, and that as far as any real conventual life went they may have been friaries by intention more than as fact. Overt persecution aside, they were still rough and turbulent times. It was certainly a turbulent enough congregation that the new Provincial and the newly restored Province had to manage. Their historian, Peter O'Dwyer, cites from the Roman archives one description of the Carmelite Irishmen of that time, as follows:

> Because of persecution they are born in the fields like grass, they
> grow up like animals, are admitted [to the Order] like soldiers; when
> professed [they are] without discipline, when sent to study abroad
> they do not bear to be subjected to the bridle of obedience; they become
> a burden to all …[1]

It is evident that indiscipline was a problem: these men had got used to fending for themselves and while some may have longed for the closed conventual life with its common services as customary in the traditional Continental Carmelite houses, others were too used to their own independence. Consequently, the Roman authorities, in 1751, laid down that postulants were no longer to be professed in Ireland but had to subject themselves to a canonical novitiate on the Continent. The problem was far from unique to eighteenth-century Irish Carmelites: it applied equally to all the Orders of regular clergy — hence the decree from *Propaganda Fidei*.

It is, at this remove, ironic, that just as the institutional Church in Ireland was gradually escaping the worst of the persecution, that institution should have inflicted so damaging a decree. As Hugh Fenning has put it, this disastrous decree constituted 'practically a death sentence for the Mendicants'.[2] The Carmelites were particularly hard hit as, unlike the others, they had no native novitiate on the Continent and the cost of getting their novices to Europe, and of getting other Carmelite houses there to accept them, constituted a serious impediment. At the time of the decree, there were some 64 Carmelites in the Irish Province: by 1767, this had fallen to 34. *Propaganda Fidei* relented in a practical way — in 1774, they agreed to the creation of novitiates in Ireland but limited the Carmelites to a maximum intake of fourteen every three years, and these to be not less than 25 years of age. This was hardly the remedy the Order needed. By 1801, the Province was down to 10 friaries with 28 priests.

The nineteenth century saw a great Catholic revival in Ireland but for quite some time the Carmelite presence was relatively weak. Its leading house, in Dublin, which moved from Ash Street to French Street in 1806, before moving to Whitefriar Street in the 1820s, had as late as 1820 a modest complement of six priests. Nevertheless, from 1822 the Order managed to run St Patrick's School on Longford Street, for a very large number of boys. By that stage, according to one of its most famous members, Dr John Spratt, the whole Province in 1820 numbered only 21 members. Spratt was central to one of their most important moments, symbolically and practically: in 1825, he acquired the site of the historic Carmelite foundation on Whitefriar Street and had consecrated there the famous Whitefriar Street Church in 1827, constructed at the substantial cost of £4,000.

Even so, for the Province as a whole, over the next 20 or 30 years, there was little evidence of dramatic growth ahead. By 1840, the Dublin house still only had eight friars, and, on the island as a whole there were still, in 1840, only 26 Carmelite priests in seven friaries. Furthermore, of those 26, some 7 lived outside of any Community, surviving independently. In 1850, Dublin still only had eight Carmelite priests and the country still had only seven friaries. The numbers of priests at Kinsale, Kildare, Knocktopher and Moate remained at two each, morale was not particularly high, and the conventual life, even in Whitefriar Street, was not universally well-observed.

However, despite the intensifying crisis of poverty in the Irish country-side, culminating in the devastating Famine, improving change was on the way. It has already been seen in the great work accomplished by Fr Eugene Cullen in Knocktopher and in what Fr Spratt had accomplished in Whitefriar Street. A significant turning-point came in 1850–2. For the Catholic Church the appointment of Paul Cullen as Archbishop of Armagh in 1849 — taking up his appointment in 1850 — proved a major event as he was both a committed reformer and a strong leader. From Armagh, he was transferred to become Archbishop of Dublin in 1852. His summoning of the

Synod of Thurles, in August–September 1850, was a defining moment: the first synod of Catholic bishops in Ireland since the twelfth century, it was hugely significant in giving a new emphasis to hierarchy, authority, centralisation, uniformity and disciplinary reform — not least in respect of clergy themselves. It gave a considerable impetus to the promotion of education, especially at secondary level. Cullen himself — in 1866 the first Irishman to be made cardinal — gave great encouragement to Catholic teaching Orders and to the building of churches, schools and colleges.

Paul Cullen made a distinctive contribution to the history of the Carmelites at that time. Having close connections with, and very direct access to, the highest levels of hierarchy in Rome, he was almost certainly linked with the appointment of Fr Thomas Albertus Bennett as Carmelite Provincial in 1851. As already noted, Bennett had been Cullen's theological adviser at the Thurles Synod and when it came to Carmelite reform itself, Cullen and the Carmelite Prior General, Lobina, sang from the same hymn sheet. Lobina was determined to reform the Irish Province and to bring the Irish Carmelites into regular conventual observance. He had already appointed Bennett as Visitator General with full powers to inspect and reform every house and to try to impose strict observance. The fact that Bennett was a character of energy, dynamism and zeal for correct living and that he was reappointed Provincial, holding that office for twelve unbroken years, greatly contributed to a changed climate in the Order. A few of the brethren, of course, proved to be almost incorrigible, whether given to drink or refusing to keep Community or to observe the vows of poverty and obedience. Even as illustrious a figure as Fr John Spratt, like some other older members, perhaps cherished his independence over the restrictions of Community observance. So too, apparently, did Fr John Albert Hopkins, sole member of the Carmelite house of Tohergar, Co. Roscommon, since the death in 1853 of his confrere, Fr John O'Connor: Hopkins refused to abandon Tohergar or his own independence and was suffered to remain alone there until his death 25 years later, in April 1873.[3]

Nevertheless, the Carmelite commitment to education was manifest in a marked way during this period: Knocktopher College was opened in January 1852, St Kyran's Academy at Moate in 1854, the Academy of St Mary in Dominick Street also in 1854, culminating in the establishment of Terenure College in 1860 — all with the dual mission of preparing Irish youth for the world and securing vocations for the Order and the Church. By 1856, the Whitefriar Street Community had grown to sixteen members and vocations were on the increase. Bennett was re-elected Provincial at the Chapter of 1855 but wanted to refuse the post until effectively ordered by Archbishop Cullen to take it. When Bennett ceased to be Provincial in 1863, the efforts for fraternal reform, recruitment and church expansion were continued by his successor, Spratt. He insisted upon a stricter conventual life, forbidding friars to go from one friary to another, insisting that they be in their friaries before bedtime, with full silence from then, all to be present for early morning meditation, and to observe readings from the *Lives of the Saints* during dinner. Spratt's Provincialship was not universally popular within the Order: his many outside charitable commitments gave rise to dissension and charges of neglect within. Nevertheless, with his sudden death in 1871, Dublin's poor had lost a champion and the Carmelites one of their most distinguished members. His death came just a few months before the Provincial Chapter of 1871 — in some ways the most significant gathering of Irish Carmelites in the nineteenth century.

The Provincial Chapter of 1871 was held at Terenure College. It was convened at the instigation of Prior General Angelo Savini. He attended in person, the first Prior General to visit Ireland in over four centuries. From its proceedings it emerges that there were now 40 Carmelite priests in the Province. Of the three men who had acquired Terenure, Bennett was absent due to illness, but, to acclaim, John Carr was elected Provincial and Eugene Cullen became his Vicar.

Important decisions were taken in matters of discipline and organisation; as to the former, no friars were to visit socially outside with lay people after dinner; as to the latter, a novitiate was to be established in one of the Dublin houses and special dedicated examiners were to be appointed to interview potential novices prior to acceptance or profession. Subsequently, Savini sent a long list of specific instructions for and regarding the novices themselves. As for Terenure, on 30 November 1871, Savini appointed Andrew Elias Farrington as Terenure's president in succession to Michael Gilligan. A new chapter in the history of the college and the Carmelites had commenced.

42

43

Above: Staff and students in the grounds of Terenure College, *c.* 1878.

Left: Thomas Albertus Bennett, John Carr, John Spratt, J. Hall and J.L. McCabe, 1880s.

Chapter 4

Terenure — District and Demesne to 1914

Terenure House lake and grounds from
a wood-carving by George Petrie, 1820.

AS IT ENTERED THE NINETEENTH CENTURY, TERENURE WAS AS YET HARDLY A village, rather a townland with the fine houses of the resident gentry and the gate-lodges and cottages of those who served them. At the historic turning point between Cromwellian *interregnum* and Restoration, in 1659–60, between Rathfarnham and Harold's Cross there was no village and a mere ten people occupied the townland. The first 'construction' that approximated to any road that put Terenure on a map was an avenue linking Terenure to Rathfarnham which was created *c.* 1753. This by-way running east–west became what today is Highfield Road, Rathgar, running into Terenure Road East. Heading in the direction of Crumlin it became the first part of the intersection that in time became Roundtown or Terenure Village.

That village, developing gradually in the course of the eighteenth century, consisted of the cottages of the artisans and labourers who served the Big Houses arising over that century and the next: Connor's, Farrell's, Harrison's cottages, Healy's and Howard's Lane — later known as Yewland Terrace. Constituting a circle of dwellings, as they developed, in effect, they created the core of the village of Roundtown from the beginning of the seventeenth century. Some of these were built by the Shaw family of Bushy Park for their workmen. In one of them, Harmony Cottage, there lived from the 1840s a Mrs Shaw, grandmother of George Bernard Shaw. In another, Jubilee Cottage, at that same time lived Richard Hitchcock, an early scholar of the Ogham script.[1]

As for the Big Houses, the largest of them had existed for long before this. Terenure House, the oldest of these stately houses, existed in one form or another from medieval times, and, as seen earlier, was re-built as a residential castle in 1592. Its nearest neighbour, Bushy Park, was built in the seventeenth century. It was known as Bushe's House up to 1772, so-called after its founder, Arthur Bushe of Co. Kilkenny who held the post of secretary to the Revenue Commissioners. From 1772 it was owned by John Hobson of Tobber, Co. Dublin. He changed the name to Bushy Park. Abraham Wilkinson purchased it before the end of that century and, as previously noted, gave it to his daughter, Maria, as part of her dowry when she married into the Shaw family in 1796. As seen earlier, Robert Shaw, her husband, inherited Terenure House that same year. Terenure House was then temporarily forsaken, until taken for a time by a prosperous gentleman, Henry Edmond Taaffe before being taken over by the Bournes.[2] Descendants of the Shaws continued to live in Bushy Park until its last occupant, another Maria, sold it and its land to Dublin Corporation in the 1940s. The next important residence was Fortfield, constructed in 1785 for Barry Yelverton, MP, attorney general and chief baron of the Irish exchequer: he was promoted to the peerage as Viscount Avonmore in return for supporting the Act of Union. Little expense was spared in making 'Fortfield' one of the finest mansions in the county set in magnificent grounds boasting a splendid ornamental lake. For all that, one con-temporary commentator remarked of its name, critically, that 'it was so-called from a tasteless fort erected on the lawn'.[3]

Yelverton did not long enjoy his elevation, dying in 1805. The house and estate passed through a succession of highly placed owners, from Lord Clanmorris until 1811 to Master of the Rolls Sir William McMahon who, in turn, sold it to a judge, the Right Hon John Hatchell in 1858. It remained in the Hatchell family until its last owner, Miss Mary Margaret Perrin, passed away on 15 November 1929. The residence was then razed to the ground to make way for the house-building of the 1930s that saw the construction of the Fortfield houses.

In the first decade of the nineteenth century, 'Olney' was built, close by Terenure crossroads. Other fine dwellings followed over the next 40 years. Along Terenure Road West came 'Horton' and 'Minnowbrook' on its south side; on its north side came 'Cozey Lodge', later called 'Netherby' and as will be noted shortly, was destined to end up as the Presentation Convent and School. Next to it were built 'Laurel Lodge', 'Bessborough', 'Temple Howell' and 'Hazelbrook'. The latter was the home of Lord Chancellor Maziere Brady whose nephew, William, an Anglican clergyman and ecclesiastical historian, famously converted to Catholicism in Rome in 1875.

Along Terenure Road East were constructed 'Heathfield', 'Rokeby' and 'Rockview' on its north and 'Sylvan Lodge', 'Beechfield', 'Palermo' and 'Green Mount' on its south side. Down Terenure Road North came 'Montevideo' on its east, 'Elm Park' and 'Ashfield' on its west. Finally, along the east side of Terenure Road South were constructed 'Frankfort', 'Beechfield', 'Rosanna', 'Westbourne' and 'Eastbourne'; on its west side, there developed 'Moira Lodge', 'Rose Villa' and 'Everton Villa'.[4] 'Eastbourne', off Bushy Park Road, in time became the family home of High Court President George Gavan Duffy, the last on the Irish side to append his signature to the Treaty in 1921. The Gavan Duffys lived there until in 1951 it was sold to the religious order of the Sisters of St Peter Claver to become their convent.

Only in the first decade of the nineteenth century did a road pass by Terenure House, cutting it off from Bushy Park. That road which was a toll-road from 1801 to 1848 led from the city to Templeogue and beyond that, to Blessington. Its first tollgate was on the corner of Fergus Road and Templeogue Road. Apart from this, there was little enough to ruffle the rural calm of the area. There was no church in the immediate area before the coming of the Carmelites with their creation of the Oratory within the college, and Terenure was still part of the parish of Rathfarnham. The Church of Ireland followed immediately after, when the stockbroker, John Gold, purchased in 1860 the site on Zion Road where he had erected a fine Gothic church, with residence, meeting hall and school which opened in 1861.

Five years later, the new Catholic parish priest of Rathfarnham, Canon Daniel Byrne, procured the site at Terenure for a chapel and schools for boys and girls. The Presentation Sisters moved into the area at the same time. They had purchased the house on Terenure Road West originally known as 'Cozey Lodge' when it had been owned by city wine-merchant Richard Heinekey; it had been renamed 'Netherby' when purchased by a Mrs Solomon. In 1866, it was purchased for the Presentation Sisters who converted its coach-house and stables into a school for girls. It proved an immediate success and its provision for over 100 local girls meant that Canon Byrne was able to dispense with his plans for the girls' school and used the site to create a Catholic chapel alongside the boys' school. As for 'Netherby', in 1889, the Sisters erected a new redbrick building of two storeys with eight classrooms.

Successive Ordnance Survey maps chart the slow, gradual growth of residential housing and businesses while successive censuses serve to underline how gradual the process was. From 1841 to 1871, for the district of Terenure, the census recorded the numbers of inhabitants and dwellings as follows:

TABLE 1: INHABITANTS IN THE DISTRICT OF
TERENURE AS RECORDED IN THE CENSUS 1841–71[5]

Year	Houses	Persons
1841	162	582
1851	190	1,060
1861	165	930
1871	184	1,004

The census of 1891 retrospectively recorded the two areas of Terenure townland, with its 569 acres and Roundtown with its 26 acres as follows:

TABLE 2: INHABITANTS IN THE DISTRICTS OF TERENURE AND
ROUNDTOWN AS RECORDED IN THE CENSUSES 1851–91

Year	Houses		Total	Persons		Total
	Terenure Townland	Terenure/ Roundtown		Terenure Townland	Terenure/ Roundtown	
1851	190	145	335	1,060	851	1,911
1861	165	178	343	930	939	1,869
1871	184	182	366	1,004	903	1,907
1881	191	205	396	1,021	1,143	2,064
1891	191	237	428	1,032	1,282	2,314

Clearly there was growth in both numbers of houses and people, but it was modest rather than dramatic. Looking at various maps, one of 1837 reproduced in MacGiolla Phadraig's *History of Terenure* shows how truly rural Terenure House was. Between it and Roundtown, which was renamed Terenure (Village) in 1868, there was but the solitary house, 'Olney'. The same held for the other side of the Templeogue toll-road where there was no dwelling between Bushy Park House and 'Rose Villa' opposite 'Olney'. To the west there was 'Fortfield' and to the north, bar Eden Cottage, nothing as far as Terenure Road West.

From the 1840s, the general area saw substantial new houses being erected for members of the professional classes. They included 'Horton', Minnowbrook House and Oriel Cottage to the northwest of 'Olney' and 'Terenure Terrace' between 'Olney' and Terenure College. Civilisation was advancing: 1849 saw the arrival of the Dublin Metropolitan Police, setting up a police station opposite 'Olney', replacing the old toll-house. Here they remained until 1878 when they removed to 'Eglinton' on Terenure Road North for the next century.[6]

By the time of the 1912 Ordnance Survey map, not a great deal had changed along either side of Terenure Road from the college and Bushy Park to 'Olney'. A few houses had appeared at Lakelands Park, half way between 'Olney' and the college. As Fr James Carmel O'Shea recalled, when he first set foot on Templeogue Road, in the fateful autumn of 1914, there were only four houses along this stretch, namely 'Parkfield', 'Lockerbie', 'Ruthville' and 'Avonbec'.[7] Further down, at the crossroads and beyond towards Harold's Cross to the north, Brighton Square and Eaton Square had been heavily developed; similarly, to the west, towards Kimmage crossroads and to the east, towards Rathgar, significant development had occurred. Within the centre of Terenure Village — its name restored in 1868, although Roundtown lingered as an alternative both in print and folklore — significant small-scale development had taken place over the period 1850 to 1900.

Socially, the nineteenth century saw the gradual penetration of the professional middle classes of judges, barristers, solicitors, medics, financiers and bankers into the area to join the pre-existing gentry at the top and the artisans and labourers who served them, at the bottom. In tandem with this social change came infrastructural improvements, most notably in transport. The horse-drawn omnibus developed in Dublin in the early 1840s and a route serving Terenure and Rathfarnham was operating by 1846, running three times daily. Within ten years of this they were passing the college every fifteen minutes, at a charge from the city, of 6d inside and 4d outside.

In 1872 a horse-drawn tram service was inaugurated, running from Nelson's Pillar to Rathgar and soon after this extended to Terenure; eventually becoming the longest line in the city and suburbs, running from Rathfarnham to Dollymount.[8] Within a decade these were to be joined by the first roadside steam tramways when, in 1880, the Dublin and Lucan Steam Tramway Company was formed and the first section of its service began in June 1881. A month later the separate tram companies of the city were amalgamated to form the Dublin United Tramway Company. In Terenure, they had two depots or stables, opposite the church on Terenure Road North.[9] Seven years later, in August 1888, Terenure entered the picture when it became the terminus of the Dublin and Blessington Steam Tramway. The first steam tram from Terenure to

Blessington commenced on that sunny Sunday morning of 1 August at 8.45 a.m. and took 90 minutes for its sixteen-mile journey.

From its depot at the end of Terenure Road, at the crossroads, city-bound travellers from Blessington, Brittas, Tallaght and Templeogue could link up with the trams from the nearby Terenure tram depot and likewise this new service brought day-trippers to Blessington and Wicklow from the city. The Dublin and Blessington tram passed the college running along Templeogue Road on its Bushy Park side. For all its blessings, benefits and romance, it was not without its tragedies and fatalities. So much was this the case, that it became known as 'the longest graveyard in the world' from the practice of the bereaved in placing white crosses at the scene of these fatal accidents.

One of these unfortunates was a college tenant and employee, Matt Duncan. Sixty-seven-year-old Matt had lived in the three-roomed gate-lodge at the main entrance to the college, with his wife, Elizabeth, nine years his junior, and their two sons, James and Patrick. Matt was a Carlow-man, Elizabeth a Wicklow-woman. They had married in 1857 and he had become a farm labourer in the college. His elder son, James, in a twist of bitter irony, was an unemployed tram conductor, while the younger lad worked as a messenger boy for a local grocery store. On All Saints' Night, Sunday, 1 November 1915, Matt — who was hard of hearing — was walking along the tramway outside the college and not hearing the approaching tram, he was knocked down and killed. The tram-driver, Michael Horn, was charged with causing Matt's death: a passenger witness, Patrick Brazil of Templeogue, claimed that he for one could see the unfortunate man walking along the track and that while the driver rang his warning bell, the tram kept going and proceeded about 170 yards after fatally striking the unfortunate.[10] His death was far from exceptional. Further down the tramway, The Inn in Templeogue Village became known as 'The Morgue': passing The Inn, the Dublin and Blessington tram knocked down and killed locals and travellers whose bodies would be laid out at the hostelry as the nearest decent repository.[11] Despite all of these tragedies, the development of these transport facilities over 1840 to 1914 contributed gradually to the commercial growth and social diversification of the area.

However, when the Carmelites founded the college in 1860, it was still very much an Arcadian retreat. Fr J. Peter Wheatley, a Dubliner born in 1836 who was ordained in 1864, recalled that in his early years as a priest, once one crossed Portobello Bridge from the city one was 'amidst green fields'.[12] For the Carmelites and their young charges, it must have been a wonderful setting in which to begin their new venture.

The area was still a scene of woodlands, streams, lakes and ponds. Three waterways were within a stone's throw. The Dodder with its origin in Kippure in the nearby Dublin Mountains rose within a mile of where the Liffey rises but made a much more direct descent to the sea — and, though short enough in its journey — it could be perilous in sudden flood. Over time many bridges over the Dodder along the way from Terenure to Rathfarnham were swept away. The one finally built in 1765 lasted until replaced in 1953 by the present Pearse Bridge. Along its banks over the eighteenth and nineteenth centuries, grew up numbers of mills, from cloth and paper to corn and timber: nearby Terenure College the Ely Cloth Mills employed up to 100 workers in the 1830s and survived in business until 1880.

The Poddle — or more accurately the Timon River, which feeds into it — originated beyond Tallaght, flowing to Perrystown and on through Kimmage and Harold's Cross to join the Liffey near Capel Street Bridge. To enhance its use as a source of drinking water, a weir and watercourse were created at Firhouse in the thirteenth century and by means of a canal it was linked to the Poddle near Whitehall crossroads: this not only supplied the power for some 30 plus mills by the late 1870s, it also served to supply fish ponds at Cypress Grove, Fortfield House and Terenure House. This little diversion flowed on past 'Olney' to another pond at Glenpool House and onward across Harold's Cross to join the third stream, the Swan River. To prevent flooding downstream in the Liberties and Blackpitts, the authorities in 1938 created a culvert diverting Poddle water through Terenure College lake, under the road into Bushy Park and on into the Dodder. As for the Swan, originating north of the college at Parkmore, it was a streamlet dividing Terenure from Kimmage. In 1938, it was diverted by culvert into the Poddle at Mount Argus, onward to Ranelagh, entering the Dodder at Lansdowne Road. These water-ways with their associated lakes and ponds, together with the woodlands at Bushy Park and Rathfarnham, made for a marvellous surrounding neighbourhood for Terenure House and College.[13]

Then there was the demesne itself. Around the year 1830, George Newenham Wright described it thus in the volume *Ireland Illustrated*:

> The demesne covering about fifty English acres, is extremely elegant and judiciously improved. In front of the mansion is seen a lawn gradually sloping to the margin of a beautiful artificial lake whose surface is enhanced by the passage of swans and various aquatic birds, and an occasional barge with its gay and happy voyagers, steering for some of the little wood-grown islets that slumber on the tranquil surface of the waters. The plantations of woods of Terrenure [sic] are rich and luxuriant …[14]

Samuel Lewis in his *Topographical Dictionary* in 1837 celebrated

> The picturesque beauty of its grounds, embellished with stately timber of many varieties, and its garden laid out with great taste and comprehending a rich selection of choice plants and flowers. In the demesne and gardens are numerous varieties of orange trees, ash, elm, horse-chestnut, holly and hawthorn, and more than 1,750 different varieties of rose-trees; the conservatories and hothouses contain upwards of twelve thousand square feet of glass, and the whole is arranged in the most perfect order and preserved with the greatest care.[15]

A year later, John D'Alton in his *History of the County of Dublin* enthused:

> Tyrenure [*sic*] succeeds with its magnificent gardens, hothouses, groups of trees and shrubberies of evergreens, its grottoes, urns and rustic seats, disposed through all the grounds; its fine sheet of water, insulated banqueting-house, fishing temple, winding walks, and picturesque bridges.[16]

A great deal of this was clearly due to the Scottish landscape gardener James Fraser whom Frederick Bourne hired as his head gardener and who was to be one of the major garden designers in Victorian Ireland.[17]

As for the house and demesne, shortly before the Carmelites opened their establishment here, the 'lawn' in front of the house comprised eight acres which boasted green and copper beeches over 100 years old, together with many other ornamental trees. This area was separated from an eighteen-acre paddock by a 'Ha-Ha' or concealed ditch with invisible wire fencing, that division thereby hidden from view of the house. To the rear of the house was another lawn — used for grazing — some five acres in extent and separated from the front lawn by another concealed fence. To the immediate north of the house was a private garden of some two acres and boasting a great variety of splendid trees from Italian cypress and American tulip to cedars of Lebanon: amidst them all, a magnificent native chestnut whose girth was then fifteen feet. It was onto this garden of delights, with fountain, conservatory and temple that the dining room of Terenure House looked out.

In the western corner of the property, at the rear of the building, lay a one-acre fruit and vegetable garden that supplied the kitchen — facing the sun and protected all the way round by high walls, and entered by way of a grotto-arch from the pleasure garden. Finally, to the south of the kitchen garden was another paddock and orchard of some three acres, also entirely walled round.

Crowning all was the splendid lake with its islands, bridge, boat-house and fishing temple — a lake that was to feature long in the history of the college and in the memories of generations of its pupils.

As for the house itself, when Alexander Hall had restored it, to its front was a porch some 20 × 8 ft, doors at each end: essentially an outer hall leading to the inner and larger reception hall which was some 27 × 14 ft, and some 20 ft high to ceiling. To either side of this were two matching ante-rooms, 16 × 17 ft, the one a library, the other a breakfast room. These in turn opened into a drawing room to the left and dining room to the right, each some 27 × 30 ft. With their projecting bay windows, these two rooms looked out onto the finest views.

A corridor on the right linked the dining room to the main kitchen, while another to the left led to a staircase to the first floor master bedrooms: the largest was an elliptical 28 × 26 ft, above the dining room; to the left, two smaller bedrooms, one 20 × 16 ft and the other 16 × 13 ft. On this first floor were also a bathroom and servant's room. Above them, on the second floor were the attic rooms, comprising some five family bedrooms: to the centre and front, with pride of place, lay the 23 × 19 ft nursery, flanked by two smaller bedrooms each 16 × 13 ft: all had their own doors but all were also interconnected. Behind all these to the rear were another two bedrooms at 23 × 17 ft, with dressing rooms and a toilet. Finally, a large staircase from these led down to the kitchens and store-rooms while another staircase, of stone, led up to the roof.

The extensive main kitchen contained, in addition to ranges, modern boilers supplying the entire house with hot water. At the rear of this there was a scullery and back kitchen serving, among other things, as a bakery. Added to these were wine-cellars, store-rooms and a heated dairy and enclosed kitchen yard. On the floor immediately above the kitchens was a large ballroom and attached refreshment room. The water supply to these extensive premises came by way of a steam engine pumping it up to large cisterns in the roof, supplying both house and fountains. The house was gas-lit throughout, from a gasometer in the back yard.

When the property passed from the Bournes, it fell into some neglect, but, when Alexander Hall acquired it in 1854, he expended a large sum in restoring the grounds and dwelling to their former glory. The pupils who enjoyed this place over the following decades must have been fortunate indeed, even if, as must have been the case, the Carmelites were hard-pressed at times to maintain so rich a purchase.

John Simon Carr and J. Peter Wheatley, *c.* 1870.

55

AEREO POSTAL:

VERY REVEREND R

TEREN

IRLANDA

REPUBLICA ARGENTINA

LINEAS AEREAS DEL ESTADO

CORREOS
REPUBLICA ARGENTINA

LINEAS AEREAS DEL EST

CORREOS
REPUBLICA ARGENT

LINEAS AEREAS DEL ESTADO

CORREOS   15ᶜ
REPUBLICA ARGENTINA

DUBLIN

CHAPTER 5

The Farrington Years,
1871–8

Envelope enclosing William Peakin's
nineteenth-century reminiscences
of the college, 1952.

THE COLLEGE ENTERED THE 1870S WITH A NEW PRESIDENT IN FR ANDREW Elias Farrington. Born in west Wicklow on 13 January 1840, he entered the Carmelites in 1859, was professed in 1860 and was ordained in December 1865. He was a complex character who, in the course of a long life, had many achievements to his name. Two years after his ordination he was made Prior and Principal of Knocktopher. In the following year, the General, Angelo Savini, wanted to send him to help with a mission in Wales, which Dutch Carmelites had established in Merthyr Tydfil in 1864. He was sent there in May 1868 but was brought back to Ireland the following year. In 1870 he was appointed Rector of the Dominick Street Academy. Described by Provincial John Carr as 'a young, wise, prudent and learned man',[1] it was at Carr's recommendation that Savini appointed him president of Terenure College on 30 November 1871, in succession to Fr Michael Joseph Gilligan who now became Master of Novices in the college.

Farrington was indefatigable as well as learned. Even as he ran the college, he was actively engaged in social evangelism as well as research, writing and publication. As to the former, he took a special interest in one of Dublin's toughest black spots, Hammer Hill in the Coombe, in Dublin's Liberties. The local Francis Street curate, Fr John Behan, 'easy-going, trampish and eccentric', had interested Fr Farrington in sending in his Carmelite troops, 'laden with brown scapulars' to bring the place to some kind of redemption and in the course of the 1870s and 1880s, Fr Farrington on occasion could be found surveying the 'Hillites' like 'a general surveying a battlefield' — with the hot-tempered Fr Cornelius Crotty, the 'neatly-garbed, level-headed and go-gettish' young Fr James Behan, and the gentle and golden-voiced choirmaster, Fr Tom Doyle, as his troops.[2]

As for writing and publication, he somehow found time to produce, in 1873, lives of St Andrew Corsini, Florentine Carmelite of the fourteenth century, and Blessed Frances d'Amboise, founder of the Carmelite nuns in France in the fifteenth century, working on other Carmelite lives at the same time. His work sufficiently impressed his superiors in Rome to secure for him the award of a doctorate in April 1873. It is testimony to his energy, that in that very month he also had to take on the position of Master of Novices in Terenure when Fr Gilligan's ill health forced him to retire. There were six novices there by the autumn of 1873, eight by mid-1874 with a further four by that autumn. This was at a time, as will be addressed in more detail later, when the college reportedly had some 80 lay-pupils and the Provincial was reporting to Rome that the college was at last beginning to prosper so that it was full.[3] Admittedly, in the matter of the novitiate side of the college activities Farrington had the support of his Assistant Master of Novices, James Davis, who was also college vice-president. A Dubliner, born in 1836, Davis entered the Order on 14 July 1858, and was professed on 16 July 1859. In his early 30s when he was in Terenure, he had been a restless and uncertain soul, wishing, at different times, to go on the missions to America or to be permitted to leave the Order altogether, in the early 1870s. He suffered from ill health too, with suggestions of consumption. For all that, in addition to his teaching duties, he pursued formal study at Trinity College in 1874 and at the same time busied himself in research and writing that saw, among other works, the publication of a life of St Elias in the same year. In that year, too, he secured his masters in theology from Rome. He ceased to be on the college staff from 1876 but in later life was for a time, Rector of the Dominick Street Academy or Seminary, as it was also styled.

At no stage during the Farrington presidency did the numbers of Carmelite priests on the Terenure teaching staff exceed half a dozen. They came and went frequently enough too. When Farrington took over from Gilligan at the end of 1871, they numbered six priests. Two of these — concerning whom more later — Frs Michael Moore and Thomas Bartley were themselves to be presidents of the college subsequently. The remaining two, in 1871, were John J. Brennan and Thomas Osmond Cullen. Within a year Cullen had gone elsewhere and the brilliant but troubled 30-year-old Fr Tom Reddy had come in as professor of Greek, which he taught the boys and the staff. He had been Vicar-Prior in Knocktopher at the time, but within two years he had moved on and by the end of the 1870s sought to leave the Carmelites. He was secularised in 1878 but was later re-admitted to the Order. A problem with drink caused him to be moved from one friary to another, as far afield as America in the early 1880s and Spain by the late 1880s.

By 1874, the charismatic Fr Joseph Vincent Butler had joined the staff. Born in Limerick in 1844, he entered the Carmelites in 1861, made his solemn profession in 1864 and was ordained in 1868. He was sent to Rome for further study, returning in late 1873 and was then assigned to teach in Terenure. In 1878, he was sent to Rome for further study. Three years later he led the pioneering group of Carmelites who set out to establish their mission in Australia. Known as the silver-tongued orator, he was hugely successful in their first parish of Gawler, South Australia, and as Prior of Melbourne from 1882 to 1888. As the complement of religious teaching staff did not exceed six, it is almost certain that some of the novices were also engaged in teaching duties. A press report of 1875 spoke of the Carmelite Community of Terenure as comprising fifteen members and since only six priests were named as the permanent teaching staff at that time, one must conclude that some nine novices or unordained professed confreres made up a significant element of the teaching team. In addition, confreres from Whitefriar Street were almost certainly involved. With regard to lay teachers, there is no evidence that they were employed in any great number. There were some, of course, in specialised areas such as the drawing master Mr Rogers in the early 1860s. In the 1870s, there was the music master, J.J. Johnston, who trained and conducted the college orchestra, and an elocution master, R.J. Ball.[4]

The range of subjects offered in the mid-1870s was extensive: it included Christian doctrine, English, elocution, Latin, Greek, French, history, geography, mathematics, and science, together with drawing, music and dancing — all this apart from games, mainly handball and cricket at this time. Given the scope of this syllabus and that it was a boarding school requiring 24-hour supervision, seven days a week, it was no sinecure for those who lived and worked there.

Numbers

It is clear enough from disparate sources that the college grew significantly in the number of its enrolments in the decades after 1870 despite the vagaries and gaps of the surviving registers. It has been seen that at the end of the 1860s the numbers were steady at around 50[5] and that by January 1871 the figures had risen to 70, comprising 52 boarders and 18 day-boys.[6] In the summer of 1875, a reporter was informed that the numbers were between 70 and 80 of whom 44 were boarders and in the summer of the previous year the Provincial informed the General that Terenure had some 80 pupils on its books.[7] It was at this stage that the decision was taken to build an extension to the premises. Work on this must have commenced in late 1875 or early in 1876 and it was nearing completion by the middle of 1876 — so the new Provincial, John Bartley, reported to Rome in April of that year. The date of completion is variously stated: the commemorative *Annual* of 1960 refers to it in one place, as 'The 1874 Wing' while O'Dwyer states that it was completed in 1878.[8] However, a press advertisement of August 1877 observes that 'The College has been considerably enlarged recently by the addition of a new wing. There is consequently, accommodation for an additional number of pupils', while a report in the *Freeman's Journal* of July 1877 describes a new concert hall or 'Grand Hall' attached to the college as have been 'created within the last two years'.[9] Looking out from the front of the original house, the new extension was constructed to its right, facing the main avenue. It was a substantial undertaking, some three storeys in height. On the ground floor this provided for a large study hall with a raised platform at one end, which allowed for its use as a theatre and it doubled also as an examination hall, which latter purpose it served until 1948. On the first floor, new dormitories were created and on the second floor, separate rooms were constructed with a corridor down the centre, which layout remained in place until 1925 when the corridor was removed and the entire area reconstructed for additional dormitory accommodation.[10] One of the historical curiosities of this development was the fact that the clerk of works for the project was James Carey, member of the 'Invincibles' who murdered chief secretary, Lord Frederick Cavendish, and under secretary, Thomas Henry Burke, in the Phoenix Park on 6 May 1882. Notoriously, Carey turned informer, leading to the execution of five accomplices and was himself murdered by a Fenian, Patrick O'Donnell, in Capetown to which he had fled. The magistrate charged with investigating Carey and unravelling the conspiracy was Judge John Adye Curran whose son John, twenty years, later became a student in the college.[11] The new wing was undoubtedly a welcome development for priests and pupils alike and would appear to support the claims that the place was 'full' and that there were some 70 to 80 pupils there in the mid-1870s. The extant documentary evidence, however, is misleading. The so-called *Daily Roll of the School, 1869–1885* shows different figures. For March 1871, it shows 51 boarders and 15 day-boys and in September of that year they are at 36 boarders and 14 day-pupils. By 17 January 1874, there were 43 boarders and 24 day-pupils. The boarding numbers appear to have peaked at 51 by 21 March 1874 but from the new session in September 1874 the numbers went from 33 to 40 by December 1874, peaking at 42 by May 1875. Over October 1875 to March 1876 they fell to 35 and rose to 40. By September 1876, the number returned, presumably boarders only, was 42. By the beginning of the 1880s the number of boarders and day-pupils appears to have fallen noticeably. Whatever the exact picture may be, the college recruited its fair share of colourful characters and was busy with their entrances and their exits. Despite the college's having a formal commencement date to its academic year, pupils could and did enter at any odd time of the year and from far and near. In December 1873, Gordon Stewart of 14 South Great George's Street, Dublin, enrolled three months into the year at '£32 including extras': he entered the annals thus: 'He was a very small fellow — had a great deal to say, but was not very fond of learning'.[12]

Another diminutive scholar was John Travers, a boarder from Dublin's Upper Wellington Street, who commenced in June 1872 when the school year was at its end: he did not stay long or leave a deep impression, his account entry reading: 'Left for business, where I do not know. Oh he was a little fellow, small —'.[13] Masters Michael and Patrick Byrne from Abbeyleix, Co. Laois, came in as boarders at £60 the pair in the middle of a year, in February 1874. They came from near and far, local boys from Terenure as boarders as well as day-pupils, and lads from all counties and other countries. There is no pattern or clusters of country or county towns from which they came: a random sample from around 1876, from a college accounts book, shows the Byrne brothers from Sorrel Hall, Co. Tipperary; L.J. McConny from Bray, Co. Wicklow; John McCormack from Dernegra, Collinstown, Co. Westmeath; Masters Willie and Michael Coyle from Cashel; Matthew Muldarry from Athy, Co. Kildare; three Murphy brothers, John, Michael and Thomas from Athleague, Co. Roscommon; another set of his Murphy brothers from Edenderry, Co. Offaly; and Daniel Lunny from Belfast.

They came from all quarters of Dublin City and county: a Master Carey from Kinsealy House, Malahide; Robert and John Wall from 19 Stephen's Green North; and James Fleming from 25 St Stephen's Green, son of a Stephen's Green wine-merchant who supplied fine Italian wines to the establishment of the lord lieutenant and who lived in a fine house in Killiney, young James entered as a boarder at £30 'with extras' on 7 October 1873, but soon after 'left for Blackrock'.[14] Others were Joseph Kenny from Wexford Street; the Bailey brothers from Duke Street; Joseph Taaffe from the Collector General's Office, Fleet Street; and Master Dolan from the Royal Irish Yacht Club, Kingstown; Jonathan Arkins from Tolka Lodge, Drumcondra; and Master Roberts from the Kildare Street Club.

From further afield came John Brophy from Wavertree Station Cattle Depot, Liverpool, who enrolled as a boarder in the middle of the college academic year, in

January 1874, and David Mullen from High Street, Dunfermline who came in on 7 September 1872, followed later by his brother George and Michael Gallagher from Seacombe, Cheshire, who entered at the end of the 1870s. In some cases, the boys were sponsored or paid for by guardians or patrons. Most notable among them, perhaps was the case of Denis McCarthy of Cork City, and later with an address in Victoria Street, London, who entered on 31 January 1878. His sponsor or fee-payer was none other than Dion Boucicault, the Irish stage Irish actor and dramatist, author of the *The Colleen Bawn* and *The Shaughraun* and whose own life was as colourful and as commented-upon as his theatre productions. In addition to Denis's standard boarding fee of £15 per half year, Boucicault was billed for Denis's piano lessons at £2 and £1 for drawing: however, a note on the account addressed to Boucicault at East 15th Street, New York, added, 'Nov 19 … He is not to learn music in any way after the date of the above': perhaps to forestall any youthful ambitions for the stage.[15]

For boarders whether sponsored or not, the uncertainties of life at the time could intervene precipitately: sudden deaths and bankruptcies of parents or guardians could terminate their college careers. Typical was the case for the brothers John and William Marten: 'to six months pension ending Aug 1878 — £27-0-0 — Bankrupt'. Similarly, for boarder Thomas McCarthy of Great Britain Street who studied in the college from 1876 to 1880, there was the comment 'Mr Fallon who paid for this boy, did not pay, became bankrupt'. Illness too could intervene such as to terminate college attendance as evidenced by Jeremiah Fagan of Ballinglen, Co. Wicklow, who managed two years from March 1878 but who went home at the end of a period when he had had 24 visits to the college doctor at 5s a visit. Less typical a cause for departure is found for the Egan brothers, Francis and Patrick of Synnott Place, Dublin, who joined in 1879: 'March 1882 — Masters Francis and Patrick Egan left College on Wednesday 8 March to join their father in Paris'. More sombre and mysterious were the departure and fate of young Dominick Tallon of Lacken Lodge, Dungarvan, Co. Waterford: he commenced in September 1874 as a boarder but after December 1877 it is recorded: 'Paid in full and is gone to South America et mortuus est, R.I.P'.[16]

The premature exits were as frequent as untimely entrances. Master McDonnell from Water Park, Carrigoline, Co. Cork, who had entered in October 1873 left pre-cipitately in 1874: 'Gone on board a merchant ship'. More often than this the reason for premature departure was to pursue careers in commerce: when Patrick Sinnott, boarder *c.* 1875–76, left the records noted: 'Left for business, to his brothers, Francis Street, Dublin, where I am sure he will cut a figure … he was very stupid but good-natured and obliging but very backward'. For Patrick Walsh, in October 1874, it was remarked: 'Paid in full, left for home having finished his Education, but tall and strong enough for the farming business'.[17]

Some premature exits were by virtue of expulsion, as in the following report:

> On the 8th December, G Lawless, J Hagan, J Maloney, Thomas
> Murphy and M Lennon having received permission to go to

Kingstown with two prefects, Messrs O'Donnell and Dunne, refused to return when ordered and only came back towards midnight under the influence of drink, for which conduct they were expelled. M.A. Moore, 18 Dec 1880.[18]

Most often, however, the reason for premature departure was not for expulsions which were rare enough in the records, but by reason of removing to rival establishments. Most frequently these transfers were to Blackrock, Clongowes Wood and Castleknock but sometimes also to local rival educational establishments such as 'Mr Campbell's, Rathmines'. However, the transfer could be to their own fraternal institute in Dominick Street: such was the case with the Holohan boys, Henry and Charles, Terenure day-pupils from October 1876 to 13 February 1878 when it is reported, 'The boys left for Dominick School [*sic*] on this day'.[19] Such traffic between competing institutions, however, was in both directions.

Often enough, too, the college saw students move on to Clonliffe and All Hallows College. One such case was that of James Mahon of Valleymount, Co. Wicklow, who boarded at Terenure from September 1873 and left for Clonliffe on 6 September 1875; another was that of the two Harrington brothers, day-pupils from Brooklawn, Kimmage Road, who left for Clonliffe in 1879 after having come to Terenure in September 1878. As for All Hallows, Terenure student, J.J. O'Connell, entered on 1 September 1881, destined for the South Australia Mission. More importantly for the history of the Carmelites and Terenure College itself, a small number of students in the 1870s, and a greater number thereafter, moved on to enter the novitiate there. From the 1870s the most significant such figure was John Daly of Mooretown, Kilcullen, Co. Kildare. Born in 1864, he first came to the college as a boarder on 30 May 1878 and entered the novitiate in the spring of 1881. First professed in 1882 as Brother Laurence, he was ordained in Rome in 1887, at the age of 23. Subsequently assigned to the Kildare Priory, he was moved to Terenure College and Community in 1893 and he became an institution in himself, spending the rest of his days and some 53 years of his priestly life there.[20] Here he was professor of religious knowledge and had special responsibility for preparing students for Holy Communion and Confirmation. In that capacity he became one of the best known of the college Carmelites to generations of their students. Celebrating his golden jubilee in the college in October 1937, he passed away there on 22 January 1940.

The Terenure College of the 1870s may be distant in time, but it is remarkable that those days were remembered and briefly recorded by one of its earliest pupils. William Peakin first came, as a day-pupil to the college in the early 1870s, certainly by August 1873 and was joined there a year later by his brothers Patrick and Thomas, all now boarders. Their father conducted a victualler's business in Thomas Street in the city.[21] The Peakin boys had uncommonly long association with the college, as pupils. Although Thomas was no longer recorded after 1884, another brother Joseph had joined them by 1882: the boys were still boarding there to 1885 at least, even over at least one vacation, and Mr Peakin was still paying by instalments from December 1886 to November 1889.

Subsequent to his Terenure years, William ended up in Argentina. Writing from Buenos Aires in his eighty-fifth year, he penned the following brief reminiscences:

Reminiscences of TERENURE COLLEGE in the year 1873

By an old pupil.

It is a long way back, but the memories are very pleasant, and if my memory does not fail me I entered as student in the grand old college in the year 1873. I was a small boy, so small that I was instantly dubbed with the name of FIN MA COOL (the Irish Giant).

The property now of the college formerly [sic] belonged to SIR JAMES BOURNE [sic] a distinguished traveller and lover of nature, who never came back from his journeys without some novelty, which accounts for the magnificent collection of trees from various countreies [sic]. A fine cork tree (perhaps the only one in Ireland, a magnolia wallnut [sic] trees, mulberrys, a collection of cypreses [sic], splendid copper beeches with their great harvest of nuts, large shady chestnut trees with their beautiful flowers etc. The splendid little artificial lake with its island and teeming with fish. Not forgetting the stately mansion, a splendid example of arcitecture [sic].

In the time of Sir James an Italian arrived in the country and started the first mail coaches, and as the line passed by his gates he gave permission to Bianconi to tie up his horses in the grounds, in the wall of the playground remained the rings to which he tied his horses. In the seventies another Italian arrived who moulded little religious statues, carrying them round in a basket for sale. His name was Nannetti and I believe his son afterwards [became] Lord Mayor of Dublin. Speaking of mail coaches, later came the Blessington coach which passed the college gate, this was about the most unconfortable [sic] vehicle invented by man. After one trip the passenger knew exactly how many bones he had in his body; the coach had no springs and the roads were rather rudimentary. If Oliver Goldsmith had known Terenure he might have dedicated the first lines of his fine poem to it,

Sweet Auburn loveliest village of the plain
Where health and pleasure cheered the labouring swain
Where smiling Spring its earliest visit paid
And lingering summers parting blooms delayed …

The Rev. Prior of the college in those days was Father Farrington a splendid type of man. tall [*sic*] dakrk [*sic*] curly hair, dark complexion which perhaps may have come from Spanish ancestors. Then came the scholastic Donegan, Dunne, Hart, Mulholland etc. All these took Holy Orders … How I remember our walks round Templeogue, Kimmage etc. and some leader — usually me — sneaked out of the ranks to buy sweets or other contraband.

I would now like to look back to the games we played; hand ball [*sic*] predominated there was a spacious alley; football gave place to strong rivalries which were generally displayed after the rain when the ground had several pools and the main object was push your opponent head first into the water, this was taken as part of the game. Cricket was rather incipient, then came hurley which we played with clubs like grandfathers walking sticks. We also played a strange game originated by the Canadians LACROZE [*sic*] this we played with long bent sticks with a net of raw hide attached, and when one became proficient it was possible to throw the ball over 100 yards.

Regarding my fellow students I forget most of them, however there was Willie Flanagan (whose father was a town councillor) and I am sure young Flanagan shined in after life as he had a great gift of the gab, then Larry Kelly from the Argentine who took his title of medical doctor in Dublin, James Mooney from the town of Terenure. Amongst the day boys were the twin brothers Hoolihan who were so alike that Edward often paid for the sins of his brother and vice versa. If any of my old companions still exist I send them my heartiest congratulations. We got military drill given by a retired German officer who put us through right about face — eyes right etc. his English was rather guttural and caused many a laugh. Then we had John the bootblack, a great friend of the boys, who I believe afterwards joined the Popes' Army.

I will relate a small anecdote before concluding my not very literary lines. One afternoon in one of my various escapades in grounds of the college I discovered in the farmyard an old wooden pig trough and it instantly occurred to me to imitate the American Indians in their canoes. I launched the fragile bark on the placid waters of the lake and with [the aid] of a small plank as a paddle I reached the middle of the lake and in a false movement my bark turned over and I found myself at full length in two feet of water; reaching the shore like a shipwrecked sailor my next trouble was to get back to the college without being seen. I dodged behind trees wriggling along the ground here and there when suddenly I ran into the Reverend Prior, Father Farrington. 'Well Finn, you look like a drowned rat'; as we walked together I told him the tale — 'go and change your clothes and come and see me'. When I changed my clothes I put on two pairs of trousers in case of doubt and slowly walked to my doom. The Reverend Gentleman had on the table a glass of port wine and a piece of cake — now he said take that, and the next time you thing of taking a sea voyage take a canal boat. All is well that ends well.

WILLIAM J. PEAKIN
FINN MA COOL

Peakin led an adventurous and colourful life especially in the years after leaving college. In a subsequent letter to the Prior in 1952 he recounted some of this and added that while the Terenure boys of 1953 might read his 'vagaries' he hoped they would not imitate them — some hope:

> I was a boarder in the College for about a year. What I did when I left the College is a long story. Not married. Paid a short visit to Dublin in 1914.
>
> Now you give me a tough job to recount my peregrinations since I left Terenure, and I begin to think that Jack London the famous novelist must have followed in some of my tracks. However I will do my best in a condensed manner.
>
> When I left Terenure I was sent to the French (now Blackrock College). This College was founded by French Priests who had to leave France when the Germans took over Alsace and Lorraine. All very distinguished gentlemen. The Superior, Father Leman, was Doctor of Divinity and Doctor in Medicine, His assistant, Father Bottrel, was an accomplished musician and he was also a fine painter as might be seen by the Stations of the Cross which he painted in the College Chapel. I remained in Blackrock until the middle of '79. As a student I was not a shining light, dedicating myself more to games than books. I managed to secure a few cups in the Athletic Sports. In '79 I entered for the Intermediate Examinations Junior Grade, and when I got my block of writing paper I felt like the youth in the same predicament who wrote on his paper:
>
>> Take back this virgin page pure and unsullied still,
>> some hand more sage this page must fill.
>
> The results came out in the Newspapers, and to my complete astonishment I passed the Exam taking honors [sic] in Latin, The only reason I can give for this was that we had to study Caesar's Gallic War and the question to describe the Bridge over the Rhine for me fell like manna from heaven as during the term I had to [pay?] for some of my vagaries to write a description of the bridge 20 times so

it was absolutely printed on my memory. I knew every beam and nail in that bridge. That finished my studies [in] Blackrock.

With this I will conclude with my Scooldays [sic], and dive into my wanderings.

In the middle of the eighties the roving spirit overtook me and I embarked for the United States visiting Boston, New York, Philadephia [sic] and Brooklyn, in the latter I got a place with a wine merchant, wages were not mountainous but living was extremely cheap.

While in the States I met three Irish Champions Johnny Lawlor who had made a match with Alderman Casey of Brooklyn of 21 games, ten to be played in Cork and eleven in Brooklyn. Lawlor won the 10 games in Cork but in Brooklyn he had not a look in as Casey won the 11 games easily.

Peter Maher the Irish heavyweight boxer made a great show winning several fights [I?] assisted at one in Madison Square when he knocked two out in 30 seconds each match, later he had the misfortune to run up against Bob Fitzsimmons who wiped the floor with him. The other champion was Patsy kerrigan [sic], who was so appreciated by the Irish Community that they presented him with a set of pipes which cost over one thousand dollars.

A call from the paternal roof called me home again. However the spirit of roving got me again and in '89 I embarked for Buenos Aires. A short time after my arrival there a revolution broke out and when I saw a number of dead and dying in the streets I came to the conclusion that it was an unhealthy place so I left for Montevideo in the next Republic.

A few days later the English Consul asked me if I would like a sea trip. In a few days I was aboard the steamer JAMES WATT as supercargo of a load of two hundred mules, bound for Port Louis in the island of Mauritius in the Indian Ocean. I had 4 lusty helpers, and we arrived with good weather except off the Island of Tristan de Acunha [sic] where we nearly rolled over. Well the James Watt left me in Port Louis and went on her way to Australia. I spent a short time in Mauritius, during which i [sic] met a Mahoommedan money changer who spoke English extremely well; and I visited a mosque with himm [sic], I had to take off my boots and stockings and bathe my feet in the sacred pool. There were about 60 devotees on there [sic] knees with their foreheads touching the ground. I was in the temple about 15 minutes and not one moved to see who the stranger was, somewhat different to our congregations. One day in my walks round the town I met a tall youth in a military uniform, by his aspect ginger hair, face highly freckled. I accosted him he said 'yis I spake

English' with a strong Hibernian Accent [*sic*]. He was there with his regiment the Connauht [*sic*] Rangers, he invited me to the barracks and there we quaffed Guinness porter at two pennies per pint exactly the same as in Dublin, this by special order of Guinness. Another thing which drew my attention was the water cress, long stalks covered with leaves and tender as lettuce.

As few vessels touch Mauritius I took a passage on a British India Steamer bound for Calcutta. We touched at Colombo, Ceylon and duly arrived at our destination about 120 miles from the mouth of the Ganges. I passed some weeks in Calcutta, played in cricket matches, saw the English soldiers, Bengal Cavalry, Sikhs and the fierce little Gurkas. Funds running low I embarked before the mast in a fullrigged sailing ship the 'HEREFORD' bound for Port of Spain, Trinidad, WEST INDIES [*sic*]. We had as passengers some 500 Hindus, men women and children and a large cargo of rice.

After an uneventful voyage, touching only at Santa Helena for fresh water, we reached Trinidad, discharged the passengers, went north to the island of Guaduloupe [*sic*], unloaded the rice and back again to Trinidad to load PITCH [*sic*] in the inexhaustible lake, also 500 cases of Angostura Bitter, and left for Bremerhaven, Germany. From there I was glad to get home and have a rest. Not for long however as I was back in the Argentine in the beginning of the nineties.

Never losing his sense of humour, William concluded:

Very reverend Father you must excuse my delay in sending this. Autumn came in rather bruskily [*sic*] and I was laid up for sometime. In fact I felt like the old lady of whom thev [*sic*] poet wrote

'The bales groan the sideboards crack
old Bettys [*sic*] joints are on the wrack'.

With all the magnificent advances in Medical Science it is wonderful that no Doctor can oil our joints as the mechanic oils his machine.

Now to hasten things I send you a rigmarole of my wanderings until the beginning of the nineties. If you think it interesting I will send Chapter II , 'SI DIOS QUIERE'[*sic*].

I trust that if your boys read my vagaries, that they will not attempt to imitate them, as no matter how humble there is no place like home, and with dedication, work, patience and perseverance there is always a place in the old country to keep the home fires burning. With this I conclude my narrative and remain very respectfully

William J. Peakin[22]

Peakin provides a tantalisingly too brief picture of the games the students played in the 1870s. It is interesting that neither rugby nor tennis is mentioned but that cricket and a form of hurling are. It is curious too that he should have called the cricket in the place 'incipient': odd because it is the one game for which both the surviving internal and external records of the college for the 1860s and 1870s (and beyond) provide clear evidence. In the pupils' accounts for these decades, a recurrent charge is that for cricket or for cricket gear: throughout the 1870s various pupils were being charged 1s 6d for cricket — in what precise connection is not stated. The Manron brothers, Patrick and Richard from Spitafields in Dublin's Liberties, were billed a sizeable 6s in July 1881 for a 'cricket club' while Joseph Gallagher, in the same month, was charged 6s for 'cricket shoes' and exactly a year later some 10s 6d for 'cricket trousers'.[23] In the early 1880s there are a few records of pupils being charged a fee for a combination of football and cricket, as with the boarder James Carey, in June 1882, when he was billed 'football and cricket — 7s 6d' and before that, in February 1880, boarder James Healy of Great Brunswick Street, Dublin, was also being charged 7s 6d for 'football and cricket'.[24] For the period 1860–80 there are few press reports in relation to competitive sports engagements between Terenure and other colleges or outside bodies. Such few as there are invariably are accounts of cricket matches. Typical is this report from May 1871:

TERENURE COLLEGE (PAST AND PRESENT) v.

FRENCH COLLEGE, BLACKROCK

This match came off on the College ground, Merrion, and resulted in a victory for the home club by 27 runs on the first innings. High figures were scarce, the bowling of Howard and Molony for Terenure, and Taaffe and Cahill for Blackrock, being too good for long scoring. For the visitors Howard got 5 wickets and Molony 3. For French College Taaffe obtained 7 wickets, Cahill an equal number, Ryan 4, and Magrath 2.[25]

Whatever the boys may have got up to in terms of sports there is no question that the college was well known and respected in the 1870s. Its annual prize days were attracting great numbers of parents and friends as well as some very estimable people. One register entry records, 'The summer vacation commenced on 13 July 1871. His Eminence Cardinal Cullen presided at the Examinations'.[26]

Then there was the following press report from the summer of 1874 when the annual prize day was attended by, among others, Dr Bartholomew Woodlock, then rector of the Catholic University, and Very Rev. Dr Michael O'Connor, Bishop of Ballarat: a Dubliner, ordained in 1854 by Paul Cullen, he had just become bishop of this newly formed diocese in 1874 and whose St Patrick's Church was to be the first Catholic cathedral consecrated in Australia:

TERENURE COLLEGE

The annual academic exercises at this excellent institution, so admirably conducted by the Carmelite fathers, under the presidency of the Very Rev Mr Farrington, DD, came off yesterday in the presence of a very large and fashionable audience.

It is now fifteen years since the college and extensive grounds came into the hands of the Order, and session after session the pupils have distinguished themselves in a marked degree. The numerous visitors yesterday were agreeably surprised at the successful efforts of the boys, and Mr J J Johnston, the music master, has every reason to congratulate himself on the effectiveness of his tuitions. The declamation was singularly good. Masters O'Connell and Byrne acquitted themselves most creditably, and well deserved the plaudits of the audience.

The visitors numbered 300. Amongst those present were Most Rev Dr O'Connor, Bishop of Auckland; Rev Monsignor Woodlock, Rector, CA; Rev Thomas Burke, O P; Very Rev Father Towers; Very Rev Mr Hall; Very Rev Mr Hall, Very Rev Henry Magee, Rev Mr Hanley, C C; Rev Mr Walshe, Very Rev Dr McDonald, Prince Edward's Island, America; Dr O'Leary, M P; Captain Byrne, Dr Dywer, Mr R M Levey, Mr Fleming, Mr Stapleton, Rev Mr Maher, O S F; Rev Mr Gilligan, Rev Mr Moore. An excellent *dejeuner* was provided for the visitors.[27]

Three years later with their new hall brightly decorated with banners and flowers a considerable assembly gathered to be entertained by a concert of music from the college band, trained and conducted by Messrs Johnson and Tighe, and of singing by the college choir. Dramatic presentations of scenes from *The Merchant of Venice* and *Julius Caesar* followed and then the prize giving ceremony in which the prizes were presented by the Lord Mayor. Thereafter, strolling through the grounds and premises, parents and friends numbered several hundred. One commentator concluded 'at no previous period has the College been in so flourishing and successful a condition'.[28]

Entering his final year as president over 1877–8, Andrew Farrington left to his successors a considerable legacy of achievement, promise and — as will emerge later — of difficulty.

Joseph Vincent Butler, *c.* 1880.

72

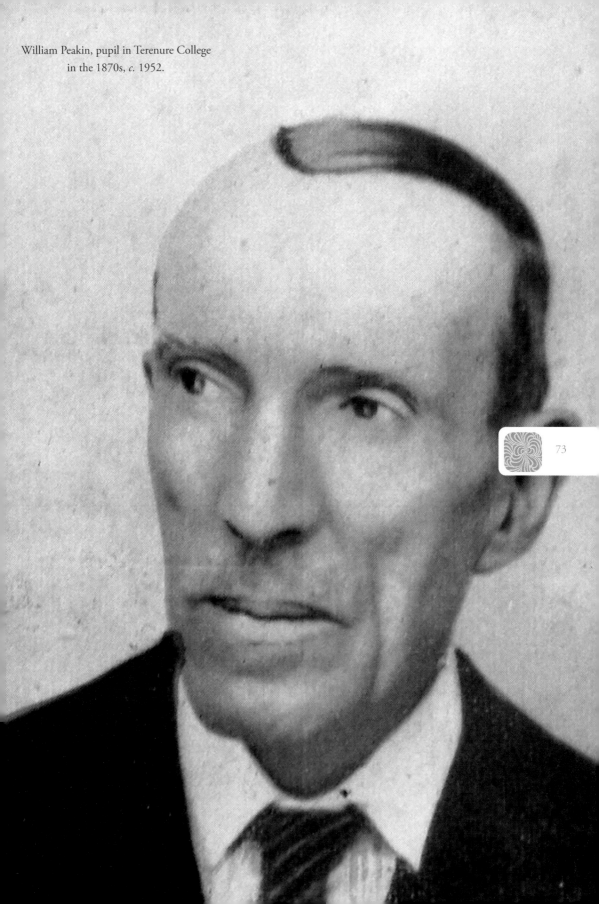

William Peakin, pupil in Terenure College
in the 1870s, *c.* 1952.

73

74

Terenure College concert room and gymnasium, *c.* 1920.

'The Irish Invincibles and their Friends', *Belfast Weekly Post*, 21 April 1883. Courtesy of the National Library of Ireland.

THE IRISH INVINCIBLES AND THEIR FRIENDS.

P. EGAN.

J. FITZHARRIS.
"SKIN THE GOAT"

P. TYNAN.
"NUMBER ONE"

P. J. SHERIDAN.

JAMES CAREY, T.C.

PRESENTED GRATIS WITH "THE BELFAST WEEKLY POST."
. 21ˢᵗ April, 1883.

75

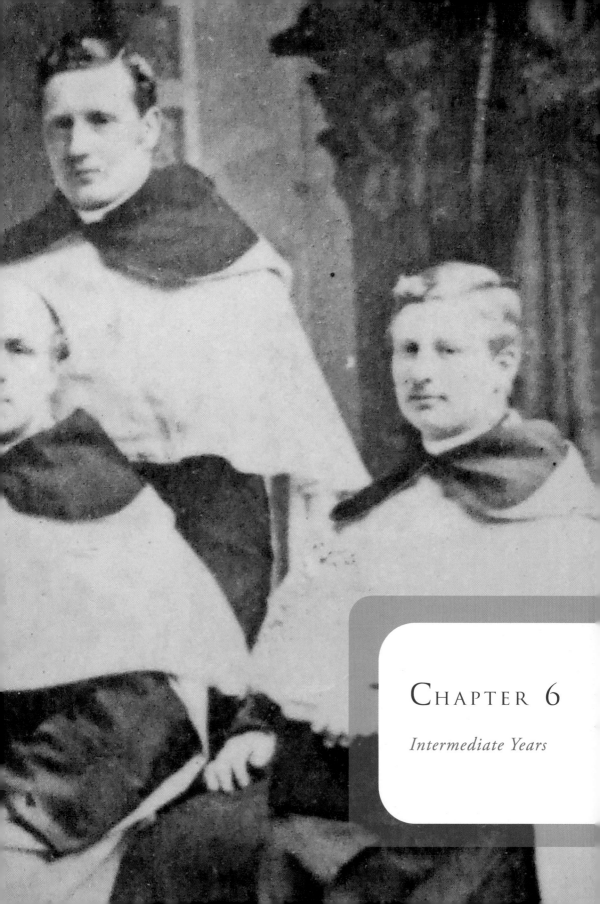

CHAPTER 6

Intermediate Years

John Simon Carr, J.V. Butler, John Leybourne, Hilarion Byrne and Patrick Shaffrey — the Australian Mission quintet, *c.* 1880.

WHEN ANDREW FARRINGTON CEASED TO BE PRESIDENT OF TERENURE IN 1878, he seems to have been succeeded for a short time by Fr John Elias Bartley: although not named as such in any other extant source, he appears as president in an advertisement for the college, which was published in the *Catholic Directory* for the year 1878.[1] A Kildare-man, then 46, he had joined the Order in 1853; ordained three years later, he was made Prior of Kildare in 1864 and was elected Provincial in 1875. Described by John Carr as a good man 'but was lazy and inactive as Provincial',[2] and, whether unfounded or well-founded, he was, unusually, re-elected Provincial in 1884 and again in 1887 to 1891; subsequently being re-elected Prior of Kildare in 1895. However, of his work in Terenure nothing extant is documented. The succession of Michael Aloysius Moore to the presidency, also in 1878, brought in another Kildare-man, five years junior to Bartley. He already had school management experience as vice-president of the Dominick Street Academy from early February 1872 and was appointed Prior of Whitefriar Street by Bartley — as Provincial — in 1875. In the same year as he became president of Terenure, he was elected head of the Irish Province and so held an arduous dual mandate. In that year of 1878, too, he had the gratification of admitting eight young Carmelites to solemn profession, among them two future presidents of the college, Michael Avertanus O'Reilly and Thomas Patrick Kelly. Moore was deeply committed to education at all levels — concerned to ensure well-educated Carmelites for the college and the Province — he was hardly in office when he arranged for Thomas John of the Cross Doyle — a talented musician and later choir master at Whitefriar Street — and Joseph Vincent Butler, the 'Orator', to be sent to Rome for further studies. At Terenure from 1878 to 1881, he became deeply engaged in the promotion and supervision of the pupils' and novices' studies. He was himself, first educated at the famous school attached to the Carmelite friary in Kildare which produced a cohort of significant Carmelites — the Bartley brothers: John Elias and Thomas Stanislaus; the Cullens: Eugene and Felix John; Tom Kelly; John Dunne; and James Daly — his passion for education was natural and his presidency concluded with an important development in education when the government at last provided a form of financial support to secondary, or, as it was then sometimes called, 'superior' education.

Before turning to that development it may be appropriate to mention here some other features of Moore's career. During his Provincialship, he was planning to establish a school in Kinsale. Under pressure of finite resources, he had to resist the requests of the Archbishop of Dublin, later Cardinal, Edward McCabe, to send out three Irish Province Carmelites to India and to take over responsibility for a college in Trinidad. However an appeal for help to establish a Carmelite mission in Australia was entertained. That appeal had been made by Dr Christopher Augustine Reynolds, fourth bishop of Adelaide. A Dubliner himself, on a visit to Rome in 1880, Reynolds sought out the Carmelite General, Savini, with an appeal that Savini establish such a mission. The Carmelite General referred him to Whitefriar Street. As it happened, a member of the Community there was Terenure's first president, Michael Gilligan who had been a boyhood friend of Reynolds, and Gilligan, introducing him to Moore, the appeal received a positive response. The result was the initiation of the Irish Carmelite mission in Australia.

THE AUSTRALIAN MISSION

Early in 1881, Moore, as Provincial, sent out five Irish Carmelites to Adelaide, to found the Community in the parish of Gawler. They were led by 37-year-old year Joseph V. Butler, as Superior. Then there was Ignatius Carr, Irish speaking scholar and theologian, described by one source as 'a solid, religious, prudent man'.[3] Ignatius, born in 1834, was brother of John Carr though eighteen years his junior. He had been the last of the Irish Carmelites on the Welsh mission in Merthyr Tydfil, before it closed down.[4] He became Commissary General for Australia in 1898, and, returning to Ireland was, under self-protest and diffidence, elected Prior of Knocktopher in 1909, in his late 70s; he held the post until August 1913 and died there in 1914. The third of the group was Patrick Shaffrey, one of the earliest of the Terenure novices in 1873. He was solemnly professed in 1878 and became both an impressive speaker and moral theologian. He was to spend ten years on the Australian mission before returning to Ireland.

Another was Moses Hilarion Byrne, urbane and talented in secular and sacred music; born in Naas, Co. Kildare, in 1853 he died on 14 October 1906. He had received the habit in Terenure in 1873, was solemnly professed on the 16 July 1878, and was less than three months a priest when he set out on this mission. Finally there was John Brocard Leybourne, a 43-year-old Dubliner who had joined the Order in September 1858 and was ordained in Maynooth on St Patrick's Day, 1864. A talented speaker and a literary man involved in translating French spiritual works, he was attached to Whitefriar Street from the mid-1860s until his departure for Australia. He was back in Ireland by 1887 and became Master of Novices from 1898 to 1900 and Sub-Prior in Terenure. It was not a happy time for him there as he did not get on well with his Prior, Richard Colfer, who, he complained, treated him rudely and failed to let him fulfil his Sub-Prior duties. He consequently resigned his office in Terenure and returned to Whitefriar Street.[5] Suffering from heart trouble in later years, he died suddenly in August 1911 at the Maryborough home of his friend, the Parliamentary Party MP, P.A. Meehan, where he was taking a recuperative break.[6]

These five left Dublin on 25 February 1881 and arrived at Port Adelaide on Holy Saturday, 16 April. The next day, Fr Butler preached the first Irish Carmelite sermon in Australia in their new parish of Gawler, 25 miles north-west of Adelaide. They arrived there with £2 between them and lived in a four-roomed cottage. The adjoining garden was a large one with vines and orange, lemon and fig trees. Within a few months they managed to extend their dwelling with the addition of three bedrooms, bathrooms and a refectory. Subsequent purchases gave them a complete quadrangular establishment with the church at the centre of the square known as Parnell Square. Their parish community consisted largely of labouring people — many Irish Catholics of Co. Clare extraction — who worked in the iron and flour mills of Gawler. The mission soon expanded with a new school and convent by 1883 and a new church in neighbouring Mallala in the same year under Hilarion Byrne. In addition, in April 1852, J.V. Butler and Patrick Shaffrey went on to found a new Carmelite house in Melbourne. Among the priests and Priors who worked at Gawler in the twenty years from 1882 were a number of men who feature in Terenure College history: T.P. Kelly, Prior of Gawler from April 1882, was to be president and Prior of Terenure from 1905 to 1906; James Cogan who was college president from 1909 to 1913 and again in 1916; and Michael O'Reilly, president from 1891 to 1899. Fr Cogan arrived in 1900 and became first Prior of Semaphore Parish — a huge parish including Port Adelaide. As for the mission in Melbourne, one Terenure pupil to be encountered later, F.X. Ronayne, became Prior there in 1919 before being appointed Assistant General from 1920–3 and was succeeded as Melbourne Prior by another Terenure man, Peter Elias O'Dwyer who laboured in the Australian Mission until returning to Ireland in 1932.

THE INTERMEDIATE

The origination of the Australian Mission came at a time of strained resources and changing times back home in Ireland. When Michael Moore became Terenure president and Carmelite Provincial in 1878 an important milestone was reached in the history of Irish education when the Intermediate Education Act was passed. This gave some state finance to the sector for the first time. Based on a similar precedent in Trinidad, it introduced a state competitive examinations system involving payments to school managers dependent on the results. Widely welcomed at the outset, it eventually invited serious criticism for encouraging a culture of cramming and rote-learning. Nevertheless, for the first time it gave significant encouragement for the expansion of access to education.

The first examinations were held in 1879 and Terenure College became, from the outset, an official examination centre. Despite Catholic fears that with their limited school resources and endowments they would fare badly in contrast to their Protestant counterparts, the results brought surprise, even to the Education Commissioners, with a few of the top Catholic boarding schools excelling in their results and in the numbers of their prizes and exhibitions won. Three Catholic and three Protestant institutions shared the first six places out of the total participant schools, with Blackrock College heading the list with 48, followed by St Stanislaus, Tullabeg, with 40, then the Royal School Armagh with 28, the Royal Academical in Belfast with 26, St Vincent's Castleknock and the Academical Institution, Coleraine with 23 each.

Over the next two decades the numbers presenting for the examinations were as follows:[7]

TABLE 3: NUMBERS OF STUDENTS PRESENTING FOR STATE EXAMINATIONS, 1879–90

Year	Boys	Girls	Total
1879	3,218	736	3,954
1880	4,114	1,447	5,561
1881	5,147	1,805	6,952
1882	5,153	1,461	6,614
1883	5,037	1,125	6,162
1884	4,143	1,001	5,501
1885	4,123	1,058	5,181
1886	4,343	1,199	5,542
1887	4,613	1,318	5,931
1888	4,551	1,507	6,058
1889	4,838	1,695	6,533
1890	3,913	1,293	5,236

How many Terenure students took these examinations is not always clear either from its own or government sources but from 1880 there are some figures for the numbers sitting the examinations in the college as an examination centre: perhaps it is reasonable enough to assume that the vast majority, if not all, of these were students of the college, although it is clear from the following advertisement in the national press in June 1880, that others were invited to take their examinations there:

> Carmelite College, Terenure
> Intermediate Examinations
>
> Students from Rathgar, Rathmines etc, who have selected Terenure College for their centre, will kindly forward name and address to the Very Rev. President, in order to have a suitable place assigned them in the Intermediate Examination Hall of the College.[8]

From 1880 to 1884 the number sitting state examinations in the college were:[9]

TABLE 4: NUMBERS OF STUDENTS AT TERENURE COLLEGE PRESENTING FOR STATE EXAMINATIONS, 1880–4

Year	Junior	Middle	Senior	Total
1880	24	13	0	37
1881	42	5	1	48
1882	45	7	1	53
1883	36	4	1	41
1884	26	0	0	26

For the examinations of 1885, Terenure ceased to appear as an examination centre and consequently it is unclear how many may have presented. The same holds for the next year, and it may well be that Terenure students began to sit their Intermediate Examinations in another location, very possibly at the Royal University centre where the number of candidates presenting suddenly rose from 249 in 1884 to 278 in 1886. Another possibility is that the Terenure boys may have taken their examinations in the Carmelite Dominick Street Academy: in 1887, it was recorded for the first time as an official examination centre and some 41 candidates took their examinations there in that year: this on the one hand, seems a high number for the Academy; on the other, however, Dominick Street would have been a relatively long-distant centre for Terenure students. However, from 1888 to 1909, Terenure was again continuously listed as a centre, ceasing to be so thereafter. Unfortunately, the official reports from the Commissioners for Intermediate Education from 1888 no longer indicate the numbers of candidates presenting from each institution.

What there is, instead, is the record of the sums paid to the various participating schools and colleges in terms of payments for passes or to their individual scholars in terms of prizes or exhibitions. As regards prizes and exhibitions from the start of the 1880s, Terenure had its share of successful candidates: not many in number perhaps but some of them to feature significantly in future life whether for Terenure, the Carmelites or the country. Their distinctive accomplishments in subsequent life will be considered later; here it suffices to name them by year:[10]

1880:	John McNerney
1881:	McNerney, Dillon Cosgrave and Thomas J. Lenehan
1882:	McNerney and Lenehan
1883:	McNerney and James J. Furlong
1884:	Francis C. Lenihan
1885:	–
1886:	John J. Cosgrave
1887:	John J. Cosgrave
1888:	Charles J. Gavin
1889:	William Gavin and W.J. Walsh
1890	James J. Reynolds, James Cogan, Charles Gavin and Walter J. Walsh
1891:	James Cogan
1892:	William A. Walsh, Patrick J.M. O'Reilly
1893:	–
1894:	–
1895:	–
1896:	Louis J. Walsh and David F. Conway
1897:	Louis J. Walsh and David F. Conway
1898, 1899, 1900:	–
1901:	John S. Maxwell, Thomas Kavanagh, Richard J. Fitzsimons

From 1902, the publication of the names of prize winners was discontinued. From 1905, the national press published lists of institutions and the numbers of awards they received. More often than not the Christian Brothers O'Connell Schools on North Richmond Street, Dublin, topped the list or featured in the top three:[11]

TABLE 5: AWARDS RECEIVED BY STUDENTS IN THE SCHOOLS LISTED, 1905–09

School	1905	1906	1907	1908	1909
O'Connell	18	53	37	49	40
CBS Cork	15	34	39	32	57
Clongowes Wood	11	33	43	41	47
St Andrew's	8	33	18	21	14
Royal Academical Belfast	7	27	25	43	30

In none of the years listed above did Terenure feature in the lists. Even in the years 1880 to 1901 their winners, though distinguished, were few and far between. In what for Terenure was a 'good' year, 1890, it had only 4 prize winners compared with Blackrock's 25 and Clongowes 55. A question arises whether the college was in fact putting forward few or many of its students as examination candidates at all, and if more than just a few, were they failing to secure passes. We have seen the figures of candidates in Terenure rising from 37 in 1880 to a peak of 53 in 1882 and then falling to 26 in 1884 when the college ceased to be recorded as a discrete examination centre until 1887 and how from 1888 the numbers presenting were not issued to or by the press.

However, from 1886 to 1894 inclusive, the Commissioners provided lists of schools whose managers were paid fees based on results from candidates who passed, and indicated the numbers of those passing and the sums they brought for their school managers: for Terenure College the numbers and sums were as follows:[12]

TABLE 6: DETAILS OF STUDENTS PASSING AND SUMS BROUGHT
FOR THEIR SCHOOL MANAGERS, 1886–94

Year	Students Passing	Amount to Nearest Pound
1886	3	£14
1887	8	£36
1888	9	£34
1889	10	£35
1890	8	£34
1891	5	£27
1892	13	£92
1893	7	£32
1894	6	£60

From 1895, the number of students who passed was no longer published, only the amount a given school received. For Terenure to 1905 these amounts were:

TABLE 7: SUMS BROUGHT IN BY TERENURE STUDENTS
PASSING FOR THEIR SCHOOL MANAGERS, 1895–1905

Year	Amount
1895	£61
1896	£123
1897	£99
1898	£98
1899	£14
1900	£22
1901	£114
1902	£76
1903	£167
1904	£107
1905	£46

Then, from 1906 to 1908 the numbers of boys on the roll, and the amounts their schools received were provided:

TABLE 8: NUMBER OF STUDENTS ON THE ROLL IN TERNURE COLLEGE
AND SUMS BROUGHT IN, 1906–08

Year	No. on Roll	Amount
1906	30	£34
1907	50	£76
1908	67	£81

Finally in 1909, the numbers presenting and passing were given, in addition to the numbers on the roll and the amount; for Terenure the figures were:

TABLE 9: NUMBERS OF TERENURE STUDENTS ON THE ROLL,
PRESENTING AND PASSING, 1909

Year	No. on Roll	No. Presenting	No. Passing	Amount
1909	73	38	6	£35

The contrast between Terenure and certain other schools and colleges could hardly be greater. In 1886 when Terenure College recorded 3 students and received £13 14s, Blackrock College had also 3 students and received £8 18s, Castleknock with 25 students received £126 and O'Connell Schools with 103 students passing earned £293 18s 6d. Blackrock's passing numbers took off from 65 students earning £297 in 1887, and maintained numbers of this order thereafter. O'Connell Schools continued to dominate annually: 1887 showing 93 passes and £281, 1888 some 120 passes and £282, in 1905 it brought in £2,279 against Terenure's £46, in 1906 some £2,212 against Terenure's £33 and in 1908 some £1,752 against Terenure's £81.[13]

It is clear that whatever Terenure may have been over 1880 to 1909, a grind school it certainly was not. Although the different categories of all these statistics can make informed estimations hazardous, no consistent pattern seems to emerge in the numbers of students that the college was attracting or admitting over the years 1880 to 1909. There is one internal source which records the numbers taking house examinations over the years 1884 to 1891 and these are as follows:[14]

TABLE 10: NUMBER OF TERENURE COLLEGE
STUDENTS TAKING HOUSE EXAMINATIONS, 1884–91

Year	No. taking house examinations
1884	50
1885	Not recorded
1886	54
1887	57
1888	45
1889	52
1890	57
1891	45

If it may be safely assumed that the vast majority of the college's students sat for these house examinations then all that can be ventured is that total enrolments rose and fell over a small range of close on 45 minimum and 57 maximum from the early 1880s to the early 1890s, and, allowing for ambiguities or uncertainties in the surviving sources, that they may have reached a new low point of 30 in 1906 and a new high of 73 in 1909.

T.P. Kelly, Patrick Shaffrey and Michael Moore, *c*, 1870.

CHAPTER 7

Staff and Students
of the 1880s

WHATEVER THE TRUTH ABOUT ITS NUMBERS THE COLLEGE CONTINUED TO attract students from near and far and to enrol some of exceptional ability who would make important contributions to college, community and country in the decades ahead. Before recalling some of these it may be appropriate here to mention Moore's immediate successors as presidents of the college, namely Philip Paul McDonnell and Edward Patrick Southwell.

Fr McDonnell, from Garristown, north Co. Dublin, was ordained in 1863 on the same day as Michael Moore. He was Prior of Moate from 1863 to 1881, and, according to Spratt, was 'a very zealous and hard-working man': highly regarded by the local bishop, clergy and people of Moate, he had a new church built there in the 1860s and a new monastery for his Community in the course of 1870. He was renamed Prior there in 1878 and in 1881 he set out for Argentina to raise funds — presumably from its Irish settlers — and collected £10,000 to help clear the Irish Province's debts. Later on, he was one of four Carmelites who set out for America to set up their foundation Community in New York where he was appointed Bursar in September 1889. He returned to Moate where he passed away on St Patrick's Day, 1902.[1]

With McDonnell on that fund-raising trip to South America was Edward Patrick Southwell who held the Terenure College presidency from 1883 to 1885 in direct succession to McDonnell. A Kildare-man, he was 42 when appointed president. Before that he had been Prior of Kinsale from 1881 where he had been responsible for the opening of St Mary's Intermediate School the previous year. Subsequent to his term in charge of Terenure, he was one of the pioneering four Irish Carmelites who, as noted above, left to found their Community in New York in 1889 where he was elected Vicar Prior. In 1895, the Chapter elected him Prior in New York and he was re-elected to this position in 1903. An extremely hard-working man, he was appointed Prior of the new Dublin house of studies, 'Ardavon', from 1908 to 1909 and was elected Provincial in 1909, serving in that post until 1913. He then was re-elected New York Prior from 1913 to 1919 and died in Tarrytown, New York, on 11 May 1922.

The commitment of Moore and McDonnell to the new environment created by the Intermediate Education Act is evident in a publication produced by the Terenure College in these years. This was *The Annual Record* which was produced as a 30-page booklet-cum-prospectus for the years 1881–2 and 1882–3. There may have been issues published before 1881 and after 1883 but if so they are no longer extant. Much praised by the national and provincial press of the time, the *Annual* was remarkable for the detailed manner in which it supplied the exact results of its examination candidates in their various subjects. Before turning to this, it is timely to mention also the insight the *Annual Records* provide into staffing at the college at the beginning of the 1880s.

The *Record* for 1881–2 showed the college headed by four officials, as follows:

President — Very Rev. Paul McDonnell O.C.
Vice President — Rev. P.T. Donegan, B.A. O.C.
Dean of Studies — Rev. J.P. Reilly O.C.

Spiritual Director — Rev. J.P. Wheatley O.C.

P.T. Donegan, received into the Order in 1873, taught English and Classics in the college from 1881 to 1884: in the following year he became president of Dominick Street Academy: here, he was described, somewhat unkindly, by J.F. Byrne who was enrolled there in 1888, as 'a little nondescript man chiefly distinguished by being Chaplain to the Lord Mayor of Dublin'.[2] True or not, Donegan was discerning enough to assess his new pupil's abilities and promote him to a class higher than warranted by his years. Fr Donegan's own career thereafter was far from undistinguished, becoming Prior at Knocktopher in 1895 and Assistant General for the Order in 1906. Later, he went to Kinsale but, suffering greatly from cancer of the mouth, he ended his days at Terenure where he passed away on 29 January 1916.

The Dean of Studies John Stanislaus O'Reilly, in addition to teaching English, also taught drawing and elocution. He was then 25 years of age. Finally, among these college officers was Spiritual Director John Peter Wheatley (sometimes Whately). A Dubliner, born in 1836 and ordained in 1864, he had been appointed Master of Novices at Terenure in 1876 and held that post until 1885 when his request to be allowed to relinquish it was acceded to by the Chapter of that year. He was reassigned to Whitefriar Street where he had charge of the altar boys. One of these, the already mentioned J.F. Byrne, in later life recalled Wheatley as 'a holy little man … pale, thin, wrinkled and dyspeptic'. Byrne added that he generally 'appeared sad' but on occasion could be joyous, especially when any of the altar boys would be received into the Order. In Byrne's recollection, such occasions were not all that infrequent: four of his own altar boy pals became novices within the space of five years, the brothers Denis and Hugh Devlin, Bob Power and Paddy Wade. Their interweaving lives brought them in and out of Terenure and Carmelite history over the next several decades.

Denis, born in Dublin in 1873, joined the Carmelites in August 1892, taking the name Berchmans. He was ordained in Rome in June 1900. Having been a novice in Terenure he became Master of Novices from 1902–03. His younger brother, Hugh, followed him into the Order in March 1895, graduated from the Royal University in 1902 and taking the name Dominic, spent his life there until he passed away on New Year's Day, 1953.[3] As for Denis, by 1912 he was a member of the Community in Port Adelaide at the very time when his fellow Whitefriar Street altar boy, Bob Francis Power, was Prior there. A year later, Denis was attached to the Carmelite friary at Albert Park, Melbourne, before coming back to Ireland as Prior of Terenure from 1913–14. By 1915, he was back at Whitefriar Street where in 1916 he was involved in providing moral support and spiritual counsel to the insurgents holding out in that area. At the Irish Provincial Chapter of that same year and in contrasting geographies, Denis was elected Prior of Port Adelaide while the Australian Carmelite and former Terenure College pupil, Michael Louis Gerhard, was elected Prior of Terenure — a post he held until 1922. However, Devlin's plea to decline the post was granted and ironically, his old pal Bob Power was appointed again to the Priorship of Port Adelaide in his place. Three years later, in another ironic re-link to their boyhoods; Devlin was elected Prior of Whitefriar Street while his fellow altar boy Paddy Ambrose Wade became his Sub-Prior. While Denis had been Prior of Terenure in 1913, exactly ten years later, Paddy Wade became its Prior, and, like Devlin, held the post for just a year. Devlin went on to become Irish Provincial from 1929 to 1934 and at the very Chapter that elected him he himself opened an important discussion on the future of the college — a discussion which will be referred to later in this work. As for Bob Power, 'a truly splendid fellow' according to Byrne who gives a graphic description of Bob's entry into the Carmelites at Terenure College in the summer of 1894, he spent his priestly life in Australia on being appointed Prior of Port Adelaide from at least 1912, and was reappointed until 1919 when he transferred as Prior to Middle Park, Melbourne, becoming Pro-Provincial of Australia in 1925 and again in 1929. He was remembered as a Newman-like figure in his sensitivity and magnanimity and when he died in May 1933 he left a gaping hole in the mission and in the hearts of young Australian and old Irish confreres alike.[4]

As for the fourth of the group, Paddy Wade, born in Dublin in 1880, he was received into the Order in March 1897 and although not ordained until 1905, he is described as a professor in Terenure College in the census of 1901. After ordination, he was assigned to the New York house on East 29th Street, Manhattan, until 1913. In 1914, he transferred to Albert Park, Melbourne, until 1919. A year later, he was back home in Whitefriar Street where he was Sub-Prior until 1923 in which year he became Prior of Terenure.[5] He was listed in this capacity up to 1925 in which year he became Prior of Knocktopher.[6] By 1932, he was back in Whitefriar Street, but in 1933 was again in Knocktopher where he passed away on 7 December of that year.

So much for just four of Wheatley's altar-boy vocations: subsequent to these Whitefriar Street years, Wheatley was elected Prior of Moate over 1898 to 1909 and again from 1913 to 1919. He does not appear to have been engaged in formal classroom teaching during his Terenure days in the 1880s. Carmelite historian O'Dwyer characterised him as 'a deeply spiritual' and hard-working man of 'somewhat narrow views and judgements'. For all that, were he to be remembered for one thing only, it surely would be that it was he who recruited for the Order — during a mission in Belfast — its future and first ever Irish General, Peter Magennis; an achievement at once historic for the Order and disastrous for Terenure College as a secondary school. This is a matter for later. In the meantime, in the historic Chapter of 1909, Wheatley was elected Sub-Prior of Terenure and Master of the Professed there: and, it was in Terenure that he spent his final days, passing away there on 4 August 1919.

These college office-holders apart, in 1881–2 there were five other Carmelite priests on the teaching staff and one priest from outside the Order : the Carmelites were J.B. Hart, J.P. Cowley, S. Mulholland, J.J. Dunne and A. Greaven. The non-Carmelite was M. L'Abbé Polin. Joseph Berthold Hart had been admitted to solemn profession in the college by Moore in 1878. Never in great health, he taught English and mathematics in the college until 1884 when he was located in Whitefriar Street for the next ten years: thereafter he spent time in the New York friary but went out on the Australian Mission in 1894 until his death in 1909 at the age of 52.

His Terenure confrere, Joseph Cowley, had been a Terenure pupil of the Royal University in 1882, taught English, maths and Classics in the college. Like Joseph Hart, Cowley suffered poor health. Despite this, he also spent years working on the Australian mission before being appointed Assistant to the General, Pius Maria Mayer, in Rome in 1902. His ill health forced his resignation from the post in 1905, to be succeeded by his Terenure College confrere, P.T. Donegan, and Fr Cowley died four years later on 17 February 1909. John J. Dunne, a Kildare man born in 1859, professed in 1880, and matriculating in 1881,[7] taking Greek as his special option, was science master to the pupils in the 1880s and also taught Greek, maths and religion to the clerical students there. He did a great amount to build up first-class laboratories in the college and was deeply disappointed at being transferred to Moate in 1909. He died aged 60 in March 1919.

Also teaching science with him at the start of the 1880s was Fr Stephen Mulholland who, like Cowley, had been a Terenure student of the Royal University in 1882, and who later, in 1886, left for Gawler in Australia. Finally among these Carmelite teachers was Fr Alfred Leo Greaven, another Terenure College Royal University student who had joined the Order in Terenure in 1878 and soon found himself teaching Classics to the juniors. In the late 1880s, he was sent to Rome for further study, though in yet another case, ill health forced his premature return to Ireland, and by 1896 he was located in Knocktopher.

As for the non-Carmelite L'Abbé Polin: he was one of the college's two modern languages professors, in his case teaching French and German. George Polin came from Alsace to Ireland around the year 1870 when that territory was annexed by Germany in the course of the Franco–Prussian War. Gifted in languages, he was on the staff of Blackrock College from at least 1875, in which year he is listed in its prospectus as teaching French and German. He was connected with the Catholic University at Stephen's Green, from soon after his arrival and, apart from teaching in Terenure College, he was elected to a lectureship in modern languages in UCD in May 1884 and was a Fellow of the Royal University up until his death in Harold's Cross Hospice on 29 July 1889.[8] In regard to lay teachers, there were four at the time: J.R. Leahey for Piano and Singing, J.H. Lowe in charge of orchestra, Professor Burke for dancing. Finally, for Italian there was Signor Francesco Morisini. Like L'Abbé Polin, Morisini taught on the staff at Blackrock College. A former pupil of the college with impeccable Roman connections, Morisini was apparently a close relative of Pope Pius IX.[9] These apart, the college in 1881 had the services of a matron — unnamed — a dentist, M.J. Bloom, and a medical officer, Surgeon O'Dwyer. By 1882, the college had employed another lay teacher for French and English, Richard Cassan Greer, who also prepared senior students for the Royal University classes. As a Terenure pupil, he became a high-achieving undergraduate of the Royal University; taking his matriculation, he won an exhibition and by 1882–3 had passed his first arts degree with honours in Latin, English, French and natural philosophy. Eldest son of District Inspector of National Schools, James William Greer, MA of Tuam, before the decade was out Richard had married Mary, sister of William Peakin, the Terenure pupil whose reminiscences featured earlier in this work.

These *Annual Records* of the early 1880s presented the college in a positive light and there was much to be positive about. In 1882–3 it became a constituent college of the Catholic University.[10] Reviewing the results in the Intermediate Examinations over the years 1879, 1880 and 1881 the college was proud that the numbers securing success and the quality of those successes were growing. It was reported that for 1879 the numbers presenting were 15, with 3 overall passes, 8 passes in particular subjects and 2 obtaining prizes. In 1880, 19 candidates presented, 9 obtained overall passes, 8 secured passes in particular subjects and 1 secured an exhibition of £20 for three years. In 1881, the numbers presenting had risen to 30, consisting of 25 for Junior Grade, 4 for Middle Grade and 1 for Senior Grade. Of the 25 juniors, 15 passed in 3 or more subjects and 6 others in 1 or more subjects; in Middle Grade, all 4 passed in 3 or more subjects; and in the Senior Grade the candidate passed with honours in two subjects.[11]

Reviewing these results leads to a consideration of some of the students themselves who sat for these examinations or who may have shone in other respects. Among the juniors of 1881 was Patrick Manron, one of the two brothers of Spitalfields who had come to the college from Newbridge in August 1879 and whose father Patrick ran a local bacon and butter business in the Coombe. Another was Thomas Cosgrave from North Circular Road, a boarder along with his brother Jonathan who came in October 1880. Thomas was something of a star pupil, topping the Terenure Intermediate results of 1881 with passes in all seven subjects in which he presented, securing honours in three, he left the college at the end of the following year.

One who had a much longer stay in the college as a pupil was Laurence (Larry) Kelly from Suipacha, Buenos Aires. Larry arrived in April 1880. Undoubtedly he had been recruited during the visit to Argentina by Frs McDonnell and Southwell who had advertised Terenure College in the Buenos Aires press before they left Argentina for Ireland on 7 March 1880.[12] Laurence took his intermediate in 1881 with passes in three subjects: and if that was hardly exceptional, in the following year in the house examinations he excelled — winning a silver medal, second place, for 'exemplary conduct' and a prize in the senior classes for one of the highest percentages obtained in the house's general examinations.[13] Larry's parents or guardians saw to it that he was well cared for — apart from his annual boarding fee of £31 10s he was charged 6s for 'extra lunch', 4s 6d for eggs and 4s and sixpence for 'porter'. (Porter was often served to pupils in boarding schools at that time as a safer, cleaner alternative to water although there is no evidence or suggestion that there was then anything wrong with the waters of Terenure.) Such charges recur during the length of his stay and are joined by others such as his Intermediate fee of 2s 6d and large enough sums of 7s 6d and 15s, all for photographs. And a long stay it was: in October 1884 Fr Edward Patrick Southwell noted that 'Laurence Kelly is to commence as a Gentleman Boarder from

October 1884 at £40, without piano',[14] and his various payments continued until May 1891. To judge by F.J. Byrne, he was much loved by his fellow students. Later on he graduated in medicine, practising in Ireland and in Shropshire, in England. Another who originated in a far-distant place was Thomas Reynolds who was born in Ceylon in 1871. His father, T.J. Reynolds, had worked in the Ceylon Civil Service but had retired home to Highfield Road, Rathgar, from where, through Terenure, young Thomas had matriculated in the Royal University in 1888.[15]

Among the most brilliant of the early 1880s students was John McNerney. A local lad, from Ashfield Terrace, Terenure, born in 1865, he came to the college as a day-pupil in September 1876 at £6 per annum fees. In March 1878, he became a boarder. He was paying additional fees for drawing and singing lessons within a year; fees for piano lessons, scapular, beads and prayer book followed in November 1881, and for cricket and football. In the Junior Grade Intermediate examinations in 1881, he was the college's star pupil winning a three-year exhibition; he secured fifteenth place out of 173 exhibitions offered country-wide, and a first-class prize of £4. He had already topped the Terenure list for juniors in the 1879 Intermediate, and again in 1880. He continued to win cash and book prizes in the years ahead. What his subsequent career might have been is not certain: there is a John McNerney recorded for the area in the 1911 census who gave his occupation as 'journalist' and who was born in the same year: then again, in the 1936 the *Irish Times* recorded the death of a John McNerney late of Browne and Nolan, the publishers, and whose obsequies were conducted by Fr Troy, curate of Terenure parish.[16]

Other outstanding students included Thomas and Francis Lenehan who, although they lived in Garville Avenue, Rathgar, entered the college as boarders in September 1880. Like McNerney, Thomas secured a three-year exhibition in the Junior Grade Intermediate examinations in 1881. He was not the completely sainted scholar however: a note of 12 November 1881 by Fr Michael Aloysius Moore observes that 'Thomas Lenehan has neglected his music for some time'. However, he continued to shine, winning a book prize in the Intermediate Examinations of 1882, while his brother, Francis, was a prize winner two years later.[17]

One of the most remarkable of the students of these years and with the longest association with the college was W. Dillon Cosgrave. Born in 1864, Dillon Cosgrave first went to the Dominick Street Academy where he won an exhibition in the Intermediate Examinations of 1880.[18] Following on that success he and his brother, Thomas Cosgrave, entered Terenure College around October 1880 where Dillon distinguished himself further.[19] In the state examinations of 1881, he was Gold Medalist in Modern Languages in Middle Grade.[20] In these examinations, he presented in six subjects and secured honours in all six, particularly excelling in Latin, French and Italian. He stayed on with the college and the Carmelites, being accepted for the novitiate there in November 1886, and received the habit on 30 January 1887, taking the religious name of Brother Augustine. Despite his academic brilliance which he continued to express in copious historical works for the rest of his adult life, he never went forward to ordination as a priest, and, in some ways was eccentric. J.F. Byrne provides a fascinating account of him, as follows:

> One of the oddities in Whitefriars [sic] Street was a person named Dillon Cosgrave, an advanced novice who remained that way. He had been ordained deacon but there he stopped. He either wouldn't, or wouldn't be let, go on; and he couldn't go back. Apparently he had reached the point where 'returning were more tedious than go o'ver'. For Dillon even the most elementary mathematics and physics had no meaning; and possibly on that account, he was in a way the most extraordinary genius I have ever met. His knowledge of general literature and of the arts, including the literature of music, was extraordinarily comprehensive. He knew such tomes as *Burke's Peerage*, and *Thom's Dublin Directory* from cover to cover. Whenever a street band struck up, he couldn't resist following it. Occasionally, he asked me to go on one of these peregrinations; and on our way through the city he would keep up a ceaseless prattle about incidents, historic, memorable, notorious or infamous, connected with the neighbourhood we were in, or even individual houses we passed.
>
> Dillon Cosgrave was an elder brother of the 'Lynch' in Joyce's *Ulysses* and the *Portrait*. He was of medium size, blond [sic], and near-sighted; and always he remained as simple and trusting as an unspoilt child. At sacerdotal ceremonies he was a complete failure. Often they tried him out at the 7 o'clock First Friday High Mass on the side altar to the left of the church, he would literally fumble and tumble, himself and missal, all over the steps of the altar.
>
> I was told that it was his practice when eating dinner always to eat his potatoes first. His fellow novices were constantly playing practical jokes on him, like the time they said to him, when they saw a for-midable-looking female at a fruit stand, 'Dillon, ask the woman how much are the penny oranges'. And Dillon did. He went over and, peering at the lady, enquired, 'How much are your penny oranges'. She gazed at him sharply, and being quite certain that he, cleric or no cleric, was trying to cod her, she stooped and picked up from a bucket a green moldy [sic] orange and holding it menacingly in her hand she screamed, 'Go 'long wid yourself, y' unholy spalpeen. If ye don't get out o' me sight a wanst, here's a penny orange I'll let ye have, where ye won't like it, fer nawthin.'

Following on his solemn progression as Brother Augustine in April 1891, he was attached to Whitefriar Street but also taught in both of his *Alma Maters*, Dominick Street Academy and Terenure. He was a graduate in arts of the Royal University and was involved actively in university politics, serving on the election committee for the

Senate candidate, Edward Magennis, in 1906. He became a 'character' among Dublin's antiquarians. The historical article which he published in the *New Ireland Review* in 1906 on 'The True History of the Phoenix Park Murders' received a rather mixed reception from a reviewer who conceded: 'he corrects many mistakes in a recent work by Tighe Hopkins, but might, we think, have devoted his talents to something more useful. The blackest page in recent Irish history is better left unturned'.[21]

Brother Cosgrave was unfazed: in the same year he published *A History of Ireland* followed three years later by his definitive *North Dublin, City and Environs* and was almost certainly the authority behind the 1927 centenary history of Whitefriar Street Church. Remembered as wonderful conversationalist and a walking encyclopaedia — almost literally so — he was active in a number of historical and cultural societies devoted to Dublin history. As a venerable white-haired Carmelite Dubliner, he deserved better of his city than to be killed by one of its trams while crossing Jervis Street in April 1936 in his seventy-first year.[22]

One of Cosgrave's fellow pupils of 1881 who did not enter the Order but had an important association with the college in later life was Edward Joseph Mallins, a ten-year-old day-pupil from Grosvenor Road, Rathmines, who entered the college in 1881. The latter secured his MA from Trinity, became a solicitor and country court registrar for Cavan and Letterkenny and was a founding member of the Terenure College Past Pupils' Union in 1925. Entering with the Mallins lad in September 1881 were the O'Reilly brothers, James and David from Eadestown Naas: in his adult life, David became a prominent figure in equestrian circles in Naas in the decade after 1905. Another contemporary of theirs who did follow Dillon Cosgrave into the Order was Richard Colfer who shall figure in more detail later. From Tinraheen, outside Gorey, Co. Wexford, where his father, John, farmed over 650 acres, Richard came to college as a boarder in August 1883 and would in time become a president of the college three times, over 1900–02, 1906 to 1909 and from 1922 to 1923. Richard was followed by at least one other pupil of the 1880s before whom there lay a similar path. Charles Gavin, a Dubliner from Clonliffe Road, entered the college with his brother William in September 1887, and as will be detailed later, became college Prior and president from 1924–5. It is possible that there was another: a James Cogan who entered the college in 1889 and a James (Joseph) John of the Cross Cogan was college president from 1909–13 and again in 1916. The college register entry for James Cogan in 1889, however, gives his middle name as Michael, not Joseph.

Before going on to consider some of the students of the 1890s and 1900s, it may be appropriate to note a few general features of life in the college in the 1880s. In May 1882, the ex-president Fr Moore said farewell to his pupils as he set out for the mission in Australia. He took with him Fr T.D. Kelly who would one day return and become college president from 1905–06. Also departing from the college with them was Fr Edward Romaeus Stone — a great loss to the boys as he was effectively their coach and games' master. There is evidence that the field team games played there in the early 1880s were principally cricket, rugby, handball and possibly soccer. As to the latter, there is a little uncertainty here: one record refers to 'the annual foot-ball match between the "Past" and the "Present"' as was played on Tuesday 21 December 1881 to mark the end of the Christmas term. It was followed that evening by a dinner for the Past Pupils after which a prize-giving ensued, in particular for those who had been successful in the 1881 Intermediate Examinations'. There is no detail as to how this 'football' was played but when the recently ordained Fr Edward Stone, left for Australia his departure was lamented not least because 'under his guidance the cricket and football clubs have reached the highest state of efficiency and distinction'. He was remembered as one who had 'for many years' been 'President of the Games' and his loss was a grievous one: under his management 'the Football and Cricket Clubs had acquired no inconsiderable reputation'.[23] Referring to recreational activities in the winter of 1881–2, it was reported that 'Handball and Football were the most favoured out-door amusements. Club matches of football were played regularly every week'. The report went on to state that there had been three 'public or "out" matches' and represented them as follows:

> December 21st
>
> Past versus Present, at Terenure. Played according to the Association and won by the PRESENT.
>
> —
>
> February 21st
>
> St Gall's College v Terenure College. Played according to Rugby Rules. The victory was undecided.
>
> —
>
> Terenure College v Academy, Dominick-Street. Played at Terenure according to Rugby Rules, and won after a warm contest by the College.[24]

Since the Gaelic Athletic Association was not founded until 1884 and as the soccer 'Football Association' was established in 1863 when the 'Laws of the Game' were adopted, and the Irish Football Association was founded in November 1880, we must assume that the football played at Terenure in 1881–2 was that which later became soccer.

In the following winter of 1882–3, which must have been a hard one, the 'two chief outdoor pastimes, Football and Skating' were duly practised. It was noted that 'Football was even more popular than ever'.[25] The annual match of 'Past' versus 'Present' came off at the end of Christmas term with victory going to Present by two goals scored by none other than Richard Cassan Greer. What happened to Terenure soccer thereafter is not on the college record.

Cricket is the game most widely referred to in the surviving records of or about the college from its inception. By 1882, there is formal reference to Terenure College Cricket Club with J.H. Gallagher as captain — in his second season as such — and Secretary John Byrne. Their season began officially on 27 April and it closed on 3 July with the usual match between Past and Present selections. Gallagher, Byrne and Joseph Duncan—an American student who went to the States in the Autumn of 1882—had acquired considerable reputations as bowlers and in their season of open competitions with other schools and teams they played six matches, winning three, losing two and drawing one. Their first match was against 'French College' as Blackrock was known at the time, with a substantial victory of 138 runs for 9 wickets against French College's 17. Not to take away from the Terenure boys' glory it should nonetheless be noted that their star batsman was actually Fr Romaeus Stone who scored an impressive 82, with Gallagher making 15 and Byrne 15 not out. It was the only match Fr Stone played in that season, as only three days later he was off on the *Rose* to London, heading for Australia with Frs Moore and Kelly. It is not clear if French College enjoyed the counterbalancing skill and experience of a clergyman of their own. In their second match, this time against a team from the civil service, the match was tied at 42 with a certain E. Thornton, for the college not out at 14. (One wonders if he may have been a forebear of more famous athletic Terenure Thorntons almost 100 years later.) In that same month of May 1882, they lost to Blackrock at the latter's sports grounds in Merrion as they did again, in June, to the civil service in the Phoenix Park. However, their season ended successfully at home in July when Terenure's Present beat their Past 167 for 6 against 43. In the following year, 1883, the Terenure XI again played six matches and again winning three, losing two and drawing one, the latter being the match between Terenure and Carmichael College on 13 June 1883. Indeed, despite the fact that 'an exceptionally large number of the distinguished cricketers of the last season having left school' such was the popularity of the game and the extent of the pool of participating talent that for the first time in the club's history they were able to field a second eleven.[26]

The earliest reference to Terenure rugby as encountered by this writer appears to go back to 1881 and the matches played between St Gall's College (Belfast, presumably) and Terenure, and between Terenure and Dominick Street, both on 21 February, and 'as played according to Rugby Rules'. Interestingly in a section of the 1882–3 *Annual Record* devoted to sports and recreation, there is specific mention of association football but no reference whatever to rugby. The next reference to the latter is not till an *Irish Times* report of November 1907 concerning a match between the college's third XV and Mornington, with the college victorious in a tough match, by three points. This was followed by another victory in December over King's Hospital by three tries to no score.[27] The 1907–09 teams included a number of pupils who would have significant later careers and significant connections with the college who will be referred to later: they included Robert. J. May, J. Sheil and R. Albert Metcalfe, in later life a doctor, a lawyer and a Carmelite friar respectively. They were also the teams associated with Fr Peter Elias O'Dwyer. Born in Co. Kilkenny in 1881, he was schooled in Knocktopher, greatly influenced there by one teacher in particular, Fr Elias Magennis. That influence led Peter O'Dwyer to Terenure College in 1897. Going on to a brilliant undergraduate career in the Royal University, studying Greek and mathematics, he was appointed to the teaching staff at Terenure and was ordained in 1898. He was described as a professor in Terenure in the 1901 census and was still teaching there until 1909. Despite his own serious ill health, he took an active interest in college sport and according to Fr Norbert Heaslip, writing in 1958, Fr O'Dwyer 'introduced Rugby as the official school game'. If this is too large a claim, nonetheless under him Terenure rugby certainly reached a new level. It appears that the Prior and president, Fr Colfer, deputed him, then known as Brother Elias, to promote the game in the college. He obtained the help of well-known rugby referee, J. Magee who coached the team every Sunday, ahead of a match held every Wednesday. Their first year was a very successful one. They easily defeated the Catholic University School in their first outing on 5 October 1907 and by 21 December they had won all eight of their matches. In the ensuing cup tournament, however, they fell victim to Wesley in the first round. Among the members of that 1907 team were the Becker brothers, George and Michael, sons of a well-known tea importer and merchant. George would later study medicine while his older brother Michael would join his father in the tea business and the family would later produce another famous rugby Becker in Vinnie. On this team too was young Robert May, destined to a great career in medicine and a co-founder of the Past Pupils' Union. Another founding member of the union who played in the 1908 Terenure rugby cup team was Bob Metcalfe who would later spend his life as a Carmelite priest.[28] It would be another half century, in 1958, before it secured it's most famous triumph in the double schools cup victories — Senior and Junior — a triumph he lived to see in the year of his own golden jubilee. His own career over, that time heralded change too — leaving Terenure in 1911 for Knocktopher, and then to a new Carmelite Community in Middletown, New York, in 1912. The following year saw him move to Australia for seventeen years, where he supported Irishness in a number of forms — from playing the bagpipes, to organising Irish-language classes and promoting Sinn Féin ideals and its movement prior to independence. Following spells as Prior at Melbourne and Adelaide, he was back in New York in 1930 before returning to Ireland and various assignments at Knocktopher, Kinsale, Moate and to the Gort Muire House of Studies, until passing away on 18 April 1965. [29]

Apart from the rugby tradition which emerged in the college over the 1870s to the early 1900s, there was also the GAA. In the year after the formation of the Gaelic Athletic Association, Terenure was one of the first, perhaps the *very* first college to affiliate to the organisation. By the end of 1885, Terenure College was one of only six GAA clubs in Dublin City and county, along with Faughs, Davitts, Metropolitans, Dunleary, Dalkey and the 'All-Ireland Hurling Club'. When the Dublin County Board produced their centenary *Official Brochure* in 1934 they recorded that Terenure foundation thus. The resolution of the students and professors establishing a GAA Club in the Carmelite College is quoted as follows:

> That believing it to be one of the functions of educational establishments to provide for the physical no less than the moral and intellectual training of the rising generation of Irishmen, in accordance with the instincts and traditions of their ancient race we hereby form ourselves into a branch of the GAA to be called the Terenure College Branch of the GAA. [30]

However, it is not at all clear that Gaelic football took any firm hold in the college at that stage or at any other over the 25 years after that. The college GAA club is not listed in the official return of Dublin clubs affiliated to the GAA in 1888: the Terenure GAA club that was listed thereafter was the local Terenure Sarsfields, founded in 1892 and recruited mainly from the workers of the local tramway depot.

However, one tradition laid down — off the field — in these years, was that of the dramatic. While the earliest reports from the 1860s and 1870s refer to those annual prize-giving occasions when star pupils declaimed passages from Shakespeare and other literary worthies or presented a scene or two from his plays, by the early 1880s they were clearly staging more elaborate productions. This became practicable when, as noted earlier, a new concert hall became available from the mid-1870s. By 1881, the press reporting on Terenure plays was referring to 'these annual theatricals now so much looked forward to each recurring Easter holiday time'.[31] In the case of the production of Easter 1881, the newspapers spoke of tram cars from the city filled with visitors on their way to the college and in that year some 400 were reported as having attended a production of *The Merchant of Venice*. Here Master James P. Devlin as Shylock stole the show while John McNerney excelled as Portia. Two years later, they produced 'a very successful rendering of *Hamlet* ... before the most crowded house ever witnessed in Terenure. Fully six hundred of the students' relatives and friends were present'. In this production, Larry Kelly from Buenos Aires played Claudius while the star role of Hamlet was played by recent past pupil, James Devlin. Horatio was played by none other than William Peakin, while his brother Patrick played Marcellus. Others of the star pupils in this production included McNerney as Polonius, Richard Cassan Greer as Rosencrantz and John Byrne as Laertes. Devlin played Hamlet with 'supereminent success' — and, as the *Irish Times* reported, 'he is essentially an actor, and his rendering of the "Crazed Prince" would reflect credit on many of our professional tragedians'.[32] It was with tragic irony that this budding actor was to die very soon after, following a sudden illness, at the age of 21. By the 1890s, it appears that the annual play had been brought forward from Easter to the end of the first term before the Christmas break: in 1893, for example, W.S. Gilbert's *Rosencrantz and Guildenstern* — a skit upon *Hamlet* — was staged at Christmas.[33]

College of Our Blessed Lady of Mount Carmel,

TERENURE, DUBLIN,

UNDER THE PATRONAGE OF

HIS GRACE THE ARCHBISHOP.

ANNUAL RECORD,

1880-81.

103

DUBLIN:

BROWNE AND NOLAN, PRINTERS, NASSAU-STREET.

1881.

1883.

College of Our Blessed Lady of Mount Carmel,

TERENURE, CO. DUBLIN.

ANNUAL RECORD,

1882-83.

Annual Record of Terenure College 1882–3.

Philip Paul McDonnell, 1880s. McDonnell was Prior of Terenure in 1882–3.

CHAPTER 8

*Priests and Pupils
from the 1890s*

Sketch of 'Ardavon', today Mount Carmel Hospital.

IT WAS AT THIS STAGE, DURING THE PRESIDENCY OF MICHAEL AVERTANUS O'Reilly, that the college's second big extension was undertaken. This may have been a case of the new broom sweeping clean or of a new man ushering in a new regime. Fr O'Reilly became president in 1891 and it was in the Definitory meeting of September of that year that the decision was taken to undertake this second extension.[1] The work was commenced soon after and was completed in 1894. It became an impressive three-storey addition, from the corner of the old chapel — at the end of the 1870s extension — stretching in the direction of Fortfield. On the ground floor this provided for classrooms and a new oratory, known in later times as 'The old chapel'. The new first floor supplied a science hall and additional classrooms. According to tradition this science hall was, through the good offices of Frs John Dunne and Thomas Kelly, extremely well-equipped by the standards of its day. Above it, on the second floor, provision was made for a new study hall and separate rooms for members of the Community.

This development would hardly have been undertaken if the numbers of students and staff had remained at the level obtaining in the first half of the 1880s. While there is no Terenure College register to provide detailed, consecutive evidence of the numbers of enrolments through the 1890s and 1900s, Richard Colfer who was appointed Prior there in 1899, told the Carmelite General in November 1900 that the college had some 70 pupils, as well as novices, and that they had been forced to resort to the employment of lay teachers to cope with the number of students. Furthermore, corroborating Colfer's remarks, there are in the archives of the Department of Education and Science some school roll-books relating to Terenure College for various years from 1890 to 1906. Some of these lists are partial, listing only those boys who as examination candidates were returned in order to claim payments for results, under the operation of the Intermediate Education Act of 1878. For example, that for the year 1890 returns only 19 names; that for 1896, 45 names; for 1897, 46 names and that for 1898, 42 names. However, when it comes to the next extant roll, that for 1904, the list appears to be a total one: over the signature of Thomas P. Kelly, Prior since 1903, it now provides numbers for specific age ranges, as follows:

Under 13 years of age: 11
Between 13 and 19 years: 28
Over 19 years: 1
Total: 40.

Again, the comparable return on 15 October 1905 shows:

Under 13 years of age: 16
Between 13 and 19 years: 30
Over 19 years: 0
Total: 46.

Suddenly, in the next year, 1906, there is an apparent steep rise:

Under 13 years of age: 25
Between 13 and 19 years: 50
Over 19 years: 0
Total: 75.

It is possible, of course, that the lower numbers before 1906 arise from a practice that the college had significantly more students than those for whom they were claiming results. It is likely that the figure of 75 was a total figure because, besides returning these numbers by age group, the Prior in 1906 also included names and dates of birth of various boys within these age groups: however, whereas he returned 25 boys as the total of under-13s, in the list of actual names and dates of birth which he provided, he supplied only 18. Similarly, out of the total of 50 between 13 and 19 years, he supplied only 31 names, 23 of them in Junior Grade, 7 in Middle Grade and 1 in Senior Grade (Junior Grade referred to examination candidates 16 years of age or under, on 1 June of the examination year; Middle Grade candidates were to be 17 years or under, and Senior Grade 18 years or under). In effect, he seems to have claimed for only 49 out of 75. If that could be applied to the earlier figures it would suggest total annual enrolments in the region of 70 for the 1890s and 1900s. To some extent the census of 1901 may support this point. It records the college as having in residence on census night, apart from 6 professors and 13 clerical students, 48 boarders. If one hazarded say 20–30 day-pupils then the total enrolment in 1901 would have been from the high 60s to high 70s.

PUPILS AND TEACHERS:

Whether bright or not so bright, the 50 to 80 students per year attending Terenure College from the 1860s to the 1900s were an élite — the tiny élite of boys who received any education beyond basic primary in Ireland in the nineteenth century. In 1870, it was estimated that there were about 5,000 pupils in 'superior' or secondary schools: Terenure's boys were therefore one in a hundred of that secondary school population. Over the course of the next three decades that secondary school population was to rise significantly from a total of 25,000 boys and girls of all denominations in 1881, of whom some 12,000 were Catholics, to close on 39,000 in 1901 of whom close on 26,000 were Catholics. Placing Terenure in context, in the year 1881 it was one of some 220 'superior' schools for males providing education to 15,494 boys.[2]

When the college was founded in 1860 there was no state aid of any kind for secondary schooling, not for buildings, equipment nor teachers' salaries. There was no provision for the training of secondary teachers, whether religious or lay. As for lay teachers, of whom there must have been few — Terenure certainly had very few before the 1920s — conditions were grim and career progression non-existent. University graduates were the exception. Teaching itself was frequently a second choice calling at this level, either for those aspiring to better careers in another profession such as law or for those who had not continued in their first choice especially if this had been the pursuit of a religious vocation. For the latter in particular, their position could be one of gratitude, deference and obligation, entirely dependent on the goodwill of their superiors whether diocesan or regular.

Salaries of those 'living out' ranged from £40 to £80 per annum between 1860 and 1914 at a time when carpenters were on the yearly equivalent of £75 to £90.[3] At Tullabeg in the later 1870s the salaries ranged from £40 per annum for the piano teacher, Mr Turner, to £80 per annum for the graduate teacher of mathematics, Mr John Collins.[4] In a 1905 government-commissioned report into Irish secondary and technical education by T.A. Dale and F.H. Stephens, it was noted that 'From every source from which we obtained information we learnt that no Irish graduate, save in exceptional circumstances, will enter the teaching profession if any other career presents itself to him'.[5] As late as 1911, the chairman of the Intermediate Board of Education, Dr William J.M. Starkie, was to remark that 'no layman wilfully takes up [intermediate school] teaching as a permanent occupation'.[6] From the landmark of 1878, it would be a very long time before conditions improved significantly for lay teachers and the provision and control of secondary education would rely almost exclusively on the energy, commitment and resources of clergy and religious orders. For Terenure College from the mid-1880s that commitment depended on four persons in particular: Bartley, O'Reilly, Colfer and Kelly.

From Southwell to Colfer:

The presidency of Terenure passed in 1885 from Edward Southwell to Thomas Stanislaus Bartley. He was younger brother to John Elias Bartley. Able, handsome and genial, he was 41 when he took up his new role in the college where he was fondly remembered for his command of French and equally for his command of a splendid wax-ended cane, for blackboard demonstration purposes only. Subsequently he would become Provincial from 1903 to 1906 and critically, Bursar to the Province in the decisive year of 1909. It may have been seen as a position which well-suited his talents as he had already played a significant role in raising some £2,000 in funds for the restoration of Whitefriar Street in 1905.[7] His successor in 1891 was Michael Avertanus O'Reilly. A native of Moate, he had been received into the Order in June 1873 on the same day as his Terenure College confreres Patrick Donegan and Edward Stone and was solemnly professed with them five years later. He became Prior of Kinsale in 1884 and following a period of study in Rome he was still only 34 when he became Prior and president of Terenure in 1891. Presumably he was seen as effective in office as he was re-elected to it by the Chapter of 1895 until 1899. His most visible legacy to the college is the 1894 extension but it was one where shortage of funds prevented its complete development. Like his predecessor, he went on to become Provincial from 1906 to 1909. With the numbers of students and of novices growing in Terenure in

1907–09, he came under pressure to move the novices out — initially to Knocktopher — and, in 1908, he presided over the purchase of 'Ardavon' (Mount Carmel Hospital today) as a potential Dublin novitiate: but, for both Terenure and 'Ardavon' a different immediate future was soon to unfold. Following the end of his term as Provincial in 1909, he was appointed Bursar to the Province.

O'Reilly's successor in Terenure was a former pupil, Richard Colfer who, it will be recalled, came to the college as a boarder in 1883. Son of John Colfer and Alice née Redmond, he was born in 1866, joined the Order in 1885 and was ordained in 1891. He was only 28 when, in 1894, he was appointed Master of Novices in Terenure, a post he held for four years, and, a year later, in 1899, at 33 he became one of the youngest-ever presidents of the college. Before becoming president for a second time, for the period 1906–09, he was elected Vicar-Provincial (1902–03). Later on, from 1912, he spent seven years as Prior of Middletown, New York, and then returned to Ireland as Prior of Kinsale from 1919 to 1922. He became president of Terenure for an unprecedented third time in 1922–3 before being elected Provincial from 1925 to 1929.

During his first term, Colfer found himself to some extent in the wars. He lost his Master of Novices, Leybourne, who complained that he was being treated badly by Colfer and that the latter, as Prior, was too frequently absent on outside business. However, Leybourne also complained bitterly about his Provincial, Farrington — second president of the college — as being rude and unreasonable and seriously at odds with his own confreres in Whitefriar Street. Colfer soon found himself caught in the middle between the discontented friars and their Provincial. Andrew Farrington tried to run a tight ship, not least in regard to the use of alcohol, and faced a minor rebellion, which Colfer was called upon by the General to try to defuse. By 1902, he appeared, according to O'Dwyer, 'to all intents and purposes to have replaced the Provincial'.[8] By that time Farrington was insisting that neither the General nor Colfer should send him any more communications. In the end, in March 1902, the General, Bernardini, actually deposed Farrington as Provincial and appointed Colfer as Vicar Provincial. To Colfer's credit, it was a post he did not seek or want but which, having accepted, he was almost certainly glad to relinquish in 1903. This did not, however, spare him from further responsibilities: in 1906 and until 1909 he again found himself presiding over the fortunes of Terenure. He did so at a time of great growth and, in the end, of danger. During these three years, the college appears to have enrolled its largest number of pupils since its foundation and it attracted growing numbers of postulants and novices.

In between Colfer's terms, however, Michael A. O'Reilly also served a short second spell as president, in 1904, followed by Fr T.P. Kelly in 1905 and 1906. The latter had entered the novitiate in 1873 and was solemnly professed in 1878. Six years later he found himself Prior of Gawler in Australia and from 1895 Prior of Melbourne before returning to Ireland. Following Colfer's second term in 1909 the Chapter of that year elected Louis Nolan as Prior. This did not work out due to his ill-health and he was suddenly replaced by James Cogan of whom more later. However, at the time of Nolan's appointment he was not president of the college as a secondary school but rather Prior of the Terenure Community and novitiate, for Terenure had ceased to be a place for lay-pupils. Before turning to that decisive disjunction, in the chapter which follows, it may be appropriate to conclude this one with reference to some of the pupils who walked the corridors and played the fields of Terenure over the 1890s and early 1900s.

PUPILS OF THE 1890S AND 1900S:

The backgrounds and later careers of the boys were extremely varied. Gerald Keller from Co. Cork, who enrolled in 1897, was the son of a Kanturk solicitor. James Duddy who came from Belfast in 1896 at the age of fourteen returned there to become a commercial traveller for a brewery. Also associated with the drinks trade was a much more local lad, John Ryan. He lived with his family on the college property. His father, Patrick, originally from Co. Wexford, was a spirit-merchant with a public house on Thomas Street. His pub boasted a splendid clock and he became known as Pat 'The Clock' Ryan. Their home on college grounds — eventually demolished and land-scaped to provide an all-weather pitch and fast track — rejoiced in a large garden, long known as Ryan's Garden. In this large, twelve-roomed house was born the father and aunts of future Archbishop of Dublin, Dermot Ryan.[9] Young John entered the college in 1898 at the age of nine, but did not stay long, deserting in 1899 for the Christian Brothers — presumably at Synge Street — and went on in later life to be a clerk. Sons of famous racehorse trainers there were too, from William Paley of Lark Lodge on the Curragh in the late 1870s and 1880s to Hyacinth Frederick William Burke Cullen — who boarded from the mid-1890s — from the famous Cullen horse-training family of Rossmore Lodge on the Curragh.

Also enrolling in 1898 was ten-year-old Albert LeBrocquy from the house called 'Horton' on Kimmage Road, Terenure. Albert's father, Louis Le Brocquy, was born in Liège, Belgium, in 1861 and grew up in Dusseldorf, returning to Belgium in 1878 where he became a clerk in the War Office. He resigned from this in 1884 and returned to Dusseldorf to manage a family business in the manufacture of lubricating oils and greases, and in this setting he developed a deep interest in chemistry. Having met and married an Irishwoman, he came to Dublin in 1886. He set up an oil business in Ringsend and in 1896 moved it to a disused whiskey distillery at Greenmount, Harold's Cross. They rented 'Horton' to be near to the business and in the following year, Albert was enrolled in the college. In later life, he married Sybil who acted and wrote under the *nom de plume*, Helen Staunton. Together they were active in public life, in the League of Nations Association, and were founder members, in Ireland, of other bodies such as Amnesty, Irish Civil Rights and Poets, Playwrights, Editors, Essayists and Novelists (PEN). Their children were the artists Louis and Melanie, and Noel who became managing director of the Greenmount Oil Company.[10]

Others who were to feature as the first of several generations of Terenure boys included the Bobbetts, Patrick and William, from the late 1880s: in addition there were the twin brothers, Joseph and Ignatius Bobbett, born in 1871 who both entered the Order; Joseph in 1892 and Ignatius in 1894; Joseph passed away in 1893 at only 22, while Ignatius left the Order in 1895 before being solemnly professed. A family originally of Huguenot descent, their father, James, farmed over 130 acres at Creekstown, Ashbourne, Co. Meath.

Also from farming backgrounds, but more local, were the McGrane boys, James, Leo and Christy who were day-pupils. James and Leo enrolled in 1901. Their father, also James, was a successful farmer from Knocklyon Castle, the family managed over 200 acres of the property, which they acquired in 1826 and held until 1964.[11] A person of considerable local standing, James Snr was a magistrate, a distinction, perhaps, for a Catholic at that time. He also undertook to manage the farm of the Carmelite nuns at Firhouse. James Jr was twelve when he entered the college and upon completing his education, he went back to work the family farm. His two brothers saw active service in the First World War. Leo who was a lieutenant did not survive the conflict; Christy, however, who joined the Royal Flying Corps, did and spent the rest of his life in the Colonial Service in what then was Southern Rhodesia. James's son Dennis, born in Knocklyon Castle in 1933, also went to Terenure in the 1940s, followed a generation later by his own son, Jaime who was born in 1974.[12]

One member of the final cohort of Terenure lay-students coming up to the 1909 closure was Maurice MacGowan. Following a fine scholastic record in the college, Maurice went on to the law, qualifying in 1918. He was appointed to the Land Registry, going on in time to become its Deputy Registrar and Chief Examiner. He took a great interest in the college in later life, taking particular trouble in promoting its Boys' Club. An active member of the Past Pupils' Union, he established the union's Golfing Society, was a vice-president and trustee of the Terenure Rugby Club and was union president in 1942–3. He had the honour of being the rugby club's first president on its promotion to senior status.[13]

Among the most brilliant of that final cohort was Henry Lappin. A gifted Classics scholar, he also had a great interest in English literature and in his early adult years was something of a Shakespearean scholar who was on terms of friendship with the Irish Shakespeare expert and poet, Professor Edward Dowden. Born in Belfast in 1890 or 1891, he entered Terenure in 1906 and was a pupil until its closure. After that he remained on in the college, for he is returned as a twenty-year-old resident there on the census night of 1911. At that point, he was studying in University College Dublin and was either staying on in Terenure as a hostel resident or it may be that he was considering a vocation to the Carmelites. Whatever the case, on leaving Terenure College he emigrated to the United States. He worked for a publishing firm in Minnesota for a time and then went on to lecture in English literature as an instructor at Cornell before becoming a professor at D'Youville College, Buffalo, in the mid-1920s. Married to a girl from Belfast, he kept up a friendship and correspondence with Fr Peter Louis Nolan who had been Prior in 1909. Lappin was one of the early literary critics to have published on the poetry of Gerard Manley Hopkins.[14]

Among the many others were men whose lives were to be spent in and for the Carmelite Order and often enough in the service of the college itself and some of whose stories will appear later: they include Richard Brocard Taylor, Charles Gavin, Martin Farrington — nephew of Andrew Elias, Robert (Bob) Metcalfe and Louis Gerhard to name but a few. Striking among them, however, was a Terenure pupil of the 1890s who went on to become Prior of the college from 1914 to 1916, William Joachim Brennan. A Knocktopher boy, born in 1880, following his Terenure schooling he entered the Order in 1898 and was ordained nine years later. A friar renowned for his kindness and charity he taught in the college from 1907 to 1909. Following his term as Prior there, after 1916, he was assigned as Prior of New York and was subsequently Prior at Kinsale, 'Ardavon', Whitefriar Street and finally Kildare where he celebrated his golden jubilee. He died there in February 1953.

One concludes, however, with a lay memoir. The Swayne boys from Merrion Avenue, Blackrock, Co. Dublin: Edward, James and Jack came to the college in 1889 and studied there through the 1890s. Over 60 years later, one of them penned the following:

> A few enthusiasts were playing a somewhat lethargic [game of] cricket on what was then called the top walk. The season was over long ago and it was now an unusually warm day for October. I had tired of my companions and now I went off alone, and climbed a big laburnum on the left-hand side of the field. Most of the leaves had fallen, most of the branches were quite bare but on an occasional twig were the withered seed pods. Idly I explored a few of these blackened pods and meditatively chewed a few of the seeds. I was a long time up in that tree and maybe had eaten a dozen of them when suddenly I grew a trifle ill and dizzy.
>
> I descended and strolled into the Library and took down a large volume of the *Boys' Own* paper, for I was then much interested in a serial entitled *The Fifth Form at St Dominic's*. My head ached and I think I must have drowsed when I was awakened by a heavy hand on my shoulders. I looked up and was staggered beyond words. Of all people, there was Fr Quigley beside me, his face haggard and for once his nose somewhat pale. Fr Quigley was then possibly thirty-five years of age and my connection with and knowledge of him was in my mathematical capacity for he taught us the six books — how often have I thanked God there were no more of the late Mr Euclid's geometrical publications extant — and his famous abstractions. I am thankful to say that I do not remember one of these paralyzing puzzles now, for life is sufficiently complicated. Fr Quigley had a cork leg. I forget which leg it was and there were amongst us boys many incredible legends about it, the most acceptable to his frightened pupils being that a Tipperary boy, driven to despair with the Second Proposition in the third book of that classis, had bitten off

the reverend gentleman's limb, for which, the legend ran, he was burnt in a public place and amidst much applause from an admiring crowd of schoolboys. I was to know this much understood gentleman much better in later years but then, as I turned my gaze to him, I was alarmed to see real tear in his big eyes. His hand rested heavily on my shoulder and he said in tragic tones, 'Boy, Parnell is dead!' The day was the 6th of October, the year 1891. I was eleven years of age.

With us at that time, Parnell figured in our mental national galleries with Julius Caesar, Napoleon, Dan O'Connell and Jules Verne. Fr Quigley bade me kneel and pray for the eternal rest of the lost leader and then I ran away to the only man I loved in all the College, Brother Cosgrave, for this gentle soul was not ordained. I found him, as I expected to, in the dusty music room where there were three pianos. These I loathed for I was stumbling through *Hemy's Second Tutor for the Piano* at the time and had already a species of youthful rheumatism in the last two fingers of my right hand as a result of my efforts with a ghastly composition entitled *The Swallow's Return*. Brother Cosgrave was still trying to play the *Marseillaise* with one finger. He never managed to play it entirely, or indeed, any other tune, but what he did know of the French National Anthem, gave him infinite satisfaction. I broke the news to him and he slammed down the lid of the piano and dragged me away to the Refectory. There we met the placid Fr Colfer to whom Bro. Cosgrave stuttered out the news. It was taken calmly.

At that time the College had not received the additions which now adorn the building, and owing to some infantile complaint I suffered from, I had to sleep all alone in a very small bed in a vast room, I believe, on the third storey, where heretofore a few selected and more advanced boys, were introduced to elementary chemistry, the principal results of which were a perpetual odour about that part of the College, of ancient and long-forgotten eggs.

There were two tall old-fashioned windows to the room where I slept. These were curtainless, never opened, had brown painted shutters fastened back with a small hook and were never used. The windows looked out on the front of the College and if you crawled to the end of your bed, and the moon shone, by nearly getting a permanent crick in your neck, you might see the Dublin and Blessington Steam Tram clatter past on its way to the cannibalistic regions of Templeogue, at that time, firmly believed by the smaller boys to be the abode of giants, savages and witches.

One never-to-be-forgotten night, I wakened. The moon shone full into the room so that I could see things clearly. What persuaded me to hop out of bed will never be known, but I left the bed and went to the window nearest me. I stared out at the lawn and saw nothing but the still trees. I have no idea what time it may have been for time meant nothing to me as it means less to me now. I went to the other window and leant against one of the shutters. I could go to that shutter at this minute if it is still there. It was at my left hand and I idly fiddled with the little hook which kept it back in position. Suddenly the shutter flew open and I froze with horror! A human skeleton hung from a wire in the recess and possibly due to the door or the shutter being flung back, this grisly apparition slowly gyrated. There were many tiny labels fixed on it here and there and of course it was merely a relic of days past maybe when anatomy was taught. Whatever the reason, the spectacle was too much in the moonlight for an eleven-year-old boy and I promptly dropped down unconscious. It seemed centuries later when I was discovered by Miss Cox (Housekeeper), whom I loved whole-heartedly in spite of her snow-white hair and advanced years. I was never put to sleep there again, of course, and in class next day, plodding through that appalling French Classic, *La Jeune Sibrienne*, I whispered my terrible experience to Messrs Leonard and Grahame who refused to credit my tale.

Terenure College, fifty-nine years ago: I remember the meals I had, I can recall the kitchen, I remember the study hall, I vividly remember the appearance of some of my books. I have one still — *The Lady of the Lake*. I recall the godlike Fr McCabe and that handsomest of men, Fr Bartley whom we privately had nicknamed 'Biblioth'. He was a brilliant French scholar and he taught us the language of the Gaul with a highly efficient cane wax-ended and conducive to a good memory. He was much like Daniel O'Connell in the best accepted portraits of that versatile genius.

I was about four years in Terenure and I think left in the year 1893–4 and have never been there since but have seen it from the road about twice.

Some dozen years ago, looking into a bookseller's window in Westmoreland Street, a small, white-haired cleric came beside me. He wore a soft low black hat and thick glasses. He peered eagerly into the window and I took a peep at him, for there was something faintly familiar about him. I whispered into his ear, 'Can you play all of the *Marseillaise* yet?' It was Brother Cosgrave who had written one of the most readable histories of Dublin. He turned to me. He had got incredibly old but his eyes twinkled as much as ever. He knew me at once and chatted a long time when he had to go and severed one of the last links I had with a school I loved and feel happy to remember.[15]

College extension in progress, it was completed in 1894.

Albert LeBrocquy enrolled as a student in the college in 1898. Albert's son was artist, Louis LeBrocquy.

Thomas Stanislaus Bartley, Prior of Terenure, 1885–91.

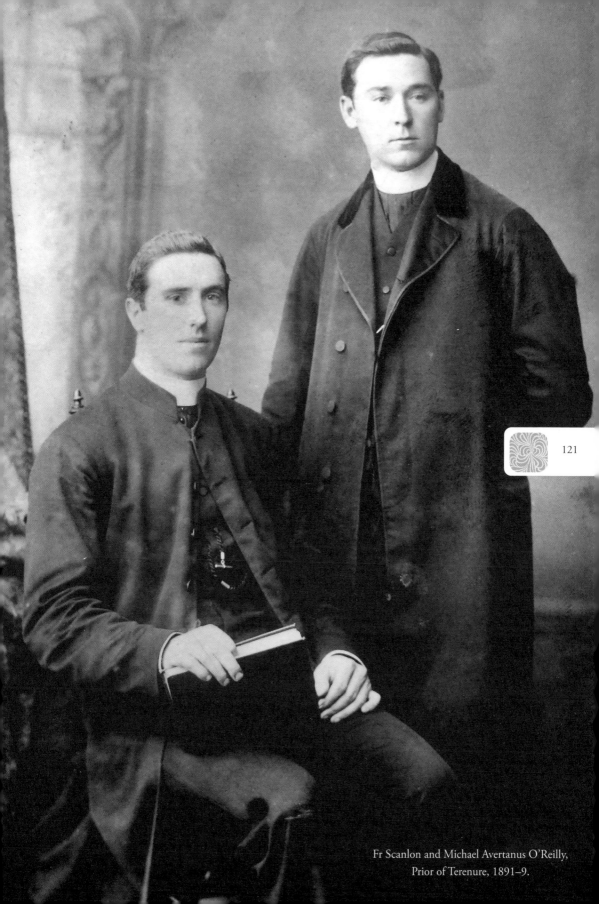

121

Fr Scanlon and Michael Avertanus O'Reilly,
Prior of Terenure, 1891–9.

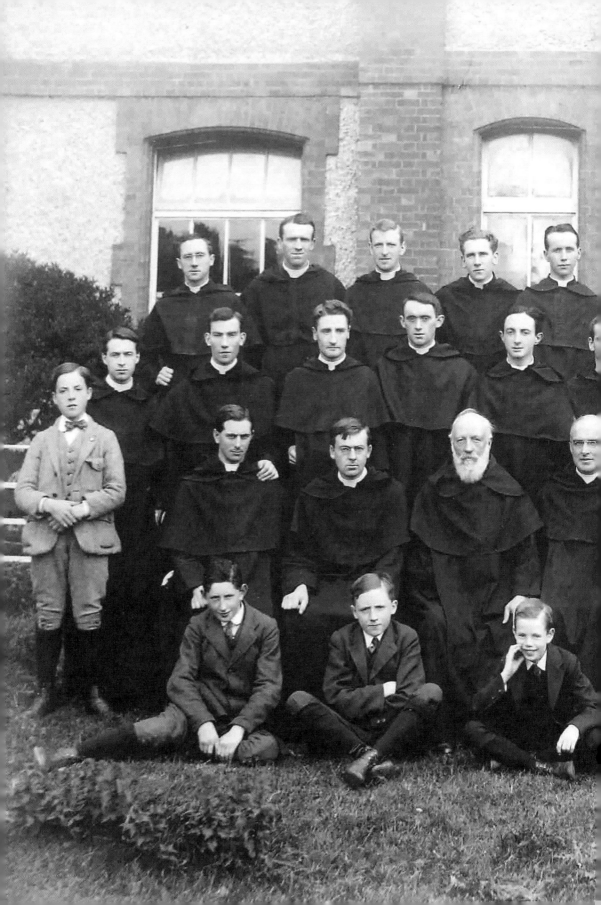

CHAPTER 9

Closure

Group photograph, 1916. It includes in the first seated row (starting second from the left): L. Gerhard, P. Butler, J.J. Cogan, W.J. Brennan, and J.S. Meganetty. A young J.C. O'Shea stands to the right.

IN 1910, TERENURE AS A COLLEGE FOR LAY-BOARDERS AND DAY-PUPILS WOULD have celebrated its golden jubilee. The college could also have celebrated the fact that in that year, no fewer than thirteen of its recent students enrolled in UCD, then only in its own second year of existence: an impressive record.[1] Alas, jubilee celebrations were not to be. On 10 May 1909, the decision was taken to close the college and it would cease forthwith to be a secondary-education institution. Given that in 1909 it had reached its maximum enrolment since 1860, it was an extraordinary decision. That decision was taken by the Order at its Definitory meeting in the college itself. What lay behind this dramatic determination?

There is tradition that the decision was an imposed one — taken by a continental Prior General who had no knowledge of, sensitivity to or sympathy with the cause of secular secondary education in Ireland: that his exclusive priority was to promote vocations and to use the college as a kind of juniorate for postulants, as well as novitiate. This view is an extreme one and not particularly fair to the General. A less severe but still critical view was given in the middle of the 1920s by the Terenure Prior, Fr Brocard Taylor. In a letter written by Taylor in November 1926, he recounted the college's history and observed: 'Fr Mayer, being baldly advised, closed it in 1909 to the dismay of the people with consequent loss of prestige by the Order'.[2]

Pius Mary Mayer, however, who became Prior General in 1902, was no stranger to the Irish Province or to Ireland and matters Irish. He had presided over three Chapters of the Irish Province before that decision was taken. Furthermore, his Assistant General at the time was none other than Peter Elias Magennis who had served his early novitiate years in Terenure from 1887.

It is hard to escape the judgement that the decision owed a great deal — but not everything — to the problem of indebtedness. It had been earlier suggested that, when Andrew Farrington ceased to be Terenure president in 1878, he left behind some difficulty as well as considerable achievement. His 1870s' extension had placed the college in debt. That indebtedness was compounded to an undisclosed extent in 1881 when the Order bought more land for the college, acquiring an additional field on its northeastern boundary.[3] It is remarkable that from the 1870s to 1909 the college fees changed very little and although the evidence is circumstantial rather than direct, the fees income never allowed the college to balance its books in these decades.

When the May 1881 Chapter was over, its president, Fr Carr, confided in the General regarding his fears: unless the debt problem was overcome, Terenure College would have to be sold.[4] It was possibly against this background that Fathers Edward Southwell and Philip Paul McDonnell set off for Argentina in a bid to raise funds to clear or reduce the debts of the Irish Province, raising only £900 of a needed £10,000.[5]

It was certainly the case that the following summer, when Fr Michael Moore and his confreres, Thomas Kelly and Edward Stone, left for Australia, it was 'on the quest' and that quest was explicitly to raise funds to reduce Terenure's debt. It was a quest that was resented by his Carmelite colleagues in Australia who were hard pressed to raise the resources they needed for their own mission.[6] What the outcome to this quest may have been is not clear, but three years later, in September 1885, the Provincial, John Bartley, expressed his anxiety about the college's serious financial problems and blamed his predecessors for this state of affairs.[7]

It is not clear if matters had improved any in the times immediately after. Still Provincial four years later — in his third term as such — John Bartley in March 1889 informed the General, Savini, that Terenure, Whitefriar Street and Kinsale — all with attached schools — were barely self supporting. At that stage in its history it is certain that the Irish Carmelite Province — despite the rise in vocations and professions — was severely stretched. Apart from their five houses in Ireland — the country ones hardly able to make ends meet — they had founded and staffed their two Australian houses in Gawler and Port Melbourne. As if this were not enough, Bartley then set off with Frs McDonnell, Southwell and Michael Baptist Daly to establish their new Community in New York, with only himself returning.[8] It was all the more surprising then that, as seen earlier, a decision was taken by the Definitory in September 1891 to authorise an extension to the college; either some financial miracle had occurred or they were living in great expectations: possibly the former, for in the very next year they agreed in principle to purchase Carmichael College for a proposed £3,100 with a view to creating a new national school. Matters must have been improving in the early 1890s — the Terenure extension was progressed to completion in 1894 and, in addition, in that same year they laid the foundation stone for a new national school in Whitefriar Street which cost £8,847 in the end. A year later they extended their North American commitment by setting up a new mission at Tarrytown, 30 miles north of New York, which the Definitory approved at an expected cost of £5,000. Then early in 1902, the Definitory agreed to a request from Vicar-Provincial Colfer that they purchase an additional small property near Terenure College.[9]

It was in this year, 1902 that the General Chapter in Rome elected Pius Mayer as Prior General in succession to Louis Michael Galli who had died in May 1900. Mayer lost little time in visiting his Irish Province. In May 1903, he conducted a visitation of Terenure College: on the monastic observance aspect of matters he found little cause for concern but when he presided over the Province's Chapter in the college, with Fr Joseph Cowley as his Assistant General, he found no other cause for rejoicing: the college, it transpired, had an income of £1,000 but an expenditure of £5,250 — with no cash in hand. Mayer presided over the next Irish Chapter three years later in 1906 and did so for a third time in May 1909. On that second occasion, in 1906, it is not clear if the financial problems persisted: perhaps not, for in September 1908, the Order purchased a new Dublin property — 'Ardavon' — today the site of Mount Carmel Hospital. The intention was that this would serve exclusively as a new novitiate and house of studies while Terenure College would be exclusively devoted to the education of lay-pupils.

Built in 1847 and including four acres of land above the banks of the Dodder River between Churchtown and Rathfarnham, it was purchased from the Devine family for around £2,000 and on 24 September 1908 was opened as a novitiate with

Fr Patrick O'Dwyer as Prior and Fr Stan Meganetty as Master of Novices.[10] The first to be received there, James Angelus Rabbitte and Bob Metcalfe had been Terenure boys, both being on the Terenure rugby team the year before. The plans for 'Ardavon' as novitiate and house of studies, and Terenure for lay-pupils, did not endure. 'Ardavon' was retained but leased out to a family called Howard, and it did not return to Carmelite use until 1917.[11]

This dramatic turnaround in its fortunes was dictated by events in which Terenure College was central. In the same year as the purchase of 'Ardavon', Peter Elias Magennis was appointed Assistant to the General, Mayer. His brief was to advise Mayer on all matters relating to the English-speaking Carmelite areas of Ireland, America and Australia. At the fateful Irish Province Chapter held at Terenure in May 1909, Mayer presided, with Magennis as his secretary. In his opening speech, Mayer referred to the financial difficulties and deficiencies of the Irish Province and of Terenure College, in particular. Kildare, New York and Tarrytown were found to be in debt, but was Terenure heavily so. The Definitory therefore decided to close Terenure as a lay college or secondary school and to convert it to a novitiate and house of studies. It was decided to sell 'Ardavon' in the hope of recouping its £2,000 purchase price but that decision was not followed through. However, considerable confusion in direction and some division of opinion appear to have prevailed from May to November 1909 and beyond. By 1 November 1909, the college's debts stood at a sobering £11,737 and on 11 November it was decided that each of the ten houses in the Irish Province would be levied to help meet the interest payments on this debt. The levies varied from a humble £7 10s charge to impoverished Kildare and Knocktopher, to modest charges of £35 to Kinsale and Moate, and £40 to Port Adelaide and Port Melbourne to a sizeable £100 each to Whitefriar Street and New York.[12]

The Provincial, Fr Southwell, reported that some of the Carmelites wanted to retain 'Ardavon' as being large enough to accommodate both novices and professed, and to sell Terenure College. In one respect, this would have been easy enough: by the end of June, the halls of Terenure had fallen relatively silent: practically all the lay-boys had left and Fr Stan Meganetty was supervising the novices. In the end, however, by what process is unclear, Terenure was retained and it was decided to sell 'Ardavon'. That decision, however, was not persisted in; by the spring of 1910 the best offer of £1,200 fell far short of the original purchase price.[13] In the event, they decided to let the 'Ardavon' house and farm.

In the course of 1909, Terenure's financial situation had become extreme. By the end of the year, the Order had to raise £4,000 to meet the most pressing demands and was forced to double the levy on the country houses. In order to keep the most clamant of the college's grocers, provision merchants and suppliers at bay, Whitefriar Street provided an emergency £2,500. The following year, it gave an additional £1,200 to try to reduce the outstanding loan. Slightly better days came in the years immediately ahead: from 1910 to 1913, the Order managed to reduce Terenure's debt from £10,901 to £9,820, but the damage had been done.

One of the strangest aspects of the closure of Terenure as lay-college is the apparent silence surrounding it. The decision was sudden and its implementation immediate, all occurring within the space of a month. No notice appears to have been given — and no phasing-out years provided for, especially in respect to boarders. No extant documents in Terenure itself, or in other Carmelite archives, record protests or dismay of parents, guardians, public or past pupils. Stranger still, close searches of diocesan archives disclose no letters of concern to or objection by the Archbishop of Dublin who, only eighteen months before, had reluctantly allowed the opening of a new Carmelite novitiate (at 'Ardavon'). The boys simply left, and that was the end of it.

As noted earlier, folklore attributed the cause and the blame to an insensitive or ill-advised Continental Prior General. And, while a financial crisis was clearly at the centre of the 1909 decision and precipitated it, it is difficult to believe that the Carmelites, so well-regarded in the city and country, and so well-connected with a potential network of successful past pupils, could not have arranged an emergency appeal to bail out the college if that were their sole and exclusive concern. However, the Carmelite agenda or vision was perhaps significantly more complex than simply the solution of a financial crisis however daunting. Unlike, say, the teaching orders of De La Salle and Irish Christian Brothers, or even of an Order like the Jesuits for whom education was central; the Carmelites in Ireland and everywhere else, were in spirit contemplatives and, in practice, mendicants. Their monastic ideal was central in this regard and formal provision of education to lay society was an acquired rather than an original or inherent vocation. To some extent, indeed, the adoption of formal education provision as part of their mission could serve, as a primary purpose, the attraction of young men to the Order's monastic life and the provision of education to lay-pupils for secular purposes it could be argued might be a secondary purpose.

When one takes the long view, from 1860 to 1909, it transpires that the closure of Terenure was not only not unique in modern Irish Carmelite annals, it was not even the first such case: rather, it was the last closure in that era before the First World War. The renowned Carmelite school in Kildare, which had 300 pupils on its books at the start of the 1870s and which produced a cohort of illustrious Carmelites was closed in 1884 when the De La Salle Brothers arrived.[14] Older, but equally renowned, was the college in Knocktopher, opened on 1 January 1852, and which Fr Bennett had wanted to close in 1859. Affiliated to the Catholic University in 1875, it closed its doors in 1899.[15] Then, three years later, Fr Bennett's Dominick Street Academy founded in 1854, was closed in 1902. Terenure came at the end of a list of closures. Why Dominick Street and Knocktopher were closed is not evident in the surviving literature. Like Kildare, it may have been because teaching orders of brothers had opened in competition in their localities.

Such closures must have eased the pressures on a clearly overstretched Order from the 1880s to the First World War. Certainly, there were tensions and differences in the Order on the issues of missions versus lay education on the one hand, and within the Order and the college on the issue of spiritual formation of novices versus lay education on the other. This is why one suggests significance in Magennis's appointment as Assistant General to Mayer, a year before the decision to close. The combination of novitiate and secular college on one premises caused tensions. At the end of the 1880s, for example, students preparing themselves for a lifetime vocation in the Order were so discontented with the type of formation, and training they were receiving that they took the audacious step of writing in complaint to the General. Improvements followed in the next year when the students were enrolled in the Catholic University for their philosophy and were given formal lectures in theology by one of the Terenure fathers. Nevertheless, when a year later again, the General, Galli, visited in September 1890, he too concluded that the college was not suitable as a novitiate and until finances made it possible for a more suitable alternative to be secured, the novitiate there should be cloistered and clearly sequestered from the college activities and students. To what extent this may have been accomplished is not certain but, perhaps not very far, since Richard Colfer in September 1901 introduced a new reform regime for Terenure's novices. This involved a compulsory two-year course in philosophy and a wide-ranging syllabus of studies in preparation for university courses.

While this new attention was being directed to novice formation and education, the foreign missions exercised a more intense centrifugal pull on the operations and resources of the Irish Carmelites. Two examples from the Australian Mission in 1904 illustrate this. Take the case of James John of the Cross Cogan. A Terenure student and one of its prize winners in the Intermediate in 1890 and again in 1891, he was received into the Order the following year and was ordained in Rome in 1899.[16] In September 1900, he was sent on the Australian mission along with Patrick Paul O'Dwyer and Francis Joseph O'Reilly. Stationed in South Melbourne, in 1904 his frustration at the lack of adequate personal support from Ireland led him to write to the Prior General to complain at the way this was hampering their endeavours.[17]

Even more forcefully, his younger confrere, Paul O'Dwyer, who was made Prior of Port Adelaide in 1903, wrote to the General, also in 1904, to tender his resignation as Prior because the Irish Provincial, Stan Bartley, was not sending him sufficient Carmelite priests: as far as O'Dwyer was concerned, it was difficult if not impossible to have a viable monastic observance. He went to the extreme position of advising the General, Mayer to close Terenure to lay-pupils so that it could concentrate on the formation of Carmelite vocations.[18]

On the Australian mission with them at the time was Peter Elias Magennis. He had been persuaded as a nineteen-year-old Belfast youth, to enter Terenure College, as a postulant, by John Wheatley, in 1887. Ordained in 1894, he was assigned to teach at Dominick Street and within a year was principal there, a role which lasted until 1896. Following a year in Knocktopher, he was sent out to Australia in 1898 to the mission at Gawler where he became Prior the following year. Shortly after this, he moved to a new foundation at Port Adelaide where his confreres included Cogan and O'Reilly. In June 1903, the Irish Provincial Chapter elected him Prior of Port Melbourne but he declined to accept the appointment — possibly because he too, like Dwyer, was frustrated at the lack of personnel for an effective Community life.

Wheatley regarded his protégé, Magennis, as profoundly a reformer and as one 'who will yet be a redeemer of the Order in Ireland'.[19] Wheatley was anxious to see him back in Ireland and realised that wish. He told General Mayer, that the religious in Terenure needed Magennis's commitment to formation and observance, but added, significantly, that Magennis would only agree to take charge of the novices and professed there if Terenure were closed to lay-pupils. Magennis was brought back in the autumn of 1906 to become Master of Novices at Terenure. Two years later, he became right-hand man to the General and the decision on closure taken at the 1909 Chapter, where Mayer presided and Magennis advised, takes on a meaning beyond the problem posed exclusively by debt. That ambivalence in the Order about mission and education did not cease with the closure. Even when Terenure was reopened to lay-pupils in 1917 that uncertainty continued as will be seen in due course. In the interval, with the boarders departed and the day-pupils no longer crunching their way up the main avenue, the novices and professed who remained after 1909 must surely have been rattling about the silent corridors. While little of the post-closure sequel has survived, the census of 1911 captures the place and its occupants as if in freeze-frame. The census records 'The Residents of house, 18.2. in Terenure'. They numbered some 26 and included fourteen-year-old John Coffey, fifteen-year-old Bernard McDermott and sixteen-year-old James Fallon — the latter dying as a Carmelite priest in his eighty-sixth year in 1981. At the upper age limit was to be found 74-year-old Fr John Wheatley and 70-year-old Fr Tom Reilly: and those young and middle-aged whose Carmelite careers — even in the restored Terenure — were just unfolding; these included future Prior Presidents Louis Gerhard, Charles Gavin and Richard Brocard Taylor. Prayer, formation and farming operations continued in the quiet years that followed, but the place could not be entirely cut off from a world at war and an Ireland heading for revolution.

131

Peter Elias Magennis, first ever Irish Prior General of the Carmelite Order.

Ordination group at Terenure College, 1915.
Louis Gerhard and James Angelus Rabbitte are second and third from the left in the back row.

132

133

THE REB
DU
Apri

LLION IN

LIN,

1916.

CHAPTER 10

*Carmelites and
National Revolution
from 1916*

Cover of *The Six Days' Rebellion*,
a souvenir of the 1916 Rising, *c.* 1916.

THE CLOSURE OF THE COLLEGE IN 1909 WAS SUDDEN AND DRAMATIC: IT LEFT little by way of evidential wreckage in its wake. The re-opening in 1917 was just as sudden and was preceded by little or no floating evidence to indicate that the tide had turned: whether those within the Irish Province, who never wanted the college closed in the first place, now predominated in the councils of the Order and carried the day, or whether those at the top — specifically Magennis, Southwell, Provincial at the time of closure, and Stan 'The Da' Meganney, Master of Novices, had had a serious change of mind and heart the evidence does not emerge. Even the possibility that some powerful and external official source, such as the Dublin Archdiocese, successfully prompted the reconsideration and restoration is not in evidence. However, there was one event at that time which interrupted the quiet, contemplative tenor of its ways — the remarkable Carmel Bazaar.

The Carmel Bazaar was a great fund-raising fête held to raise badly needed finance to meet the cost of major building works at Whitefriar Street. Fr Joseph McCabe was Prior there from 1913 to 1919; on his return from his years as Prior in New York, he found the old Community house in a ruinous condition, condemned by the corporation with a compulsion to repair. He, therefore, conceived a grand plan to create a new house and upgrade the original church. Onerous debts were incurred in undertaking this work, some £13,000 of which £3,000 had been collected when the war broke out in August 1914.[1] He developed the idea of this great fête or bazaar, to be held in the grounds of Terenure College. Originally planned for September 1916, it had to be postponed until May of the following year. Opened by the Lord Mayor on 19 May 1917 and running until 28 May, it was by any contemporary standards quite a major undertaking with multiple diversions and entertainments. Over 70 stalls lined each side of the main driveway, with grand archway and bandstand. Each evening there was ballroom-dancing in the main hall and concerts in a Café Chantant pavilion; there were also half-hour whist drives, boating on the Lake, funfairs, show-jumping, miniature golf and tea gardens; the college experienced some metamorphosis from a seat of contemplation to a forum of entertainment. Not all Carmelites were edified or amused. The ageing Fr Andrew Farrington, who took over the presidency almost a half-century before when Fr Gilligan resigned over boating on the lake, was not impressed: with the Band of the Dublin Metropolitan Police playing a medley which included *I'm Through with Roaming Romeo's*, *Love's Own Kiss* and *Tingle-ingling* he could hardly be blamed: 'And now there is a Bazaar with dancing and singing Café etc— all diabolical undertakings. If things continue like this I will write to Cardinal Vanutelli' he fulminated.[2]

For all that, funds were raised, Whitefriar Street's debts were reduced and the college was opened up to the public again in a way that it had not been for almost a decade. Doubtless very many local residents patronised the event along with the citizenry at large. In that context, James Carmel O'Shea, fourteen-year-old Kinsale lad when he came to the college as a postulant in 1913, and living there as novice and student when the bazaar took place, offered one interesting comment when thinking back on those years: 'During the Bazaar the Provincial, the Very Rev J J Cogan, O. Carm., received very many petitions to re-open the College, and so it was decided to do so'.[3]

Such petitions on that occasion can well be believed, but similar representations must have been well in train before that since a full-page advertisement announcing the re-opening of the college appeared in the programme published to advertise the bazaar. Whatever its genesis, all that is certain was the decision to reopen the college on Tuesday, 4 September 1917, as a 'High-Class Day School and Boarding College'.[4] What prompted the decision is unclear.

In one sense nothing had changed since 1909 — substantial debts still remained — almost £8,500 in 1916 and over £7,300 by 1919 and in its Chapter of 1916 the Irish Province was complaining of the shortage of personnel as well of as finance.[5] If a reason for the original closure was somehow to concentrate on vocations it certainly had not worked, to the extent that no significant increase in vocations had been suddenly forthcoming: just a little more than a month before the college reopened the Provincial admitted to the Prior General that at that very moment they had no novices at all — this at a time when they were planning to move the novitiate out of Terenure and down to Kinsale. Against this background the closure has some appearance of futility rather than utility and the quick succession of Terenure Priors over a short space of years — apart from James Cogan's tenure — suggests some instability: Colfer in 1909 was succeeded very briefly by Peter Louis Nolan. Cogan followed, from 1909 to 1913, when he took up the Provincial's Office for a remarkable four successive terms from 1913 to 1925, followed by another two terms from 1934 to 1940. Denis Devlin — ex Terenure boy — succeeded Cogan as Terenure Prior for one year from 1913 to 1914, followed by William Joachim Brennan from 1914 to 1916 and Charles F.X. Ronayne for a brief period in 1916 before a new Prior was appointed.

THE NEW PRIOR PRESIDENT:

Among those left behind in the wake of the 1909 closure was a remarkable young Australian Carmelite, Louis Rudolph Gerhard. Born in the Carmelite's Gawler parish in October 1889, he received his main secondary schooling with the Marist brothers in Semaphore, a suburb of Port Adelaide. He came to know Peter Magennis when the latter became Prior of Gawler from 1899 and when Fr Magennis was summoned back to Ireland to be Master of Novices at Terenure, he brought the seventeen-year-old Gerhard with him. The college role of 1906–07 records him there as a Junior Grade Intermediate student.[6]

He entered the novitiate, made his first profession on 15 October 1907 and was solemnly professed in October 1910. The first ever Australian Carmelite, he was ordained on 6 June 1914 on the same day as the Dubliner Ronayne who was to become Prior of Melbourne.[7] He had already secured his BA and HDip at the newly established National University of Ireland in Dublin and had completed his theology studies at the Jesuits' Milltown Park. One former pupil remembered him as a 'cold, austere disciplinarian'.[8] By contrast, a Carmelite contemporary, who was then a university student and Terenure prefect, Fr Thomas C. Murphy, clearly remembered 'there was something special about him which endeared him to the boys, a magnetism which attracted them and called for mingled respect and admiration'.[9] Fr Murphy well remembered Gerhard's magnetism and personal kindness and recalled of the re-opened Terenure College that 'it was indeed a happy school, largely owing to the affability and happy personality of the Prior'. Likewise, his Australian Carmelite contemporary and historian, Frank Shortis, described him as an energetic enthusiast who could tell a tale against himself. Teaching in Terenure for many years, Fr Gerhard recalled the story of overhearing a pupil asking 'Where's that bloody old fool, Gerhard?' and Fr Gerhard remarking that he didn't mind being called a bloody fool, but he objected to being called old when he was only 27![10] This was in 1916, in which year he was elected Prior of Terenure, a post he held in the vital re-opening years to 1922.

THE CARMELITES AND THE IRISH REVOLUTION:

These, of course, were vital years also in the history of the country, from the 1916 Rising through the 1918 election and War of Independence to the Treaty and formation of the Irish Free State. The Carmelites were to find themselves in the midst of this turmoil and were, indeed, to forge friendships with leading men of the Irish revolution that served them well and gave them a significant standing when the young revolutionaries later found themselves statesmen.

That relationship was forged from the outset with the 1916 Rising. One young Carmelite, James Carmel O'Shea, already just encountered, was serving his novitiate year in Terenure College when he had direct experience of the Rising, even if unintentionally: on Easter Monday 1916, he and fellow-novice, Mick Mansfield, had gone into town to visit the museum and were caught up in crossfire on St Stephen's Green. On being advised to make their way home, they were unable to secure public transport and having to walk, they were again caught up by the fighting at Portobello Bridge, from which they had to crawl to escape.[11]

The Carmelites' Whitefriar Street house was at the centre of the area of that insurrection, between the neighbouring Jacob's Factory and the Royal College of Surgeons, which had both been occupied by the insurgents. The redoubtable Fr Louis McCabe had climbed into Jacob's Factory to minister to the insurgents holding out there, while his confrere, Fr Denis Devlin, who had recently been Prior of Terenure, offered 'spiritual and patriotic' encouragement to those involved that came to Whitefriar Street. There was no hesitation in the Carmelites' response to the Rising. In June 1916, Fr Cogan, the Provincial, celebrated a Requiem Mass in a packed Whitefriar Street for the executed Joseph Mary Plunkett — with a congregation which included Plunkett's parents and widow.[12] On 15 May 1916, at their New York Friary on 29th Street, the Carmelites held a solemn Requiem Mass for 'the souls of the men who had died for their country in the recent Sinn Féin Rising in Dublin'. Offering that Mass were Frs Magennis, Southwell and Flanagan. Southwell urged the congregation to pray for the patriot dead, expressing his own admiration for their heroism and sacrifice.[13] As for Magennis, his deep and important involvement will be touched on shortly. In regard to the Australian president of Terenure, he was to have direct experience of the War of Independence on more than one occasion. At the onset of the Rising a section of the 4th Battalion of the Volunteers under W.T. Cosgrave and which included Vice-Commandant Cathal Brugha, entered the South Dublin Union at St James's Street and occupied the three-storey nurses' home, to prevent the British relieving Dublin Castle. On Thursday of Easter Week, the British launched an attack on the nurses' home where Brugha was seriously wounded by gunfire. On the next day, Fr Gerhard, dressed in stole, led a procession carrying the wounded Brugha to the Union Hospital.[14] Later on, he was in charge there on a night when the British raided the college because they believed that the Carmelites there were hiding Republicans. Prior Gerhard and a confrere were stood up against a wall while the college was being searched. Believing he was going to be executed, Gerhard asked the British Commanding Officer for permission to make a last confession to his fellow Carmelite. This was agreed but as soon as Fr Louis began to do so a soldier moved closer to overhear, and was ordered away. Fr Gerhard and colleague survived.[15] As it transpired, British suspicions about the college and hiding insurgents were apparently well-founded. The college Community provided a safe-house for Michael Collins during the War of Independence. This might smack of convenient folklore were it not for the fact that one member of the Community, Brother Canice Cuddihy, was specifically charged by Prior Gerhard with the task of hiding the Big Fellow in the college grounds.[16] There were at least two raids on the college by British Forces during these years, on 21 December 1920 and on 21 January 1921: according to Brian J. Heffernan, the instructions to the officers leading both raiding parties were to capture the IRA men, Richard Mulcahy, Cathal Brugha and W.T. Cosgrave, and though none of them was apprehended, ammunition was found during the second raid.[17]

Louis Canice Cuddihy was a Kilkenny man, born in 1878 and educated in St Kieran's College before moving on into his father's business. However in 1916, he felt called to the monastic life and was received into the Carmelites where he was professed in 1921. A great sportsman and champion of the underdog he had a special concern for the junior school boys in the 1920s and 1930s. In later life, he was assigned to Moate, Kildare and Kinsale but his formative Carmelite experience was in Terenure. He passed away in 1949. As for Fr Gerhard, one gleans a sense of his nationalist sympathies in his own reminiscence of directing his Terenure boys in a staging of Lady Gregory's play, *The Rising of the Moon*.[18] Following upon the end of his term as Prior and president of Terenure he was, in 1923, appointed Prior of Tarrytown, New York and it was in America he stayed for ten years, retiring to his Australian homeland in 1933. Here he taught and ministered for many more years in Melbourne until his death in May 1960. His Terenure years led to close friendship with William Cosgrave and others.

Terenure College was not the only Carmelite friary to be subjected to raids by British Forces. At the end of December 1920 they raided the Whitefriar Street house and found a revolver, ammunition and 'seditious' literature. The Deputy-Adjutant-General, J.B. Wroughton, complained to the Provincial, Fr Cogan, in a letter of 3 January 1921, as follows:

GENERAL HEADQUARTERS, IRELAND,
PARKGATE, DUBLIN
3rd January, 1921.

Reverend Sir,
I regret to inform you that, as a result of a search recently carried out by Military at the Carmelite Monastery, Aungier Street, Dublin, a revolver, a considerable quantity of miscellaneous ammunition, Military equipment and an amount of seditious literature were found on the premises.

I am commanded to request that you will be so good as to investigate this matter, and forward an explanation to these Headquarters for the information of the Commander-in-Chief.

Further, I am to ask that you will state exactly what steps you propose to take to ensure, in future, that Monasteries, Churches, buildings or grounds under your control, are not used to secret arms, ammunition, equipment or seditious persons or literature.

I am to say that it is not the wish of the Commander-in-Chief to cause Sacred edifices or Monastic orders to be subjected unduly to search or interference. Unless, however, the Commander-in-Chief can feel assured that such buildings are strictly confined to purely sacred uses, you will doubtless agree that he has no alternative but to treat them on the same footing as putative centres of rebel action.

I am,
Sir,
Your Obedient Servant,
Colonel on the STAFF
Deputy Adjutant General

The Provincial's response, if any, is not extant.

THE AMERICAN CONNECTION:

The forging of friendships between the college, the Order and the leaders of the emerging Ireland from 1916 was not confined to Ireland. We have already noted the Requiem Mass offered in New York's 29th Street Priory in May 1916 and the sentiments of support expressed by Edward Southwell. That priory was to become haven and refuge for Irish political fugitives over 1916 to 1924, notably Liam Mellows and Eamon de Valera. One of the key figures here was Fr Laurence Denis Flanagan — an old Blackrock school friend of de Valera and even longer than the Long Fellow. When de Valera made it to the USA after his escape from Lincoln Jail, he was given refuge in the 29th Street Priory by Fr Flanagan, even to the extent of being given the Long Friar's seven-foot bed. A Moate man himself, years later — in 1947 — when Fr Flanagan returned to Ireland on vacation he was not forgotten as de Valera had a state car put at the Friar's disposal. De Valera's Carmelite connections began in schoolboy friendship with Flanagan and ended in the late 1970s when he specifically requested of the Provincial, Fr Joe Linus Ryan, that he be buried in the Carmelite habit, as was duly done. However, the key connection and friendship was that which developed between Fr Southwells's concelebrant — Fr Peter Elias Magennis — and the revolutionaries.

THE FIRST IRISH GENERAL:

Of them all, Magennis became the most publicly identified and actively engaged Carmelite in the cause of Irish freedom. He was prominent at the major demonstration of support in Madison Square on 10 June 1916 in honour of the executed insurrectionaries. He was elected president of the Friends of Irish Freedom. At one of their public gatherings, he recounted how he had been close friends with leading figures of the Irish Parliamentary Party and had been a keen support of their Home Rule movement: but the Rising and its executions had converted him into a supporter of physical force and Irish Republicanism. He described their leaders, Pearse, McDonagh and others of the executed as personal friends who had done more for Irish freedom in one week than the constitutional movement had done in 100 years.[19] Over the course of the next year, he was deeply committed to endorsing Irish–American public demonstrations in support of the cause and pulled no punches in condemning the New York police authorities for their breaking up of these demonstrations. He was at the centre of the formation of the Carmelite branch of the Friends of Irish Freedom in New York in June 1917 where some 800 attended to hear him, other Carmelites and the redoubtable Judge Daniel Cohalan of Clann na Gael. In addition, he became actively involved in promoting the Gaelic League and its cultural agenda in the United States. Indeed through his work in particular the Carmelite House in 29th Street became, in one contemporary view, 'a headquarters and a rallying point in the noble work for the independence of Ireland'.[20] In May 1918, he was elected president of the Irish Race Convention held in New York with 2,500 delegates from across the United Sates.[21] At the same time he was busy as treasurer in helping to raise funds for Pearse's St Enda's School. By November 1918, he was to the fore of a movement to secure American intervention on behalf of Ireland and which was instrumental in getting the American Catholic hierarchy to press President Wilson to apply his principle of self-determination to the Irish cause. From there he went on to join the movement calling for Irish representation at the Versailles Peace Conference. Perhaps the high point of the public recognition of his role in Irish–America's support for Ireland came at the Irish Race Convention in Philadelphia in February 1919 where a gathering of 5,000 saw him re-elected president. When he left New York in August 1919 to attend the Orders' General Chapter in Rome, Liam Mellows, who had been given refuge in 29th Street after the Rising, was among the 500 who gathered on the quayside to see him off. Despite American and British press attacks on Magennis, these did not prevent him securing the unique distinction of being elected Prior-General of the Carmelites, the first Irishman to hold the top position. It was indeed a remarkable endorsement and he was now placed in a position of some influence in the diplomatic quadrangle of Rome, London, Washington and insurgent Ireland. Monsignor Hagan, Rector of the Irish College in Rome, was delighted at Magennis's elevation, as were his old comrades in the Friends of Irish Freedom who rejoiced in the fact that they had such a champion in Rome. This was to be evident when British diplomatic pressure was exerted on the Vatican to condemn Terence MacSwiney's hunger strike. Papal Under-Secretary of State, Monsignor Carretti, consulted Magennis for information and advice which resulted in a thwarting of the British quest for a condemnation. Back in Ireland to preside at the Chapter in September 1922, he attended the funeral of Harry Boland, shot in the Civil War. Indeed, as Boland's biographer, David Fitzpatrick notes, the Carmelites who had provided Boland with 'extensive practical as well as spiritual support in New York', now came to the rescue again to allow his remains lie in Whitefriar Street where his funeral Mass took place, after the Pro-Cathedral and another Church were refused.[22] Magennis recalled his memory of seeing Boland's remains in Whitefriar Street in an article entitled 'An American memory of Harry Boland' in the *Catholic Bulletin* in 1922.[23]

In this, he lamented the deaths of Boland, Collins and Griffith and more tragedy and regrets followed with the execution of Liam Mellows on 8 December 1922. In his own final letter to his mother, on the morning of his execution, Mellows wrote 'Tell Patsy I send my love to him and Fr Feeney and Fr MacGuinness'.[24] Meanwhile, Magennis had played an important role with Monsignor Hagan in enabling Seán T. O' Kelly, early in 1920, to gain an audience with and the sympathy of Pope Benedict XV for the Irish cause, and in explaining the context of MacSwiney's hunger strike.[25]

The connection with O'Kelly was to develop into one of enduring friendship. O'Kelly had been the Irish Provisional Government's representative in Paris when they were trying to gain recognition at the peace conference. In the debates on the Treaty and in the Civil War which followed, O'Kelly sided with de Valera and was one of the founding members of Fianna Fáil in 1926. Ten years later when this committed member of the Knights of Columbanus, and then Minister of Local Government and Vice-President of the Executive Council, married Phyllis Ryan, daughter of Agriculture Minister Dr Jim Ryan, it is Fr Magennis who officiated at the wedding in the University Church St Stephen's Green. They in turn were at Fr Magennis's bedside in St Vincent's Hospital when he passed away a year later, on 26 August 1937. In 1995, O'Kelly fondly recollected some 60 years of friendship with the Carmelites and remarked: 'Fr Peter, to my mind was the greatest Irish Republican of his time'.[26]

From Truce, Treaty to Civil War and beyond, Magennis continued in his efforts for his country. The execution of his friend Liam Mellows caused him great grief and led him to be hostile towards Cosgrave as a result. However, it compelled Magennis to involve himself in a proposed Vatican mission to try to bring the Civil War to an end. Dermot Keogh has described in some detail the way in which Magennis pressed the Vatican authorities in this matter: he succeeded to the extent that a mission was sent, but to no avail.[27] Finally, another factor serving to re-enforce the political and cultural nationalist orientation of the college in the years that followed its re-opening was the fact that young men and women who had grown up and served in the nationalist revolution chose in due course to send their sons to Terenure College. There were many such examples, but two will suffice here to illustrate this.

The parents of David Kennedy — whose passage through Terenure over the years 1946 to 1956 will be noted later — are a case in point. David's father, Paddy, a Dubliner of Tipperary origins, had joined the British Civil Service after leaving school *c.* 1912. He worked in London where he joined the Gaelic League, got to know Michael Collins there and had actually admitted to its Hampstead Branch in 1917, one Alfred Wilmore, known to later generations as Michael MacLiammór. Paddy soon after was transferred by his employers from London to work in Dublin in the last years of British rule from 1919. He turned up as usual at the Custom House on the very day it was burned — knowing in advance what was about to happen. He remained in the civil service after the transfer of power and ended his career, long after, to head up to the newly formed Department of Health after the Second World War.

David's mother, Mairín Ní Mhuiríosa had graduated in Celtic studies from UCD and became a well-established author. Well-known and highly-regarded as the author of *Stair Litríocht na nGael*, she and Paddy Kennedy had met in the Gaelic League and both came to have strong connections with the Ring Gaeltacht where he was a trustee.[28] Very recently, in his magisterial *Gaelic Prose in the Irish Free State, 1922–1939,* Philip O'Leary has recognised her as one of a select band of contemporary Gaelic critics who moved beyond the 'benedictions, blasts and banalities of Irish prose writings of the 1920's', singling out her '*Filíocht Ghaedhilge an Lae Indui*' as a contribution of special merit.[29] The second example is that of the father of Hugh, Tom and John Gunn, with Tom entering Terenure in 1936 and graduating from the college with the class of 1946. Their father, a Corkman born in 1902, joined Na Fianna in 1913 and during the War of Independence had become one of the youngest, if not the youngest, members in the Old IRA and possibly the youngest commissioned officer in the Irish Free State Army. He was only seventeen when given full-time duty as a lieutenant and company commander of the 3rd Northern Battalion. In 1922, he brought his battalion from the North, dropping off one company at Dundalk to take over the garrison being evacuated by the British there. He arrived in Dublin with 200 men to Wellington (later Collins) Barracks. From here, in December 1922, he was assigned by the chief of staff to take his battalion of three companies through the city with the rear company taking over Victoria Barracks, the second taking over the Hibernian Military School and the third, under his direct command, taking over the Vice-Regal Lodge from the British. In the act of raising the tricolour, he was at the effective birth of the Irish Free State.[30] With many boys of similar parental political backgrounds, with the Carmelite National commitment, and, as shall be seen later, with ex-pupils of the 1880s and 1890s who were prominent in the national movement, like Louis J. Walsh and J.J. Sheil, Terenure College was reborn and grew up with strong nationalist credentials.

THE week commencing Easter Monday of 1916 will
of Dublin in particular, as the " Black Week." T
the Bank Holiday, at which hour armed "Sinn
St. Stephen's Green Park, the College of Surg
houses commanding the leading thoroughfares. A
Government, but although the policeman on duty at the gate was
uniform were shot at sight, and motor cars were seized to form
Irish Republic. The number of soldiers in the city was not suffici
the streets, the ▓▓▓ and the hooligan element of the population
up reinforcements. The ▓▓▓ held out until Saturday afternoon,
unconditionally surrendered, recognising that his forces were hope
ty, did not surrender for some days afterwards.

The Photographs that are reproduced in this booklet will
during the Black Week. Fire rather than military operatio
many of the shops were set fire to, and from Tuesday evening un
Fire Brigade was powerless to perform its accustomed duties, as
of buildings were burnt to the ground. The damage done was e:
buildings destroyed was the General Post Office, a portion of
£60,000. Next to the Post Office, the most historic building tha
its priceless art treasures. Both buildings were erected from the
Royal Hibernian Academy being built and endowed by him.

The rebellion was mainly confined to Dublin, but there w

During the operations 125 police and military were killed,
Thirteen of the ▓▓▓ leaders, including the seven signatories to
and executed after trial by Field Court Martial, and over one hu
year to life.

REBELLION.

REBELLION.

Interior of *The Six Days' Rebellion*,
a souvenir of the 1916 Rising, *c.* 1916.

be remembered by the people of Ireland, and by the inhabitants
ouldering embers of disaffection broke into flame at mid-day on
" (ourselves alone) parties seized the General Post Office,
and many other public buildings in the city, as well as private
mpt was made to capture Dublin Castle, the seat of the Irish
dead, the gates were closed and the attempt failed.   Soldiers in
ades across the streets.   A proclamation was issued setting up an
deal with the outbreak, and as the police were withdrawn from
left in possession of the city until the military authorities brought
the " President of the Provisional Government," P. H. Pearse,
outnumbered.   Some of his followers, holding outlying parts of

147

y more eloquently than words the damage that Dublin suffered
s responsible for most of the damage.   After being looted
end of the week the heart of the city burned itself out.   The
persistently fired on them, and consequently whole blocks
d at three million pounds.   The most important of the public
interior of which had been recently reconstructed at a cost of
red was the Royal Hibernian Academy, in Abbey Street, with
s of the celebrated eighteenth century architect, Johnston, the

lated risings in the south and west.

ounded, while 180 civilians were killed and over 600 wounded.
oclamation of the " Irish Republic," were sentenced to death
were sentenced to terms of penal servitude ranging from one

Terenure College

WILL

RE-OPEN

Tuesday, Sept. 4th, 1917,

AS

A High-Class Day School and Boarding College.

For Terms, Prospectus, etc., apply to
The VERY REV. PRIOR.

Advert for the re-opening of Terenure College, 1917.

148

"CARMEL"

THE BAZAAR OF 1917.

Under the Patronage of

HER MAJESTY,

QUEEN AMELIE OF PORTUGAL.

AND

The Lady Mayoress.	Lady Catherine Berkeley.	Lady Kelly.
The Marchioness of Head-fort.	Mary Baroness Mowbray and Stourton.	Lady Glynn.
The Countess of Denbigh.	Baroness Ashbourne.	Lady Doran.
The Countess of Kenmare.	Baroness McDonnell.	Countess Plunkett.
The Countess of Gains-borough.	Lady Bellingham.	Mrs. Redmond Barry.
Viscountess Gormanstown.	Lady Murphy.	Mrs. O'Connor.
Lady Sophia Grattan-Bel-lew.	Lady O'Brien.	Mrs. Molony.
Lady Chance.	Lady Redmond.	Mrs. Ada Curran.
	Lady Lynch.	Mrs. P. J. Brady.

Right Hon. the Lord Mayor.	Sir Thomas J. Lipton, Bart.	The O'Donoghue of the Glens.
Right Hon. Earl Nelson.	Sir James Murphy, Bart.	The Attorney General, K.C.
Right Hon. Viscount Gor-manstown.	Sir Arthur Chance.	His Honor Judge Curran, K.C.
Right Hon. Lord Ash-bourne.	Sir Joseph M. Redmond.	P. J. O'Neill, Esq., J.P.
Right Hon. Lord McDon-nell.	Sir John P. Lynch.	W. M. Murphy, Esq., J.P.
Right Hon. Michael F. Cox, M.D., P.C	Sir Joseph Glynn.	W. Field, Esq., M.P.
Sir H. Bellingham, Bart.	Sir Henry Doran.	P. J. Brady, Esq., M.P.
	Sir P. Shortall.	
	Count Plunkett.	

Advert for the Carmel Bazaar of 1917 held at Terenure College.

BALL ROOM.

Entrance off Main Hall, College Buildings.

DANCING EVERY EVENING.

FOUR SESSIONS:

6.30 p.m to 7.15 p.m.
7.30 p.m. to 8.15 p.m.

8.30 p.m. to 9.15. p.m.
9.30 to 10.45 p.m.

MR. CLARKE-BARRY'S BAND.

Committee:

Messrs. J. A. Smyth, C. Coakley, P. J. Cleary, M. Gorevan, J. C. Hynes, C. Travers, J. J. Sheil, E. M. Lloyd, Dr. G. J. O'Farrell, Dr. W. Hooper, Messrs. E. C. Walker, J. M. Sheil, J. P. Conry, F. Coyle.

Hon. Secretaries:

J. P. Kenny, Esq., B.L.; J. L. Hatch, Esq.

Assistants:

Mrs. Coakley, Mrs. Hooper, Miss McCabe, Miss D. McCabe, Miss J. O'Connor, Miss P. O'Connor, Miss Hatch, Miss C. Hatch, Miss Lyons, Miss Doyle, Miss Davy, Miss A. Davy, Miss J. Mooney, Miss M. Mooney, Miss Keating, Miss Lennon, Miss O'Neill, Miss Doyle, Miss McMahon, Miss T. O'Keeffe, Miss Smyth, Miss R. Smyth, Miss Lalor, Miss V. Lalor, Miss K. Fitzgerald, Miss M. Fitzgerald, Miss Coyle, Miss Curran, Miss Broderick, Miss Ronayne, Miss M. O'Donohoe, Miss Coleman, Miss Bourke, Miss Molloy, Miss L. Byrne, Miss Cussen, Miss R. McMahon, Miss M. McMahon, Miss Masterson, Miss Alice Meagher.

Stewards:

Messrs. J. J. Meagher, C. J. Fallon, Dr. H. J. Barniville, Messrs. D. O'Keeffe, E. L. Fitzpatrick, C. J. Cashin, W. Fanagan, J. R. MacMahon, B.L.; Dr. E. A. Magennis, Dr. J. B. Magennis, Mr. J. J. Doyle, Dr. P. V. Dolan, Messrs. J. F. Lalor, A. Glynn, J. Gaynor, T. P. O'Connor.

E

Advert for ballroom dancing, 1917.
This is an example of the entertainments available on the college grounds during the Carmel Bazaar.

'The Bing Boys': Donald, Bradley, Perry, Butterfield and Smith, ex Terenure pupils taken in Belgium following the end of the First World War, 5 February 1919.

E. C.
-*-

GENERAL HEADQUARTERS, IRELAND,

PARKGATE,

DUBLIN.

3rd. January, 1921.

Reverend Sir,

I regret to inform you that, as a result
of a search recently carried out by Military at the
Carmelite Monastery, Aungier Street, Dublin, a
revolver, a considerable quantity of miscellaneous
ammunition, Military equipment and an amount of
seditious literature were found on the permises.

I am commanded to request that you will
be so good as to investigate this matter, and forward
an explanation to these Headquarters for the
information of the Commander-in-Chief.

Further, I am to ask that you will state
exactly what steps you propose to take to ensure, in
future, that Monasteries, Churches, buildings or grounds
under your control, are not used to secrete arms,
ammunition, equipment or seditious persons or literature.

I am to say that it is not the wish of
the Commander-in-Chief to cause Sacred edifices or
Monastic orders to be subjected unduly to search or
interference. Unless, however, the Commander-in-Chief
can feel assured that such buildings are strictly

To:-
Provincial,
Carmelite Order,
Carmelete Monastery,
Aungier Street,
DUBLIN.

confined to purely sacred uses, you will doubtless
agree that he has no alternative but to treat
them on the same footing as putative centres of
rebel action.

I am,

Sir,

Your obedient Servant,

J B W...ghton

COLONEL on the STAFF,
Deputy Adjutant General...

Letter from the deputy adjutant general's staff to
the Prior of Terenure College stating that the
British Army would have 'no alternative but to
treat ... [the college] ... on the same footing as
putative centres of rebel action', 3 January 1921.

TO:—

Provincial,
Carmelite Order,
DUBLIN.

E.C.

UACHTARÁN NA HÉIREANN
(PRESIDENT OF IRELAND)

BAILE ÁTHA CLIATH
(DUBLIN)

28th July, 1960

Dear Father O'Callaghan,

I send you herewith a reconstruct of the little speech I made at the dinner here. I have dictated it from memory. As I told you, I had neither manuscript nor notes on the occasion. I am sorry for the delay in sending it to you, but I knew it was not urgent.

I am looking forward to seeing you here again very soon.

With all good wishes.

Very sincerely yours,

Eamon de Valera

154

Letter from Eamon de Valera to Fr O'Callaghan
enclosing a transcript of a speech he gave about his
relationship with the Carmelites, 28 July 1960.

"When referring to the Carmelites of 29th Street on the occasion of the dinner here I said something like this:

It is a great pleasure to me to have here the Prior-General and the other representatives of the Carmelite Order.

The Carmelite Order has been in this country almost seven hundred years, but for me the Carmelites have always been, in particular, associated with 29th Street, New York, and with Fr. McGuinness, Fr. O'Connor and Fr. Flanagan, and the other members of the Community who were there forty years ago. The night before I appeared at the Waldorf Hotel, in June 1919, when I was being sought for by the journalists all over America, I spent at 29th Street.

It was at 29th Street that Liam Mellows stayed, and it was there that he found his most steadfast friends when he arrived in America after 1916. Fr. McGuinness and he regarded each other as comrades in the campaign for Irish independence.

Father McGuinness was President of The Friends of Irish Freedom, and used his position to see that the views of the Irish in Ireland were steadily kept in mind in the activities of that Organisation. Soon after my arrival, however, Father McGuinness was called to the General Chapter in Rome. He was elected Prior-General, and so was no longer able to act as President of the Friends of Irish Freedom. That was a setback to the Cause of Irish freedom. Had Fr. McGuinness been able to continue as President I am confident that many of the later disastrous differences which arose in that Organisation would never have occurred. Bishop Gallagher, whose views were quite different, succeeded Father McGuinness.

Father McGuinness was a true Irishman, who loved his country and his people. He won the regard of everybody. His speeches and his writings were an inspiration. His death was an uncalculable loss.

After his death, however, the Fathers in 29th Street continued the work for the Irish Cause. Liam Mellows, Harry Boland, Seán Nunan, Liam Pedler and I were constant visitors there, and were accepted almost as members of the Community. Harry and I had our games of handball and Liam Mellows used us as a butt for some of his practical jokes.

The tradition of love and service to Ireland has been faithfully followed at 29th Street. The old and the new are represented here tonight. Father Coffey was a member of the Community at 29th Street back in 1919/20. He is with us here. We regret that the veteran, Fr. Flanagan, could not be with us, also. Fr. Coffey, Seán Nunan and Liam Pedler have been exchanging reminiscences of the incidents of that period. It is pleasant to see them all assembled here.

UACHTARÁN NA HÉIREANN
(PRESIDENT OF IRELAND)

BAILE ÁTHA CLIATH
(DUBLIN)

(2)

Father O'Connor, Fr. Hugh Devlin, Fr. Slattery, Fr. Medcalf and Fr. Hastings, who figured so prominently in the Community forty years ago, are now gone from us, but their spirit has not left 29th Street.

Their successors, with the present Prior Provincial, Fr. Donald O'Callaghan, whom we are so happy to welcome here, and Fr. Reid, loyally carry on the old tradition, and when we need advice or help from friends in New York the first friends we think of are our friends in 29th Street - I should, I suppose, now say 28th and 29th Streets - and we have never found them wanting. May it remain so, and may those who in the future are responsible to the Irish people for the conduct of Irish policy and Irish affairs always find such willing co-operation as has been given us by the Carmelites during the last forty years.

I give you the toast of the past, the present and the future. On God's right hand be those who have gone, and may those of the present and the future be always in His keeping."

Éamon de Valera

156

157

Whitefriar Street Church on Aungier Street, 1914.

CHAPTER **11**

Restoration, 1917–31

Display by pupils of the oft-publicised
Swedish drill, 1928.

CARMELITE COMMITMENT TO IRELAND'S CAUSE ENSURED THAT WHEN THE college re-opened its doors in 1917 that it would find ready favour with those who would come to power in the half century and more following the foundation of the Irish Free State. Nevertheless, little enough is known about the college in the twelve years from its restoration. One may surmise from the substantial advertisement that the Terenure authorities published in 1917, and reproduced frequently thereafter, that there was a new zeal in promoting the college.

Indeed, within a year of the restoration, Fr Gerhard was announcing that, in response to queries from neighbouring residents, the college had embarked upon providing a 'preparatory course' for boys aged nine to twelve. The numbers of those neighbours began to grow in the course of the 1920s — and those neighbours were close: in 1926, the firm of Fitzgerald and Leonard had just completed 22 substantial, five-bedroomed houses on part of the college grounds facing Templeogue Road, and others were to follow in the decade and more ahead. In that same period, the college authorities made intensive and extensive use of advertisements in the national press each summer and autumn. Some could be fairly basic, but at times they were quite lively and aggressive. One, for the autumn of 1923, presented an unusually spirited message, offering 'Health—Happiness—Success' and proclaiming among Terenure College's attractions and merits 'an ideal situation; own farm, fifty-five acre sport-field, boating, swimming' in addition to 'a distinguished Irish professor' and 'a matron' who was 'a qualified nurse'.[1] Its general tone was a marked departure in terms of positive self-promotion: it catered for entrance examinations to 'University, Banks, Pharmacy, College of Science and Veterinary College, etc', and boasted among its records since 1920 'First Place in Arithmetic and other distinctions' while paramount in its sporting achievements was 'winning the Dublin Football Championship and Cup twice'. While this novel approach was not sustained in college publicity through-out the 1920s, by 1930 the college was able to add that it was 'A Distinctive Educational Establishment, standing in 60 acres, including 10 acres lake and woodland' and boasted the crowning attractions of 'Electric lighting, Steam heating'.[2]

Furthermore, given their close involvement with the national struggle, it was hardly surprising that the authorities encouraged a new or stronger commitment to matters Gaelic. It was certainly evident in the more obvious commitment to Gaelic games, as will be seen later in this chapter. In the first public advertisement of re-opening, which he placed in the daily press in the autumn of 1917 Fr Gerhard gave prominence to Irish language, literature and history in the college's syllabus and also to the fact that they had brought in a lay professor of Irish to promote this in the curriculum. In addition, Irish dancing now appeared for the first time, alongside physical drill and music.

THE TEACHERS:

As to the teaching staff, three Carmelite priests were listed — Frs Taylor, Griffin and Gearon. Fr Peter Thomas Griffin was born in Templetouhy, Co. Tipperary, in 1887.

He studied at the National University where he secured his MA, and then was sent for further study to the Gregorian University in Rome. He was professed in 1909 and ordained in 1917 after which the greater part of his active life was spent teaching at Terenure, although, he also devoted some seven years of his priestly days to the Chaplaincy of the South Dublin Union — for long, a great Carmelite commitment. He was appointed Bursar to the Province in 1922 and Assistant Provincial to Richard Colfer in 1925, and again to Denis Devlin as Provincial in 1931 and to James Cogan in 1937. Between 1931 and 1941, he returned to the Terenure teaching staff where he was a senior professor of Latin and English. Affectionately nicknamed 'Uncle' by his confreres in the Community, he was the most popular of them all among the pupils in the 1930s: tall, balding, 'slow of step but quick of wit ... and at all times most gentle', he passed away in December 1941.[3] As for Fr P.J. Gearon, after three years teaching in Terenure, he departed for the Australian mission at Port Adelaide in 1920. He became Prior there in 1923 and gained a reputation for active involvement in conservative politics. By the 1930s, he was back in Europe, based in the new Carmelite house at Faversham, Kent, and was actively producing various well-received devotional and apologetic publications up until the 1950s.

However, most striking perhaps, in Fr Gerhard's first advertisement of 1917 was the mention of a small but significant number of lay-teachers. Some of these, it transpires, were very distinguished in their fields, nationally and even internationally. The professor of Irish of whom the college was proud to boast in its advertisements, was Éamon Ó Tuathail. Born in Dublin in 1882, he was reared with a maternal uncle on the Dufferin Estate in Co. Down. In his teens, he learned Irish through Conradh na Gaeilge and took to it so readily that in his twenties Éamon became a travelling teacher of Irish in Co. Monaghan before returning to Dublin in 1910. Here, in UCD, he earned his MA in Celtic studies in 1914. He became a great collector of folklore, song and verse in Irish from the northern counties of Antrim, Armagh, Cavan, Monaghan, Tyrone and Co. Meath. He was one of the early collectors of ediphone recordings and for a long time was associated with Coláiste Uladh at Cloghaneely in Co. Donegal. He published extensively on various aspects of Irish literature and folklore. Notable among his publications were *Rainn agus Amhráin* — a collection of songs and verse from counties Meath, Louth and Armagh, which appeared in 1923 and *Scéalta Mhuintir Luinigh*, or *Munterloney Folktale*, published by the Irish Folklore Institute ten years later. By the time he joined the Terenure staff in 1917, he was already described as president of the Leinster College of Irish and professor of Coláiste Uladh. Before the 1920s were over, he had become professor of Irish at Trinity College Dublin in a chair that had been reformed into a new, more vibrant professorship of Irish literature in 1919.[4]

For Terenure College, Ó Tuathail was clearly some catch: when Fr Richard Colfer, succeeding Louis Gerhard as president, placed his advertisement in the national press in August 1922, for the college's re-opening, he had selected only two issues to highlight, namely 'Modern Business Methods' and 'Irish Classes under the direction of Eamonn O'Toole Esq M.A.'[5] Eminent in his field too was the college's elocution teacher, none other than Frank Fay, 'late of the Abbey Theatre'. Fay and his younger brother, William — both Belvedere boys — were major figures in the emergence of an Irish national theatre movement. They were co-founders of the Dublin Dramatic Society and the Ormonde Dramatic Society in 1898 before establishing their National Dramatic Company, which later merged with the Irish National Theatre Society. In 1904, Frank was one of the founders of the Abbey Theatre, and, apart from his practical role there in speech-training, he was central to the creation of the Abbey's distinctive ethos. He had the distinction of acting — as Shawn Keogh — in the very first production of Synge's *Playboy of the Western World* in 1907. He and Willy went to the United States for several years until they returned to work in England in 1914. Frank, however, later returned to the Abbey and to teaching elocution, and found himself on the Terenure College staff.

Another significant teaching colleague was Eugene Moynihan who taught higher mathematics, physics and chemistry. He had begun his teaching career in 1904. A Corkman educated there by the Christian Brothers, Eugene was a brilliant student who took his primary degree in science while also excelling in French and English. He taught in a number of Dublin colleges before joining the Terenure staff: this was before its closure in 1909 and he came back in 1917 immediately upon its re-opening. Here and in Kevin Street Technical College, he spent the rest of his professional career, retiring from Terenure in 1943. He was an energetic, lively individual and very popular with the senior boys in particular. He possessed a 'sparkling wit', a hearty laugh and great sense of humour. Sadly, he had not long to enjoy his retirement, passing away after a heart attack in early January 1946.[6]

THE PRESIDENTS:

Following Louis Gerhard's assignment to America from 1922, there was a quick succession of three Prior Presidents: the ever-patient and gentle Richard Colfer (1922–3), then ex-Dominick Street Academy and Terenure College boy, Patrick Ambrose Wade (1923–4), and Charles Gavin (1924–5). These rapid changes, arising from serious problems of ill-health,[7] cannot have been conducive to the stability and growth of the college and they coincided with significant changes in the government's approach to secondary education. It may be noted, however, that in the years immediately after the First World War and the War of Independence and Civil War similar institutions experienced difficulty and decline: Clongowes entered a period when its morale was 'at its lowest ebb', while Blackrock College in the same period has been described as 'performing below its potential in many spheres and had suffered from diminishing numbers due to lack of staff dynamism'.[8]

With Fr Richard Brocard Taylor, known affectionately as 'The Doc', becoming the president, Terenure College entered a period of some continuity since he held the office until 1931. It is difficult to avoid the judgement that with the homecoming of 'The Doc', Terenure entered a new era. Indeed, in a somewhat giveaway observation, one of his presidential successors, Fr Dunstan O'Connor, confessed of Terenure that 'there was no serious effort to run it as a school until Doctor Taylor, with minimal resources, became Prior in 1925'.[9] For one thing, the chopping and changing at the top ceased. He became one of a succession of presidents who not only held the office for long enough to make significant impact but who were in themselves remarkable and distinguished individuals — for Fr Taylor was succeeded by Fr James Carmel O'Shea and Fr Andrew Eugene Wright. Between them they gave almost twenty years' unbroken leadership from 1925 to 1943.

Born in Dublin in 1888, Richard Taylor was a Junior Grade Terenure pupil in 1904[10] and entered the Carmelites in 1906. He took for his religious name, that of the thirteenth century first Prior of Mount Carmel, Saint Brocard, who laid the foundations for the Carmelite Order by securing, in 1195, their monastic rule of life from Albert of Jerusalem. In 1909, Richard was a Royal University prize winner and, academically gifted as the young Carmelite was, Fr Wheatley saw a bright scholastic future for him and sent him to Rome where Wheatley hoped Magennis would guide his future studies. He had already obtained his masters degree in Classics along with fellow student, Charlie Ronayne, and in November 1911 both were sent for further studies to Rome where Magennis, as Assistant General, would maintain a mentoring interest. Here, three years later the two, together with Louis Gerhard, were ordained on 6 June 1914. Returning to Dublin and Whitefriar Street in 1915, the following year he was assigned to Terenure where he taught until 1921, becoming successor there to Gerhard from 1919. There followed some four years in the Carmelite International College of San Alberto in Rome under Magennis and Ronayne as Assistant General. It was a prestigious assignment and a significant preparation for taking up the appointment as Terenure's president and Prior in 1925. Regarded as one of the finest minds in the Carmelite Order in the twentieth century 'The Doc' Taylor was described by O'Dwyer as a 'reticent and mildly caustic character'. There was also more than a hint of intellectual snobbery, a suggestion that Taylor saw intellectual prowess as almost more of a desideratum for would-be Carmelites and for Terenure pupils alike than any other consideration. Certainly, as will be noted shortly, Taylor himself made no bones about his insistence that in effective student formation, the intellectual dimension was paramount. He came into his office at a propitious moment for the college and its future.

It appears that when the Provincial Chapter of the Order was held in July 1925, Charles Gavin had ceased to be Terenure Prior and the post apparently had been left vacant for a time. Not only that, when the General, Magennis, came to preside at this Chapter, in his opening address he placed the future of Terenure as a lay secondary establishment at the very top of his agenda. It appears that a long debate was held about the college's past, present and future — a debate which went over two sessions without decision. Then, at the opening of the Chapter's third and final session, Magennis put the question 'should Terenure be retained as a College?' to which a majority vote for retention was recorded. It may seem extraordinary that the matter should have ever arisen as it would appear to do so again momentarily in the 1930s when economic depression and uncertainty of enrolments led some members of the Order to question the wisdom of keeping Terenure College going and urged that it would be closed down.[11] Certainly its comparative academic performance and the number of its pupils from 1917 to 1924 may not have been great. This, and debate over what should be the Irish Carmelites central mission may have lain behind this momentous questioning. Again, it is hard to avoid the speculation that Magennis may have been the moving hand that initiated a debate on closure versus continuation in 1925, just as he was almost certainly the one behind the decision to close in 1909.

THE NEW STATE EXAMINATIONS:

As to academic performance, its measurement — as ever — is a complex and contentious area. What cannot be contested is that the number of Terenure pupils taking the state examinations was small and their success rate hardly inspiring. In 1924, the first year of the new Intermediate and Leaving Certificate examinations, for example, in a list of 103 boys' schools presenting candidates for both the Leaving Certificate and Intermediate Certificate, Terenure was not to be found: it had no Leaving Certificate candidates. It was featured in a list of 39 boys' schools and colleges, which presented for the Intermediate Certificate only, coming twenty-first out of those 39, in terms of numbers of candidates: Terenure had 7 presenting, 1 securing honours and 3 securing passes.[12]

In fairness, of course, the Leaving Certificate was a new examination in 1924, a product of the significant government legislation or administrative innovation in secondary education from 1922 to 1924. Even before the formation of the new state in 1922, it was officially acknowledged that the old Intermediate system with its payment on results was not satisfactory. The overall national failure rate was problematically high. The Intermediate Education Commissioners, in their report for 1919–20, found that 49% of all candidates failed to secure a pass in a single subject, while a Vice-Regal Committee on Education in 1919 complained of the adverse nature and effects of the payment by results system.[13]

That committee proposed the ending of the old three-grade system of junior, middle and senior, and the substitution of an Intermediate Certificate examination for pupils aged 15 to 16 and of a Leaving Certificate examination for those aged 17 to 18. The government of the new Irish Free State put an end to the old National and Intermediate Education Boards in 1922 and 1923 and created the new Department of Education in 1924.[14] Then its Intermediate Education (Amendment) Act of 1924 put an end to payment by results. This was replaced by a capitation grant for every student between the ages of 12 and 20 who had passed an entrance examination for admission to the secondary system and who fulfilled a requirement of at least 130 attendances in the school year: £7 per pupil following the Intermediate Certificate course and £10 for those taking the Leaving Certificate program. In addition, an increased grant of 10% was paid for schools teaching through Irish for a least half the instruction and 25% for those teaching fully through Irish. Further emphasis on Irish followed in the years ahead with a pass in Irish being essential to secure the Intermediate Certificate, and the honours Leaving Certificate from 1928, and to secure the Pass Leaving Certificate from 1934. Furthermore, from 1922 the rigid adherence to prescribed texts was abolished, and a more flexible programme introduced. In addition, for the first time, secondary teachers' salary increments were paid for by the state so long as each school employed registered teachers proportionate to the number of pupils.[15]

As mentioned, Terenure appears to have had no candidates for the first Leaving Certificate Examination in 1924 and had few enough thereafter but it certainly was not unique in this. In 1926 — when 441 boys took the Leaving Certificate and 249 passed — Terenure had 11 presenting for the Certificate examinations with no successes. At the same time Rockwell with 48 presenting secured 9 honours and passes in the Leaving Certificate; Castleknock with 24 presenting had no honours and only 1 pass in the Leaving Certificate; Belvedere with 55 presenting had only 5 honours and passes in the Leaving Certificate; and Blackrock with 44 presenting but only 5 securing honours and passes. In 1927, Terenure appears to have had no Leaving Certificate students and likewise St Mary's, Rathmines; while Blackrock had 13 with 9 successes; Castleknock 9 with 6 successes; Belvedere 16 with 8 successes. In 1928, Terenure and St Mary's again appear to have had no Leaving Certificate candidates; while Blackrock had 11 successes out of 12; Belvedere 16 out of 17; and Clongowes 18 out of 18. In 1929, in the Intermediate Certificate Examination, Terenure had only 7 presenting, with 4 successful. Again, though this looks minimal, it was hardly exceptional: in that same year St Mary's, Rathmines, had just 6 presenting, with 5 successes; Blackrock 34 with 26 successes; and St Columba's, Rathfarnham, had 13 presenting with 3 successes. As for the 1929 Leaving Certificate, Terenure again had no candidates.[16] In 1930, the college had 2 Leaving Certificate candidates, both failing while St Mary's, Rathmines, had 4 with 2 failing.[17] Thereafter, the press ceased to publish the schools' lists as the Department of Education changed its method of communicating results. It was hardly a glorious record for the college but by 1936, it had 8 candidates, 7 passing, 3 with honours, and in 1937, 10 sat the examination with 8 passing, 5 of them with honours.[18] It might be argued that the Terenure authorities preferred their students to sit the Matriculation rather than the Leaving Certificate examinations in the 1920s, but unfortunately the official figures for Terenure candidates for the Matriculation Certificate examinations do not bear this out. The numbers of its candidates for this examination over 1925 to 1930 were as follows: 1925 — 2; 1926 — 4; 1927 — 0; 1928 — 0; 1929 — 0. Not till 1930 was this trend reversed when 7 Terenure candidates presented.[19] This was despite the fact that nationally at the time, the Matriculation Examination was less demanding and it emerged that pupils were successfully taking it at the end of the first year of the two-year Leaving Certificate programme: indeed, there were instances of pupils successfully taking the Matriculation immediately after their Intermediate Certificate. It is hard to escape the judgement that, academically, the college was not thriving in the early to mid-1920s and that it took some time for the endeavours of a reforming Prior and president, in the person of Richard Brocard Taylor after 1925, to have effect.

Within five years of the institution of the new state examinations, the spirit of latitude and the freedom from prescribed texts that appeared to mark the scheme's inception was being undermined as far as some commentators were concerned. For one of them, writing in 1929, the Department of Education, through the new state examinations for Intermediate and Leaving Certificate had 'obtained a stranglehold on the school authorities, and practically, if not theoretically, dictate exactly what is to be taught, and how, and when …'.[20] This divorce between latitude in theory and narrowness of curriculum in practice, as a result of the format of the Intermediate and Leaving Certificate examinations, was commented upon, at times trenchantly. A particularly detailed critique was offered by the Jesuit, Fr John Joy, in the *Irish Monthly* in October 1930 where the narrowing of the curriculum and the decline of modern Continental languages was decried.[21] With such concerns, some of the older, traditional colleges may have preferred to direct their pupils towards the Matriculation examination rather than the Leaving Certificate. It was certainly the case that at Clongowes during this period, 'the courses remained virtually intact' and 'the values of the traditional classical education which the school offered were underlined'.[22]

In this context, Terenure's Fr Taylor had his own strong views about the nature of education and the new system with which he was unhappy. Speaking in February 1926, he deplored 'the make-believe in education' and attacked the government's new secondary-education programme, observing that as a result, his own college had changed very greatly over the previous few years and that the pace of educational programme change had been so fast as to constitute a revolution. Viewing education as a three-dimensional entity, involving the moral, the physical and the intellectual, he felt that the first two were adequately catered for. Indeed, in Terenure they had 'modified' the physical training aspect: they had introduced rugby football 'and had enhanced this dimension also by introducing Swedish drill'. In regard to the physical and moral dimensions, Irish colleges under the new regime were free from interference, but when it came to the intellectual dimension — in his view the most important of the three — they were not. There was a certain measure of government interference that was not for the best. 'The Doc' remarked that he had known the old Intermediate system very well, both as a 'pupil victim' and as a teacher. In the twenty years since he had sat his Intermediate in 1906, a number of regrettable changes had occurred. For one thing, examinations had come to be seen as a nuisance and had now 'been watered down'; for another, most boys only sat for the new Intermediate Certificate which was a cross between the old junior and middle grade examinations: 'very few boys at all entered for the Leaving Certificate examination'. He deplored the dropping of traditional, in-house, end-of-year examinations which, in themselves, were a form of education. As he saw it, the object of the secondary educator was to prepare his charges for a university career: to which university would 'put the finishing touches'. Government interference had led to serious damage to the classical tradition: 'Latin had suffered and Greek was defunct. French, of course, was gone'. In his experience, in the old days the junior honours grade boys had been able to read French novels and newspapers.

Dr Taylor took what amounts to a very elitist view of the nature and purpose of secondary education. In respect of the role of the ancient and modern languages for example, he remarked:

> People would say that those languages would not help a man to earn more money. He would not deny that to a certain degree. But secondary education was essentially an affair of the middle class who are, in a sense, the leisure class. … Today secondary education still remained in the hands of the clergy. It was a small body, but if secondary education was in the hands of a lay body one could shudder to think of the result.[23]

Almost two years later, in November 1927, he returned publicly to these concerns and criticisms. Referring to 'an amount of unspoken uneasiness', he asserted that effectively 'there was no secondary education'. Latin and Greek should have had 'premier place' in the curriculum and the teaching of modern languages had become 'a dead letter'. Noting that 'English, Maths, Irish and History were compulsory' he went on to add that 'Science would soon be compulsory: where then was the liberty with regard to the details of the programme and teaching?' and he deplored the fact that no individualism was to be left to either teacher or pupil.[24]

This time, his remarks did not go unchallenged. In December 1927, *The Irish School Weekly* took him up. It contradicted the validity of his view that in effect Latin and Greek should be compulsory, that without them there was no secondary education. Remarking that since the vast majority of secondary pupils on leaving school went out to earn a living, it was not unreasonable that the curriculum should be broad and practical as well as cultural and that the classics

> must not be over-emphasised: the Leaving Certificate examination was not the matriculation examination and served a different purpose. Just because Latin and Greek were not compulsory did not mean they were ignored or neglected: in the 1927 Leaving Certificate examination, 72% of 517 boy candidates took Latin and 85% of those that did so were successful in it.

As to Dr Taylor's charge of lack of liberty, *The Irish School Weekly* countered that the courses of study had now been conceived on a very broad basis — so much so that some secondary teachers complained that the programme was too indefinite and offered too much latitude: as far as *The Irish School Weekly* was concerned 'an enormous degree of freedom was inherent in the basis of the new programme'.[25]

One suspects that Dr Taylor may not have got the better of the argument and that his views were selective if not eccentric: certainly, to view the Irish middle class of the 1920s as 'a leisure class' was hardly accurate. Nevertheless, if Taylor on education was eccentric and elitist, at least he was consistent. He was determined to make Terenure a special institution, a member of the inner circle of élite colleges at the time. He deplored the decision to close the college in 1909. In 1926, he remarked on the enormity of the problems he faced in restoring the college fortunes; problems that he attributed broadly to the mistakes of previous presidents, Provincials and Chapters.[26] These problems persisted in the years ahead: when the Irish Province held its 1929 Chapter, the new Provincial, Denis Devlin, raised a discussion on the college in which a shortage of pupils was mentioned as one factor hampering the college's development.[27] This notwithstanding, Fr Taylor's efforts to enhance its standing and prestige cannot be gainsaid. It even extended to his determination that the president of Terenure College should have his own motor car. In his last year as president, 1931, the Provincial Chapter took issue with possession and use of automobiles. 'The Doc' had no scruples about or hesitation in the matter. He told historian, Peter O'Dwyer, that he had acquired a car not only for reasons of practical efficiency but as much for the social status it would entail as he sought to enhance the college's image among peers and parents and to increase thereby its attractiveness and enrolments. It may also be seen in his support for the introduction or reintroduction of rugby.

Gaelic Games and Rugby Union:

The restored college in 1917 embraced the new sporting culture of Gaelic games promptly and earnestly. So too did Blackrock, this being a return to Gaelic games for the first time since the 1880s for both colleges.[28] Looking back from the 1960s, Fr O'Shea had a distinct recollection that a definite decision had been taken by the college authorities that 'only the national games of Gaelic football and hurling should be played'.[29] The college certainly encouraged these games and enjoyed some competitive success in fielding both senior and junior teams. In May 1918, its junior hurlers had reached the final of the Dublin Colleges League at Croke Park, but lost to St Vincent's, Castleknock, by 6-0 to 2-6. The college's sporting fate in Gaelic games in 1919 is not clear but considerable success attended their efforts in 1920. On 8 May, again at Croke Park, in the Dublin colleges' semi-final, Terenure defeated Belcamp College, Raheny, who were themselves destined to be a formidable force in colleges' GAA games for much of the next ten years. Terenure won the match by 1-1 to 0-1: it was sweet revenge for having been defeated by Belcamp in the Dublin colleges' hurling final. From that football victory they went on to meet St Enda's, Rathfarnham, on 15 May 1920. In a remarkable performance, they trounced the Pearse boys by 6-3 to 0-

0, to win the cup.[30] They then went on to meet Knockbeg College in the Leinster final. Although Terenure put up 'a great effort' they were defeated by 1-6 to 1-2.[31]

The college's GAA credentials were well-established by then: in March 1921, for example, they had provided the venue for the Ladies' Intervarsity Camogie Competition — the Ashbourne Cup — when Dublin defeated Galway by 3-2 to 0-0.[32] In that same year, Terenure again fielded a senior football team good enough to reach the Dublin colleges' final where they went down to Belcamp.[33] In December 1922, the college senior football team again got to play at Croke Park in the colleges' competition but to no great effect since they lost to Belcamp again, this time by 1-6 to 0-0.[34] In hurling, however, some consolation was derived the following year when Terenure defeated Clondalkin College, 4-0 to 0-2: the match was played on Terenure's grounds after overnight rain had made Croke Park unplayable. The press reporter conceded that Terenure, unexpectedly on home ground, had 'the advantage of being familiar with an uneven sod'.[35] Sometime thereafter Terenure's GAA lights seem to have dimmed, and, for the remainder of the decade the faltering colleges' championships came to be dominated by Roscrea, Knockbeg, St Ciaran's, Kilkenny, Newbridge and Belcamp. While the junior hurlers are mentioned as having met Clondalkin College in May 1924, thereafter Terenure is not connected with Gaelic games in the leading national newspapers and sports' journals. When, in March 1926, the Leinster Colleges' Competition Committee met to settle the fixtures schedule, Terenure College was not among the participating teams. Carmelite historian, Peter O'Dwyer, remarked that there were various schools of opinion as to why Terenure went over to rugby from Gaelic games. He recorded Fr Paddy Walsh as saying that he could get no competition in the latter at the time, and continued: 'Others refer to the incident between Blackrock College and Terenure when the names of the Blackrock team are said to have been embossed on the medals even before the match'.[36]

It has to be added, however, that as the late 1920s wore on, the GAA Colleges' Competitions went into an obvious decline. Although Clongowes Wood — which had only entered a short time before — won the 1926 Leinster Colleges' football final for the first time, the press admitted that, as to fixtures, 'the list discloses defections in both hurling and football which reduced the competition to a very insignificant state'.[37] By 1927, these championships had become 'nothing more than a skeleton competition and with just as much vitality'.[38]

In 1928, Dr E. O'Sullivan, secretary of the GAA Colleges' Central Council, bemoaning the lack of competition, referred to that lack as the standard excuse 'of our Seoinín schools which are rigidly boycotting our games with a persistency that is a tacit "BAN" in itself', but he hoped that 'many lost sheep will return to the fold'.[39] He did not mention if Terenure was one of those lost sheep or if it was to be counted among 'the Seoinín schools'; but, as a matter of fact, by 1925, its presence in Leinster or Dublin GAA competitions was non-existent. A similar development appears to have arisen in Blackrock concurrently: although 'its exit from the inter-schools hurling competition at this stage is shrouded in legend, it is reported that, having experienced frequent unpleasantness at the hands of the organisers of these games, it was decided to opt out of the competition from 1925'.[40] Likewise at Clongowes Wood, when Gaelic games were introduced in the early 1920s, they did not prosper, though that institution's historian, Peter Costello, attributes this to 'social reasons'.[41]

At the same time, the surviving evidence appears to bear out the accuracy of Fr O'Shea's recollections: Rugby does not appear to have been played by Terenure — at least competitively and inter-collegially — from 1917 to 1924. According to O'Shea — and he was directly involved in trying to organise Gaelic matches with other boarding schools and colleges — these efforts fizzled out as the traditional rugby-playing institutions found the GAA ban on playing 'foreign games' was something that they could not support. It appears, therefore, that rugby was re-introduced to Terenure in 1925–6 for the first time since 1909. Fr O'Shea stated the case simply as follows:

> In 1926 Terenure again took up Rugby. The chief reason was, I think, to secure a regular succession of games each week, and also because the pupils, the majority of whom were day pupils, opted for Rugby. This much I do recall, that in the school year 1924-25 only two [GAA] matches with outside schools were played, one at home and one away, and this fact had a very great weight in the decision to go over to Rugby. Gaelic games were not banned in the College, they continued to be played, but of course, owing to the 'Ban', no part could be taken in the organised games with other schools.[42]

Independently corroborating this was a public address of February 1926 by Fr Taylor. In the course of his speech, he spoke of rugby as 'having just then been introduced' to the college. It is difficult to reject the conclusion that the re-introduction of rugby was on the initiative of 'The Doc' Taylor and that it was part of his vision to enhance the standing of the college by integrating it into the inner circle of élite colleges. It is certain that when he left Terenure in 1931 to take up appointment as first Prior of the new Irish Carmelite College of Pio XI, in Rome, he had left behind in Terenure a considerable legacy, not least as shall be shortly seen, in its social standing. Furthermore, if the college under his presidency appeared to manifest antipathy or indifference to the new state examinations, it still managed to attract young men who would become distinguished in their fields and older men — former pupils — already distinguished.

The Past Pupils' Union:

Of a decade of the college's history of which relatively little is known, one development of singular significance was the foundation — or reformation — of the Past Pupils' Union. The first intimation of this came in a press report of December 1924. With the blessing of the Provincial, Fr Cogan, a meeting was held in Terenure of past pupils of the college and of the Dominick Street Academy, the object being 'to re-establish the Union' of the former pupils of both institutions. It is not clear from any available evidence when the original union had existed but this meeting's unnamed secretary asked any pupils 'who are interested in the project, to get in contact'.[43] Clearly a respectable number did, for, on 23 April 1925 some 80 former pupils of 'Dominick Street Academy, Terenure College and the Allied Carmelite Colleges' met in Jury's Hotel, Dublin, for what was the inaugural dinner of the Past Pupils' Union. Fr Cogan, as Provincial, presided and others who spoke included J.H. McLaughlin and J.J. Shiel, and the surgeon, Leo Keegan.

Within a month of this, a meeting of the union was held in the college for the purpose of electing officers and a committee. J.F.L. Keegan was elected president with five vice-presidents, namely H.S. Meade, John Murray, J.L. Malone, G.P. Sheridan and V.P. Tighe. Then followed the joint secretaries, Fr P.A. Walsh and Michael Cole with Bernard Cannon being elected treasurer. Finally the ten-member general committee consisted of Seán Ó hÚadaigh, J.J. Shiel, Frs Denis Devlin and T.J. Kelly, together with C. Culhane, J. Finnegan, P. Duffy, M. Kiernan and F.J. Donnellan.

Their first president was the noted surgeon John Francis Leo Keegan, a Dubliner born in 1878. It is ironic, therefore, that he was known as a Belvedere man — to which Belvedere's own records attest, but presumably he must earlier have attended the Dominick Street Academy. He qualified as a doctor in 1901 and became a fellow of the RCSI in 1904. In 1906, he was appointed visiting surgeon at Jervis Street and through involvement with the Red Cross he became visiting surgeon at the Castle Hospital during the First World War. Later he became resident surgeon at St Vincent's Hospital and a council member of the Royal College of Surgeons. One colleague recalled him as 'a not too tall, dapper figure, quintessentially a man of Dublin; uncomplicated of mind, he typified the extroverted surgeon-figure. He gave an example to all in punctuality, loyalty and moderation'.[44]

That he was almost certainly a Dominick Street Academy alumnus is supported by the fact that his fellow-surgeon, co-founder and vice-president of the Terenure Past Pupils' Union, Harry S. Meade, had been a Dominick Street pupil before transferring to Terenure where he studied in the 1890s. 'One of the most brilliant surgeons in Ireland', Henry Sords Meade was born in China in 1884 where his father was a civil servant. As a child he was sent back to Ireland to be educated, first in Dominick Street and then in Terenure. From there he went to Cecilia Street Catholic University Medical School, qualifying in 1909 and two years later became assistant surgeon in St Vincent's. When war broke out in 1914, Henry Meade joined the French Army Medical Service and was decorated for his services with their 17th Army. He then transferred to the British Royal Army Medical Corps, serving on the Western Front from 1916. At the war's end he returned to Ireland and became consulting surgeon to the infant Army Medical Service of the Irish Free State. In 1928, he succeeded to the Chair of Surgery in UCD. A great traveller, he was well known in many overseas clinics, notably in Vienna, and was one of only seven Irish presidents of the Association of Surgeons of Great Britain and Ireland. He was elected president of the Royal

College of Surgeons in Ireland in 1948. Described as a 'craftsman' surgeon, his name was a byword for integrity; remembered by a St Vincent's colleague as 'once my teacher, later my colleague and ever my friend', many recalled 'his fondness in telling each of us what he thought of us' yet remembered too 'his complete inability to tell a joke … and a complete incapacity to resent the joke when told against himself … [a man] of generosity unbounded'.[45]

There were at least two other prominent medical men among the founding members of the Past Pupils' Union, Vincent Paul Tighe, who succeeded Leo Keegan as PPU president in 1927, was born in Dublin in 1868 and after his Terenure College days, he graduated from the Royal University and from the Royal College of Physicians of Ireland (RCPSI). For many years he was house surgeon in Temple Street and a governor of the Royal Hospital for Incurables; in what little free time he had, apart from helping the college, he was a keen golfer, sometime captain of Carrickmines Golf Club. He worked right up to the day of his death, in his eightieth year, on 31 October 1948. His elder son, Henry, also a doctor, had predeceased him by ten years; Tighe was survived by his only other son, solicitor Paul.[46]

Then there was Robert May who played on the Terenure rugby team from 1906 to 1908. He was a son of the Mayor of Drogheda whose family history in that town went back over for centuries. After his Terenure days, Robert studied medicine in the Royal College of Surgeons, qualifying in 1923, and became one of the best known general practitioners in Ireland. In his limited spare time, he took a great interest in the breeding of Irish wolf-hounds on which subject he became an internationally recognised authority.

Among the first vice-presidents one of the most distinguished professionals of his time was the architect George P. Sheridan. He was born in Larchfield, Dundrum, in 1868, son of Peter Sheridan, carpet and bedding warehouse proprietor of Parliament Street. Peter moved his family from Dundrum to Granby Row in the inner city, from where the young George was educated at the Dominick Street Academy. Following his schooling there, he was apprenticed to the architect James Hargrove Bridgford and served time with a number of others before moving to London in 1892 for further training. Two years later, he was elected an Associate of the Royal Institute of British Architects. He returned to Dublin to establish in 1895–6, the architectural practice of Morley and Sheridan. Following Frederick Morley's death in 1896, Sheridan was in sole practice until he took his nephew, Liam Tierney, as his partner in 1945. He was a bachelor who was very much a gentleman architect, regarding his profession not as a money spinner but a 'pleasant occupation' at which 'he loved to potter'. For all this self-deprecation, he was sufficiently esteemed among his peers to become president of the Royal Institute of the Architects of Ireland (RIAI) from 1923 to 1925 and during his tenure of that position was responsible for securing its splendid headquarters on Merrion Square. As president of the RIAI, he was invited by the Dublin City Commissioners in October 1924 to act as advisor in the reconstruction of O'Connell Street's buildings destroyed in the War of Independence and Civil War.[47] Held in the highest esteem and affection by his colleagues, a friend recalled that 'G.P' used to brighten every function he attended.[48] Apart from becoming Terenure PPU president in 1929 he was generous to a fault for many years in his professional capacity as College Architect, up to his death in July 1950. At that stage he was the oldest member of the union which he contributed a great deal to establish on a sound footing.

With him in that enterprise were three legal men, John J. Shiel, Seán Ó hUadaigh and Louis J. Walsh. Seán studied in Terenure c. 1900 and subsequently became a solicitor and was active in the movement for national independence. He went into a law partnership in 1914 and was George Gavan Duffy's election agent in the critical general election of 1918. Active in Kingstown municipal politics, he was one of the key figures in having the name changed to Dún Laoghaire. His offices were raided and wrecked by the Black and Tans and he was taken prisoner by them and jailed in Mountjoy and Kilmainham. He managed to turn the tables by becoming a judge in the Republican courts and capped his legal career by becoming president of the Law Society of Ireland for 1947–8. Apart from his huge contribution to various Gaelic language activities he was to become first chairman of Aer Lingus and a Director of Aer Rianta over the years 1937 to 1944 — heading two semi-state bodies in which many leading Terenure past pupils found their careers in the years after that. Ever patriotically wearing his blue tweeds and Fáinne, he succeeded George Sheridan as PPU president in 1930.[49]

Closely paralleling his career was that of John J. Shiel who was a contemporary of his in the college in 1900. A native of Rathcoole, Co. Dublin, he came to Terenure from Mount St Joseph's, Roscrea. He may well have had divided loyalties when in February 1909, in the second round of the Leinster Schools Junior Cup, Mount St Joseph's defeated Terenure by three goals, six tries and thirty three points to nil, with Terenure's ultimate indignity that the Roscrea College was fielding its first ever Junior Cup team.[50] On leaving Terenure, he proceeded to study law and qualified as a solicitor in 1910. He was both deeply religious and ardently nationalist. A member of the Irish Volunteers, he took part in the Howth gun-running of July 1914: a year later, he was a founding member of the Knights of Columbanus. With his tall and commanding presence, he was widely known and respected in law and local politics. He became, at various different times, chairman of Dublin County Council and of the General Council of County Councils, and built up an extensive legal practice in Dublin and Co. Kildare. Apart from acting as the college's solicitor, he was particularly devoted to the activities of its PPU, yet somehow also found time to become president of the Leinster Motor Club.[51]

The third of the lawyers who was a PPU founding member was Louis J. Walsh. Born in 'Walsh's Hotel', Maghera, Co Derry, in 1880, he was the son of another Louis who made his small fortune in post-gold rush California before coming home to take over his widowed mother's hotel. Young Louis went to school locally and to Derry's St Columb's before going on to Terenure as a boarder. One of the most brilliant Terenure students of the 1890s, he was an Intermediate Junior Grade

Exhibitioner in 1896 and followed this in 1897 as a Middle Grade Exhibitioner.[52] Of his 1890s Terenure days, he vividly remembered Fr John Reilly, an ardent Parnellite to the end, despite the Church's turning against the Chief in the wake of the Parnell–O'Shea scandal. This memory apart, Walsh was no sports' lover and this did not make for happy schooldays. However, his academic excellence and achievements were ample compensation. Following his entry to UCD in 1898, he enjoyed a glowing scholastic career and shone in its Debating Society which was luminous with talent at that time — Sheehy-Skeffington, Tom Kettle, Hugh Kennedy and others — while in Louis's own matriculation class he had for classmates James Joyce and future UCD history professor and minister for education, John Marcus O'Sullivan. The challenge of such talents did not stop Walsh from winning the President's Gold Medal for Oratory during his first year there.[53] He secured his BA in 1902 and law qualification in 1905 and, entering legal practice, he also entered into the nationalist movement, in 1921, spending time in Ballykinlar Internment Camp and Derry Jail for his troubles. In October 1922, he was appointed a District Justice. Apart from his judicial work in Donegal Northwest, he became a prolific author and playwright — whose works included *The Yarns of a Country Attorney*. For all that, he found time to be a committed supporter of the college and its union until his death in December 1942.[54]

Regarding the first joint secretaries, Michael A. Cole, a nephew of Fr Cogan, came to the college as pupil on its reopening in 1917, was in the licensed trade after his Terenure years and at one stage had been president of the Licensed Grocers and Vintners' Association. Devoted to the union, he was to become its president in 1934 and again in 1938. His co-secretary of the union was Fr Patrick Anastasius Walsh, a Dubliner born in 1889 who attended the college in the late 1890s and early 1900s. On completing his studies there, he entered the Terenure novitiate in 1907 and graduated with his BA from UCD before going on for theology studies at the Jesuits' Milltown Park. He was ordained in 1915 and after a short stay in Whitefriar Street was assigned to New York and Tarrytown until his return home in 1919. Here he taught at Terenure and was involved in the preliminary foundation meeting of the PPU in November 1924. He was made Sub-Prior at Terenure in 1925 and from 1929 served the Carmelite Communities of Kildare, Moate and Whitefriar Street until his death in June 1963.

At Homes and Reunions:

With such an array of experience, talent and professional standing the college and its PPU were well-placed to attract the positive recognition and the social support which they did. From the second half of the 1920s and well beyond, their annual dinner reunions and the annual 'At Home' days in the summer were well-patronised and publicised. In June 1925, the first reunion of the Old Boys, organised by Fr Walsh and his committee, was a great success. Apart from the union worthies, Keegan, Meade,

Sheridan and company, some 300 attended in glorious weather. They witnessed President Cosgrave present the medals and prizes, with music supported by the band of the ITGWU. The guests were greeted by the Provincial, Fr Cogan, and other Carmelites present included Fr Megannety and Fr T.P. Kelly, Prior of Ardavon.[55] In June 1926, for their second annual 'At Home' the union and college attracted a massive 500 members and guests to the college grounds on what turned out to be a splendid day. A wonderfully colourful occasion, with the Garda band under Superintendent Delaney, saw the traditional cricket match between past and present pupils, as well as the finals of the tennis tournament and the junior sports. President and Mrs Cosgrave presented the various scholastic and athletic medals and prizes as they had done the previous year, with tea served on the lawns. Fr Taylor praised Cosgrave for his 'yeoman service' to the young state while Cosgrave in turn praised the college and its president and the Carmelite Order — which had a very big place in their hearts. Leading figures in the Order and in the college union were prominent and by all accounts it proved to be a memorable occasion.

SOME PUPILS OF THE RESTORATION:

Just how many students the college had between 1917 and 1929 is by no means certain. Referring to the years 1917 to 1919, Fr O'Shea thought there may have been upwards of 100 in the school between boarders and day-boys.[56] That figure seems rather high. There is a remarkable photograph of students and staff of the college taken in the early summer of 1920. It shows 73 people, comprising 58 students and 15 staff. Presumably a significant minority of students are missing from this image. For all that, some students, destined to have a long association with the college, were featured. They included Joe Bobbett, born in 1905, who was enrolled in Terenure over the years 1919 to 1922 and went on to a lifetime career with Hibernian Bank until 1969. At one point, in the 1990s, he was the oldest living Terenure past pupil. He passed away in 1995 but not before leaving a brief memoir of his college days:[57]

> I was at school in Terenure College from 1919–1922. The school was then, in the main, composed of boarding boys and I was one of a small body of day-boys.
>
> We would go to Terenure Cross Roads by tram and a ten minute walk through mainly unbuilt upon land brought us to the College gates. We passed a group of Edwardian houses and UCD sports grounds on our   right and the rails of the steam tram to Blessington were on the left of the road. From our classroom windows we could see the tram puffing past several times a day.
>
> Gradually during the 1930s onwards housing estates appeared all around the College grounds and as a consequence the school boy numbers swung over to a preponderance of day-students.

It was a GAA school though some of us kicked around and 'unofficial Rugby ball'. The staff, I can recall, were Fr Gerard [*sic*], the Australian Prior, a cold austere disciplinarian; Fr Griffin, a warm, outgoing, very likeable person; Fr Daly, very elderly and bearded, he seemed to spend most of his time working in the garden. He drove off in a pony and trap to say Mass in Firhouse Carmelite Covent accompanied by two Mass servers.

Other teaching staff I remember were Mr Butler- English and Latin; Mr Moynihan, Maths and Science; Mr O'Toole; Irish. Also Miss O'Brien and Miss Stapleton — very unusual I feel sure to have lady teachers at that period in a boys' school.

On Saturday mornings we had only one class, I think, drill or P.E. and then Benediction in the small College Chapel. My father was at school there about 1885. In his day the College consisted of the 'Hall Door' block facing the new church. The wing at right angles had been added before I went there.

Fellow-pupils of Joe's in 1920, who later became prominent in professional public and commercial life and who feature in the photograph, were Paddy Duffy, Michael Cole and Dr John Cussen. Paddy Duffy, like Bobbett, became a Hibernian Bank Official, in Portumna, Co. Galway, and was one-time honorary secretary of the PPU; Michael Cole as already seen, was prominent in the licensed trade and John Cussen, medical superintendent of a large clinic in Switzerland, was a brother of a Dominican Provincial and of the noted Terenure College athlete, Ray Cussen.

However, among the eminent in that class of 1920 were a number who became Carmelites or clergymen of other orders. Especially notable in this case were brothers, Gary and Barry Cogan. Gary was a pupil from 1918 to 1920 and later joined the Columban Fathers' Maynooth Mission to China, after being ordained in 1928. Assigned to the Philippines he was there when the Japanese invaded and still there when the Philippines were liberated. His twin brother, Barry, joined the Carmelites. Taking the name Louis, he was ordained in Rome in 1933 and went on to become Prior of the Community of Sittingbourne in Kent. Also destined to great things was Edward Lynch. Born in Ballymanus, Co. Wicklow, in 1902, he came to Terenure in 1919 and two years later entered the Carmelites there. Following study at San Alberto, he was ordained in Rome in 1928 and went on to gain his doctorate in philosophy at the Gregorian. Following three years in Tarrytown he was elected Prior there from 1934 to 1943 when he became New York Provincial. In May 1947, he had the distinction of becoming the second only Irish Prior-General of the Order. Two of his brothers, Malachy and Elias, preceded him into the Order and made memorable contributions to its development in England and Wales: Fr Elias, the eldest of the three was the prime mover in and Fr Malachy the first Prior of Aylesford, Kent, restored in 1949 after 400 years. Another Carmelite great who came from that time was Gerald

Fitzpatrick who was ordained as Fr Celestine in Rome in 1929; he was based at one stage in Terenure before going to America in 1935.

Another brilliant student of that time, destined for a life in the Jesuits, was Frank Shaw. Son of Westmeath TD, Patrick Shaw, who ran a large drapery business in Mullingar and was a member of Dáil Éireann from 1922 to 1932, Frank came to Terenure in 1922 and indeed played in their hurling team. Following his graduation from the college, he entered the Jesuits. As a brilliant UCD graduate, he won a travelling studentship in Early and Medieval Irish in 1930. Ordained in 1939, he was not long after appointed to the chair of Early and Medieval Irish in UCD, in succession to Osborn Bergin, and was Superior of the Leeson Street Jesuit Community from 1945 to 1951. Despite suffering ill health for most of his life, he was an extremely witty, playful and good-humoured, dedicated to visiting the sick in hospitals. Highly acclaimed as a medievalist, with a particular expertise in the study of St Patrick, nonetheless, he made a major contribution to modern Irish historiography with his celebrated essay 'The Canon of Irish History — A Challenge'. This was commissioned by the influential Jesuit periodical, *Studies*, for an edition of 1966 to commemorate the Easter Rising of 1916, but his contribution was judged too controversial for publication then. It was not until 1972, two years after Fr Shaw's death, that it was published: perhaps no Terenure boy turned-historian has made so great a turning point: the writing and interpretation of modern Irish history could not be the same thereafter.

Among notable alumni of the second half of the 1920s was Gerry Carr who was a pupil of the college from 1925 to 1930 where he became a committed cricketer. On leaving, he went into insurance, eventually becoming a director of Coyles's Insurance. He was deeply interested in Catholic Action — that movement of Catholic laymen in supporting the hierarchy in apostolic work, as promoted by Pius XI in the 1920s and 1930s.[58] His commitment to the PPU is evidenced by his unusual distinction of serving three successive terms as its president, in the years 1953 to 1955.

Not all were as fortunate in the security of their careers. Joe O'Connor who left Terenure in 1924 — his twin brothers Sean and Noel leaving in 1927 — was a noted national track cyclist, contemporary of the great Bertie Donnelly. There was little work in Ireland after Joe left and he headed for America where he rode for the world famous Raleigh Touring Team. In this capacity he cycled North and South America — even to Australia, and found himself cycling for Raleigh in Italy when the Second World War broke out. Making his way to London he then went to work for the Admiralty as liaison officer with the great Vickers Armstrong engineering firm. He was assigned to Scapa Flow, working repairs on the Home Fleet for the duration of the war. Demobbed, he secured employment dismantling army camps. Coming back to Ireland after that and again finding no work here, he set off for the Scottish shipyards and worked there and in engineering until his retirement. His story is worth recalling if only to point to it as the tip of an iceberg of old Terenurians who — like so many others — had to leave the country for work and who seldom leave much, if any record, in the annals of the college, apart from the memory of cherished friends.

John J. Sheil, R. Colfer (Provincial) and George Sheridan
(president of Past Pupil's Union) at Terenure College, 1927.

TERENURE COLLEGE

(Conducted by the Carmelite Fathers).

HEALTH   HAPPINESS   SUCCESS

30 minutes from centre of National Capital.

Ideal Situation.
Own Farm.
Fifty-Acre Sport Field.
Boating, Swimming.
Nature Study, Science.
Music, Art, Languages.
Distinguished Irish Professor.

Best equipped and largest Class-rooms.
Highly qualified and experienced Teachers.
Commercial Course—Business Methods.
Book-keeping, Shorthand, Typewriting.
Resident and Day Pupils.
Preparatory Department.
Matron—Qualified Nurse.

Intermediate and Entrance Examinations to University, Banks, Pharmacy, College of Science, Veterinary College, etc., etc., etc.
Records since 1920:—First Place Ireland in Arithmetic and other distinctions.
Dublin Football Championship and Cup Twice.

COLLEGE RE-OPENS TUESDAY, 11TH SEPTEMBER.

Further Particulars and Prospectus on application to

VERY REV. PRESIDENT.

Advert published in the *Irish Times*, 18 August 1923.

180

Staff and pupils at Terenure College, *c*. 1920.

181

Past pupils event, c. 1960. © Irish Press.

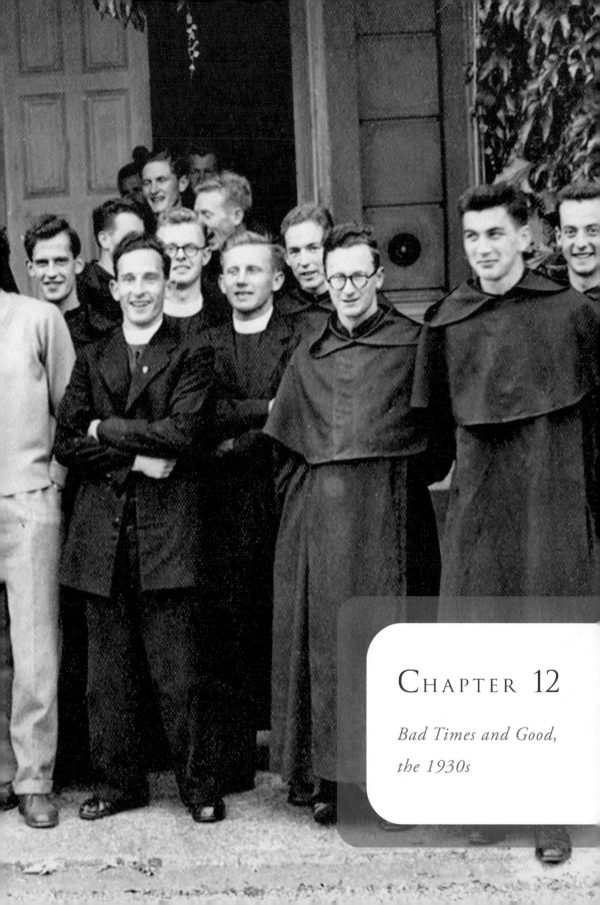

CHAPTER 12

*Bad Times and Good,
the 1930s*

Carmelites pose with a
past pupil, 1930s.

THE DECADE OF THE 1930S NEITHER RECEIVED NOR DESERVED FOND remembrance. Characterised in some places as 'The Devil's Decade', globally it was a time of political extremes and economic woes.[1] It saw growing tensions created by the spread of communism and fascism and the spectacular failure to create a viable new world order culminated in a conflict of unparalleled ferocity and slaughter.

More locally, it seems it did not deserve to be better remembered. The world economic depression reduced the opportunities for Irish emigrants in search of work unavailable at home. It almost stemmed the Irish exodus to the USA in that decade; emigration to that country fell from over 220,000 in 1921–30 to a mere 13,000 in 1931–40. Indeed, such was emigration's decline that the country's population rose in the early 1930s from 2,927,000 to 2,971,000 by 1935.[2] By 1936, 145,000 people were registered as unemployed, with a 50% rise recorded from 1927 to 1931,[3] the number doubling over the period of 1926 to 1935. Towards the beginning of the new decade, a supplementary budget was introduced in November 1931, in which the Cosgrave administration cut the salaries of public servants, including teachers, and increased the income tax by sixpence in the pound.

Hard times were compounded by the Economic War of 1932 to 1938. A contemporary could be forgiven for viewing 1930s Ireland as fearful, conservative and comfortless. Yet, all was not negative. Industrial development under tariff protection was fostered to a significant degree. New semi-state enterprises were founded: among these were the Sugar Company and the Industrial Credit Corporation in 1933, the Turf Development Board (later, Bord na Móna) and Ceimicí Teoranta in 1934, Aer Lingus in 1936 and in 1939 the Irish Life Assurance Company and the Irish Tourist Board, the latter destined to a productive long-term future despite the calamitous ill-timing of its foundation year. According to Seán Lemass, 800 factories and workshops had been set up since 1932, and 78,000 people were employed in tariff-protected industries by September 1936.[4]

As to the fate of education within this context, it also had a very mixed experience. While the total number of schools and the total number of pupils on their rolls had fallen over 1921, and subsequently in 1931 and 1939, the recorded number of average school attendees had risen, and then fallen, as presented in Table 11:[5]

TABLE 11: AVERAGE NUMBER OF (PRIMARY AND SECONDARY) SCHOOL ATTENDEES IN 1921, 1931, 1939

Year	No. of Schools	Pupils on Rolls	Average Attending
1921	5,746	498,000	365,000
1931	5,378	509,000	417000
1939	5,127	470,000	385,000

Presumably the decline in the number of schools was due to consolidation and a reduction in the number of smaller schools. However, at secondary level there was a significant expansion in the amount of government capitation and in the number of schools, pupils and teachers as illustrated in Table 12, covering the years from 1924 through 1931–2 to 1937–8.[6]

TABLE 12: AVERAGE NUMBER OF SECONDARY-SCHOOL ATTENDEES
IN 1924, 1931–2 AND 1937–8

Year	State Funding	Schools	Pupils	Teachers
1924	£320,000	278	22,897	2,133
1931–2	£386,000	300	28,994	2,643
1937–8	£488,200	329	35,890	2,969

In effect, the number of secondary schools had increased by 18%, the number of teachers therein by 39% and the number of pupils in secondary education by 57%. Among male secondary teachers a slight majority were religious — in 1930–1, they numbered 636 to 601 lay men. One development of concern, however, was the growth in the numbers of unregistered teachers. The situation over the years 1924–5 to 1934–5 can be seen in Table 13.[7]

TABLE 13: RATIO OF REGISTERED TO
UNREGISTERED SECONDARY-SCHOOL TEACHERS

Year	Registered Teachers	Unregistered Teachers	Ratio
1924–5	1,398	735	100:52.6
1931–2	1,446	1,197	100:82.8
1934–5	1,513	1,348	100:89.1

As a consequence, twenty years after the establishment of their Registration Council, a substantial and growing number were unregistered and therefore not entitled to increments: however, Terenure stated that its entire teaching staff in 1936 was registered.[8] On a more positive note, a long-sought pension scheme for secondary teachers finally came into operation from 1929. In addition, the highly contentious and sensitive issues of security of tenure and appeal against dismissal, contested for longer than the pension, finally had some resolution over 1936 to 1940.

This conveys something of the complex context in which Terenure College and similar institutions found themselves in the 1930s. Half of the secondary schools in the country at the time catered for boarders as well as day-pupils and it was a very considerable struggle to keep them going. Fr Dunstan O'Connor, president and Prior from 1952 to 1958, recalling the 1930s years later, did so without joy: 'It was a dire struggle to live. Enrolment dwindled and the future looked bleak. Some members of the Irish Province urged that the place be closed down'.[8] However, as he generously acknowledged, the doubters were defeated by the commitment and belief of two great Priors, James Carmel O'Shea and Andrew Eugene Wright. Before discussing them it may be worth reflecting that, for boys entering at that time rather than for old men later remembering darker days, the perspective may well have been different, lighter and less grim.

ONE PUPIL REMEMBERING THE EARLY 1930S:

One such pupil was Patrick Anselm Corbett. Born in 1914 in Clonmel, where his family had a printing business, young Corbett came to Terenure as a boarder in 1931. He gave a vivid account of his arrival, of his new surroundings and of the boarding regime that was in effect at Terenure in the 1930s:

> On a day in early September 1931, as a young man of 17 years, I first set foot in Terenure College. My brother-in-law, a Free State Army Officer had met me at Kingsbridge (Heuston) Station and we lunched in the Officers' Mess at Collins Barracks. Afterwards we went to the Savoy Cinema to view a film and hear the splendid organ. The sheer size of the theatre astonished me: I had never seen the like. He pointed out the glittering lights in the vast ceiling as they blinked in and out like stars in a clear night sky. The show over, we had high tea in the old, magnificent Savoy Restaurant where a string and piano ensemble played the soft music of the thirties. Then we took a taxi to the College.
>
> Previously, and after some thought, I had made up my mind to join the Carmelites. The school I attended in my home town went only as far as Intermediate Certificate in its curriculum. For that reason, the Carmelite Provincial at the time (I think he was Fr James Cogan) wrote to me and suggested that I should enrol at Terenure for a few months in order to take Matriculation without which I would not be able to enter University.
>
> Thinking that the College was some sort of Junior Seminary, I had brought with me a soft, black hat which the Prior, Fr J.C. O'Shea immediately confiscated when he received me at the old entrance late in the evening.
>
> He must have been in his early thirties at the time and I noticed how dark and foreign-looking he seemed, though he was most gentle and welcoming.
>
> There was another young Carmelite standing in the lovely hallway whom Fr O'Shea introduced as Brother Raymond and to

whose care he straightaway left me. This was the first time I met the future Bishop Lamont.

The sound of a violin remains in my memory ever since my arrival as a boarder in Terenure. It came from behind a closed door of a little room to the right of the entrance hall. This I learned later was the Masters' dining room in which was also a small piano. The boy taking a violin lesson from Mr O'Reilly, the music teacher, was John R. Kenny, a tall, plump and amiable young fellow who afterwards became a secular priest in the USA and died there a Monsignor, a few years ago. John R. as he was generally called, was one of over seventy boys boarding at that time. They and the day-boys together numbered about two hundred pupils in both junior and senior classes. When I crossed the threshold that Friday evening school had already begun. The following Sunday morning, after Mass and breakfast, I was accompanied by a couple of senior lads on a tour. I viewed what the College Prospectus had described as 'seventy acres of woodland and lake'. It was certainly picturesque and the lakeside pathways were idyllic; decorative wooden bridges led to a couple of small islands. At the end nearer the College there was a little boathouse inside which were moored two well-kept punts. At the farther end was the ruin of an ancient Coffee House, a relic of eighteenth century gracious living.

That morning I found out from my companions that only on Sundays were the boarders permitted to walk around the lake. Going out of bounds, 'over the wall', was strictly forbidden. In my innocence I wondered why, but they only laughed …

The boarders' dormitories were on the first and second floors of the middle building, the second oldest of the pile. Including washrooms and other services, they ran the full length and width of the place, bright, airy accommodation, without cubicles. Next place to me on my left-hand side was John Lamont (brother of Raymond). The Prior and some members of the Community lived in the central Georgian edifice adjoining the dormitories, a sliding panel in the wall facilitated surveillance on both floors. The Prior's room controlled the seniors. The top floor of the largest building housed the ample study hall and the remainder of the Community, along with three live-in lay teachers. The College Chapel was situated on the ground floor of this section; now it is the boys' library dedicated to the memory of Joseph Griffin, the late and much-respected 'Mr. Chips' of Terenure.

Altogether taking care of us were five Carmelite Fathers, four student brothers, all at University, one lay brother, Anthony McGreal

— a tall, red-headed young man who, though he was stone-deaf, was unfailingly cheerful. There was also Brother Rupert, middle-aged and severe-looking, who (it was said) had advanced some way in his theological studies and had chosen not to become a priest. The resident teachers included the afore-mentioned Joe Griffin (nicknamed 'The Hooley' by the boys) and Eddie O'Hanlon (who was called 'The Bear'). Besides them and living outside the College were three middle-aged teachers; a Maths man known as 'Twots', an outstanding English scholar, Mr 'Choicer' Macauley and an all-too-gentle native-speaking Irish teacher, Mr Séamus Ó'Searcaigh [*sic*]. The latter, who bore no nickname, was father of our late Fr John (Earnan) O'Sharkey and, afterwards, became lecturer in Donegal Gaelic in the Irish Department at Earlsfort Terrace.

Prefecting and general supervision were done by the student brothers, Raymond Lamont, Canice McCarthy, Ambrose (Jackie) Roche and a brother called Campbell whose first name I have forgotten (he left the Order later) …

Writing of the dormitory reminds me of the quick retribution that inevitably followed any major abuse of the rule of silence. We'd hear the wall-slide being pushed back, then Fr O'Shea, the Prior, would emerge from his room and switch on the lights. The sentence, delivered sternly, was always the same: an hour's extra study early next morning before Mass; and, ascetical as he was, he'd be up on the dot routing us out of bed.

Once a month we were allowed to go into the city for the pictures. Strictly out of bounds was a place called The Fun Palace on Burgh Quay; it was supposed to be full of temptation for the corruption of youth and that, naturally, aroused our curiosity. Yet I never heard of anyone who broke the rule, for expulsion was the penalty. If we had the money to spend, a favourite cinema plus variety theatre was the Capitol in Princes Street beside the GPO. A ticket could be had for a shilling, a lot of money in those days. One ditty we picked up from a show there was a lugubrious song that went: 'Ain't it grand to be bloomin' well dead'. It became a favourite in the college on wet days especially. The Capitol was a lovely little theatre with opera boxes. The first time I was in it was in 1966 to see the film of England's victory in the World Cup. Later, it and the grand old Metropole were demolished to make way for a hideous superstore. We got into Dublin from our 'country' suburb of Terenure by way of the Blue Bus line situated at a depot in the village on Harold's Cross road. The small vehicles were faster than the electric trams which trundled into the city centre from a terminus at Terenure also. Every day in school we heard cars of another transport system rumbling up the Templeogue Road — the Blessington Steam Tram, running on an open railway track. Its HQ was in a large shed on the spot where now stands Terenure Public Library and the first stop was in Templeogue Village outside a pub popularly known as The Morgue.

For boys with enormous appetites the food was pretty good. Still, there was a bit of class distinction at breakfast and teatime. Porridge with tea and bread and butter were served to all in the morning. Those boarders whose parents paid extra got a fry as well; those who didn't pay and postulants to the Order, like me and a few others, had to do without. The same practice obtained in the evening, but at lunch we were all equal …

… At that time the large field wasn't used for games; the college cows which provided milk grazed there for most of the year. In summer it became a vast meadow. There was no rugby club then and the present pitch used by members was given over to ploughing or meadow alternately … Mellow autumn drifted into frosty winter and the two rugby pitches by the Templeogue Road were soon ploughed up by football boots. Sixty years ago Terenure JCT and SCT couldn't boast the proud reputation they have today. Blackrock was the bogey, even then! The return from Donnybrook was usually fairly sad, though the spirit of the College never wavered. Fr O'Shea and Brother Raymond Lamont saw to that. The school jersey was of two colours then, purple and black, rather dour! After a few years a white stripe was added. Another seasonal activity was rehearsing for the Christmas play. Now I have forgotten the title of the drama which Bro Raymond helped produce. I remember that it was a comedy of the 'Charley's Aunt' genre and was greatly enjoyed by the pupils and parents. The feminine parts were taken by the boys, for there was no convent school across the Templeogue Road where Our Lady's is at present. … the concert hall was situated where today is found the Cardinal Newman Lecture Theatre and it was used also on Sunday mornings in wintry weather for our physical training class of which the director was a Dubliner who was an ex-British Army Sergeant Major. We nicknamed him 'The Bowler'. He wore a waxed moustache, had a red face, a ramrod back and a strident voice. When he roared 'Jump over the horse!', we jumped. Occasionally he took us for a short country run out of the college grounds and through fields off the modern Fortfield Road.

Of course there were the usual holiday periods when the school boarders who were mainly from the West of Ireland took off for home by train; not many motor cars so long ago! After the Easter vacation the expected pressure was turned on for the menacing June examinations. In the meantime, however, we had cricket (the crease was between the senior and the junior rugby pitches on the Templeogue Road), the tennis championships and the Annual Sports. The latter was quite an event. In 1932 the ex-President of the Executive Council, Mr W.T. Cosgrave, was welcomed by the Prior and the Community, all in their brown habits, and the National Anthem was played by the No 1 Army Band which provided rousing music throughout the games. All the boys wore white shirts, ducks and blazers. The Sixth Year Leaving Certificate lads standing at the main gate handed out tickets for tea (in the marquee) to parents and families. The weather was fine and warm so that there was a good deal of 'style' on the field; the Fifth and Sixth years were quick to notice that! Ah, but 'The Bowler' had a great day when he marched a big mob of us over the grass for a Drill Display, to the sound of martial music; he was in his element! That evening we got a high tea in celebration. The President had *his* tea in the Big Parlour …

The final event of the year was, as ever, Prize Day held on a Sunday afternoon in the concert hall. Gold medals were in abundance; there was one for best English Essay, one for best Irish Essay. Three gold medals for religious knowledge and good conduct. In '33 the latter was won by a good-humoured young man, a boarder from Scotland. It cannot be surprising that he was called 'Scotchy' Maginn. What keeps him in my memory is the fact (as he confessed afterwards to us) that he arrived to receive his gold medal just in the nick of time. He had gone AWOL over the College wall and down to Terenure village!

On the last night before the end of term the junior dormitory descended, armed with pillows, to make a raid on the senior dormitory, hoping to find us asleep. They were easily repulsed. Luckily for all of us the Prior was out late, probably at some function. Anyhow, we tidied up and went back to bed. I relate this innocent episode merely in order to contrast the kind of 'high jinks' we had with the more robust end-of-term activities of modern times.

We did our Matric examination in the Convocation Hall at University College. It is now the National Concert Hall. Every day, between tests, we had our lunch at a nearby restaurant. Soon we were packing our bags and saying farewell to Terenure College. I don't think there were any tears!

In saying farewell to the college at that stage, one wonders if he imagined that for much of his later life he would return to it. He entered the Order in 1932, taking the name Anselm, and was preceded in this by his older brother, John (Jack), who took the religious name of Ephrem. Described by one confrere as a pompous man, Ephrem was for some reason — lost in Terenure lore — nicknamed 'the gunner' while his junior, Anselm, was known as 'the young gunner'. Ephrem, however, was remembered by one pupil of the class of 1945 as 'a pleasant and friendly man despite specialising in a splendid bamboo cane and being very strong on rules'.[10]

In his novitiate year, Anselm was greatly influenced by his Novice Master, Malachy Lynch who particularly engaged his interest in Latin and in Gregorian chant. While Ephrem was remembered as a very active and energetic individual, greatly devoted to the cause of Terenure rugby, memories of Anselm present him as a very devout and otherworldly soul who really seemed too gentle for the rough and tumble of life in Terenure. On completing his novitiate, he was later sent to Rome, only to have his studies interrupted by the outbreak of the Second World War. Ordained in 1940 and assigned to Whitefriar Street, in 1946, he was one of the pioneering three sent out to establish the Carmelite mission in what was to become Zimbabwe. A decade later, he was back in Ireland, chaplain to Cathal Brugha Street Catering College, poet and esteemed preacher, Prior at Whitefriar Street and Kildare, until returning to Terenure where he lived through the 1990s until his death in June 2004.

STUDENT ENROLMENTS FROM THE EARLY 1920S TO THE EARLY 1940S:

Vivid though Fr Anselm's memoir is, it is surprising that he thought there were as many as 200 pupils, seniors and juniors, comprising 70 boarders and around 130 day-boys there at the beginning of the 1930s — surprising because Fr O'Shea reckoned on around 100 c. 1920 and Fr O'Connor counted only 159 boys in 1938. Furthermore, an account of the visit to the college by Carmelite General Dr Hilary Doswald in December 1935 referred to the fact that 'the students, numbering 150', presented him with an address.[11] Additionally, a press report of the 1936 sports day stated that 125 boys participated: assuming that as many as 20% of all the pupils did not participate, that would give a total enrolment of 150 boys.[12] Indeed, if house examination statistics are to be relied upon, then the college archive volume, *Results of Examinations, 1883–1942*, shows that Fr O'Shea's estimate of 100 for c. 1920 may have been slightly generous but perhaps not too wide of the mark. Furthermore, this source suggests that enrolments might have suffered a disastrous decline from 1925 to 1928. There is some uncertainty in all of this: the figures for the years 1922 to 1924 clearly show that all students from elementary to senior were recorded; from 1925 to 1934, it is not clear if the boys in the junior school were included, while from 1935 to 1941 they are included. These returns, which bear all the appearance of having been carefully and methodically registered — with the exception that no returns appear to have been made for the house examinations of 1927 — show the following:[13]

TABLE 14: STUDENTS AT TERENURE
COLLEGE REGISTERED FOR
STATE EXAMINATIONS, 1922–41

Session	Candidates
1922 (winter)	88
1923 (winter)	86
1924 (winter)	82
1925 (winter)	50
1926 (winter)	37
1927	–
1928 (summer)	34
1929 (summer)	61
1930 (summer)	63
1931 (summer)	67
1932 (winter)	98
1933 (summer)	105
1934 (incomplete)	–
1935 (incomplete)	–
1936 (incomplete)	–
1937 (summer)	*c.* 135
1938 (summer)	*c.* 144
1939 (summer)	167
1940 (numbers on roll)	176
1941 (numbers on roll)	170

That there appears to have been a precipitate decline over 1923 to 1928 may well explain the discussion at the 1925 Chapter regarding the closure of the college. The gradual recovery from 1929 to 1931 was followed by a marked growth from 1932, perhaps attributable to the energy and efforts of the new presidents of the 1930s and early 1940s, James Carmel O'Shea and Andrew Eugene Wright. As with other institutions of the time, the number in the Leaving Certificate final year may seem very low: just 5 in 1932; 4 in 1933; 7 in 1936; 10 sat it in 1937, 8 passing and 5 of these with honours. No figures were given for 1938 or 1939 but in 1940, 8 presented, 7 passing and 6 of these with honours; while in 1941, some 4 presented, 3 passing and 2 of these with honours. As against this, a slightly larger number presented for the NUI Matriculation in these years: 13 in 1937 with 12 successes, 3 in 1939 with 2 passing, 8 in 1940 with 7 passing, and in 1941, 10 candidates presented for Matriculation as against 4 for the Leaving Certificate. This appears to bear out the point made in the previous chapter that the college tradition predisposed it to favour the Matriculation Certificate over the Leaving Certificate examinations in the interwar period.

SOME PUPILS OF THE 1930S:

Entering the college in the same year as Anselm Corbett was Dubliner and day-pupil, Harold (Harry) Woods, probably the oldest past pupil today. Born in Rialto in 1922, son of legal cost accountant, Michael Woods, a peace commissioner, Harry first attended St Louis Convent School, Rathmines, until, in 1927, he went to Synge Street where one of his classmates was Liam, son of W.T. Cosgrave. When Harry enrolled in Terenure three years later, in 1931, he had the impression that the boarders numbered around 60 and the day-pupils around 45, figures more consistent with Fr O'Shea's earlier and Fr O'Connor's later estimates than Fr Corbett's reckoning.

Although a day-pupil, there was one period of the year when the young Woods temporarily became a boarder: this was on the occasion of the annual college retreat running up to Good Friday, and this despite the fact that the family home was then just around the corner in Fortfield Road, before moving to Ranelagh: attending the retreat became a lifetime yearly undertaking. As for getting to school from Ranelagh, the one halfpenny given to him each day for his fare was preciously saved for other purposes as he chose to race the Blessington-bound steam tram out of Terenure Village and up Templeogue Road to the college gates. Harry was to become the patriarch of a Terenure dynasty: his four sons: Anthony, Paul, Declan and Henry (Jr), and three grandsons: Ronan, Killian and Shane (Maguire) all followed in his wake.

As Harry remembers it, there was no strident emphasis on outstanding academic success; rather, the emphasis was on a sound, religious formation, good deportment and excellence in English speaking and presentation. These accomplishments apart, what also was acquired in thirties Terenure was application to study and commitment to sport. Both stayed with him when he left in straitened times in 1937 to take up a junior office employment. Night classes in accountancy, four evenings a week for four years in the College of Commerce, Rathmines, then became the foundation for an outstanding career in commerce and marketing. Within ten years of leaving Terenure he had been invited to serve on the Business Studies board of the National Council for Education Awards (NCEA), the beginning of a ladder of professional affiliations that saw him become the very first lecturer in sales and marketing in the Irish Management Institute. In 1964, and again in 1965, he had the distinction of being chairman of the Irish Marketing Institute. In the first of these two years, he led the first Irish delegation to a European Congress of Marketing and Distribution, in Barcelona, and seven years later he became the first Irishman to hold the presidency of the European Marketing Council. Thirty years later again, in his seventy-eighth year, he wrote and published the first history of marketing in Ireland.[14]

In all of this professional advancement, sport, that other side of Terenure's formation, stood to him. His interest in rugby followed him out of the college and he found himself playing for the 3A Terenure Collegians on Saturdays. He recalls the members of that modest outfit clubbing together their sixpences to buy tea and biscuits for the opposing visiting teams while there never seemed to be enough in the kitty for themselves. However, it was his commitment to cross-country running that most captured his spare time energies, winning his first medal with Clonliffe Harriers in 1947 in a six-mile road race to Finglas. Forty-two years later, he took second place in the over-65s group in the Brisbane, Queensland Marathon of 1989. He completed the last of his 25 marathons with the Dublin City Marathon of 2001 when, at 79, he was its oldest competitor.

In a life so full Harry never lost touch with his *Alma Mater*. He became PPU president in 1962 when he researched the previous history of the union and its presidents and personally provided the gold-lettered board, of Honduras mahogany, that bears their names on the college walls to this day. He was later made an honorary life-member of the union, on the same day as that other famous Terenure man, and Carmelite, Bishop Donal Lamont.

Following Harry into Terenure two years later was another Dubliner and local lad who was to be the first of another dynasty of Terenure families, the Doyles. Terence, born in 1925, was the eldest of five Doyle boys who entered the college. Terence did so in September 1933 and, somewhat to his surprise as the decision for Terenure was never clear to him. The local school, St Joseph's, may have been closer but perhaps too downmarket for a father who was Macmillan publisher's sole representative in Ireland, and for a mother who had been a schoolteacher herself. In two critical ways, Terence's memories corroborate those of Harry Woods.

Firstly, he convincingly recalls the student enrolment as being very small and in his view would not have exceeded 120 boys in total: in his entrance class in the junior school there were only five boys and the junior school as a whole 'was a very small place at the time'. He records that it was not until about or after 1935 that it began to expand significantly with the extensive house-building programme on Fortfield and Butterfield Avenues. Secondly, while he might well have been sent to Synge Street, CBS, instead, he remembered, perhaps with relief, that Terenure Junior School, and indeed its senior counterpart, were far from the CBS regime of grinding the boys to career success in local government and civil service; far from it, laid back as it was, it was quite possible to slip without academic trace, in the busy round of sports. For Terence himself, the question arose whether he would ever have made the grade academically had it not been for the tutoring of his mother and uncle who were both schoolteachers, the latter especially in regard to maths. In senior school, he recalls being taught French by Mr Macauley, reputedly a former master of Rugby School in England. In this, Terence excelled, securing first place in Intermediate French, though the level of that excellence and competition he calls into question when he ruefully acknowledges that he secured that first place with a mark of 51%. To his credit, he also secured first place in Terenure's Intermediate history examination with an impressive 84.8%.

To Terence, and doubtless to many others of the 1930s, the place was not so much a scholarly academy as an idyllic farm and place of perpetual sport. From handball to rugby, especially in the junior years, sport was all-consuming, played at every available break in the school day or the school year.

As for still being very much a farm in the 1930s, in autumn 1936, it was advertising '164 Cocks of well-salvaged hay for auction' and it still had its ploughman who lived in the entrance lodge at the main gate and who had charge of shire horses used for ploughing, 'Sandy', 'McGregor' and 'Tom'. There were then two gate lodges on that boundary of the college grounds fronting Templeogue Road. The second lodge was further down the road towards Terenure Village and was occupied by William Kerr and his family. William was a cobbler by trade and did the boot and shoe repairs for the entire college. Cattle aplenty grazed the grounds, providing extensive deposits of dung: playing rugby there had this as an additional special hazard: Terence's heartscalded mother used to berate a younger brother who was prone to landing in it on a regular basis. For Terence and his classmates the highlight of the year was sports day: to them this was Terenure at its best, marshalled to perfection by that martinet of a man, Sergeant Major Dominic Hastings.

That commitment to sport and commitment to the college was well in evidence after departing from the college with his Leaving Certificate in 1943. Not that study was abandoned thereafter: a Diploma in Public Administration from UCD's Commerce Faculty was successfully pursued in 1947–9, followed by the equally successful pursuit of his BA, through UCD's evening programme, in 1956–7 and graduating in 1960. All of this was achieved while earning a living, first at Bord na Móna and soon after at the Department of Defence. The commitment to Terenure continued all the while through involvement in its Boys' Club. Having played both junior and senior rugby in the college, for ten years after leaving he played regularly for the Past Pupils until 1953. He became active in the PPU in the course of the 1960s and was elected president in 1970. In this, he oversaw the golf outing, annual dinner and staging of a play, all delivered on a shoestring budget.[15]

Coming into college at the very end of the 1930s was a young man from Ardara, Co. Donegal: Seán Logue, born in January 1926, was the son of local draper, Patrick George Logue — a descendant of Scots Presbyterians — and Letitia Cassidy, a Donegal woman who had trained as a teacher in Glasgow before returning home to teach at Inver and then at Ardara. Terenure College was unfamiliar to him until he arrived there in September 1939, the most likely reason for the choice was that his cousin John Sweeney had enrolled there earlier in the 1930s, had done well and had played rugby with great success there. For Seán, the journey was an expedition, down from Donegal to Dublin, overnighting in Alderman Clerkin's Hotel in Eccles Street and then taxi next day to the door of the college where Fr W.J. Ardiff — who later taught him chess — took him under his wing. When he arrived he found that the college had up to 60 boarders. Quick and enduring friendships were soon formed, notably with the Roche cousins, Charlie and Joe, with Jim Barnes, Dick Fleming and Tom Gunn, to be encountered later.

Seán, for a memorable reason, did not finish the full term to Leaving Certificate in Terenure: clowning about on the stone staircase at the Study Hall on the third floor, he fell when trying to affect a rapid descent on the balustrade, falling three storeys and ending up, severely injured, for several months in St Vincent's Hospital. When fit again, he concluded his schooling to Leaving Certificate at Summerhill, Sligo. The episode, however, did not appear to lessen his love of heights and flights: Seán Logue went on, after a period working on the Irish language newspaper, *Inniú*, to a highly successful career with Aer Lingus until retiring in 1988.[16] As for the stone staircase and its balustrade, shortly after this incident it was fitted with impeding wooden blocks, still there to this day.

Entering the college between Harry Woods and Terence Doyle at the start of the 1930s and Seán Logue at their end, was one of Seán's college friends, Joe Roche. Joe entered in 1937 at the age of ten, 'going up that avenue in the longest walk of his longest day'. Joe's early days were indeed marked by a keen sense of how long the school day now seemed, after halcyon earlier days in Beaufort Kindergarten and despite its formidable Mother Margaret — how now, when the clock finally reached 2 p.m., instead of getting out they had to endure at least another half hour of religious instruction.

Born in Dublin in 1927, son of William Henry Roche who ran a retail pharmacy in Rathmines — one of three Roche brothers who were well-known pharmacists — Joe was the eldest of three boys who all attended Terenure. Like Harry and Terence before him, Joe greatly enjoyed his sport and, like them, retained vivid memories of that great institution, sports day. Along either side of the avenue two great marquees: in one of them, the Army Band tootling away; in the other, rows of tables providing mugs of tea and Johnston, Mooney & O'Brien's currant buns — free. In a smaller, more exclusive pavilion were to be found the eminences of the Past Pupils' Union, bedecked in medals and dressed to the nines — typically, Maurice McGowan, Dudley Fisher, Jack Hearne of TWA and P McGivney Nolan — grandees all and viewed in awe by the diminutive young athletes of junior school.

Joe's sporting days almost came to a premature end when, like Seán, he suffered misadventure. In his case, an unsupervised dive into the lake almost cost him his life. Suffering serious head injury, he was part rescued by schoolmate Jim Barnes who, showing that compassion that led him later to an illustrious medical career, brought young Roche to the Barnes home in 'Lakelands' before despatch to a Portobello nursing home where he received the last rites. Despite hospitalisation of many weeks, however, this was a mere interruption to a life of passionate commitment to a variety of sports, but especially to rugby. From college teams to Past Pupils' Collegians, he played the game for another two decades until his peers declared him rugby-redundant in his forty-fifth or forty-sixth year. As to the minor consideration of making a living, Joe went into engineering, starting in the family firm of Roche-McConnell, moving to Chloride in Manchester and then returning to join the Insurance Corporation of Ireland as an engineering assessor from 1956 until his retirement in the late 1980s. Like the Woods and the Doyles, Joe was at the start of a Terenure dynasty: his two sons, Billy and Peter, followed in his footsteps and grandson, David, to follow shortly. Not only that, Joe himself — dubbed 'Musso', after Mussolini, by his schoolmates, was one of three Roche cousins who came to Terenure in those days, the others being Jim and Charlie.

Charlie Roche, indeed, preceded him, enrolling in 1936. Born, like Joe, in 1927, but in Belfast and moving to Longford and Dublin as his father pursued his career with Bank of Ireland, Charlie's first experience of school was in Roscommon, his mother's home county, and then it was on to Holy Faith in Skerries before landing in Terenure for what would be a nine-year stretch. The decision for Terenure arose from a family connection: his uncle, J.J. Roche, had a Carmelite friend in New Jersey, Fr Fitzpatrick — who has earlier been encountered as Fr Celestine, himself a pupil of the restored college from 1917. Charlie's introduction to the college was when he was greeted by the Prior, Fr O'Shea, whom he recalled as a devout, other-worldly man. Like his cousin Joe, Charlie was greatly caught up in rugby: he well recalls — when playing for the Junior Cup team against the formidable Blackrock, in Bective's grounds — the tiny band of maybe 150 Terenure boy supporters outnumbered and outroared by the mass voices of some 500 Blackrock followers. In his final Terenure year of 1944–5, Charlie was vice-captain of the seniors and captain of the college 2nds.

In his last years there, he remembered the stern-looking Fr John Conleth Fitzgerald, coming to them as Prior, fresh from his previous role as Novice Master in Kinsale. He has it that Prior Fitzgerald was an innovating administrator who introduced the positions of Dean of Studies, Dean of Discipline and the system of House Captains. Stern-looking he may have been, but realist he was too: noting the perennial problem of the seniors smoking in the school toilets, he allocated the rugby pavilion to smoke in, located between the Concert Hall and the yard.

As for Charlie, on leaving Terenure he was apprenticed in the family pharmacy business, qualifying in 1950. Subsequently he went into the marketing side of the industry for 24 years, becoming general manager of Warner Lambert. On leaving this company, he set up his own pharmacy in Greystones, which is still going strong today. Retaining his links with the college, he became president of the union in 1964 and again in 1965. The esteem in which he was held professionally was evident when he was elected president of the Pharmaceutical Union from 1982–4, while a classmate, Dermot Nolan, became president of the Irish Dental Association and a younger friend and ex-Terenure man, Joseph Cahill, became president of the Irish Medical Union.[17] Coming through those hard times in the 1930s and early 1940s, it reflected not a little credit on the college that in a single year, half a century later, three of its alumni should hold the presidencies of leading professional bodies in the world of Irish medicine.

'JAZZ' DALY:

For these young men and their 1930s fellows, one abiding and beloved presence was that of Fr Laurence John 'Jazz' Daly. He was the teacher one who, when the clock struck two, kept the young juniors back for that half-hour extra of religious instruction. Diminutive though he was, and ancient though he seemed — he was in his seventies in the 1930s — he made an indelible impression. A former Terenure boarder of the 1870s himself, he had spent longer in the college than perhaps any other Carmelite in its history. Terence Doyle certainly could not forget him since, bedecked in a top-hat, Fr 'Jazz' was the first person to greet him on the day that he enrolled. Joe Roche, too, remembered the arresting figure:

> The imposing Fr Jazz … wearing a remarkable stovepipe hat and carrying an equally remarkable cane, but for all his forbidding appearance he was known to the boys as a kind man who characteristically would produce an apple from the deep pockets of his Carmelite habit, to slip to a surprised young lad.[18]

Among other temporal responsibilities, Fr Daly had for a long time been in charge of the weekly doling out of oil for the oil-lamps used by the students to study in their rooms at night. This he stored for safe-keeping in an old shed between garden and farmyard, and, as Fr O'Shea recalled: 'Woe betide any student who forgot the particular day and hour when it was distributed — he had to await another week and, failing the charity of those "who had oil in their vessels with the lamp", to abide in exterior darkness'.[19]

Apart also from supervising mealtimes and overseeing the tuck shop in the 1920s and 1930s, his major temporal responsibility was for his imperial domain, the kitchen gardens and orchard. As to the latter, another young contemporary, Tom Gunn, recalled that Fr Jazz 'commanded the orchard, where apart from apples and gooseberries and the like, he kept beehives'.[20] Ever the object of a daring raid, preserving it from intruders was one of Jazz's main concerns and it was not only the boys that he kept sternly at bay: the occasional daring intruder could also betimes include that colossus of the college, Prior Andy Wright. The most vivid remembrance of 'Jazz' was given by Fr Anselm Corbett. Recalling his boarding days in 1931 he remembered that:

> On Sunday afternoons we were given tea and biscuits with old Fr Daly, switch in hand, supervising us. He wasn't a cross priest by any means, but any recalcitrant boy got a smart, stinging belt on the bottom that quickly brought him to heel … He was indeed low-sized, had white hair and short beard, was gentle with twinkling blue eyes. As a boy, watching him, I concluded that 'Jazz' really loved being with the boys. He had his favourites too, particularly among the 'daydogs' and boarders who volunteered to help him in his autumn harvesting of apples. Clad in his brown habit, as we altar servers observed, he came down to say Mass every morning before all the other priests at one of the small side-altars. During the day he doffed the habit and appeared in an old-fashioned black 'tailed' suit, wearing a stovepipe hat. There were deep pockets inside the coat tails wherein he kept rosy, ripe apples for his 'sucks' as the rest of the

school named his favourites. The college garden, an enclosed fortress in our eyes, was his domain, the gate of which he kept tightly padlocked to keep marauders out.

I recall, in later years, Fr Daly as busy as ever waging war vigorously against intruders on the school grounds, tinkers in the Green Lane (now Greenlea Road) and courting couples in the summer. He had one cunning ploy in dealing with the latter. Having found their 'nests' under the leafy hedges, he went round with a bucket of tar and a brush, daubed the grass and awaited results. Sure enough, a good deal of romance was knocked out of the young hopefuls when they came to ground on their favourite spot. Now, wasn't he the little killjoy? But, it worked. Jazz's garden provided all the vegetables needed and from his orchard came the apples which he stored in the vast loft called The Turret, from a little edifice that once adorned the roof of the college.

Fr Daly celebrated his golden jubilee of ordination in 1937, surrounded by the glowing affection and admiration of friars and pupils alike. He passed away after a short illness, but peacefully, in January 1940. Even in death he continued to make an impact. Laid out in the college infirmary, his remains were brought in there when, as it happened, there was a single sick pupil: poor Charlie Roche was there recovering from mumps when the hallowed remains came in and, as the evening wore on, Charlie was convinced that he saw Jazz's ghost. Recovering quickly enough, Charlie, who was then an altar boy, was present at Fr Daly's removal to Whitefriar Street before burial in Glasnevin Cemetry: Charlie still recalls the breath of the funeral cortege horses on the back of his neck as he walked before them in the funeral procession that winter's day.

However, perhaps the most striking memory of him was that of Fr Anselm Corbett on the day he and his classmates left Terenure for the last time as pupils, back in 1932: 'The last thing we saw was the tiny figure of "Jazz" making his way slowly towards his beloved garden'.

DEVELOPMENTS IN THE 1930s:

Fr Dunstan O'Connor remembered Terenure's 1930s as a tough time and was to add that 'improvement in the thirties was minimal'.[21] However, just as the situation for the economy as a whole and that of secondary education were mixed, so it was too for the college itself. Numbers may have remained low until the mid-1930s, facilities may have been limited, and, for some boys, in winter, the place may have seemed cold, nevertheless there were positive developments in the interwar period.

For one thing, if numbers were low there was some growth in the enrolments of boarders in the very early 1930s. The evidence for this is indirect but persuasive: when the college was given over entirely to vocations, from 1909, the boys' benches in the little chapel were removed and replaced by choir stalls; however, in 1932 these had to be removed to make room in the chapel for an increased number of boarders. The old choir stalls eventually found new homes in the Kinsale novitiate and later, in 1944, at the new House of Studies at Gort Muire, Dundrum. As for the old nineteenth-century concert hall, it had to be changed into a refectory for the lay-pupils when they returned from 1917 until, in 1922, a refectory was provided in a room converted for the purpose at the rear of the old kitchen. In 1925, this old room was extended to double its original size. In due course, when the boys got their new dining room over 30 years later, in 1958, their old refectory became the workshop for a later legend of the college, Brother Stephen Reynolds. The college was gas lit in the 1920s: Fr O'Shea recalled the joys of staging the annual school play in gaslight, with all the challenges of flickering and dimming. The Shannon hydroelectric scheme of the later 1920s eventually gave the college its electric lighting by 1930. The year 1935 saw several physical improvements to facilities including new cloakrooms and toilets 'on the most up-to-date lines, being placed in a new building in the quadrangle'. These extensive alterations and additions were undertaken 'to cope with the increasing number of students' and the junior school was having to place a cap on places.[22] By 1940, the seasonal threat of cold and of chilblains had been removed by the installation of a new, elaborate central heating system.[23]

In more temperate weather there was always the joy of the lake. The boathouse at the college end was still secluded by trees and shrubbery as was the eighteenth-century 'Coffee House' at the other end. In 1931, a new boat was procured from Athlone and the new Prior himself, Fr O'Shea, was not shy in using it. Then, in the summer of 1935, the lake was drained and dredged and generally cleaned up. The opportunity was taken during this operation to construct a swimming pool at the far end of the lake, with concrete base and walls with two different depths for beginners and experienced swimmers. Better was to follow when a Dublin City Corporation drainage scheme in the vicinity was undertaken in 1936. A large culvert was cut through the college grounds into the lake at the college end and out of it at Lakelands end: some of the water of the Tymon River was diverted by way of this culvert through the lake and out into the Dodder River nearby. By this means a strong supply of pure water into the lake made 'ideal conditions for the swimming pool recently completed'.[24]

In addition to all this, two new grass courts had been laid down for tennis in the course of the winter of 1935–6. Then in 1936, the college's first dedicated sports hall, the Pavilion, was provided.[25] Designed by George Sheridan, it was formally opened by Seán T. O'Kelly, vice-president of the Executive Council, in an official ceremony on Monday, 18 January 1937. Blessed by the Fr Provincial, the attendance included the major figures from the union, including college solicitor, J.J. Sheil, college physician, Dr Seán Lavan, and H.F. Brennan, renowned Irish international water polo player and president of the Leinster Branch of the Irish Amateur Swimming Association.[26] All of these developments were happening in the college around its seventy-fifth anniversary. This diamond jubilee was marked by visits from the former

Prior General, Peter Magennis for the prize day in June and by his successor as Prior General, the Swiss–American Dr Hilary Doswald, in November 1935. Following a spirited and wide-ranging address by Fr Magennis, which stressed the 'magnificent inheritance' they had as Irishmen, Fr O'Shea rejoiced in the 'very successful year' they had had and in the rapid growth of day-pupil numbers. The high-point of the ensuing prize-giving came when a special award was presented to Fionán O'Sharkey who achieved first place in Ireland in music at the Intermediate Examinations.

As for the Prior General, he came to the college on Sunday, 1 December where he was guest of honour at a special concert put on by the boys. Indeed, before that, three of them presented an address of welcome in English by Joseph Clarke, in Irish by John Corrigan and in Latin by Richard Hearne.[27] Dr Doswald returned the compliment with a warm address of appreciation for all that Terenure and the Irish Carmelites had done and he was followed in this by the Lord Mayor Alfie Byrne and the president, Fr O'Shea.

The spirit abroad in the college was very far from one of gloom. The annual sports day of 1935, for example, had been an impressive one. Over 500 attended the event on 29 May. They witnessed P.J. Clarke win the college's Senior Challenge Cup while young Harry Brennan and Tommy Wright tied for the Junior Cup, with Harry equalling his previous year's junior 100 yards record. A month later came prize day, presided over by the Provincial, Fr Cogan. The event witnessed the 'strenuous battle' for the Senior Tennis Championship between Jim Brennan and Michael Ardiff. Michael was then in his final year in the college after enrolling in 1930, was its House Captain in 1934–5 and had been the first Terenure boy to be capped for Leinster Schools in 1933–4 and again in 1934–5[28] — at least since Jack Hart and Jim Colfer way back in 1909. On leaving the college he immediately joined the Carmelites at their Kinsale novitiate and was ordained in 1942. Two years later, he came back to his *Alma Mater* as a member of the teaching staff for ten years. In 1954, he went on the African mission where he spent the next 25 years.[29]

The annual union dinner, held on 9 January 1936, was equally spirited and had broken with tradition when the occasion was held on the college premises for the first time. A huge effort was made to ensure success. Despite the appalling weather, incessant rain all that day culminated in a fierce storm which hit Dublin from 6 p.m., lasting four hours and causing widespread and severe damage all over the city, there was not an empty chair or free space in the dining hall when college president, Fr O'Shea and union president, J.J. Sheil welcomed the guests, including representatives from several other PPUs.[30]

On this diamond jubilee occasion, Fr O'Shea took as his main theme the subject of the Irish language and the experiment of teaching and learning all subjects through its medium. Though careful and qualified in his remarks on this 'vexed question', he was forthright in his insistence that it was an experiment doomed to fail if forced too fast and if applied too indiscriminately: 'they had tried to apply it in Terenure College and found … that they had had to give it up in the end'. For all that, he reported that the college was in 'a flourishing condition' and that it 'could look to the future with confidence'.

Two months later there was an even greater turnout of some 800 people, including Lord Mayor Alfie Byrne, for the annual school play held over two nights on 17 and 19 March.[31] Equally, on the rugby front, College rejoiced in the brilliance of their young Jim Brennan, one of the very few schoolboys selected to play for Leinster in all three of their interprovincial matches and who scored three of Leinster's four tries against Connacht. In addition, they shared the excitement of seeing their own Hugh Milroy gain his interpro cap against Ulster that March. The Milroy family, destined for fame in Terenure rugby annals, were already well-known to the boys of the college since their tuck shop was stocked by Milroy Confections of Drumcondra. As for Brennan, he was a star Terenure athlete of the mid-1930s, breaking the school's 220 yards' record in the 1936 sports day, and going on from that to win the 100 yards and take the Senior Challenge Cup while his younger brother, Harry, had the distinction of coming second to big brother in both events and going on to win the 880 yards.[32] An even more distinguished achievement in athletics had been realised the year before that by another Terenure star athlete, Dermot McAuley. In the June 1934 sports day, in what was described as 'the wonderful all-round display by D. McAuley who won every senior championship event — five in all — and put up new College figures in three of them': he broke the college records for the 100 yards in 10 3-5 seconds, the high jump with 5-5 and the 12 lb shot with 41-10.[33] It was his third time to become college champion athlete, having already done so in 1930–1 and in 1931–2. He was All-Ireland Schools' Champion for the 12 lb shot in 1933 and set a new Irish Youths' Record in the event in 1934 with a throw of 42 ft 11 in. The sporting decade was to end on a high note too with the June 1939 sports day, 'one of the most successful ever held by the College'.[34] Three college records were broken and two more equalled on a glorious day of blazing sunshine: Cecil Gale broke the Senior Long Jump in 20-9 and won the Challenge Cup, P. Cooney broke the junior 7 lb shot record with 46-6 and D. Clarke the Junior High Jump with 4-111/2.[35]

Taken all together, the memories of annual reunions, sports days and prize days of the 1930s convey a sense of joy, pride and achievement far removed from the general gloom of that difficult decade: and, for all Fr Dunstan's recollections of a grim time, he was generous in his praise of the critically positive role played by its two presidents from 1931.

JAMES CARMEL O'SHEA:

Son of a Kinsale seaman, James, born in November 1899, would little have known his father who died in hospital in faraway Montevideo, Uruguay, in 1904. His mother made ends meet by running a fish shop in Kinsale and managed to educate her sons, James and his elder brother Daniel, at the Mercy Convent and then the Presentation Brothers in the town. Through connections with the Kinsale Priory the young James came to the attention of the Provincial, Fr Cogan, who arranged for him to come up to Terenure as a postulant in 1913. James was admitted to the Order in 1914, taking the name Carmel. He matriculated in 1916 and began studying in UCD, taking his BA, and then became the first Irish Carmelite to take the Higher Diploma in Education (HDE) in 1920. From there it was off to Rome where he was solemnly professed that November. It was here that he was ordained in July 1923. Among those who taught him there was Fr Taylor who gave him a ferocious grilling in the orals for the Licentiate in Theology: Fr James still remembered that gruelling ordeal 60 years later. He left Rome for good in 1924, receiving his doctorate just before his departure. On arriving home he was assigned to Terenure's teaching staff and within a year found himself elected Sub-Prior to Fr Taylor, and was re-elected to that post in 1929. Then in 1931, aged only 32, he succeeded Taylor as president and Prior and for the next six years did a great deal to try to enlarge the numbers and improve the facilities of the college.

Following these Terenure years, he became Master of Novices in Kinsale, then Provincial over 1940 to 1946 and then Prior of the House of Studies at Gort Muire. In light of Terenure's difficult financial history, perhaps one of his more important practical and symbolic achievements for the college came while he was Provincial: in 1944, he succeeded in paying off the final college debt of £5,000.[36] Capping his contributions were his critical roles in the foundation of Gort Muire and in the creation of the Irish Carmelite mission to Africa, as will be seen later. He was re-elected Provincial in 1958 and again in 1961 and so, was in a central position when the college came to celebrate its centenary in 1960. Subsequently, he became Prior at Whitefriar Street and it was here, after some years of poor health, he passed away on 12 October 1984. He left behind the memory of having been, juridically, the outstanding Irish Carmelite of his century.[37]

ANDREW EUGENE WRIGHT:

At the very time the young O'Shea was studying for his BA in UCD there was another young man living in Terenure and also studying in the university. Andy Wright, from Ballitore, Co. Kildare, was then studying medicine and was boarding with the Carmelites as one of the 'hostel students' when he decided to enter the Order. He was professed in 1922 and, resuming his university studies, he secured his Masters in Science and his Higher Diploma in Education, both with distinction. Following his theology studies in Rome he was ordained in 1928 and was then assigned to teach in Terenure.

Something of a giant of a man, at least in the eyes of his young charges, he became a Terenure legend in his own lifetime. Larger than life, great raconteur and wit, while trained as a scientist and teaching physics and chemistry in the college, he also became effectively Terenure's farm manager, sports organiser and grass cutter supreme. On the annual sports days, he was ever to be seen in the thick of it all, measuring, recording and commanding. Terenure lore has it that he had a great fondness for the shotgun which he was wont to discharge at the oddest times in the oddest places. On one remembered occasion he crept into a classroom armed with the gun and, urging total silence on the startled boys, quietly opened a window to discharge his weapon at a flock of crows attacking his potato and turnip crop.

Despite his large stature he was given to creeping about to surprise boys acting out of order: on one legendary occasion, on anti-smoking patrol in the vicinity of the new toilets at the back of the building, he was creeping along silently, followed at a short distance by a foolhardy young lad, Spike Moroney, carrying a firecracker which he discharged behind Fr Wright to the latter's consternation.

Known among the boys as 'Shylock', possibly because of his great head of black, curly hair, he threw himself into the preparation and production of the school plays with as much zeal as he put into his ploughing and mowing. Joe Roche recalled how his uncle, John, used to look forward to these drama productions under Fr Andy so greatly as much for their happy chaos as for their contents: supposed to commence at 8 p.m., at half-past eight Fr Andy could be heard, behind curtain, desperately hammering the finishing touches to the stage scenery.

A greatly practical man, who succeeded James O'Shea as Terenure's president and Prior in 1937, he embodied muscular Christianity as much as Carmel O'Shea embodied contemplative Christianity. On more than one occasion, his public comments on secondary education caught national attention. Speaking in January 1939 at the annual union dinner, he was critical of the government Department of Education's policies and practices. He deplored its publishing the lists of candidates sitting for the Intermediate and Leaving Certificate examinations, asserting that it encouraged 'window-dressing' by schools who put forward candidates who were 'virtually certain of getting through … Terenure put all its goods in the window'. He went on to criticise the existing programmes as being overloaded and with 'an unnecessary multiplicity of textbooks: if there were fewer books and those few books were profoundly studied, education would benefit …'.[38] Two years later, in another address to the union, which was picked up and strongly lauded in an *Irish Times* editorial, he called for a complete change of outlook in regard to 'land education', and deplored the way that young men from the land were encouraged to pursue secondary schooling as a way of escaping from the land and into safe careers in the public service, the law and the professions: 'secondary education would bestow precisely the same benefit on the boy about to become a farmer as it gave to a youth who was about to embark on a professional, business or civil service career'. His remarks were commented on extensively, in detail and very positively by the *Irish Times* editor who praised his deploring the 'curious snobbery' that attached to the white-collar job and the 'invidious distinctions between town and country'.[39]

Andy Wright was the supreme encourager. He used, betimes, to encourage and assist the boys to disassemble and reassemble an old, bull-nosed Morris Minor as a project for getting to know mechanics of the motorcar; at other times, encouraging them to construct a raft for the lake. He was the one who oversaw the draining of the lake and the construction of its little swimming pool in the 1930s. A kind, avuncular and sympathetic man, some remembered his tenure of the presidency as a utopian time when the whole atmosphere of the place was joyful.

Many pupils recalled his great gifts of practicality, humour and justness. So too did some of his confreres. He had a legendary wit. When the young Seamus Hegarty, future Bishop of Derry, was pursuing his HDE teaching practice in Terenure, he was remembered for his booming voice and his habit of phoning his mother who lived in Donegal. When the young trainee teacher spoke to his mother he could be heard all over the place: "'Who is that?" asked Fr Andy on first hearing this performance … "Oh, it's only Seamus Hegarty talking to his mother"….. "Well", says Fr Andy, "Would you tell him to use the phone!"'.[40]

For all Andy's sense of fun and the absurd, there was in his character, a sense of the sadness in life that made him especially gentle and kind to those in trouble or illness. Notwithstanding his bonhomie, he was a deeply conservative man who in later years in the Terenure Community could use his brilliant gift of wit and repartee to demolish the arguments of younger liberal-minded friars and colleagues. For all that, it was greatly to his credit that when he finished his time as Terenure president in 1943, the college enrolments had grown to such an extent that physically the place was then full. To have accomplished this in a time of world war following upon a decade of depression was no minor achievement and due in large measure to the leadership of O'Shea and Wright. Some of the challenges and features of those war years will feature in the pages which follow.

J.C. O'Shea, Prior of Terenure College, 1931–7.

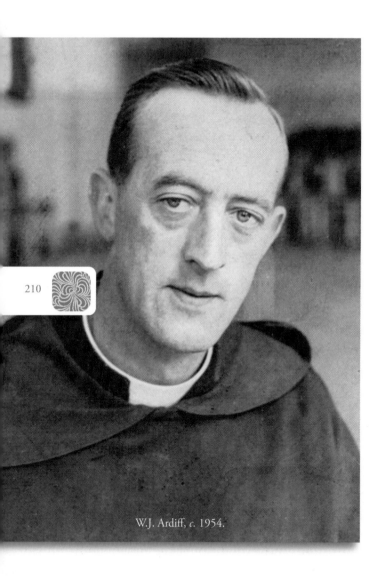

W.J. Ardiff, *c.* 1954.

Harry Brennan wins the 100 yards junior championship, 1935.

Students help in the college farm by saving hay, *c.* 1940.

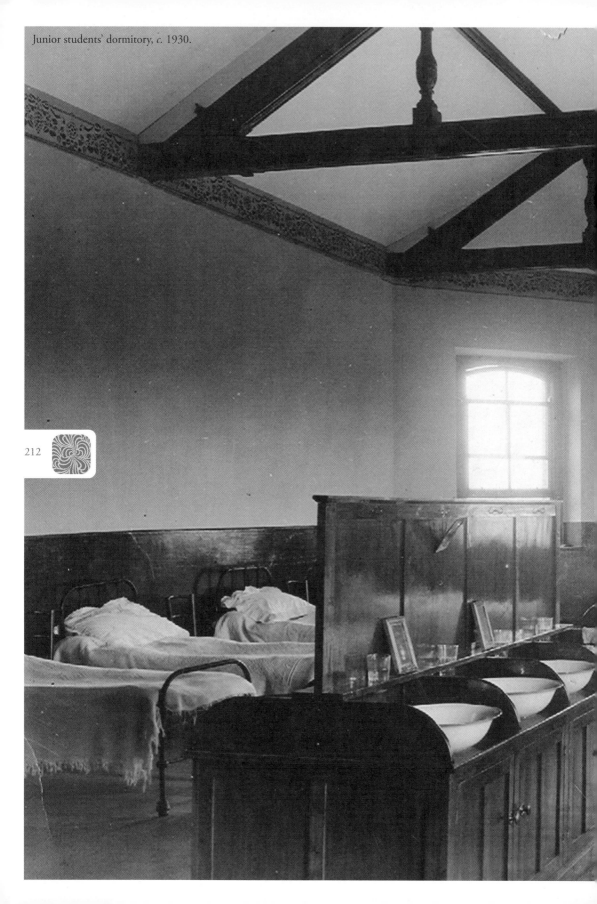

Junior students' dormitory, *c.* 1930.

212

J. Griffin and A.E. Wright in contemplation
in the college garden, *c.* 1940.

215

CHAPTER 13

College in a Time of War,
1939–45

Terenure's junior tennis champions
walk on court, 1941.

Deprivations and Dangers:

'When the kicks were more frequent than ha'pence' is how Fr Dunstan O'Connor described the Terenure experience during the Second World War. The kicks referred to were not on the field, but in the teeth, as the hard times of the 1930s became even harder in the first half of the 1940s.[1] Not that Terenure was unique — simply that, as a community like any other in neutral Ireland — it experienced hardships of scarcity even as it fortunately evaded the worst hardships of the war-time devastations suffered by so many people.

National war-time shortages of food and fuel were what most affected the country and begot the most responsive change. The old Shaw Estate on the other side of Templeogue Road, opposite the college, had been taken over by Dublin Corporation and in the course of the war was converted to greatly sought-after allotments. Presumably within the college, too, the crop-growing, kitchen-gardening and other horticultural operations were intensified under farmer, Prior Andy Wright. One thing is for sure — and by whatever means it was procured — the college took to digging turf in the Dublin–Wicklow Mountains. James Doyle, younger brother of Terence, and of whom more will be learned later, came to Terenure from Beaufort in 1940. One of five brothers who went there — at the start of a Doyle dynasty that later comprised James's three sons, five nephews and two grandsons — he mused on the impact of the war:

> I suppose on reflection that the 1939–45 war must have had a profound impact on us all, boys, priests, parents, teachers. Everything was scarce and rationed. Cars went off the road because there was no petrol/oil to fuel them. Not that many of us had access to motor vehicles. The boarders came and went on what must have been harrowing journeys. The trains usually travelled on power provided by wet turf.[2]

Speaking of turf, his brother Terence clearly recollected that 'simpler age … these war years were given over to stacking turf in the Dublin mountains and to picking potatoes in the College grounds: anything was preferred to class'.[3] Richard 'Dick' Fleming, from the home place of Fr Andy Wright and Fr Dunstan O'Connor, Ballitore, Co. Kildare, was born in 1928. He came to Terenure in 1941 as a thirteen-year-old boarder — only 14 boys were in the junior dormitory and 38 in the senior at the time, he reckoned. Keeping the boarders warm in winter — so it seemed to Richard — was the big challenge for the Terenure Fathers: and, to this end, he distinctly remembered that even the day-boys were enlisted to join them [the boarders] on a trip out to the Dublin Mountains, to cut, stack and gather in turf from the Feather Bed:

> when the end of Summer holidays brought all the boys back in September a meitheal of boarders was organised to go out and load the lorries that brought in the turf: indeed, at the worst, some trees

had to be felled in the College grounds and under the supervision of Fr Wright some boarders became experienced loggers. However, the boiler was kept going.

Richard added that 'The day boys were more useful than for just helping with the turf ... they were depended upon to keep the boarders up-to-date on the progress of the War'.[4]

Another pupil, whose family moved to Terenure in October 1935 as one of the first occupants of the new houses in Fortfield Road, was Tom Gunn who started at the college in 1936. He too recalled the turf-cutting expeditions to the Feather Bed and notes that the cutting and stacking part of the operation was done by the day-boys since it was conducted at a time when the vacation meant the boarders were at home. Presumably, it was the bringing in of the turf later on that involved the boarders also. These, as Tom remembers, were major expeditions: the transport was provided by the Michael Casey Senior and Junior, builders with the big 'Federal' trucks parked in the college where the Scout den is today. On these exciting outings, the chief cook was Fr 'Dulcie' Flanagan — so-called after his celebrated playing of the role of Dulcie, daughter of boarding school headmaster, Dr Grimstone, in the Victorian novel and play, *Vice Versa*, staged in the college at a much earlier time.[5] Dermot Columba Flanagan, a Galwayman, born in 1913, attended Terenure and was received into the Order in 1931, being ordained in 1937. Teaching in the college and Sub-Prior of the Community there up to 1946, he then went on the Welsh Mission. Here he was Prior at Llandeilo from 1946 to 1948 and became Prior of Aberystwyth twice during his 21 years there from 1958 until his retirement in December 1979; remembered as a gentle and cultured person and a patient and effective teacher of his pupils.[6]

Charlie Roche as a boarder remembered the gathering of the turf operations directed by Fr Andy. These operations petered out as coal began its return to the market in the aftermath of the war. There were darker memories than those of cutting and collecting turf. Charlie remembered too the night of the bombing of the North Strand: all the boarders were awakened and watched the fire glow in the direction of the city; and they recalled stories of other bombs falling — at Rathdown Park and at Donore Avenue: and, among the boys there circulated the rumour of a German named 'Held', living at the corner of Fortfield and Templeogue Roads, in a house with a flat roof with, allegedly, a swastika painted on it as a guide to the German bombers.[7] Charlie's memory of the night of the North Strand bombing is supported by Seán Logues's recollection of how they were all awakened by the noise and moved quickly to the windows until ordered back to bed by an agitated Fr Andy. For one Terenure alumnus who did not enrol in college until a month after the war's end, that bombing had its own indirect impact: young Sé O'Connor of the class of 1954, born in Dublin in 1936, was sent with his older sister, down to Fermoy in the wake of the Dublin bombing.[8] A Rialto-born lad, Paddy Ward, who entered Terenure in 1943 and whose father was a Guinness employee from Donore Avenue, recalled these rumours about the

'German' called Held with the roof-top swastika. Paddy's father took the war threat seriously enough to build a beehive air-raid shelter in the back garden of their Herberton Road family home. Paddy himself remembered the searchlights in the night sky and the sounds of aircraft overhead and recalled the bombing of Donore Avenue on the South Circular Road, on the night of 3 January 1941 and of the Phoenix Park on the night of 30–1 May 1941.[9] Whatever about swastikas on roofs, there certainly was a Stephen Carroll Held, whose house was raided by the Gardaí on 23 May 1940 where they discovered clear indications of German–IRA collaboration, including maps of harbours along the south-west coast. Indeed, Stephen Held whose house near Templeogue Road was called 'Kronstanz', was held and tried *in camera* — the Gardaí having found a parachute, wireless transmitters and receivers, and a box containing US$20,000, as well as documents relating to Irish aerodromes, harbours, bridges, landing grounds, and the disposition of Irish defence forces.[10] He was sentenced to five years' penal servitude.[11] Schoolboys may have vivid imaginations but, in this case, they were well-grounded in fact. However, they also had their own more immediate priorities and concerns: for many of them during the war it was the shortage of sweets and cigarettes and the curtailment of rugby matches 'away' from home that rankled: they might have added to this little list of woes, the curtailment of the annual Christmas play, at least for the first three years of the war: all these in time became their abiding memories.

PRIESTS, EX-PUPILS AND THE WAR:

If the war made its imprint on the memories of the boys of 1939–45, it also had an impact on the lives of the Irish Carmelites. This was particularly the case for those of them who had been sent to Rome for further studies in the late 1930s. These included Anselm Corbett, Enda Devane and Dominic Reale. Enda — 'Tim' to his family and 'Teddy' to others — was born in Tralee in 1916 and was educated locally. Fr Conleth Fitzgerald enlisted him as one of several from the county who came to make up Fr Conleth's 'Kerry team', as Peter O'Dwyer remembered it.[12] Enda entered the Kinsale novitiate in 1933. He secured his BA at UCD in 1937, and his higher diploma in education in 1938, with teaching practice in Terenure, before setting off for Rome that year, for further studies leading to his Licentiate in theology. The onset of the war brought him and his confreres back to Dublin to complete those studies at Milltown Park. There were further years of study at Maynooth until, in 1946, he returned to Terenure where he taught mathematics with great success for three years to 1949 when he finally got to have an extended study period in Rome. In 1952, he returned to Terenure for nine more years and here he became Bursar in 1958. Apart from his gift for teaching mathematics, he was recommended also as a gifted junior rugby coach and was president of Terenure Rugby Club over 1955 to 1959, during a decisive time in Terenure's rugby history.[13] A young John McClean in the late 1950s remembered him as 'an incorrigible maker of puns'.[14] With Anselm and Enda in the hasty departure from Rome was Dominic Reale, who led the retreat. Another Tralee man, born in 1910, and the senior of this group, his was a slightly later vocation than most. Educated locally at Tralee CBS, he then entered the civil service where he worked for five years before deciding to enter the Order where he was professed in 1932. Like Enda, but a few years before him, he studied at UCD for his BA and HDE before being sent on to San Alberto in Rome where, in July 1939, he was ordained. When the war was inevitable, he led his confreres to the Irish embassy to secure a visa to travel through France on the way home, and managed to expedite the visa business with a timely use of tips. A rough and stomach-churning passage followed, from Calais to Dover, before safe arrival home. At that stage he was assigned to the Terenure teaching staff where Fr Chris O'Donnell, a pupil in the early 1950s, remembered him for the great grounding he gave them all in grammar.[15] He became Prior from 1949 to 1952.

Less dramatic, perhaps, but no less disruptive to Community life, was the experience of the Irish Carmelites who had set up their twentieth-century mission to Wales. In 1936, the Order had accepted an invitation from the Dr Michael Joseph McGrath, Archbishop of Cardiff, to take over the then closed former diocesan seminary at Aberystwyth; by September 1936, its new Prior, Fr Malachy Lynch, transferred from Kent, had St Mary's up and running as a juniorate for the Order and the diocese. However with the impact of war the postulants and novices had to be transferred to Kinsale from September 1943.[16]

The war of course had a more tangible impact on such Terenure pupils and Carmelites who became directly caught up in it. Such was the case with Brendan Holden, son of William and Christina Holden of Moate, who came to the college as a third year student in 1932, in the same class as Michael Ardiff, Richard Hearne and Hugh Milroy. A well-organised and punctual individual, he had good academic ability, coming third in a class of 20 who sat the Christmas examinations of 1932 and sixth in a class of 24 in the summer of 1933. He left the college in 1936 and joined the RAF where he rose to rank of sergeant in the 612 Squadron — a general coastal reconnaissance outfit formed in Dyce, Aberdeen, in 1937. He was killed over Glasgow on 22 March 1941 and his remains were brought home for burial in Kilcurley Cemetery, Co. Offaly.[17] He was then only 23 years of age. Interestingly, when his mourning parents placed a death notice in the national press, it mentioned his being in the RAF and that he had been killed in action.[18]

A similar fate befell James Kelly, who was a first-year Intermediate student in 1933–4 and an extremely able one at that: with top marks for good conduct that year and altogether excelling in mathematics, science, Latin and Irish; he was still on the straight and narrow four years later when, in 1937, he won the Good Conduct Medal and secured his Matriculation.[19] A strong rugby player, on leaving the college he played for Bective Rangers and at the same time went to work in a firm of coal importers. On the outbreak of the war, he joined the RAF, becoming a fighter pilot. He was killed in an attack on the *Scharnhorst* and *Prinz Eugen,* presumably during the latter's famous dash from Brest to Wilhelmshaven on 12 February 1942. His heroism was recognised by the posthumous award of the Distinguished Flying Cross. He may be one of the Kellys commemorated on the RAF's Runnymede Memorial.

Then there was young Noel Murphy, whose father ran Murphy's Brewery in Bandon. A constant prankster in his Terenure days, from 1928–33, he joined the brewery on leaving the college but then joined the British Army on the outbreak of war and died in a tragic accident in his army barracks.

There were some, Carmelites and ex-Terenure students, who, entering the war, lived to tell the tale. These included the Carmelite chaplains Fr Thomas Cyril Murphy and Fr Joseph Bulbert. Fr Murphy with his unforgettably pure Oxford accent — derived naturally from his family, his father having been a senior official in Dublin Castle in the last decades of British Rule — taught in Terenure from 1933–4 on returning after five years or so in Australia; he taught in the college again from 1938–40 until volunteering for chaplaincy in the RAF. Here, he was accorded the titular rank of squadron leader. He and his confreres, Joseph Bulbert and Fr McNamee, found themselves serving from Iceland to North Africa.[20]

As to the number of ex-Terenure pupils who served in the Second, or indeed the First World War, there is at this point, no certain reckoning but, among those who served in and survived the Second World War were Giltrap, Timoney, Hill, Lambert, Constantine and Price. Willie Giltrap, one of four Giltraps in the college in the 1930s, was a very well-conducted young lad in the first-year Intermediate Certificate class of 1933 and did well in his summer examinations of 1934 to 1936 when he was in third year. He was also remembered as a useful rugby player in the college. He joined the RAF and reached the end of the war in one piece. He was with the Allied Forces in the occupation of Japan, stationed at one point some fifteen miles from Hiroshima.[21]

Jim Timoney had a creditable academic record from joining the college and is first mentioned in the Christmas of 1932: in his summer examinations of 1933, he came second in a class of thirteen. Joining the RAF, his first overseas posting was to Iceland and he served subsequently with the 232 Squadron in the Middle East and in South East Asia. He might have counted himself fortunate to have gone as far as Asia as, earlier, his plane was shot down when on bomber patrol over Reykjavik, from which episode he escaped with minor injuries. He continued to serve after the war and kept in touch with the college, providing Fr Bill Ossie McGrath with colourful accounts of his various adventures in India, Ceylon and the Cocos Islands. The affection in which he held the college was clearly evident in his inquiries after Frs Wright, Lamont, Ardiff and the Prior, and lay teachers 'Uncle' Joe Griffin, Eddie O'Hanlon and Christy Collins. Jim Timoney subsequently went into a career in civil aviation.[22]

Another ex-pupil was Jack Hill, brother of Carmelite missionary to Africa, Fr Mel Hill of whom there will be more later on. Following his schooldays, Jack joined the Irish Guards and fought in North Africa and after that at Anzio. Here, his platoon was captured by the Germans and he became a prisoner for the rest of the war, but he emerged unscathed to tell the tale.[23] Another survivor was Paddy Lambert who was in Terenure's first year Intermediate class in 1932 and was still on the books as a fourth-year student in 1936. He joined the RAF, trained as a wireless operator and saw active service in India and the Far East.[24] Then there was Willie Constantine who was enrolled over 1923 to 1926 at the least and who became a leading light of the College Dramatic Society *c.* 1930. He later qualified as a dentist and served for many years in the Royal Navy.[25]

In some ways, Thomas Gerard Price had the most varied and interesting career of any, whether before, during or after the war. He was born in London, in March 1920, but when he came to Terenure in the autumn of 1932, he had come from Wales, joining the same class as Timoney. Following his Terenure years, he returned to Wales to study architecture and was midway through his studies when the outbreak of war brought him into the Royal Engineers. The most gruelling part of his war service was experienced in the Italian campaign of 1943 where his 'great courage and initiative' in the face of enemy machine-gun fire earned him the Military Cross, followed by a bar to it in the next year, in this case for what his citation recorded as 'his outstanding bravery'. He did not escape unscathed, being injured when a mine exploded under his scout car. This happened on the Sangro Front in the winter of 1943, yet he continued to serve until demobilised in 1946. He then completed his architecture studies, went into practice and subsequently into partnership in 1948 until his retirement forty years later. A devout Catholic, most of his professional career was bound up in the construction or reconstruction of Catholic churches in the principality. In 1984, he was honoured with the Knighthood of St Gregory for his services to the Church in Wales. He maintained his war-time contacts by active membership of the British Legion and also served as a magistrate in Newport. He passed away in 2001 at the age of 81.[26]

GROWTH IN A TIME OF SCARCITY:

The war's privations and disruptions in no way halted the recovery and the growth of enrolments experienced from 1935. Over the years of the late 1930s to the mid-1940s, the numbers expanded as follows:

TABLE 15: ENROLLMENTS IN TERENURE COLLEGE IN 1937–8 AND 1944–5

Year	Senior School	Junior School	Total
1937–8	90	69	159
1944–5	161	90	251

This 57% increase brought new organisational and physical pressures. For the first time a process of dividing classes into As and Bs commenced in 1944 and was completed by 1948. It was in face of these pressures too, that in 1941, the college authorities introduced the positions of deans of senior and junior schools and dean of discipline.[27] The growing pressures on space necessitated the division and subdivision of classrooms. At the same time, with the pressure of numbers, the original school chapel became exceedingly cramped. When Fr Conleth Fitzgerald succeeded Fr Wright in 1943, holding the presidency until 1946, he earnestly wanted to build a new church but was frustrated in this by the pressure of competing demands.

In one way, however, the persistent problem of an earlier time — the shortage of priests to meet all needs — was no longer one, or, at least, not so frustrating. Although Fr Magennis, the Prior General in the 1920s, may have been saddened by 'the dwindling number of novices in the Province', as reported by Peter O'Dwyer, by the beginning of the 1940s this was no longer the case. Perhaps the Second World War had perversely assisted by compelling the repatriation of some young Irish Carmelites and by preventing greater freedom of movement overseas. By 1938, the Irish Province, according to O'Dwyer, had 68 priests, 11 lay brothers, 26 clerical students and 5 novices.[28] In the course of half a century the situation for the Irish Province had been transformed. A photograph of Terenure College teaching staff in 1936 shows eleven Carmelite priests and five lay teachers. By 1944, the number of lay teachers had risen only to six, but the number of clerical teachers had grown to seventeen with total staff increasing by 43% since 1936. They still may have been hard-pressed but they were far from the perilous days of the 1890s and 1920s. Furthermore, the majority of these Carmelite priests were young, energetic men with long careers ahead of them.

As country and college moved through their war years there were positive developments to encourage optimism and a sense of achievement. One was the restoration of the tradition of the annual play, a second was their considerable achievements in sport, notably in tennis, and a third was the foundation of the *Terenure College Annual.*

THE SHAKESPEARE CHRISTMAS DRAMA:

Discontinued at the start of the war, the annual Shakespeare play was revived in the winter of 1942 when Fr Donal Lamont and the 'Voice Instructor', P.P. Maguire, produced *Macbeth*. Lamont, from Ballycastle, Co. Antrim, had been a student of the college in the mid-1920s; he entered the Order in 1929 and was described by one former pupil as 'a bumptious, in-your-face-character'.[29] He was to have much more drama in real life subsequently, as will emerge later. After his profession in 1929, he secured his BA and MA in English at UCD where his masters was on the English poet, Richard Crawshaw. He was then sent to Rome where he secured his Licentiate and was ordained in 1937. He taught mathematics in the college until 1946, at which point a new Carmelite life beckoned.

His co-producer, P.P. Maguire, another Terenure legend, was an affable individual who earned a national reputation in radio-broadcasting, producing and scriptwriting.

Like many another dramaturge and thespian he was not deficient in ego and, apart from producing or co-producing the college dramas, he liked to play the leading role as well. A pupil in the early 1930s, he had been involved in the production side of college drama from at least 1937.[30] Apart from entertaining with dramatic readings in his Rathfarnham home in Crannagh Park, purchased in the 1940s, it is rumoured that he did absolutely nothing to the place from the time he moved in until the time he moved out many years later. Typically, for long he would regale his Terenure boy visitors there with test readings from his long-gestating, schoolboy novel, *A Certain Doctor Mellor*, published in Dublin in 1946. However, his national reputation was made with a radio series, *Saints You May Not Know*, starting in December 1939 and running until December 1947. He was elected president of the PPU for 1947 and 1948, and again for 1951. He ceased to be on the college staff as 'voice instructor' after 1946 on becoming a permanent employee of Radio Éireann and, later on, its head of drama. A determined defender of his radio department's reputation, he did not suffer its critics lightly, and, as late as 1978, following a testy exchange of letters in the *Irish Times*, could dismiss one critic, finally and crisply, thus:

> Certainly, I have no desire to waste any further time dealing with misstatements, illogic and a patent determination to avoid coming to grips with reality.
>
> You will, therefore, Sir, learn with relief that you have heard the last of me. – Yours, etc.,
>
> P.P. Maguire.[31]

As to his and Fr Lamont's first revival production of *Macbeth,* both Charlie Roche and Terence Doyle, separately remembered their roles, however modest: Terence as Lennox and Charlie as the Nurse with the never-forgotten sole line, 'His Majesty is gone into the field'.

However, it was the Lamont–McGuire December 1943 production of *Hamlet* that secured extensive attention and unprecedented plaudits in the press. With P.P. — inevitably — in the principal role, every facet of the production earned the highest praise. A wide-ranging review article in *The Leader* enthused:

> Rarely if ever have we seen such word perfection in a cast and as a result we did not hear a misplaced syllable even in the most quickly-spoken lines in … To our mind it was perfection in presentation and we raise our hat to Terenure College in tribute to and acknowledge-ment of a performance that could not be bettered … there is not a single boy of the forty whose name does not deserve honourable mention …

Furthermore, there was a special tribute to P.P. Maguire: 'An old boy of the College … he has been the life and soul of every Play staged in the College since his first entrance as a pupil'.[32]

THE SPORTING LIFE:

In sports too there were significant developments in the period. Basketball had been introduced in 1938 and proved extremely popular with the boys.[33] Then came the memorable sports day of June 1940: five college records were broken and two equalled on that remarkable day. Seán Ruttledge broke records in the junior 220 yards and the long jump; John Riordan secured two more in 880 yards' events while Aengus McMorrow secured the fifth record in the 12lb shot. Tom Scanlon equalled the junior 100 yards and Colm Condon, with triple wins, equalled the record in the senior 100 yards. The President's Cup for the junior champion was won jointly by McMorrow and Ruttledge while the accolade for the outstanding senior athlete went to Condon as winner of the Union Challenge Cup.[34] Not too long after this he was to matriculate, was called to the Bar in 1945 and proceeded to a distinguished career in public life thereafter, holding the office of attorney general from March 1965 to March 1973. However, back in his Terenure days Colm had already excelled as senior tennis champion, in 1937–8, while Aengus and his twin brother, Colm McMorrow, described in 1942 as 'really dangerous centres' were to go on to greater sporting heights in the years that followed. Aengus became the first Terenure alumnus to be capped for Ireland, against Wales in 1951 — although the college's 1930s pupil, Jimmy Joyce, vice-captain of the Terenure senior team in 1936 and later of Galwegians, was capped for a match between an Irish fifteen and a British fifteen at Ravenhill in January 1943.[35]

RUGBY:

As noted earlier, Mick Ardiff over 1933–5, and Jim Brennan and Hugh Milroy over 1935–6 had been the first three Terenure boys to gain interprovincial caps and were followed in this by Joyce in 1936–7 when he was capped against Connacht. From 1937–8, both at Senior and Junior Cup level there was a slight improvement in the customary fortune. At senior level they managed, in 1937–8 and in 1938–9 to draw their first round matches, only to go out in the replays, against Wesley and Presentation Bray, respectively. Then in 1939–40 they managed two wins, against Kilkenny by 20-0 and against St Mary's by 5-3 before going down heavily to Castleknock by 0-27. Although losing to Blackrock in the first round in each of the following three years, in 1942, under Aengus McMorrow the Senior Cup team made four attempts to play Blackrock only to be foiled by the weather, before finally going down on the fifth attempt in a grimly-contested battle where they lost 0-9. It would be some years more before a creditable Senior Cup team emerged. However, at Junior Cup level there was some promise at the start of the 1940s. As Fr Dunstan recalled it: 'When the Junior Cup Team defeated Newbridge 6-0 in 1944, held Blackrock to a draw and lost by a mere 0-6 in the replay, we felt we had definitely established a bridgehead' but, had to add ruefully: 'We had, too, but it took almost ten years before it was finally exploited'.[36]

That first 1944 match against Blackrock was a landmark in another respect: it was the first time the Terenure boys began to stand and sing their own cup songs. These martial efforts were written by lay teacher Christy Collins and Fr Dunstan and, as Paddy Ward remembered it, they were coached in these efforts by Fr Ossie McGrath who took the junior boys in the concert hall for cup match song practice. One of these original cup songs, to the tune of *Men of Harlech*, went:

> Come on you lads and let's get cheering
> As the Leinster Cup we're nearing
> On the road to Glory cheering
> 'Onward Terenure!'
>
> It all depends on you men
> To show that we are true men
>
> Play the game and fight for fame
> That's what we expect from Terenure men!
>
> As the battle drums are beating
> This is our war cry and our greeting
> No surrender and no retreating
> 'Onward Terenure!'
>
> [Big roar, then ...]
>
> *T.E.R.E.N.U.R.E..................!* [37]

Before the war years were over there had been another significant development in college rugby. In 1941, the past pupils began to play on Sundays to see if it were possible to field a team every week. According to Fr Dunstan, they called themselves the 'Collegians' and he recalled refereeing eleven of their thirteen games that season. At the end of 1943, they secured official affiliation and, remarkably, won the Minor League in their first season: but, that is a larger story that merits separate attention later. While, retrospectively, rugby has dominated the Terenure historical memory, at least when it came to sport, a more dispassionate consideration of the actual record of achievement would suggest that it was in tennis that Terenure actually shone from the late 1930s into the mid-1940s.

TENNIS:

The Leinster Junior Tennis Cup had been established in 1936 and Terenure's juniors captured the trophy for the first time in June 1941: at Fitzwilliam they defeated Belvedere by 8 sets to 6. The Terenure champions were F. Byrne, Gerry Clarke, Tom Moroney, Arthur Fitzpatrick, S. McElroy and Hugh Gunn.[38] It was a close and thrilling final where Belvedere's Irish Junior Champion, J.D. Hackett, partnering B. Collins, dropped one set which proved fatal for Belvedere and vital for Terenure.

The Terenure juniors proved strong enough again to reach the 1942 finals where, alas, they fell to Blackrock.[39] By 1944, the victorious juniors of 1942 had moved up to the senior ranks and this time Gerry Clarke, Tom Moroney, Joe Roche, Hugh Gunn and Arthur Fitzpatrick reached the senior finals at Fitzwilliam against High School in June 1944. They won the Leinster Senior Cup for the first time that year — the fifteenth such final — with Fitzpatrick and Gunn having an impressive 6-4, 6-0 triumph in the final doubles match.[40] Better was to follow when the college's juniors won their final a few days later with a 4-2 victory over Belvedere. They thereby secured the college's first ever Leinster double in any sport.

In all of this the remarkable figure was the young and exceptionally gifted Arthur Fitzpatrick: as Terenure's No. 1 he achieved the rare distinction of winning junior and senior medals in the same season. He was then in his fourth year on the junior team.

Further triumphs followed when two months later he won the final of the Irish Junior Tennis Championship, on 26 August 1944, in a hard-hitting battle with R. Davis of CUS.[41] Fitzpatrick had had a remarkable record. He won the College Juvenile Cup in the three years 1940, 1941 and 1942; then, in 1944 the College Junior, the Leinster and the All-Ireland under-15's Cup. He took the College's Senior Cup in 1946, 1947 and 1948 and won the under-18's All-Ireland in 1947 and in 1948 he was chosen by the Irish Lawn Tennis Association to represent Irish schoolboy tennis at Wimbledon. In that same year he entered the Order, was ordained in 1956 and spent many years in Africa. He passed away while serving in the Knocklyon Parish in September 2001.[42]

THE *ANNUAL*:

One of the most significant initiatives in the war years was the establishment of the college *Annual*. It proved to be an important factor in enhancing that sense of college as a family and in creating a historic awareness of the college and its multi-facetted contributions to community and country.

On that sense of the college as a family, one of the most able of the boys of the war years was Richard 'Dick' Fleming who hailed from Ballitore and came to the college in 1941. Playing a memorable role as Polonius in the famous *Hamlet* production of 1943, he recalled that strong familial atmosphere, centred on the personality of the Prior and president, Andy Wright, reinforced by the kindness of his Carmelite confreres, notably Fr D.C. 'Dulcie' Flanagan. A gold medal winner in English, Richard attributed his love of the subject to Fr Flanagan, and this was the man who effectively founded and edited the *Annual* in 1944.

As Fr Flanagan recalled it himself, the decision to produce an *Annual* was taken by the Prior and Community early in 1943.[43] It was partly a matter of felt necessity, to provide some kind of permanent record for an institution whose population of pupils, teachers and priests was, for the most part, in constant flux. There is also a suggestion that the original idea for a magazine came from two sixth year students of 1944,

Malachy Slevin and Hugh Gunn and that it was either to support or to forestall this that the Carmelites then took the initiative.[44] It was also, however, a matter of pride and prestige since several rival institutions boasted official annual records. A committee of three of the Community, Frs Dunstan, Lamont and Flanagan, were delegated to the task. The initial cost of £400 was to be met from sales at 2s6d per copy and from advertising: the first edition of the publication carried nineteen pages of advertisements, hard won in some cases. That first edition recorded in photographs some fondly remembered features — the cricket crease, boys playing in the lake — and some features long gone such as the rustic bridge and coffee house. From the outset it carried that much-loved and still-enduring feature, *Day by Day*, special because it was compiled and produced by the boys themselves. Its first compilers were sixth years, Hugh Gunn and senior rugby captain, Willie Buckley, followed in 1945 by classmates Joseph Griffin and Richard Fleming.

SOCIAL ACTION:

A more serious side of past pupil and extra-curricular activity was The Boys' Club. The Mount Carmel Branch of St John Bosco Boys' Club was established in the course of 1938 on the initiative of the Terenure Past Pupils' Union. Based in Whitefriar Street National School, its first practical meeting was held in October 1938. A direct product of that contemporary movement, known at the time as Catholic Action, it was set up to provide recreational outlet and social support for unemployed youths of the ages from fourteen to eighteen. The college dentist, John F. Leonard, one of the foundation members of the PPU and its president in 1939 and 1940, presided at the early meetings. Among others who joined in this work at that stage were Fr Ephrem Corbett, college solicitor J.J. Sheil and P.P. Maguire. The club progressed well for a time until it lost its premises and fell into a brief trough. In the course of 1943 the then PPU president, lawyer Maurice McGowan and his successor, optician P. McGivney Nolan — later president of the Opthalmic Institute as well as record-holding four times president of the Past Pupils' Union[45] — made strenuous and successful efforts to revive the club which reconvened in the Whitefriar Street school hall. It provided support to some thirty-five disadvantaged local boys — board games, debates, talks and book-lending in the winter, swimming and outings in the summer. Terenure boys just graduating from the college were encouraged to join the PPU and to come into the work of assisting with The Boys' Club, and a number from the classes of the 1940s did so: among these were Liam Mangan who became club secretary, Seamus Hennigan who later joined the Carmelites, Terence Doyle, Brian Rush, Richard Fleming and Joe Roche, to name but a few. Over the next year the local boys' membership rose from 35 to 50 and medals to mark their various achievements were organised by and presented by McGivney Nolan and McGowan. By the end of 1945, a considerable programme of events, from retreats to competitions, from films to outings had been successfully arranged. Ken Monaghan, a prize-winning Terenure pupil himself over each of the years from 1939–40 to 1941–2, had become secretary in the course of 1945–6 and was able to report considerable progress, opening two evenings a week and now catering for up to 70 boys. Organised visits to Tara Street Swimming Baths had been arranged and a football club had been set up. At this stage it had become one of the major aspects of the life of the PPU but it dangled from a financial shoestring and dwelt in borrowed premises.

PRESIDENT AND PUPILS TO 1945:

Despite the deprivations and difficulties of the war years, the leadership of Andy Wright and Conleth Fitzgerald was steady and confident and contributed greatly to the success of the college in these years and notwithstanding their greatly contrasting styles of government. Enrolments had never been greater and the atmosphere of the place was a happy one. A much more serious individual than Wright, Fitzgerald placed new stress on academic achievement. One former pupil, nearing the end of his time at the college in the last years of the war, clearly recalled the 'profound change in atmosphere' in 1944 — Fitzgerald had succeeded Wright in 1943 — as a new academic regime was inaugurated and a new seriousness of academic commitment emerged. Certainly, the numbers successfully taking the state examinations from the mid-1940s outdid those of ten and twenty years before:

TABLE 16: TERENURE COLLEGE EXAMINATION SUCCESSES, 1943–5

Year	Leaving Certificate	Intermediate Certificate
1943	16	19
1944	12	11
1945	17	12

As for Fr Fitzgerald, stern-looking he may have been and been remembered, yet, he was obviously respected enough by his confreres to be elected Provincial on ceasing to be Terenure president in 1946, an office which he held for two terms to 1951.

As for the boys of the first half of the 1940s theirs were still happy memories, mainly of fun, games and adventure, much less of examinations, still less of detentions. Even for the boarders whose one free day out was one Sunday a month, it was perhaps that day rather than most others that was fixed fast in their recollections — the trip to town and the afternoon tea-dances in the Metropole or the trip to Dún Laoghaire to hire a boat at 2s an hour and spend the afternoon rowing around the harbour. Dick Fleming well remembered such days with his pals Charlie Roche, Hugh Clarke from Lifford who later became a Carmelite with long service in America, Austin 'Boysie' McDonald from Toomebridge, Co. Antrim, and Willie Buckley from Moate who became a diocesan priest in Australia. As for Richard himself, leaving Terenure in

1945 with his Leaving Certificate, he first took up a CIE clerkship before embarking on a lifelong career in banking, from 1947, at first with National City Bank and ending with Bank of Ireland International. As with others, he never lost touch with the college: helping the Boys' Club, then being actively involved in the founding of the Past Pupils' Dramatic Society, and becoming president of the union in 1968. His big innovation on that occasion was to return the holding of the annual dinner to the college premises, for the first time since 1936, a practice that was maintained until 2008.

He and others remembered the matron, Miss Scanlan, who took care of coughs and bruises with great kindness. Tom Gunn and Dick Fleming remembered her as being nicknamed 'Queenie', apparently because she applied quinine as the universal remedy. The name 'Queenie', however, may have been eponymous as a later generation of boys, such as Felim Corr of the class of 1958, (Fr) Des Kelly of the class of 1956 and Frank Gildea of the class of 1973 attached this name to her successors, Miss Costello and Miss Beirne.[46] Matron Scanlan retired in 1947 and was succeeded by Miss Costello in 1948: Corr recalls the formidable Miss Costello still presiding over the refectory at lunch-times with as much firmness as she ruled over the infirmary until 1957 when, as a late vocation, she entered the Medical Missionaries of Mary and served in Africa.[47] Clearly, the name 'Queenie' was passed on down through the generations.

Despite the shortages of the times, pals like Richard 'Dicky' Dunne and Charlie Weakliam recalled the 'tuck shop': once the domain of Fr 'Jazz' Daly, it had passed in their days into the hands of Fr Elias 'Jumbo' Elliott. The two boys were classmates from the outset of their first encounter until they left Terenure in 1948. Richard was born in Skerries in 1930. His father was a civil servant in the Department of Industry and Commerce and his mother a remarkably gifted student and teacher who pursued her degree from Eccles Street Dominican College where one of her teachers had been Eamon de Valera. Charlie was born in Ranelagh, also in 1930. His father was a customs officer while his mother's family owned the Mountainview Dairy in Terenure.

These parents were perhaps representative of the modestly aspiring young families who were settling in the area from the mid-1930s. The two pals well remembered the general kindness of their priests and teachers and recalled that boys who were not great at sports or at the books did not suffer as a result: they confirm the view of another 1940s lad, James Doyle, that there was a notable absence of punishment or persecution and a notable presence of encouragement. Even if the college, in the years to 1945 and beyond, failed to win much-coveted Junior and Senior Cups, as Tom Gunn recalled, there was still the joy of the film shows screened on the nights of cup matches — *Laurel and Hardy*, *Our Gang* and *The Keystone Cops*.

Past pupils relax in each other's company at a sports day, 1940.

233

Terenure pupils eagerly line up for the start of the sack race, 1930s.

234

Attempted block of a clearance kick
in the Junior Cup final, 1944.
© Independent Newspapers.

236

Ecstatic Terenure rugby supporters celebrate a
college try, 1945. © Irish Times.

238

239

Terenure's U-14 cricket team swaggering onto the field, *c.* 1945. © Independent Newspapers.

Final final of the Lein

er Schools' Junior Cup

Cartoon published in the
Dublin Opinion, 1949.

Fr Joseph A. Kelly followed Conleth Fitzgerald as president in 1946. Known as 'Bugs' Kelly, from his habit of absent-mindedly scratching his head, he had been a primary school teacher in Northern Ireland before entering the Order as a late vocation at the age of 42. This gentle successor faced considerable change and challenge on several fronts. The changes, almost all positive, nonetheless generated their own particular pressures. The number of students in senior and junior schools rose steadily each year, as follows:[1]

Table 17: Number of students enrolled in Terenure College, 1944–50

Year	Senior School	Junior School	Total
1944–5	161	90	251
1945–6	166	111	277
1946–7	205	130	335
1947–8	212	130	342
1948–9	228	139	367
1949–50	234	149	383

A total increase of 53% in the space of six years was both welcome and unprecedented as was the steady rise in Leaving and Intermediate Examination successes:[2]

Table 18: Number of Terenure students sitting state examinations, 1944–50

Year	Leaving Certificate	Intermediate Certificate
1944	12	11
1945	17	12
1946	9	26
1947	14	27
1948	14	27
1949	12	29
1950	18	39

Fr Flanagan, editor of the *Annual*, could remark that by the end of 1943–4, the numbers already constituted a record, one which would be broken in each of the succeeding years to the end of the 1940s and beyond. That increase was especially marked by the spurt in enrolments in September 1946, just as Prior Kelly came into office. The overall growth in these years was matched by a growth in the complement of teaching staff, as follows:[3]

TABLE 19: NUMBER OF STAFF IN TERENURE COLLEGE, 1944–50

Year	Religious	Lay	Total
1944–5	15	6	21
1945–6	17	6	23
1946–7	17	7	24
1947–8	17	10	27
1948–9	17	10	27
1949–50	20	11	31

While the end of the decade saw the number of Carmelites teaching in the college at its highest up to that time, it was more striking that the number of lay teachers during the same period had almost doubled.

DEPARTURES AND ARRIVALS:

There were, of course, the inevitable departures after long service. The well-liked science teacher, Eugene Moynihan, had already just retired in 1943 after long service that had seen him teaching there even before the First World War, and sadly, he passed away three short years after retiring. The core group of lay teachers — long there by the 1940s and destined, happily for the students, to serve for decades more, were Joe Griffin, Eddie O'Hanlon and Christy Collins. Of these there will be more anon. In addition, there was the long-serving music master, V.S. Pentony and the voice instructor, P.P. Maguire. Then, too, there was the PE teacher — 'Physical Culture Instructor' or 'Drill Master' as they were called in those days — once the formidable Sergeant Major Hastings had left, in his place came J.J. O'Rourke, then Lieutenant Pat Cashin from 1945 to 1948. From the 1920s, Pat Cashin had learned the diverse methods and practices of physical culture, whether SOKOL[4] or Swedish drill, in the Irish Army. He received his Lieutenant's commission at the start of the First World War and became training officer at the Army School of Physical Culture in the Curragh. He was a significant all-round army champion, from Gaelic, soccer and rugby, to basketball, fencing and swimming. He deplored the neglect of physical culture in schools and the absence of any college in Ireland in which to train PE teachers.[5] Widely travelled, and, though married with five children, in 1949, he emigrated again, this time with his young family, to take up a post in the United States. One of his most important contributions to Terenure College was to foster and promote swimming and life-saving among its pupils and he would have rejoiced when on the eve of his departure young Jimmy O'Connor brought home Terenure's first-ever Leinster swimming title in the Juvenile Championship in September 1948. In addition, Cashin introduced basketball and boxing to college to some effect. A young lad then in First Year 'A' would be remarkable proof of that — one Henry, later revered as 'Harry', Perry. Winning both the respect and affection of the boys, Pat Cashin's loss was a sore one, his departure a matter of genuine regret.[6] His place was taken by T.E. Goddard for a year and then by the well-regarded John Kavanagh who was remembered thus:

> John Kavanagh was a successful and well-loved Drill Instructor in the College who served for ten years and, literally, died on the job, on Sunday 14th June during a drill display witnessed by priests, pupils, parents and past pupils. Expert in his craft, he was a very little man in stature, but a live-wire with a big heart and incomparable patience and generosity.[7]

Then, when P.P. Maguire left in 1947, to join Radio Éireann, his replacement, in 1948, was Rosalind Dunne, now deemed 'elocution' teacher, until 1950, after which the Abbey actor, Eddie Golden, came on board for a short time. Two new teachers, who made a considerable impact from their arrival in the autumn of 1947, were Des McMorrow and M.J. Keane. McMorrow, who taught modern languages, was a brother of the twins, Aengus and Colm, and like them contributed greatly to the college's rugby. Keane was an exciting and innovating teacher of science: he took classes on guided tours to manufacturing enterprises such as The Irish Glass Bottle Company and Guinness's Brewery and used film to illustrate aspects of his subject. He left Terenure in 1949–50 as, unfortunately, did Des McMorrow who moved on to take up a post in education administration in the British Army in Nigeria, while his successor P. Henry stayed for only one year. However, there was one lay teacher who starting in 1946 was destined to have an enduring and distinguished role in the history of the college: Michael O'Connell had joined the staff as lead English teacher from O'Connell CBS and would crown a long career as Terenure's first deputy principal. Although he will feature later in this volume, it is worth recalling the young man's recollection of just how small and intimate a group the established lay teachers were at the time. 'V.S.P' (as music teacher, V.S. Pentony, was known), Eddie O'Hanlon, Christy Collins, Joe Griffin and Michael O'Connell constituted a community with a community ; friendly, yet still formal in an old-world way, even in their staff room they addressed each other as 'Mr'. Although each one was a legend in his pupils' lifetimes, one in particular merits special mention at this point — almost an institution in himself.

JOE 'THE HOOLEY' GRIFFIN:

In October 1945, Joe Griffin celebrated his twenty-fifth anniversary as a member of the college's lay-teaching staff. Enthusiastic Professor of Latin, friend to many hundreds of boys, priests and fellow teachers, Joe Griffin left his home in Glin, Co. Limerick, during the years of the First World War to study at UCD. This is corroborated by Fr P.J. Cunningham who came to Terenure as boarder-postulant in September

1950 and who learned that Joe had probably arrived as a resident student as early as 1917, even before commencing his university studies. As Fr P.J. and others confirm, it was at this time that he struck up what became a life-long friendship with another young student, Kildare-man, Andy Wright: both were, or became, residents in Terenure College at a time when it also served as a university hostel. Fr Cunningham described how the two were very much given to playing practical jokes on each other. Joe had a black suit for his 'Sunday best' and, when Andy went off to the Carmelite novitiate in Kinsale; he swapped his own suit for Joe's, in order to arrive in appropriate attire, without telling Joe until after the event.[8] Andy, one presumes, must have been some sight arriving at Kinsale, a young giant of a man in the suit of the diminutive Joe. Graduating in Classics he joined the Terenure College teaching staff in 1920. Known by some as 'The Knight of Glin' he was more generally known as 'The Hooley Griffin' — the origins of that strange and strikingly inappropriate nickname; assuming it refers to a *céidhlí*, boisterous party or wild celebration — lost in time. Even Donal Lamont, a pupil of the 1920s — later a Carmelite and a bishop no less — who had direct classroom experience of 'The Hooley', confessed that he could not explain how Mr Griffin came by that name, but it stuck. A diminutive five foot four, with a high-pitched voice, prominent upper teeth, black-gowned with dandruff — until years of pupil wear-and-tear left him with little enough on top — it was far from parties and wild celebrations that the 'Hooley' Griffin paced the passages of his years. A man of remarkable routine, he took afternoon tea in the parlour to the right of the entrance hall and, like clockwork, every evening walked down the avenue to post the daily letter to his parents in Limerick. Unusual, unique even as a lay teacher who lived in college all his professional life, he was a very private person who, only on the rarest of occasions could be prevailed upon to share his meal with the Carmelite Community. For all that, he held court in the same parlour with any member of the Community who came in to tease or regale him with the latest college gossip. While to the boys, he was 'The Hooley', to his Carmelite teaching colleagues, he was known as 'The Gink' — presumably after the character from *The Wubbulous World of Dr Seuss*. Courteous and gentle to a fault, it is suggested that not in 50 years of teaching did he order more than an exceptional one or two pupils from a classroom. His rare and serious admonition was to threaten a miscreant with the dean of discipline. For all his gentleness, he declined to be overawed by rank, especially when the holder of it had been a former pupil. Consider Bishop Lamont's return visit to the college in 1957 as described by Lamont in the school *Annual*:

> If you think, Doney, that I am going to get down on my knees and kiss your blooming ring! ... when I think of the times when I could have walloped your behind or had the Doc Taylor or Jimmy O'Shea deal with you! ... Kiss your ring, indeed! ... And then, of course, when there was no one around, he would ask for a blessing and kneel for it. Vintage Mr Griffin.[9]

'The Latin teacher whose whole life was just that — teaching Latin', as Fr Cunningham fondly remembered him, nevertheless a few more critical commentators who, as former pupils, experienced his teaching, recalled him as

> a real character who taught Latin, but not very well ... never under-
> stood the difference between the gerund and the gerundive, could
> not parse Latin verse and never really understood Roman Civilisation
> — hopeless at Latin in some ways, but devoted to his pupils.

It was that devotion and his personal generosity and concern that they all remembered.

Charlie Weakliam of the class of 1948 found Joe Griffin to be

> the most popular lay teacher ... in some ways innocent and gullible
> and some of the characters in class could lead him on red herrings by
> irrelevant questions. Taking all students seriously, especially in their
> questions, he could become the victim of mischief[10]

Over 25 years later, another pupil and afterwards a teacher at Terenure, Charlie O'Sullivan independently confirmed Charlie Weakliam's memories of the man; recalling that the boys used to annoy him with inane questions like 'Sir, what was Julius Caesar really like?'

Fr Des Kelly, class of 1956, recalling this 'Mr Chips of Terenure' as a shy man, continued:

> his birthday fell on the 8th December and the custom grew up among
> 6th Year Boarders that they would gather outside his door on that day
> and sing the Stephen Foster refrain, 'Poor Old Joe' for his birthday
> ... he would never come out to hear it but it was well-known that he
> loved that custom. Perhaps it was his by way of reciprocation that he
> had his own custom: on the first day of Leaving Cert exams he
> would, out of his own pocket, provide oranges and apples on every
> boarder's place in the Refectory.[11]

A classmate of that same year of 1956 who first encountered 'The Hooley' in 1950, David Kennedy, remembered this

> exceedingly kind person who gave many a love of Latin: such was
> his dedication and concern that he would bring his Latin exam classes
> into special Saturday three-hour sessions to cover all possible angles
> and after exams would be on standby to quiz the emerging candidate
> on their progress[12]

His private and personal generosity touched many of his former charges and stretched over decades. Dennis McGrane, a 1940s pupil, graduating in the class of 1951 described the 'always dapper, white shirt, stiff collar, Charlie Chaplinesque' character who, after Dennis's time in Terenure, took him to dinner in the old Jury's Hotel on Dame Street. Almost a decade later, Eugene McNamee of the class of 1957 was struck by the kindness of his former teacher who, on the occasion of Eugene's twenty-first birthday in 1960, telephoned the young man at home with congratulations and soon after treated him to dinner at the Dolphin Hotel and drinks afterwards. In this, Joe never changed. Almost a decade later, former pupil, John McClean, of the class of 1963 had completed his HDE in 1967, pursuing his teacher-training practice in the college and then joining the teaching staff in 1968, recalled how Joe 'in a characteristic act of generosity, took the novice teacher for dinner in town, with a few drinks after'.[13]

What perhaps is as remarkable as the sheer span of Joe's teaching career at the college are the span and the specificity of his pupil's remembrance of him. When the young David Kennedy first encountered him in 1950, Joe seemed, even then, to be 'aged and ancient' although only about 50 and still exuding 'incredible passion and enthusiasm' for his subject. Twenty years later he was still there, active in the classroom and Charlie O'Sullivan remembered him as 'seeming ancient': indeed, Frank Gildea of the class of 1973 recalled as a fourteen year old, how Joe, 'almost blind and very frail', seemed 'to be all of a hundred years old' and yet 'for all of his frailty he was an exceptional teacher'.[14] It was typical of Joe that when he finally retired in the mid-1970s, he presented the college with a gift — a barometer that graced the Entrance Hall where the college's Reception is today and opposite two splendid eagles either side of the fire-place: sadly, eagles and barometer disappeared in a practical joke escapade c. 1979–81.[15] Sadly too, it was in August 1979 that Joe himself stole away just two or three weeks before what would have been his sixtieth year at the college. He had suffered an incapacitating stroke a few years before this and continued to be sheltered and cherished by his Carmelite colleagues. Although unable to sustain a conversation, he retained sufficient of his schoolmasterly self to be able to respond with 'Correct' or 'Bosh'! In his memory, the Past Pupils' Union with Michael J. Pender as president committed to creating the Joe Griffin Memorial Library and raised an impressive £10,000 at a special dinner in October 1981 to inaugurate the quest.[16] In the course of the following year, under PPU President Eugene McNamee a special library covenant fund was organised, which raised £2,000 a year for six years.

CARMELITES ON THE MOVE:

Inevitably, too, there was a constant changeover of personnel when it came to the Carmelites. It would be dizzying to detail the changes of personnel in all their fullness in the course of these years but a few salient ones ought perhaps to be noted.

First among these was the story of one who came to Terenure as a student in 1919: Edward, later Kilian, Lynch, born in Ballymanus, Co. Wicklow, in 1902, was one of three brothers who entered the Carmelite Order: Michael, later Elias, and William Malachy who both preceded him, had distinguished careers especially in the Order's

UK Mission. Elias became successively Prior of Ardavon, Sittingbourne and Faversham while Malachy was first Prior of the restored Aberystwyth from 1936 to 1946. Kilian went on to outshine them: joining the novitiate in 1921, along with Andy Wright; he was ordained in 1928 in Rome where he had studied at San Alberto. Academically brilliant and obtaining an MPhil, a DD and a DPhil, he was assigned to the American mission in 1931, soon becoming Prior of Tarrytown and then Provincial of New York. In May 1947, he was elected Prior General of the Order, the second Irish Carmelite to hold this highest office and returned to his *Alma Mater* a month later for the college prize-giving on Sunday, 15 June. A man of huge energy and administrative ability, he played a major role with his older brother, Elias, in the purchase and restoration of the historic Carmelite foundation of Aylesford, Kent, in 1949. Five years later, he realised perhaps his greatest contribution to the Carmelite Order when he founded the Carmelite Institute in Rome as the core body for the study of international Carmelite history and set up its multilingual review journal, *Carmelus*. A hard taskmaster, he neither spared himself nor others, and, for all his scholarship and retreat-giving, was much given to physical hard work until his death in 1985.

Then there was Fr Earnán O'Sharkey who had been a prizewinning student from1934–6, returned to college in 1946–7 as Carmelite priest and bursar, before going on to foreign fields. He and his brother, Fionán — another prizewinning pupil of the thirties and, later, a Dublin diocesan priest, were sons of staff member, Séamus O' Sharkey, who had succeeded Eamonn Ó Tuathaill in teaching Irish, from 1928 to 1933, and then Séamus joined the lecturing staff at UCD. Another former pupil who returned to teach briefly — in the late 1940s — was Fr Richard Hearne. Born in Dublin in 1917, he was a Terenure pupil from 1932, at least, and completed his Leaving Certificate there in 1936 in which year he entered the Order. After securing his primary degree in science from UCD and then his licentiate in theology from Milltown Park, Richard was ordained in 1945 and then taught science in Terenure until, in 1948, he was assigned to the UK mission. Here, he spent the rest of his life. A man of great energy and administrative ability he was elected Prior of St Mary's, Aberystwyth, from 1956 to 1962, and then Bursar at Cheltenham until 1965 before becoming Prior of the Carmelite Community of Aylesford. Many other challenging positions came his way, notably in London and the south-east, until his passing in 1987.

One of Fr Hearne's classmates in the 1930s, who became one of his Carmelite teaching colleagues in the 1940s, Fr Mick Ardiff, was encountered earlier. Like Richard, Fr Ardiff taught in Terenure in the 1940s — he greeted the young Paddy Ward and his mother on Paddy's induction day in 1943, putting Paddy through his paces in Irish and mental arithmetic before declaring him Terenureable — was to spend 25 years of his life on the missions — in Fr Mick's case, in Africa. His rugby reputation outlived his pupil days: 'Dicky' Dunne and Charlie Weakliam — soldiering together through the college in the 40s — marvelled at this man who, as they recalled it, could kick the ball the entire length of the rugby pitch.

Many of the Carmelites who taught in the college from the mid-1940s, we shall encounter later; however, there were a few who lived in, but never taught at, Terenure; nevertheless, they could be as profound an influence on, and as much of an institution to, the boys of the time as any of their teachers whether clerical or lay. These were the Carmelite 'lay brothers' who served the Terenure Community without using blackboard and chalk. Two of them who were to be found there in the period 1946 to 1950 were Brother Franco Hicks and Brother Gerard Traynor. A third, Brother Stephen Reynolds, will feature later. Brother Gerard was a Dubliner — 'a true Dub' as some deemed him. He was born in 1903 in the city and grew up in poverty. He managed, as a young man, to gain employment in the projection box of the Metropole Cinema before entering the Order to be professed as a brother. For all the decorum that would be deemed appropriately Carmelite, he loved his music and to sing, his favourite party piece being *The Trumpeter*. In his early Carmelite years, he was attached to the Community of Ardavon in Rathgar–Churchtown until he was transferred to Whitefriar Street from 1934 to 1938. In 1939, he came to Terenure where he served the college Community for many years. A deeply devout friar, he was a friend to the boys at all times — Fr Cunningham as a 1950s boarder, remembered that precisely because he was not on the teaching staff, he could 'lend a kind ear or offer a consoling word to despondent young scholars' and though a Dubliner, was always especially kind to young lads from the country.[17] He was 85 years young when he passed in November 1988.

His Terenure confrere, Brother Franco Hicks, conjured up in the boys' imagination as General Franco's brother — as Joe Roche in the 40s and Felim Corr in the 50s remembered — a gentle man, well-liked by the boys, he was born in Malta in 1899, came to England in his teens and decided to join the Irish Carmelites. Following his solemn profession in 1926, he was sent to the new friary at Faversham in Kent. Then in 1934, he was assigned to Terenure where, as sacristan, he served for 23 years until his death in 1957.

DEVELOPMENTS IN THE LATER 1940S:

Fr Fitzgerald's hopes to see the construction of a new church for the college were not to be realised during his presidency: pressure of rising enrolments pushed alternative priorities to the top of the agenda. By the end of the war, accommodation problems had become acute in both boarding and day schools. Despite the scarcity of building materials and related difficulties, in 1945 the Community asked George Sheridan, the college architect, to draw up some plans to meet these accommodation needs. By September 1945, an extension to the junior dormitory was realised and by the following summer, the erection of a completely new wing was in train. It would constitute a two-storey extension to the redbrick wing that had been realised by Fr Hall in the 1890s. The ground floor was to comprise the Crush Hall and a new theatre or concert hall with a projection room: the second floor was to consist of a new laboratory, music room, classrooms and a boys' library. As Hugh Church, Con Smith and Paddy Dooley reported in their school diary: 'Thurs 19th September ... the building of the new wing. It's all very mysterious at present and seems to consist chiefly of holes of different sizes and pyramids of sand. We are told that it will contain a new theatre but it doesn't look much like it yet...'[18]

The new wing came into operation at the start of the school year in September 1948. Providing seven class rooms and two music rooms and cloakrooms upstairs, and the new theatre and dressing rooms, modern in design and equipment including a large cyclorama downstairs. The old concert hall thereupon became available for other uses and was converted into a study hall and examination venue with a splendid pulpit-like observation feature: this remarkable crow's nest or look-out point for invigilators did not go unremembered by the boys. The venue also came into use for the College Debating Society. Then, at the very end of this decade, work commenced on a new recreation and gym hall.

GAELIC REVIVALS:

Presidents Conleth Fitzgerald and Joseph Kelly over the six years to 1949 had done a great deal to promote the Irish face of the college. The first trips to the Gaeltacht started in 1946 and became an annual descent on Spiddal and its neighbourhood in the years which followed. Fr Fitzgerald had a particular concern for commitment to An Gaeltacht. He had spoken publicly on the threat posed to its very fabric by the scourge of emigration. Speaking at the PPU annual dinner in April 1946, he had called for a scheme of public works in land reclamation to provide young men with the paid employment essential to save them from the need to go abroad and thereby also to save the language in the communities.[19]

In a related development, the college had come to support the spread of Irish among its pupils by promoting the movement associated with An Fáinne. Some 47 boys were conferred with it in 1944 for proficiency in spoken Irish, almost another 60 two years later when the first trip to the Connemara Gaeltacht was inaugurated, with Frs Dunstan O'Connor and Dominic Reale taking a central part in the undertaking. The Gaeltacht trips were well-subscribed to, some 53 seniors spending part of the summer of 1947 at Cois Farraige.

Consistently with these developments, Fr Fitzgerald sought to revive Gaelic football in the college. Richard Fleming recalled these introductory efforts while David Kennedy remembered it being played into the late 1940s, if mainly by the boarders. Indeed, Fr Joe Ryan remembered organising GAA team matches in the college in the 1950s and 1960s and in arranging matches with the likes of Clann na nGael. While Conleth Fitzgerald had a strong interest in Gaelic games, it was probably the arrival on the staff of Fr Tom Brennan in 1945 that generated a revival. In the spring and every summer, Fr Brennan put together a Terenure GAA football team that secured a number of outside friendly matches: under their captain, Michael O'Keefe, they defeated Coláiste

Mhuire 4-2 to 1-2, went down to O'Connell Schools 3-7 to 2-3 and then were victorious over Westland Row in a close encounter, 2-5 to 2-4. The tall and polished Fr Tom, in later decades nicknamed 'The Spoof', owing to his interminable African tales, would become best-remembered in a different capacity, that of Radio 'Ham' and founder of the College Radio Club or Society — but that is matter for later. For now he was well- satisfied with this relatively successful Terenure return to Gaelic football. Bad weather the following year meant a much shorter season but with a number of rugby stalwarts that included Maurice O'Kelly and Con Smith, and with Hugh Church as captain, they secured an absolute victory over a strong Synge Street of 4-7 to 2-7. It would seem that the playing of the game between schools faltered in 1948 and 1949 but in the school year 1949–50 a match against Clontarf in September 1949 resulted in a resounding victory for Terenure of 6-1 to 3-3: then the opening of the rugby season put an end to GAA activity until May 1950 when victories were secured against Westland Row and Clontarf again. However, with the primacy given to rugby and the fact that Terenure was barred from competitive Schools League GAA matches because of 'The Ban', Gaelic Games could not, and did not, secure a competitive place in the life of the college. The boys of 1950 were grateful to Frs Brennan and Ardiff for trying to get 'friendlies' for them but it was an uphill struggle.

THE RUGBY YEARS, 1946-50:

While rugby was the dominant sport among the boys of 1946–50, a trophy at Leinster senior and junior schools level still eluded them. Not that these years were without ambition or excitement. Fr O'Connor's hope that a bridgehead had been established appeared to have had some substance — as far as junior schools rugby went — in the remarkable story of 1948, which, in a number of ways, was a special year for Terenure sport. As for the rugby juniors, the bridgehead consisted of playing nine semi-finals in the previous five years and the JCT opened their 1948–49 season with a win over Blackrock. Under the management of Frs Ardiff and Devane, and with the coaching of J.J.C. Bermingham and Liam Searson, they defeated CUS 11-0 at the start of March 1949, and defeated Newbridge 17-0 two weeks later to reach the semi-finals. Then came the first of an unprecedented four ties with Blackrock for the cup: on 28 March, Blackrock were saved from defeat two minutes from final whistle when they went over for a try to make it 3 all. On the last day of March came the replay and Terenure, again scoring first, Blackrock equalised a minute before half-time: with a scoreless second half, it again ended 3-3. The final against Clongowes, due to have been held on Wednesday, 6 April, had to be postponed. In the third replay at Donnybrook, on Monday, 4 April, both sides were scoreless in the mud at the final whistle and with the schools due to break up for Easter the next semi-final and the final had to be put back until after Easter. On this third occasion — as on the former two — Terenure were the stronger side but couldn't deliver the knockout score. Finally, on 29 April, the marathon was decided with Blackrock winning by the narrow margin of 3-0. When it came to the actual final, there may have been some consolation when the old enemy was defeated 9-0 by Clongowes: it was an outcome that even made the pages of the renowned *Dublin Opinion*.

It may have been a heartbreaker for the college but many of those who fought through the mud of four junior semi-finals would live to see a better day at senior level in the not too far off future.

As for the college rugby seniors, their fortunes for most of the 1940s were on a distinctly downward direction, best recalled many years later by James Doyle:

> Inspiringly led by the famous McMorrow twins, we came within a whisker of beating 'Rock in the Cup first round each year in 1941 and 1942. Subsequent to 1942 our record was ghastly. I saw all our matches in that period and our results are morbidly worth repeating:
>
> 1943 lost to Newbridge (2nd Round).
> 1944 lost to Pres. Bray (2nd Round).
> 1945 lost to St. Andrews (1st Round).
> 1946 lost to Mountjoy (after 2 drawn games 1st Round).
> 1947 lost to Blackrock (2nd Round).
> 1948 lost to Belvedere (1st Round).
> 1949 lost to St. Columba's (1st Round and I played in that game).[20]

It was perhaps some compensation that the Past Pupils, by contrast, in their own rugby endeavours, were putting the college on the competitive map in decisive fashion.

TERENURE COLLEGE RUGBY FOOTBALL CLUB, 1940-9:

Before the war years were over, there had been another significant development in college rugby. Anselm Corbett's brother, Jack, or Ephrem in religious life, was the key initiating figure in this. Known at times as 'Tibs' Corbett, he was remembered by some for his ready wit and bonhomie and as 'a pleasant and friendly man' despite specialising in a splendid bamboo cane and being very strict on rules; he was remembered by others as a 'pompous man'. He had been on the college teaching staff since 1934, and, more generally, while he filled a variety of roles from bursar and dean of junior school to Sub-Prior, he had also developed a keen interest in rugby. With a view to encouraging students who had left college to maintain an interest in playing the game, he gathered together a group of relatively recent past pupils. These included Hugh Clarke, Johnny Corrigan, Dudley Fisher, Jack Hearne, Hugh Milroy, Sean Ryan and others: in 1931, Clarke, Corrigan and Fisher had been classmates in 2nd Year Intermediate, Hugh Milroy in 1st Year, Sean Ryan in 3rd and Jack Hearne in 4th.

From their initial meeting in the Lenehan Hotel on Harcourt Street, on 5 November 1940, emerged the Terenure Collegians Rugby Football Club. Fr Jack became its first president with Joe Clarke as secretary, Johnnie Corrigan as treasurer and Hugh Milroy as Club Captain. Three weeks later they produced fifteen for their first match, on Sunday, 24 November, taking on the college's own Senior XV with the latter winning by 8 points to 3. Not yet recognised by rugby officialdom, they managed nonetheless to secure some fourteen matches in that first season of 1940–1 against a motley run of competitors that ran from Castleknock Past Pupils to Chemists XV to the Local Defence Forces — all played on college grounds with borrowed college footballs and even borrowed Carmelite referees in the persons of Dunstan O'Connor and Donal Lamont.

As for a clubhouse and home, the college authorities generously gave the use of Lakelands Park for a pitch and a partly demolished cottage on the grounds, close by Greenlea Grove, for a pavilion, made habitable by local builder, John Townley. Each man of the collegians then played in whatever strip came most readily to hand, making for a multi-coloured XV until 1943–4 when they all managed to turn out in plain white and changed their name from Terenure Collegians to Terenure College Rugby Football Club. Then, in 1944–5 they adopted the purple, black and white worn ever since, with black shorts.

The year 1943 was significant for the infant club aside from the adoption of new colours and a new name. At a meeting of its 29 members that March, a formal constitution was adopted, Fr D.C. Flanagan was appointed president, and application for recognition was made to the Leinster Branch of the IRFU. Their initial rejection was successfully appealed and Terenure College RFC's First XV, starting at the bottom, took part in the Leinster Minor League. They were victorious in their first-ever official contest, against Malahide. From there they went on to a remarkable season, competing in 17 matches, victorious in 16 and winning the Minor League at their first attempt under captain, Joe Milroy. Their record that first season was a formidable one, scoring 245 points and conceding only 26.[21] Their victims included UCD, cup holders the previous three seasons. With the halo of success around them, they next applied for promotion to the Leinster Junior League, for 1944–5. This was rejected, but they were successful in their application a year later. They now played in the Junior ranks while having more than a sufficiency of active, playing members to still field a second XV, for the Minor League. Under Colm O'Nolan, this 2nd XV won through to the final where they triumphed over unbeaten Suttonians, thereby giving the infant club its second Minor League trophy in three seasons.

Although money and materials were severely in short supply, the enthusiasm of the club was in inverse proportion to this. With growing membership, the pressure on resources grew so that the need for alternative premises soon became urgent. However, in April 1947, a new pavilion was acquired at a cost of £2,000. A celebratory inaugural, seven-aside match between club and college resulted in victory for the latter: the college players included Tom Duggan (captain), Hugh Church, Maurice O'Kelly, Des Doyle, Charlie Weakliam, Jim Sheridan, Cormac Collier, Paddy Magee and Con Smith. While on the playing fields, 1947 was not especially memorable for the club; the season 1948–9 provided a very different outcome. In that year, the First XV achieved the remarkable record of winning the double, the Junior League and the Metropolitan Cup, under Paddy Murphy as captain. No club in Leinster RFU history had ever before accomplished this, nor did any ever thereafter. The league final was won over St Mary's on 5 April 1949 in what ended as a mud bath, with a final score of 8 points to 3. Winning the Metropolitan Cup was an even greater achievement since the Junior League team faced competition, which included the 2nd XVs of all the Leinster Senior Clubs. The final of that campaign was against Blackrock, with a historic victory of 6–0. It was one great way to end a decade and it prompted the club's decision to seek admission to Leinster senior ranks. That application, lodged on a wave of justifiable euphoria and optimism, was rejected: a new long decade of disappointment and rejection was to follow.[22] But for now, at the end of the 1940s, Terenure College Rugby Football Club had unquestionably made its mark.

Other consolations there were too, more immediately in the triumph of the Terenure junior tennis squad when they brought home the Leinster Schools trophy for the third time in eight seasons. And they did it in style, winning their section without the loss of a single point, to come through then to a thrilling final against Belvedere, which they won after a five-hour contest. Further cause for rejoicing came in swimming where Jimmy O'Connor had captured the Juvenile Championship at the Leinster Schools Gala at Beechwood at the start of the 1948–9 school year, just as coach Pat Cashin was leaving for the States.

THE CHESSMEN:

However, it was in chess that the college pupils secured their most significant victories in those years: it was Fr Mick Ardiff's brother and fellow Carmelite, Fr W.J. Ardiff, a keen chess-player himself, who established the game on a sound footing in college in the autumn of 1942, and it was he who first entered the college into the Secondary Schools Senior Chess League.[23] Helping also in developing the game in Terenure was Fr Ossie McGrath and between them, in the course of the 1940s, Terenure established itself as a significant force, but not without an initial struggle, as the following report of 1944, from the pen of the ubiquitous P.P. Maguire conveys:

> So far the club has had a short, crowded, but not particularly glorious life. It held its General Meeting in the college on Tuesday, 3 October, 1944. At this meeting a Constitution was formulated and the following Officers were appointed — Chairman: Fr McGrath, Hon. Secretary: P.P. Maguire, Committee: L. O'Mongáin, M.H. Carroll and Seamus Hannigan.
>
> A great debt of gratitude is due to Fr McGrath: indeed, it is not too much to say that, without his unfailing, enthusiastic co-operation the club would not be in existence today. During our brief life we have played roughly twenty matches, regrettably losing the majority;

however, since this appears to be the common fate of newly-formed chess clubs, we are not unduly disheartened. Our membership is still small, but, since all are enthusiastic, we have great hope for the future.[24]

So well they might: within the college itself, many boys took to the game, with Des Wheeler, Brian Colivet, James and Fintan Doyle, Charlie Weakliam, Joe Roche and Tom Gunn to the fore. As senior boys initiated their juniors into its mysteries, it became a unifying factor in college life. By 1944–5, the college was represented at both Senior and Junior levels in the Leinster Colleges competitions. By 1947–8, the Juniors had been Leinster runners-up for the second year in a row. In the 1947–8 season, the college had a good senior team, although it had to include the two best juniors to make up the standard six. Two names stood out — James Doyle who went through that whole season undefeated and Charlie Weakliam, gifted athlete and rugby player besides, who held the Irish Schools' Champion to a draw. In Brian Colivet, the college provided the individual runner up in the Leinster Senior Individual Championship.

The 1948–9 season for Terenure chess proved to be special: it was an altogether triumphant one for the college who almost completely swept the board. Fintan Doyle proved the hero of the year, bringing their first-ever chess trophy to the college when in October 1948 he won the Oireachtas Junior Championship. This followed on only two months after becoming the first Terenure boy to play international class for Ireland. Better was to follow when Captain James Doyle and Vice-Captain Peter Conlon led a team to victory in the Leinster Senior Championship, securing an impressive 41 out of a possible 48 points on the way. While Conlon won all his matches, the Doyles, James and Fintan, had their distinctions too: James tying with the Irish Champion of the day and Fintan dropping only one half-point in eight matches. Young Fintan went on from there to captain the Juniors to victory also, winning all eight of their matches and putting up 40½ points out of a possible 48. The younger Doyle, John Gunn and Patrick Cooke had the distinction of being undefeated in this entire campaign. The chessmen thereby became the second competitive sportsmen to bring Senior and Junior Championships to the college in a single season. The climax to this great year in Terenure chess came when Fintan went on to become Leinster Junior Individual Champion; the first Terenure man to bring this title home. While the decade ended with the Seniors just failing to retain their title in the final against O'Connell Schools, the Juniors went on to triumph again in a brilliant display.

The college chessmen, despite their wins, were to suffer one grievous loss — this came when their inspiration and mentor, Fr Ossie McGrath, was sent out on a different mission. On his departure one journal observed that 'in the short space of six years he has built up the Terenure College Chess Club from beginner's grade to that of international, thus putting Irish schools on the chess map'.[25]

Fr Oswald 'Mugger' McGrath — a singularly inappropriate schoolboy nickname for one universally remembered as a superb and gentle teacher — one of two Belfast brothers who became Carmelites, he and Emmanuel were nephews of the illustrious Carmelite Prior General, Peter Magennis. Short in stature and hair glistening with Brylcreem, Fr Oswald was remembered as an energetic, good-humoured head of junior school, a great conversationalist and decent, humane person. He would, before long, head off to Moate where he founded a new school in 1955 and was idolised by the local people for his kindness and good works.

His was but one of many Carmelite translations in 1949–50. The end of this decade saw extensive and far-reaching changes. The Prior, Fr Kelly, his term of service over, was assigned to an entirely new role as parish priest of the Carmelite parish of Faversham, Kent. Fr Devane was off to Rome. However, perhaps the most significant of the departures had already occurred in 1946 when a trio of pioneering Terenure Carmelites left Ireland for Africa.

Con A. Smith, *c.* 1972, member of the Terenure College Gaelic football team, 1948–9.

Hugh Clarke and Mr Griffin, *c.* 1950.

Leinster secondary schools senior and junior chess champions, 1949. At back: B. Rogers, P. Cooke, P. O'Donnell, J. Doyle (senior capt.), F. Doyle (junior capt. and Leinster junior champion), P. Condon, D. Dufferin. In front: J. Gunn and F. Cusack.

262

Half time in the Junior Cup match, 1951.

Chess club members deep in concentration, 1945. Photo taken by C & L Walsh.

CHAPTER 15

The African Mission
from 1946

Bernard Clinch plays with a local child
in Southern Rhodesia, 1950s.

> If Terenure ever starts giving prizes to its heroes, I hope Fr Anthony
> Clarke of Katerere will get the first one. Most men can be a hero
> for ten minutes in the heat of battle or for sixty minutes in a rugger
> match, but it takes a very special man indeed to be a hero in
> Katerere and to stick it day after day. Katerere is simply miles from
> nowhere or to be more precise, if Fr Clarke wanted to cash a Postal
> Order he'd have to go 100 miles to do it. As it is he has to go seven
> miles to fetch drinking water and then has to transport it seven
> miles back to his hut.[1]

So wrote a Carmelite confrere, Fr Mel Hill, in 1955. What may have been true of
Terenure past pupil, Des Anthony Clarke, was just as true of the author Mel Hill,
another Terenure pupil of the 1930s, and of many more Terenure men, besides,
between the 1940s and the present day.

Des Clarke was an exceptional man in an exceptional family of Terenure students
and alumni. By 1945, there had been at least six Clarke family past pupils stretching
back over twenty years and even then, in 1945, yet another, Paul, was in fourth year
while at that stage Frank was in final year medicine at UCD — a year later, as Dr
Clarke, he would be on standby for every Terenure RFC match to monitor and
minister to the rugby battle casualties. Joe, an ESB official, was another club stalwart
while Hugh and Gerald (Gerry) became insurance executives. Many of these Clarkes
had turned out, year after year, as college rugby full backs and Gerry became, for life,
a skilled tennis player and No.1 for Templeogue — having served on the Terenure
juniors that brought home the first Leinster trophy in 1941. Meanwhile, in 1945,
brother Noel was on the eve of ordination in the Carmelites, while Des, who entered
in 1942, would be ordained in 1949.

Born in Galway in 1924, Des enjoyed an academically successful period in
Terenure, both at junior and senior level: in the summer of 1935, he was second to
John Searson in Elementary B and over the next six years to his Matriculation in 1941
he would always be in the top three of his class, exchanging places from time to time
with John Searson and Dan Moroney. Following graduation from UCD and his ordination in July 1949, Fr Des joined the teaching staff at Terenure, with special
responsibility for sacred music and choir.[2] He would not be long there, for, within a
year he had volunteered for the Irish Carmelite mission to Southern Rhodesia,[3] and
by November 1950 was on his way to the northern mission station at Mount Melleray,
not far from Mozambique border. He was to spend the rest of his life in that country,
quickly acquiring expertise in Shona — the language native to the area. He was to see
through the dark days of Rhodesia/Zimbabwe from the Unilateral Declaration of
Independence (UDI) to a republic: in the late 1970s, he became Apostolic
Administrator of the Diocese of Umtali (today Mutare) upon the deportation of
Bishop Lamont due to his open opposition to the regime — he had in fact been
Lamont's assistant for many years. He took on the top position in the diocese despite

suffering a heart attack in the early 1970s. It was a complaint, which led to his death in 1999 after almost 50 years of pioneering evangelism in Zimbabwe.[4]

While the story of the Rhodesian Mission is more strictly a chapter in the history of the Irish Carmelites, it is not one that can or should be divorced from the history of Terenure College: so many of the college's former pupils, future priests and laymen came to play a central role in the development of the mission and in the development of that region. A very great many of the almost 100 Irish Carmelites who served there, or had direct involvement there, had been and have been Terenure men either as pupils, teachers, priests or all three.

ORIGIN OF THE MISSION:

As the Catholic Church emerged from the devastation of the Second World War, the issue of foreign missions acquired a fresh urgency and Rome became increasingly anxious to develop its global evangelical calling. In Ireland, it found a ready response in religious orders and missionary societies that grew rapidly over the twenty years after 1945. The Carmelites of the Irish Province were not found wanting when it came to responding to this impulse. By late December 1944, the Province, in all its components, had some 80 priests, 28 clerics, 14 lay brothers and 6 novices. James Carmel O'Shea, Provincial since ceasing to be Terenure's president in 1940, was strongly convinced that the time was now ripe for a new missionary initiative, despite existing commitments in England and Wales. He remarked to Assistant General Gabriel Pausback at that time that

> all our houses have a full complement of priests and there is needed some outlet for the immediate future. The young men are especially anxious for the mission work, [and]…a goodly proportion of the men who are due for ordination within the next five or six years should be available for this expansion and it's imperative that we should plan for it now[5]

He added that providing a good example through missionary endeavour would be a means of attracting 'the very best type of vocations to the Province'. Fr Malachy Lynch, the premier Carmelite authority in England and Wales was by no means so keen: any distant undertaking might threaten the supply of Carmelite support from Ireland and the authorities in Rome were cautious in the face of the Provincial's zeal. O'Shea could justly counter Lynch's concern by pointing out in March 1946 that they had seven Carmelites earmarked for Wales — all, impressively, with a sound grasp of the Welsh language and soon to be ordained.[6] By that stage, having taken soundings in Ireland, he found there were 44 Carmelites volunteering for overseas service, 22 of them priests. At this point, in regard to possible destinations, several were being considered, including suggestions for China, the Philippines, Mauritius, Nigeria and Angola. In the end, the final destination for a possible overseas development was decided by a fortuitous event: it happened that the Irish Jesuit Provincial, Fr John MacMahon, was at dinner in Whitefriar Street one evening when the subject of overseas ministry came up. Knowing that his own Society were thin on the ground in Southern Rhodesia, he suggested that this might be an appropriate goal for a Carmelite mission. Having contacted the Jesuit Bishop Aston 'Chick' Chichester of Salisbury (now Harare), the latter welcomed Fr O'Shea's overtures and effectively extended the Carmelites an invitation to help out in Manicaland — the homelands of the Manyika people in the eastern region of Southern Rhodesia. His welcome was hardly surprising, as he explained in a note to O'Shea in March 1946: '… we have twelve priests over seventy (two of them arrived last century) and another ten over sixty all of whom have been in the country for over fifteen years and the vast majority over thirty years …'.

O'Shea lost little time in convening a Definitory meeting to consider this offer: on 11 April — the very day he received Chichester's offer of Manicaland — the Definitory unanimously agreed to accept. The authorities in Rome followed with approval on 26 April 1946.

THE PIONEERS:

The Province, following Bishop Chichester's advice, adopted the strategy of initially sending out just three of their brethren to work with the Bishop and the Jesuits on the ground in order to gain experience, learn the appropriate dialects of the Shona language and to begin to come to grips with the local culture and circumstance before venturing to take direct control of territory whether already evangelised or previously untouched.

The country — self-governing colony since 1924 — was as large as France and, while it had its busy capital of Salisbury, much of its interior was little known and underdeveloped. With a population of close to 4 million at the time, it was an ethnically and socially divided society: 3.5 million native Africans; 150,000 whites and Afrikaners; and perhaps 20,000 Asians. Of the 3 million-plus Africans, only 20% were then Christian. Of the colonials, the largest religious body were Anglicans; then Methodists; followed by the Dutch Reformed Church; and then Catholics, with fundamentalist Christian sects making up the remainder. Of the colony's Catholics at the time, around 24,000 where European while there were some 180,000 native Catholics.

While the Irish Carmelite volunteers for Rhodesia were many, the first of the chosen were few — Frs Luke Flynn, Anselm Corbett and Donal Lamont. Of these pioneers, Luke Flynn was the 'youngster': born in 1918 in Westport, Co. Mayo, he had joined the Order in 1935 and had been ordained in 1943. He was, therefore, only ordained three years when at 28, he found himself setting foot in Africa. Next came Anselm Corbett who was encountered earlier as a Terenure boarder and diarist at the start of the 1930s. Despite his gentle and otherworldly nature, he proved a valuable resource through his rapid mastery of the Shona language, and in particular of its Manyika dialect. Then came the senior of the three, Donal Raymond Lamont.

As previously detailed, he was a Terenure pupil of the 1920s and teacher there to the mid-1940s, he was 35 when chosen as Superior for the African enterprise. On his last Sunday in Ireland, on 29 September, Fr Luke took strenuous part in a soccer match between sixth year and the 'rest' — his love of the game would stand to him when, in 1946 and 1947, he would be stationed with Anselm at Mondoro, Manicaland, and took the boys there for football — then on the following Thursday the three men celebrated High Mass in College before their departure on the SS *Asturias*. They reached Capetown on Monday, 28 October to be greeted by the Jesuit Fr Gavan Duffy.

For the first Carmelites to come to Africa, the Rhodesia they encountered presented a deeply divided society. Anselm was quickly taken aback by the practical apartheid he encountered in the capital, Salisbury. Within days of arrival, on entering a pharmacy to procure film for his old camera, his insistence on not being served ahead of a prior queue of native people caused much annoyance and objection from the pretty blonde shop assistant who automatically accorded him priority.[7]

Everywhere about them there was discrimination in practice, in all places of public-gathering from shops and cinemas to transport. Although many worked in city and town centres, the Africans were assigned to live in townships or their outskirts. The Carmelites found a multi-division society of colonial whites, Afrikaners, Asians and then the African majority. Apart from the Afrikaners, few of European origin spoke any of the native languages. The colonial elite over decades had expropriated the native people from large expanses of good land by a series of land acts designed to attract Europeans into farming there. The Africans were thereupon assigned to reservations and African males were obliged to register and carry identity documents.

The three Carmelites stayed initially with Bishop Chichester at Campion House where the Jesuit Community numbered around twenty. Their Jesuit predecessors had first successfully established their Manicaland Mission in the 1890s at Triashill. It was, however, at Umtali (now Mutare), capital city of Manicaland, on its eastern boarder a few miles from Mozambique that they established their most significant centre: the Jesuits' Church founded there in the 1920s, which eventually became the site of Umtali's Catholic Cathedral. Four years after their own arrival the town of Mutare became a Carmelite parish and Donal Lamont its first parish priest. This, in practice, became the Carmelite headquarters from which they went out to distant mission stations and to which they returned for communal occasions and occasional rest. By that stage, to the north of Mutare, the Triashill Mission and the 100 acre St Killian's Mission at Makoni, had been entrusted to the Order — both in 1948, the St Barbara Mission in between them, a year later, and St Benedict's, Mount Melleray, north of Triashill by 1950. In 1951 the St Anne's Mission at Wengezi to the south, had been added and in 1952, the St Simon Stock Mission in Rusape, to the west. It was in 1953 that the Carmelites founded their own first mission station, the Avila Mission of Katerere in the far north of which would become Mutare Diocese, built in fact by Fr Des Clarke and Brother Simon Noonan.[8] It was to be the first of four missions that Des Clarke established, the others being St Peter's at Chisumbanje; St Patrick's

Nyanyadzi and Chimanimani; all south of Mutare. It was in 1953 also that the ecclesiastical status of Mutare was raised to Apostolic Prefecture with Fr Lamont, now Monsignor, becoming Prefect. He was installed in May of that year and he named his own residence there 'Drumfad' after the Co. Down bay of which he had fond memories. Four years later again, Umtali became a diocese and Donal Lamont became its first bishop. His consecration was appropriately conducted at the steps of the newly built Marymount College which opened for its first students in 1958. By the end of the following decade, the Carmelites were administering some twenty missionary commitments, the first five of them including the core parish of Mutare, being entrusted to them by others, the remaining fifteen having thereafter been established by themselves. These varied from the tiny and primitive station of Avila, set up by Des Clarke in Katerere in the far north, to the more substantial and elaborate St Charles Lwanga Mission and Minor Seminary in Chimanimani established in 1961. Priories too had been created at Mutare in 1954 and in Hatfield, Salisbury, by 1958.[9]

By that stage, Terenure and the Carmelites had established a tradition of sending out new men, lay, religious and priests to aid the work. By the mid-1960s, there were over 50 Carmelites working in the country, the vast majority of them from Ireland. In the half century from 1946 well over 70 Irish Carmelites had worked there for long and short periods, some very long indeed: Peter Toner, Bartholomew McGivern and Des Clarke each had served over 45 years there, the latter two arriving in 1950 and the former in 1953. It would not be practicable to detail the histories of the more than 70 Irish Carmelites in Rhodesia/Zimbabwe, nor even the stories of the many Terenure men among them, but it would be appropriate to touch on a number of them if only to underline the links between Terenure College and Africa.

The three pioneers of 1946 were followed in October 1947 when Br Angelus Kinsella and four Terenure men left the college for Rhodesia: Frs Andy Wright, Jackie Ambrose Roche, Mel Hill and Brother Bernard Clinch.[10] Fr Wright has already featured prominently in previous pages and it suffices to say here that his practical bent, energy and genuine interest in farming operations made him a most useful addition to the Irish Carmelite mission to Rhodesia. He was assigned to co-operate with the Jesuit Fr Ketterer in the development of the two parishes of the Holy Rosary and St Robert's in Mutare. These two men, each famously good-humoured individuals, got on exceedingly well with each other and their parishioners, with their friendly easy-going dispositions. Andy's Terenure colleague, Mel Hill, painted a memorable picture of the Kildare-men in action:

> The father of all Terenure men out here is (you guessed it first time) Father A.E. Wright. He was on the staff of Terenure when some of us were running around in rompers. He was playing for Blackrock 2nds before some of us were born, but he still has plenty of kick left in him … Fr Wright with his co-disciple, Fr P.G. Meagher, lives in the native location in Umtali. They are the only white men allowed

to live there and that makes a great difference to the prestige of the Church in the eyes of the African … The last thing you see Fr Wright doing any night is going up from the location to the presbytery in the town, putting a bottle of milk and a heel of bread into the basket and pushing his old Ford car down the hill with tomorrow's breakfast under his arm … Needless to say he is hail-fellow-well met with everybody in the town, Catholic and Pagan alike.[11]

Fr Andy spent six hard but good years in Umtali. On returning home on holiday in the early 1950s, as his confrere Fr Jarlath O'Hea recalls, he was sent off to the new college at Moate where he worked eleven years with Jarlath until 1963–4 when he returned to his real home of Terenure for the happy rest of his days.[12] His being re-routed from Mutare to Moate may well have been a blessing as there is a suggestion that he very greatly missed the rich, green fields of home.

As for Fr Mel Hill, he became one of Terenure's legendary Rhodesia hands. Born in Athy in March 1914, he became a pupil in the college in the late 1920s and early 1930s where he had an excellent academic record. Matriculating with Honours in 1930 he secured honours in his Leaving Certificate in 1931. Received into the Carmelites in 1932 and ordained in 1940, following his ordination, Fr Hill became Superior of St Mary's, Aberystwyth, for six years. He then became one of the most colourful and assiduous chroniclers of the Rhodesian years where he spent the greater part of his life from 1947. A great storyteller and wit, he was both poet, essayist of style and a prodigious spinner of rhymes. Prior of Triashill from 1950, he was promoted to Commissary Provincial for the six years 1955 to 1961, and in time was Mission Superior at Triashill and at St Benedict's and Prior of the Carmelite Community in Hatfield, in the outskirts of Harare, at different stages. Following the best part of his life spent for Church and people in Rhodesia/Zimbabwe, Mel Hill passed away in 1984 and was interred in the Carmelite mission at Triashill: he was one of twelve Irish Carmelites laid to rest in Africa up to the end of the twentieth century. Laid to rest in Triashill also — almost twenty years before him was fellow Terenure man, 'Jackie' Ambrose Roche who went out to Africa just one week before Mel in 1947. A Kinsale man, Jackie was born in 1912 and was ordained in 1938. He taught on the Terenure staff after graduating from UCD, was at Ardavon at the end of the 1930s and then back in Terenure both as teacher and Bursar from 1942 to 1945. Having gone to Rhodesia — and never enjoying the best of health — he died there in June 1963 at the relatively early age of 49: he was only the second Carmelite to die on mission in Africa, the first being the Australian Fr William Morganti, in 1961. 'Jackie' was the first Irish Carmelite to die there and the first Irish Carmelite to lie in the graveyard of Triashill Mission.

Before the 1960s were out, Africa had, sadly, claimed another famous Terenure alumnus — Fr Patrick M. Hipwell. From Bagnalstown, Co. Carlow, Paddy was the oldest brother of a clan of Hipwells who studied at the college — David, Derrick,

Michael, Gerald and Brendan followed. Paddy came to the junior school in 1946 and, by 1948, he, David, Derrick and Michael (or Mick) were all on the rolls. Mick became the most famous of the clan through his rugby exploits, as will emerge later. Paddy had a modestly successful academic record in the college, winning the arithmetic prize in 1946–7 and securing four honours in his Intermediate Certificate in 1951 but then let other classmates win the academic laurels. However, although younger brother Michael had many celebrated rugby exploits, it was Paddy who had the distinction of being on the Terenure cup team who brought home the college's first ever Leinster senior trophy in 1952. After completing his Leaving Certificate in the following year, Paddy entered the Carmelites and was solemnly professed in October 1957 and ordained in July 1961. Assigned to the parish of Rusape on the western border of Umtali Diocese, Fr Paddy was fortunate in the support his missionary efforts secured from home. On first going out to Africa he had been 'adopted' or sponsored by a group of printers from Independent Newspapers. They raised the funds that enabled him to build two new churches in his region. On a visit home in 1966, they held a function for him at Wynn's Hotel where they made him a presentation. As a result of their, and his, efforts the first of these churches was opened in 1967. The second, that of Our Lady of Fatima at Inyanyuzra, was completed in 1968 and was due to open when Fr Paddy was killed on 2 November, his motorcycle colliding with a car. A huge loss to his Order and its mission, he was only 33 when he died and was laid to rest at Triashill.

Another of the Terenure missionary exiles of 1947 was Brother Bernard Clinch who travelled out with Fr Roche. He was one of two brothers by blood who also became brothers and later priests in the Carmelite Order. The Clinches were true Dubliners, of Clinch's Court, off Bride Street, famous as a family of coopers and carpenters.[13] Joseph, older by four years, entered the Order in July 1939 at the age of 20 and Bernard followed in November 1940 when not quite 18 years old. Both, because of their construction skills, played a key role in the physical development of the Carmelite missions. Arriving in Africa first, Brother Bernard was stationed in Triashill but 1954 — when Fr O'Shea was Mission Superior — found him busy at St Benedict's, a mission station founded by the Marianhill missionaries in 1913. Taken over by the Jesuits in 1929, this mission was passed on by them to the Carmelites as the last of six such mission transfers in 1953. Here Bernard looked after all building and farming operations and taught manual skills to the senior pupils of its school.[14] In the early 1960s he found himself starting a new farm and mission at Chisumbanje in the Sabi Valley. Later on he was to be ordained and returned to Ireland.

Even as Br Bernard left Terenure for Africa, his own brother, Joseph, joined the Carmelite Community in Terenure, having first been in Whitefriar Street in the early 1940s. He remained in Terenure until, in November 1950, he too set out for Africa, with Frs Des Clarke and Tommy Brennan. Fr Tommy would prove a godsend to missionary endeavour not just by virtue of his vocation but because of his passion for all things electrical from wiring to the wireless. It would not be long before he would enable many

a mission house to dispose of oil lamps of ancient memory and switch to electricity —
and also to put themselves in touch through radio. Similarly, Brother Joseph, with his
own practical manual skills — like Bernard — was to make much possible.

Born in the Liberties in January 1919, baptised in St Nicholas of Myra on Francis
Street, Joe became a Synge Street boy until he abandoned desk-work for woodwork.
Then in 1939 he entered the Carmelites at Moate and was assigned to Whitefriar
Street from 1940 to 1947. Just as Bernard left Terenure, Joseph arrived there, providing
all its woodworking maintenance needs, not least in the important matter of providing
stage props for the annual college play. On arriving in Africa with Frs Clarke and
Brennan in 1950, he spent the next twelve years at Triashill. Here, in the early 1950s
with the encouragement of Donal Lamont, he opened a carpentry school. Here too,
along with the Terenure men, Fr Martin McMahon who ran a teacher-training school,
he contributed greatly to the hum of progress in Triashill. A carpenter by trade he
became a farmer by necessity and Fr McMahon — recently arrived from Terenure in
1952 — remembered Joe busy atop a new tractor at Triashill; but perhaps Mel Hill's
pen picture best captures the real Brother Joe *in situ:*

> To get to Triashill Mission station you drive through something
> unique in Zimbabwe — an avenue of pine and cypress trees two
> miles long … When you get to the end of the avenue you can see a
> block of buildings to your right. Go in and meet Br. Joseph Clinch.
> He'll take the pipe out of his mouth when you enter and drop the
> saw that he has in his hand and give you a very warm handshake that
> will make you wince. I expect his hands get hard from holding the
> tools. By this time his dog, Chips, will be generously making a mess
> of your clothes and an African lad will come over to take him off
> your shoulder. Chips is part and parcel of the Carpentry School. He
> fools around there during the day and sleeps there at night on the
> wood shavings. That's why they call him Chips. The students like
> Chips and they often write about him in their compositions which
> I have the privilege of correcting. Br Joseph is tall, dark and slim and
> like most of our men out here, he hails from Dublin … Now Bro
> Joseph has his new carpentry school with fifty carpenters under his
> watchful eye and between the demands of the nuns and the demands
> of the missions, they never have an idle moment.[15]

Indefatigable, restless and inexhaustible, he supplied all kinds of local needs
through his workshops, from chairs and desks to wagons and roofs. Within the
growing education system of that developing country, he learned as much as he taught,
taking courses from catechetics to mathematics that enabled him to become a recognised teacher himself. Following the years 1962 to 1966 at St Benedict's, he was
assigned to teach at Kriste Mambo, north of Triashill, southeast of St Benedict's. Here
a new school had been founded in 1963 and here the tall, slim, pipe-smoking Br Joe

came to teach between 1966 and 1970. One of a cohort of Carmelite Brothers in Africa from 1946 to 1970, there was a perception that somehow they occupied a lesser place in the pecking order: with a touch of wry humour they called themselves 'The King's own Rifles', first into battle, and expendable it seemed. But Joe and his confreres were living in the time of a changing Church and in the wake of the Second Vatican Council there was a gradual attenuation of such distinctions. It was perhaps in the context of these changes that Br Joe at the end of the 1960s thought of becoming a priest. He entered a seminary in Pretoria in 1970 and was ordained Carmelite priest in December 1972. Returning to Ireland not long after this, he then went out to South Africa as priest of a parish in Lavistown, below Table Mountain. Emphysema, however, took its toll and, returning to Dublin, he spent his five years from 1982, reunited with old African confrere Martin McMahon, back in Terenure. Well-known and loved by the folk of Fortfield, and regaling his young Carmelite Community brothers and college pupils with many tales of his African days, he crossed over his last Zambezi in September 1986. In later as in earlier life, Br Bernard followed in Joseph's path and was ordained priest in April 1974. He outlived Joseph by twelve years, passing away in March 1988.

The example of the first Carmelite missionaries from the college to Central Africa proved infectious and fairly soon a tradition in this regard developed. Nor was it confined to Carmelite priests and brothers: laymen too became involved. Most notable here was the case of Jim Barnes. From a Belfast family who came south, setting up a famous textile business in Tallaght and settling in Lakelands, the Barnes boys were destined for illustrious careers in medicine. Jim's older brother, Joseph, became internationally recognised for his work in tropical diseases while another brother, Fergus, who graduated in medicine from UCD in 1946, became a highly regarded psychiatrist in North America. Taking up a position with Haven Sanatorium in Detroit in 1951, three years later Fergus was appointed assistant professor of psychiatry at Georgetown University as well as teaching on a visiting basis at Seton Institute, Baltimore. Jim joined Terenure in Elementary B in autumn 1937, sharing the class with other college worthies including Tommy Gunn, Ronnie Marsh, Eamonn O'Nolan and Brian Rush, but moving a class ahead of them by 1940 and sharing third year in 1942 with Seán Logue and the Roche cousins. In 1944, he was one of the twelve successful Terenure Leaving Certificate candidates and soon went on to UCD. Qualifying in medicine, he spent a year in Dublin and then for one more year, he went for further experience in Yorkshire.[16] In 1950, having married Joan O'Loughlin, they went straight to the mission field in Southern Rhodesia. Here they spent some four years, with their young family, working at the Mount Melleray Mission in a three-roomed hospital — one room for the doctor, a second for women patients and a third for the men. As young Dr Jim's reputation spread, the queue of women grew so that the men's place had to be transferred to the shade of a nearby tree: the tree coming to be called 'the men's ward': so Mel Hill described the situation there in 1952. However, Jim's own medical mission was not confined to the station at

Mount Melleray but ranged over an extensive area of Nyanga to the north, involving long days and nights of travelling. Joan must have been some remarkable woman in these circumstances, far from home and bringing up the first three of their African-born children in a family of six. When in 1955 they returned home to Ireland, it was to set up a family practice in Finglas — no sinecure either — and where they soon commanded the respect and affection of countless patients. Forty years of service followed until, with Joan's death, he returned to Zimbabwe in 1997. Here he worked for two years at the hospital of the Regina Coeli Mission in the north of Mutare Diocese. He played a major role in securing a new operating unit and equipment for the hospital, which was run by the Dominicans. He finally returned home in 1999.

From these Irish pioneers in 1946 up to and beyond Jim Barnes's first tour there, there grew up a whole succession of Irish Carmelites who went out there from 1947 to the early 1960s. By the end of the 1950s, there were at least 30 Irish Carmelite priests and brothers at work in the Umtali Diocese — the vast majority of them had been Terenure pupils and/or teachers. A purely random selection would include John O'Sharkey; Templeogue-boy, Cormac Kennedy; college captain in 1951 Pius Kiernan; the remarkable Senan Egan; then Gerry Meagher who had been the college's dean of discipline in 1946 and president of the Past Pupils' Rugby Football Club from 1946 to 1950; Cormac Collier, class of 1947 and his brother Conal, class of 1949; and Patrick (Fred) Lally, member of the 1952 Terenure Senior Cup winning team. They ranged from humblest Carmelite Brothers such as the sharpshooting David Fintan O'Connell — who like the Clinch brothers, was to be ordained Carmelite priest in the early 1970s — to the highest office holders such as Prior and Provincial James Carmel O'Shea.

A remarkable, if unsung, hero, of these times, and for long after, was Fr Michael B. Kenny. A Dubliner who started his schooling at Synge Street and then transferred to Terenure in 1944, he had an excellent academic and indeed, sporting record in the college, before completing his Leaving Certificate in 1947. He entered the Carmelites that year, took his BA at UCD in 1951 and was ordained in 1954. Two years later, he went off to the Rhodesian Mission and spent some 43 years there: not only was such a span remarkable, equally so was the fact that for most of that time he was a solitary Carmelite, working in isolated, one-priest missions and spent some 23 years at St Barbara's, Makone. Indeed, he spent the entire period of the War of Liberation in Zimbabwe and only came back to Ireland in 1999, spending his very last days in Mount Carmel Hospital, the place where he had resided when it was Ardavon, the Carmelite House of Studies, which he had left, 43 years before, to go out to Africa.[17]

Within a decade, Terenure had established what now amounted to a rich tradition of commitment to the spiritual and material welfare of its Rhodesian responsibility. It was therefore natural that numbers of Terenure boarding and day-pupils who experienced the college in the 1950s would not only join the Carmelites but go on to form a new generation of Terenure men in Africa.

THE TERENURE AFRICAN GENERATION FROM THE 1950s:

This new generation of 1950s Terenure boys included, among others, Frs Michael
Hender of the class of 1953; Stan Hession and David Weakliam of the class of 1954;
and Bob Kelly of the class of 1956. None of these would necessarily have joined the
Carmelites from Terenure College solely or primarily to go on the Umtali Mission, but
there is a persuasive sense in which by their time in the college, Rhodesia had become
part of Terenure's culture. One has only to note the boys' own record of the comings
and goings of their Carmelite teachers back and forth from Africa, the occasions of
welcome, presentations and farewells, as recorded in the pages of their section of the
college *Annuals* to appreciate this. In addition, of course one has to acknowledge the
deep Catholicism of their own family lives and backgrounds at this time and the
general commitment of Irish Catholicism to overseas missions. Before going on to
reflect on the life experience of some of these boys of the 1950s, it may be appropriate to explore the evolving situation they would encounter. Unlike their predecessors
of the pioneering generation of the 1940s–1950s, the boys of the 1950s and 1960s
who became the Carmelite missionaries from the mid-1960s to 2000s would arrive
at a Southern Rhodesia/Zimbabwe that differed in two fundamentals — in practical
infrastructure and in political and social climate.

As to the first, there had been a notable extent of development in Southern
Rhodesia in general as a result of the international Christian missions there after the
Second World War. In Umtali, in particular, there had been great advancement as a
result of the Irish Carmelite commitment. From the modest beginning of the 1940s
pioneers when they took over five under-resourced Jesuit missions, by 1970 Irish
Carmelites — mostly Terenure men — were organising and serving some fifteen
missions in Umtali. Between 1946 and 1996 a total of 93 Carmelites had worked in
Zimbabwe, 29 of them dying there. Following the setting up of their own first mission
stations at St Anna's, Wengezi in 1951, and Fr Simon Stock at Rusape in 1952, came
the building of the Church at Rusape, the teacher training and carpentry schools in
Triashill and the new most northerly mission of Avila — all in 1953. Founded by Des
Clarke and Simon Noonan, Avila in Katerere, was remote, being sixty miles north of
Nyanga: by 1996 it had primary and secondary schools, a clinic and the most beautiful
church in the country, built in vernacular style, by Senan Egan when he served the
VaHwesa people from 1964 to 1976.[18] The year 1954 saw the construction of the
first purpose-built Carmelite Priory in Mutare City, the foundation of the Regina
Coeli mission at Nyamaropa and the purchase of 'Drumfad' for Apostolic Prefect
Donal Lamont. In 1956, the new mission of St Therese in Chiduku was established,
followed in 1958 by that of St Joseph at Sakubva township outside Mutare. In 1959
came St Andrew's mission at Marange; St Columba's in the Honde Valley bordering
Mozambique; and the establishment of the Carmelite nuns' novitiate of St Benedict's
in the north-east. In 1960, to the south, came the formation of St Patrick's, Nyanga,
and a year later St Peter's at Chisumbanje and the Minor Seminary of St Charles

Lwanga in Chimanimani, the major college at Kriste Mambo followed in 1963, and finally Carmel College, Mutare, in 1964.

The year 1965 was momentous for three quite different reasons. Firstly, Bishop Lamont ordained Fr Edward Matura as the diocese's first Manyika priest in the country's history. Secondly, as if to underline the racially inclusive nature of the Catholic Church in Africa, the first African Carmelite, Francis Kennedy, came back home from Ireland. Born in 1929 in Salisbury, he came to Ireland to follow his Carmelite vocation in 1948. A very gifted and charming man, a linguist and great storyteller to boot, he was received into the Order as Br Cyprian and was solemnly professed in November 1952. By that stage, he was teaching on the staff at Terenure. In 1956, he was ordained in the Cathedral in Salisbury. He returned to Ireland for further study before coming to have his first assignment at St Therese's, Chiduku. Over 30 years of service to the people followed, until his death in June 1996 and his burial in Triashill.

Thirdly, the triangular relations between the native people, white colonial settlers and their titular masters in London reached a crisis with the Unilateral Declaration of Independence by Ian Smith and his associates. This brought an entirely new dimension to life in the colony and a new strain in relations between the Smith Regime and the Catholic Church, especially in the person of Umtali's Bishop Lamont. Once he became Bishop in 1957, he could no longer endure in silence the inequalities and discrimination practised against the native majority and felt the need to challenge this situation. In 1959, his pastoral letter, *Purchased People*, publicly denounced the system of discrimination and called on white Rhodesians to consider their attitudes in the matter. He brought his fellow senior ecclesiastics with him over the next twenty years in a series of critical joint pastorals, from *Peace through Justice* in 1961 to *A Crisis of Conscience* in 1970, from *Reconciliation in Rhodesia* in 1974 to *A Plea for Reconciliation* in 1978. Typically forthright was his *Open Letter to the Rhodesian Government*, 11 August 1976:

> Conscience compels me to state that your administration by its clearly racist and oppressive policies and by its stubborn refusal to change, is largely responsible for the injustices which have provoked the present disorder and it must in that measure be considered guilty of whatever misery or bloodshed may follow.

But little — or more properly — no reconciliation resulted, certainly not between the Church and the Smith regime, especially from 1965. Missionary activity was curtailed, the government forbade the opening of new mission schools; much was lost, including 100 diocesan primary schools taken over by the new 'state'. Lamont himself was placed under house arrest, and, in 1976 was tried and sentenced to ten years' hard labour before being expelled in 1977. His place was taken by another old Terenure man, Des Clarke, as Vicar Apostolic of Umtali. With the winning of independence in 1980 and the declaration of the Republic of Zimbabwe, Lamont was able to return, until his retirement in 1982. That retirement saw his return to Terenure where, in 1987, he celebrated the golden jubilee of his ordination in his *Alma Mater*. Not many Terenure men, nor indeed Irishmen, have figured on a national postage stamp as he did in Kenya, in 1978, nor have that many been nominated for a Nobel Peace Prize as he was in the same year.[19] He remained in the college along with his confrere and Rhodesian pioneer, Anselm Corbett, until Donal died in August 2003.

It speaks volumes for the success of the Carmelite mission that despite all the turmoil of the fifteen years to 1980, the ground work for a native church structure had been successfully laid. Apart from the growing number of native religious vocations and ordinations, two years after Lamont's expulsion the diocese had consecrated its first native bishop, Auxiliary Bishop Patrick Mutume. Two years after Lamont's return to Ireland, it consecrated Bishop Alexio Churu Muchabawia as his successor. By that stage, the general church infrastructure was greatly developed from what it had been 50 or even 20 years before. By 1988 diocesan clergy were sufficiently numerous for eight of the original fifteen missions of 1946–70 to come directly into their responsibility.[20] In 1982, the visionary Cork-man, Tom Power, who had served and survived in St Peter's, Chisumbanje, during the war years, undertook responsibility for a Zimbabwean Carmelite vocations programme.

However, the years of the Zimbabwean War of Independence had taken their toll on both structures and individuals. Lamont's prediction that armed rebellion would result from a continued denial of justice and equality came to pass. By 1976, many of the Carmelite mission school pupils had absconded across the border with Mozambique only to return as trained freedom fighters. No Carmelites died directly in the liberation struggle from 1976 to 1979 that resulted in ceasefire and then formal independence in April 1980. Two were, however, injured by gunfire; Tom McLoughlin, born in Leitrim in 1928, came to Terenure in 1943, matriculated and joined the Order in 1946, and, after his UCD BA in 1950, went on to Rome and was ordained in 1953. By 1955, he was on the Rhodesia Mission. Fifteen years later he succeeded Seán Coughlan as Mission Superior, a post he remained in until 1976. In January 1977, he was shot and severely wounded in an ambush in Chimanimani. The episode forced his abandonment of Zimbabwe and his return to Ireland where he ministered as chaplain to the Adelaide Hospital and then to St James's Hospital until his sudden death in July 1992. His non-Terenure confrere, Gerry Galvin, was sixteen years in Zimbabwe where he was also shot and wounded in that war, when visiting St Columba's. He transferred temporarily to South Africa and then Ireland but in 1986 returned to Zimbabwe to work in a new climate. Others like Lawrence Lynch suffered imprisonment and deportation for failing to report on the movements of African insurgents. Bishop Patrick Mutume also suffered a harrowing imprisonment in Nyanga during the war. In Avila, Senan Egan was attacked and that assault broke his spirit — he left for Harare, never to return to Avila.

Apart from deaths, injuries, imprisonment and deportations of missionaries, the war brought destruction: St Benedict's Mission was obliterated in the conflict and the seminary at Chimanimani was forcibly closed in 1978. It also brought a temporary halt to Carmelites coming from Ireland: the last to arrive during these troubled times were Frs Tommy Fives and Ambrose Costello, who arrived in 1972. As a consequence, for the Terenure boys of the 1950s and 1960s who became Carmelite missionaries from the mid-1950s to the early 1980s, it was a very different socio-political climate they experienced from that of their predecessors.

Fr Michael Hender:

To return to some of these, consider the experience of Ashford lad, Michael Hender of the class of 1953. He came from Wicklow De La Salle in 1949 to board at Terenure College. He was persuaded in that direction from a vocations visit by Fr Conleth Fitzgerald. Greatly enjoying his boarding days, he had already decided on entering the Order even before sitting his Leaving Certificate and indeed entered the Kinsale novitiate in September 1953 with four other Terenure lads, one of whom was Paddy Hipwell. He obtained his BA from UCD and in 1957 he went on to the cultural melting pot of San Alberto in Rome until 1963. He then returned to Terenure as teacher of history, English, French and religion. Following a year of studying Catechetics in London in 1969-70, Africa beckoned. A year of learning Shona ensued, at the St Therese Mission on the western border of Umtali Diocese, and then it was north to Kriste Mambo (Christ the King) — a major boarding school until it opened to day-pupils after Zimbabwean Independence in 1980. For Michael Hender, moving from Kriste Mambo in 1974 to a decade at the St Columba Mission in Honde Valley in the far east of the diocese brought dangerous years as the guerrilla war against the Smith regime intensified. Death was then a close companion, unforgettably at Mutasa in October 1977 when quick-thinking and fast-talking spared him and the catechist John Sunwa from the wrath of the guerrilla army. In 1976–7, during an appalling period, he, Sunwa and Carmelite sisters carried on their work in the Honde Valley, travelling by bicycle since landmines in the roads precluded the use of their truck. Then in November 1979 at St Joseph's Mission, Mutare, he and fellow-Terenure alumnus, house captain of 1951, Fr Pio Kiernan; who had come out to Africa in 1960,[21] were taken out at gunpoint to be shot at midnight on the veranda of their house but miraculously were spared — again due to some fast talking. They survived the terrors of those years. In 1984, Fr Michael was given a transfer to the Minor Seminary at Chimanimani in the south. It was 1992 — over twenty years — before he had a year's break to visit family and recover from a serious operation. Then it was back to Zimbabwe, to Triashill, to build St Michael's Primary School — one of 50 buildings he initiated and brought to completion. Still no rest, in December 2000 it was off from Triashill to the remote region Coeli Mission in the far north of the diocese for five years before transferring to the Hatfield suburb of Harare to minister with Fr Norbert Heaslip, to the very great needs of the township of Epworth.

Michael Hender's life and experience — though he would recoil from such recognition — is at once unique and yet representative of those Carmelites and Terenure boys who gave up so much for Zimbabwe. Perhaps he would disown the idea that he especially, together with Leo Gallagher, had been largely responsible for preserving the memories of that remarkable contribution, through his *Carmeletter*, *Celts Among the Shona* and other publications.

FR STAN HESSION:

Graduating from Terenure in the year after Michael was another Wicklow lad, Stan Hession, from Blessington. He came to Terenure as boarder in 1947 and in one way it was almost inevitable, for Carmelite blood was in the family veins. His widowed mother, from Blessington, had as cousins that illustrious trio of Carmelite brothers: Malachy, Elias and Kilian Lynch. Furthermore, she and her son, Stan, came from a part of Wicklow that had long and strong Carmelite associations that included the Farringtons as well as the Lynches.

From those years of the late 1940s and early 1950s, he remembered many a prank and minor mischief that boarders got up to and recalls the election by acclamation in 1949 of classmate, Brian Kiernan, as house captain and with the giant Enda Ryder as his vice-captain and 'minder'. In days when food was not over abundant, he found much refuge in the tuck shop then located under the old stone stairs. It was by happy chance that in September 1953 he and fellow sixth year, Peter Kelly, were put in charge of the tuck shop. Stan Hession, self confessedly, was not greatly attached to playing sports and no more greatly into the books, but, like any boarder, was glad to get going to away matches, in Donnybrook, and then heading for the Roma Café on Talbot Street for fish, chips and vinegar which stank out the bus on the way back to the college. Happy days — he looked back after Leaving Certificate in 1954 to a place that was maturing and enlightening, to a college where there was kindness without cosseting; yet, it was a place where one had to stand on one's own feet, sink or swim on one's own. This kind of experience would be some preparation for what lay ahead. Six of that class went on to novitiate in Kinsale, including David Weakliam, Paddy Graham and Chris O'Donnell. The usual comings and goings to and from Gort Muire, UCD and Milltown Park followed, until, a year after ordination in 1963 he was off to Zimbabwe, with Joe Neville, Martin Farragher and Willie O'Regan. Stan Hession felt the political tension of the place from first arrival — like a slap in the face. He was assigned for eighteen months to St Benedict's — which the Vicar General called 'Disaster Area No. 1'; it was politically charged area, subject to a military which was constantly on the move, especially under cover of darkness; suspicion and hostility pervaded all around. As Fr Stan put it, in retrospect, 'without necessarily being in terror one lived days of apprehension'. Ten years in the Eastern Highlands of Chimanimani followed —

difficult in a different way, living without the support of a regular Community life. Following a year's sabbatical at Chelsea College, London, from 1977–8, he was due for return to Chimanimani but, with war still raging in the region, he had a forced domicile in Gort Muire, chaplaincy duties at St James's Hospital — that long-enduring responsibility of Dublin Carmelites — and then parish duties for three years in Scotland before returning to Harare for a final tour of duty at the student house of Mount Carmel. Then, in June 1993, Stan came back to Whitefriar Street until, in December 1994, he found himself again in Kinsale as a member of its Carmelite Community, 50 years from the days when he first arrived there after leaving Terenure.[22]

Such were the lives of just some of the college alumni and teachers who had extensive experience in Zimbabwe. However, it would not be far from the truth to say that a great many more Terenure Carmelites had some practical and direct experience whether on shorter stay substitutions, official visits or retreat-giving: there were well over twenty such individuals from Conleth and Bonaventure Fitzgerald, through Paddy Burke, Simon Grace and Eltin Griffin, to Chris O'Donnell, Micheál Ó Néill, Billy Langan, Jimmy Murray, Bob Kelly and others.[23]

Furthermore, the indirect contact from Ireland could in ways be critically important — from the sales of work that supplied the finances for the mission and the funds raised by the Terenure Past Pupils' Union from their own drama produc-tions from 1953; to moral support and diplomatic interventions. Critical here, for example, and yet to be fully chronicled was the work of David Weakliam — Terenure pupil (class of 1954), teacher, Prior and Provincial — in the 1970s. As Provincial, through the worst of the war years into the peace, from 1976 to 1982, he and Terenure Prior Bob Kelly and their confreres organised the moral and material support crucial to the survival of the Carmelite mission in Zimbabwe. It must have been altogether heartbreaking for them to see that free country from 1980 deterio-rate politically and disintegrate economically in more recent years. In particular, this must have been the case for the former Prior of Terenure and Provincial, Fr Bob Kelly of the class of 1958: after serving as Provincial from 1994 to the year 2000, and, after a life of teaching and service in Ireland, he headed out for the Zimbabwean mission but returned in 2007 with direct experience of the catastrophe which had befallen the people of that Republic. For all that, Terenure's closeness to that com-mitment did not dilute or decline: on the contrary, in 1994 the college was twinned with Kriste Mambo Secondary School as part of a process whereby the Carmelite Communities and parishes in Ireland and Scotland were partnered with twelve missions and institutions in Zimbabwe. In 1995, as a result of that twinning, two of Terenure's fifth year students, Feargal O'Connell and Bernard Broderick, and their teacher, Brendan McCauley, went on behalf of the college on a formal visit to develop the links between Terenure and Kriste Mambo College, Rusape. As a fact-finding mission there was much that was learned from Zimbabwean students in a valuable cultural exchange.[24] That journey took them to other Carmelite locations that have featured prominently in that fifty-year relationship, from Hatfield in Harare to St Killian's and Mutare, from Rusape to Regina Coeli in Nyamaropa and to Triashill. Along the way there were memorable meetings with Zimbabwean Carmelite priests, novices and pupils and indeed, with missionaries whose lives of service have in whole or part been spent there: Frs Coughlan and Kiernan, Joe Neville and Des Clarke, Fred Lally and Paul Graham, Jim Doyle and Jim Kinahan among others — many of them Terenure men, former pupils and priests who remain actively involved right up to this day.

Fr Mel Hill supervising works
in Rhodesia, 1950.

Local woman performing day-to-day chores in Southern Rhodesia, 1950s.

Local women go about their day's work, Southern Rhodesia, 1950s.

Local children in the school at Triashill, 1950s.

Benny Clinch left for the Rhodesian Mission in October 1947
and saw out his days in the company of his colleagues in Terenure.

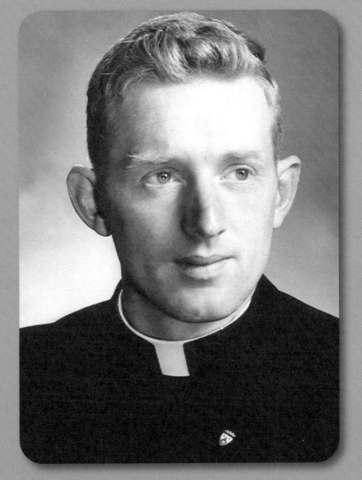

Patrick Hipwell, 1962. He was a very popular and productive
missionary. He died in Africa following a motorbike accident
in 1968 and is buried in Triashill.

CHAPTER 16

*Staff and Structures,
1951–65*

Carmelites process to the dedication
ceremony for the new chapel, 1957.

THE DECADE OF THE 1950S PRESENTS AN IRELAND OF STARK CONTRAST: ON the one hand, a society in stagnation, a wasteland of unemployment and emigration — in a decade of despair for the 'vanishing Irish';[1] on the other, a militant Church and so confident as almost to be the Church triumphant.

From 1926 to 1961 the population went into uninterrupted decline by decade, as follows:

TABLE 20: POPULATION OF IRISH FREE STATE/REPUBLIC, 1926, 1936, 1946, 1961

Year	Population
1926	2,971,992
1936	2,968,420
1946	2,955,107
1961	2,818,341[2]

During the same period that spectre of a vanishing Irish nation was manifest in the records of emigration: averaging 33,000 per annum in the 1920s, it fell to an average of 14,000 per annum in the 1930s. It then more than doubled to average 33,000 per annum from 1940 to 1945, rising to over 41,000 per annum from 1945 to 1948; it continued averaging 40,000 per annum from 1950 to 1956 and rose to over 42,400 per annum from 1956 to 1961, so that over 400,000 left Ireland in that dreadful decade — the highest since the appalling 1880s.

By contrast, the Church was never stronger, opening more places of worship and education than ever before, attracting more vocations than previously recorded, sending forth more missionary priests, nuns and brothers than Irish history had ever known. At a time when the Irish Carmelites were sending out many of their very best men and very best Terenure men, there were 7,000 Irish religious working overseas, over 4,000 of them in Africa. Even if the country's population was falling the percentage of Catholics within it was rising as the total number of adherents to other religious persuasions went into decline:

TABLE 21: PERCENTAGE OF CATHOLICS IN THE IRISH FREE STATE/REPUBLIC, 1926, 1936, 1946, 1961

Year	Population
1926	92.6
1927	93.4
1946	94.3
1961	94.9[3]

While formally the Church was presided over from Armagh, by Cardinal John D'Alton from 1946 to 1963 and Cardinal William Conway from 1963 to 1977, the really formidable presence was that of John Charles McQuaid, who reigned as Archbishop of Dublin, from December 1940 to January 1972.

For all that the country stagnated economically through the 1950s, it is remarkable that, in education provision, resources expanded despite the absence of innovation in that area by the government. At primary level, while the numbers of schools declined the numbers of pupils and teachers rose steadily, even remarkably, in the twenty years from 1945:

TABLE 22: PRIMARY SCHOOL PROVISION, 1945, 1950, 1955, 1960, 1965[4]

Year	No. of Schools	No. of Pupils	No. of Teachers
1945	5,009	463,000	12,800
1950	4,886	464,000	12,900
1955	4,872	495,000	13,200
1960	4,882	506,000	13,900
1965	4,847	473,000	14,500

TABLE 23: SECONDARY SCHOOL PROVISION, 1945, 1950, 1955, 1960, 1965[5]

Year	No. of Schools	No. of Pupils	No. of Teachers
1945	393	43,000	3,600
1950	434	49,000	3,800
1955	474	59,000	4,400
1960	526	77,000	5,200
1965	585	99,000	6,500

While the absolute increases in each category spoke of considerable expansion, significant pressures built up: with the number of pupils increasing by almost 230% the number of schools had increased by almost 50% and the pupils-teacher ratio rose from 12:1 to 15:1.

What was true for the country at large became true also for Terenure College. Its number of pupils increased steadily through the 1950s into the mid-1960s as follows:

TABLE 24: TERENURE COLLEGE PUPIL NUMBERS, 1950, 1955, 1960, 1965[6]

Year	Senior School	Junior School	Total
1950	234	149	383
1955	268	141	409
1960	333	207	540
1965	495	276	771

Over these fifteen years, Terenure College enrolments doubled: the numbers in junior school almost doubled while the numbers in the senior school more than doubled. Furthermore, this 100% increase had followed upon a 50% expansion over the earlier five years 1944–5 to 1949–50. In some contrast to the position from the 1920s to the 1940s, the numbers taking the state examinations grew, with those taking the Leaving Certificate almost trebling:

TABLE 25: TERENURE COLLEGE LEAVING AND
INTERMEDIATE CERTIFICATE EXAMINATION
CANDIDATE NUMBERS, 1950–65[7]

Year	Leaving Certificate	Intermediate Certificate
1950	18	39
1955	34	38
1960	43	34
1965	51	52

To meet this considerable growth, there was a corresponding expansion in the size of the college's teaching staff:

TABLE 26: TERENURE COLLEGE TEACHING STAFF,
1950–65[8]

Year	Religious	Lay	Total
1950	20	11	31
1955	19	13	32
1960	26	15	41
1965	24	21	45

It is interesting to note that the numbers of Carmelites on the teaching staff had reached their highest-ever number *c.* 1960, but more striking is the almost doubling in the number of lay teachers and also the changing ratio of religious to lay from almost 2:1 to near parity by 1965. As the 1950s began, there were far reaching changes in the composition of the teaching personnel. It was over to Fr Kelly's four successors as president, Fr Dominic Reale (1949–52); Fr Eugene Dunstan O'Connor (1952–8); Fr Thomas Patrick Burke (1958–61); and Fr Patrick Cornelius Keenan (1961–7) to oversee these transformations.

Fr Reale was last encountered as a young priest leading the exodus of Irish Carmelites from Rome back to Ireland following the onset of the Second World War. When he became Prior and president in 1949 he was 39 years old. He was remembered by former pupils as a gifted teacher who excelled at encouraging students to think out problems and to debate controversial issues: a man who may have been kindly forgetful too: he once spotted Wicklow boarder John Brady, French boarder Arnaut Slowey, and future Carmelite P.J. Cunningham of the class of 1955, transgressing the rule against frequenting the lake, ordered them to report themselves to 'KAC' — Fr Kevin Andrew Clarke, dean of discipline — and then 'forgot' to check if they had done so, which, of course, they had not. Stan Hession, already encountered on the African missions, recalled how Prior Dominic would regularly inspect the classes, coming to that of the placid, idiosyncratic ex-Christian Brother, 'Buffalo Bill' Cody, not the greatest of teachers, and intoning, 'Tell me , Mr Cody, and just *how* are these boys doing?'

When in 1952, he was succeeded by Fr Eugene Dunstan O'Connor, Fr Reale went on to nine years in Knocktopher — three as Prior — and then six years in Moate until 1967 when he returned to Knocktopher as Prior. At Knocktopher he restored the Carmelite Church of 1832 and added a fine community hall for the area. Moate, under Fr Reale, became one of the largest boarding schools in the country. Moate too enabled him to indulge his passion for developing Gaelic games and to realise some golden years as that College won three All Ireland and six Leinster colleges' championships.[9] His Terenure successor held the office of Prior and president for six years until 1958. Already encountered as a chronicler of the college's past and a promoter of its rugby future, E.D O'Connor was a formidable character in a number of respects. One can read between the lines in reviewing the very first entry in the 'Day By Day' section of the *Annual* for 1953: 'Sept 4th: Paper strike or no paper strike, we return to-day. Congratulations to Rev. Fr. E.D. O'Connor, O. Carm., on being appointed Prior of the College. We all know Fr O'Connor, but worse still, he knows us'.[10]

Mutual acquaintances indeed, for he had been in the college for over thirteen years, yet he was still only 38 when he took over that large and growing responsibility. A man of few words, little given to casual conversation, and never to petty gossip about others, he was a good listener with a knack for the caustic quip. Born in Ballitore, his father William and his mother Catherine Aylmer were both teachers. He was ordained in 1940 and had been appointed as Assistant Provincial from 1949 to 1952. For the boys in general, most Priors were perceived as distant eminences and 'Dunny' was no different. Apart from his commitment to rugby, learned and loved in his own Rockwell student days, his three great academic commitments were to promoting Irish, endeavouring to find young scholars who would pursue Greek and teaching German. Felim Corr, a Cavan boarder who came to Terenure in 1953 and who left in 1958, even as 'Dunny' completed his second innings as Prior, recalled that he himself was a not-too-keen member of the class of six who had been assigned to honours Irish, a subject on which he and Fr Dunstan did not see eye-to-eye. He found him a somewhat distant personality but conceded that he was very career-oriented on the boys' behalf. Likewise Richard 'Dicky' Dunne remembered Fr Dunstan selecting certain students to study Greek, whether they liked it or not! A pupil contemporary of theirs and himself later a Carmelite, Des Flanagan found Dunstan to be a tough individual who would brook no contradiction. Likewise, that great missionary man, Fr Michael Hender, himself of the class of 1953 would say that although very small in stature, Dunstan had only to look at a rowdy class and there would be instant silence. Another past pupil would recall Dunstan's character-istic and unique habit of emitting frequent and ominous growling sounds, as though a volcano were ready to erupt: to some he appeared, irascible, difficult and unyield-ing — yet others remembered him for his tolerance and kindness.

Following Dunstan's term of office the college presidency went next to Fr Thomas Patrick Burke over 1958 to 1961. Better known to a wider world as a scientist, in that connection he will feature later in more detail, Fr Burke was a Dubliner, born in 1923. Known in academic and family circles as Tom or Fr Tom, to his Carmelite confreres he was always Paddy or Fr Pat. Like some of those great late nineteenth and early twentieth century Carmelites, Tom Burke had, as a boy, seen altar service at Whitefriar Street and indeed his uncle was Brother Gerard Traynor of fond Whitefriar Street and Terenure memory. The young lad went to school at Synge Street CBS in the 1920s and 1930s and entered the Order in October 1941, taking final vows in 1945. He joined Terenure's teaching staff in 1952 — in the same year as Frs Cyprian Kennedy, Eltin Griffin and Jim Kinahan; Chris O'Donnell well remembers Fr Burke introducing him and his classmates of 1953 to the joys and mysteries of calculus and co-ordinate geometry.[11] The headship of Terenure College was hardly a position he would have sought but his legendary energy would not have been spared on it and it may well have been with relief that he would relinquish it after three years and return to his profes-sion of science, within the conventual life of faith and prayer.

One of Terenure's best-remembered and best-loved sons was his successor, Patrick C. Keenan, otherwise known as 'Patsy' to his colleagues and as 'Mex' to his pupils. Son of a blacksmith, he came from that heartland of great Carmelites, Co. Kildare, more specifically Ballymore Eustace where he was born in December 1916. He arrived in Terenure as a boarder in 1931 and found himself in the same third year Intermediate class as John Lamont, the Clarkes, the O'Sharkeys and Dudley Fisher. Having been received into the Order in 1934, as a novice in Kinsale in 1935, he had the treasured privilege of meeting that great Carmelite martyr, Titus Brandsma, who died in Dachau Concentration Camp in 1942. Patsy was solemnly professed in 1938 and was ordained four years later. There followed what was almost a lifetime of teaching in Terenure — he was one of those few Carmelites who spent the greater part of their priestly and professional lives there. In the course of time, from joining the college staff in 1948, he held almost every office in it including dean of studies from 1952 to 1961 as well as Prior and president for the six years following. After he became college Bursar, until 1982, having finally retired from teaching, he moved to Kinsale. Here, he enjoyed a rich life in the Priory and in the wider community for twenty years until his passing in 2002. Patsy Keenan made an abiding impression on the pupils of the close on 40 years who passed through his classes or who learned from his devoted coaching in Gaelic games and rugby. As to the latter, Fr Fintan Burke recalled Patsy's phenomenal memory for rugby players and rugby match statistics as well as his presidency of Terenure College RFC. He liked to appear 'fearsome' to the boys and indeed was known among generations of them as 'Mex'. Boys' nicknames for teachers have at times been mysterious but in this case there is no great mystery: he was a man of swarthy complexion and his early teaching years coincided with the appearance, on children's television in the early 1950s, of the cartoon character, 'Mexican Pete', a black-bearded hombre whose party-piece was the Mexican hat-dance. Jim Blake of the class of 1964, and subsequently PPU president in 1992, vividly remembers the way the energetic Fr Patsy would stand outside the classroom door, winding himself up and bracing himself for the battle that lay ahead and within. Others recalled that his concern to communicate, his passion to educate could generate frustration, and it was not unknown to them that blackboard dusters could take sudden flight across a crowded classroom on occasion. 'Mex' was remembered by Patsy's confrere in later life and his pupil in the early 1950s, P.J. Cunningham, 'with his black stubble like a beard waiting to burst out' — a friar with a fearsome look and loud voice but soft as anyone behind that 'forbidding front'. As another former pupil and later confrere was to put it, Patsy Keenan was 'the man with the booming voice and the heart of gold'. In 1954, three young Carmelites just back from Rome were sent to join the teaching staff: Joe Linus Ryan, Tom McLoughlin and Des Flanagan; the last named recalled Patsy at the time as 'a revered, respected and wonderful soul … a kind and welcoming spirit for new young teachers'.[12]

Carmelite New Arrivals:

There were new teachers a-plenty, priests and lay alike. Many of the new Carmelite teachers will be encountered in later pages, such as Frs Lar Hegarty, Paddy Grace, Jim McCouaig, Jarlath O'Hea and others; but, two who were not so new and who ought to be mentioned at this point were Kevin Andy 'KAC' Clark and Jim Kinahan. Andy would become a pillar of the Terenure teaching staff and Carmelite Community, strong and enduring. Like Patsy Keenan, he had joined the staff in the school year 1947–8. From Avoca, Co Wicklow, and nephew of the famous nationalist rector of the Irish College in Rome, Monsignor O'Hagan, Andy was just 28 when he came on the college staff, having previously been a Terenure pupil.[13] He was to serve the college as teacher of Latin and English for a marvellous 43 years, for 15 of which he was to be dean of discipline. Despite the terrors often associated with the title, 'KAC' was famously a kind man: as Felim Corr put it so well, recalling this teacher of the 1950s, 'Fr Clarke, Dean of Discipline, whose good nature and positive outlook belied this forbidding title'; he was greatly interested in the welfare of the pupils and was equally famous as a man of great good humour and sense of fun. As another Wicklowman and pupil of the 1950s, Michael Hender, experienced it, discipline under the dean, Fr Kevin Clarke 'was exercised in a very fair way and without favouritism'. He and Patsy Keenan became great friends and within the lore of the Carmelite Community there is the oft-told and worth-retelling story of their divergent political interests and allegiances: on the occasion of a general election Patsy and Andy decided since they were on opposing sides they might as well not vote since their votes in that constituency would merely cancel each other. This was fine until Patsy, working away in the Bursary, spotted Andy all dressed up and exiting the college. He quickly followed and caught up with him at the polling station: as their confrere and later long-serving Provincial, Fintan Burke, remarked, 'Patsy was too long on the road and too shrewd a man to fall for that kind of electoral pact'.[14]

Typical of his kindness was Andy Clarke's insistence on travelling to Sligo for the funeral of the mother of former pupil, Eugene McNamee, in 1988, although by then he was unwell himself: typical too that when that great servant of the college, Pat Walsh, retired and went to move out, it was Andy's insistence — along with Fr McCouaig — that prevailed on him to take a room for life in the college.[15]

Joining 'KAC' on the staff for years later was Jim Boniface Kinahan whose career was to be more changing and varied. From Ballycumber, Co. Offaly, where he was born in 1923, Fr Jim was ordained in 1945. First assigned to Aberystwyth, he joined the Terenure staff in September 1952 and taught there for eight years, becoming Sub-Prior there from 1958 to 1960. He was expert in the teaching of Irish, French, German and Italian. He subsequently served in Kinsale, Beaumont Parish in Dublin, Africa and the Scottish Mission in Glasgow where, from 1978, he worked with Fr Des Kelly.[16] Coming back to Ireland — to Moate — in 1982, he again found himself on Terenure's staff, teaching in the junior school from 1985 until 1993 and now bearing the burden of the nickname 'Bozo' — who, like 'Mex' — was another comic character of early 1950s television. Apart from his priestly duties he had the task of giving voice instruction and drama training following the departure of the Abbey actor, Eddie Golden who left in 1955. It fell to Fr Jim and his colleague Michael O'Connell to produce the 1955 *Macbeth*. In some respects an unlikely drama director, he was a very quiet soul but one always in support of the 'underdog', ever-ready with a kind word to any who seemed down, and gently successful in persuading reluctant pupils to take to the stage.

As already noted, to the original core of the six lay teachers of 1945 — Griffin, Collins, O'Hanlon, O'Connell, Pentony and Maguire — came significant additions over the next twenty years so that, by 1965, they constituted a significant minority of 21 staff. Inevitably, a number of these would be transitory: Ms Dunne in elocution; Ms Kane, Mr Forrester and Mr McKenzie in instrumental music; M. Layton, J. Doyle and J. O'Connor, for example. Others would be young teachers at the outset of a long — even life-long — career in the college. Notable here is Vinnie Morris who first started in the junior school in 1962 as teacher, having attended in 1949 as pupil, and he would spend some 40 years there as a teacher until retiring in 2005–06 having been deputy principal on the way. One of the young laymen, who joined the staff, just as Vinnie Morris and his classmates were going through the second year seniors in 1954–5, was Pat 'Buster' O'Brien. A wonderfully gifted Irish teacher at a time when the language was compulsory to pass the Leaving Certificate and dreaded in many places, Pat O'Brien was a remarkably humble man with little to be humble about and certainly not about his teaching success —'... to get the lads through the Leaving [Certificate]' as he used to put it. Kindness and constant good humour expressed the tenor of his professional life. Pupil and future colleague, Vinnie Morris remembered Pat's 'totally original sense of humour — a mixture of home spun wisdom and feigned ignorance presented to us in a feast of words'.[17] Coming to the college for his first teaching post in the autumn of 1974, Frank Gallen, business studies master and later deputy head, recollected the warmth of the welcome that Pat extended to him. His passing after a protracted illness, in May 1974, was a great and greatly lamented loss.

Some of the lay staff of that period had been retired, experienced national school teachers like the tall, gruff, but decent Eamon O'Sullivan who taught Irish for ten years from 1955; his great jowls, large moustache, hang-dog look and strong interventions inevitably bought him the nickname 'Bull Dog'; but a benign bulldog, remembered by Charlie O'Sullivan of the class of 1970 as 'not fierce, but big, jolly and with a beguiling growl'.[18] With him from the 1956–7 was the diminutive, pipe-smoking Mr Henry, with his unforgettable, copperplate blackboard writing, and, so ancient that he seemed to some of his pupils to have been a relic of the 1920s, but a tough relic at that. One story of disputed authenticity involved Mr Henry and a senior school pupil who as such was proud and perhaps unique as the owner of a splendid Morris Minor convertible which he took to school and parked by the building's side below the class were Mr Henry taught. On one occasion, the normally placid Mr Henry seized a school bag and sent it flying out an open window only for the projectile to descend in speed and force, crashing through the canvas roof of the unfortunate's convertible.

Not all that generation's masters were necessarily qualified in their craft yet became famous both inside and outside of school. Two of them were Maguires and one — P.P. — has already featured, larger than life, in what has gone before. A decade after P.P.

Maguire left, Leo arrived. Leo Maguire came to the college in 1956–7 to assist with choir and singing.

At that stage Leo, 53 years old, was becoming a national institution when, from 1952, he became the presenter of the famous Walton's sponsored radio programme of Irish music: this was broadcast and presented for fifteen minutes every Saturday afternoon from 1952 until 1981 when all sponsored programmes were terminated. His became one of the most famous, partly from the rich timbre of Leo's baritone presentation, the sound patriotism of its themes and for its unforgotten opening 'weekly reminder of the grace and beauty that lie in our heritage of Irish songs — the songs our fathers loved' and with its equally memorable sign-off: 'If you feel like singing … do sing an Irish song'.

Born at home on Watling Street, Dublin, in 1903, Leo's career of public performance commenced in 1913 when Michael Mallin put him up on a table to sing at the Irish Citizen Army inaugural rally. Later, he was trained by John McCormack's tutor, Vincent O'Brien, and would go on to perform with the Dublin Operatic Society. In 1927, he commenced his Radio Éireann career while working for Dublin County Council. By the 1940s, he had taken up music full-time, teaching in the School of Music before going on to teach part-time in Dublin schools and colleges. His Terenure commitment, beginning in November 1957, lasted until 1981 when he retired from the college and from national radio. He was a talented songwriter, some of his compositions becoming nationally and internationally well-known, including *The Whistling Gypsy, If You Ever Come Across the Seas to Ireland,* and his *Dublin Saunter* with its famous refrain,

> For Dublin can be heaven with coffee at eleven
> and a stroll through Stephen's Green,
> There's no need to hurry, there's no need to worry,
> You're a king and the lady's a queen

He wrote this song especially for the famous bearded actor, Noel Purcell. In his eighty second year, Leo passed away — as well-remembered by Terenure alumni as much as by anyone. In a fine verse song that he wrote in Terenure in April 1959 — entitled *To A Possible Reader One Hundred Years Hence* — he unintentionally wrote what might have been his own most fitting epitaph:

> O men to come, who walk beneath the sun
> By Shannon's banks or Liffeyside along,
> Do not forget the great deeds gladly done
> By men who loved the right and hated wrong:
> And, maybe in your prayers you'll think of one
> Who tried to pay the reckoning with a song.[19]

Over his 25 Terenure years he used to take choir and teach speech and poetry to the juniors every Wednesday, sitting at the piano, imparting and rehearsing Irish and religious songs. Bernard Kenna and Fr Joe Mothersill of the class of 1974 well remember Leo trying them out for singing and voice training. Two classmates of 1970 who would end up as Terenure teachers, Carmelite and lay, Fr Michael O'Neill and Charlie O'Sullivan share that memory too, though Charlie would confess that gifted though Leo was and hard although he tried, he failed miserably to put a musical note into his young head. These were only some of the lay teachers whose careers in Terenure commenced in the 1950s or early 1960s.

'The Bear' O'Hanlon:

There was however one of the lay old guard with many years behind him and with many still to follow: on 16 October 1953, Eddie 'The Bear' O'Hanlon celebrated 25 years of teaching in the college. Hard though it may be to envision, he had by then been teaching almost as long as 'The Hooley' Griffin, and longer than any member of the Carmelite staff by 1953. It was in 1927 that this shy and self-effacing lay master with his frank and engaging smile, who was so inappropriately named 'The Bear', joined the staff just after graduating from college. One of the college's great teachers, devoted and loyal, imparting enthusiasm and cultivating curiosity, he became, outside the classroom, one of the college's institutions as records steward of the college's sports days. Remembered by many as a gentle man, Joe Roche recalled how 'The Bear' never resorted to physical retribution and never needed to since his gaze and his irony were 'sufficient to quell the most boisterous and silence the most bumptious'.[20] The only hammering Eddie ever engaged in at the college, as Fr Joe Linus Ryan observed, was the relentless hammering home of his lessons, with fidelity to that ancient adage, '*Repetitio est mater studiorum*'. Another Carmelite colleague recalled how the thin, sharp-nosed O'Hanlon with black hair turning silver, could silence and petrify an unruly class with that fearsome stare that could put the fear of God into boys: a wonderful teacher and devout man yet one for whom, in this man's recollection, the glass of life was half-empty rather than half-full. Perhaps this was with some cause since tragedy was a close companion: he and his wife lost two children to infant deaths; then he was badly injured in a car crash that also injured his wife and only son, and killed his parents; and then came the sudden death of his daughter, Patricia, on the eve of her marriage. Yet, with 25 years served in 1953, he went on to serve a remarkable 43 until he retired in 1970–1 — but continued dutifully in that role as steward of the college sports day records. As James Carmel O'Shea pointed out, Eddie O'Hanlon served no fewer than ten Priors and presidents, from Richard Brocard Taylor to Paddy Simon Grace.

Christy 'Wiggy' Collins:

In 1959, the third of the old guard of laymen marked his twenty-fifth year in the college. Christy Collins was unique among them in at least two respects. For one, he was an unregistered teacher; for another, he was known as a man of encyclopaedic knowledge. When he was recruited to the college by James Carmel O'Shea in 1933, he had no teacher training qualification, but had received some kind of training with the Christian Brothers in Marino,[21] and never acquired one bar the exceptional one of learning in and succeeding in the classroom. When one inquired of the students from the 1950s to the mid-1970s what it was he taught them — in terms of subjects — the answers ranged from Irish and English, to history, geography and mathematics precisely because the range of his interests stretched more widely even than their own memories of the man. As Dunstan O'Connor put it, 'Perhaps one of the secrets of his success as a teacher is that he always remained a student. He was never content to let his vast body of knowledge remain static. There were always new things to learn, new worlds to conquer'.[22] It was a clear sign of the way he was treasured that, being unregistered, the Carmelites topped up his salary for those 42 years of his remarkable service. Fr Bene O'Callaghan of the class of 1960 recalled the 'bachelor genius, teacher of Irish in an easy-going humorous way'.[23] Fr Des Flanagan who taught with him in the mid-1950s observed: 'Christy Collins, unqualified in formal letters but by far the most outstanding and gifted teacher in the College; a master of English, quiet and distant but most pleasant who cycled into College every day ... they were fortunate and proud to have him on the staff'.[24]

Yet, typical of Christy Collins's range, Fr Des Kelly remembered him as 'the terrific Irish and French teacher, a great character who taught his 6th Years as though they were university students ...'. This impression of this beloved man with his John Lennon type spectacles and his great mop of hair was confirmed by several other pupils of the time; for Sé O'Connor of the class of 1954 he was that 'teacher of Irish and French, superb in stimulating interest, focused on the subject rather than on examinations', while for David Kennedy, Christy Collins was 'this most interesting and highly intelligent man, at his best with a small honours class with whom he could discourse on almost any subject ... an exceptionally well-educated man who passed a lot on to his students'.[25] And to Fr Chris O'Donnell he was 'this really brilliant mind and teacher who taught virtually everything except Latin, an amazing teacher'. So too his talent for teaching was recalled by Tony Scott of the class of 1957 who described 'Wiggy's gifted way of interesting them in the Irish language, taking some minutes before the end of classes to read chapters from the Irish-language thriller novels by Reics Carló': but most memorable is Tony's pen-picture of the man, approaching his next class with advance soundings, drumming his fingers on his attaché case on the way down the corridor in advance notice to the boys.[26]

Such were some of the staff, clerical and lay who found themselves in a college meeting rapidly expanding demands and growing pressures in the decade and more from 1950.

STRUCTURES:

Inevitably those pressures compelled change: 'This year saw the completion of a vast scheme of improvements to the amenities of the College and its surroundings which have made this an historic year'.[27] So wrote the editor of the college *Annual* in 1952. He added that 'Further progress may be necessary in the years ahead but all that can be done without changing the old look of the College, has been done'. It wasn't clear whether this was a promise to preserve or a caution to transform. Nor is it clear from surviving sources what 'the vast scheme of improvements' was in 1952: they included the provision of a new recreation hall behind the handball alley,[28] certainly there is evidence that the lake was drained and cleaned up, but beyond this, the other improvements are not recorded. However, one change that was introduced to give order and a sense of identity to a body of boys that had expanded so greatly in number was the introduction of the 'house system' in 1952–3: initially applied to all sporting activities in order to encourage a total participation and to strengthen a sense of more local identity, the entire school was divided into four 'Houses', namely, St Patrick's, St Elias's, St Colmcille's and St Simon's, with every boy, independent of grade or year, being assigned to one 'house', each house therefore comprising one quarter of all the boys of every grade. It aimed to afford an opportunity to every boy to competitively participate in the college's own games and sports since every boy could not hope to appear in intercollegiate, representative games. It aspired to cut across the divisions or barriers of years and grades and afford an opportunity for groups of younger and older boys to share a more local in-house sense of community.

THE NEW CHAPEL:

Before long, too, Fr Conleth Fitzgerald's wish of 1943 was to be realised with the decision to construct a new church or college chapel. The preparatory work was begun on 9 May 1955, to the great excitement of the boys with the arrival of the bulldozer and the commencement of site clearance, followed by the blessing of the site by the Prior General of the Order. A year later, on 25 May 1956, Archbishop McQuaid laid the foundation stone for a church designed to hold from 800 to 1,000 worshippers.[29] It was a ceremony he would gladly perform since only three years before that the Carmelites in Terenure had gifted his archdiocese with a good plot of college land to enable him to build a new parish church off Fortfield Road and which was consecrated as St Pius X, at Wainsfort Grove.[30] The new college chapel — Our Lady of Mount Carmel — was designed by architect Stanislaus Nevin in modernised Romanesque and built by Sisk, at a cost of approximately £60,000, the college's largest outlay in a very long time. The design created an impression of an interior far more spacious than the exterior suggested — the nave being very high-ceilinged with a coffered-barrel vault, offering a view along its 135 feet to the altar, uninterrupted by any supporting pillars. As befitted what was both a Church for a sizeable public congregation with that fine nave, it was simultaneously an oratory for a monastic Community and so, within the chancel, were the choir stalls, double-ranked, in mahogany. In addition, five side chapels were located either side of the nave. By that stage, the foundation stone for a new wing linking the college to the chapel had been laid. Together, once constructed, these two developments would profoundly alter the landscape, not least by cutting off the view of the lake and its woods from the old Terenure House and by occasioning the felling of some huge 300-year-old trees, including a great cedar of Lebanon. For all that, the new chapel was a magnificent structure in traditional layout for the pre-Vatican II liturgy, with congregation on two sides facing the altar which in turn faced east, the celebrant with his back to the congregation. The new edifice made it possible for the entire school population to be accommodated for all collective religious occasions. Furthermore, it freed up space by releasing the old in-house chapel which came into use as a badly-needed recreation room. The new interconnecting wing and cloister provided accommodation for the Carmelite Community who could now vacate the old house, releasing the upper story of the main building which was transformed into classrooms ready for use by the start of 1958. This in turn enabled the junior school to be transferred to the top of the theatre wing. This new wing was blessed on completion by Prior General Kilian Lynch on 26 October 1957, ten years after he had returned to Terenure's prize day, on the occasion of his election to the highest post in the Order. Then at 11.00 a.m. on 27 October, the Feast of Christ the King, Archbishop McQuaid began the formal blessing of the new chapel in a major ceremony attended by a great throng of pupils, staff, past pupils, parents and friends. The first Mass in the beautiful new building was celebrated by Prior-General Lynch before the High Altar, above and behind which was placed a splendid wooden statue of Our Lady of Mount Carmel, illuminated by concealed lighting within the apse. It was built with a view to the future since its 900 seats were in excess of the actual requirements in 1957 — a strong expression of confidence in a future that was realised. One other construction, not of bricks and mortar, but nonetheless of moment, was to emerge in this period, as sign of the times, the Parents' Association.

THE PARENTS' ASSOCIATION:

It was early November 1956 that the meeting was convened which led to the foundation of the Parents' Association. In a very direct sense, it represented a milestone in the maturing of the college, a product of its growing size and of the need therefore to establish an effective three way communication between parents, pupils and teachers. The idea appears to have been first raised publicly by Prior Dunstan O'Connor in his speech at the annual prize day in June 1956. There he remarked that an active participative role by parents in the education of their children should not be the prerogative of the few and urged that the formation of some sort of parents' association might be worth consideration. His suggestion was taken seriously to the extent that a few interested parents got together to form a Provisional Committee, with a view to eliciting a more extensive expression of interest. Apart from the president, lay figures included Jack Bermingham, Michael Flynn, John McCann, J. Church, P. Tormey, J.P. Clarke and M. Hall-Carroll, among others. Jack Bermingham from Rhode, Co.

Offaly, was actually a Blackrock College man, but by 1956, he had had a long and varied association with Terenure College: a brilliant 'Rock rugby player, he was capped for Ireland at 21 and won five Leinster Cup medals. An inspector for the Land Commission, he settled in the newly developing Fortfield area as it started up as a suburb beside Terenure College in the 1930s. Frs O'Connor and Ardiff persuaded him to come over to coach their new rugby teams from 1943 — with some success in the long term. Ten years later he organised the college's first horse show and from then till his sudden death, he made it one of Dublin's most successful gymkhanas. He became the chairman of the Provisional Committee and the first chairman of the Parents' Association. John McCann was an alderman and a former Lord Mayor of Dublin, very successful as a popular dramatist and father of one of Terenure's many great actors, possibly its greatest, Donal McCann. M. Hall-Carroll, J.P. Clarke, J. O'Farrell and M. McNamara had all been active in the union at various stages, Clarke being president in 1952 and again in 1956. Another of the founding members was joint honorary treasurer, Tim Cahill, a former president of the Labour Court, whose three sons: Joe, Paddy and Tommy, Terenure boys all, became doctors. Their mother was one of several who were to have an active involvement in the association and whose presence, was, oddly and interestingly, to link the founding of the association with the Junior Cup triumph of 1955. The Terenure Junior Cup campaign had been closely watched and supported by a group of formidable mothers, among them Mrs Cahill, Mrs McNamee, Mrs Tormey and Mrs Hollingsworth: their role in that campaign was well-caught by Fr Grace who dubbed them 'The Selection Committee'! Following that victory, as a group they played no small role behind the scenes in generating the Parents' Association.[31]

That Provisional Committee convened a general meeting in the college theatre in November 1956 at which the Parents' Association was established. It was none other than Leo Maguire who opened the meeting where the formation of this body was successfully proposed to an audience in excess of 100. The association aimed to assist members in problems confronting them in regard to the education and careers of their boys, sought to make social and other contacts and to organise events to help the college in its efforts to provide additional accommodation for the pupils. It was envisaged within the last objective to raise funds to help with the new chapel, the library, a new science hall and swimming pool, to provide career talks, and to promote social events for the parents.

In the course of its first twelve months, the association had successfully organised the first formal series of career guidance lectures, a prize fund had been inaugurated and contributions organised for the new chapel. Their fundraising had also helped the college budget, preventing what would otherwise have been the first fees increase in seven years. The secretary, Michael Flynn, was able to report that the membership had reached 360, a substantial increase on the numbers at the foundation meeting. By 1959, while the weekly fund-raising collectors were proceeding well, there was some suggestion of a waning of interest in public social functions and in careers lectures.[32]

In fairness, there was a strong revival of interest and activity over the following year. This owed much to Jack Bermingham's work in having the annual horse show support the funds of the association and was aided also by Mrs Sparks' organisation of an annual card drive, which proved a great fund raiser. There was a very diverse programme of events including a special 'What Does the Panel Think?', organised with great success by Michael Harrington, the panel including Andy Wright, Sean Óg Ó Tuama, Gerry Wheeler and Dr Karl Mullen: altogether a combustible combination. Finally, in connection with the centenary year of 1960, the association organised a hugely successful formal dinner attended by almost 300 and with Donal Lamont, Bishop of Umtali, as guest of honour. By the time of the AGM of 1962, the efforts of the association had resulted in the raising of some £2,000 for the college building fund, and despite the passing of their great chairman, Jack Bermingham, the future of the association appeared promising.

310

T.M. McLoughlin joined the teaching staff at Terenure in 1954.

Long jump in progress at the sports day, 1952.

Terenure supporters watch a rugby match, 1952.

M. Healy, junior rugby captain (in the college strip) and J. Cahill, senior rugby captain (right),
at a Terenure junior match, 1957.

Parents, pupils and past pupils wait outside the
new chapel following its dedication, 1957.

314

Presentation of the Junior Cup by the
captain's mother, Mrs T. Cahill, 1955.

THE TWENTY YEARS FROM 1945 WERE DECIDEDLY YEARS OF CHANGE AND growth. It is possible, however, in chronicling change, to overlook continuities. Some of that continuity, admittedly, has been witnessed in reference to the working lives of that central core of lay teachers whose key members had, already, celebrated silver jubilees at Terenure by the mid-1950s or who, joining the staff in the late 1940s, were destined to long lives of service, with close on twenty years behind them by 1965.

Continuity reinforcing a sense of community was also borne out by the persistence of dynasties or clans of leading Terenure families and their boys, whether day or boarders. Some of these have already been noted: there were seven Clarkes from 1927 to 1947: Frank, Joe, Carmelites Noel and Desmond, then Hugh, Gerald and Paul; the five Doyle brothers from 1933 to 1952: Terence, Paddy, Joachim, James and Fintan, as distinct from the three Doyle brothers of Baltinglass: Joseph, Brendan and Kevin who flourished from 1951 to 1963. Quickly following the earlier Dublin Doyles, some of whose own sons and grandsons joined in later times, were the five Searson brothers from 1934 to 1959: Jack, Liam, Frank, Noel and Arthur. A more enduring presence still was the 21 year stretch of the five O'Nolans from 1932 to 1953: starting with Colm, then Fergus, Eamon, Gearóid and on to Fr F.J. O'Nolan from 1943 to 1953. Well-remembered too were the Church boys from 1937 to 1954: Paddy, Hugh, Ray, John and Brendan, rugby lads all, whose number and presence led a sports reporter of their time to ask the college games-master if there were ever a Terenure rugby team that did not have a Church in it. Perhaps the same question might have been raised of a later clan, the five Tormey boys and their eighteen-year span from 1948 to 1966: starting with Kilian and on to Gerry, Simon, Peter and Pat. Almost, but not quite equalling them in range and numbers were the McMullen brothers originally from Bray, four of them from 1940 to 1946: Louis, Frank, Noel and Vincent; there was a foursome of Roches: Michael, Johnny, Patrick and Brian from 1948 to 1969 and a foursome of Blakes: David, Peter, Jim and John from 1949 to 1966; likewise, later came the Sparks clan of four boys from 1953 to 1971: Niall, Pat, Conor and Brian. Others clans were to follow in the decades ahead.

It is perhaps some compliment to the college that old dynasties continued well beyond the original invaders and that new ones developed in later years, such as the O'Connells, sons and grandsons of lay teacher and first vice-principal, Michael.

For the moment, we will depart from these dynasties but remain focused on the sense of community, family and continuity which was borne out in other simple, taken-for-granted ways from the late 1940s to the 1960s, in ways as simple and obvious as the track of a typical day or the trace of the seasons through a typical year. In this regard are two points, so obvious as to be easily overlooked: firstly, Terenure College for its boys as much as its Carmelites, was a distinctly religious environment where the days and the seasons were marked by the conventions and practices of the liturgical year; and, secondly, the college for a long time held on to its pastoral ways, even as it became a green enclave surrounded by the ever-growing suburbs.

A Day in the Life:

Many who arrived, or left, in the course of the 1950s would have recalled the place as Mike Murphy did so fondly and memorably:

> ... a spacious yard for playing in, an orchard for robbing, a gymnasium with a tuck shop, two handball alleys and the bicycle shed, where those boys who were disturbingly sophisticated and daring could go for a few pulls of a cigarette during the breaks.[1]

Nevertheless, despite the familiarity of place, reconstructing a typical day out of fifteen or twenty years might seem beset with difficulty and, admittedly, there would be different contours visible whether viewed from the perspective of a boarder on the one hand or a day-pupil on the other; yet, these boys though living somewhat different lives had strong elements in common within the confines of a single day or the boundaries of a given year. The fact that day-boys had virtually the free run of the place out of school hours and school terms — in an era before 'no win, no fee' litigation and automatic insurance claims — diluted that difference of experience. In the memories of many day-boys, this was one of Terenure's most cherished features all their schooldays: it was both adventure playground and home from home, as it proved too for boarders, especially those who departed last on vacation and returned first, happier to be here than at some colder domestic hearths. However, it does not serve to romanticise too much the joys of the place: it was an institution and as such run according to routine and regulations, however benign.

For the boarder, the typical day began at 7.30 a.m. with rising and ablutions; then it was Mass in Latin, at 8.00 a.m. in the oratory and on to breakfast in the refectory half an hour later: porridge, bread, butter and tea from the great urn, supervised by 'Cook' and 'Queenie' the matron. New boys, lost on their first mornings, found their way to the refectory by following the waves of voices. One who sat down to breakfast on his first day, and asking a fellow boarder to pass the sugar for the porridge was greeted by a roar of laughter: luxuries were in short supply or, if they existed, they did so through the largesse of parents and relatives and were safely stored in the boarder's locker. One such experience was that of Fr Des Kelly of the class of 1956: he received butter from home and kept it safely in his locker. As time went by and he and his mates became more experienced, they realised that Fridays were an especially lean day for grub; pooling their pennies, they would requisition a day-boy to purchase a barm brack, and, with scant regard for use-by-dates, Des's unlockered butter would then find its best purpose.

Morning classes started at 9.00 a.m. until a break in the yard two hours later when handball and football would materialise in an all-too-brief frenzy. Then back to classes before lunch and then the dreaded double-class from 2 to 3.45 — the class that would ever drag. Wednesday, admittedly, brought the relief of a half-day when the morning classes ended with 'Benno' or benediction and where the real challenge to the adventurous was to dodge it without being detected: so successfully, perhaps, that in September 1964, Fr Clarke had issued a decree that 'One and all had to attend Benediction. An early appointment with the dentist will not be accepted as an excuse'. Class-end at 3.45 p.m. brought the inevitable rugby or alternative recreational break, followed by private study or piano with Mr Pentony from 5.20 to 6.00 p.m., this latter a crucial hour-mark of the day when the entire flock of up to 100 boarders would be gathered in with strays being checked for: then, to 'tea', of beans on toast or fried bread. The rosary followed, taking them up to around 7.00 p.m. for further study till 8.30 p.m.: a final recreation break, for juniors till 9.00 p.m. and for seniors till 10.00 p.m. — and so to bed, if not to sleep.

Saturdays in those years entailed morning classes, even in junior school, up to 12.15 p.m. and then the great march down to confession, with benediction too on that day as on Holy Days, as Dennis McGrane recalled; and, for the day-pupils it was then off home for lunch but only to be soon back up to college again for the afternoon of rugby matches.[2] Sundays brought Mass at 9.00 a.m., breakfast, more study, as Felim Corr recalled; after that came the letter-writing home and the dash to the letter-box set in the boundary wall by the main entrance, the letter being deposited by leaning over the wall and so not violating the rule of being off the premises.[3] One Sunday in four brought the free day out — or half day more like — out on the 54A bus to town and the cinema or the match in Croke Park or Donnybrook or more daringly for seniors, to the afternoon tea dance at the Metropole. Alternatively, it might be a trip to Dún Laoghaire, or, better still for those whose domicile was within reach, a quick dash home and back, be it to Skerries or Bray or Blessington from whence lockers could be replenished for the month that lay ahead. It was rare indeed for that Sunday free time to be abused by failure to return by six or seven: there was an occasion, as one of the class of 1953 recalled, that a boarder who came in late — and probably the worse for the wear — was condemned to expulsion, with the sentence, uniquely and sadly, being proclaimed in front of the whole assembly of boarders.

For the other three Sundays there was permission to wander to the far side of the lake — as Felim Corr and P.J. Cunningham separately remembered — and to watch Terenure College Rugby Football Club matches in the playing fields beyond it: then it was back to tea and prayers and to the delights of the Sunday film show. Because the boarders' life was so relatively confined, such confinement proved an added incentive to seek selection on the rugby teams since selection entailed getting off early to travel to away matches.

One remembered grief of Sunday mornings was that they could be reserved for a sermon of stern remonstrance and reprimand for any serious mischief or misdeeds perpetrated in the course of the previous week. Against this, one remembered treat — after the letter-writing was done and posted — was securing the Sunday paper of one's choice (or political preference). The legendary general *factotum*, Pat Walsh, of whom more anon, would be commissioned to head off after 11.00 a.m., out the Fortfield Road side-gate and down to Smith's newsagents in Greenlea, at the back of the college;

his return precipitated the usual mad scramble for the papers and the coveted seats at the wall by the orchard.

Dormitory diversions were few enough in the 1950s and 1960s although the dorms could be lively places of muted and occasionally not-so-muted debate, after lights out — and this despite a changing weekly rota of senior prefects occupying the strategic beds at the four corners of each dorm; and, before the opening of the new rooms for the Community as a result of the 1957 construction work, the Community rooms and sleeping quarters included a friar's room, with sliding hatch, at one end of a dorm.

One boarder who much later came to share a missionary life in Africa with that continent's first native white Carmelite, Cyprian Kennedy, was Fr Michael Hender. Michael was boarding when Cyprian was at the Carmelite brother stage of his vocation, based in Terenure and doing night-duty in the dorms despite teaching and studying during his days. A sense of the boys' night-time clowning is well-rendered by Michael:

> Our very large senior dormitory was often a lively place even after we had settled into the blankets and when the ten o'clock time for silence had passed. Discussions and arguments were loudly expressed about the events of the day that had occurred in the classroom or on the sports field. Humorous threats and remarks would be thrown at those who showed no sign of changing their stubborn opinions. During one such noisy commotion the shadow of a tall figure was spotted outside the glass door at the entrance of the dormitory. Suddenly there was complete silence everywhere except for one or two pretending to be snoring. The door handle clicked: the shadow entered; it was Brother Cyprian Kennedy. He stood there motion-less. Were we going to be rebuked severely for being so rowdy? Everyone seemed to be holding their breath. Then he moved in the darkness, walking slow-step by slow-step to the centre of the dormitory. He stopped there; now maybe we were going to hear a harsh harangue. Then, without saying a word, he left through that door. As soon as Brother had exited, Jude McGovern of Cavan, who was in the bed next to mine in the middle of the dormitory, stood up on his bed and imitating a guitarist began to sing quite loudly this popular song of that era,' If we know you were coming we'd have baked a cake, baked a ...'. The door by which Brother had left opened and he re-entered. Jude disappeared at high speed, head and all, under the blankets. Now, were we, and especially Jude, in for thunderous fireworks? No; after an elongated thirty seconds of sus-penseful silence, with not even a snore this time, Brother left again and we all slept happily ever after.[4]

The penetration of contemporary popular songs into the sacred time and place that was the college in those days owed not a little to one item of then modern invention — the transistor radio. Scarce and expensive though they initially were, one made its way into Terenure's night corridors through the person of an English boarder, Timothy Wallace. Michael Hender recounts:

> In the 1950s a transistor radio was a great novelty. The only pupil with one was Timothy Wallace who was English. On a Saturday night there was always a very popular musical programme called The Top Twenty, at 10 p.m. By that time we were supposed to be asleep in our very large dormitory or at least keeping the rule of silence. Timothy had his head and the transistor under the blankets listening to the top pop songs. Others in the dormitory could barely hear them ... just a very muffled sound. Then a student's loud, threatening voice would come through the air, 'Look, Wallace, turn that thing UP or turn it OFF'. If he turned it up it might be heard outside the dormitory, thus attracting the attention of the authorities. So it was usually turned off. At daytime Timothy liked to get involved in discussions and arguments even when his presence at times was not very welcome. He liked to express his opinion in arguments that were sometimes quite serious and heated. He gave the impression that what he said was quite decisive and final. Usually this did not go down well with the others. Then Vinnie Nolan, in a nice, slow Kildare accent, would bring things to a conclusion by saying 'Well, Timothy, there's a lot in what you say but by no means everything!' The others felt quite satisfied with this pronouncement but it usually left a puzzled expression on Timothy's face.

The inevitable high jinks apart, the pupils whether boarder or day, were well-grounded in the religious practices and liturgical passage of the year. Those who spent even a few years, and many spent up to ten between junior and senior cycles, soon became accustomed to that unfolding pageant: Mass for the opening of the academic year; then the three-day school retreat, around the feast of St Therese on 1 October; Advent and the preparation of carols and Christmas hymns; the blessing of the throats on the feast of St Blaise every 3 February; Lent with its self-denial and the dramatic liturgy of Holy Week; the Easter vacation and then the celebration of Whit: and steadily throughout the year came the learning of sacred song and plain-chant, the daily routine of prayers at start and finish, with Angelus at midday. Such cycles were there from foundation in 1860 and endured for a long time, certainly well into the 1960s when Vatican II heralded a time of profound and far-reaching liturgical change. There was, of course, also that secular and sometimes mysterious seasonal cycle of boys' games, from marbles and push-halfpenny to conkers, together with the more official cycle of rugby to spring, then some GAA and soccer, cricket and tennis from spring to summer, and handball all year round.

ARCADIA IN SUBURBIA:

Well into the 1960s, the place remained a pastoral retreat with its still extensive fields and gardens, and its farming and horticultural rituals from autumn through winter to summer. There were now the electric fences to keep the cattle corralled and so often the source of pranks by pupils and Carmelites alike. From the routine harvesting of the hay to the occasional helping to douse the fires that mysteriously beset the odd hayrick; from assisting with bringing in the apples; to the regular yet excited recording of the arrival of the threshing machines; and on to the November picking of the potatoes, this last no great attraction perhaps, though for some anywhere was better than class. Better still was to be sent out into town to the Mansion House to help with the annual sale-of-work for the Carmelite Missions each October. And best of all, perhaps, was the excitement of preparation and production of the annual school play, staged just before the Christmas break: such diversions came around with the same regularity as the operations of the college farm. Farming activities were still very much in evidence in the early to mid-1960s: so Fr Bob Kelly clearly recalled when he was pursuing his teaching practice there in the 1962–3:

> The College was still a farm in 1962–63, with two men working it fulltime, one from Cavan and the other, the herdsman Harry Daly; there were only a few pitches at the time, the great part devoted to crops: there were still five or six cows providing the College's milk, one or two sows and their litters; and a tractor, an early David Browne model driven by the Cavan man: there was still a vegetable garden, and the field along the Fortfield Road provided oats, turnips and hay.[5]

Others too, like Fr Joe Ryan and actor Michael Grennell, as late on as the class of 1976, remembered the grazing cattle, mowing machines, the birthing of calves and the squealing of piglets at the back of the farm.[6]

SERVANTS AND RETAINERS:

Adding to the homely atmosphere and the seemingly timeless continuity of the place in these decades was the background presence of the long-serving college servants and retainers. For many years, two cooks and the matron or nurse not only presided over the vital concerns of feeding, caring and curing, but actually lived on the premises until the mid-1960s at least. Even after that, when Nurse Eileen O'Beirne joined the staff in September 1965 and served until her retirement at the start of the 1990s, she continued to reside in the college until sadly she passed away in 1992. As to the farm, there were still its ever-faithful draught horses, Sandy and McGregor, and herdsman

Jim Heenan who lived with his family in the gate lodge closest to the main entrance. Jim had been land steward and grounds man for twenty years from 1935–6 when he decided to retire home to Tipperary following the passing of his wife.[7]

Others who seemed to be a permanent part of the landscape were Percy and Mrs Austin who lived in the old 'Yellow House' on the grounds. Percy was somehow involved in grounds upkeep while Mrs Austin organised the college laundry: many recalled the newly washed rugby jerseys blowing in the wind in her garden. Another abiding presence was that of old Jim King, carpenter, maintenance man and traditional fiddler *par excellence* who lived in what once had been Ryan's house on the grounds at the rear of the college and which later was known as King's house. Other retainers ranged from the college dentist, J.W. Thornton, in the 1950s and 1960s, the doctor, Sean Lavan, college medical adviser from at least 1944 to 1966, William Kerr the cobbler who lived in the other gate lodge on Templeogue Road, and the long-suffering and long-shearing college barber, Joe Doran. However, the most enduring of its corporeal presences that created that timeless sense of continuity was the college's most eminent of grey eminences, Pat Walsh.

The Saint Peter of Terenure College:

Pat Walsh came to work in the college from at least 1946. Some say that he was 26 when he came there: others believe he was much younger, a mere youth who came to Terenure as a houseboy. Whatever the truth, he was there for at least 50 years until he finally took his keys to the Kingdom in 1996. Houseboy perhaps, but janitor certainly to the junior school: however, as time rolled on it seems his duties simply grew year by year. With his bunch of 100 keys, he became the general custodian of the college where his vigilance was combined with great diligence and his honesty with courtesy: the 'St Peter of Terenure College' is how another legendary college retainer, Ita Clancy, described him.[8] An immensely fussy man who shuddered at the thought of ever being taken by surprise, he needed to know everyone's plans or changes of plan long in advance, in order to be prepared. Such was the range and yet regularity of his routines that pupil and priest alike could tell the time by Pat's place and purpose. Walking with a limp, and thereby nicknamed 'The Duck', he came up from Kerry where he had received a very good primary education to become either houseboy or janitor, at everyone's beck and call. He set and lit the fires early in the morning and kept them going all day, served the priests in their refectory; he did their rooms, spreading the dust about with his busy duster. In time his empire extended, spreading to take control of the ordering and supply of copy-books, text-books and stationery which he dispensed from the fortress that was his copy-book office, that Holy of Holies into which none dared trespass. He tended to the boiler house and manned the phones, or rather the phone, as, for long, there was only one such apparatus in the place: it was, after all, that other Ireland where possession of a phone was a rare and greatly prized privilege. Fr Jackie Madden, a Dubliner born in 1932 and educated at St Vincent's CBS, joined the

Carmelites in 1949 following an interview with Conleth Fitzgerald in Terenure College and then pursued his teaching practice there in 1954. He was well-placed to discern Pat Walsh's comings and goings and vividly recalls how assiduous Pat was in the matter of phone calls, as in all else. When Fr Jackie came back to college in 1958 as a full-time member of the teaching staff and spent the next 22 unbroken years in Terenure, there was still only one phone and Pat was still manning it.[9] Then in 1974, when Ita Clancy came in as receptionist, there was a more elaborate switchboard system and Pat would take over control of an evening or during Ita's annual vacations. She and Fr Jackie separately remember him manning it with such attention to duty that were a friar for whom there was a call not immediately in evidence, Pat would search out the missing monk in whatever distant corner or corridor of the premises: he did so with such relentless success that he came to be called 'the Mounty', since he always got his man.

A diminutive figure, yet one never to be bested, Pat Walsh had all the boys in his sights and little escaped his alert gaze. He knew all the trouble-makers only too well and would not desist from besieging the poor, preoccupied Priors, following them doggedly, regardless of what urgent business they might have in hand or to what latest emergency they might be heading, and Pat would persist until they heard from him which miscreant had perpetrated which latest mischief. Dutiful as he was, he was also a man of great independence. He took his two-week vacation every summer and either spent them cycling the far corners of Ireland or else spent one week helping some friend make hay and the other helping Miss Lawlor of Naas at the Horse Show in the RDS where she had an annual catering contract. A great man for exercise, as if he did not get enough of it traipsing the corridors in his long and crowded days, every Sunday after lunch he would walk into the city and walk back in the evening. On reaching his retirement in his sixty-fifth year, he was moving out of the college of his own volition, quietly and quickly, and had to be persuaded by Frs McCouaig and Clarke to accept the invitation to stay in what long been his home: so there he remained until a stroke in his last years brought him into hospital for an extended period. As befitted the closeness of his relations with the college and the Carmelites, Pat donated one of the new stained-glass windows for the chapel; in turn, in 1993, the Carmelites admitted him as an affiliated member of their Order and when he died, in 1996, he was interred in the Carmelite plot in Glasnevin — a unique distinction, then and since.

CENTENARY COMMEMORATIONS:

With characters such as these colouring the landscape of their days and years the boys and their Carmelite mentors could well feel at home in some timeless place where routine and regimen ruled their lives. For all that, however, there was one event of these times that proved the exception: in 1960, the college reached its centenary. A time for reflection and retrospection, it was also one for rejoicing: the most difficult years, it seemed, were behind and nine decades of ups and downs had culminated in a decade of unprecedented growth and success: new staff, religious and lay, rising vocations, unslackening demand for pupil places; new chapel, new concert hall, new classrooms and facilities now joined old certainties of faith and season.

The impact of that one hundreth birthday is today seen perhaps most lastingly in the pages of the college *Annual* for 1960: larger than ever, with more images than ever, in some ways it should be a collector's item. Yet, in compiling it for the occasion and in trying to reconstruct that previous 100 years, the editorial team and the college authorities admitted the difficulties of the task:

> We had to wrestle with gaps in the records, defective records, pictures without names attached, feeble memories and traditions that could not be substantiated, and a hundred and one other enemies of authentic history ... How easy it would be if we could publish the apocryphal with the authentic![10]

Nonetheless, it was with justifiable pride that their opening pages included special greetings from Pope John XXIII, through his secretary of state, Cardinal Domenico Tardini, as also from their own Prior General in Rome. From here, the American-born Kilian Healy congratulated the college and his Irish Carmelite confreres for the special place they had achieved for faith and fatherland:

> The Carmelite Order is justly proud of its oldest school in secondary education which has given to Ireland God-fearing young men, who have fought for their country's freedom, worked diligently for its educational and social advancement and valiantly defended and preserved the Faith.

He singled out for special mention Terenure's remarkable contribution to missionary activity in Australia, America and Africa: by these endeavours alone, 'Terenure College has every right to rejoice on the occasion of her centennial anniversary'.[11]

While all associated with the college might indeed rightly rejoice, one might surmise that for one individual in particular that 1 May 1960, assigned as the special day for the centennial celebrations, must have been especially treasured — James Carmel O'Shea. Now Provincial for his third time in four terms, as college president from 1931 to 1937, he had kept his faith in the college and his confidence for its future at a time when some of his confreres were losing heart and might have left it to founder.

When he described the occasion as 'an event of very special joy for the whole Irish Province of the Order', it cannot be doubted that it was an event of very special joy for himself also, even as he wrote movingly of the founding fathers: 'These were men of mercy whose godly deeds have not failed' (*Eccles*, 44:10).

At a time in Ireland when Church and state dwelt in conspicuous harmony the formal celebration of the event brought their leaders in some strength to the college. From Church officialdom on that Sunday, 1 May, feast day of the college's patron saint, Joseph the Worker, came Apostolic Nuncio Antonio Riberi, and from Rome directly, the Prior General Dr Healy and his Assistant General the modest but distinguished historian of the international Carmelite Order, Joachim Smet; from Dublin, Archbishop John Charles McQuaid, and out of Africa for the occasion, Donal Lamont, now Bishop of Umtali. There were also among the high clergy present Dr Daniel Conway, at that time Auxiliary to Cardinal D'Alton the Archbishop of Armagh. Finally, from the Church side an extensive presence of leading Carmelites from Ireland and overseas as well as the Provincials of several other Irish religious orders and presidents of Irish Catholic colleges.

Representing the state there came one of many old acquaintances, Eamon de Valera, now president of Ireland, and, with him, his predecessor in that office, Seán T. O'Kelly. An Taoiseach, Seán Lemass, headed the government party which included Minister for External Affairs Frank Aiken. There came, too, another old friend of the college, W.T. Cosgrave, together with Dublin's Lord Mayor, Seán Brady, and UCD's president, Michael Tierney, with his colleague, Professor Tom Wheeler. The army top brass included Colonel S. Brennan and Captain J. O'Brien, the aide de camps to the president and the Taoiseach respectively. Friends of the college, officers of its various societies, notably the PPU, and the whole student body crowded the college chapel for the High Mass where the Prior General was celebrant.[12]

The various dignitaries were met on arrival by the 100 strong guard of honour from the 20th Battalion, FCA, together with the No. 1 Army Band, while the avenue was lined by the college Boy Scouts and the pupils smartly turned out in dark blazers and crisp white slacks. Inside the chapel, the sacred music, concluding with *Te Deum*, was gracefully provided by the choir of clerical students from Gort Muire Carmelite theologate, their singing conducted by Fr Joe Ryan.

If the occasion had special meaning for Provincial O'Shea, it must also have had rich resonance for the preacher on the occasion, past pupil and past teacher, Donal Lamont. Speaking to the text 'You are the Light of the World', his sermon was electric in substance and delivery. At this remove, the Ireland of which he then spoke now seems another country in another time:

> Our country that is like no other — no fretful, anxious hurrying to
> and fro ... no frequent evidence of great luxury or wealth ... an unusual
> unworldliness, a peacefulness, a benediction ... [with] this singular
> sense of the Divine, this national awareness of God's Presence ...

all of which, he felt, was greatly due to the work of the country's Catholic schools. Adverting to the deep contemporary divisions between East and West, between communism and democracy, he observed these as transitory states where inherited prejudices were daily losing the battle against the 'more obvious truth of the brotherhood of men under the fatherhood of God'. He urged trust in the special role of Ireland as a place of faith and a culture which despises 'the shallowness and half-heartedness of the largely unbelieving West no less than it despises the tyranny of the professedly atheistic East'.

Unencumbered by colonial possessions and unembarrassed by their memory, Ireland had a faith that could 'renew the face of the earth'. Terenure College, he asserted, by continuing to inculcate in its boys, reverence for God, true scholarship and that 'reasonable patriotism ... which has regard for the rights of other nations in the common family of men', would ensure its contribution to that renewal. In his conclusion, he asked his hearers to 'think of those whose charity had founded this College, whose faith carried it on and whose hope was to this day'. One pupil of the class of 1960 who stood in line to greet the dignitaries and who heard this sermon was Fr Bene O'Callaghan who recalls clearly to this day that moving and brilliant homily.

After the Mass, the college theatre was the venue for a VIP lunch for some 200 guests, with Fr Dunstan O'Connor as toastmaster. The opening toast, to the president of Ireland was the occasion for its proposer, Prior General Healy to recall the friendship between the Carmelites, the college and de Valera, going back to the days of Prior General Magennis, especially over the years 1919 to 1921. Growing up in Worcester, MA, as a young boy whose father hailed from Kerry, Dr Lynch recalled hearing his father singing the praises of de Valera and his work for Irish freedom. The toast, 'The College', was proposed by Tom Wheeler, Professor of Chemistry in UCD from 1945 to 1962 and who paid tribute to the quality of the education that his son, Desmond, received in Terenure: Desmond had already gone on to a distinguished science career and was already professor of chemistry at the University of Southern California even as the proud father was proposing this toast. He took the opportunity to point out to his audience, including Taoiseach Lemass, how the Carmelites and other Orders had built, equipped and staffed their schools 'without a halfpence of expense to the State'. In the speech which followed, Prior Patrick Burke paid a special tribute to the lay teaching staff of the college, while Provincial O'Shea spoke warmly of the college's old friends, Seán T. Ó Ceallaigh and W.T. Cosgrave 'who as a rebel on the run had [once] taken shelter in Terenure College'. Finally came the reading of the many telegrams from the mightiest to the humblest, and perhaps the most touching coming from far-off former pupil, teacher and now missionary, Mel Hill in Africa.

Against the background of that memorable day in the life of the college, other celebratory developments of that year would seem low-key by contrast. The Committee of the Past Pupils' Union, under the presidency of Joe Milroy, remained in office for eight months longer than their usual annual term: they decided to postpone the AGM so that there could be continuity of experience in assisting the college with its centenary activities. In late April, the union marked its own place in those activities with a huge attendance at its Pontifical High Mass, celebrated in the chapel by Bishop Lamont. Later, some 200 past pupils and their guests were entertained to a formal lunch in college at which they made a presentation of a new sanctuary lamp for the chapel.

Later on that year, a modest history was produced to mark the centenary; the boys were given a special free day in May; and, in the autumn, in recognition of all that Terenure had done for education, the Prior and president, Fr Burke, was conferred with an honorary doctorate in laws by the National University of Ireland and that special year was brought to a close in December with a Solemn High Mass and *Te Deum* sung by the Prior General of the Order.

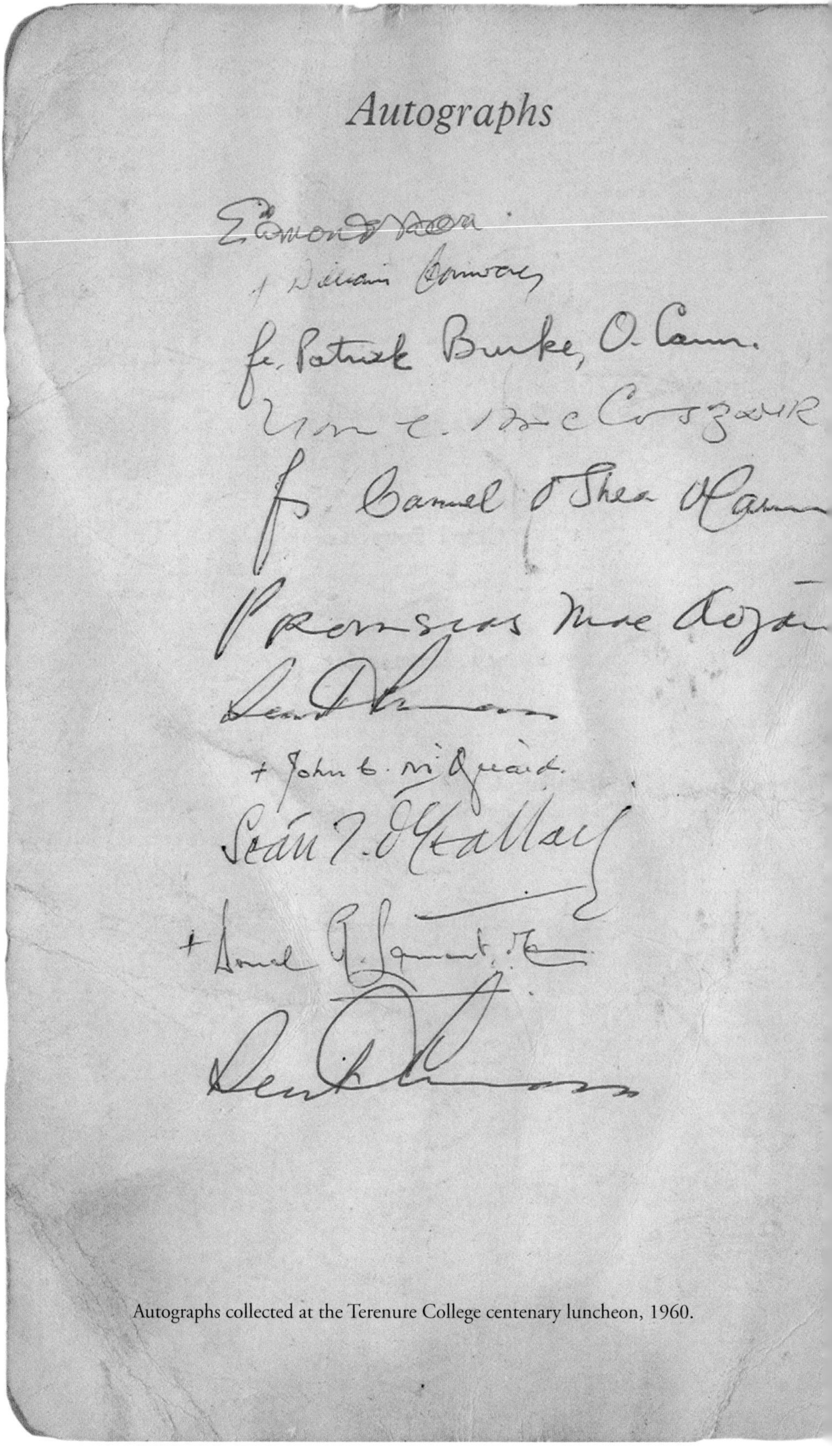

Autographs

Edward [?]

+ William Conway

fr. Patrick Burke, O. Carm.

Wm C. McCormack

fr. Carmel O'Shea O'Carm

Proinsias Mac Aogán

Seán [?]

+ John C. McQuaid.

Seán T. O'Ceallaigh

+ Donal R. [?], [?]

[?]

Boys line the avenue in welcome of President de Valera to the centenary celebrations, 1960.

335

Frank Aiken and W.T. Cosgrave leaving the
centenary Mass, 1960. © Irish Times.

336

Past pupil of the year, David Kennedy (centre), with Fr A.D. Weakliam and Mike Murphy at the PPU annual dinner, 1975.

TERENURE COLLEGE

1860   1960

Centenary

COMMEMORATION

Luncheon

1st MAY, 1960

Cover of the Centenary Commemoration luncheon booklet, 1960.

CHAPTER 18

Pupils and Past Pupils,
1951–65

Tree fallen on the Templeogue Road
outside the college, 11 July 1955.
© Irish Press.

IF THE CENTENARY CELEBRATIONS CAPTURED A SENSE OF ACHIEVEMENT AND pride, there was much to be proud of: a college once surviving and now thriving. It may not have placed academic triumph as its exclusive and all-consuming goal, but its students over these years were achieving significant success in Church, commerce and academia.

CARMELITE VOCATIONS:

As to Church, it was hardly surprising that from a college so imbued with the culture of Carmel that there were many and significant vocations to the Order in particular and to the priestly life in general. Some of these young men of the 1950s and early 1960s who entered the Order have already been encountered: Michael Hender and Stan Hession, for example, who left the college for the Order following the completion of their Leaving Certificates in 1953 and 1954 respectively. Then there was P.J. Cunningham of the class of 1955. From Timahoe, Co. Laois, where he was born in 1936, he was third in a family of eight whose father Patrick was in the defence forces. After schooling in Mountmellick, P.J. entered Terenure in September 1950 as a boarder and postulant: he did so in a context in which numbers of religious congregations at the time were actually visiting schools, though in his case, despite overtures from Franciscans and De La Salle Brothers, it was a recommendation from his headmaster in favour of the Carmelites of Kildare that led to the initial and decisive contacts with Provincial Conleth Fitzgerald, which led to his enrolment in Terenure. Taken up to the college in a car his father borrowed, he was warmly welcomed by Frs Kevin Clarke and Prior Dominic Reale.

Completing his Leaving Certificate in 1955 — with special success in science — he entered the novitiate at Kinsale, with another Terenure alumnus of the same year, Martin Farragher: as with any novitiate, a tough year, having no social contacts with the town and no letters home except at Christmas and Easter. The one diversion was a walk outside the walls every Sunday and then back to the routine of prayer, study and work under novice master Claude Tyndall — himself once a teacher at Terenure. The Tyndalls of Naas had been Protestants who converted to Catholicism and gave two sons to the Church and the Carmelites. From Kinsale it was on to the House of Studies at Gort Muire — opened by the Order since the mid-1940s — and from where he cycled daily to UCD to study for his BA. If Kinsale was tough, Gort Muire was hardly less so — even while out at UCD, Gort Muire lads, like other clerical students, were discouraged from fraternising with the lay undergraduates. From BA and HDip in 1960 — with teaching practice at Terenure, and then back to Gort Muire for five more years of theology and philosophy, and ordination in 1964. On finally finishing his formal religious studies at Gort Muire it was back to Terenure for an extended period on the teaching staff — in P.J.'s case, until 1973 and then with periodic transfers to other Carmelite houses. This, while P.J.'s own experience, was very representative of the kind of career path followed by many of the Terenure vocations to the Carmelite Order in the 1950s and 1960s. But, anticipating changing times from the 1970s, when Fr P.J. was assigned to the quietly contemplative Carmelite Community at Knocktopher in 1973, under Fr Teddy Devane, that Community was to find itself being asked to break with tradition in the very next year when it became the first Irish Carmelite Priory to take over responsibility for the care of a parish. A sign of the times, perhaps, that would repeat itself in P.J.'s later life, when in 1992, he accepted temporary appointment as parish priest of Ballyhale, and then in 1993 finding himself in temporary parish ministry in Glasgow.[1] Neither he nor his confrere, Fr Des Kelly, would have predicted such a trajectory in the early 1960s.

Des Kelly of the class of 1956 was a Dubliner born in Drumcondra who grew up in Skerries and whose civil servant father had taken up the unusual career of patents agent. Des's arrival at Terenure in 1950 was partly due to the fact that the local De La Salle secondary school in Skerries was only in its infancy and unable to provide the full range of subjects that Des's father thought appropriate; but it was also due to the example of a neighbour, Milo Reddy, then studying engineering and whose Terenure experience had been extolled by his family. Milo had had an excellent record during his Terenure years from 1947 to 1952 and graduated from UCD as an engineer in 1956.[2] Des quickly came to enjoy his Terenure years, especially the Shakespeare productions and the elocution classes given by gifted elocution teacher, Corkman and Abbey actor, Eddie Golden. As befitted a master of his craft, Eddie was adept at identifying accents and teasing the boys about them: on Des's first day at elocution Eddie got him up to speak and immediately interrupted him: 'North Dublin — Rush — but we'll soon knock that out of you!' For the young man from Skerries, life after the Leaving Certificate was not dissimilar to Fr P.J.'s, the Kinsale novitiate, the further years of study, and, like P.J., and indeed anticipating him, he experienced the changed times post 1960s, of being a contemplative Carmelite in an active parochial ministry, for, in 1978, the Order sent him as parish priest to their new responsibility in Glasgow.[3]

A contemporary of Des in the class of 1956 was another Dubliner with a Carmelite vocation — Fr Billy Langan, eldest of three boys in a family of four. There is not a person who passed through Terenure over the eighteen years from 1982 who would not have known and loved this legendary figure: teacher, sportsman and illustrious coach in tennis and badminton: but this is matter for a later place. In a way, he was almost a local, growing up in Harold's Cross and later Templeogue, but his earlier schooling was in St Louis's, Rathmines, and then Synge Street. The change from Synge Street to Terenure was a practical one, with its greater proximity to home, but while that may have been the prime parental consideration, for young Billy Langan the irresistible inducement was that Terenure's sports grounds were on the premises: an athletic youngster has to have his priorities right. Were Fr Billy to be fully believed, in Terenure he 'engaged in everything that wasn't study': wing forward in rugby for the seniors, but more important still — inheriting the mantle of the great Archie Fitzpatrick by becoming college No. 1 in both juniors' and seniors' tennis at various stages, apart from not being short of a step or two for success in the long jump.

Mysterious indeed the ways of the Lord — this tennis supremo had earlier been a Harold's Cross altar server and when the Leaving Certificate finished he represented Leinster against Ulster in the Irish under-18 interprovincial championships on 13 August: three weeks later, he entered the Kinsale Carmelite novitiate, on 31 August 1956. Along with Des Kelly, he was one of five Terenure alumni out of sixteen young men who entered that year. Like Des's and P.J.'s, his was a similar path, UCD for a BA, Terenure for teaching practice, Gort Muire for theology years, but then, to Moate where he was on its teaching for seventeen happy years and where he became a major Community presence, before returning to his old school at Terenure, as chaplain and later as Bursar.[4]

Another alumnus who joined the Order in these years was Cork-born (Thomas) Cyril O'Callaghan, known to confreres and later pupils as Fr Bene. Middle child in a family of two boys and a girl, Bene and his older brother Seán, both found themselves in Terenure College in the 1950s and did so indirectly through a family loss: the death of their sister Mary, aged only four, brought the bereaved family into contact with the Carmelites through Fr Declan Sugrue who offered great comfort and support at that time. Parents Cornelius and May — who ran a grocery shop on the Bandon Road — having heard good things of Terenure from friends and neighbours, consulted Fr Sugrue with the consequence that Seán entered the college in 1956 and then, after his Intermediate Certificate in 1958, Cyril came too as one of almost 120 boarders. The inevitable homesickness eventually left and close classmate friendships soon formed. Among his contemporaries of that year were Chris Crowley, a Valentia Island lad, destined to a senior position in the Order three decades later, as Provincial for two terms from 1982 to 1988, and Don Moore whose son, Eoin, a generation later would be Terenure pupil, teacher and Carmelite Community member.

As a Terenure pupil, Fr Bene was perhaps refreshingly different — he was not a hero at sports, played rugby without shining, and played tennis for a while till his rackets disappeared. Instead, he performed at the piano under Mr Pentony and played the harmonium for Fr Joe Linus Ryan when the latter was trying to cultivate the charism of Gregorian chant among Bene's classmates. Nor did he neglect the theatre, anticipating his own role in later life by taking the role of Friar John in the December 1959 Romeo and Juliet — opposite Donal McCann's Fr Laurence.[5] The Terenure of his college days was a friendly place, its friendly atmosphere being greatly enhanced by the presence and the kindness of its young Carmelite clerical students. It came as no surprise, therefore, to family, friends or teachers, that after his Leaving Certificate, he too joined the Order. He started his novitiate year of 1960–1 with Fr Chris Crowley and Tony McDonald who spent so many years in Zimbabwe. He followed the by-then well-trodden path to Gort Muire, UCD, teaching practice and the classroom, except that, in his case, having started in UCD Arts in 1961 he switched to UCD Science from 1962 to 1965, the Order then needing science teachers. Following his ordination and years of further study and after a year in Whitefriar Street he was posted back to Terenure for a year to teach science and religion and later to pursue other responsibilities as well, including a major role with Terenure Scouts as will later emerge.

Two boys who preceded him in Terenure and who were destined for distinguished roles in the Order were Chris O'Donnell and Adrian David Weakliam. Like Billy Langan, Chris was almost a local: born in 1936, a Ranelagh lad who first went to school in Harold's Cross, he served as an altar boy and was known as 'The Bishop' from his dignified way of processing in Church. His father, from Killybegs, worked for the ESB, while his mother, Eithne Coyle from Gortahurk, was well-known as president of Cumann na mBan: something of a romantic desperado of a revolutionary, revolver in hand she had once, during the War of Independence, held up the Letterkenny mail-train to see who was writing to the police. Given what has been said, much earlier in this work, about the Carmelites and the national struggle, Chris clearly had impeccable antecedents. It was not these, however, which dictated the parental decision to transfer him to Terenure; rather it was the national strike of primary teachers in 1946. Here he enrolled in preparatory or, in effect, the third year of junior school, where other classmates also then joining included two future Carmelites, Paul Graham and David Weakliam. Greeting Chris on his arrival was gentle Ossie McGrath who, with his brother Emmanuel — also a Carmelite — were nephews of the illustrious Peter Elias Magennis. Fr Ossie's commitment to chess and his gift of inspiring others to take it up and excel passed to Chris, as to others, as Chris and classmates went on to junior and senior prizes in the Leinster schools: by his own final year, 1954, Chris was on the Irish international side. Such impressive diversions apart, Chris's heart was set on becoming a priest and he was sought out in that regard by the Redemptorists. However, with his Leaving Certificate behind him in 1954 and the memory and experience of the kindness of Frs Paddy Burke and Tommy Brennan to the fore, the Redemptorists had no hope — it was Kinsale and the Carmelites or nothing. His post-Kinsale years followed the standard after that: Chris pursued a masters in English in UCD on the subject of the great fourteenth century English mystic, Richard Rolle. Not many can say that they had for external examiner on their research dissertation the great J.R.R. Tolkien: Chris, in all frankness and humility, confesses the great Tolkien's stern judgement and backhanded compliment: 'this young man is not to get a first class honours because of the arrogant way in which he writes', he decided. The judgement did not stop Chris O'Donnell's brilliant scholastic career, but eventually, he did learn his lesson. One of the first Irish Carmelites to secure his PhD at the Gregorian University in Rome some twenty years later, the PhD examiner for that occasion not only recommended the award of the degree but complimented the candidate on 'the courteous manner in which he treated writers with whom he disagreed'. Well-before then Chris's career path had diverged significantly from the pattern of learning at Terenure and coming back to teach at Terenure — in the late 1960s, he studied Hebrew and Syriac under the scholar and future archbishop, Dermot Ryan, before being assigned to teach theology at Gort Muire and then to Rome for doctoral studies. It was a short-lived sojourn in the Holy City on this occasion as the new Provincial, Fr Joe Ryan, brought him back to act as Assistant Provincial for what turned out to be the best part of six or seven years.[6]

The last of their classmates who would be a future Carmelite, to be considered at this point, was fellow-Leaving Cert student of 1954 — Adrian, younger brother of the formidable athlete, Charlie Weakliam. Another Harold's Cross native, and like Billy Langan, Adrian started off in St Louis's, Rathmines, before moving on to Terenure in 1945. Here like so many other contemporaries, he found a 'home from home', in part through the very friendly relations of pupils and priests, and in part because of the wide range of recreational diversions, from sport to chess to camera club and much else besides. As he and his many classmates of 1954 recalled, 'what a good time and what a good place in our lives it was'. After UCD, where he took science and philosophy, and after ordination in 1963 and the obligatory Milltown theology years over 1960 to 1964, it was, for Adrian, now Fr David, back to Terenure, teaching science and training rugby. By the end of the 1960s he was Sub-Prior and at the start of the 1970s dean of studies, effectively college principal. By that stage he was well on his way in a vocation that led, as shall be seen later, to the leadership of the college and the leadership of the Order in Ireland.

THE MEN OF COMMERCE:

For those in Terenure, as elsewhere in secondary education in Ireland at the time, who did not feel called either to serve Church or state, the options were mainly to commerce or to college, and on from the latter to academe or the professions. Many of the other 1930s and 1940s predecessors had made their way gradually into the hitherto impenetrable preserve of banking and insurance and would go on to leading positions in the major commercial banks or insurance companies. So it had been with Harry Woods (1937) in accountancy and marketing; Charlie Weakliam (1948) from insurance into banking with the Royal Bank; James Doyle (1949) into insurance — ending as head of Royal; Richard Fleming (1945) into banking, for a long period with National City Bank; and Richard Dunne (1948) with Hibernian Insurance for 28 years. Many lads of the 1950s and early 1960s followed in their footsteps: Felim Corr and Brendan Kelly both of the class of 1958 into accountancy and likewise John Cotter, Patrick Moore and the rugby great, Brendan Sherry, both of the class of 1961; so too Brendan Dolan (1953) who gained worldwide experience in a short time, joining Alcan in Oxford and subsequently being sent to Nigeria and later British Guinea, and Michael O'Keeffe, a brilliant student of Irish and Classics in his Terenure days who, on qualifying as an accountant, became the first chief executive of the O'Flaherty Volkswagen Group. Jim Blake of the class of 1964 went into business and commercial travelling for the Barnes's Glen Abbey Group before later going into business for himself. Similarly in insurance, to take but two names from a host, there was Brian Fennell of the class of 1953 who became inspector for National Mutual Life in Australia; and Val Murphy of the class of 1955, committed secretary of the college's Boys' Club and who went on to a successful career with Norwich Union.

One area of commercial and semi-state activities where Terenure boys progressed from an early stage was Aer Lingus. Among its earliest, most successful and senior personnel were the McMorrow twins from Crossboy, Co. Sligo, who had entered the college in 1937 and left with their Leaving Certificate honours in 1943. A formidable force on the senior rugby team in their day, they became a formidable force in the infant national airline also: Aengus became manager at Shannon and Colm manager at Dublin: the quip soon arose that one could be seen off at Dublin Airport by one McMorrow only to be greeted at the other end by an identical McMorrow.[7] Other Terenure alumni in the early Aer Lingus years were Seán Logue of the class of 1944 and Des Doyle who was a pupil from 1936 to 1945; the latter rose to become its sales representative in Europe, having joined the company earlier and then become Middle East sales rep for Coca Cola before returning to the national carrier. They were followed into the company over the following decades by several former Terenure pupils among whom were Gerry Lawler of the class of 1948; John J. O'Donnell and Donagh Harrington of the class of 1954; Barry Fitzpatrick of 1955; David Kennedy of 1956; and Niall Herbert and Eugene McNamee of the class of 1957. The first three had entered Aer Lingus as pilots via the Irish Aer Corps while Eugene, a future PPU president in 1982, was to enter it at first in a temporary capacity during the Lourdes centenary of 1958, when the company was exceptionally busy and boasting in the securing of its first Constellation aircraft. Three years later, he was recruited into it and went on to serious studies in flight navigation and flight operations. He was soon promoted to flight operations officer and later to operations controller for the next 22 years. The Terenure–Aer Lingus tradition was passed on when his eldest son, Paddy of the class of 1985 went on to become airline pilot. In all of this, and keeping in mind the talents and abilities of those who were recruited, it will not have been unhelpful that the first chairman of Aer Rianta, and the first chairman of Aer Lingus was none other than Seán Ó hÚadaigh, one of Terenure's oldest past pupils, a founder member and former president of its Past Pupils' Union.[8]

The last of this Aer Lingus group considered here, David Kennedy, came to Aer Lingus by a very different route. From Terenure he went to UCD, and upon completing his degree, secured his master's in science. Accomplished in much that he undertook in Terenure, whether as student, actor or chess player, he went on to a distinguished career both commercial and academic. He was teaching at Kevin Street School of Technology while taking his MSc when he was recruited by Aer Lingus who promptly sent him to the USA, to the renowned Case Institute in Cleveland, where he developed expertise in operations research. By the late 1960s, Professor Michael McCormac of UCD had recruited him to teach on his pioneering MBA programme — then a major innovation in Irish business studies — and it was not long after this that David found himself heading up Aer Lingus operations in the States. Before too long, he had achieved the distinction of becoming CEO of Aer Lingus and shortly after that President Paddy Masterson of UCD had recruited him to the newly established professorship of strategic marketing. In all of this he remained a loyal and engaged Terenure past pupil, becoming president of its union in 1988.

In respect of all the major professions, to review the students of the college who went on to university to study for them in the 1950s and 1960s is to form an impression of a college that was now flourishing. To take but the two examples, of engineering and medicine: into engineering went, among others, Lorcan Murphy of the class of 1950; Dennis McGrane and Denis Quinlan of the class of 1951; Anthony Conlan, Milo Reddy and Eamonn Sweeney of 1952; Peter Kelly, John Riordan and Cormac McHenry of 1954; Mel Healy of 1959 — who went to work in computer engineering with General Electric in the United States — and Johnny Roche of the class of 1963. In medicine, among others were Peter Conlon of the class of 1950; the three O'Connor brothers Chris (1950); Hubert (1952) and Eugene (1953); there were George Matthar of the class of 1952 who went to practise in San Francisco; and his house captain, John B. Dillon, also of the class of 1952; Tim Wallace-Murphy (1953); Loman Cusack (1955), who had then been house captain; then there were the three Cahill brothers, Joe (1957) — captain of the first ever Terenure Junior Rugby Cup victors in 1955 — and his brothers Paddy (1960) and Tommy (1963); Seamus Healy in 1958 and his brother, Peter (Tony), in 1962; Philip Williams in 1959; Neville Smith in 1962; Dermot O'Brien in 1964. Finally from the class of 1960, T. Joseph McKenna. Born in Dublin on 5 August 1942, Joseph entered Terenure College's Elementary A Class in 1950 where among the first to greet him was Fr Ephraim Corbett, Dean of the junior school. Others he soon encountered were Frs Jim McCouaig, Patsy Keenan and Lar Hegarty, the latter so long-serving there that he was still going strong when Joseph's son, Peter, enrolled in the college a generation later. Among the well-remembered lay teachers were Michael 'The Liberator' O'Connell who lived near Templeogue Bridge, Eddie O'Hanlon and Joe 'The Hooley' Griffin. The original Terenure College supporters' rugby chant had been 'The Hooley, The Hooley, The Hasha, Hasha Hooley' and whether Mr Griffin acquired the nickname from the chant, or vice versa is a matter of conjecture.

From an early stage Joe became caught up in college sports and in time proved to be no mean rugby player. Indeed, he was selected for and played second row on the team that won the Junior Cup in 1958 in the year of that memorable double cup victory: 'a sound, heavy forward [he] used his weight to good purpose both in pushing to gain a scrum and in holding the push against a heavier eight' was how the college *Annual* reported his role. His classmates Peter Grant and Michael Black also featured on that team as did good friends , the gifted place-kicker Paddy Cahill, Dermot Herbert, the fullback with the devastating tackle, the superbly athletic Gerry Martin who captained that victorious XV, and those later legends of field and stage, respectively, Brendan Sherry and Donal McCann. Most of them continued to play rugby after leaving the college. Joseph himself was on the Senior College XV when it came to the 1960 season but lost out from playing in the final due to an eye injury.

In the wake of their Leaving Certificate examinations in 1960 some five of that class, including Chris Crowley, Tony McDonald, and Bene O'Callaghan entered the Carmelites. While Joe may have been tempted, he opted instead for medicine at UCD. He played rugby all the while during his six medical years there and then turned out for Terenure RFC in the Senior Cup teams of 1968 and 1969. He became an intern in St Vincent's over 1966–7 and then a research fellow under Frank Muldowney in 1967–8. The years 1969 to 1971 saw him become a resident at Georgetown University's medical school where he worked under Larry Kyle, before going on to Vanderbilt for seven years to 1979. Here he worked in the team of the pioneering endocrinologist, Grant Liddle who, among other achievements, developed the adrenalin gland test that now bears his name.

In 1978 Joseph returned to Ireland, to research and practice at St Vincent's and to lecture at UCD, where he became professor of investigative endocrinology. From 1996 to 2003 he was registrar of the Royal College of Physicians of Ireland and, over the same period, he held the important post of secretary to the Irish Committee for Higher Medical Training. Then in 2003, he had the distinction of election as president of the RCPI. He is currently chairman of the Irish Committee of Higher Medical Training and of the Forum of Irish Medical Training Bodies.

THE SCIENTISTS:

Finally, one of the little acknowledged strengths of Terenure from the 1950s and 1960s was that in the sciences of physics and chemistry. Little recognised it may have been, but when one considers the succession of young men who matured to form a cluster of brilliant scientists from the late 1960s onward, one can only conclude that Terenure College was a highly productive scientific incubator. Apart from people who went on to study science initially, like McKenna in medicine and Kennedy in operations research, there was the run of scientists that included Sé O'Connor of the class of 1954; Edward Keogh of 1955; Tony Scott of 1957; Patrick Flanagan of 1958; and Peter Mitchell of 1963. Of these, Edward Keogh went on to UCD to take his honours degree in chemistry under Tom Wheeler: he secured his DPhil in 1963 specialising in spectroscopy and nuclear magnetic resonance before moving into commercial scientific life.[9] Sé O'Connor had gone on to secure his MSc in molecular spectroscopy in 1960, following his BSc at UCD in the field of physics. After a year with Irish Ropes in Newbridge, he was persuaded by Professor Tom Nevin to return to UCD to take up an assistant lectureship and to resume his research in the field. He secured his PhD in the area in 1965–6 and went on to a brilliant career in research and teaching in physics there. However, he retained the closest links with Terenure College which he had entered in September 1945, thoroughly enjoying all his days there. Having attended a small local private school before that and seeing — as he journeyed along the Templeogue Road there — the Terenure lads besporting themselves on the college's extensive playing fields, he decided that he wanted to go and actually asked his parents to let him, though he suspects his father would have wished it in any case. Like so many others he came to enjoy the spontaneous fun-loving nature of the place, unfettered access to its sports fields and facilities at all times and the many spontaneous, sporting challenges that made the place a magnet for its boys. It also helped that Sé excelled at mathematics and it must have been to the chagrin of many of his mates that he enjoyed it so much and that it was to him a relaxation and recreation compared to other subjects. However, it was a strong anticipation of his future career that he took the college's science prize in his final year. It says everything for the loyalty that the institution engendered that Sé, like so many others, not only never lost contact with it, but remained actively and deeply committed to it — from the Charlemont Street Boys' Club project in the 1960s through careers guidance and the Parents' Association, on to the presidency of the union in 1994.

A later Terenure star, Peter Mitchell of the class of 1963, followed a not dissimilar path. His stellar transit through Terenure senior school suggested as much: the science prize in first year 1957–8; the honours list in second year 1958–9; the science prize in third year; the science and mathematics prize in fourth year; the class prize in fifth year and the class prize in his final year of 1962–3 suggested a brilliant career and that it might lie in science. As if that was not enough to excite equal exclamations of admiration and envy, young Peter was no mean figure on the college stage: making for a menacing Lady Macbeth in 1961: 'Peter Mitchell was a fine choice as Lady Macbeth. He lived the part, nothing less. His sleepwalking scene was magnificent and having seen it once one wanted to see it again'.[10]

His accuracy in physics, chemistry, mathematics, and mathematical physics transferred to the golf course: he led the college students' golf team to the Leinster final in 1963 and then won the captain's prize at Portmarnock in his first year out of school. When it came to after-school career however, it was science which triumphed. At UCD he secured a first-class honours BSc in experimental physics in 1967 and then went on to his MSc and then his PhD in spectroscopy in 1972. By then, he was at the start of an illustrious teaching and research career in UCD. By 1981, he had embarked on an exciting new field specialising in radiation physics and radioecology and also developing the applications of technology to medicine, especially in the area of radiotherapy. His international reputation was acquired in various roles, through over 140 published research papers, work for the EU Commission's Euratom Group, nuclear fission safety research programmes and for his state-of-the-art radiocarbon dating facility, which he established at UCD in 1992. An earlier of his Terenure contemporaries and then colleague at UCD was John Anthony Scott known as Tony.

Like Billy Langan and Adrian Weakliam, Tony was a Harold's Cross native and his first taste of elocution was with the formidable Miss Kenny in the local national school. Helping out the Carmelites with their famous annual Mansion House sales of work for the missions was Tony's mother, Elsie, and it was through that link that he came to move up to Terenure College. Starting in September 1947, he came and went on a tricycle made for two: perched behind him on the back of that contraption was another junior and classmate, John Cronin, who later in life studied law and went to work for

Guinness in Cork: up they went on the Templeogue Road, back they came down Mount Tallant Avenue, taking their lives in their hands and the corners on two wheels. Following a happy passage through his ten Terenure years the final one of 1956–7 was especially unforgettable for Tony, Eugene McNamee and their 32 classmates: it was the famous or infamous year when Leaving Certificate mathematics (and other) papers were leaked, with resulting national newspaper headlines and the ghastly need of resits. Not that either one of them either needed or benefited from the leak: Tony's progress had been admirable and culminated in his winning the 1957 Gold Medal for Religious Knowledge, to add to his third, fourth and fifth year honours list citations from 1954 to 1956. From there it was on to UCD, completing his honours degree in 1961: he had received first class honours all through his undergraduate years and went on to his MSc and PhD, working in the field of atmospheric physics at UCD, with its internationally renowned Professors P.J. and J.J. Nolan. As with Sé O'Connor, Tony was recruited to the UCD teaching and research staff by Professor Nevin, and despite a full teaching load, he delivered his PhD successfully and on time in 1966. While, thereafter, Tony Scott went on to a distinguished academic career, becoming vice president for communications in UCD, and later president of the RDS — a position only ever held by one other Terenure man, the UCD agricultural scientist Austin Mescal — it is appropriate here to backtrack momentarily and to suggest that what this brilliant cohort of Terenure alumni had in common, apart from their own high abilities and commitment, was the good fortune of singularly impressive science teachers at their *Alma Mater* in the 1950s and 1960s. While most of them will be referred to in more detail later, and in a different context — namely, Frs Paddy Simon Grace and James J. McCouaig — there was also the earlier-mentioned young and creative science lay teacher, Mr M.J. Keane, and the decisive figure of Fr Tom Patrick Burke.

Fr Burke had already featured as president of the college during its centenary year but, in some ways, the most interesting part of his public life had yet to come. During the 1950s he had been a profound influence on Terenure's teaching of science, fulsomely acknowledged by past pupils as such. It was no strange fate that brought him and one of his prize pupils into a professional association friendship that resulted in their — and one of Terenure's — most significant contributions to Ireland. On leaving aside the burden of presidential office in 1961, Fr Paddy Burke with his expertise in atmospheric and radon physics in which he had taken his PhD as far back as 1948 was brought in to UCD to join the Nolan Group in 1962, just as Tony Scott was in the early stage of his postgraduate research there. Fr Burke arrived at a critical stage given that Professor Nolan was close to retiring and Tony was the only other person specialising in atmospherics, and he was to remain active in the staff until 1988. For all that invaluable and world-wise work, Fr Paddy's fidelity to the Carmelite way of life never faltered: even though they lasted only five minutes or so, he would cycle back every lunch-time for the midday prayers of his Community at Gort Muire.

Former teacher and pupil now began a collaboration which at one stage in 1963 found them both in New Mexico one summer — Tony on his way to a science conference in Berkeley, Fr Burke double-jobbing by giving a local parish priest a vacation break and doing collaborative atmospherics research with colleagues in the University of Albuquerque. During that summer they both visited a schools' science fair in Albuquerque: standing in a school-yard in Socorro watching an American teenager successfully demonstrating the flight of a home-made rocket as part of his science project, they both wondered if it might be possible to launch a similar schools 'science fair' back home. Out of that visit and that shared musing came the Young Scientists' Exhibition. With the critical support of Aer Lingus Chief Executive, J.F. Dempsey, they launched the first ever Irish Young Scientists Exhibition in January 1965. The success of that first exhibition was very great, although the climate and the timing was right since, just two years before that, in October 1963, the more general RDS Scientific and Technical Exhibition in Ballsbridge had elicited a promising response.[11]

This notwithstanding, there is no gainsaying that the first Young Scientists Exhibition in 1965 was an outstanding success; it captured the imagination of the young and their teachers, and the rest, as they say, is history. Tony Scott, in the midst of his UCD duties and research, carried the main organising burden but acknowledged just how crucial it was then and for many years after to have had the support of national airline sponsorship. Critical too was the fact that he had become a member of the RDS where Professor Nolan sat on its Science Committee in the 1960s: Tony became the key figure in securing the RDS as almost the national home for the annual Young Scientists. Their own college of Terenure had its participants in that first exhibition and has gone on to enjoy success there at various stages ever since. Noteworthy in this regard were three projects: in 1988, the trio of Gareth Ó Murchú, Colin Kelly and John Menton won the Group Runners-Up Award for their economics study of 'Private Consumption and Savings relative to Income and its Effects on the Main Economic Indicators'; in 1991, John Bohill, Cillian de Gascún and Brian Kelly, for their project 'Equating Myth and Fact: a history of the Hell Fire Club', won a special commendation and, in addition, the *Irish Times*' Young Historian of the Year Award; and in 1996, Donal O'Connell won the Young Scientists' Best Individual Project for his study of 'Earthquake Patterns in Great Britain'.[12]

It would be difficult to underestimate the contribution the two Terenure and UCD men, Burke and Scott, made to the promotion of a science culture in Ireland and its schools; their colleague, Peter Mitchell, was to support their efforts by leading the Irish Youth Science Group of the RDS to the London International Youth Science fortnight. No more than Tony, and despite his advancing years and frailty, Fr Paddy never missed a single annual exhibition. The great contribution by Burke and Scott, teacher and alumnus, was fittingly recognised as recently as October 2007 when Dublin City University awarded them the honorary doctorate for their creation of this 'national treasure': it was a timely recognition for Fr Paddy Burke who passed away soon after, in March 2008 at the age of 85. As for Tony Scott, he had already risen to become UCD's dean of science from 1987 to 1993, to which he added the portfolio of the University's directorship of public affairs to 2004 and then capped it all with the distinction of becoming president of the RDS from 2007 to 2010.

353

College supporters, 1950s.

OH BOY !

aren't they good!

354

It's the glucose in Brookfield sweets that makes them so good . . . so exquisitely different. Ask for them by name and accept no others, for they're pure as pure can be.

BROOKFIELD
Sweets of Distinction

MADE AT THE BROOKFIELD GARDEN FACTORY, BLACKROCK, CO. DUBLIN.

I

SHEAFFER'S

Writing Instruments

Your choice of a Sheaffer's pen assures unbounded years of service, pleasure and pride in owning one of the few ultimately precise products of craftsmanship in the world to-day.

TRADE ONLY : COSTUME JEWELS LTD.

Everything you need for Sport—

From a tennis racquet to a golf tee, from a boot stud to a goal post—you'll find them all at Elverys.   Under one roof we have every item of equipment the sportsman needs, and as well as that, the right clothes for each sport. The name "Elvery" is your guarantee of satisfaction — bear in mind that it is backed by a reputation built up by more than a century's trading.

—you'll find at

O'Connell Street & Nassau Street, Dublin

P. Mitchell in the old chemistry laboratory, 1960.

356

David Kennedy (PPU president), Eltin Griffin (Prior) and James V. Doyle (guest speaker), Brian Cotter (president of St Mary's PPU), 1988.

Text on poster within image:

PRIVATE CONSUMPTION & ITS EFFECTS
ON THE MAIN ECONOMIC INDICATORS

AIMS: TO EVALUATE THE CONSUMER MULTIPLIER.

...D: A RANDOM SURVEY (500 FORMS)
WITH ANALYSIS OF ALL RELEVANT
AND AVAILABLE DATA

...CLUSIONS: LOW MULTI...
...HIGH TAXATION AND
...NDENCY ON IMPORT...
...NG DEMA...

359

John Menton, Gareth Ó Murchú and Colin Kelly at the Young Scientist Exhibition, 1988.

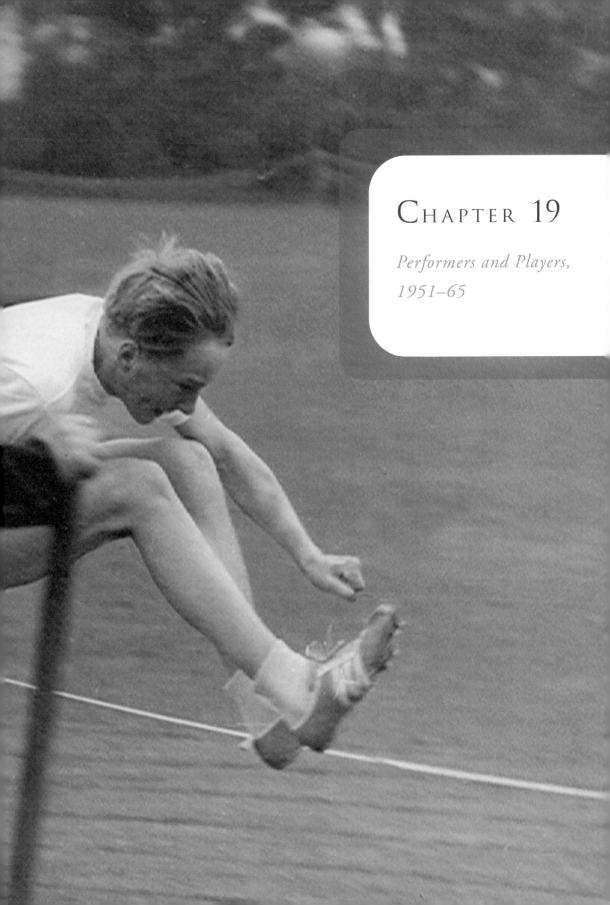

Pupil competing in the
long jump, 1950s.

> For unceasing effort without the rewards which bring the plaudits of
> the crowds, it would be hard to beat the battle of Terenure College
> in Leinster sports. Almost twenty years of trying has failed to bring
> the Leinster Senior or Junior Cups to the Carmelite Institution and
> Athletic titles have yet to shower on it.

So wrote columnist John D. Hickey in December 1949:[1] 'always the bridesmaid,
never the blushing bride' it must have seemed to the college's staff, pupils and alumni.
However, at the start of the decade to follow, matters were about to change and, in
1951, that change came through quite different exploits of three individuals in three
quite different arenas over the course of its first six months.

At the end of January 1951, a young lad from Harold's Cross, then in fourth year,
Harry Perry, boxed his way to victory in the Leinster youth championships. He went
on to complete a great year by winning the national title at featherweight level that
December after a superbly fought victory over Paddy Martin of St Vincent's, then one
of the best featherweights in Ireland, North or South.[2] This was a first for Terenure
but only one of many firsts for the remarkable Perry. As the *Times* pictorial put it:

> A 17-year old scrapper whom this column mentioned early last year
> as one of the best prospects in Irish amateur boxing, has justified
> himself and gets my vote [as Boxer of the Year]. He is Harry Perry ...
> at present in Terenure College ... in the four days of boxing in the
> [national] championships, Perry fought five times, winning four
> times on points and once by a knock-out.[3]

For Perry, it was only the beginning of a legendary career, which saw him become
Irish national champion nine times over the next ten years at various weights, contest
the European championships at Lucerne and Berlin, two Olympics at Melbourne and
Rome, and fight for Europe in Chicago against the renowned American Golden Gloves.[4]

In a much quieter, though no less intense and mentally aggressive discipline, from
27 to 29 of March 1951, Leinster secondary schoolboys battled it out in the province's
Chess championships. Here Fintan Doyle, then in final year, fought his way successfully through five preliminaries to reach the final and sixth match against Hussey of
St Mary's. It was ironic in that Hussey had been his opponent in the first round match,
which they had drawn, after it had gone to adjudication. Doyle's previous form had
not been his best and few, even among his schoolmates, were prepared for what
followed. He faced a tough, but successful encounter against Norris of Synge Street;
trounced Carney, also of Synge Street CBS, in the third round; and saw off O'Brien
of O'Connell Schools in the fourth. His fifth-round match against the very strong
and undefeated Conlon, also from O'Connell Schools, saw young Doyle gaining in
confidence, to defeat his opponent in the twenty-fifth move. Then it was the final
and Hussey again, each with four wins and their draw. Surprisingly and courageously,
Fintan declined to play a safe game and with great aggression vanquished his opponent

on the twenty-first move. His victory brought the first of two Leinster championship titles back to the college, in a year which also saw him captain the Irish boys' international team against England that December. Even before this victory, the gifted seventeen-year-old had already represented Ireland three times that year.

The final triumph for the college in 1951 came in athletics. Here, in the Leinster intermediate championships, Larry Byrne, then in fourth year, came fourth in the high jump at 5ft 2in; however, in the 220 yards sprint, he excelled: he cruised into the semi-final which he won with ease; then, in the final, he ran as never before and, with a final explosive burst, he snatched victory by a foot from Moloney of Roscrea. For Larry and for Terenure it was a first-ever Leinster in the 220 yds, adding a new achievement to Charlie Weakliam's 1947 great victory in the 100 yds, which had been the college's first-ever sprint title in these championships. Few would have guessed, however they might have wished, that Terenure College was soon to enter a very special time in its history in athletics. However, before exploring the glories of that golden age, it behoves to consider this: that for the general run of 'ordinary' students who may not have been rugby monarchs or chess kings, the college at this time was still a very exciting and interesting place to be. There were, after all, activities and engagements, whether as revivals or new arrivals, which made it so.

REVIVALS:

Among the alternatives to rugby, athletics or chess there were diverse activities, commitments and societies that could closely engage the college community, whether staff, parents, pupils or past pupils. They ranged from the College Drama Society and the College Past Pupils' Dramatic Society to the Geography Society, Sketching Club, Golfing Society, Debating Society, the Scouts, the Camera Club, the Radio Society and the Orchestra: all these and more, apart from the usual run of outdoor activities from handball and Gaelic football to cricket, swimming, tennis and rugby. One of these was unique and special in that it sought, on the one hand, to involve past pupils and pupils together, and, on the other, to reach out beyond the contented walls that kept the college something of a haven. However, all of these had in common the tendency or the fate of ebbing and flowing, faltering or reviving as time passed and personnel came and went. Some, in the 1950s and 1960s, were revivals; others, new arrivals.

THE DEBATING SOCIETY:

In the course of the late 1940s under Fr Lamont, the Debating Society — for every college an essential training ground for confidence and display — was in a flourishing condition, with well-supported meetings and some memorable moments and performances. Not least among these, and very popular with the boys, were the mock trials. Most memorable of them, perhaps, was that final session of 1944–5 when

Macbeth and Lady Macbeth were charged with murder. It was a tough one for the defence, Liam Dunne and Michael O'Keeffe whereas prosecutors Des Doyle and Dick Fleming had a blissful brief and for them it was an easy victory when the house, by acclamation, carried the conviction. Nevertheless, presiding judge, Fr Lamont, decided to apply the Probation Act as it appeared to be a first offence.

The society appears to have foundered or fallen silent over the years 1945 to 1948, only to revive in January 1949 with all four years of seniors, from third year upwards, becoming involved, with Fr Dunstan O'Connor presiding. Although it was active in 1949–50, it appears to have faltered in 1950–1. It made an effective reappearance in November 1951 with a lively opening session in which Joe Cahill, J.J. O'Donnell and Milo Reddy were to the fore: with Bernard Rogers as secretary and Dunstan in place again as president a very successful season followed. And so it went: failing in 1953, reviving in 1954 through Fr O'Connor's direct intervention and the encouragement of Fr Jim Kinahan when names that would feature prominently in college life, and later in public, came to the fore, among them Eddie Gowing, David Kennedy, Adrian Weakliam, Brendan Church, Stan Hession and Cormac McHenry. Then, in the late 1950s, it appears to have disappeared for quite a number of years but, it would seem, reviving in 1962–3 when sixth year's Charles Hayes as chair and fifth year's John Maguire as secretary, became involved. Maguire became a leading light in the intellectual life of the college before going on to an outstanding scholastic career.

Another good year followed for the society, in 1963–4, when for the first time ever, the college entered an intercollegiate competition: while not triumphing, the society had now developed a momentum that proved lasting and influential in involving many students who might not have stepped on to a playing field.

THE BOYS' CLUB:

During these same years the Boys' Club exhibited a similar pattern of revival, slump and revival that characterised a number of the societies. It was, nonetheless, important in developing a spirit and habit of outreach — an important consideration for any college where a relatively privileged position could combine with a self-concerned and self-contained existence. From its foundation as a college Past Pupils' Union initiative in 1938, the Boys' Club had a chequered history, but by the mid-1940s it had an extensive range of activities and a strong membership. However, in the early years of the 1950s, it had become moribund. Then, by 1954, with Bobby Fallon of the class of 1948 as secretary, and Gerry Carr as PPU president, the club was revived — through the good offices of an unnamed past pupil who lent the homeless club a premises on Westland Row. It now restarted with some twenty boys meeting for recreation once a week. Plans to realise a purpose-built hall were drafted and a building fund instituted. Fallon's committee received great support from the Prior, Fr Dunstan O'Connor, and from Fr Michael Ardiff and the Rugby Club had generously granted use of its premises and playing field.[5] Whatever woe befell, by that September they were back on Aungier Street and having to fork out a high rent, which was met from the proceeds of film shows and motorcycle grass-track meetings that were popular at the time. They had lost the services of Fr Ardiff who had gone on the Rhodesian Mission, and of Bobby Fallon whose own livelihood took him first to South Africa and then to England for a few years. His loss was a serious one as he had been the mainstay of this charity. Without permanent premises, the club operated only fitfully in 1956–7. In December 1957, Fr O'Connor called a meeting to try to reorganise, by having the club converted into a 'conference' or branch of the St Vincent de Paul Society. It was then largely owing to the efforts of Peter Tormey that this succeeded, with access to new premises on Ranelagh Road.

Over the early part of 1958, it had enrolled some 30 young lads and was hosting two evenings a week for them with indoor games and Sunday morning soccer matches in Lakelands Park. By this stage, Niall Herbert had taken up the secretaryship and over the period 1958–9, the numbers rose to in excess of 50 but the number of volunteers to help out had fallen. Despite this, the activities were successfully sustained, including the provision of a week's holiday for twenty of the boys, and even more being accommodated the following year. Furthermore, the range of activities had been extended, to the staging of their first play and the organisation of competitive football and athletic teams and at that stage a number of recently graduated past pupils had come aboard to assist. Niall Herbert continued to act as secretary up to 1961–2 and then his Terenure and Aer Lingus colleague, David Kennedy, took over.

At Ranelagh Road, through St Vincent de Paul, they had the use of a large house, quite adequately catering for their 40 to 50 boy members. It was no mean feat to have faithfully sustained the schedule and programme, without faltering, for four years, managing two evenings per week, plus weekend and summer vacation activities. By 1964, the club was going from strength to strength; some 60 youngsters benefitted and by the summer of that year, a record 42 boys had enjoyed the annual holiday camp sport vacation at Ronan Murphy House in Sallins, Co. Kildare. At that stage, five of the 1964 sixth years had rallied in support and Niall Herbert had once again taken up the job of Boys' Club secretary. Over the rest of the 1960s, these volunteers, with some new initiatives, enabled the club to expand greatly and to achieve a very great deal for its growing number of members.

NEW ARRIVALS:

If the Boys' Club was a creditable and worthy survival, the 1950s' college also experienced a significant number of new arrivals, too many to chronicle here in detail. One was that of the Boy Scouts, beginning in 1957 and whose story will appear later in this work. A second was the College Orchestra.

In the autumn of 1952, the junior school was justly proud of its new initiative — the production of an operetta and nativity play for that Christmas. For them it took choral practice out of the classroom and on to the college stage. It was largely down to a new arrival, Fr Thomas Luke Flynn, who specialised in sacred music and who had joined the college staff in September 1950. This was a large venture to undertake, though magical for its young participants. However, to make it happen properly required among other things, in his view, an orchestra, something which the college does not appear to have had before in that century. Then, somehow, out of eight boys 'doing the piano', some five 'doing the violin' and five or so others who had 'tried the violin', an orchestra was put together from that November. However hair-raising, teeth-grinding and nerve-wracking this orchestral enterprise may have seemed, it managed to back the Christmas operetta and then, *mirabile dictu*, it went on to take first class honours in the Department of Education examinations of March 1953. This was no mean feat especially when it is noted that one of the two external examiners was the illustrious Professor J.F. Larchet.[6] The infant orchestra acquitted itself so well that under Fr Luke it went on to stage a highly successful orchestral and choral concert the following Whitsun evening. The College Orchestra had arrived, with skilled performers in Peter Held, Brian Walshe and Ray Farrelly and with a talented new arrival at the cello, James Cahill.

It was a big reversal then to lose Fr Luke to Moate, in September 1953, yet the orchestra repeated its early successes in 1954 and 1955 under the new tuition and leadership of Maurice Kane to 1956 and, thereafter, under John Mackenzie and Liam Forristal to the mid-1960s. By the time of his own departure to the principalship of the Limerick Municipal School of Music in 1961, John Mackenzie had brought the orchestra to a new level, achieving a first-class honours of 91% in the state examinations.[7] By that stage, it had long 'developed beyond all expectations and become an institution in its own right'.

THE FIELDS OF PRAISE:

To revert to commentator John D. Hickey and his observations on Terenure College as 'a great sporting institution' that had as yet failed to be truly 'great': in fairness to him, he nevertheless acknowledged that the 'College has won for itself a place in Irish sport of which any school might be proud'.[8] The decade and a half which was about to commence when he penned these comments in December 1949 would go on to show that prouder still it would earn the right to be. Not that it had been completely devoid of success before this, as the exploits of its junior tennis players had already demonstrated, but, in athletics and rugby it had still to nail the lie or defy the past: nail it, defy it, it did.

The early years of the 1950s in the college did not give much evidence of promise nor of triumphs to come, either in its own annual sports days or in its inter-collegiate endeavours. Its senior relay four in 1951, for example, were defeated 'by vastly superior teams' and neither then nor in the following year was there any victory to show at Leinster schools. On the contrary, in 1953, the college had a smaller number of participants in the Leinster schoolboys' championships than usual, and, unsurprisingly, no victories then, either. By that stage, it may be recalled, the 'house system' had come into operation, putting an end to individual cups and the traditional notion of 'the best all-rounder'. Furthermore, no pupil was permitted to compete in more than three events. No records were broken and one wonders if the system may have acted as a brake or damper even as it was designed to foster team spirit and identity. Matters were not helped by the wretched weather in the Mays and Junes of the early 1950s, but sunshine was not far off: 1954 saw the emergence of two lads at junior and intermediate levels who showed great promise and would deliver great performance in the future, Eddie Thornton and Kilian Tormey.

Eddie Thornton had come to the college from the Dominicans, Cabra, at first year intermediate in 1952, while Kilian had entered at pre-intermediate in 1949 from CBS, Synge Street.[9] Eddie qualified for the junior 220 yds and Kilian for the intermediate high jump and long jump in the 1954 Leinster schools championship, while Alfred Regan secured his place in the intermediate 220 and John Mulvaney in the senior discus. While no victories were secured, these were signposts to better days. By 1955, the college had upped its presence at the Leinsters, participating in sixteen events. Tormey excelled in the high jump and became Leinster senior champion in this event and then went on one week later to equal the Terenure College record in the high jump: he achieved for the first time since the 1930s, the 5 ft 5 in reached by the great Dermot McAuley in 1934. Adding to that sense of better days was the emergence that summer of young Kevin Flynn, to win the intermediate 100 yds and the 220 yds in 10.8 and 22.5 seconds respectively; and, crowning that memorable college sports day was Eddie Thornton again: he won the intermediate high jump at 5 ft 1 in when the corresponding Leinster senior maximum that year had been 5 ft 2 in. Kilian Tormey went on to win the Leinster senior hurdles in 1956 and came second in the same event in that year's All-Ireland colleges competition. In Terenure's own sports day that same year, Kevin Flynn easily won the senior 100 and 220 sprints while Eddie won a treble in the intermediate 100 yds, 220 yds and high jump. There was now a real sense emerging that the college was building to significant breakthroughs in provincial and national athletics. Adding to it was young Robert Keogh who became Irish Open junior champion in tennis.

The year 1957 brought the equalling of two college records, by Flynn in the 100 yds at 10.5 seconds and by John Lysaght in the high jump at 5 ft 5 in. It brought, also, one of the college's largest contingents to the provincial championships. Now in his fifth year and so, his first senior grade, Eddie won his semi-final in the hurdles and finished second in that final. However, best of all was the college's first victory in the glamour event, the senior relay. Here the senior quartet of Flynn, Thornton, Joe Doyle and Bobby Keogh brought home in triumph the Fr Austin Murphy Perpetual Challenge Cup, against the formidable opposition of Blackrock, Monkstown and O'Connell Schools. This victory saw Flynn selected to contest the All-Ireland relay for Leinster and so earned for a Terenure man the then unique distinction of being chosen interprovincial in three different codes, athletics, cricket and rugby.

Thornton suffered an unfortunate setback in that year's All-Ireland senior hurdles final when, running well, he pulled a muscle, but courageously continued, to finish third. Undaunted, the following year of 1958, and despite bad weather, in the senior 100 yds, he broke the college record of 10.50 seconds, set by Kevin Lawler in 1947: Eddie finished in a storming 10.15 seconds. More remarkably, he flashed past Bobby Keogh in the 220 yds to set a new college record in 23 seconds, overturning Charlie Weakliam's, which had held since 1948. This was to be *annus mirabilis* for Eddie Thornton: on Saturday, 17 May 1958, in the Leinster senior hurdles' heats, he set a new record of 15.5 seconds; four days later, in the semi-finals he won and broke the record again at 15.4 seconds and then went on to win gold in the final with a 15.2 second finish, his third record in a few days. From there, he was chosen for Leinster in the All-Irelands, again won gold in the senior hurdles and yet again broke his latest record with a 14.8 second victory.

Happy Days:

It was in September 1958 that two young men arrived in the college late in a secondary-school career: one was Albert McCarthy who arrived in fifth year from Synge Street; the other was Dominic Smyth who came into the same grade from St Mary's, Dundalk. Terenure could hardly believe its luck: the former was already All-Ireland senior 100 yds champion, the latter already All-Ireland intermediate 100 yds champion. One evening in the spring of 1959 when the athletic season had come round again, on his first training session on the college grounds, young McCarthy turned to athletics overseer, Fr Patsy Keenan, and asked: 'Could I bring along my coach on the next evening we have practice?'. So, as that great in-house coach and rugby strategist, Fr Jackie Madden recalled, the next night a guy called Joe Doran arrived to put young McCarthy through his paces. It was to be the beginning of a remarkable coaching relationship between Doran and the college that brought Terenure's athletes in general, and not just McCarthy, to a new level.

Terenure entered 23 events in the 1959 Leinsters, with newcomers Philip O'Sullivan qualifying for the senior javelin and Jim Lane for the intermediate pole vault finals. It was, however, in the sprints that the triumphs came: McCarthy became Leinster champion in the 100 yds at 10.4 seconds and in the senior relay that year the record was broken five times: twice by High School and three times by Terenure. The final proved an unforgettable spectacle: Albert McCarthy, 'Doc' Hurst, Ned Browne and Dominic Smyth proved unbeatable as they stretched the gap at each transfer, until Smyth finished, to complete that meeting's fifth record-breaking time of 44.7 seconds. It was then on to the All-Ireland where McCarthy retained his crown with a 10.1 second finish in the 100 yds. He then led off the senior relay to a cracking start, with the Doc, Ned and Dominic finishing brilliantly to win in a new record time of 44.6 seconds.

It was a memorable year that saw the college bring home both Leinster and All-Ireland trophies, and, by then another new star was ascending: Eddie Coleman, in third year in 1958–9 had reached the Leinster finals (junior section) in the 100 yds and 220 yds in 1958 and had gone on to the finals of the Leinster intermediate relay in 1959. Then, in 1960, this future rugby star and president of the IRFU, won the Leinster intermediate 100 yds and went on to win the All-Ireland championship in that event, in a memorable year when Jim Lane took home gold in the pole vault.

The year 1960 was in one real sense a coming of age for Terenure athletics. It is some credit to the talents of that year's teams and to the skill and faith of their trainers, Joe Doran and Jackie Madden that for the first time in Terenure's history, the college won the All-Ireland Shield for the best all-round team at intermediate level.

As for Joe Doran, he not only continued successfully to coach the college's athletes but went on from there to serve Terenure College Rugby Football Club. From there he was recruited to the Leinster branch of the IRFU and went on to be physiotherapist to the Irish international rugby teams. As for college athletics, new talents emerged in the early 1960s. Especially notable then was high jumper, Eddie Keelaghan; hurdler, Declan Whitney; and sprinter, John Thornton. In 1963, these three brought home three All-Ireland golds, in the intermediate high jump, intermediate hurdles and the 200 yds, respectively. Then, at their own college sports day that year, Keelaghan produced a new high jump record of 5ft 5in while John Thornton won three events, setting new college records in two of them, the junior 220 and the long jump. The next year, 1964, witnessed three more college records. Keelaghan broke the 30-year high jump record, held by Dermot McAuley since 1934 when he cleared a then remarkable 5ft 8in: it was the last of Dermot McAuley's many college records to fall.

The climax to this golden age of college sports days came in 1965 when there was, as reported at the time, 'an orgy of record-breaking':[10] eight new college records were established and a ninth equalled on that remarkable last Sunday in May.

The newly-emergent star was Jack McNamara who won in three events, setting records in two of them: he beat Eddie Thornton's 1958 record in the senior 220, and then set another of 53 seconds in the 440. Likewise, John Staunton, winning in the long jump and the triple jump, set a new record in the latter. However, most remarkable of them all, and unprecedented perhaps, was young John Thornton who ran in four events and won all four, setting a new record in each of them. He bettered Charlie Weakliam's 100 yds of 1947 by one tenth of a second, with a 10.4 second finish; beat his own 1959 record in the 220; then bettered his own hurdles' record of the previous year, and capped it all by outdoing John Staunton's 1964 record in the 440 with a time of 55.8 seconds.

In that same year of 1965, the college went on to its best-ever Leinster schools championship up till then, winning three first, two seconds and three thirds. The first-place victories went to Jack McNamara in the senior 220 yds and to John Thornton in the intermediate 220 and hurdles. As if their college's cup was not already overflowing, Terenure then went on to bring home three All-Ireland cups: Jack again in the senior

220, John again in the intermediate 220 and finally, to crown that golden age came the splendid victory: a new Whitney, Brian, and a new Tormey, Pat, passed their baton brilliantly to John Thornton and he to Jack McNamara, and so to glory with a record-equalling All-Irelands senior relay, last set in 1959, appropriately, by Terenure College.

RUGBY:

For Terenure rugby, whether college or club, the 1950–1 season did not augur particularly well for the future. The college Senior XV went out of the Leinster Cup in the semi-final against King's Hospital and the juniors fell to CUS in what was effectively only their first cup match. At junior-school level, some solace might have been found in the under-12's playing of a certain K. Flynn, praised even then as one who could 'weave his way through any defence'.[11]

As for the younger veterans of Terenure Rugby, the RFC had no competition wins to register and secretary, Joe Milroy, could only report the doleful news that their application for promotion to senior ranks in Leinster had been rejected. No one was hazarding what better might befall for the following year. Elsewhere in college sport, as previously noted, Harry Perry had been boxing to glory and the under-14 cricket heroes had brought home their cricket cup for the first time ever. That unique cricket triumph of 1952 was well-remarked upon by the secretary of the schools' section of the Leinster Cricket Union when, on presenting them with the cup, he remarked: 'I have umpired 14 of the 15 League Finals played but have never seen bowling so accurate as that of Kevin Flynn or fielding so keen and so good as that of this Terenure XI'.[12] He might have added a mention of the extraordinary bowling record of David Kennedy on that XI when, on their very first competitive outing, he bowled 6 maidens in 10 overs and took 6 wickets for 6 runs; he continued, against St Andrew's, by taking 4 wickets for 7 runs, against Blackrock some 6 wickets for 16 and crowned all of this against Avoca with 3 maidens in 5 overs and 5 wickets for 2 runs; in all of that season he took 30 wickets for 66 runs. It would be many a long year before Terenure's cricketers might come close to the under-14 team of 1952.

Nonetheless, it was at college level that the long-sought Holy Grail of Leinster rugby was finally captured. Terenure had been in its quest since the restoration of its own senior rugby squad in 1925–6, to no avail. In the 1951–2 pre-Christmas warm up matches they had done well enough to encourage some slight hope, were unbeaten in these contests, winning twice against Blackrock, and had the comfort of retaining twelve of the previous year's team who had not fared too badly. The Terenure rugby squad was fortunate in the judicious mentoring of Maurice O'Kelly, in some eyes the greatest all-round sportsman Terenure could ever boast. One of the college's rugby 'greats', he played on the under-18 team when he was only fifteen; in each of the three years that he played for the Seniors he was also capped for Leinster. He excelled in other sports as well; along with Archie Fitzpatrick, he was one of Terenure's and Leinster's finest tennis players, was capped for the Leinster cricket team and was a force to be reckoned with in Leinster schools' athletics. Apart from playing League of Ireland soccer for Bohemians, for years after graduating from the class of 1948, he devoted a huge amount of time to training Terenure's rugby teams; later on, when working in the Far East, he captained the Hong Kong XV against the All Blacks.[13] Much later still, on his return to Ireland he also returned to the service of Terenure through its Past Pupils' Union, as will be seen.[14] Back to the 1951–2 college rugby season, under Maurice's guidance and led by John O'Connor, their passage to the final in the new year was impressive in the sheer margins of their three preliminary victories: 22-3 against Wesley, 22-0 against Masonic and 14-0 against Belvedere. Jack O'Donnell proved the old reliable, especially when it came to conversions while newcomer Jack Hayes went over twice against Wesley, only to be concussed out of match with Masonic, twenty minutes after the start. The Church brothers: John and Brendan, proved crucial try-getters as did Hubie O'Connor and Ken Mulvaney who went over twice in the last three minutes in the semi-final against Belvedere.

The final against Castleknock, on 22 March 1952 at Lansdowne Road, was a closer call. Although the latter had produced the greater pressure in the first half, at the turn their forwards 'gradually crumbled before the devastating Terenure pack' who had grown in confidence after a nervous start.[15] Jack O'Donnell's great strength and pace and Ken Mulvaney's kicking accuracy took their toll, while Paddy Hipwell's and John Hayes's deadly tackling proved critical in blunting the Castleknock attack. In bearing away the cup with a 9-3 victory that first-ever triumph almost left its chroniclers lost for words — but not quite:

> When the Senior XV brought home the coveted Leinster Schools' Cup, the hopes and dreams of countless Terenure rugby players, present and past, were at last realized. This achievement stamps the team and the season as the most successful in the history of Rugby in the College. It was the crowning glory of the team's record of being unbeaten throughout the season.[16]

Indeed, as ever, results spoke more tellingly than scribes: they played seventeen matches, won sixteen, drew one, lost none and scored 275 points with only 30 conceded. One outcome of that great season was that four of the victorious team were then selected for Leinster: Seamus Connolly, Hubert O'Connor, John J. O'Donnell and Captain John O'Connor who, having already been selected for Leinster against Munster and Connacht, now captained Leinster against Ulster.

While the juniors that same year could claim no glory, the further future held promise in the commendable record of the junior school's under-12s who, out of nine matches, won seven, drew one and lost only one.

However, glory for the Junior Cup XV was not too far away. In 1954, the under-14s, with an impressive season under Fr Enda Devane and with Kevin Flynn as captain, recorded eleven wins out of twelve matches and racked up 222 points with a mere 12 against. A remarkable fourteen of this squad featured in the Junior Cup team of 1955, including Captain Joe Cahill, Mick Hipwell, Gerry Tormey and Niall Herbert. Under the skilful and dedicated coaching of Michael Hall-Carroll, Hugh Church and Fr Jim McCouaig, that team fought its way to Terenure's first-ever Junior Cup final. Hall-Carroll, or 'Micko' to his friends, had come from Beaufort, Rathfarnham, in 1935 and graduated from Terenure in 1943; apart from training the Junior Cup team of 1955, he became a stalwart of the Rugby Football Club from the early 1950s, led their Second XV to victory in the Metropolitan Cup in 1958 and went on to become the first Terenure man to climb the administrative heights of the game, becoming Irish selector, chairman of selectors and president of the Irish Rugby Football Union. As for the pre-cup friendly season before the real battle, it did not augur well, with an opening defeat to Blackrock followed by four other failures to win.

For all that, their first-round contest against Monkstown revealed a different and menacing fifteen, with a 26-0 victory in which the powerful and deadly accurate Joe Cahill produced 17 points, including two tries. To these Mick Hipwell added two more tries and Bobby Keogh a fifth. A scoreless draw against Masonic led to a grinding replay in which Terenure emerged victorious by 8-0. Only three days passed before they were into the semi-final against Castleknock which, being drawn, required a rematch with Terenure emerged victorious. Excelling in great sweeping movements, led by Cahill, and incisive openings by out-half, Gerry Tormey, the outstanding player in that game, they came away the better, 9-3. So it was that a battle-hardened team faced Blackrock in a final for their first time ever, on 1 April 1952, only three days after the semi-final and in an era when substitutes did not feature once a match had started. With 'a mighty pack' Terenure swept Blackrock aside with a 9-0 victory that was rendered all the sweeter in that it thwarted a historic and unique treble of Senior and Junior Cup doubles in succession. Two penalty goals from the sharp-shooting Cahill and an altogether thrilling last-minute try by the brilliant Eddie Thornton brought Terenure's juniors to triumph. It was a triumph all the worthier since they had contested six cup matches inside three weeks. The college songwriter could not be restrained from singing, to the tune of *Fr O'Flynn*:

> In Terenure College there was a collection
> of youthful aspirants to football perfection
> and Fr McCouaig picked out a selection
> and sent them to play in the Schools' Junior Cup.
>
> So here's a health to the men big and small,
> the Backs and the Forwards, the trainers and all;
> their plans scientific, their play so terrific,
> the Cup-winning Champions of Junior Football.

Calm was soon restored and reality re-established by the immediate start of examinations, but not too many years later the college came into bliss unblemished in the unforgettable 1958.

It was not just that the magic of Eddie Thornton won the Leinster and All-Ireland hurdles championships, or that the junior tennis team had won the Leinster junior brought off their first — and to-date — only cup double. For seniors and juniors alike it was an especially sweet double victory after the bitterness of seniors' defeat to Blackrock in the finals of 1956 and 1957, and the juniors' defeat to them in the latter year. Now the seniors were led by prolific scorer Gerry Tormey and included not only the veteran Eddie Thornton and Mick Hipwell, but future college vice-principal, Vinnie Morris. They had an impressive run, bar one blip, up to the final; they defeated Monkstown 21-0, High School 12-0, then the blip of a 0-0 with St Mary's until a replay yielded an impressive 21-0 victory; and so, on to a gruelling final against Belvedere. Poor conditions hampered scoring and Terenure suffered a major blow when its captain, Gerry Tormey, had to leave the field with a twisted knee. However, as the *Irish Press* reporter recorded: 'Seldom have I seen such a display of lion-hearted courage and sustained endeavour as Terenure displayed in winning this Leinster Senior Schools Cup Final at Lansdowne Road'.[17]

Luckily, before the damage had been done to him, Tormey had done the only damage that mattered on the day by 'dodging his way through a sea of defenders' to score a superb try and the college hung on to a grim but glorious 3-0.

Then followed the juniors who had reached their final under the able Captain Gerald Martin, with victories over Monkstown by 21-0, St Paul's by 3-0 and Castleknock 10-3. It may have been a lucky omen, but their final against Blackrock was held on 1 April again. It was a thrilling final in which Martin, ably assisted by scrum partner Brendan Sherry, proved the architect of a historic victory over their arch-rivals by 13-9.[18]

TERENURE COLLEGE RUGBY FOOTBALL CLUB:

The historic double of 1958 became a historic treble with the victory of the past pupils in capturing the Leinster Junior League that same season. It was their fourth junior league triumph in five years. For Terenure RFC, it was a sweet victory tinged with bitterness, made so by the quite remarkable fact that over fifteen seasons ' they have contest sixteen finals, including the final in every competition in which they were entitled to compete ... the most successful junior club in Leinster' but, as the editor of the college *Annual* expostulated:

> surely success in any sphere merits reward, yet that reward is being
> denied. How can any clear-thinking person who has the interests
> of Rugby at heart, reject their application to enter the senior ranks?
> Such rejection argues that there are some who do not wish 'to
> promote, foster and develop the game of Rugby.[19]

By any measure, the record of the Past Pupils' Rugby Club from its foundation in the 1940s was a remarkable one and that history over the years to 1949 has already been noticed. It will be recalled how their remarkable run of victories in their first official season, 1943–4, competing in 17, victorious in 16 contests and winning the Leinster Minor League at their first attempt, brought them to apply for promotion to the Leinster Junior League in 1944–5: rejected then, they were accepted in 1945–6. Their unprecedented double victory of 1948–9, in the junior league and in the Metropolitan Cup, had now placed them in a seemingly unassailable position in their bid for promotion to the senior ranks. Ten years later, their plea for promotion was still being made in vain. This was despite the astonishing record of its fifteen years in competitive rugby in Leinster. Here now was, for them, a two-edged tragedy: on one side was the fact that, in the team's anxiety to play seniors competitive rugby, quite outstanding player alumni like Kevin Flynn, Jack Hayes, Fergus Doyle, Hubie O'Connor and Jack Mulvaney, for example, would have to forsake Terenure and forage elsewhere for a senior game: on the other edge, brilliant young prospects like Tormey, Cahill and others, as Brian Burke wrote in December 1956, if they chose to remain loyal to Terenure after graduation would have to remain in junior ranks and thereby deprive themselves of a chance of selection for interprovincial or international rugby honours down the road.[20]

As if to reinforce the injustice, such senior teams as Galwegians, Corinthians and UCD who had the decency to give them the occasional friendly match came off second best, and, over the three years 1955 to 1959 the club had a record that would have left most Leinster senior outfits green with envy:

TABLE 27: TERENURE COLLEGE RUGBY FOOTBALL CLUB RECORD, 1955–8

Year	P	W	L	D	For	Against
1955–6	30	28	1	1	443	112
1956–7	30	22	6	1	365	93
1957–8	27	24	2	1	403	119
1958–9	29	26	3	0	538	127

All this was accomplished while sustaining the haemorrhage of some of its greatest players. As columnist Joe Sherlock observed, in 1956:

> No club has ever done more to earn promotion ... in thirteen years since its affiliation it has contested fourteen finals, it has won the Junior League three times running and it is the only club in the past twenty years to achieve this distinction. Three times it has reached the Metropolitan Cup Final and won it twice. It has contested the Minor League five times and won it three times. Last season its first XV won twenty eight of its thirty matches, drew one and lost one; and, in the process, scored 457 points, including 297 from tries, against 112.[21]

As late as November 1957, a leading article in a popular sports journal lamented: 'Poor old Terenure! Last Sunday at Lakelands Park they gave the mother and father of a hiding to Connaught Senior Rugby side ... but for all the good it did them, they might as well have been playing a team from Banteer, Co Cork'.[22] On 8 January 1959, the Leinster branch of the IRFU finally relented or reluctantly caved in to the pressure of the irresistible: Terenure would play senior rugby, starting in the 1959–60 season, and as if to underline the injustice of what had gone on for so many years before, Terenure capped its 1958–9 season with yet another junior league triumph.

Terenure RFC entered the senior ranks, under Captain Jim Walsh with a match against Bective on 12 September, just short of the club's twenty-first birthday. And, despite losing the match it was a team well-topped with talents that included Kilian Tormey, Mick Pender, Brendan and Hugh Church, Ken Mulvaney and Mick Hipwell, to name but a few. Better was to follow in their next encounter when they tied 6-6 with Wanderers, the then Leinster Senior Cup holders.[23] They then secured their first senior season victory against Clontarf, winning 13-6. That first season, with sixteen victories, one draw and six defeats certainly justified that promotion — the drawn game against Wanderers had been secured with only fourteen men, and the recognition of their quality came with Eddie Thornton, Mick Pender, John Dillon and Denis Geary securing caps for their respective inter-provincial teams. While it was true that comparatively lean years followed as far as trophies went, by the mid-1960s the Senior XV had reached the top of the class, capturing the Leinster Senior Cup in 1966 and again in 1967. By that stage, Terenure College RFC had well come of age — a new clubhouse erected in 1962 at a cost of £7,000, a new and very active social life associated with it thereafter, a first overseas tour in 1964 and club player, Mick Hipwell, becoming its first player to secure an Irish international cap, against England in 1962, followed in this by Brendan Sherry, five years later.

Harry Perry, winner of the junior national featherweight title, 1951.
© Independent Newspapers

LEINSTER BRANCH
IRISH RUGBY FOOTBALL UNION

PROGRAMME

SCHOOLS' JUNIOR CUP FINAL

BLACKROCK COLLEGE

v.

TERENURE COLLEGE

AT LANSDOWNE ROAD

On Friday, April 12th, 1957

KICK-OFF AT 4.30. P.M. SHARP

Replay April 17th

PRICE THREEPENCE

John T. Drought, Ltd., Printers. 5 & 6 Bachelor's Walk, Dublin.

Programme for schools' Junior Cup final, 12 April 1957.

Programme for schools' Senior Cup final, 16 March 1958.

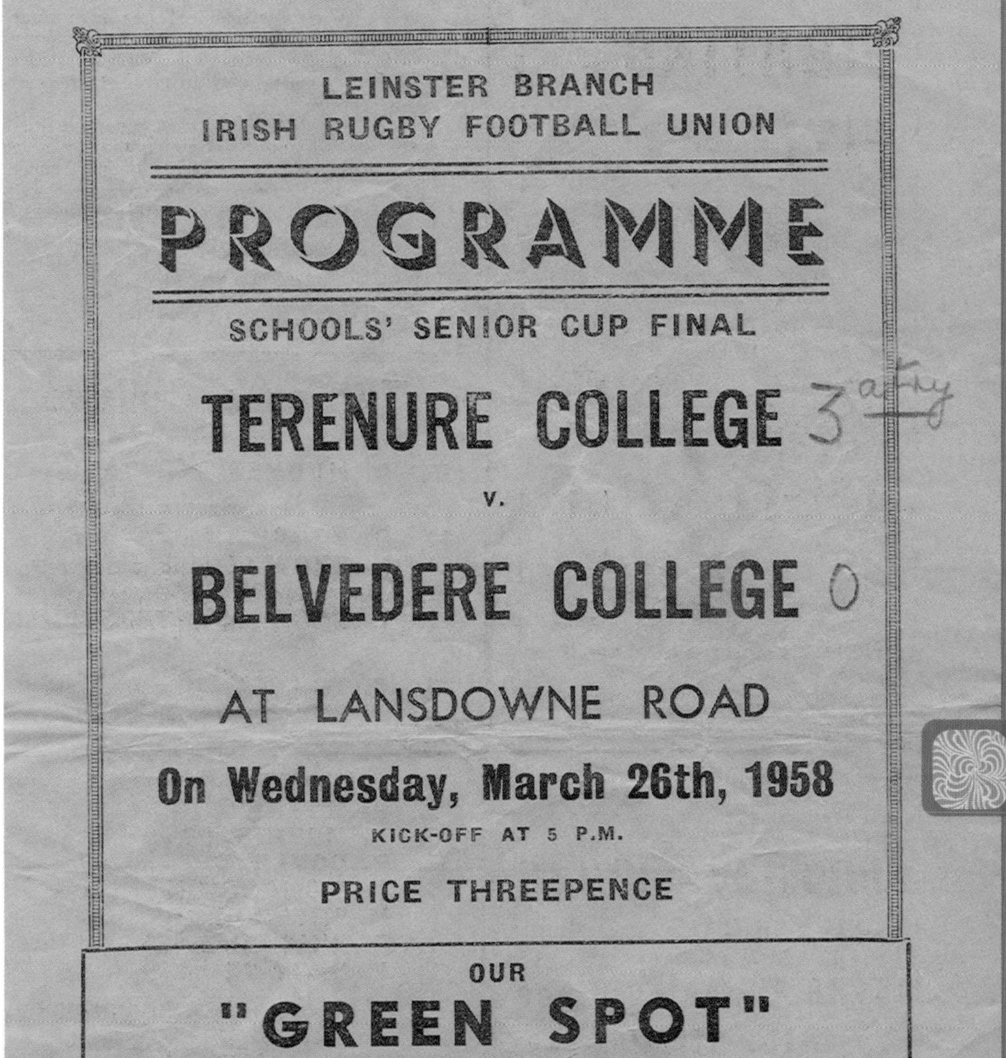

LEINSTER BRANCH
IRISH RUGBY FOOTBALL UNION

PROGRAMME

SCHOOLS' SENIOR CUP FINAL

TERENURE COLLEGE 3 a try

v.

BELVEDERE COLLEGE 0

AT LANSDOWNE ROAD

On Wednesday, March 26th, 1958

KICK-OFF AT 5 P.M.

PRICE THREEPENCE

OUR
"GREEN SPOT"
J. J. & S. 10 Years Old
is matured for a minimum period of 10 years in our own sherry casks in our own warehouses and bottled under expert supervision.

There is no finer whiskey!

MITCHELL & SON
21 Kildare Street - - Dublin
'Phone 62377

John T. Drought, Ltd., Printers, 5 & 6 Bachelor's Walk, Dublin.

57 v 6

Terenure Line never crossed in Cup. Mal

Dermot McAuley winning the 100 yards senior championship, 1934. McAuley set many college athletic records in the 1930s, the first of which was not to be bettered until the 1950s.

Mc Cauley Winning
yds. Senior Champs:
at
enure College Sports

381

CHAPTER 20

Turbulent Times,
1965–85

Fr Lar Hegarty coaching the
under-8s, 1982.

FROM THE MIDDLE OF THE 1960S, THE COLLEGE EXPERIENCED TWO DECADES of unprecedented change. Much of this it shared with most colleges, the country and the world at large; some of it was particular to Terenure; all of it generated challenge and promoted new directions and responses. By the mid-1980s an older generation of staff — some seeming immortal in the longevity of their careers — was going or gone and a new generation of boys, who entered after 1965, inhabited a universe profoundly altered from that which had cocooned the class of 1965 and its predecessors.

EDUCATION:

Irish education at post-primary level had been virtually untouched by state policy or serious innovation since 1924: it was now about to be greatly shaken up by structural change and the introduction of 'free' education from 1966. Under the pressure of economic imperatives since 1959, the government had flagged for the first time its intention to become actively involved in education policy. Dr Patrick Hillery as minister for education had signalled as much when he set up a major investigation into the system in 1962. The resulting report, *Investment in Education*, published in December 1965, highlighted the gross inequality and inadequacy of post-primary participation nationally and stressed the necessity for change. Then, in September 1966, Education Minister Donagh O'Malley, without consulting management or teacher organisations, announced the intention to introduce 'free' education for all in secondary level — and this proposal became reality in the next school year, from September 1967. Upon implementation it went beyond his original announcement of applying up to Intermediate level by actually providing a fees-free system up to Leaving Certificate. Secondary schools could opt in or out, as they chose: parents could send their children to either 'free' or fee-paying establishments as they preferred or could afford. Widely acclaimed, the O'Malley initiative transformed the take-up of secondary education: whereas in 1966 there were under 10,000 students sitting the Leaving Certificate, by 1991 there were over 60,000 candidates. Though widely welcomed, it was hastily contrived and implemented, creating stresses and strains both infrastructural and relational. From 1968–9 to 1973–4, the numbers of pupils in secondary schools alone rose by 25% from 133,591 to 167,309. Simultaneously, the numbers of their teachers rose from 6,684 (of whom 1,325 were full-time unregistered) to 9,377 (with, 1,201 unregistered), an increase of 40%.[1] Schools opting in would receive an additional grant of £25 per pupil — a maximum that did not keep pace with inflation and thereby necessitated the need for those 'free' schools to raise voluntary additional funds. Other changes of significance predated this major one. In 1964, all secondary schools became eligible for building grants in order to encourage them to extend their provision; and, in May 1963, Patrick Hillery had announced the intention to create post-primary community schools and regional technical colleges. Other contemporaneous changes included important curriculum reform, the emergence of curriculum committees and teachers' 'subject' associations — as for the example, the Mathematics Teachers' Association in 1964 — and the 1970 government initiative to consolidate post-primary provision in certain areas by the creation of community schools.

Terenure and the 'Free' system:

As for the O'Malley free education scheme, the authorities in Terenure, as indeed in other boarding and fee-paying colleges, decided not to opt in. For the Terenure Carmelites it was a straightforward decision: the Community decided to stay out. Subsequently, the Provincial Chapter of the Order considered the matter in 1967 and its decision endorsed that of the Community; it was prompted by practical considerations as much as by tradition or sentiment. For one thing, the college had ongoing financial liabilities, which would only be exacerbated were they to enter the free scheme. For another, there was a growing urgency to expand physical and personnel provision, with a strongly felt wish to upgrade facilities. They thought, and no doubt rightly in view of the failure of the grant *in lieu* of fees to keep pace with inflation, that to enter the scheme would preclude any significant upgrade in the foreseeable future.[2] Furthermore, it was not as though Terenure College was beating the bushes to find pupils. As Fr Des Kelly recalled, the amount on offer to enter the scheme was 'insignificant for an establishment with the size and overheads of the College, with its extensive grounds and other expenses', and he was to add that wisdom dictated staying out of the scheme initially, to see how it might work in practice: if time revealed this original decision to have been unwise they could always reverse it by entering at a later date, whereas, once in, whatever befell, they could never leave it.[3] His recollection is separately and fully reflected by the memories of Fr Jackie Madden who felt then and still feels it was the right decision: they may have lost out on capitation grants but to some extent this was offset by fee income. Terenure didn't get very much from the department anyway, and it had to fund — and was used to funding — its junior school entirely from the Order's and the college's own resources.[4] Fr Grace, Prior at the time, having succeeded Fr Keenan in that significant year, 1967, was greatly exercised by the need to make the correct decision, fearing that an opt-out would cause them to lose students.[5] The opposite however, proved to be the case.

Expansion:

If the period 1945–50 had seen a 50% increase in student numbers and the following fifteen years a 100 % increase, it did not stop there. Over the twenty years to 1985, there was a quite remarkable further increase in student enrolments, with a consequent demand for increased teaching and administrative personnel. This development is summarised in Table 28.

TABLE 28: STAFF AND STUDENTS, 1965–85[6]

Year	Religious	Lay	Total	Senior School	Junior School	Total
1965	24	21	45	495	276	771
1970	26	37	63	622	344	966
1975	27	50	77	749	308	1,057
1980	22	51	73	805	371	1,176
1985	21	63	84	758	336	1,094

Far from Fr Grace's fears being realised, within three years of the arrival of the 'Free Scheme' and Terenure's opting out, pupil numbers rose by over 25% and in the twenty-year period, 1965–85, they rose by over 41%: indeed, they had peaked with a 52% increase by 1980. At the same time, the staff numbers had risen by over 86%. Most remarkable in the latter was the changing ratio of lay to religious teachers. The Carmelite Community still made up the majority of the teaching staff at the start of this period and interestingly, despite the vocations' decline that set in throughout the Irish religious landscape from the 1970s and 1980s, their numbers had fallen only from 24 to 21: yet, it was the first decline in their numbers since Terenure had been founded. This brought its own challenges and changes as shall be shortly seen. By 1970, the lay teaching staff already constituted a notable majority at 37 to 26. By 1975, they were twice the number of Carmelite teachers; by 1985, three times that number. The change in the balance of vocation, lay or religious, did not leave to a change in the balance of power: the college remained a Carmelite College in authority, management and ethos. Nevertheless, the rising student numbers and the reversing ratios of Carmelite to lay staff, led to very significant structural changes. Before examining these, it may be appropriate to consider some of the personalities who manned the vessel as it found its way through strong tides and stormy waters, as Church and society underwent respective and related revolutions.

CHURCH AND SOCIETY:

The history of the 1960s and after was dominated in Church by the Second Vatican Council and in society by the youth revolt and cultural revolution that expressed itself in diverse and disturbing ways. As to the council, opened in 1962 and ending in 1965, its ten commissions of enquiry touched almost every major aspect of Catholic faith and practice, from scripture and morals through liturgy and the missions, to religious orders, the Eastern Churches, Christian unity and the lay apostolate, in a quest for renewal and modernisation. Most obvious perhaps, and especially at local level, would be the replacement of Latin by the vernacular in all sacramental rites; the consequent efforts would be seen in everything from the physical layout of the church to the rise of the Folk Mass and lay Eucharistic ministry. Even as the Church was addressing the need for a responsive relation to the modern world, that world, at least in the west, was convulsing itself with the rise of pop culture, rock music, flower power, psychedelic experimentation, the folk movement, student revolt, and anti-war protests. It would be easy to exaggerate the extent or depth to which these convulsions affected the young of Ireland: to look at the pictures of the Terenure class of 1970, and more strikingly of 1975 onward, and to compare them with those of the classes of 1950 and 1960, is to be immediately struck by the long hair and the flared slacks. There is the anecdote of Fr Grace and a hirsute fifth year of 1973: Fr Grace, not being 'a dedicated follower of fashion', according to one account secured the young man in a headlock and, producing a pair of scissors from his habit, he gave the trendy teenager an in-class, on-the-spot haircut. Myth or otherwise, its very existence as a story illustrates the point. However, most students of the late 1960s, 1970s and 1980s were in reality probably more conservative than they themselves were prepared to admit. Nevertheless, there was a new spirit abroad and it took some effort for the Terenure authorities of the time to adapt to and to manage it. A majority of the Carmelites themselves in the college and the Province were not getting any younger and faced their own internal convulsions as they came to grips with Vatican II's *Perfecte Caritatis* or 'Adaptation and Renewal of Religious Life'. Within the Order in Ireland, lively debate and a strong search for renewal developed. Under Provincial Fr Joe Ryan, who held office over three remarkable terms from 1969 to 1976, significant change was encouraged and led, and consultation and discussion encouraged. There was a limit, however, and when the spirit of youth revolt began to infiltrate seminary life — even of Carmelites — he promptly and decisively sent all his clerical students out from Milltown to Rome in 1971.[7] The Irish Carmelite response to societal change and Vatican II came with the Extraordinary Chapter of 1968, to work on the Carmelite Constitution in the light of the council, and in one sense culminated in the memorable Provincial Chapter of 1976 — the first 'open' Chapter, with large attendance and freer debate than any friar had experienced before. Such change was reflected in the running of the college as much as of the Order, and it may be appropriate here to consider some of those who staffed and ran the college over the decade or so from 1965.

THE PRIORS:

When Fr Patsy Keenan stepped down from the increasingly demanding office of Prior in 1967 — doubtless with a sigh of relief — he was succeeded by the legendary Fr Patrick Simon Grace. Like his contemporary and a former president, Dunstan O'Connor, Fr Grace was, by some accounts, a tough man, yet, for all that like Dunstan he was perceived as one for whom the glass of life was half-empty rather than half-full. By other accounts, he was actually a shy person and one remembered for many acts of personal kindness. For all his complexity, he proved a reliable force during this time of turbulence, and in one way, he was one of Terenure's élite band of seeming immortals:

retiring from the classroom in 1996, no Carmelite or lay teacher had before or has since surpassed his record — his whose professional life was spent solely in Terenure and he taught there for an unequalled 46 years. Born in Aglish near Villierstown, Co. Waterford in 1921, but a Kilkenny man in heritage and allegiance, he was educated in the North Monastery, Cork. He joined the Carmelites in September 1940 and was ordained in 1948.[8] It was in the next year that he joined the staff of the college, at the same time as Fr Des Clarke, John Romaeus Lamont — younger brother of Bishop Donal — and Fr Lar Hegarty, another legend and another of the seeming immortals. Nicknamed 'The Cow' — ungraciously — he acquired this *sobriquet* not from his general behaviour but from a peculiar mannerism, a strange guttural utterance that marked the beginning of his speaking. He taught religion and science and to very great effect. He was one of that small but significant cluster of science teachers from the 1950s that produced a string of able young science students some of whom became distinguished scientists. He was a strict disciplinarian and not averse to the practice of 'wiggings' whereby he would elevate some unruly or reluctant scholar on to their tiptoes by an upward leverage of their sideburns, as several pupils remembered. One former pupil, and later a Carmelite confrere, recalled that if it came to a question of slacking or neglect of study, he 'took no prisoners' — he was the teacher whose homework was always done first and never forgotten. For all that, he was a gifted teacher. Even when well-advanced in career and years, a student like Joe Cleere of the class of 1983 — and PPU president exactly twenty years later — who led no special love of science, found him to be a superb teacher with a gift for making the subject interesting.[9] Apart from teaching science and religion he was also games master in the 1950s, as befitted one who had been a Co. Cork and a Co. Kilkenny Minor hurling ace in his day: in Terenure, he became a formidable trainer of the school's senior rugby team — respected enough in this regard to have been chosen for the Leinster selectors.[10] He coached the seniors over the years 1955 to 1963 and therefore coached them to victory in 1958, the year of the historic double. In his unorthodox way, it may well be that he coached them to courage and victory in the manner of King Frederick the Great of Prussia encouraging his troops to battle — 'Onward you fools, do you want to live forever?'. Nevertheless, one insightful former pupil, recalling his own rugby days and Fr Grace's coaching, remarked that he manifested an unusual combination of being very tough yet very indecisive, hesitating and verging on the side of doubt. This complex combination was later evident when as Prior he had to lead the discussion and the decision in respect of the free education issue. For all his toughness and propensity to deliver a clip on the ear, he was remembered with respect and affection and was the one that so many alumni kept in contact with in later life: he was asked to officiate at their marriages, and the baptisms of their children, more so than any other member of the Community, and was a frequent presence at the unhappier events of their family bereavements.[11] Perhaps his complexity is best caught by another former pupil who remembered him thus: 'a uniquely caring man with an extremely short fuse, bearing a great bunch of keys which he could suddenly launch, rocket-like at an errant pupil'.[12]

For all his hesitations, he presided over the greatest changes and challenges the college until then had ever seen. As one commentator put it succinctly:

> He began teaching Religious Knowledge when the Maynooth green Catechism was still in print; Hart's Christian Doctrine and Sheehan's Apologetics were the staple texts in the years before Vatican II. We then had a period of no texts and plenty of questions, followed by new text books and still more questions.[13]

One of those major challenges has already been noted — the decision to opt out of the free education scheme. A second was soon to follow.

THE END OF BOARDING SCHOOL:

In this time of many changes, one of the most contentious was that ending the century-long tradition of educating and catering for boarding pupils. Although their numbers were around the one hundred mark, at the end of the 1960s their numbers were beginning to fall, largely because the rapid spread of decent new secondary schools throughout the country made such education more locally accessible. Furthermore, the cost of keeping boarders probably far exceeded the fee income they generated. Whereas in the 1950s boarders made up some 40% to 50% of the student body, by the mid-1960s, they had declined to constitute only about 10%. Nevertheless, the decision to terminate the system caused great concern, disquiet and debate among the friars of the Terenure Community and among the Carmelites of the Irish Province. Many of the older Friars — and indeed, some of those not so old had been Terenure boarders and they had a naturally protective and defensive commitment to that tradition. Nonetheless, for a generally ageing Terenure Community, the task of properly caring for and supervising the young boarders seven days a week was an exhausting one — and increasingly so in an age of increased educational pressures and cultural change. The days of supervision were long and draining, from 6.00 a.m. until 10.00 p.m. and later at times: to go out for an evening required one to have cover. With the beginning of numerical decline in the boarding population, and in the face of the palpably growing pressure from the locality to admit ever more day-pupils, the matter came to a head at the end of the 1960s. The debate began in Terenure but spread upwards and outwards into the wider Irish Province. Fr Joe Ryan, as Provincial, felt it best to let the debate proceed with meetings, position papers and more meetings, and finally the Terenure Community decision to opt to terminate the boarding system was endorsed by the Province in general. Perhaps one of the factors that helped Prior Grace to overcome his hesitations was the fact that he had at his side, from the commencement of his term, the young and decisive Fr Adrian David Weakliam. Here was one who knew Terenure inside out, as a distinguished former pupil of the class of 1954 and a highly regarded teacher. Born in 1936, he was received into the Order in October 1954, taking the name David, and ordained in July 1963. Graduating from

UCD with a BSc, he returned to Terenure where he taught physics with great success from 1964, while Frs McCouaig and Grace specialised in teaching chemistry. Becoming the Community's Sub-Prior in 1967, he then, in 1970, was appointed to succeed Fr McCouaig as dean of studies, a position which effectively made him college principal over the years 1970–3. These were the years which saw the complete phasing out of the boarders. While something of a Terenure tradition had been lost, it was, certainly in retrospect, a merciful release for the hard-pressed friars. As already seen from Table 28, it did nothing to damage the intake to the college: on the contrary, even as the available space increased, so did the number of day-pupils who arrived as quickly to fill it. As dean of studies, Fr David effectively ran the day-to-day business of the college — doing so with matchless efficiency — while Fr Grace as Prior, was effective manager of the college with the key power and responsibility of interviewing and securing teaching staff for the growing student body.

In 1973, on Fr Grace's relinquishing the position of Prior, David Weakliam was elected in his place both as Prior of the Community and principal of the college. He led the college in the period of continuing change over 1973 to 1976 when he was elected Provincial of the Order in succession to Fr Ryan — a position he held for two terms until 1982. Thereafter, Fr Chris Crowley succeeded as head of the Province, up to 1988. On Fr David's becoming Provincial in 1976, he quickly recommended that the position of principal of the college and Prior of the Community be separated as the dual responsibility had become intolerably onerous. This recommendation, which was accepted, became one step, but an important one, in a succession of structural changes which had already been in train since Fr David took up the reins in 1973. Before reverting to these, this particular change led Fr Bob Kelly to succeed as Prior in 1976 — while the day-to-day running of the senior school was entrusted to Fr Paul Graham as its Provincial, and the running of the junior school to its dean, Fr Lar Hegarty. In 1979, the title of head of junior school was also changed from dean to principal.

The pressurised nature of the teaching day for teachers in general and for Carmelite friars in particular in the profoundly altered 1960s is well seen in the typical day of Fr Bob Kelly, nine years before he succeeded Fr Weakliam as Terenure Prior. Born in Moyvoughley, Co. Westmeath in 1939 and first educated locally in Moyvoughley and Ballymore, by two wonderful schoolteachers, Ina Flanagan and Patrick Cooney, Fr Bob went in 1953 to the Carmelite College, Moate, then only in operation for four years. Here, he was to experience the humane influence and inspiration of two former Terenure Carmelite legends, Frs Ossie McGrath and Andy Wright, each one larger than life and, in partnership in Moate an improbably wonderful combination for any school. Entering the Order after Leaving Certificate in 1958, he pursued his studies in Ireland until 1964 and, from October of that year, in Rome. Returning to Ireland in 1967, the Provincial assigned him to teach religious education in Crumlin Vocational School. Apart from the conventual life he observed in Whitefriar Street, he now taught seven classes a day of 45 minutes each, five days s a week together with confessions in Whitefriar Street on Thursdays and Saturdays, Masses on Sundays, and on top of all this there was his ministry to Mercer's Hospital. It was a regime that well-prepared him for the pressures of Terenure with its 1,000 plus students and 77 teaching staff. Returning to Terenure in 1970 to teach in the junior school, he was witness to the phasing out of the boarders and to the new lease of life it gave to the Community. However, he also encountered the rapid expansion of the day-pupil population which saw the first appearance and then the proliferation of pre-fabricated buildings. He himself, in the later 1970s, was to play the key role in infrastructural developments that would finally eliminate the prefab scourge. That, however, is a matter for later: for now, it is timely to consider the expansion of the number of staff and the structural changes that came as a consequence.

Expansion and Frustration:

In the Terenure lore of this period are the years of the great surge, 1966–71, when the number of lay staff rose from the 21 of 1964–5, to the 27 in 1969–70, and finally 37 in 1970–1, as the college responded to the relentless rise in student numbers. Another such surge came in the period 1980 to 1985 when the lay teaching personnel rose from 51 to 84. The sheer size of the place, with its close-on 1,000 students in 1970 and staff of over 60, brought unprecedented stresses and strains. Terenure was far from unique in this: the explosive take-up of secondary education in the 1960s, and the radical changes, well-intentioned but pushed through without too much forethought for consultation or resources, created pressures and frustrations in the system and in the teaching profession. These resulted in three strikes by the three separate teacher trade unions in the first few months of 1969, with the secondary-school union, ASTI, bringing out its members that February. As the historian of ASTI, John Coolahan, remarked, strikes in 1969, and the ever-present threat of strikes over the period of 1968 to 1971, led to 'a traumatic period for Irish education'. The history of that conflict has been written elsewhere.[14] It suffices to say here that with Terenure College's lay staff fully or almost fully unionised in ASTI, they became totally involved in the secondary strike which brought the senior school to shut down from 1 to 24 of February 1969. The strike was precipitated by the report of the Ryan Tribunal in May 1968. This recommended a common scale for all teachers, which dismayed ASTI by lowering the maximum point in the scale for future secondary teachers. It was the first strike by them since 1920 and the first such event to close Terenure. Surprisingly however, relations between the lay teachers and Carmelite management emerged unscathed, partly because of the huge ASTI vote in favour of strike, partly because the unity of the Terenure lay staff on the issue, and partly because the Carmelites were not unsympathetic to the teachers' cause: they were, after all, teachers themselves. It also greatly helped that the Joint Managerial Body, representing all religiously run secondary schools, Catholic and Protestant alike, had agreed to pay the basic salary in the course of the strike.[15] The strike ended on 24 February when ASTI accepted a government offer of increased pay for special function allowances. These special functions or posts of responsibility were to have their own impact on Terenure, in assisting it to adapt to the pressures of a new era.

STRUCTURAL CHANGE:

The basic management of Terenure College had been unchanged since 1941 when the deanships of senior and junior schools and of discipline were introduced. From then until 1972–3, the college was run exclusively by the Carmelite management structure of Prior, Sub-Prior, dean of studies, dean of discipline and the deans of the two schools. Then, from the start of the school year 1972–3, the senior lay staff was brought into management to a significant degree, and a series of management changes unfolded to the end of the 1970s. The lay teachers' quest for the creation and recognition of posts of responsibility had been first adopted as a policy item by ASTI back in 1962 and it first pressed its claim in this regard early in 1968. In May 1968, the Ryan Tribunal had recommended the formal institution and financial recognition of the posts of principal, vice-principal and eight other grades of responsibility. It had further recommended that in schools owned by religious either the principal or the vice-principal post should be held by a lay teacher. By February 1971, following complex negotiations, the Joint Managerial Body had accepted posts of responsibility as an inevitable feature of the Irish education world and final agreement between it and ASTI had been concluded by June 1972.

However, even before this, the Terenure Community faced the realities both of their own actual situation and of lay teachers' aspirations. For them, 1971 was the last year when all the management administrative positions of responsibility were held by Carmelites. In 1972, a new position of vice-principal, together with a system of form master, was inaugurated. Michael 'The Liberator' O'Connell, then in his twenty-fifth year of service, became the first vice-principal in the college's history. It was certainly not a case of 'Buggins Turn', for, although he was now the senior lay teacher, he was also deeply and immensely respected in the college. It was an extremely happy choice, until his retirement at the end of the school year 1979–80. His successor, Tom Byrne, was an equally well-received appointment and one which he held until 1996. The simultaneous introduction of the form masters' positions, saw six such posts assigned in 1972, three going to the Carmelite Frs McCouaig (fifth form), Madden (fourth form) and Doran (second form), while three went to the laymen, O'Connell (for sixth form), Tom Byrne (third form) and Pat O'Brien (first form) — a past pupil (class of 1958) and long-serving teacher from 1962–3 who shared the staff room with namesake Pat 'Buster' O'Brien, the tall Pat 'Thumber' O'Brien was a talented artist as well as being a gifted teacher of English. At the same time the headship of the senior school was held by the dean of studies, in this case, Fr Weakliam, and the headship of the junior school by Fr Lar Hegarty.

In 1976, further devolutions of responsibility and title came when Bob Kelly had become Prior and Fr Weakliam Provincial: and a new title, principal of the senior school, was introduced, the post being filled by Fr Graham. At the same time, the head of the junior school was still entitled dean and the post still held by Fr Hegarty. While still holding the responsibility, in 1979, Fr Hegarty's title as post holder was changed from dean to principal of the junior school. By that stage, the new structures were bedding down and were doing so with a pronounced degree of goodwill and good order. They had done so before the next surge of lay-teacher recruitment, which brought the total teaching staff to 84, comprising 63 lay and 21 religious teaching staff. For all the turbulence of these times, it should be noted that, as in earlier periods of change, the sense of the rapid unfolding of events, of unpredictability and of turmoil even, was counteracted by those abiding presences who, to the boys of the 1960s, 1970s, and 1980s, seemed part of a timeless continuum. Foremost among them then was that legendary dean of the junior school.

'Heggo':

When Fr Lawrence F. Hegarty, Fr Lar to his friends and confreres, or 'Heggo' to the boys, had his title changed from dean to principal of the junior school, in 1979, he already had 30 years of Terenure teaching and pupil-minding behind him. Seen on the playing fields surrounded by the little boys at rugby, or in the schoolyard at break-time, frustrating their efforts to retrieve the soccer ball as he dribbled it expertly and concealed it under the hem of his voluminous habit, Fr Hegarty seemed a permanent presence of support and encouragement in a world now more than ever in flux. Like Fr Grace, and exceptionally, all his priestly and professional life was spent in and devoted to the college. It showed. From the beginning to the end of his teaching days, no Carmelite was more universally loved and respected. The boys simply adored him. Frank Gallen, just commencing his teaching career in Terenure in 1974, and destined one day to become deputy principal, vividly remembers Fr Hegarty 'ever present in the school yard, surrounded by the Junior boys, always there for them',[16] while actor, Michael Grennell, of the class of 1976 recalled that he remembered the name of every boy he ever taught, while architect, Paul Joyce, of the class of 1971 remembered him as 'tough, and kind and invariably fair'.[17] For a long time, he occupied his office on the top floor of his junior school, up seven flights of stairs above the crush hall and its tuck shop, across the corridor from Elementary 3A's classroom. From here, too, he wrote himself indelibly into his pupils' memories and their dreaded school reports, forever written with his favourite fountain pen and its never changing and unmistakeable turquoise ink: so Ronan O'Connell of the class of 1973 and Bernard Kenna of the class of 1974 remembered him. Entering Terenure in 1975, his former pupil and later Community colleague, Fr Eoin Moore, well remembered Fr Hegarty announcing his arrival at the class by thumping a hollow spot in the architrave which would resound with a loud and striking bang, and how, on Friday afternoons, he would read to them a chapter from Enid Blyton's *The Wishing Chair*.[18] Another one of those marvellous Carmelite Kinsale natives who returned to their home place only for their novitiate year, Fr Lar was born in 1921, eldest of five in a family of four boys and a girl who lost their father early in their young lives. Their widowed mother managed to educate them with a heroic success. Lar completed the Leaving Certificate in Cork in 1940 and entered the novitiate in September 1941. After his UCD BA, he made his final profession in October 1944 and then on to the well-trodden paths to Gort Muire and Milltown until ordination in July 1948. In September 1949, he was welcomed to Terenure where he served his Community for 49 years. All of his teaching years were spent in the junior school where he left an indelible impression on the minds and in the memories of its alumni pupils. He took up the headship of that school in succession to Ephrem Corbett as early as 1952, and only relinquished it, exactly 30 years later, when he was succeeded in 1982 by young Fr Martin Kilmurray, now Carmelite Provincial in Ireland, but for seventeen years junior school principal.

Lar Hegarty's life was, above all else, shining in its simplicity. Never in an aircraft, never having a passport, his trusty bike was he preferred mode of travel, which grew old gracefully with him. When not minding the boys or saying his prayers, his preference for relaxation were his Sunday visits to Glenmalure Park — then the home of Shamrock Rovers: he was an ardent 'Hoops' supporter, was a regular frequenter of Irish international soccer matches in Dalymount Park and a devoted collector of soccer and rugby match programmes.

As to his own field activities, he was in succession to Andy Wright — the great grass-cutter of Terenure College and the untiring painter of its many goal posts. As former pupil and later (and still) Terenure teacher, Charlie O'Sullivan of the class of 1970 observed, Fr Hegarty trained the under 11s at rugby for 25 years and, when Charlie himself joined the staff, Fr Hegarty remarked that he would give it up if only Charlie himself would take it over.[19] That deal was struck and Fr Lar at last took a well-earned rest. A big man with a big heart, he must have had even bigger lungs: most pupils, in remembering him, typically see him blowing up interminable footballs, at every boy's beck and call. As one Carmelite friend recalled: 'for about thirty years he pumped and laced every football that was used'.[20] Jim Blake, recalling his first day at the college in 1954, recounted how fortunate he was to have first been greeted by Fr Lar and how he came to epitomise much that was special about Terenure: 'in particular, that happy optimistic spirit that "everything would be alright on the night"'. Affable and devoted, he would spend hours on end simply mending rugby balls or tending to the condition of the pitches. This was from a man who was expert in Greek, Latin, Irish and English, and yet, renowned in the college for his concern for those not academically high-flying. He had an ocean of patience for those not great at the sums or the Irish. It was therefore fitting that after his passing in 1988, there was instituted through the good offices of the Past Pupils' Union — under its president, Des Lamont — the Fr Laurence Hegarty Bursary, the first dedicated bursary in the college's history, awarded annually to a fifth year pupil or pupils for interest and progress in a modern language on the curriculum.[21]

A Changing Place:

For Terenure, as elsewhere, these years were not only a case of changing times — they saw, too, for Terenure, a greatly changing place. Unannounced and undetermined at any moment, the period 1965 to 1986 saw the gradual decline and disappearance of the farm. No one can point to any definite moment which precipitated this since there was none. The orchard and kitchen gardens lingered longer but only the rose garden survived in any recognisable state, carefully tended by Fr Martin O'Malley, especially against the occasional raids by Fr Andy Wright when he wanted to take flowers for hospital visits. As to the farm, when Frank Gildea arrived as a boarder in 1969, his recollection was that there was no great farming activity going on, although cattle still grazed the rugby pitches to such effect that visiting teams were known to call the place 'Termanure'. And the orchard was still in use when he left with the class of 1973. Likewise Michael Grennell, who was a pupil from 1966 to 1976, recalled in his earlier days the squealing of piglets and the birthing of a calf.[22] Ronan O'Connell who left Terenure with the Leaving Certificate class of 1973 thought the farm was still functioning in some kind of manner, but Joe Mothersill who left in 1974 — and became a Carmelite — thought that by then it was no longer a going concern.[23] The gradual decline of the farm over the early 1970s was also accompanied by the rise of the 'prefab', as the college sought to cope with the growing enrolments. By the time Frank Gallen arrived on the staff in 1974, the first Years — all 125 of them — had to be accommodated in these prefabs. They simply did not exist a decade before that when Fr Bob Kelly arrived to pursue his HDip in 1962–3. In September 1966, the first of them had arrived to provide three new classrooms and even more followed in 1969.[24] It would fall to Fr Bob as Prior and manager two decades later to put an end to the prefabs with a major building development. Before turning to that, two major developments of the late 1960s and 1970s were realised. One was the construction of the swimming pool, the other the redesign of the college chapel.

The Swimming Pool:

Until the early 1970s from when it was taken very seriously as a sport in the college, swimming — like cricket — was one of those activities that had a very up and down history. Fr Micheál Ó Néill's reflection that 'great things happen in Terenure due to individuals' was certainly borne out in respect of swimming: it has been seen how important was the role of Pat Cashin in promoting it in the mid- and late 1940s, producing in Jimmy O'Connor, Terenure's first Leinster champion, in September 1948. All this was without benefit of any suitable college pool — the lake pool not being remotely adequate — and had to be achieved by organised visits to Tara Street or Blackrock Baths. For a decade and a half, it appears to have ceased as an organised activity in the college. By 1962–3 however, with the support of instructor B. Halpin, a swimming club appears to have re-emerged and a successful gala was held at Iveagh

Baths in May 1964 for the junior boys. At that stage, as a number of former pupils recall, Fr Heaslip took up the challenge of promoting swimming in a college with no pool: he took groups into Tara Street weekly, arriving there in his clapped out Hillman Minx, loaded down with six or seven boy swimmers — all this on a Sunday evening, after which he would be prevailed upon to treat them to chips in the nearest Wimpy Bar, all at his own expense. By 1967, it had been re-established as a popular activity in the college, with some 150 of the boys taking part in that year's competition, and with some from the senior school taking it up seriously. By 1968–9, the college's first trophy since 1948 had come its way: it won the Duffy Memorial Shield, awarded to the college or club that had made the greatest progress in the Life Saving Awards. At that stage, the college authorities were committed to try to create their own pool.

Once committed, it was surprising how quickly it came about — even if it were in two stages. Trucks began to arrive in late December 1968, to the delight of the boys, and in January 1969 work began on demolishing the old 'Yellow House': here, once the site was cleared, excavations for the pool were commenced and, by mid-March, the process of tiling was well under way.[25] One good turn begot another: the old 'Yellow House', long falling into decay, had somehow been kept adventurously negotiable by the efforts of Br Stephen and was so being used by the college Scouts. Upon its demolition, they had to be and were provided with a fine new Scout hall at the rear of the college and into which they moved in 1968. On the last day of June 1969, the 25-metre outdoor, heated pool had been completed, with high hopes to have it covered within a year. Surrounded by a wooden fence and having a small concrete changing room to its side, it was fairly basic, yet represented a tremendous new facility for the college. In September, newly arrived PE teacher, Patrick O'Kane, soon had his hands full organising gymnastics and swimming for the year ahead. Meanwhile the hopes to have the pool fully converted into an indoor facility took somewhat longer than the hoped-for year. Finance was one problem, and, although the PPU had played an important pump-priming role in assisting with a new college building fund, set up in 1966 — even as the prefabs arrived — the ambitions for the college far outstripped even the singular fund-raising abilities of the union and its associates. Nevertheless, with some judicious planning and borrowing, the pool was successfully completed and opened in June in 1972, a great boost to the college and its neighbourhood.

New Construction:

The gradual departure of the boarders began to free up much needed space from the early 1970s. Already, in 1971, the senior dorm had been converted into classrooms followed by progressive conversion of the junior dorms to a similar end. The old study hall, as a consequence, was then fixed up for conversion to a lecture theatre and geography room, and the former boarders' recreation room was converted to a library.[26] This was followed in 1975 by the conversion of the old workshop in the yard into first-year classrooms, and in the following year a new kitchen and communal refectory block had been added. Some would come to regret that during these works a demolition of part of the original house resulted in the removal of the very fine original staircase that came down into the reception hall, opposite the main door — it was in some sense, a deconstruction typical of that age — it was done in conjunction with the removal of the old boys' refectory and the old kitchens. This was by way of preparation for major building work from 1978 — and a pity that it could not be undone. It was carried out apparently to prevent the pupils coming down *en masse* into the hallway, but perhaps an elegant barrier rope and an eloquent injunction would have sufficed to stop the hordes and save the stairs.

However, the most significant development at this time in terms of scale and of symbolism was the reconstruction of the church and sanctuary. Following the design of architect John Scannell, the church interior was transformed to capture the spirit and intent of the liturgical revolution that followed in the wake of Vatican II. The sanctuary was radically relocated to the main body of the church and the seating rearranged to circumscribe it, thereby creating a new sense of closeness and communion. The original sanctuary space was remodelled to provide a new chapel to Our Lady.[27] The overall effect was to greatly enhance both visibility and the sense of belonging, while the choice of furnishing materials by artist, Ray Carroll, created a wonderful sense of warmth and repose.

In a striking way, the organisational and the physical changes in the college from the mid-1970s onward were intimately interrelated. As has been noted, up to 1976 and the end of David Weakliam's tenure, the Prior had been both manager and principal of the college. With his own huge capacity for work, his gift for administration and his proverbial incisiveness, Fr Weakliam had come to see these conjoined roles as no longer viable. In this old dispensation, the one man had to look after two schools in the minutiae of their daily running, fulfil the role of strategic planning officer and, at the same time, be the father and minder of an ageing Community the needs of which were growing and compelling. This incompatibility was resolved quickly, simply and decisively by him when now, as Provincial, in 1976, the roles of Prior and principal were separated, with Fr Kelly being elected to the former and Fr Graham being assigned to the latter. The process reached completion in 1979 when, at the start of his second term, Fr Kelly became Prior and manager, with responsibility for the Community and strategic planning for the college, while the principal, from September 1979, Fr Jim McCouaig, was responsible for the running of the senior school. The rationale behind this was the major building programme that commenced in 1979: the construction of some twenty new classrooms, workrooms and laboratories, a new gymnasium and new changing rooms for rugby; six specialist rooms and offices and work places for the greatly increased lay staff whose numbers were just about to surge again from 1980:[28] and, it is wonderful to relate, the consignment of the prefabs to the past. Such a major undertaking at a projected cost of £1.2 million was way beyond the means of the college and its friends. Crucial, therefore, to its ever happening was a vital agreement with the Department of Education. The latter undertook to provide 80% of the cost, subject to the condition that the college would guarantee the offer of twenty places for boys from St Joseph's and twenty places for those from St Pius National Schools. The fact of fund-raising the outstanding 20% — done by way of a covenant scheme and traditional fund raising ventures — meant the separation of functions between Prior-manager and principals was both timely and necessary. It speaks volumes for the efforts and energies of Past Pupils' Union, Parents' Association and the fund-raising committee that so much was accomplished so quickly. The grand plans conceived in 1978 and commenced upon in 1979 were completed by the end of 1981. The process not only provided urgently needed and well-executed new facilities, but engendered a new sense of community and a robust sense of renewal after times of unprecedented turbulence.

Michael 'The Liberator' O'Connell, *c.* 1972.

Jan. 1st, 1971.

`Phone ⎰ 905804
        ⎱ 904621

Dear Parent or Guardian,

      The enclosed letter from our Father Provincial arrived with me shortly before Christmas. The contents speak for themselves.

      The phasing out of boarders from our College breaks a tradition established over the past century, but the march of time seems to make this inevitable. Those who have been associated with our Boarding School over the years will hear of the decision with a certain amount of nostalgia, and will understand that there are many compelling reasons for taking such a step.

      It is the hope of our Community that hardship will be caused to any family as a result of this d

      May I avail of the opportunity to wish you every blessing and happiness in 1971.

        Yours sincerely,

        P.S. Grace, O.Carm.

        (President.)

401

Letter from Prior Grace to parents informing them of the college's intention to phase out boarders, 1 January 1971.

Letter from the Provincial Linus Ryan to
Prior Grace stating that the Order had
decreed that boarding at Terenure should
be phased out, 16 December 1970.

The Provincial's Office,
Whitefriar Street Church,
56 Aungier Street,
Dublin 2.
Telephones 755217, 758821
Telegrams "Whitefriars, Dublin"

Dear Father Prior,

As you already know, the Provincial Chapter held this year decreed
that the boarding school at Terenure College should be phased out.
Since this decision was reached much consideration has been given
to the method by which it will be implemented. It has now been
decided that no more pupils may be admitted to the College as
boarders from to-day.

You will remember the lengthy discussions which took place before
it was decided to close this section of the School and the concern
expressed for both pupils and parents or guardians. It is now
your task, difficult as it will be, to inform all concerned that
the College will be finally closed to boarders on and from the
30th June, 1973. (This date will permit boys who have already
begun Certificate Courses to complete them.) The intervening
time should allow you to give every possible assistance to those
      will not have finished their secondary education. We feel
      that you will be able to use your good offices in helping
      .ace any pupil whose parents or guardians may wish them to
continue at a boarding school.

However, should all efforts at replacement fail and there be
proven hardship to a family we would ask you to refer individual
cases to us with a view to the possible provision of accomodation
and study facilities.

For many years Carmelites have made a contribution to education in
Ireland. The demands in the locality have led to an increasing
number of day pupils and it was felt at the Chapter that we could
contribute more at the College by extended effort in this field,
whilst continuing to fulfil our role as educators of boarding
pupils at Carmelite College, Moate.

We fully realize that our decision may cause upset in some
families but we feel sure that the parents and guardians of our
boarding pupils will understand that this difficult decision was
not made lightly.

On behalf of the Definitory,

Fraternally,

J. Linus Ryan O. Carm.

J. Linus Ryan, O.Carm.,
Provincial   16th December, 1970.

To The Very Rev. P.S.Grace, O.Carm.,
    Terenure College,
    DUBLIN 6.

402

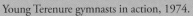
Young Terenure gymnasts in action, 1974.

404

Pele during his visit to Terenure College, 1979.

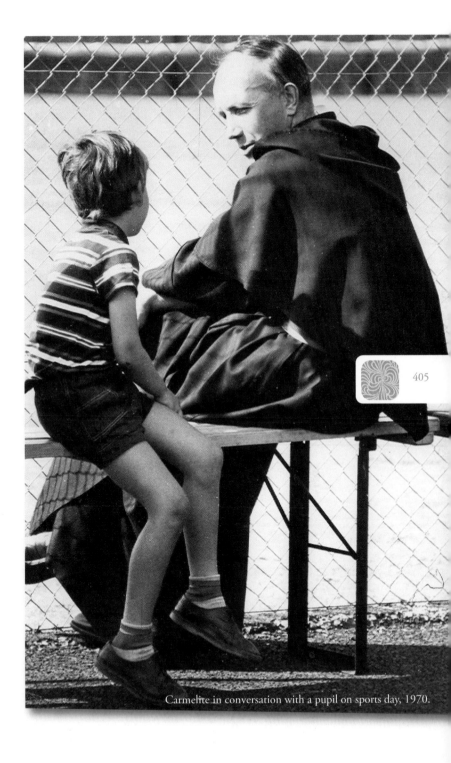

405

Carmelite in conversation with a pupil on sports day, 1970.

Sixth years, 1966. *Above left to right*: R. Walsh, A. Nolan, L. Chuang, H. Herkner, F. Duggan, J. Treacey, P. Sparks. *Below left to right*: A. Abel, E. Bedford, G. Walsh, P. Kearney, B. Harrington, T. Morrissey, P. Robinson.

Sixth years, 1966. *Above left to right*: D. Keogh, B. Mooney, M. Glynn, D. McCafferty, J. Gleeson, D. Joyce-Glynn, C. Jenkinson.

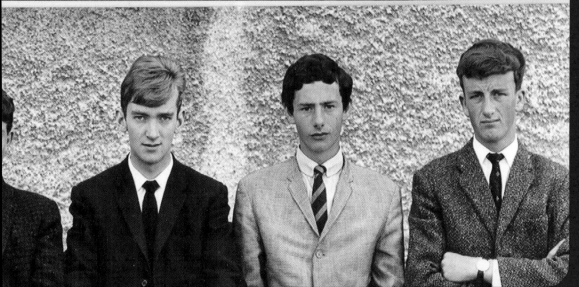

CHAPTER 21

Masters and Scholars,
1965–85

Terenure students, M. Colley,
S. Daly, J. Henchion and
J. O'Grady-Walshe, 1979.

IN THE GREAT SURGE IN LAY STAFF NUMBERS THAT CAME IN THE LATE 1960s and early 1970s, some who arrived came to stay, or to stay for a very long time; others, by choice or perforce, served more briefly. Among the latter was one whose career exemplified that the teacher's lot was not always a happy one.

Patrick O'Kane came to Terenure in 1969 as a qualified but unrecognised teacher of physical education. On finishing his secondary education at St Columb's, Derry, he proceeded in 1966 on to a scholarship to Trinity and All Saints in Leeds, where the broad liberal arts curriculum and the special programmes in PE made for highly professional graduates in physical education. On graduating in 1969, he applied for and succeeded in securing the position of PE teacher in Terenure, following an interview with Fr Grace. Patrick was all set for a successful career in the college. Unfortunately, the Department of Education refused to recognise his qualifications, despite strong representations by Fr Grace and Michael O'Connell: the department representatives on the Registration Council refused to accede to recognition — to have done so would have required the state to fund his salary and increments and to provide a very substantial capital grant for a gymnasium and a full range of equipment. It was in the years before the foundation of the National Institute of Higher Education (NIHE), Limerick. It says a great deal for the generosity of the Carmelites that they paid his basic salary and dean of studies, Fr McCouaig, purchased whatever equipment he needed; however, as long as recognition was refused, no security or career progression was possible for Patrick O'Kane. After three years of continued refusal of recognition, Patrick had to abandon Terenure for a teaching position in Folkestone, Kent, where recognition and progression were guaranteed and where, within a year, Patrick became acting deputy head: however, having to work for Kent Local Education Authority before they could convert any 'acting' position into an actual position, he moved on to the headship of a Mining Trust School in Zambia. Here Margaret, his wife, and he had their first two children and here they taught for four years before returning home to a career in engineering.[1] While the problem of non-recognition and the status of being an unregistered teacher would over the next decade or so become a declining one, it was no solace to its victims.

Among other new lay staff to join Terenure in these years was a group of senior school teachers who would have long and distinguished careers in the college. Among them were former Terenure pupils: John McClean of the class of 1963, Charlie O'Sullivan of 1970, Brendan McCauley of 1976 and Kevin Williamson of 1977. Among long-serving lay teachers who had not been college alumni, but likewise, would be destined to play a very significant role in Terenure's development were Joseph McDonnell from Limerick, Seamus McCool from Donegal, Andrias Ó Danachair from Offaly and Frank Gallen from Dublin. By any reckoning, McClean was a considerable acquisition, for classroom and sports field alike. A Harold's Cross lad who first saw a classroom when he entered Mrs Ohle's famous establishment at No. 10 Fortfield Road, he entered Terenure's Elementary B in 1955. Enjoying his school days there, he later recalled Terenure as 'a school for all the people and not just one that engaged in creaming off the best' — he would experience the truth of this observa-tion directly as a teacher when, as first year form master, he would serve on the college's admission committee: here he would come to note the emphasis on the need and practice of observing social, economic and academic diversity in this regard. He was soon nicknamed 'The Doc', because of early academic success. His winning the prize as senior English essayist in 1963 was a pointer to his later teaching success, especially in English, but also in communication generally: so his brilliant success as rugby and soccer coach would testify later. Specialising in English during his UCD years, he returned to Terenure for his teaching practice and joined the teaching staff in September 1968. Twelve years later he became form master, a position he retained until 1995–6. He left Terenure to pursue a highly successful career in coaching rugby at UCD and setting up the Rugby Academy there.[2]

Joe McDonnell and his colleague, Seamus McCool, joined up in what the former aptly called 'The Year of the Great Influx', 1968. They would spend a teaching life there, finding themselves, like others, committed to a great deal more beyond teaching. Coming through Limerick CBS and UCD, where he graduated in mathematics, Joe heard that Terenure was looking out for mathematics teachers and was taken on by Fr McCouaig that September. Over 40 years later he is still teaching there, energetic as ever. On arrival, little separated him in years from the sixth form into which he was plunged on his very first day. In time, and beyond the classroom, he would find himself gifted with responsibility for organising and reorganising the debating tradition within the college and from the early 1990s as will emerge later, he would become the vital force in the emergence and success of Terenure's 'Model United Nations'. However, it was his becoming enticed into, entangled with, and passion-ately devoted to the production and direction of the annual college play that claimed such energy as might have been left after teaching full days of mathematics. It was a trust that was passed to him in 1977 by the previous guardians of the school drama, John McClean and Fr David Weakliam. As if this was not sufficient for the day — or the school year — he would also find himself closely involved in under-11's rugby and its annual encounter, the Cardiff Rugby Exchange.[3]

His mathematics colleague, Seamus McCool, had joined fresh from Clongowes Wood and spent a teaching life professing the beauty of that subject. Indeed — as Joe McDonnell eulogised on Seamus's retirement — the latter deplored the decline of 'real' mathematics: 'Maths you could get your teeth into'. Equally, Joe described him as one steadfastly preoccupied with the 'day-to-day spiritual struggle of the ordinary man…'. His intense humanity and his intense humility ensured that all life was seen in terms of the heroic ability of ordinary people to survive in the face of over-whelming odds'.[4]

Their colleague, Andy Donagher, joined the great influx a year later, in 1969. A graduate of UCG, he taught in Galway from 1959 but, ten years later, would be found teaching Irish and English in Terenure and, in all the turbulence of those times, proved steadfast as a rock in a tempest. A kind and gentle character, he came in time to head up the teaching of Irish in the college, where he served over 40 years until he retired in 2002–03. Andy arrived into a Terenure campus which included the plague of prefabs: these had classroom doors that could be lifted from their hinges, to the frequent mischief and merriment of the lads: in one episode of college lore, the Chinese boarder, Kuan-Chen Jeang — according to one disputed account — unhinged the door and placed it, precariously-poised, in anticipation of Andy Donagher's arrival. Andy was a teacher remembered for his forthright, grand entrances to class: along comes Mr Donagher, down comes the door with a bang, then comes the interrogation as to who was the culprit, followed by Jeang's confessional protest: 'But, Sir, there is no door there!' followed by retribution. In later life, the Jeangs, Kuan-Chen and his brother, Kuan-Ming, generously remembered the college — donating to the lake restoration project — when their careers opened very different and happier doors for them.[5]

The year 1970 saw the arrival of another of Terenure's own, Charlie O'Sullivan. In college memory, Charlie was one of the 'greats' even before he joined the teaching ranks: under the magical athletics coaching of Fr Jackie Madden and Joe Doran, the college had a second period of sprint and relay success down to the mid-1970s: Charlie enrolled in 1960, preceded five years by eldest brother, John, and followed three years later by younger brothers, Eugene and Philip, the latter destined for fame on a different stage. Charlie soon wrote his name into the college's record books, breaking the junior ½ mile record with a 2 min 18.1 seconds in 1967, the intermediate ½ mile in 1968 at 2 minutes 6.7 seconds; moving up to seniors in 1970, he broke two college records: the 800 metres in 2 minutes 2.2 seconds, held by P.M. Maher since 1961, and the 1,500 metres in 4 minutes 38.5 seconds, and also winning the sixth year mile at that 1970 sports day. Athletics aside, he was no mean rugby player (though self-confess-edly not a great captain); he was on the Junior Cup-winning team in 1967 and later played Senior Cup rugby for the college and Leinster, before going on to win Irish international caps for their under-19s, 21s and under 23s. Charlie may have been a little out of the ordinary in knowing what he wanted to do after the Leaving Certificate and in later life — he wanted to pursue arts in UCD and later to teach: indeed, this was borne out on his first day at university, literally, on fresher's day: interviewed by an *Irish Independent* reporter who found it so striking to discover a student who knew exactly what he wanted, his story featured in the next day's issue of the paper. Reading geography, mathematics and economics, he graduated in 1974. That summer Fr Hegarty invited him to pursue his HDip in Terenure: that September saw him back home in his *Alma Mater*, on the permanent staff from August 1976 and happily teaching away there, almost 35 years later. As with all other alumni-turned-teachers, Charlie found a warm and totally unpatronising welcome. Five years later, outside the classroom, he became Terenure's first-ever lay games master, inheriting the mantle worn to such brilliant effort and for so long by Fr Jackie Madden. Charlie held the post for a happy if exhausting seventeen years, along with senior rugby coaching that saw groundbreaking tours to the UK, France and in 2002, New Zealand. He finally relinquished his senior coaching duties in 2007–08. Sporting commitments apart, he was to become involved in the development of European studies programmes within the college and, through Terenure, with other colleges in Europe.[6]

Another Dubliner, but not a Terenure alumnus, who came on board in 1974 has been encountered already, Frank Gallen, now deputy principal. Frank was a Drimnagh Castle CBS man who graduated in commerce and tested a career in accountancy before deciding to return from London to pursue his HDip in Education. This he did in a demanding school that had already, early in the academic year of 1972–3, seen off two HDip practitioners in three weeks. Impressed by his own staying power and survival, his HDip inspector mentioned his name to the Terenure authorities who were then seeking a business studies teacher. From the college's restoration, way back in 1917, business studies in one form or another had been a feature of Terenure's portfolio; however, 60 years' later, it had developed into a more demanding, professional and substantial feature of the secondary-school syllabus. Fr Weakliam contacted, interviewed, and employed him and Fr Madden showed him around. When Frank arrived he found that, in Terenure, business studies was a standard subject in its syllabus and not just an option; and that his senior colleague in that field, Kevin Doherty, on the staff from 1964–5 to 2003–04, was the founder of the Business Studies Association of Ireland and lecturer in special methods in the UCD education programme. Kevin 'Dots' Doherty, a past pupil of the class of 1957, had gone into banking before joining the teaching staff, and, apart from his innovations in business studies, would become responsible for introducing the first computers into the college in the 1980s. He retired in 2004–05 after four decades of distinguished service. As for Frank Gallen, 35 years later — even as deputy principal — he still rejoices in Terenure's special atmosphere: on that long road he was, successfully, form master for second, transition and fifth year classes over 21 years, before becoming deputy principal in August 2006.[7]

An alumnus of the 1970s who became one of those teachers who came in on the second big recruiting wave of the early 1980s was Brendan McCauley. Preceded by older brother, Declan, in 1973 and followed by younger brother, Fergus, in 1980, Brendan enrolled into first year of senior school in September 1970, in the third last year of the boarders: he was not alone in finding them on the whole a formidable, well-built body of lads — all the better for not being crossed. However, neither caution about the boarders nor a less than stellar rugby career in college prevented Brendan from reaching the top — becoming school captain in his final year 1975–6. With him on this school-day odyssey were Ray Blake, soon after to be captain of Trinity Rowing Club, later Clongowes teacher and then wine critic for *Food and Wine*; Ray Doyle, later a general practitioner in Galway; Paddy Blake, also a GP but in Canada, and Vinnie Murphy, later a biochemist who ended up living in Denmark where he teaches his subject. With their Leaving Certificate immediately behind them, and before these diverse vocations unfolded, their first break was together on a weekend break in Murroe, Co. Limerick, provisioned by their mothers with brown bread and cooked chicken. From that weekend, they were christened the 'Murroe Gang'. The gang is uniquely commemorated with an engraved stone of the Past Pupils' Walk — of which, more anon. Graduating in 1979 from UCD, with his degree in history and geography, Brendan's professional return to Terenure was not immediate; neither was it long-delayed: securing his first teaching post in Castledermot, Co. Kildare in 1980–1, he then successfully pursued — at the recommendation of Fr Weakliam — the diploma in religious education, at Mount Oliver, Dundalk. So armed, he then took up a permanent position in Terenure, as teacher of RE — and other subjects — from September 1982. Like John McClean two decades before, and Charlie O'Sullivan, he found returning as teacher, to his second home as pupil, was in no way problematic: colleagues whom he held in awe as teachers, like McClean and Dennis Whitty, welcomed him warmly and treated him as an equal.[8]

Finally, in this matter of alumni-turned teachers, another who joined the staff in the time of this second surge was Kevin Williamson, swimming coach. It is worth recalling Kevin's unusual path from Terenure pupil to professional. Born in Dublin in 1959, Kevin's father, Larry, had been in business as a pork butcher, but his real and enduring passion was swimming and swimming instruction. This he taught part-time, including teaching blind people how to swim, in the Iveagh Baths. In 1972, he secured the position of swimming instructor and swimming-pool manager in the wake of Patrick O'Kane's departure from the college: Patrick's PE role was to be taken up by Diana Moore who accomplished much, especially in the revival of tennis over 1972 to 1982, while his swimming duties fell to Larry.[9] In that same year, Larry then transferred son, Kevin, to Terenure where he was to do for the college in swimming what Charlie O'Sullivan had done in athletics. Kevin enrolled in Terenure with an impressive swimming record already behind him, for he entered as Irish under-10 champion in four different strokes. Friends of his new-found school place came to include another impressive swimmer, Feargal Ó Nualláin, and a king of kayaking, Donal Cahill: at one stage in their school years Kevin and Donal kayaked their way from Dún Laoghaire to Wexford in four days.

More seriously, as swimmer Kevin was destined to reap a remarkable harvest of gold medals and trophies and national records: these spanned a wide range of distances in the course of a shining career that took him to an Irish hall of fame from childhood through teenage years and into young adulthood. Historian of Irish swimming, Fergus Barron, in describing Williamson's record as 'astonishing' has hardly overstated the case: writing in 1993 he was to observe:

> As a senior he won the 100 Metres Freestyle three times (1975, '76, '77), the 200 Metres eight times (1974, '75, '76, '77, '80, '81, '82, and '83), the 400 Metres an astonishing ten times (1973, '75, '76, '77, '78, '79, '80, '81, '82, and '83), ...and the 1500 Metres ten times (1974 through to 1983) . .....and the 400 Metres Individual Medley in 1975, '76, '77, '81 and '82. He was also the anchor-man on the Terenure Freestyle and Medley Relay teams which won fourteen golds between

1979 and 1989. He was the first Irishman to break four minutes for the 400 Metres Freestyle ...He was also the first to break 16 minutes for the 1500 Metres ...His long course record for the 1500 Metres, which he set on 16th November 1976, has never been broken.[10]

After boxer, Harry Perry, he was to become Terenure's second Olympian. He qualified readily for the 1976 Montreal games and four years later again was to qualify for the Moscow Olympics. While for long-unbeatable in the Irish context, within that of the Olympics and despite his best efforts, his lack of qualifying for final rounds emphasised the huge gulf between the standard of the sport in Ireland and that which obtained internationally. With the country lacking an Olympic-size pool and with its devoted and earnest coaches lacking the international experience required to bring their charges to the very highest standard, the country's best swimmers and athletes were profoundly disadvantaged at Olympic level. Within the country itself, a swimmer as uniquely gifted as Williamson was, found himself at a disadvantage in not having the crucially constant competition that would have lifted him higher still. Graduating from Terenure in 1977, Kevin won a sports scholarship to the University of Michigan from 1977 to 1979, he returned to Ireland for the Olympics preparation in 1980, and then back to Michigan in 1981 from where he graduated with a BSc in education in 1982. After the premature death of his father, Lar, who had been Irish Olympic swimming coach since 1976, Kevin succeeded as pool manager in May 1983, and became Terenure's swimming coach from June of that year. It was typical of the generosity of the Carmelites and of the gentle and direct kindness of the then Bursar, Fr Jim McCouaig, that they not only made this possible — but that they gave him the time and space to pursue his HDip in education lectures in Trinity, in fulfilment of government requirements for degree recognition — something that had not been available to Patrick O'Kane a decade or so earlier. Thus qualified, and with a record as one of the very greatest sportsmen ever to come out of Terenure, in 1984 he was entrusted with the management of the school swimming team, and a new history for Kevin Williamson and for college swimming, ensued.[11]

The generation who grew through Terenure from 1965 to 1985 were hardly less distinguished than their predecessors. Indeed, building on the education reforms and the wider opportunities, nationally and internationally, many went on to even greater successes in the world of banking and commerce, in the fields of academia and entertainment, and in the professions, whether religious or lay. As to the religious life, and despite the 'vocations crisis', the Carmelite Order continued to engage former pupils in a life of sacrifice and leadership. These boys and men, notably, for example, Micheál Ó Néill and Martin Kilmurray of the class of 1970, and Joe Mothersill of 1974, would go on to be quite outstanding contributors to the life of the Order and of the college, as will appear in due course in the final chapter.

When it comes to the worlds of business and the professions, to chronicle the roll of successful Terenure alumni in these years, whether self-employed or in major corporations, would require a book in itself. Here one can only mention a representative selection and note a few by way of example. That token list could include, from the 1960s, auctioneer Michael Jordan; Judge Iarfhlaith Ó Néill (1968); architect Paul Joyce (1971); Frank Gildea (1973); Bernard Kenna (1974); Ken Murphy (1974), director general of the Incorporated Law Society; Conor O'Kelly (1977), CEO of NCB; Colm Duggan (1978), senior partner in Arthur Cox; Cormac McCarthy (1980), CEO of Ulster Bank; Brian O'Kelly (1980) of Riada Corporate Finance; Brian Weber (1981), CEO of Citi-Quilter; Fergus Murphy (1982), CEO of EBS; John Church (1983), CEO of Arthritis Ireland; and Paul Tuite (1984) of Price, Waterhouse, Coopers; and artist James Hanley (1984).

Auctioneer and fine art expert, Michael Jordan was a likely candidate to be a Terenure pupil since his home on Templeogue Road was then only two doors from the college. Michael was to be another middle boy of three to enrol, preceded by his brother, Joe, and followed later by younger brother, Patrick. In his schooldays there, Michael decidedly preferred soccer to rugby, which he played 'as required', and played some serious soccer even after he left; yet, after leaving the college and making his way in the world of auctioneering and *objets d'art*, it was playing rugby for the club that kept his link to the college an active and enduring one. He became one of the college's most committed and imaginative of fundraisers, who included Paddy O'Reilly, Bernard Kenna, Frank Gildea, Gerry McGuinness and a host of others — and returning to rugby — he became president of Terenure RFC from 1998–9. Michael will be seen later on as a principal in one of the college's longest and most significant recent undertakings — the restoration of the lake.

One of his associates in that enterprise was Paul Joyce of the class of 1971. His welcome by Fr Lar Hegarty in September 1960 was less than fulsome when the latter fell about laughing at the then small and scrawny new boy when he told 'Heggo' that he had come to Terenure to play rugby. Many years later, Fr Hegarty would confess that he had got it badly wrong about Paul being an unlikely rugby prospect. As the first of his family to enter the hallowed halls, the young Joyce soon felt aware of

> tremendous tradition of family dynasties in the place ... the Morrisseys, Thomas, Bosco and Gerry; the Flannerys, Ray, Anthony and Gerry who only seemed to have to get the ball and it would end in a score; ... the Colemans ... the Sparks ... the Hipwells, all of them talented and influential to the extent that an isolated lad might best keep his head down[12]

Not that Paul did: having the foolhardiness to express disgust when Gerry Hipwell failed to bring home the cup to 'Nure, his outspokenness had its consequences when the diminutive Joyce was dangled by the ankles over the banisters at the top of the main school stairwell over the crush hall. For all that, incredibly, they were happy days, especially happy summer days when, with the new pool open, he and Gerry Morrissey were taken on as lifeguards for a then princely 10s note at the end of each month. Swimming, scouting and play-acting apart, one of the significant influences was the nurturing of art, by Fr Power in junior school and by Pat O'Brien and John McClean in senior. The latter put great effort into college participation in national art competitions at the time. It stood to Paul Joyce when, after Terenure, he entered the UCD School of Architecture and from there to a career in that profession. The links with the college were actively maintained, through the Rugby Club where he was captain at one stage in the mid-1980s, and through his professional expertise: he was engaged for various projects from upgrading of the tennis courts, extension to the gym and weights room, classroom extensions, laboratory and library, to the repair and refurbishment of the swimming pool and the major new community residence facility as recently as 2006–07.

The artistic dimension of college life has not been touched upon thus far in this volume. There was an active sketching club in the 1950s and the college produced some talented artists in that period, notably the French–Irish pupil, Arnaud Slowey, of the class of 1955, and Paul Egan and Robert Flatman both of 1958. In the mid-1960s, under Fr Tom Power, a revival occurred and great interest was then taken in the Caltex School Art Competitions. It was not until the big expansion of 1970–1, however, that permanent lay teachers came on board, starting with the tall, slim Ms Fitzgerald to the mid-1970s. In 1976, the college's most distinguished pupil artist enrolled: James Hanley, an able student who was a medal winner in his every year until leaving in 1984. Although a love of scouting was among his preferred extra-curricular activities, it was his skill as a cartoonist that most brought James to notice in the college: his alternative 'staff photo' of 1984 became a collectors' item, treasured even by some of its victims. Following his graduation from UCD, James, as John McClean observed, 'found his true home in the National College of Art and Design' where he secured a first-class honours degree in 1991. A year later, 'Natural Disasters' — his first solo exhibition was highly successful. From there he went on to represent Ireland at Germinations 8, a European biennale of young artists, held in Holland, in 1994. His reputation developed rapidly: his second exhibition, 'White Lies', in April 1995, was described by The Abbey's Patrick Mason as 'another milestone in what promises to be one of the most significant journeys of painters in this country', while Luke Clancy in the *Irish Times* and Medb Ruane in the *Sunday Times* gave it the highest praise, the latter referring, *inter alia*, to Hanley's 'great technical flair' and the former describing James' work as 'a star performance … allowing the eerily unreal pass itself off as reality'.[13] Since then his work and his talent have been hugely in demand, his commissions executed for the highest in the land.

Another who shared James Hanley's love of art and love of scouting in Terenure was Bernard Kenna of the class of 1974. He had come into the college from Mrs Ohle's in 1964, greeted — inevitably — by the legendary Fr Lar Hegarty. Moving up in 1968, he learned his science for Miss Mona O'Toole — the first female teacher in the senior school, as he recalls, and then had the formidable Fr Grace for science in the higher classes. It was, however, the attractions of scouting as much as of science that made the senior school experience a well-remembered and enduring one, for it would be scouting more than anything else that kept him most closely in touch with college after leaving. Bernard was unit leader from 1978 to 1983 during which time Terenure won every scout competition there was, nationally. However, domestic and business commitments had to take precedence from the mid-1980s. Following his UCD years, where he read science and was Boat Club captain in 1978, Bernard joined NCR's computing division before going into business for himself. For all that, he still managed to find time for the college and its concerns, was active in the Past Pupils' Union and became its then youngest-ever president in 1987, preceding David Kennedy (1988) and Des Lamont (1989). Further business commitments compelled a temporary withdrawal from deeper engagement, but not completely, for he was to play a major role in two developments, to be chronicled later, in the area of college drama and college environment.

Finally, among those who made their way in life through business there was one very tragic loss during those years. Con Smith, a legendary figure in the college's past, was killed in the British European Airways flight disaster of Sunday, 18 June 1972. Attending the college in 1941–7, he was only 43 when he was one of 118 passengers, including 18 Irish business leaders, to die when the plane crashed four miles from takeoff out of Heathrow. There were no survivors. The businessmen, representing the Confederation of Irish Industry, Córas Tráchtála and Chambers of Commerce, had been on their way to Brussels.[14] Con was then president of the confederation and had come a long way since his entrepreneurial days of importing used tractors and setting up petrol stations through the country from the late 1940s and early 1950s. He went on to build up the Smith Motor Group and Gowan Distributors, among the largest and most successful motor agencies in Ireland. In time, he would become a director of the Central Bank and was in his second term as confederation president when the tragedy befell. Con was greatly loved by his Terenure classmates and was, ever, a character of great charm and a person of even greater generosity. He was described by that other great Terenure alumnus, Maurice O'Kelly of the class of 1948 and PPU president in 1971 and 1972, thus:

> He will remembered, therefore, with pride by all generations of Terenure Past Pupils, perhaps specially by the sixth years of 1971 and 1972 who had the privilege of hearing him address the inaugural career guidance seminars. There are no replacements for men like him. Only substitutes. This is the measure of the greatness of one of Terenure's most distinguished past pupils.[15]

THE CARING PROFESSION:

The traditional strength of the medical profession among Terenure alumni between 1945 and 1965 continued to be a notable feature of past pupil career paths over the following twenty years and since. The litany of such success is too long to replicate or to detail here. One can but mention a few individuals by way of example. Outstanding among them and of special interest because of enduring Terenure connections is Ronan O'Connell, today professor of surgery in UCD and St Vincent's University Hospital. He and younger brother, Cormac, now an electrical engineer and microchip designer in Canada, were sons of none other than Michael 'The Liberator' O'Connell. Michael was vice-principal two years before Ronan graduated from Terenure in June 1973, and retired from the position in 1980, the year after Cormac left. The lads grew up in a scholarly household since their mother Joan was also a teacher who became vice-principal of St Paul's, Greenhills. From them, Ronan was to inherit a love of words and their origins but he was not to be caught up in this interest to the exclusion of all else, especially sport. Enrolling in 1963, he soon encountered, among others, the tough and ancient Mr Henry and the 'unforgettable Fr Hegarty with his term reports beautifully inscribed in turquoise ink'. Ronan soon found himself playing rugby as winger and full back — not brilliantly, but adequately — and cricket and athletics too: here an abiding memory is of Fr Jackie Madden marking out the running track with creosote and ordering the young lads away when the inevitable ball would land in his newly applied handiwork. The other great joy and diversion was the Scout troop, run by Fr Doran; like Fr Madden, Fr Doran was a seemingly non-stop smoker, but a dedicated hiker: memorable trips here, especially the expeditions to the Carmelite College at Cheltenham. Then there was Fr Brennan and his famous Radio Club, EI 2BY, run from the attic in the old school, it opened up a world of communications. These diversions were soon put aside as the young alumnus went on to study medicine in Trinity and to brilliant effect: he secured first class honours and first place in his finals in 1979. Going on to specialise in colon and rectal surgery at the Mayo Clinic in Minnesota and securing his MD by thesis in 1987, he became fellow of the RCSI in 1983 and of the Royal College of Physicians and Surgeons of Glasgow in 2001, before going on to the chair of surgery in UCD and St Vincent's. Widely published in leading international journals and editor of the *British Journal of Surgery* from 2002–06, he is joint editor of the bible of modern surgery, Bailey and Love's *Short Textbook of Surgery*.

In 1974, following Ronan O'Connell from Terenure into medicine was John Crown. Son of a Leitrim father and Kildare mother, emigrants to the United States, John was born in Brooklyn in March 1957. He grew up there, educated by the Sisters of St Joseph at the local parochial school, experiencing a typical New York childhood until a return to Ireland in 1967. First settling in Newbridge where he attended the local Patrician Brothers School, a move to Dublin a year later saw him enrolled in Synge Street CBS where he successfully completed his Intermediate Certificate in June of 1972. He was then enrolled in Terenure College, entering into fifth year in September 1972, where Joe

Mothersill, later Carmelite, Ronan Fawsitt, later Kilkenny medical practitioner, Patrick Long, later a historian, and Bernard Kenna were among his year mates.

John's first encounter with the Terenure staff was with Fr Grace, a man of encyclopaedic memory who prided himself on his recall of the multitude of pupils whom he encountered in his many years in the college. Despite Fr Grace's reputation for toughness, John recalled him as a very kind and gentle individual. His confrere, Fr Weakliam struck young Crown as the most intellectual of his teachers who had a special capacity for engendering a love of his subjects and who had a particular gift for communicating a sense of excitement in regard to scientific discovery and advances. Remembered too, among others, was the very cerebral, somewhat eccentric but widely loved Christy Collins. Like almost all Terenure pupils, he was soon caught up in sports, without being particularly gifted at any, though he had a particular liking for soccer.

Having done well academically at Synge Street and working fairly hard at Terenure, especially in sixth year, he had the very unusual distinction for a late arrival of being elected one of the college prefects in his final year. John had early on hoped to pursue a career in medicine, and indeed, had already felt drawn to the specialism that later made up the core of his professional life. That hope began to be realised when, following a very good Leaving Certificate, he left Terenure to take up the study of medicine at UCD. But, the academic side of university student life apart, following on his interest in debating at Terenure, he became involved in student political life at UCD and in the Union of Students of Ireland, in a period when there was a proliferation of ideologies and political persuasions, especially on the Left. Early on, John found himself adhering to or rather developing a radical centrist position even as he represented UCD at USI conferences.

They were eight busy, happy years in UCD's Medical Faculty, from 1974 to 1980 leading to graduation. In the immediate aftermath, he interned at the Mater Hospital and then in 1980–1, somewhat unusually, he immediately went back to UCD to pursue successfully a BSc in pathology. Two rotation years in Dublin were followed by continued medical training at Guy's Hospital, London, in 1984. He then returned to pursue his specialism in oncology, at St James's Hospital, joining the team led by Sean McCann and Peter Daly. Here they were pioneering the process of bone marrow transplantation made possible by the personal generosity and the fund-raising energies and acumen of Eugene Murray who had been a Terenure pupil in the 1950s and whose efforts had led to the establishment of the Bone Marrow Leukaemia Trust.

In 1985, John went back to America to work firstly at the Mount Sinai Hospital from 1985 to 1987 and then on to the world-famous Memorial Sloan-Kettering where major advances were being made in cancer research. These years saw him working with the most illustrious men in the field, most notably with the pioneer Jim Holland, the leading international expert in research into childhood leukaemia. John had been head-hunted here by another illustrious figure, Larry Norton, a leading international authority on breast cancer. Here John, therefore, came to work with the leading men in the field, including a sizeable contingent of Irish-born oncologists. He spent over six years at Sloan-Kettering before returning to Ireland in 1993 to become, remarkably — and lamentably — one of only four oncologists working in the Republic.

He had wanted to move back with his family to Ireland and to St Vincent's. At the same time, he developed a significant collaboration with Dr Dennis Slamon of UCLA, a pioneer in the use of Herceptin in cancer treatment. In addition, from 1999 he worked closely with Professor Martin Clynes who was pioneering research at Dublin City University's National Institute of Cellular Biotechnology. With two decades of world-class research and publication behind him, in 2003, John Crown became Thomas Baldwin Professor of Translational Research at DCU, then the first chair of its kind in Europe, pioneering the bridge between laboratory and bedside. Two years later, he became Newman Clinical Research Professor in University College Dublin. At the same time he was no stranger to public debate on medical and hospital treatment matters in Ireland and became a leading champion of equal medical access and universal health insurance. In recognition of his achievements, Terenure College nominated him Past Pupil of the Year, in 2006, and three years later, in what perhaps was a unique double, his previous *Alma Mater*, Synge Street, recognised his achievements with a similar accolade.

Another who made his mark in a vocation of caring was Michael Meegan of the class of 1977. Not long after graduating from Terenure and Trinity, he went to Africa in 1979 on a visit that was to change his life. Working with the Masai in Kenya, he became involved in and committed to the charity International Community for the Relief of Starvation and Suffering (ICROSS) set up in 1978. Back home, he had the considerable support of Kevin Niall and colleagues in the PPU. ICROSS sought and seeks to help marginalised East African communities to fight disease and prevent it, especially the scourge of HIV/AIDS. Meegan has become a veteran in the war against Malaria, TB and AIDS in Sub-Saharan Africa. His inspiration was the great tropical diseases physician, Dr Joseph Barnes, whose brother Jim has already featured in these pages, ministering to the people of Zimbabwe.[16]

Finally, among the distinguished medics who have been Terenure alumni of these years were Declan Keane and Sean Daly. Born in 1961, Declan was a Dubliner — indeed his Dublin roots go back directly to great, great grandparents. He, and younger brother, Brian, entered Terenure together in 1974 after a more rigorous system of assessment than would have been experienced a decade before. For all the general amiability of the place, it still had a certain strangeness for a youngster from Ballyroan National School: rugby, for a boy who had only ever played under-12s Gaelic football for Ballyboden St Enda's; priest-teachers for a boy who had only been taught by lay teachers; the sheer size of its student body and the expanses of the playing fields and premises. Still, the academic side held no terrors: excelling in class he won the sixth year class prize in 1978–9 and he greatly enjoyed the rugby despite being concussed in his very first match there. He survived to play on the Junior Cup team when they brought home the trophy against Blackrock in 1977 — the second of the unprecedented three Junior Cup trophy triumphs from 1976 to 1978: victories that owed a very great deal to that compelling motivator, Fr Brendan O'Reilly. It was a game he continued to enjoy thereafter, even through all six years of his medical student days in UCD. Equally diverting for him was Terenure drama and he especially recalls his role as Rosencrantz in the celebrated 1975 *Hamlet*, alongside the great Grennells, Michael and Nicholas, and that other great star, Lorcan Cranitch. Declan was to be one of seven Terenure alumni of the class of 1970 who pursued medicine to a successful conclusion of their studies. He paid particular credit to the career guidance and encouragement of Fr Fennell. On qualification, Declan went on to specialise in obstetrics, commencing in the Coombe and Holles Street, followed by four years in Bristol. It was then a return to Dublin for three years, followed by two more in Oxford, before interviewing successfully for the position of master of the National Maternity Hospital, Holles Street. Its youngest-ever master, he took up the position on 1 January 1998.[17] He retained the closest of links with his *Alma Mater*, being invited to deliver the annual sixth year prize-giving address in 2001 — delivering a speech to an audience that included former teachers, Carmelites and lay, was almost as daunting as delivering one's first baby. That apart, he has been a faithful attendee at annual PPU dinners and golf-outings as well as a regular contributor to the career guidance classes he so appreciated in his own days there. In 2001, Terenure signified its pride and appreciation when the college PPU President Paul Tuite, on behalf of the college and the union bestowed a joint honour of past pupil of the year on Declan Keane, master of Holles Street, and fellow Terenurian, Sean Daly of the class of 1980 and master of the Coombe.

R. Hopkins, school rugby international, goes for a spin, 1978.

Past Pupils' Union dinner, 1988.

425

Terenure College group during a private Mass with Pope John Paul II in Rome, 1980.

427

CHAPTER 22

Sports and Sportsmen,
1965–85

Gerry Flannery with his 100 and 200
metres Leinster trophies, 1971.

THE JUNIOR CUP TEAM TRIUMPH OF 1976 USHERED IN PROBABLY THE greatest period of Terenure rugby history at schoolboy level. The juniors, whose back-up coaching team, led by Fr Aidan O'Donovan, which included Denis Whitty, John McClean, Kevin Flynn, Charlie O Sullivan, achieved victory against Blackrock in a nail-biting final: in the second minute of injury time big Johnny Holloway broke through the Blackrock defence to score a superb try with marvellous coolness under pressure. It was to be Terenure's first Leinster schools' rugby victory since 1967 when the juniors had again beaten Blackrock in a tight 6-5 victory. The juniors would go on to win again in 1977 and secured their third in a row in 1978. The victory of 1977 against Blackrock, winning 12-10, was accompanied by the triumph of the senior thirds coached by John McClean, in the newly IRFU-recognised Third Senior League: they defeated De La Salle 19-15 to bring the Minor League Cup to the college. It says something for the extent of the available talent and the quality of the coaching that only one player of the 1976 cup winners, featured on the 1977 winning team — forward and captain, David Webb — the first Terenure pupil to win two Junior Cup medals. Better was to follow in 1978 when Fr O Donovan's juniors took their third cup in a row while John McClean's second XV won their senior league for the first time since 1969. Captain Kieran Harty, who played with the 1977 victors, led Terenure juniors to victory over Blackrock 10-6 in what was one of the most exciting and most sporting encounters of the decade. Meanwhile the seniors in 1978 reached the final for the first time in six years, losing out to Clongowes by 9 to 6: one of their number, Ray Hopkins that season became the first Terenure lad to play schools' international when he was selected against Australia, England and Scotland, while he and three others, Matt D'Arcy, John Holloway and Niall Williamson, were selected for Leinster in the interprovincials.[1] A year later, Fr Jackie Madden coached the seniors to their first Leinster Cup victory in 21 years. It was a team that now included the brilliant juniors of yesteryear. From the 1976 team: David Webb, Niall Williamson, John Holloway, Brian Bagnall, J. Bourke, P. Fitzpatrick, J. O'Sullivan, and from that of 1977 there were Robert Duffy, Brian Colgan, David Byrne, Kieran Harty and Mark Keogh. Then, in 1989, the Terenure seniors won their fourth Leinster Cup and their only back-to-back triumph until 1992 and 1993. Once again it was heroics against Blackrock: the close 12-10 victory was achieved after a tremendous fight-back and a sensational last minute try and conversion, courtesy of Ray O'Neill and Brian O' Kelly, respectively. Nine of these winning seniors had been on the Junior Cup winning team of 1978; four had played in the triumphant 1977 juniors while Maurice McCabe and Colm Verdon secured their first Leinster medals. Captain Kieran Harty had been the sole survivor of the 1979 victors and achieved the unique distinction of being on the four cup-winning sides, the two juniors of 1977 and 1978 and the two seniors of 1979 and 1980 and combined this record, therefore, with never having played on a losing cup team. He also, therefore, surpassed David Webb's and Gerry Hill's records of two juniors and one Senior Cup medal. The seniors would do it again in 1984 when they defeated Monkstown by 15 to 3 under Captain Michael Costello and Coach John

McClean. Michael later that season got his schools' international cap and scored two memorable tries against Scotland. In a season in which they conceded only 12 points and secured 87, they never let the burden of being favourites compromise their effort, with Peter Walsh's place-kicking being especially outstanding. Their victory was very much the case of a talented side supported by an equally talented and committed back-room team of coaches and trainers from McClean and O'Kelly to O'Sullivan and Des Thornton. It would be three years before another final came their way, and eight more before the cup came home again in 1992.

TENNIS:

Terenure's great tennis days of the early 1940s would be the long over before the college would again experience the joys of team victories. There was some consolation in the personal triumphs of individuals like tennis and badminton wizard, Fr Billy Langan, who was schoolboy interpro in 1956, the formidable Bobby Keogh, Leinster under-15 champion and interprovincial in 1957, and Ken Kelleher as interpro in 1962. At the end of the 1960s and beginning of the 1970s — in the days of Diana Moore — some very talented individuals emerged in the persons of Ray Kinsella Leinster and Irish junior champion in 1972, and, before him the great Sparks players, Conor and Brian. In 1969, Conor had won silver at the Catholic Student games in Lisbon. The victories started coming from 1966 when the then junior, Conor, won the Leinster Under-15 Open Championship. He was to be the inspirational captain of 1966–7 when the juniors brought home the Leinster Championship — Conor and Brian, with Liam Bannon, Jimmie Menton, Johnnie Cronin, Patrick Mahony and Kinsella: they defeated Gonzaga 4 to 2 in that year: this the very next day after overcoming Gormanston in the semi-final. A year later, 1968, under Johnnie Cronin as captain they brought home the junior trophy again, this time with newcomers Martin Kinsella and Gerry Flannery on board. Fallow years followed, with no joy for seniors or juniors, though in 1971–2, Ray Kinsella emerged as one of Ireland's outstanding schoolboy players. The seniors managed to reach the final in 1977 and the juniors began to come good again. In 1979, they defeated Gonzaga in the final at Donnybrook and then went on to win the boys' doubles in the Association of Independent Schools' Championships. Their 1979 win was prelude to an even more impressive schools' season in 1980: they were successively victors over Beneavin, 5-1, Wesley 4-1, St Columba's 5-1, and Malahide 6-0: it was then on to a tense semi with Gormanston under the splendid captaincy of Mark Shortall and with young superstar from the junior school, Seán Molloy: they won through to meet St Aidan's of Whitehall over whom they were victorious 4-1. There followed the memorable 1981 season when at last a Terenure seniors tennis team won their cup as did the minors and all three grades of senior, junior and minor were now promoted to the 'A' division of their sport. The remarkable Seán Molloy played that year on all three school teams and never dropped a match. Although 1982 saw no team triumph, Terenure now had three great players in Fergus Murphy, Seán Molloy and

Robin McNaughton. Then followed the great 1983 season when again they won Leinster senior and minor trophies.

It was all the more remarkable that this had been accomplished while they were bereft of college tennis courts for twelve years. Only the generosity of the Templeogue Tennis Club made it possible by providing access to its courts. All was to change in 1984 when the college, although losing Diana Moore to emigration, regained Fr Billy Langan as coach and secured five brand new tennis courts. The new facilities were quickly taken up and the college soon boasted six school teams.

ATHLETICS:

In track and field, too, there were exciting times, notably so at the start of the 1970s and in the mid-1980s. As to the former, the early 1970s were dominated by the two brothers, Anthony and Gerry Flannery, in college, Leinster and All-Ireland sprint events. The decade for college sports began with three senior records and three intermediate records also. Anthony Flannery beat Jack McNamara's 1965 record in the 200 m by 0.7 seconds with a run of 22.1 seconds. At the same event, Denis O'Connell broke Jack's 1965 record in the 400 m with a 51.9 seconds win, while Charlie O'Sullivan broke Pat Maher's 1961 record of 2 minutes 7.4 seconds in the 800 m with a time of 2 minutes 2.2 seconds. Then in the intermediates, young brother Gerry Flannery beat John Thornton's 1965 record in the 200 m by 1/5 second, in a time of 23.2 seconds: Barry Murphy beat Thornton's 1965 record in the 400 m by 2/5 seconds, and Maxwell Injeh beat Larry Byrne's 1951 record in the long jump by a magnificent 5 inches with a leap of 20 ft 3 in. Anthony's season of success continued in the Leinster 100 metres and the All-Ireland 100 metres with an impressive 10.7 seconds — the then fastest ever time by an Irish schoolboy. Denis O'Connell took the Leinster 400 and the All-Ireland 400 metres with a personal best of 50.3 seconds. Gerry too won in Leinster, in the 100 m, but was pipped for first place in the national contest. He made up for the latter by winning the All-Ireland 200 m in 23.0 seconds. The senior relay won the Leinster in 45.5 seconds, coming second in the All-Irelands.

Even better was to follow for Gerry Flannery in 1971. He now broke the college senior 100 m record with a 10.6 seconds, beating his brother Anthony's 1970 record: he went on to win the Leinster senior 100 m sprint final for the second successive year with a time of 10.9 seconds and then won the senior 200 in 23.4 seconds. In doing so, he brought home the Lynch Cup (senior 100 m) and the Thornton Cup (senior 200 m) to Terenure for the fourth successive year. The college had now won the senior 100 metres seven times in the previous thirteen years and the senior 200 metres six times in ten years. In helping the senior relay team to victory that year, he himself had now won eight Leinster titles in three years. He went on to crown Terenure's golden era of athletics by winning the All-Ireland 200 m with a personal best of 22.3 seconds and, only one hour later, came from behind to win an astonishing victory in the senior 100 metres. In winning the double, he became the first Terenure athlete ever to win the senior sprint double in the All-Ireland college championships.

It would be over a decade before Terenure would record such signal triumphs although John Sanfey, in 1975–7, turned out to be a star performer in his own right. He broke Gerry's 1970 record in the 200 m in 1977 with a 23.1 second win while in that same summer sports contest Derek McConnon beat John Thornton's junior long jump record of 1963 by a single centimetre. At the same time, David Breen broke John Brabazon's 1973 junior high jump record with a leap of 5 ft 4 in. Finally, in the same year Terenure produced its first junior pole vault champion since Jim Lane in 1963 when Brendan McCabe took both the Leinster with a 2.8 m and the All-Ireland with a 2.9 m vault. It would be a decade and more before strength and victory returned to Terenure inter-schools athletics, with bronze medals at junior, inter and senior levels in the west Leinster cross country championships in 1984. A year later, Paul Murphy was to win Leinster senior 100 metres and took bronze in the 200; the inters won the 4 × 100 relay while at the All-Irelands, Aidan Brennan triumphed in the 200 m intermediate final while the Intermediate 4 x 100 relay also went to Terenure.

SOCCER:

Finally, there was one major sport where Terenure had neither triumph nor tradition since the 1880s — soccer. This was to change as of 1966–8 and the sport at pupil and past-pupil level was to feature strongly enough over the next ten years. The story, as unearthed by Rodney Bishop and John McClean, is as follows:

> On 8th December 1966 ... an organised group of pupils of the College, complete with Manager, formed a football team, adopted the name Springfield F.C. and played an obscure football match against a team called Madonna Y.C.. The prime movers of this inaugural fixture were College's pupils Philip Jones, John Chadwick and Derek and Bobby Stewart. Other players also involved in this match were Noel Germaine, Ray McInerney and Paul Meade. This team continued to play only friendly matches as Springfield F.C., until they entered the Dublin Schoolboys Under 17 & 18 Divisions the following year. This group of pupils of Terenure College were unofficially attributed to be the forefathers in forming ... the football club known today as Terenure College Association Football Club.[2]

Their first formal venture came, in the 1967–8 school year, when the college entered a senior soccer side in the Dublin Schoolboys League and in the Leinster Secondary Schools Easter Vacation League. These first outings enjoyed moderate success in that they finished mid-league in the former, then played very well in the latter, beating CUS 7-0 and St Paul's 4-0 before going down to Chanel College in the quarter-final. To the fore among these Terenure pioneer footballers were Noel

Germaine as a very effective centre back distributor; their creative captain, Bobby Stewart; sharpshooting striker, Paul Meade, who got an interpro cap for Leinster and earned it by scoring twice against Ulster Schoolboys; the brilliant goalkeeper Michael Spillane who got an Inter-pro trial, and Gerry Morrissey. In the Leinster schools under-15, they got to the semi-finals against Sandymount High School, with Morrissey and Joe Kelly being outstanding.

Apart from the founding fathers or, perhaps, more properly, the founding sons from Springfield, there emerged, behind the scenes, in the evolution of the college as a presence and then a power in schoolboys' soccer, two young teachers of the late 1960s, John McClean and Dennis Whitty, together with Fr Joe O'Nolan: the latter had served on the staff from 1967–8 to 1971, Dennis Whitty had arrived in 1964 and John McClean, as noted previously, had joined in 1968. The latter, soon after arrival on the staff, found himself being roped in by the boys at lunch-time in the school yard to supervise their soccer efforts and being cajoled into coaching them. He, Denis Whitty and Fr O'Nolan would form the management and coaching core of the young team that evolved from Springfield, into 'Collegians' up to 1971, and which, from 1971–2, formally became Terenure College AFC. They soon after entered the Dublin Schoolboys League as Springfield United — playing at under-17 level and then, in the under-18s in 1969 they played for the first time as Terenure College or Collegians.[3] Although the competition for talent and the time available for training and matches was greatly constrained by the dominance of rugby and other sports, college soccer was soon able to field up to four teams at different levels and enjoyed success at a remarkably easy stage. The core management group would be joined later, in promoting the game, in the 1970s, by Aidan Hughes, Larry Halpin and Frank Gallen.

The seniors had a remarkable season in only their second year, 1969, when they won the inaugural Leinster Schools Cup Championship, were finalists in the All-Ireland and secured runners-up position in the youths' division of the Dublin and District Schoolboy League. Their defence was superb, with full backs Morrissey and Derek Stewart and with goalie Spillane at his brilliant best. Under the calm captaincy of Bobby Stewart and with deadly strikers in Paul Meade and Conor Sparks they pulled off this great early success: Sparks securing a hat-trick in the semi-final against O'Connell Schools and going on to score the winning goal in the final at Dalymount Park against St Paul's. It was a remarkable season, with the juniors doing well and the under-13s winning their Leinster Cup — against Chanel — with Des Thornton and Des Stafford as full backs and Niall Walsh as keeper, all excelling. In short, Terenure had won the Leinster double. Joe Cleere of the class of 1983 recalled the great strength of Terenure soccer in those years — with the under 13s, under 14s and under 15s all winning their respective cups in 1973: his brother, Brian, was as a star player for the under 13s and under 14s in that special year when the college made school soccer history[4]. Although the seniors would not repeat the achievement of 1969 in the following year, it was a remarkable year for them: although knocked out of the Leinster Senior Cup in the quarter finals, they were deemed the most consistent team in the country and were, therefore, chosen to represent Ireland in the first-ever European Schools Championships, held that summer in Kaiserslautern, in Germany. Apart from those seniors already mentioned, goalie, Paul Homan, was very effective while full back, Noel Germaine, proved to be one of the best in that European competition. Although they did not progress from the group stages of that competition, they were awarded the overall Fair Play Award for their efforts in that inaugural competition. Upon their return home from Germany and upon completing their Leaving Certificate examinations the team decided to continue on playing together. They had assumed the name Collegians, entered the Universities and Colleges League: managed by McClean and captained by Ray McInerney, the team starred with players like Pat Diffney, Aiden Farrell, Alban Colwell, Tommy Foster, Paul McGee, Pat Jordan, Terry Jones, John Walsh and John O'Connor. It was at the end of the 1971–2 season that they changed their team from Collegians to Terenure College AFC.[5] They immediately joined up to the Amateur League, Division 2, Sunday. In their very first season they won the Leinster Junior Shield, beating Mellowes BDS by 5–2 in the final: this was in a competition that contained 164 competing teams. A year later, in the 1973–4 season, they added the Division 2 Sunday title to their triumphs, a feat they were to repeat exactly 30 years later.

In the years after the early 1970s, new players of real class like John Cronin, Benny Murphy and Derek Page would enter the senior ranks but nothing in Terenure College soccer history would equal the triple triumphs of 1973. Perhaps the most remarkable here was the achievement of the under-15s: they won two of their preliminary contests after penalty shoot-outs, went on to beat Castleknock 2-0 and then, in the final, overcame Beneavin in another penalty shoot-out. Under Captain Ronnie Harrison and Coach John McClean — the only soccer coach in Ireland with the recognised FA coaching badge at the time — they brought home the O'Meara Cup. Further successes came the way of the under-15s who won their 'Blitz' Cup in 1974 for the third time in four years.

However, among past pupils, and indeed teachers, the game at AFC-level continued to attract: Frank Gallen came to play with Terenure College AFC at the time, as did Frank Gildea of the class of 1973 and Pat Jordan of the class of 1970 and some of them are still playing five-aside to this day, known among themselves as 'The Coffin-Dodgers'.[6] Indeed, within a short time after its foundation, Terenure AFC was able to field squads at five different levels of the game. Today, almost 40 years later, Terenure College AFC continues to play soccer at the top amateur level, competing in the prestigious Leinster Senior League, and its teams continues to turn out to play their matches in their 'home' ground of the college, better known as 'The Lake'.

There was, however, also a far different kind of stage on which the college had for long and would continue for long to excel.

437

Fr B. O'Reilly watches from the sideline as Terenure College plays, 1980s.

J. Barry (Cork hurling trainer), Christy Ring and Fr W. Bradley
with the Liam McCarthy Cup at the college, *c.*1950.

CHAPTER 23

The Play's the Thing,
1947–97

The audience gathers for the college's annual play, 1940s.

Away from the sports field, there was one event that is better remembered, perhaps, than any other: the staging of *The Play's the Thing*. Presented on 23 March 1997, and compèred by alumnus and entertainer extraordinaire, Mike Murphy, this event described itself, accurately as: 'A Celebration of 50 Years of Plays in the Terenure College Concert Hall'. As PPU president of that year, Ronan J. Nolan, explained:

> The occasion is the 50th anniversary of the opening of the College Concert Hall which has surely been a landmark, in many ways, for all of us who have attended the school since then. The Concert Hall has been the venue for a succession of memorable school plays and other major events in school life such as prize-givings and, indeed, examinations.[1]

If the concert hall were the occasion, there was also a cause and a real purpose: the cause was to raise funds for the Terenure College Past Pupils' Benevolent Fund; the purpose was to honour the great tradition of acting and the great succession of actors, musicians and other entertainers who brought such credit to the college down the years. Every school has its school play and some colleges in certain periods have a distinctive history in such matters, as perhaps O'Connell Schools in Gilbert and Sullivan operettas in the 1950s and 1960s. It may be averred, however, that no college dedicated to wider educational purposes has ever rejoiced in so long and rich a succession of gifted entertainers, amateur and professional, whether actors or musicians, nor in so splendid a tradition of dramatic productions. Shakespeare, for so long, was the college's dramatic forte, from foundation until 1988, with a brief break in 1970–2. Thereafter, a larger canon of modern drama was also explored. At the same time, from the 1950s, the Past Pupils' Dramatic Society provided wider offerings in the lighter drama of comedy and farce.

The college, of course, had been blessed in the services of gifted theatre practitioners such as the Abbey's Frank Fay in the 1920s and Eddie Golden in the 1950s, but it also discovered some special producers and talented storytellers, even among the Carmelite friars such as Fr Seamus Aengus Hannigan, producer and artist. Before turning to these and to the extraordinary cluster of brilliant alumni-entertainers from the 1960s, it is worth noting just how far back in the twentieth century one can find Terenure pupils destined to become international names in entertainment and theatre.

Two such were the Perry brothers, Desmond and Gerald, who hailed from Rathmines Road and enrolled in the college on the same September day in 1927, and leaving in 1932. Gerald produced a number of plays for the Past Pupils' Dramatic Society in the 1940s: later on, the society returned the compliment by staging an adaptation from his own pen — *Uneasy Money*. Born in Dublin in 1916, Des started his acting career in 1947, on the hard road, with various 'fit-up' companies touring the towns and villages of Ireland. Three years later, he went to England where he played in repertory theatres before he secured significant roles in the West End: these included *The Playboy of the Western World* and *Stephen D* in St Martin's Theatre and

A Patriot for Me, at the Royal Court. Major film roles followed later, notably in *Ulysses*, *A Portrait of the Artist*, and *Sacco and Vanzetti*. He played various one-off parts in The Abbey before joining the company fulltime in 1976. Here, he later played in *Tarry Flynn*, *The Quare Fellow*, and as Polonius in *Hamlet*.[2] In the new medium of television, Des enjoyed great success and an enduring career. Here, most famously, he became a household name as Jack Nolan in the long-running domestic serial, *Tolka Row*, based on the 1951 Maura Laverty novel of that name. The series lasted from 1964 to 1968 and was the first-ever 'soap' made by RTÉ. One of his co-stars here was Stacia Nolan, or, in real life, Iris Lawlor, who came to have the closest active participation in Terenure College's drama history: this, directly through her work in making-up the boys for their parts in the annual plays, and indirectly, but just as decisively, by virtue of being mother to two of Terenure's and the Irish theatre's finest actors, Michael and Nicholas Grennell. Iris and Aiden Grennell — a Clongowes lad himself, who had just gone straight from there into the Abbey School of Music and Drama, met when they both worked for Longford Productions. As for Des Perry, *Tolka Row* apart, he played many distinguished roles in film, television and on stage before his death in December 1985. His funeral Mass in that year was concelebrated by Carmelite friars Eltin Griffin and Dunstan O'Connor, along with local Mount Merrion parish priest, Monsignor Ardle McMahon, while the attendance included his brother, Gerald, the Grennells and another Terenure thespian, Bosco Hogan.

Another entertainer, and pre-war pupil, was Albert Le Bas from Kenilworth Road, Rathgar, who entered Terenure in 1938 from Beaufort. He went on to become, with or without the blessing of St Elias, a magician; perhaps, indeed, the most famous magician ever to come out of Ireland. Born in 1928, Albert was only three years in the college before he gave his first public performance at the age of thirteen. He went on to become a member of the Inner Magic Circle of London, the International Brotherhood of Magicians, the Society of American Magicians, and often had the honour of performing for his confreres at their international gatherings. He died prematurely, at the age of 44, in September 1972, but long-remembered for his classic trick, 'The Miser's Dream'.[3]

Two other brothers in blood and drama of that age were the Good brothers, John and Maurice. Born in 1926 and 1932 respectively, and growing up in No. 1 Butterfield Avenue, Templeogue, both had started off at Synge Street CBS before transferring to Terenure. John graduated from the college in 1944 and went into journalism; Maurice completed his pupil years there in 1950. Each was caught up in college drama and Maurice went on, thereafter, to a life in theatre and film. Described by near-contemporary, David Kennedy, as 'a seriously good actor', Maurice had played a quite outstanding role in the long-remembered and remarkable 1948 staging of *Macbeth*: 'splendidly played throughout by Maurice Good who to coolness and ease of movement added clear enunciation' was the verdict of one reviewer.[4] The next year, 1949, he played an equally highly regarded Cassius in *Julius Caesar* before leaving the college to launch a very successful career, commencing at The Gate, then moving on to film and television in England and the USA. He played leading roles in various science-fiction productions such as *Quatermass* and *Dr Who*, and went on to film-directing, writing and producing before emigrating to Canada in the mid-1970s.

Performance talent in the college in the decade or so after the war was predominantly but not exclusively confined to acting and theatre direction. An earlier chapter has noted the development of the orchestra in the 1950s. One very talented pupil of that time and who was destined for an outstanding career was violinist, Brian McNamara. Brian was a pupil in Terenure over the period 1956 to 1963 and his musical talent was quickly evident. He came, of course, from a background steeped in the art since his father, Michael, was principal of the Municipal School of Music on Chatham Street, Dublin. Nevertheless, only ten years old in 1956, Brian gave his first public performance in the college concert of that year. He made an immediate and abiding impression: the audience, including Lord Mayor Ben Briscoe, Snr, were captivated by the sheer quality of the performance of one so young. Studying violin with Jaroslav Vanecek at the College of Music, Dublin, it was to be seven years later that he made his first solo recital — with the RTÉ Symphony Orchestra — when he performed Mendelssohn's violin concerto. A German government scholarship soon followed. This took him to the Hochschüle in Berlin and then to the Hochschüle in Cologne from where he graduated with the highest distinction. It was not too long before international performances as a soloist brought him to delighted audiences in England, Scotland, Holland, Switzerland and Japan. Later, he would become a frequent performer for Irish and German radio as also for the BBC. By 1975, he had become senior teacher of violin in what is now the Dublin Institute of Technology's Conservatory of Music and Drama.

Destined to be as musically eminent, nationally and internationally, was Jim McCann who attended the college up to the early 1960s, completed his Leaving Certificate there in 1962 and then went on to study medicine in UCD. The attractions of the rock and folk scenes during his schooldays proved too strong and, during the summer vacation of 1964, in Birmingham, he started 'gigging' in the local folk clubs there. Back in Dublin, in 1965, he joined a group called The Ludlow Trio: in 1966, they scored a major success with their version of Dominic Behan's *The Seas around Us*. A solo career soon followed, as well as a time in theatre where he enjoyed an especially good run with Maureen Potter in *Gaels of Laughter* in 1968. A successful Irish television series, *The McCann Man*, came after and it was on this that he met Luke Kelly. In 1974, a temporary slot with The Dubliners turned into a five-year spell when Ronnie Drew left to go solo. Jim toured extensively with The Dubliners and then resumed a solo career that took him as far as Tokyo.

A decade after Jim left Terenure, the college, like other institutions where religion is central, saw the coming of a very different musical orientation. In the wake of Vatican II and the arrival of a vernacular liturgy, came the emergence of the Folk Mass: the guitar had entered the sanctuary. Strange though this may have seemed to more venerable Carmelites and other, older souls in college, the 1970s' and 1980s'

Folk Masses and the College Folk Group — or, to give the correct title, the Church Youth Choir — brought a new inclusiveness that helped to foster and promote alternative and popular musical talent. Effectively initiated by the dynamic Fr Des Kelly, its pupil members came to include future teacher, Brendan McCauley, his musically talented brother, Fergus, and the future 'pop' musician, lyricist and composer of film scores, Paul Bushnell: he, of course, was a son of eminent musical parents, Tony who was a multi-instrumentalist and Anne, a veteran of Irish film, music and television and an internationally recognised cabaret performer. Enrolling in Terenure in 1969, Paul became caught up in its folk group, from entering senior school in 1973–4. From then until leaving in June 1980, he was to become one of its leading figures, playing bass guitar and arranging songs and music for the Sunday Folk Mass in the college. In 1980, he was one of the company from the Terenure and Gort Muire folk groups who paid a memorable visit to Rome and who actually met and sang for Pope John Paul II at Castel Gandolfo that August. His career after Terenure took off from busking on Grafton Street to being appointed musical director for the film, *The Commitments*. This secured for him the award of a Gold Disc from MCA Records. Settling eventually in Los Angeles, he has enjoyed notable success as producer and performer, working with international artists such as Natalie Imbruglia, Phil Collins, Elton John and Sting. In recognition of his success he was awarded the accolade, Past Pupil of the Year, in 1992.

Just as not all Terenure's best performers were actors, so too not all its best performers turned professional. A special case in point here is the Hamlet of the 1953 production — Paddy Finnegan, later a dentist. His performance as the Prince of Denmark, alongside Adrian Weakliam's Polonius and David Kennedy's Ophelia was long-recalled as a quite stunning achievement. As an aside, this was to be the last of the female roles with which David Kennedy was to be saddled: his voice broke during the 1953 *Hamlet*, alternating between falsetto and baritone and it was to his own intense relief that in the subsequent 1954 *Julius Caesar* he was cast as Cassius. As for Paddy Finnegan, like many others of the decade, he subsequently kept up his acting interest, appearing with the Dublin Shakespearean Society.

It has to be said of the 1950s college Shakespeare productions that they were far more professional and serious undertakings than they had been in the years of Fr Andy Wright where happy chaos and 'it'll be all right on the night' prevailed. That 1953 *Hamlet*, of course, had been directed by the master, Eddie Golden, who knew his stage craft like few others. Indeed, there was a backstairs politics to this, worthy of the scenes behind the arras. The formidable Prior, Fr Dunstan, had not been at all happy with the standards of the 1952 *Romeo and Juliet*. Although Fr Eltin Griffin, then briefly on the teaching staff, and P.P. Maguire were technically in charge, Dunstan and Eltin became plotters in a plan of parallel production: Dunstan brought in Eddie Golden who ran unofficial parallel rehearsals, initially unbeknownst to P.P. Maguire. The latter, legend has it, on discovering same, then relinquished his involvement in the college productions. The resulting *Hamlet* and subsequent productions saw college theatre reach a new level. This was so even when Eddie had to leave for new commitments and production came back to base: yet, Carmelite stage directors and producers, and indeed, English teacher Michael O'Connell, proved very serious and close to professional in their approach. In the preparations of course it mattered a great deal that stage props and sets now had the attention of a seriously good carpenter and woodworker like Brother Stephen (Reynolds) and that the scene-painting would be accomplished by Fr Seamus Hannigan, a skilled artist as well as a superb storyteller who was known to the boys as 'Jeff Chandler', that handsome gunslinger of countless Hollywood 'westerns'.

From the mid and late 1950s, therefore, and as was the case in athletics, Terenure was about to enter something of a golden age of college theatre — three decades and more of schoolboy actors who became legends of stage and screen. Prominent among them was Mike Murphy, actor and broadcaster who came into Elementary A in junior school in 1949 and left senior school a decade later. He recalls that it was the quiet and sensitive Fr Hannigan, with his interest in literature and theatre, 'who set me on the road I was eventually to follow'.[5] Mike Murphy first took to the concert hall stage as First Murderer in the 1955 *Macbeth*, a role he relished: he was hooked, and went on to play Gratiano in the 1956 *Merchant of Venice* and, much more triumphantly, played Edmund in the 1957 *King Lear*. It was a role that won him high praise, not least from the illustrious *Irish Press* theatre critic, Gabriel Fallon. Soon after this, momentarily there was tragedy: the youngster who loved Terenure for its rugby and its drama did not excel in its classrooms and *paterfamilias* exiled him to Synge Street, and then to Coláiste Muire, in the forlorn hope of better grades; however, pleadings and protests from mother and son saw him restored to *arcadia* in Terenure. The rest, as they say, is history, and a career in theatre, radio, film and television that Fr Hannigan might have been proud of.

DONAL MCCANN:

The year 1957, which saw Mike Murphy win golden opinions for his Edmund in Fr Hannigan's *King Lear* and in which Paul McKay featured as Captain and Vinnie Morris as Gentleman, saw the role of Cordelia taken by a neophyte — Donal McCann. 'Cordelia in the middle of the front row is dodgy if you have boarders in the second row', Donal would later recall to Gerry Stembridge.[6] It says something for the talent of this third-year lad, whose classmates included future rugby great, Brendan Sherry, and star athlete, Jim Lane, that he made an immediate impact in what was a remarkable production. Philip Williams pulled off a memorable performance in the lead role — 'an amazing performance for a boy of sixteen' enthused Gabriel Fallon: or, as McCann later remarked of Williams, 'an excellent King Lear who went on to become a doctor, unfortunately'.[7] Fallon went on to offer high praise to Murphy, McCann and the other leading players and then concluded: 'Having seen *King Lear*, my only regret is that I missed this College's *Hamlet, Macbeth, Julius Caesar ...*

Merchant of Venice. What sins of omission on my part! But what a golden record for Terenure College! Long may it continue'.[8]

Having shared in the triumph of 1957, Donal went on to play Malvolio in the 1958 *Twelfth Night* and Polonius in the 1960 *Hamlet*. His early affinity for the stage was hardly surprising since his father, John, was a well-known playwright of those times. For all that would follow later, Donal did not let the early stage reputation go to his head or lead him to be anything other than a normal Terenure teenager, enjoying his rugby and especially the Scouts, as much as the concert hall. Moving up to the seniors in 1955, he was, like any fourteen-year-old lad, as excited about the prospects of scouting expeditions as of acting performances.

THE 81ST SCOUT UNIT:

It was in March 1957 that Fr Dunstan asked Fr Jim McCouaig to organise a Scout troop in the college, on foot of a suggestion to this effect from Archbishop McQuaid. In early April, Fr McCouaig called a meeting of first and second years that led to the foundation of the original unit. Their first 'hike' to the Dargle soon followed, with tea urn and billycans. Towards the end of May 1957, they were given their first permanent but precarious roof over their heads, in the rapidly deteriorating 'Yellow House' of Maggie Austin's earlier days. With the help of Br Stephen and former pupils like Raymond Cannon, Enda Ryder and several others, the place was made tolerably habitable and with much parental goodwill and jumble sales, the troop got on its feet. It held its first investiture that September, in the college chapel, with Fr O'Connor presiding. Its first-ever report, under the heading of 'On My Honour', appeared in the *Annual* for 1957 from the pen of that same Donal McCann. Scouts and McCann alike would only go from strength to strength. Each party, in time, would travel far afield: the Scouts to Munich in 1960 in which expedition McCann and his classmate, John McClean, were participants. Later, the troop went to Scotland in 1961; Lourdes in 1965; many times to Cheltenham (the Carmelite College, not the race course); Germany in 1973; and Belgium in 1978, to name but a few camping destinations.

As for young Donal, on leaving the college in 1961, he took up architecture, briefly, and then journalism, but continued to enjoy the stage through the Past Pupils' Dramatic Society. In 1963, for example, he took the part of Orangeman William McStay in *All the King's Horses*, sharing the stage with other recent past pupils, Hugh Church and David Kennedy, with Tony Scott as stage manager.[9] Apart from his being an outstanding rugby player, Hugh was a fine amateur actor in the Past Pupils' Dramatic Society and was regarded by Donal McCann as one of the best comic actors he had ever known. As for Donal, his journalistic sub-editing for the *Evening Press* afforded him the time to take up part-time acting classes in the Abbey school and, by the end of the 1960s he had joined the Abbey Players. One of his more significant roles at that time was in the 1969 production of *Waiting for Godot* where he partnered with

Peter O'Toole as Vladimir. Over a decade later, following a string of critical successes through the 1980s — especially as Captain Boyle in *Juno and the Paycock* — he went on to great effect in the plays of Brian Friel: especially acclaimed was his performance as Frank Hardy in the 1980 production of *Faith Healer*. That insightful and discriminating theatre devotee, with the extraordinary gift of recall, John Devitt, gave a memorable summation of McCann just as he was at that stage of his career:

> ... it was quite late in the day that people realized that this guy is really exceptional. It was those scenes in *Faith Healer*, where he became conscious of power. I remember him holding his hand, like that, to the audience — 'I've got you. I've got you' — followed by an incredibly long pause and nobody breathing. At that point, McCann was fully conscious of his power. But it might have taken him twenty years to get there. Cyril Cusack hadn't the name for being generous to other actors, but he was amazed at McCann in the part ... 'I've been going back, night after night', he told me. 'I want to see how he does it: it's the most amazing performance I've ever seen'. This was not Cyril Cusack's usual idiom.[10]

Even greater heights were to be reached, greater acclaim to be bestowed: his Thomas Dunne in Sebastian Barry's *The Steward of Christendom*, in 1995, won him the London Critics' Circle Theatre Award for best actor. There followed a three-month run at the Brooklyn Academy of Music where the *New York Observer* hailed 'a performance of unarguable greatness', while *Newsweek* went on to hail him as 'a world class star', with the *New York Times* dubbing him 'this astonishing Irish actor ... widely regarded as the finest of them all'. Despite the acclaim and despite his own demons, he remained unassuming and unfailingly gracious about his Terenure days. His death in 1999, at the age of 56, left a black hole in theatre but simultaneously bequeathed to some a sense that they had seen one of the greatest actors of all time. Joe Dowling put it simply: 'absolutely the single best actor I've ever seen, without question'.[11] As classmate and old pal to the end, Brendan Sherry, concluded: 'His friends in the Carmelite Order in Terenure College who had so influenced his early years, took him in as one of their own, waked him, prayed over him and accompanied him to where he now rests, with his mother's people, in St Patrick's Cemetery at Monaseed, Gorey, Co Wexford'.[12]

As young McCann was just leaving Terenure, another future stage talent had just arrived. John Bosco Hogan enrolled in prep in 1959, from O'Connell Schools, and made his first stage appearance when a third-year senior: he played an unremarked upon Jessica, daughter to Shylock, portrayed excellently by Michael Dore. Yet, Bosco must have made some impression for, in the next year's production, *As You Like It*, he played the significant role of Celia, followed in December 1965 by *Romeo and Juliet*: here, as Benvolio, cousin to Romeo, he was judged to have had 'one of the most difficult parts' and the house reviewer considered that 'Bosco's handling of the part points to genuine talent ... with ability above the ordinary'. This reviewer concluded with the masterly understatement, 'I feel we shall be seeing more of him on the [college] stage'.[13] Then, in his final year, came triumph as Hamlet where he won 'exemplary praise ... with a performance far above the level of normal schoolboy acting': little wonder then, that in that year, he also won best actor in the Dublin Shakespearean Festival. Following great success on the professional stage, he went on to make a lasting impression in film, notably in 1979 as Stephen Dedalus in Joseph Strick's *A Portrait of the Artist*; here, he starred with John Gielgud, T.P. McKenna and Maureen Potter. Other notable film performances came after, including *In the Name of the Father* in 1993. Still going strong 40 years later, his 'consummate skill' won him an acclaimed role as Bishop John Fisher in the 2007–08 television production, *The Tudors*.

Over the course of the next decade, he was to be followed into the Terenure Concert Hall and beyond into the world of professional acting by a succession of special talents — all contemporaries: Daragh O'Malley, Stephen Brennan and Philip O'Sullivan were in third year in 1969–70 at a time when the young Lorcan Cranitch was in prep year with Nicholas Grennell while Michael Grennell was in pre-inter.

In two respects, the Fr Madden and Fr O'Nolan production of 1969–70, with sets by Fr Aengus Hannigan, was special. For one, it was the college's first-ever attempt at *Richard III;* for another, three of this group of future greats, just mentioned, appeared together in it: Daragh O'Malley as Richard, Philip O'Sullivan as Duchess of York, and Stephen Brennan as Elizabeth, wife of Edward IV.

Coming to Terenure into third year in 1968–9, the young Limerick lad, Daragh — son of the then Minister for Education, Donogh O'Malley — won high praise for his first appearance on the stage of the concert hall: 'if any member of the cast has to be mentioned, it must be Daragh O'Malley', observed the reviewer. Daragh's stay in the college was brief enough, apparently moving on after fifth year in 1971. This, however, was not before starring in the 1970 production of *Juno and the Paycock*. This was the first non-Shakespearean production in the college since the start of the 1940s and it turned out to be one in which O'Malley's role as the Paycock was described as 'formidable'. He captured the audience; the stage now captured him — he soon after moved to the London Academy of Music and Dramatic Art. From there, he worked his way to a very successful career in film and television in Ireland, the UK and the USA. He became a household name through, among other productions, the *Sharpe* television series in which he starred as Patrick Harper, alongside Sean Bean as Richard Sharpe in a very popular TV series set in the time of the Napoleonic Wars.

One year behind Daragh in Terenure, Stephen Brennan had acting in his blood. His mother, Daphne Carroll, had been one of the Radio Éireann Players: these were described by John Devitt as 'really something special ... the actors in that company, they were really prodigiously gifted'.[14] His father, Dennis Brennan, was a well-known actor and broadcaster with that distinctive voice which had made him as unmistakeable and as popular to radio listeners as ever Leo Maguire had been. Stephen made his own college debut in the 1968 *Julius Caesar,* as Calpurnia, and then played beside

Daragh as Jerry Devine in the 1970 *Juno*. A year later, he took the lead role as Fr Mallon in Joseph Tomelty's *Is The Priest At Home?*, in which Philip O'Sullivan played McLaughlin, the 'curate'; and Michael Grennell took the part of Marona, the house-keeper. It was not long after leaving Terenure that Stephen's professional career commenced. He was involved in several musicals before he joined The Abbey, in May 1976, for what turned out to be a long run: 8 years and over 60 leading roles later, he went to the National Theatre in the UK. By then, his career had brought him into working with outstanding, established professionals such as Cyril Cusack, Ray McAnally, Eamon Kelly and, indeed, old schoolmate, Donal McCann. Film roles later on included *The General* and there were substantial appearances in television series such as *Ballykissangel* and *The Tudors*. In more recent times, too, he acted regularly at The Gate Theatre, notably in *Waiting for Godot*.

As for Michael Grennell, he had already established a record in the history of drama in Terenure: in the 1970 *Juno* he became the then only first-year student to have appeared in a senior-school production.[15] This cannot be said to have been, by any means the best production in Terenure College history, but it harmed not one of them as they all pressed forward to highly successful professional careers.

What followed, for college dramatics, in 1972, was seemingly a ropey time. An attempt to stage another non-Shakespeare play — this time, Shaw's *Joan of Arc* — had to be abandoned, followed by an emergency substitution of O'Casey's *Shadow of a Gunman*: here, appropriately, Philip O'Sullivan and Michael Grennell saved the night with two great performances as Seamus Shields and Michael Davoren. Philip, brother of Terenure athlete, teacher and games master, Charlie, had already appeared in the 1968 *Julius Caesar*. Whatever revolution was going on, or being attempted, behind the scenes is not clear, but, in the next year, 1973, there was a return to Shakespeare with a new production partnership of Fr Joe O'Nolan and John McClean, the latter being the first lay co-producer since the days of Michael O'Connell and P.P. Maguire in the 1940s; and another key lay figure had also arrived, in the person of Denis Whitty as set designer. The two Grennell boys appeared in this, Nicholas as one of the Musicians, and Michael as Sir Andrew Aguecheek — a performance praised as 'a piece of finely-drawn camp'.[16]

Lorcan Cranitch was then a third-year pupil when he made his senior school debut as one of the Officers in that production. His star rose quickly: in the 1974 *Julius Caesar*, he won high praise for his introspective presentation of Brutus, to Michael's Cassius and Declan Doyle's Julius. What was to follow, in 1975, was probably the college's greatest ever drama production. The *Hamlet* of that year saw Lorcan in the lead role, with Michael Grennell as Claudius, brother Nicholas as Bernardo, William Letmon as Laertes and Gary Mountaine as Ophelia. The performances over four nights were so successful that the word spread and, unprecedented in college drama annals, it was decided to extend the run for another full week for the benefit of other Dublin schools and colleges. In the end, the production was seen and acclaimed by over 3,000 people: 'Lorcan Cranitch was intensely moving as the shocked and disgusted young prince of the early play while later, his sardonic taunting of Claudius was masterly'. So the reviewer went, adding high praise too to Michael Grennell: 'giving his last performance on the College stage, [he] was an excellent Claudius, a scheming murderer with a conscience. Michael has great presence on stage and his Claudius was the most mature of his many roles'. Nor was Ophelia overlooked: 'a much younger actor with something of the same talent is Gary Mountaine. He played Ophelia with an assurance that was amazing in a boy so young'.[17] It was recalled, long after, by some who saw that performance that his rendering of the crazed Ophelia and his singing of her songs reduced the concert hall to tears.[18]

Following this *Hamlet*, Lorcan could not look back. Further stage triumphs followed in his UCD years and from these it was on to the Royal Academy of Dramatic Art, in 1980, where his fellow students included Kenneth Brannagh. Lorcan's early professional years saw him on the stage throughout Ireland and Great Britain, playing a wide range of roles from Irish anti-heroes to English aristocrats and Russian dissidents. In 1991, he secured a major role in the BBC's *Parnell and the Englishwoman*, playing Tim Healy. In more recent times he became a household name and face with his darkly brilliant portrayal of Detective Sergeant Beck in the TV series, *Cracker*.

As to the ongoing story of the college drama productions, the return to Shakespeare continued until the *King Lear* of 1988, with new talent emerging all the while. Notable among the talented new arrivals were Michael McElhatton who was in Terenure from 1971–82 and Steve Nealon who was a pupil from 1977–88. Michael played a memorable Horatio in the 1979 *Hamlet* and then followed it with the lead role in the December 1980 *King Lear*. He soon after went on to a highly successful professional career on stage, and in film and television, in addition to script-writing. His film and television roles included that of Johnner Doyle in Paddy Breathnach's *I Went Down*, and, more recently, as Sam, in John Crowley's 2003 film, *Intermission*, and most recently in the RTÉ drama, *Single-Handed*. As for Steve Nealon, his portrayal of Claudius in the *Hamlet* of December 1987 was equally memorable:

> The character of the coolly treacherous King was excellently captured by Stephen Nealon in a restrained, very mature performance. His Claudius was a dignified, authoritative figure, a man whose charm and ability might have made for a good ruler, had he not murdered for the throne. Stephen presented an impressively kingly figure throughout.[19]

On leaving Terenure Stephen pursued his craft at the Samuel Beckett Centre in Trinity College and has filled many Shakespearean roles since then.

Securing his Leaving Certificate from Terenure a year after him, Aidan McArdle was the King Lear of the 1989 production, played with 'great sensitivity'. Aidan went on to UCD and The Abbey Theatre, and then to RADA. He graduated from the latter in 1996 and has since played significant roles in leading theatres such as the Royal Court and the Hampstead in London, while his work with the Royal Shakespeare Company has included the title role in *Richard III*.

Regime Change:

By the time Steve and Aidan first trod the Terenure Concert Hall boards significant changes had come about. One was the passing of the producer/director baton from John McClean to Joe McDonnell. Joe took over in 1977. It was no sinecure; rather, an all-consuming commitment for the first three months of every school year. When Joe took over he was a man of limited drama experience: he had not been engaged with it during his Limerick years but, admittedly, had played the lead role in UCD in its production of Yeats's *At the Hawk's Well*. Nevertheless, to follow in the footsteps of Fr David Weakliam and John McClean, in the era of the great talents, was no joke: Joe had witnessed the stellar talents of the Grennells, O'Malley, O'Sullivan and Cranitch. Furthermore, the annual play was not just a kind of extra-curricular encounter with the Leaving Certificate English syllabus: it was an institution and a cultural landmark in the social calendar of Terenure and west Dublin. All this notwithstanding, Joe McDonnell broke the mould — several moulds in fact. For his first venture, the 1977 *Merchant of Venice*, he introduced radical changes to character and to speeches, all tantamount to sacrilege: he presented a new kind of Shylock, and one with much shorter speeches. His mould-breaking brought departures and new arrivals: Iris Lawlor, who for so long had laboured at doing the boys' makeup, departed. Furthermore, in a move of outrageous innovation, he introduced real, live girl actors from Our Lady's School, just across the road. This radical new departure must have been a huge relief to such red-faced, adolescent boys who, from Terenure's time immemorial, had been saddled with female roles, to the taunts of the muscular young men in the audience front rows: a huge relief this, and, now an even greater attraction awaited the lads in the auditorium as much as those on stage or behind the scenes. Further shocks followed, a decade later: from 1989 he broke with the Shakespearean tradition that had only ever before been breached for the three years from 1970 to 1972. This was to good effect: the talent of the new thespians did not depart with the classical canon. The 1992 *Plough and the Stars* was a triumph: it was so much so that even the discriminating McClean, never given to flattery, praised it as 'a wonderful production'.

Although the responsibility for the annual play is a major one, Joe McDonnell undertook it for a remarkable 30 years, 'despite the nightmare of organisation and the ever-present threat of looming disaster'. It was, presumably, with some relief, that the chalice and the challenge passed eventually to staff member, Graham White, and past pupil, Darren Kinsella.[20]

Memorable though those 30 years of skirting disaster and achieving triumph were, nothing could underline the strength and rich accomplishment of that tradition than the major event of 23 March 1997, with which this chapter commenced.

THE PLAY'S THE THING:

The idea originated with staff member Brendan McCauley who thought it might be appropriate to mark and to celebrate 50 years of drama in Terenure College. It would be a fitting testament, not only to what had been achieved over those years, but also a remarkable demonstration of the affection and loyalty of the Terenure alumni, and especially of those who had paced that stage and gone on to make a life of entertainment for others. All of those, whose talents and stage careers have featured in the foregoing pages, turned up to act and to participate in making an unforgettable evening and an enduring and priceless memory.

The marketing, promotion and sponsorship was superbly organised by Bernard Kenna, Jim Blake, Frank Gildea and Barry Dooley, all leading lights in the Past Pupils' Union. The show was devised and directed by Michael Grennell, produced by Brendan McCauley, Declan Murphy, J.P. Doyle and Jamie Doyle, and was brilliantly cast in the format of an 'Oscar' ceremony. Video narration was done by the venerable Aidan Grennell and the live presentations were made in person by Donal McCann, Philip O'Sullivan, Michael McElhatton, Lorcan Cranitch, Steve Nealon, Aidan McArdle, Tom Farrelly, Greg Magee and Jonathan Browner. In addition, there were video presentations by Jim McCann, Dave Allen and Paul Bushnell, while Anne Bushnell participated as a special guest. All tickets were sold out and all proceeds, in excess of £5,000, went to the Past Pupils' Union Benevolent Fund. It would be invidious to single out performers or performances; nevertheless, there was, at the end, one *tour de force*, when the recently ill and then recuperating Donal McCann produced a wonderful *ad lib* performance at the occasion's end.

This event entered the lore of Terenure College: a magical moment for the college, so rightly proud of its progeny, and they of it.

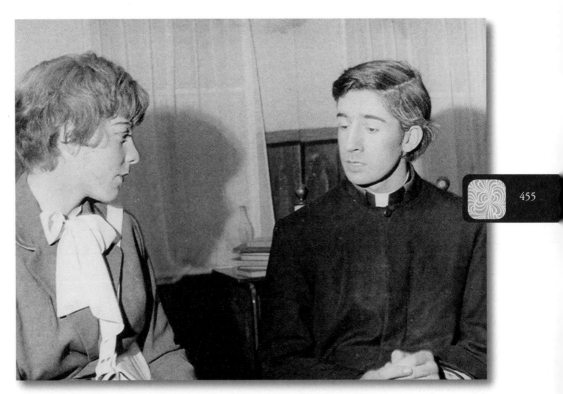

Martin Donnelly and Stephen Brennan in *Is the Priest at Home?*, 1972.

Lorcan Cranitch – pupil at the college in the 1960s–70s went on to success onscreen in *Cracker* and *Ballykissangel*.

457

Cast

Lear, King of Britain	PHILIP WILLIAMS ✔
King of France	VERNON O'BYRNE
Duke of Burgundy	PAUL DELANEY
Duke of Cornwall	PATRICK FLANAGAN ✔
Duke of Albany	SEAMUS HEALY
Earl of Kent	DAVID BLAKE ✔
Earl of Gloucester	IAN SEXTON
Edgar ⎫ Sons to Gloucester ⎰	PATRICK FLYNN ✔
...nd ⎭ ⎱	MICHAEL MURPHY ✔
Curan, a Courtier	EDWARD TREACY
Old Man, Tenant to Gloucester ...	ERIC POWER ✔
Doctor	DAVID HEARY ✔
Fool	MYLES BYRNE ✔
Oswald, Steward to Goneril	LEOPOLD BATT ✔
A Captain, employed by Edmund ...	PAUL MacKAY
Gentlemen attendant on Lear .... ⎰	VINCENT MORRIS ✔
⎱	SIMON TORMEY
Messenger to Cordelia	DERMOT CREAN
Herald	PATRICK FITZMAURICE ✔
Servant to Cornwall	CONOR MASSEY

458

Lear

Programme of the college's staging of *King Lear*, 1957,
in which Mike Murphy and Donal McCann featured.

Goneril }
Regan } Daughters to Lear } DON McDONALD
Cordelia } FRANCIS DUNNE
DONAL McCANN

SOLDIERS AND OTHER SERVANTS AND ATTENDANTS

M. Raggett, D. J. Ryan, J. Buckley, B. Clancy, L. Hollingsworth, J. Moger, E. Raggett, M. O'Doherty, L. Flanagan, J. Costigan, M. Foxe, B. Maloney, A. Searson.

Scene : BRITAIN

ACT ONE : The Castles of Lear, Albany and Gloucester.

ACT TWO : A Heath and the Castle of Gloucester.

459

ACT THREE : The Battlefields at Dover.

Music for Songs composed by *Mr.*

Produced by *Fr. Aengus Hannig.*
with
Fr. Boniface Kinahan, O.Carm., an.

Settings and Music by *Paul*

Stage Manager : *Bro. Stephen*

Lighting installed and operated under
Mr. Enda Ryder.

Costumes supplied by P. J. Bourke an.

Wigs by Madame Drag.

Terenure College
Dublin

The Pupils present

KING LEAR

by

WILLIAM SHAKESPEARE

★

DECEMBER 5th, 6th and 7th
1957

P. Finnegan as Hamlet in the college's production, 1953.

Donal McCann and Mr J. Griffin, 1970.

461

CHAPTER 24

Renewal and Restoration,
1985–2010

Carmelite Community. Seated: Fr A. Corbett, Fr M. O'Malley, Fr L. Fennell, Fr E. Griffin (Prior), Bishop D. Lamont, Fr T. Brennan, Br. Traynor. First row: Fr J. McCouaig, Fr J. Clinch, Fr J. Madden, Fr J. Murray, Fr S. Grace, Fr J. O'Hea, Br J. Reynolds. Second row: Fr. D. O'Connor, Fr W. Langan, Fr M. McMahon, Fr M. Kilmurray, Fr L. Hegarty, Fr A. Clarke.

THOSE GROWING UP IN IRELAND FROM THE 1970S ONWARDS FACED A VERY different world to those whose youth was spent from the 1940s to the 1960s. The later world was a more troubled, unsettled and dangerous one — from the plague of drugs, through threats of war and the prolonged misery of the Northern Troubles. It was, simultaneously, a more exciting and rapidly changing place, from more accessible foreign travel, computers and information technology, the whole phenomenon of popular culture and the wider possibilities of self-promotion. Whether these students of the later generation were, in reality or in perception, different or more indulged than their parents is hard to say: some who had been long enough in the teaching profession were tempted to suggest that there had been a partial revolution in parental mentality: the 1950's parent was, in situations of teacher–pupil conflict, likely automatically to endorse the teacher; the parent from the 1980s was more prone to endorse or defend the child, and not always to good effect. Issues of discipline would come to the fore even as corporal punishment came to be outlawed. It would be easy to exaggerate the degree to which this may have affected certain schools and colleges and it is probably true to say that for naturally effective and intrinsically authoritative, rather than authoritarian teachers, such change made little difference; contrariwise, teachers without the gift of presence and who might have got by in the old days, would find it increasingly difficult to survive in the new culture.

The process of change in secondary education in Ireland continued apace in the three decades from the 1970s, and did so in a context, first, of economic decline and then of rapid economic growth — all with consequent or complementary social and cultural change. The number of traditional secondary schools continued to decline, while the number of pupils attending traditional secondary education continued to grow. Whereas in the mid-1960s, there had been some 60,000 pupils in the system, by 1991, there were 60,000 sitting the Leaving Certificate alone. Furthermore, for all the economic problems of the age, those 60,000 Leaving Certificate students represented 80% of their age cohort. The number of pupils in these schools went from 167,000 in 1973–4 to 206,000 in 1983 and the number in all kinds of second-level institutions rose from 329,000 in 1985 to 370,000 ten years later. Correspondingly, the numbers of full-time teachers in the system had risen from 19,000 in 1985 to 21,400 by the year 2000. By the mid-1980s lay teachers had grown to comprise 84% of teachers and females had grown to represent over 55% of the total.[1]

Those who directly experienced the system, whether as pupils or teachers, lived through significant turning-points. Education Minister John Boland had announced the prohibition of corporal punishment with effect from 1 February 1982. Around the same time much discussion had developed around the possibility of a four-year junior cycle. As an element in the 1987 Programme for National Recovery, the 'transition year' was to be introduced. Following on that, the old Intermediate Certificate programme and examinations were abolished and the new, more flexible Junior Certificate was introduced as of 1989; its examinations replaced the Intermediate Certificate examination from 1992. Over this same period the whole area of access to third-level education became more pressurised and competitive. This came as a result of the emergence of the 'points system' for admission to third-level courses through the Central Admissions Office (CAO). The CAO admitted the first cohort of students for 1978. The CAO/CAS system was extended and tightened up from 1991 when a common points system for all third-level institutions was agreed and from 1992 when the points were applied to a student's single sitting of the Leaving Certificate examination. How far these developments rigidified the secondary-school experience for pupils and teachers is perhaps a moot point but certainly the existence of the transition year programme by that stage was some cultural counteraction.

The altering balance between religious and lay teachers in the system was reflected in Terenure as early as 1965–70. That alteration continued apace in the 25 years from 1985. Over the two and a half decades from 1985, the numbers of students and staff rose, then peaked around 1995 and declined gradually thereafter, as illustrated by Table 29:

TABLE 29: TERENURE COLLEGE STAFF AND STUDENTS, 1965–2008

Year	Religious*	Lay	Total	Seniors	Juniors	Total
1965	21	63	84	758	336	1,094
1990	20	59	79	810	278	1,088
1995	20	69	89	792	234	1,026
2000	15	67	82	761	174	935
2005	12	73	85	737	169	906
2008	12	72	84	714	158	872

* The figures in this column are the numbers of members of the Carmelite Community in Terenure
— due to retirement or ill health, not all of them would have been teaching.

The number of boys in the junior school had peaked around 1980 at about 370 and their number has more than halved between then and the present. There was one particular, if complex, reason for the extent and suddenness of the drop which occurred around 1999–2000. The decision had been taken to cease admission in second year and to commence admission with third year. It partly related to the raising of the age for making First Communion to 8 years, and partly to the closure of boy's junior admissions in Our Lady's Bushy Park and Loreto Beaufort. The numbers of senior boys continued to rise until *c.* 1990–5 and the decline thereafter was much less marked. No doubt, the overall intake was affected by the expansion of neighbouring schools and colleges in west Dublin and by the fact that the immediately neighbouring suburbs were areas of ageing population and of high-value housing that militated against any really significant inflow of young families. Nevertheless it must have been something of a relief to the staff and authorities of the college that the relentless upward rise of pupil numbers since 1950 had at last begun to stop and gently recede, 40 years later. While the vocations crisis from the 1970s and 1980s accentuated the altering ratio of religious to lay, it remained the case that by the 1990s an adequate number of able young Carmelites had come forward to help the responsibility of leadership in the college.

THE CARMELITE LEADERSHIP:

In succession to Fr Bob Kelly, from 1982 there were six Priors: Frs Eltin Griffin, 1982–8; Jim McCouaig, 1988–94; Paddy Staunton, 1994–7; Jimmy Murray 1997–2003; Micheál Ó Néill, 2003–08; and Michael Troy, 2008–present. The senior school enjoyed considerable continuity of leadership, under Fr Jimmy Murray from 1982 to 1991, Fr Fintan Burke from 1991 to 1999 and Fr Éanna Ó hÓbáin since 2000. That sense of continuity was reinforced by the long service of the lay vice-principals or deputy principals: Michael O'Connell, as first lay principal, was succeeded by Tom Byrne who held the post from 1980 for sixteen years until 1996; Vinnie Morris took over for almost ten years to 2005–06 when Frank Gallen was appointed. That strong sense of continuity in leadership was ever more marked in the junior school. Here the principalship, in succession to the almost patriarchal Fr Lar Hegarty, went to Fr Martin Kilmurray who held the post for a remarkable fifteen years from 1982 to 1997; after this, he became Assistant Provincial, based in Gort Muire from 1997 to 2009 and since June 2009, he became Provincial. On his moving to Gort Muire, the junior school secured Fr Michael Troy as Principal from 1997 to the present. When Eltin Griffin breezed back into Terenure College in 1982, as Prior — 30 years exactly since he had spent one teaching year there — six breathless years must have followed. Always a character, with a joy for conversation and impossible as only liturgists can be: hence the quip as to the difference between a liturgist and a terrorist — one can reason with a terrorist. Born in Cork in 1925, he grew up in Mayfield where Eddie Golden was a neighbour — and they were to meet up again in Terenure in 1953 to plot the great *Hamlet* production, despite P.P. Maguire. Eltin was 57 when he returned to Terenure to take over the management of a Community of twenty plus and a college of a thousand plus. Renowned as a preacher — one of the great Carmelite preachers — he was, in Fr Chris O'Donnell's remembrance, 'the most cultured Carmelite I knew'.[2] Consistent with this and one abiding legacy is that Fr Eltin was the one who commissioned the magnificent modern stained glass windows in the college chapel. For all the managerial responsibilities, he kept up a relentless pace of publication, scholarship, editing, and writing. A wonderful picture of him was painted by receptionist Ita Clancy, for years so well-placed in the lobby, to see and suffer the comings and goings of countless Carmelites, teachers, pupils and parents:

> Prior Eltin Griffin ... 'a devil for the writing' ... always writing
> articles or preparing the mss for religious broadcasts ... an affable

soul, he would come down to me at Reception, in his stately pro-
cessional stride, with his hands folded within his habit and benignly
smiling as he approached … an approach that I came to fondly dread
… 'Gooood mooorning, Dear Ita' and then out would come one
hand clutching a ream of manuscript notes that he hoped I would
type up … all this with phones hopping and callers clamouring and,
to cap it all, his handwriting not exactly copperplate. 'Are you in a
hurry for this, Father?' … 'Don't worry, Ita, … when you've got
time': and then next morning the casual and coy hovering around
Reception in the hope that I, the hapless Ita, had delivered … which
I inevitably did, despite the pressures.[3]

He came during the year of the great change when the Irish Province of the
Carmelites experienced more transfers then a premier league club in summer: former
Terenure pupil, Chris Crowley, became Provincial and Terenure Prior and teaching
Carmelites Frs Bob Kelly, Jim McCouaig, Patsy Keenan, T.D. Doran, Aidan
O'Donovan and Gerry Hipwell were all on the move. The tall, wiry, shy and gentle Jim
McCouaig was not too long away from Terenure: he had been teaching (and rugby
coaching) from 1951 without a break, becoming dean of studies in 1961 and senior
school principal in 1979. He had been ordained along with Eltin Griffin in 1950 and
their paths would intersect again: for he returned to Terenure, Eltin's successor as Prior
and manager from 1988 to 1994: eight years later, Eltin would deliver a homily for his
friend and confrere in the college chapel, in January 2002, when Jim had gone to his
well-earned rest. Fr Jim's successor as Prior and manager of the college was Mayoman,
Fr Patrick Staunton. Joining the Carmelites in 1954 and ordained in 1962, he was
soon off to the missions in Zimbabwe. Eleven years later, in 1974, he returned to
Ireland and became parish priest of the new Carmelite-run parish of Knocklyon until
1982. Three years in Whitefriar Street were followed by appointment as parish priest
of Beaumont in 1985 and it was, therefore, very much as a newcomer that he took
over responsibility for Terenure College in 1994. It was a single-term appointment
during which he made a major contribution in heading up the chaplaincy team. Former
principal of the senior school, Fr Murray, now succeeded Fr Staunton in 1997 and held
the reins until 2003 when he was succeeded by Fr Micheál Ó Néill. Fr Micheál was one
of a number of younger Carmelites who formed a new generation who came to play a
major role in the recent history of the college or of the Order — together with him in
this were Frs Martin Kilmurray, Joe Mothersill, Eoin Moore, P.J. Breen, Michael Troy,
Éanna Ó hÓbáin and Richard Byrne.

Micheál and Martin were of the class of 1970, the former from Terenure where
classmates included sprinter, Charlie O'Sullivan, and soccer stalwart, Derek Stuart,
while Martin was from Carmelite College, Moate. Micheál was Galway-born, son
of a fluent Irish-speaking Garda who, in turn, was uncle of the celebrated critic, Denis
Donoghue: the latter, now Henry James professor of English at New York University,

in his autobiography, *Warrenpoint*, recalled Micheál's father as the most gifted of a gifted family. On his retirement from the Gardaí, the family moved, in 1961, to Lavarna Road, in Terenure. It was from there that Micheál entered the college in Elementary B in September 1961, greeted by Fr Hegarty and first taught by Fr Joe Linus Ryan. Never considering himself a star player at rugby, he worked hard enough at it to gain his place, eventually, on the second Senior Cup XV in 1969: 'our least experienced forward, but always played with great enthusiasm and grew considerably in stature as the season advanced' was Fr Jackie Madden's progress report at the end of the 1969 season. The truth of this judgement was later borne out when Micheál was capped for Connacht Schools and then in his final year, with his height a plus for the line-outs, was promoted to Terenure's first XV in the august company of Anthony and Gerry Flannery, Johnnie Cronin, Charlie O'Sullivan and Noel Germaine. His teachers in senior school included geography master, T. 'Snowy' Murphy, a man of great fluency with words and who would carry a happily never-used, great lump of wood, which he called 'The Board of Education'. Micheál had a hugely successful academic record, always excelling in Irish but also bearing away the science award in fourth year and the arts award for fifth year, in 1968–9. Even as he sat his Leaving Certificate in 1970 Micheál had more or less decided on a vocation with the Carmelites, not a little helped in this way by the gentle examples of Fr Brendan O'Reilly, Br Stephen Reynolds and Fr Maurice Barry — today his confrere in Kinsale but then a priest whom he served as altar boy. Entering the novitiate in September 1970, a year later he was off to Rome with fellow-novices Martin Kilmurray and Fintan Burke, the latter destined to be Provincial from 2000 to 2009 and the former destined to succeed him in that role. Micheál's Roman years of study were to be curtailed by a request to return home to pursue his HDip in education in Trinity and then home to Terenure in September 1979 as Chaplain and head of religious education. Two years later, with Provincial Weakliam's reluctant blessing, he answered the call of the missions to remote rural Peru, ministering to the Quechua people until 1985. It was after this that he completed his studies in Rome and was awarded the doctorate for his study on 'The Emerging Spirituality of the Christian Communities of Peru'. He then went on to serve on the General Council of the Carmelite Order in Rome for twelve years. Next, a short-lived, if much-loved, assignment to Knocklyon Parish after this, was followed, in 2003, with his appointment as Prior of the Terenure Carmelite Community and manager of its schools. In case he had not enough to do, he was also simultaneously, to become Bursar, and holding all three positions until going to Kinsale as Prior in 2008.

His confreres in Rome, Martin Kilmurray and Fintan Burke, came from there to Terenure in September 1976 while pursuing their teacher-training diploma in Trinity, the first ever Carmelites to attend Trinity, as the NUI did not recognise their Roman degrees. Longfordman, Brother Martin, soon became Fr Martin and a permanent staff member from 1977, while Fintan was assigned to teach in Carmelite College Moate. Within five years, Martin would be principal of the junior school and little imagined that he would shoulder this responsibility for the next fifteen years. For all the changes in the wider world and the secularisation of Irish society, Fr Kilmurray's junior school was profoundly set in the liturgy of the Christian year, with beginning-of-year and end-of-year Mass, the serious preparation for Christmas, Easter and the key saints' days, together with the preparation for Confirmation. In 1997, Fr Martin became Prior at Gort Muire and in 2000 was appointed Assistant Provincial and then, in 2009, he was elected Provincial. His principalship of Terenure junior school passed to Fr Michael Troy.

A Westmeathman, from Ballynacargy, Fr Michael went to Moate as a boarder after his local primary schooling days. His Moate years up to Leaving Certificate in 1984 were greatly enjoyed and he well-remembered how welcoming a place it was, with Carmelites Jimmy Murray, Billy Langan and Mick Morrissey doing a great deal to make it so. He took up a pre-novitiate year at Heather Lawn, Balinteer, where the Community included Frs Gerry Hipwell and Martin Farragher, and then to Kinsale under novice master, Fr Bob Kelly. Following the years of philosophy in Milltown and of social science in UCD from which he graduated in 1991, he was assigned to the Terenure Community from where he then pursued his study of theology at Milltown. The year of teacher-training in Terenure and Trinity followed, over 1994–5 and a year later he was to be fully occupied teaching and, indeed, coaching in Terenure thereafter. He was to succeed Fr Kilmurray as principal of the junior school in 1996 and, fourteen years later has continued the great and happy atmosphere of that place unbroken since the days of Fr Hegarty.

The sense of Terenure College, junior and senior schools, being a Christian place was greatly enhanced by young Carmelite new arrivals like Frs Troy and Ó hÓbáin. Entering the Order just before Fr Troy was Fr Éanna Ó hÓbáin, principal of the senior school since 2000–01. The senior school lost the brilliant leadership of Fr Fintan Burke, principal since 1991, on his being elected Provincial in 2000. It was very fortunate, therefore, to have in Fr Éanna an able, dynamic successor. A Dubliner, from Beaumont, Éanna had attended Coláiste Muire for secondary school and entered that novel introduction to the Carmelite Order — the 'pre-novitiate', in 1985: this was a trial year in which one lived in a Carmelite house but earned a living at a job outside for a while. A year as novice in Kinsale in 1985–6 was followed by a number of years at Gort Muire House of Studies and then one year, 1989–90, teaching at Terenure junior school. There was further study in theology and pastoral leadership before completing his Higher Diploma in Trinity and finally, in 1993–4, to permanent teaching, at first in the junior and then the senior school. The great challenge which he, his confreres and his lay colleagues faced in the 1990s was how to simultaneously maintain the college's homely atmosphere and its provision of a rounded, well-balanced education in face of the mounting pressures and expectations created by the 'points' system and the 'points race'. It is a challenge that they feel they successfully faced by wise anticipation and discriminating delegation of positions of responsibility and with a strong sense of pastoral mission and care.

That sense, in turn owed much to the pervasive spirit of goodwill in general and to the work of the chaplaincy team in particular. Key figures in that chaplaincy team included other young Carmelite vocations, with Frs Eoin Moore, P.J. Breen, Richard Byrne and Ms Mary Carroll.

Eoin Moore had been a pupil in Terenure from 1975 to 1986 as had his father, Don, in the 1950s. His brothers, Colm, David and Stephen, would follow him onto the school rolls. Like so many before him, his first contact was the assessment test with Fr Hegarty and then on to first day in full uniform — purple blazer, grey shirt, school tie, shorts, sweater socks and shoes — the full regalia and the standard daily outfit of the time. Rescued into retirement from rugby due to illness, at fourteen, he denied any shining academic par excellence with the exception of a 100% in a fifth-year Maths test, to the utter astonishment of himself, his classmates and his teacher, Fr Bob Kelly. So many recalled Fr Bob, walking with a wagging cane, never used but, sweeping from side to side, clearing a path through crowded corridors like Moses parting the Red Sea. Then too, there was Irish teacher, Mr B. 'Dynamite' Devine, so-called from his short fuse, typically, standing by the window with head in his hands as if in contemplation or despair, but all-seeing nonetheless. Soon enough it was on to senior school with Fr McCouaig as principal. Here John 'The Doc' McClean was a firm and commanding figure who could scare the wits out of everyone by gaze alone, and the ever-serene Fr Jimmy Murray, never raising his voice but with that kind of face and look that made one want to confess or own up. There too was Fr Brennan of the Radio Club and the task and mystery of helping him rewire the attic spaces for his radio transmissions; and best of all, the Scouts and the liberating sense of caution to the winds with scouting trips to Cork and Galway and a deserted Castletownbere, streets empty because all the locals — and probably the whole country — were glued to their television sets watching the wedding of Charles and Diana. Like a few others before him, even before the ink had dried on his Leaving Certificate exam answers, he had hoped to enter the Carmelites, not a little influenced by the kind and inspiring example of Fr Billy Langan who, from joining the Community in 1982, had taken chaplaincy and pastoral care to a new level. Like Fr Éanna before him, and like his near contemporary confreres, Frs Michael Troy and Richard Byrne, Eoin entered the recently instituted pre-novitiate home at Heather Lawn, near Marley Park, where Fr Bene O'Callaghan was first Prior — Fr Bene himself once a Terenure boarder and classmate of Eoin's father, Don. From there, for Eoin, it was on to Kinsale for the novitiate year in 1987. Further study, then solemn profession came in 1993 with over a year in Knocktopher while pursuing the diploma in liturgy. Following some years of duty in Gort Muire and Beaumont, it was back to Terenure in 1997, as Sub-Prior, with responsibility for the church and for the work of the chaplaincy team. Here he would find new colleagues in Fr Richard Byrne and Mary Carroll who joined the chaplaincy team in 1998, after having started her Terenure career teaching English from 1992. P.J. Breen, a Dubliner, schooled with Augustinians in Dungarvan, had arrived in Terenure a year earlier as trainee teacher; he quickly got involved in promoting the Debating Society and in pastoral care. Within a year, he was on the permanent staff teaching French and religious education and, from 1994, in a new initiative, he became the only lay member for a new chaplaincy team of four. It was in January 1996 that he sought admission to the Order. In 2002, he was ordained and assigned to Whitefriar Street but, a year later, he was back, teaching and engaged in Chaplaincy duties along with Frs Eoin and Richard and with Mary Carroll. Not long after, with the retirement of Pat Cahill, Fr P.J. became head of geography: he found himself fully committed in a school where there was great respect in the classroom combined with great openness in exchange between the boys and their teachers in an environment that is proudly and unapologetically Carmelite and Christian.

If the arrival of these relatively young additions to the Order and the college bespoke a sense of revival and renewal in the history of both, it has to be said, too, that the never-ending need for physical renewal of the college was manifest in these years.

Physical Development 1985–2010:

It will be recalled that by the Christmas vacation of 1982 the completion of a great programme of building extension had been celebrated, with the blessing of the classroom extensions, practical work rooms and new gymnasium. However, as is evident from Table 28, the growth in numbers of students and staff continued apace for another fifteen years, creating new pressures on space and facilities.

By the time of the new millennium, it would have been over twenty years since there had been any significant upgrading, had it not been for the remarkable effort of confidence, co-operation and planned development over the late 1990s that resulted in the college's most significant physical renewal in a quarter of a century: a confidence that however daunting a task it could be done; a co-operation between past pupils and their union, parents and their association, Carmelites and their lay teaching and administrative colleagues; planned development that raised the proceeds that helped to realise the renewal. It was in that sense as much a renewal in spirit as in material surroundings. On 7 December 2001, returning to the college as Assistant Provincial, Fr Kilmurray, on behalf of Provincial Burke and the Order, spoke of Terenure thus:

> This College is not simply an institution of learning but a community of faith … [with a] particular ethos (which is Catholic and Carmelite) … Within such a school as this, teachers and pupils work together in acquiring knowledge and skills, but they also search for the truth about our world and the One who gives ultimate meaning to human existence — Jesus Christ. … In the Carmelite tradition we emphasise the value of community, prayer and service … and we live in one world as brothers and sisters in the knowledge and friendship of God.[4]

He was speaking at the blessing of the new development that had been conceived back in the mid-1990s when Fr Fintan Burke was principal of the senior school, he himself principal of the junior and Fr Paddy Staunton was Prior and manager. The development programme conceived then, envisaged three stages: firstly, renewal of the older buildings and recasting of the Lady Chapel into a school and Community oratory, and the modernising and re-equipping of the information technology department; secondly, an upgrading of the sports facilities involving the construction of a weights and fitness room, the laying-down of an all-weather floodlit training area and inclusive facilities for a wide range of different sports; and thirdly, construction of an entirely new wing with a spacious new entrance, a restructuring of the junior school and significant upgrading of the facilities for woodworking, technical graphics and computer-aided design. The new school wing would provide a pastoral care centre, remedial education resource room, a meditation room and additional classrooms. The concern for decent pastoral-care facilities reflected a genuine recognition of the pressures and difficulties in the lives of young people that had been of such central concern to the chaplaincy team over the previous two decades.

Those who conceived the project clearly had that faith which moves mountains. The development, originally costed at £1.8 million then, had to be revised upwards to £2.5 million within two years as a result of inflation. Nothing daunted, a fundraising team of parents, past pupils and Carmelites set about the task with dynamism and with results so that, by 1999 close on £1.7 million had been raised.[5] Architect Paul Joyce was commissioned to design the new development, starting with the gymnasium and weights room extension in 1998, moving on to the new classrooms, science rooms and library extension in 2000. In addition, the swimming pool, which had been seriously damaged by a fire in 1993, had been recommissioned but then, following a disastrous leak it had to be repaired and refurbished a second time, at very considerable cost, re-opening in 2007. Original repair estimates of 2004 suggested a cost of £250,000 to put it right: by the time this had been accomplished in 2007 it had cost £3,000,000.[6] Finally, a very different project, which completed the redevelopment plan, was the provision of badly needed new living quarters and library for the Carmelite Community, designed by Paul Joyce and completed in 2007–08. All of these developments gave evidence of the great spirit of co-operation and shared endeavour that made such progress possible. In some ways, however, perhaps the most uplifting example of that spirit and what it can achieve may be seen in the story of the lake.

THE RESTORATION OF THE LAKE:

Historically the centrepiece of the Terenure House grounds in the mid-nineteenth century, the lake had boasted its islands, coffee house at one end, boat-house at the other. From its earliest Carmelite days well into the twentieth century, as seen earlier in these pages, it had been variously a source of contention or delight, access forbidden or allowed, skated over, swum in or outlawed, depending much on the Prior of the day but depending also on its condition. Its becoming a source or victim of pollution was not new. In his diary for 1908 that charismatic Carmelite who featured far earlier in this work, Fr Joseph Butler, was to record a visit to the college in May of that year: 'May 20th: Very tired. Went to Terenure for a few days. Some scoundrel put lime in the fish hatchery at Terenure. Fr Dunne discovered. A few hundred out of 2,000 little fry killed'.[7]

Thirteen years earlier, it had been the scene of high drama when frozen over in the winter of 1895. A well-known pupil, Michael Sage, fell through the ice and would have been lost had it not been for the great courage and presence of mind of a passing twelve-year-old, Arthur Percy Phelan: as the press reported, Phelan

> lay down flat on the ice, as near as he could to Sage and threw one end of his overcoat to him, retaining hold of the other end himself. Sage caught hold of the garment, and Master Phelan, being aided by other lads, who held his heels while Sage was hauling himself up with the overcoat, thus enabled the immersed lad to regain the surface of the ice.[8]

Cleaned and drained and supplied with a swimming area in the late 1930s, it was still clean and usable in the early 1940s when Paddy Ward went to college. Yet by the time Denis McGrane, as pupil, had come in the late 1940s 'there was no question of swimming in [it]: it was an uninviting feature at the time, a dark hole, to put it mildly'. That seems to have been the case through the 1950s since Brendan Sherry of the class of 1961 could not recall anyone in his time either swimming in it or being allowed near it. It must have been cleaned up shortly after, since Jim Blake in the late 1950s remembered it as a wonderland of swans and signets, with its two islands, waterfall and 'Fr Sharkey's boat' or canoe; and, in the 1960s, Fr Micheál Ó Néill remembered it as still clean, not out of bounds and as boasting a raft. It clearly deteriorated quickly at the end of the 1960s and into the early 1970s. Two simple sentences in the pupils' 'Day by Day' diary for 1972 said as much: 'May 23. Photographs were taken for the College *Annual*. The Lake is declared "a no-go area"'.[9] The diary entry of 1972 is confirmed independently by the recall of Frank Gildea of the class of 1973: by his day it was 'dangerous' and 'off-limits'. These reported variations in condition are not necessarily contradictory: the condition of the lake from time to time owed much to what flowed in from outside. However, by the end of the 1980s, it was in such a mess of stagnation that some of the Community wondered if it should not be filled in. Indeed, so bad was it by then that the Scouts began using it as a hazard to be crossed by ingeniously constructed rope bridges, and with a very real incentive to avoid descending into the horrors below. Redemption however was at hand, in the persons of five foolhardy and visionary past pupils — Mick Jordan, Frank Gildea, Bernard Kenna, Barry Coleman and Paul Joyce. All of them had been active in achieving things already for the college, and three of them, Jordan, Gildea and Joyce, had been successful on behalf of the Rugby Club in raising funds that were substantial, in the order of £5,000, for a scrummaging machine. Each of these principals modestly disclaims originating or precipitating the moment that 'something must be done'.

There are at least two distinct accounts as to the precise origin of the campaign to restore the lake. As Michael Jordan understood it, the originating call to action came from former Bishop Donal Lamont, then living in retirement as a member of the Terenure Carmelite Community. This account has it that the Bishop in a conversation with Paul Joyce mentioned the dreadful condition of the lake, who then mentioned it to Michael. Indeed, no swan had been seen on or near the lake since 1986 and no fish survived to swim in it. The other version, and perhaps they are not mutually exclusive, comes from Paul: his father-in-law, Commandant Eoin Quinn, then chairman of the Dodder Anglers, complained to him about the state of the lake: perhaps the commandant had said as much to Bishop Lamont or the Bishop to him. Whichever the case, at the end of the 1980s, Paul raised with Michael the possibility of its restoration, and he enthusiastically responded to the idea. In 1990, an initial approach to the National Lottery was unproductive — though eventually and significantly that would change. In 1991, their efforts became more focussed and they drafted in Bernard Kenna, Frank Gildea and Barry Coleman and thereby the committee was born, formally in September 1991: Michael became chairman, Frank, secretary and Barry, treasurer, with Paul and Bernard Kenna as the other foundation committee members. The fact that all five came from different years and so had access to extensive separate networks greatly helped to broaden their influence throughout the alumni network. They drafted in Fr Grace as Carmelite representative and patron. Early overtures to the Carmelites and to past pupil colleagues were encouraging: the Order committed an initial £10,000 and in March 1991, on behalf of the Rugby Club, Joe Milroy committed £5,000 to the project. However, little did they conceive the scale of the task that lay before them; yet, from the outset, in Paul Joyce's words, it was 'a hugely committed, dynamic, electric Committee'. It fell to Paul to produce the initial plans of what was to be done and the initial estimates of what it might cost: it fell to them all to raise the money. A key factor in the early stage was to secure the co-operation and positive support not just of the past pupils but of the city corporation. Their parks' man, Christy Boylan, took a keen interest, walked the grounds with them and actually suggested a walkway round the lake. Fundraising began in earnest in April 1991 and the target was then a massive £120,000. As Paul Joyce began to detail the scale of the undertaking, he presented the project as involving three distinct phases of the 'vital, the urgent and the ornamental'. The vital phase one involved the cutting of fallen banks, the opening up of the top of the island, the reshaping of the lake shores and the creation of a number of lagoons into which the 20,000 tons of dredged silt would be placed for later drying and later redeposit. Allowing a year to dry out, the mounds of silt would be redistributed as earthworks and eventually reseeded. A massive six-foot depth of silt across the extent of the lake would be dredged and stored in the process and, to prevent recurrence, a large silt trap had to be created at the entrance to the lake. This initial phase cost in the region of £27,500 and the firm of Killeen was contracted for the work. In the first week of September 1991, the Committee authorised Paul Joyce to sign the contract. On 23 September, the students recorded the arrival on site of the heavy machinery and fleet of trucks.[10] This work had been completed by the February of 1992 at a cost of £27,500 when there was just £28,000 in the restoration fund.

However, long before Phase 2 — the 'urgent-works' had been embarked upon, the committee, with almost military planning and practice, had pushed on with its wider and more systematic funding. A three-pronged attack was devised — to target the National Lottery again, to identify and persuade major sponsors, and to identify and bring on board the long line of past pupils stretching back class by class, year by year, even to the 1930s.

In the renewed quest for National Lottery support, Michael Jordan, as chair, lobbied local politicians, Dáil deputies and ministers, to some effect. Critical in this was his securing the support of Ben Briscoe, TD, whose help and advice in targeting the National Lottery proved invaluable. The lottery's agreement in principle to provide £25,000 out of an asked for £40,000 came in the final week of October 1991. As City Manager Frank Feely observed to Michael Jordan, it was to be the single largest lottery grant to any project in Dublin that year: the promise of this grant had been given on condition that a restored lake and lakeside would become a public amenity, which was agreed, and the grant would be released in stages as bills for work done were submitted. It was critical in enabling committee to contemplate proceeding with Phase 2.

By that stage the promotional and fund-raising aspects of the project were being progressively developed. Promotional material included a very persuasive brochure that featured the print of an oil painting of a restored lake, commissioned from artist and alumnus, James Hanley — his first commission. In addition, *Irish Times* photographer, Peter Thursfield, was brought in to create a photographic record of the progress of the restoration, and environmental correspondent of the same paper, Frank McDonald, was brought on board to write a feature in due course. From Bernard Kenna came the idea of a fundraising fashion show and later on the Dodder Art Group would stage an art exhibition as a fundraiser. The fashion show, supported by the Parents' Association and the Church Fund Committee, and introduced by compère and past pupil, Mike Murphy, was held on 29 April 1992 and proved a huge success, raising over £5,500.

By that stage, Phase 2 — the urgent works — had got under way. This involved driving timber piles into the banks to prevent erosion, the construction of a number of weirs to direct the flow and oxygenate the water, and a major tree surgery operation to remove overgrown trees and branches. This phase also involved a critical additional feature — the creation of a walk or pathway. This became critical because it involved the mass engagement of the past-pupil body behind the whole project. Whoever had the original idea may be contested but it involved the brilliant concept of a Past Pupil's Way, marked by individual kerbstones bearing the name and class year of each donor.

Each stone would involve a donation of £100 per individual. It succeeded brilliantly in engaging the body of alumni and within a year some 300 such kerbstones had been subscribed to, engraved and laid down, with more to follow in the months ahead. Frank Gildea recalled how touched the committee were by the extent of the response; especially so by instances where a single individual committed to four or five stones to commemorate fathers or brothers or to cover for classmates who may have fallen on hard times.[11] The process initially raised a vitally needed £30,000 to keep the project going. The organisational work, devolving on a small committee of five, was huge. However, by identifying or persuading individuals to accept the role of class year leader, and engaging them to contact as many of their year classmates as possible and by securing the co-operative input of twenty former PPU presidents, the task began to become manageable and to pay dividends — and not just in funds. Bernard Kenna began to create a computer database of alumni and the very process of its completion had very positive effects on creating a stronger sense of shared past, and a new sense of a partnered present and future, around the college. The donations began to pour in, from near and far. Indeed, the records indicate that the very first donor for the Pupil's Way was Austrian alumnus, Hans Herkner, then living in Western Australia.[12] Others from afar included the Asian brothers, Chen Kuan Jeang and Ming Kuan Jeang, of 1968–70.

Quite effective 'project' support packages had been prepared by the committee and Secretary Frank Gildea and his colleagues began distributing these to the class year leaders. Important help in this process came from Joe Clancy, PPU president in 1991–2 who agreed to circulate up to 700 of them with the distribution of the annual PPU diaries. The early general response was so positive that by early October almost £30,000 had come in such donations, to add to the lottery's £25,000: in the week of 1 to 8 October 1991 alone, some £700 had been donated in kerb donations. By early November, some 1,000 more letters were ready to be mailed to the alumni of 1981 to 1990.

By mid-February 1992, the future was beginning to happen. The first swans had arrived and a month later, courtesy of the Dodder Anglers' Association, minnows and 200 trout would be added to the waters. At the same time, even as Phase 2 commenced with the tree surgery, costing over £3,000, and hoped for completion by August, in March–April 1992, the committee were planning and fund-raising for Phase 3. This involved keeping up the momentum on alumni donations but also now persuading major sponsors to deliver, with a particular eye to making Phase 3 — the ornamental — possible. Ornamental it may have been in terminology, but it would prove critical in bringing the whole project to an elegant, finished conclusion. It involved the provision of Japanese style bridges — to revive memories of the original splendid oriental bridges which used to span the lake — to introduce ornamental, named benches and to create a pebble beach, which would not only complete the sense of elegance but would serve even as outdoor classroom for environmental studies. By June of 1992, the progress was helped by the honouring of earlier promises: the Rugby

Club had come up with another £1,000 of its £5,000 promise, the fashion show people had lodged their £5,500, and, under Chairman Paul McGee, the Terenure Soccer Club or AFC had given £500 while a further £500 duly followed from them in January 1993. While major institutional donors, as inevitable in larger organisations, tended to be subject to delays and procedures, nevertheless, over the next six to twelve months, they came good in substantial ways, with Coyle Hamilton Insurance, Terenure AIB and Irish Shell giving £5,000 each, while some individual personal donations of a substantial nature also came such as the gift of a weir from Ophthalmic Surgeon, Hugh Cassidy, and of water pump from Paul Haycock. By September 1992, with Phase 2 over and Phase 3 under way, the committee had raised close to £80,000 and Roadstone were now on standby to complete pathways. With great perseverance the Restoration Committee kept up the effort and the pressure: by January 1993, it had raised an impressive £105,000 out of the £120,000 target; most of the kerbs and pathways were in place and they were soon to start on bridges and beach. By the middle of January 1993, they were predicting a completion date of May. So it came to pass. On Sunday 30 May, the restoration of the lake to a pristine condition was marked by extensive celebrations, the spirit of which not even the downpours of that day could dampen. When all the sums had been added and the audits completed there was a relatively minor shortfall of £10,000 out of £120,000: the Parents' Association rallied again to assist with a further £1,000, that September, and PPU added a further £500 in January 1994. On 7 January of that year Sé O'Connor, PPU president — whom we last encountered graduating exactly 50 years before — wrote to Frank Gildea to announce that these five, foolhardy past pupils who had formed the Restoration Committee were to receive the union and the college's Past Pupil of the Year Award — the first conjoint award since it had been established ten years before. At the union's annual dinner in the college, on 26 February 1994, Michael Jordan, Frank Gildea, Barry Coleman, Paul Joyce and Bernard Kenna were honoured for their remarkable initiative and achievement. In announcing the award, President Sé O'Connor explained simply how it had been given to mark 'the initiative, commitment, skill and perseverance' shown by the five alumni. To this day a plaque in the college commemorates their achievement.[13]

479

Scouts golden jubilee camp at Mount Melleray attended by An Taoiseach, Jack Lynch, 1977.

480

Funeral of ex-Mayor of Tocroyoc, Peru, December 1983.

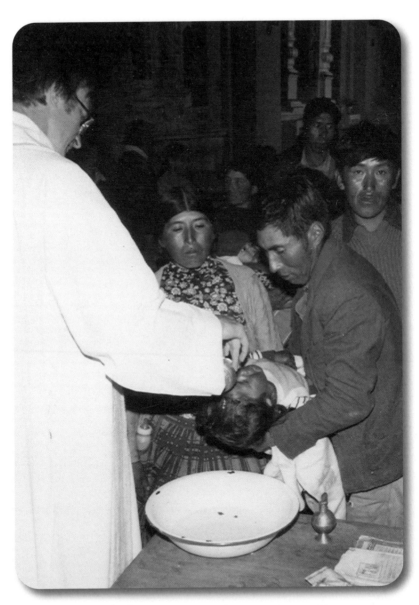

M. Ó Neill performing a baptism in Peru, *c.* 1983.

482

Procession in the parish of Espinar, Peru, *c.* 1983.
Right: Stained-glass windows from the new chapel commissioned by Fr Eltin Griffin. Photo by P. Breen, O. Carm.

483

CHAPTER 25

Towards 150

College rugby supporters, 1988.

THE NEW CAPITAL DEVELOPMENTS FROM 1998 AND THE RESTORATION OF THE lake from 1990 to 1994 exemplified in deed more amply than ever words could do the reality of the community that is Terenure College as it approaches the point of being 150 years young. For pupils and teachers who came and went over the 25 years from 1985, it was as welcoming, homely and as exciting a place as ever it had been in the 1950s when Donal McCann strode its stage or in the 1860s when Denis McAuliffe raided its orchard. Study and the pressure of points notwithstanding, there were as many diverting engagements and possibilities as ever, and more.

External events exerted their influence. The Northern Troubles, intensifying and then gradually and painfully declining, saw the emergence of Co-operation North develop its presence in the school. European integration and Ireland's participation therein, over the same period, was reflected in the growing presence of European studies in the curriculum. The introduction and evolution of transition year offered new possibilities for curricular innovation and pupil initiative. The building of self-confidence in expression and presentation was well-reflected in the foundation and growth of the Model United Nations: an international schools competitive forum where Terenure's pupils came to excel. Paralleling this was the institution and development of Toastmasters' International. In addition, some innovations of this time were designed to recall the past as much as to celebrate the present. As has been seen, such was the case with the Past Pupils' Way. It was now to be seen on a more personal commemorative note in the institution of the Terenure College Run, in memory of Fr Gerry Hipwell. Fr Gerry had been an outstanding pupil, from 1958 to 1964 and apart from being a brilliant sportsman, had been school captain in his final year and captained the college in the 1964 rugby final against Blackrock in Lansdowne. In 1981, ten years after being ordained Carmelite priest, he was assigned to Moate where his energy, leadership and rapport with pupils had an inspirational effect. His tragic death in May 2004 left a great void in Moate lives and in Terenure affections. It was, therefore, in his memory, that the Terenure School Run was instituted in 2005, its inaugural winner being Simon Taggart.[1]

Even in the field of sport, some codes which had been dormant, fitful or non-existent, revived or arrived. Notably in this context, among revivals was badminton.

BADMINTON:

In the mid-1960s, the sport became popular in the college and some individuals stood out: past pupil, Chick Doyle, was capped 37 times for Ireland and won the Irish championship nine times. Past pupils, John and Robert Taylor followed in his Irish and international footsteps in the 1970s while Aidan Murray and Niall Tierney excelled in the 1980s and 1990s. A new club was formed in the college in 1975 and the junior under 14s won the Leinster Division I at their first attempt. The sport suffered some disruption, due to building work at the end of the 1970s and early 1980s. However, before the college lost its PE teacher, Diana Moore, to emigration and marriage in the USA, it had secured its use of the splendid new sports hall. The result was that the sport became available to any boy who wished to play, from second to sixth year. It also now secured the coaching services of Fr Billy Langan, newly returned from Moate in 1982. The result of the boys' enthusiasm, the new facilities and his skilled coaching were soon evident: Terenure College became a force to be reckoned with in Irish schools junior badminton. During the 1980s, the minors won their Leinster competition in various categories some sixteen times and the seniors and juniors won their Irish cups three times each. Then, in 1986, the college juniors won the Primary Schools' Shield and won it again the next two years in succession. The college junior team of Niall Nolan, Fintan Smith, Andrew Armah-Kwantreng, Joseph Ledwidge and their captain, Cillian de Gascún, brought home the Irish championship to the college for the first time in 1990, defeating Coleraine Academy in the final match. This was in a year when the team's mentor, Fr Billy, was also Leinster manager. They were clearly in good hands and it showed when they retained the Irish championship in 1991. They won it again in 1994 and in 1999. The 1990s proved a great time for Terenure College in competitive badminton. In 1992, the college won every available Irish trophy: the unique Irish senior and junior double was captured for the first time, in what, for the seniors, was their first Irish triumph. In 1993, the seniors retained their Leinster and Irish titles. The following year, 1994, the seniors and juniors again won the double in the Irish cups while seniors, juniors and minors won treble Leinster trophies. As Fr Langan reported, the college then 'took a sabbatical from trophies' in 1995; however, the seniors came back again in 1996 and 1997 to retake the Irish cup while the juniors, Kevin Kerrigan; captain, Ciaran Murphy; and three Walsh boys, Aidan, Niall and Gavin; brought their Irish cup home in 1999. The seniors returned to triumphant ways almost; Daniel Sinnott, Ronan McDonagh and John Halligan, again won the Irish Cup; they then repeated this triumph with three of the 1999 team and with Ciaran Rogers taking over from Robert Coleman. By the measure of any Irish schools sport this was a truly impressive record and it was reflected in the fact that in the twenty years from 1989 to 2009 at least eighteen Terenure College players represented Leinster and Ireland.[2]

GAA:

A sport or group of sports that had an uneven and uncertain history in Terenure down to the 1980s was Gaelic football and hurling. Indeed, just like soccer, these tended to be squeezed by the dominant calendar of interschools' rugby and to be dogged for a long time by the fact that the 'Ban' effectively precluded Terenure and like-minded institutions from competitive participation. From the 1960s, Gaelic football and hurling had a chequered history in the college. At the start of the 1960s, during the final part of the school year, some in-house leagues in football were organised, and in the junior school there was sufficient interest in the middle of that decade for an in-house hurling league to be organised by Fr Aidan O'Donovan.

The reporting of these games could vary from the cursory to the non-existent. Rugby continued to dominate and if a rugby season were prolonged due to postponements or re-matches arising from drawn games, Gaelic games would suffer, as happened markedly in 1964.[3] Furthermore, there was no evidence of interschool contests in either football or hurling.

This was to change from the start of the 1970s when 'blitz' tournaments between schools came to be promoted by the GAA and the college. Essentially, these constituted a strategic attempt to penetrate the rugby-dominated institutions but they involved significant compromise of rules and format — teams of thirteen rather than fifteen; games of shorter duration, all played in quick succession on the same Sunday afternoon. This went a little of the way in meeting the wish of those boys who wanted to play Gaelic games once the rugby season was over, but it was hardly satisfactory to the Gaelic Athletic Association. These efforts at revival were earnest enough, and, in addition to certain individual Carmelites who showed some interest in promoting this development, teacher Pat Cahill apparently gave a lot to the project from the mid-1970s. By 1975, for example, these 'blitz' tournaments resulted in the formation of under-18, under-16 and under-14 football teams in the college, contesting for victory against the likes of Blackrock, Castleknock and some local schools and colleges. However, the recurrent refrain was that 'the season is too short'. Although the under-18 team of 1978 was felt in the college to be the best they had had in years — without actually winning a trophy — at the end of the 1970s, throughout the 1980s and for most of the 1990s even these modest competitions disappeared below the horizon. Then, in 1996–7, as a result of the enthusiasm of local St Jude's Templeogue GAA man, Joe Morrin, the Gaelic Morrin Cup competition was established, for football competition between four local schools. Coached by their teacher, Mr O'Connor, the Terenure lads entered the competition and won that cup. By the following year, an under-15 'blitz' in football took place, with the Terenure team featuring a future star of the game, one Conal Keaney. However, no reports or photographs have come to hand to record any GAA activity involving the college from 1999 to 2005. At that point, a serious revival appears to have been germinating and from that time to the present, an enthusiastic promotion of the game within the college, by teachers, Philip Wallace, Paddy Clint, Brendan O'Callaghan and Fr Michael Troy has led to a definite revival. In 2006, Philip Wallace, dubbed 'the godfather of GAA in Terenure College', could report that to their fourth year fell the honour 'of being the first Terenure College Gaelic football team to enter a Dublin GAA schools' competition. Over 2006–07, the college authorities provided a splendid new pitch for Gaelic games and the under-16 footballers reached a quarter-final. In that same year, hurling showed a strong competitive presence for the first time, with teams participating in the Dublin Colleges' Championships at senior, junior and minor levels; by 2008, this sport boasted a new profile in Terenure: the under-14 hurlers won all their games in a three-match league and the under-13 footballers won the Tom Quinlan Plate, defeating Synge Street to secure Terenure's first

GAA trophy in a century. As Paddy Clint remarked, a year before, 'most definitely the seeds have been sown for a strong future in GAA in the College'.[4]

In a work of this scope, it is not feasible to detail the history of every sport that was, from time to time, played in the college, a project for another time, perhaps. What is striking is the sheer range of sporting activities made available to, or by the pupils and made possible by the support of administrative and teaching staff, parents and past pupils. Apart from codes already mentioned, the range featured golf and handball, gymnastics and table tennis, equestrianism and canoeing, hockey and basketball, cross-country running and squash. At different times in the course of 150 years, or even in the course of ten, they would rise, recede or revive, depending on the interest and talent of pupils, the zeal of a given teacher, the infectious example of national or international success by senior practitioners or professionals; or, dependent even on a mutual interaction of one sport and another where a succession of failures or successes in one could have opposite effects on the attractiveness of another. However, whether a given sport was in the ascendant or not, the vital thing for the boys, as tennis supremos Fr Langan and Michael Smyth always urged, was to participate and, above all, to enjoy.

CRICKET:

As has happened with the GAA games — when it came to recession and revival — so it was for cricket. The first and oldest of Terenure College sports, it had entered the doldrums in the 1960s. It was described as 'still struggling' in 1962, 'still down in the dumps' in 1963, and 'not well supported' in 1964. Matters got worse before they got better. In 1976, however, 'after a lapse of several years', it made a come-back in the boys' affections. So teacher Michael Denny reported. Its revival may have owed something to a personal passion for the sport: he had joined the staff in 1973 and taught there until 1982. In 1977, the interest had grown to the extent that Terenure entered teams in the Leinster under-15 and under-14 schools' competitions. What happened in the years immediately after this is unclear at this stage, although Terenure produced the occasional fine cricketer, such, for example, as Seán Clarke who, in 1983, became a Leinster and Irish schools' international player. In the following year, the college brought home the Fr Alf O'Connell trophy for the first time. They were to repeat this achievement in 1990 when they defeated Belvedere. With the encouragement of Larry Halpin, John McClean, Fr P.J. Breen, Fr Éanna Ó hÓbáin and later of Fr Eoin Moore, the sport widened its interest among the pupils. By 1993, after a lapse of some years, Terenure's cricketers returned to interschools' creases. By 1996, they had added under-14 boys to their squad. Trophies may have eluded them, but they reached the semi-finals against Gonzaga in 1998 and 1999 before exiting at that stage. With very talented cricketers, including Rory Flanagan and Robert Carroll, they reached the final of the Alf O'Connell competition in the year 2000, losing to St Columba's, but Flanagan and Carroll were honoured with selection for Leinster. In the early years of the new century, the game's popularity was spreading to junior school, due not a little from the encouragement of Fr Moore. Higher up, the senior XI had a memorable season in 2007, winning their semi-final against Malahide, with Niall McDonnell 57 not out and Ryan Hopkins 61 not out. They fell in the final, on 21 May, to a stronger St Columba's. However, as with Gaelic games, as the decade advanced, so too did the popularity of the sport.

TENNIS:

Quite a similar history unfolded for Terenure's role in interschools' tennis. Following their great season in 1983, some fallow years ensued. Between them, Fr Langan and Pauline Dervin saw some promise in 1987 when the seniors, led by Niall Murphy, reached the Division 2 final, but lost to Newbridge 4-3 at Fitzwilliam. There was justifiable pride in the record of their captain, however, as he went on to interprovincial success and won the Irish under-16 singles later that summer. As for the college's standing in tennis at that stage, they certainly saw themselves in the top six of Irish college teams, and with higher hopes. Such hopes were boosted by the emergence of real talent down the line: young Peter Rowell, at the start of a fine career, won the Irish under-12 singles in 1988.

Then, in 1989, the minors won their first Division 1 final, against Blackrock, for the first time since 1972 when that particular competition had commenced. Starring among the victors was Rowell who won all his matches and all of them in the shortest time. In 1990, there was further cause for pride and rejoicing when the seniors won the Division 2 title and the juniors reached their Division 1 final. The college's own senior champion in 1990 and again in 1991, Paul Pounch, won all his cup matches and, in addition, the Connacht under-18, and then gold for Ireland at the European schools' competition, in the singles and silver in the doubles, at those games in Andorra in July, while Peter Rowell won the Irish indoor championship.

In 1991, for seniors and juniors alike, it was a case of so near and yet so far: both teams reached their finals, with some of the strongest teams they had fielded in decades, but each went down to their Blackrock opponents. Nonetheless, real talent continued to emerge as Terenure's Fintan and Justin Smyth won the doubles at the European Student Games in Easter 1991. However, the mid-1990s was a time when the tennis managers in Terenure felt that they had seen some of their very best prospects graduate; not till 1996 did the outlook again appear brighter. The minors, A and B, impressively won their Leinster championships and the seniors, with the coaching of Michael Smyth and the support of Carol Foster, returned to Division 1, while the juniors reached their semi-final. The next year, 1997, the juniors went on to win Division 2 and the seniors, with the quite outstanding Turlough Flood on board, reached the finals only to go out to Wesley.

Once back in Division 1, the seniors and juniors both found the going very tough indeed, the seniors recording only one victory in five contests while the juniors lost all of their Division 1 matches. Some consolation followed in 1999 when both seniors and juniors won the cup in the 'B' Divisions and five Terenure teams reached schools' semi-finals. The seniors defeated Gonzaga 4-1, under captain, Patrick Donaghy. The junior 'A's defeated Wesley 3-2, with Graham Doyle as captain and with rising stars Michael Lynch and Kevin Kerrigan undefeated in any of their matches. By 2002, Michael Lynch had achieved No. 1 ranking in Irish under-16 tennis in a season when he won the National Masters under-16 competition and represented Ireland against Scotland victoriously, later that year. In 2003, he became college champion, as he would do again in 2004, and was a member of the victorious senior A team, under Ian Daly, that reached the final of the Division 2 competition that summer. In a nail-biting battle against Belvedere, which went to the wire at 2-2 with only one match to go, Daly and Conor McDonnell clinched the match and the cup after a tie-breaker in the third set.

Two years later, college teams reached something of a high point. Entering just one team in the senior division for the 2006 interschool's' competition, they won through to the final against High School and, led by Keith Elliott, emerged victorious by 3-2. The juniors matched their older brothers by defeating Gormanston 3-2 in their final and thus ensured that Terenure brought home two tennis trophies. It must have been a bittersweet victory for coach, Michael Smyth, whose *Alma Mater* was Gormanston. His loyalties must have been stretched a little further in 2008 when, although the minor 'A's won their cup against Belvedere, the seniors lost out in the semi-final and the juniors in the final, both to Gormanston. For all that, and, with the much-lamented retirement of Carol Foster from marshalling duties and the much-appreciated arrival of Orla Devane, as it came close to the end of a century and a half of tennis, Terenure College was still a force to be reckoned with.

ATHLETICS:

Throughout the period from 1985 to 2010, the old allegiance to athletics and rugby continued to prevail. In athletics, the arrival on the teaching staff of Michael Madigan in 1979 and of Des Thornton in place of Diana Moore in 1981–2 was to have some consequence. Although it took a year or two to regain the heights of success achieved in 1984, and although Michael Madigan left in 1986 to become principal at Oatlands College, he left a fine legacy, as Des Thornton generously acknowledged: in 1987, Terenure's athletes enjoyed great success. Indeed, in some respects, that year may have been the very best all round in the course of the last quarter of a century.

The year began with over 70 lads competing in the West Leinster Schools qualifiers. Here minor, Derek Fitzgerald, won the high jump and helped his comrades to victory in the relay. The juniors' Richard O'Brien won the 100 metres. For the seniors there were victories for Brendan Keary who went on to win the Leinster 100 m final; John Menton, in the same competition, winning the shot and the discus; Donal Garvey triumphing in the 800 m and 1,500 m; Lee Devlin in the steeplechase; Cathal

O'Leary in the high jump; David Lynagh in the long jump; and Eddie Thornton in the 400 m hurdles. The crowning triumph came when the seniors secured victory in the relay with Declan Tonge, Gavan Barlow, Keith Hester and Brendan Keary. Two years later, the intermediates, Derek Fitzgerald, Richard O'Brien, Seán McAteer and John Paul O'Reilly won their Leinster relay and, in the process, broke the record with a 45 seconds triumph and then went on to win silver in the All-Ireland. Then, in 1990, in the west Leinster trials, the minors, juniors and seniors all emerged as the best overall team in their respective age groups and in the following year the minors won this accolade for the third time in a row. In the years that followed this, there were few major team triumphs in Leinster or All-Ireland competitions. By 1999, teacher and coach, Padraig Forde, was lamenting that, with standards continually rising and the time needed for training seeming to expand, they were finding it 'difficult to compete', especially at senior level. It was not just a case of growing examination pressures and the rivalry of competing sports, but also that, increasingly, talented young athletes were seeking success through their preferred athletic clubs rather than their colleges. Despite this, even in the later years of this period, individual Terenure athletes continued to excel, while in school or thereafter. Peter Garvey did so in the 1992 intermediate 800 m and 1,500 m steeplechase where he won double gold in the Leinster finals and silver in the All-Ireland 800 m. Similarly, Andrew Long won all-Ireland gold in the intermediate 100 m, and soon after this, James Matthews emerged as a significant new talent. In 1995, he won silver in the All-Ireland 400 m hurdles and, later that summer, triumphantly brought home three golds from the Fédération Internationale Sportive de l'Enseignement Catholique (FISEC) games at Budapest, where he was a member of the winning 4 × 400 relay team, while also victorious himself in the 400 m and 400 m hurdles. In 1996, he helped Terenure to victories at intermediate levels in the Leinster and then the All-Ireland 4 × 400 relays.

Individual successes continued into the new century. Keith O'Malley-Farrell won the intermediate All-Ireland high jump in 2001. Three years later, Ross Williamson won Leinster gold, in the minor 500 m while at junior level, Matthew Boland clinched double gold in the Leinster 800 m and 800 m hurdles and Paul Hickey won gold in the javelin that year. Nor was Terenure College without its Olympians. Boxer Harry Perry and swimmer Kevin Williamson have been encountered earlier in this work. Among its alumni Terenure would count two more, in 1996 and 2000. 'My sister used to do a bit of gymnastics so I tagged along one day' is how Barry McDonald laconically described his introduction to a sport where his excellence would in time bring him on to the world stage.[5] He was only eight when he walked into 'the ramshackle gym in George's Street' and began, unconsciously, on the long road that would lead to Atlanta. He had enrolled in Terenure's first year seniors in 1983–4 and left as a sixth year in 1988–9, all the while devoting hours a day to his chosen discipline. By that stage, having been British school's champion four times in six years, he secured a scholarship to the University of Illinois, Chicago. Within a year he was ranked No. 1 on the American collegiate circuit. Among the several different disciplines that challenge the gymnast, Barry had a particular skill on the parallel bars. On these, at the National Independent Colleges championships in Michigan, in 1991, he achieved the highest score ever recorded by an Irish gymnast when the judging panel awarded him a 9.95. Indeed, two of the panel actually awarded him that 'perfect and elusive 10' and his opponents, in an unprecedented gesture at the time, gave him a standing ovation.[6] There was no question of not qualifying for the Irish Olympics team for Barcelona in 1992 and it is a moot point how he would have fared had the fates or ill-fortune not intervened with an unfortunate ankle injury. He kept to his craft and four years later qualified for the Atlanta Olympic Games in 1996. While a mishap on the pommel horse in the qualifying rounds meant he did not make it to the final rounds, he had nonetheless realised a life's dream. Terenure College acknowledged as much when they conferred on this modest and brilliant alumnus the Past Pupil of the Year Award in 1997.

Three years later, Terenure College past pupil, UCD alumnus and Donore Harriers star, John Menton, was to qualify for the 2000 Olympic Games in Sydney. John attended Terenure from 1978 to 1988, and not without academic distinction: he captained the three-man team of 1988, with Gareth Ó Murchú and Colin Kelly, who secured group runners-up award in the Young Scientists' Exhibition of that year, the best result the college had received since the inauguration of the exhibition in the 1960s. It was a project of no little erudition, entitled *An Analysis of Private Consumption and Savings Relative to Income and its Effects on the Main Economic Indicators*.[7] Something of a giant at 6ft 7in, even in his late teens, he had already shown great promise in college sports when coming to the fore in rugby and in the shot put of which he became senior champion in 1987 and again in 1988. Following his study of law in UCD and embarking on a legal career with Arthur Cox, specialising in technology and intellectual property among a range of legal areas, it became a question of balancing the demands of career with the love of sport, in particular the discus of which he became a leading Irish exponent. It was in this field, while working and practising in New Jersey, that in the year 2000, he registered a personal best of 63.70 metres and thereby earned qualification for the Olympics in Sydney that year. Although a medal was not to come his way, he continued to excel in discus and shot in the many Irish championships which he pursued thereafter, contributing to the great standing of the Donore Harriers Club.

For all the range of sporting disciplines in which Terenure men found the talent to excel, it was the old romance of rugby that continued to capture the college's imagination and to inspire its hopes.

RUGBY:

Having brought home the Leinster Schools Cup in 1983, the Junior XV would reach the final in 1984 and again three years later, only to lose to Blackrock on both occasions. However, at the end of the 1980s, cause for celebration came when, under trainer Des Thornton and captained by Cillian de Gascún, they vanquished Gonzaga in 1989, after a mighty struggle. It was Gonzaga's first attempt to bring home the trophy from the final and when the two sides met, it had to go to a replay: the first contest had ended in the remarkable score of 0-0. In the replay, the hero of the day, No. 8, James McGovern, made the running for the second, winning try, delivered by Paul Sharpe; the first had been brilliantly executed by Cillian de Gascún. Although Gonzaga kept this match on a knife-edge, with a great drop goal from Philip Quinlan, Terenure, happily, held on for a victory by 8-6; all the happier, perhaps, in that the Gonzaga coach, Bobby Byrne, had once been a Terenure pupil.[8] It was a victory to cherish all the more in that it would be another twenty years before being achieved again. In between came three Junior Cup finals that brought disappointments, in 1995, 1997 and 2005, at the hands of Blackrock, St Mary's and Belvedere, respectively. In 2009 however, after a close 5-3 victory over St Michael's, the Junior Cup came home. For St Michael's, this must have been a bitter pill to swallow since it proved to be their third Junior Cup final defeat in a row, but one imagines few tears were shed in Terenure other than those of relief and joy: their ninth Junior Cup triumph was almost ample compensation for the defeat of their seniors in their final only a week before.

As for the seniors, with victories in 1980 and 1984, it would be another eight years before they triumphed again. They came close enough in 1987 when they lost to Blackrock 15-9 after a formidable fight back from a 15-3 gap. Two of that squad in 1987 were to go on to considerably greater rugby days. Niall Hogan, then in fourth year and playing scrum-half in the semi-final against Belvedere, created a brilliant opening that paved the way for a try from Gavan Barlow, leading to a 13-3 victory. In the final against Blackrock he played again, as did Conor O'Shea, then in fifth year: neither was to experience the thrill of coming home with a Senior Cup, or for that matter, a Junior Cup, during their Terenure schooldays, but they were to make up for it later. Captaining the Irish Schools International side in Terenure, Hogan went on to lead the College Rugby Club, secured his first international cap against England in January 1995, when a medical student, and was to become captain of Ireland for the first time in March 1996 when he led the Irish XV to victory against Wales. The college and its union honoured him with the Past Pupil of the Year Award in 1996.

Similarly, his college team mate in 1987, Conor O'Shea, was to go on from Terenure to play fullback for Lansdowne and secured his first international cap against Romania in November 1993. It was but the first of some 35 international caps between then and the year 2000 when injury forced his retirement from the international game, but not before a tally of 64 test points and 6 test tries. Following successful years of playing for and captaining London Irish he became director of rugby academies for the Rugby Football Union as well as becoming a television commentator on Irish international matches.

Meanwhile, in the 1990s the Terenure Senior Cup team proved a formidable force in what was, for them, a memorable decade. It was the first decade in which they brought that cup home on three occasions, and the first time since 1979–80 when they did so two years running, in 1992 and 1993. On the latter occasion, another new arrival on the squad was destined to a distinguished international rugby career for his country. Girvan Dempsey was in fifth year in 1993, when he was promoted from the second seniors and won high praise from coach McClean as 'a most accomplished player [who] displayed elements of class throughout the season'. Those elements of class only grew in the years ahead: he was to make his international debut against Georgia in November 1998 and was still playing internationals a full decade and over 80 caps later. Like Hogan before him, he was honoured by the college union in 2005 as Past Pupil of the Year. He was both deserving and fortunate to have been playing for the college in the early 1990s. 'These indeed were glory days', recalled McClean who was senior coach there from 1983 to 1996 and who left then to direct the UCD Rugby Academy. The lads brought great credit to the college's rugby tradition in that decade: Ian Blake of the class of 1990 and playing on the Senior XV when they fell to Blackrock in the semi-final, had gone on to selection for Leinster and then Irish schoolboys and had the distinction of being on their first-ever schoolboys Triple Crown winning team in 1990.[9] Ian was the first of four successive Terenure lads to serve as hooker on the Irish schoolboys' international side: he was followed by David Crossan in 1991, James Blaney in 1992, who captained them on their historic New Zealand tour that year, and Cormac Egan in 1993.

James — one of five Blaneys in Terenure College at the time — captained the team superbly in the 1992 cup triumph over Belvedere whom they defeated 19-6. He then went on to lead Leinster in their first victories over Munster and Ulster in a decade, captained Ireland in the home internationals and captained them again in the inaugural New Zealand tour where he was joined by another of the 1992 Leinster Schools Cup winners, Cillian de Gascún: scorer of a superb try in that final, he won golden opinions as 'a most accomplished player with the rare ability to produce an outside break and a change of pace' — high praise indeed since it came from McClean.[10] Also in that cup-winning team and then in the Leinster and the Irish International schoolboys was James McGovern who had already in 1989 distinguished himself in the 1989 Junior Cup-winning team: just as he had done in that final against Gonzaga, he now repeated in the senior final against Belvedere with a memorable try in that 'conclusive and impressive victory' by 19 to 6.[11] The victory was clinched by the superb place-kicking of Seán Dempsey whose final score was but one of eleven points he put over that day. It was a team that their later coach observed 'was up there with the best I have coached in ten years'. Better was to follow in 1993 when they again brought the cup home after an 8-3 victory over Clongowes Wood. It says something for the general quality available that only six of the 1992 cup winners played on the 1993 victorious XV. A new arrival destined for fame was fullback Girvan Dempsey; he was then only in fourth year but already described as 'an accomplished player of class'. He was but one of a splendid array of talent, under Tom Hennessy, that secured the second in a row triumph. While the college did not feature in a senior final again until 1997 it was then to some effect when they defeated Clongowes 22-15, with another Blaney, David, as captain, and Des Thornton as coach, to win the Senior Cup for the eighth of ten times. It fell to David Blaney to deliver a killer blow with a brilliant try in the sixty-third minute, followed by a final triumphant crossing of the line by scrum-half, Barry Healy.[12]

In the finals again in 1998 and 2000 but defeated, they secured a memorable come- back in 2001 when they overcame the old enemy, Blackrock, by 21 to 19 and finally two years later brought the cup home for the tenth time with a narrow 3-0 victory over St Mary's.

TCRFC:

The growth and successes of the rugby club in the 1960s have already been noted, as they captured the Leinster Senior Cup for the first time in 1966 and then retained it the following year. While it would be another 28 years before they recaptured it, in 1994, in the intervening years the club had much to celebrate. If success eluded the seniors at the start of the 1970s, it was happily otherwise for the juniors. The club's second XV under Bosco Morrissey captured the junior league title in 1970, by defeating Lansdowne 14-12 and only narrowly missed out on a double when they lost to St Mary's in the final of the Metropolitan Cup. There was ample consolation in the triumph of Eddie Coleman's third XV who did complete their double that year: they retained the minor league title they had won in 1969, by defeating Bective Rangers 17-6 and then won the Albert O'Connell Cup with a 6-3 victory over Old Belvedere. It was the beginning of a decade when the Terenure Club would come to dominate Leinster junior rugby, winning the minor league again in 1971, the Moran Cup in 1972, 1973 and 1974 and being Junior 3 League winners in 1975 and 1976 in addition. In May 1975, led by their president, John O'Connor, the club enjoyed a memorable tour of Bermuda, winning all six of their matches.

Under Enda Ryder as president in 1977–8, a new development programme was planned and in February 1979 was given the go-ahead to proceed. Designed to modernise the club's facilities, it involved a considerable outlay in access of £100,000: a justifiable vote of confidence by its members in a club, which over that decade would have contested 45 finals, winning 27 of them. Even so great a commitment did not circumscribe the club's ambitions as it undertook a highly successful tour in America. At the same time, while the Senior XV was in a stage of redevelopment, the second XV brought home the Leinster Junior League in 1981 and again in 1982: they defeated Lansdowne 12-6 to secure their twelfth junior league title in 37 years. In the following season, 1982–3, the Senior XV, captained by Gerry Morrissey — the third Morrissey brother to represent the club — had one of the most memorable victories ever; not in a final, but in the senior league semi-final against a powerful St Mary's. The two sides met again in the final the next year when a winning try from Paul Haycock brought Terenure its first Leinster Senior League title with a 15-13 victory. As the 1980s came towards their end, the club continued to have cause for celebration. Captained by Liam O'Dea the Junior 1 side brought home the Metropolitan Cup in 1988 for the fifth time, and the first since 1979; while Paul Haycock was selected for the Irish World Cup squad; Eddie Coleman became chairman of the Irish selectors, and, in the college itself, David Lynagh and Niall Hogan were capped for Ireland schoolboys. The 1990s brought new achievements as the Leinster Senior Cup came home in 1994 and again in 1996 when they also won the Leinster championship as they did again in 1999 and 2001. Likewise, the Metropolitan Cup took its place among the club's trophies in 1997 and again in 1999 when they also won the Leinster Junior League. As the club faced into the new millennium it could look back on a proud record over more than half a century.

Whether in victory or defeat, an illustrious history at the forefront of sport over so wide an expanse, speaks volumes for the sense of community and cohesiveness of any institution. Terenure College in this regard has been fortunate not only by a committed, professional teaching and administrative staff and a devoted teaching Order, but equally by a hugely supportive Parents' Association and Past Pupils' Union.

THE PARENTS' ASSOCIATION:

The Parent's Association, founded in November 1956 remained active for almost a decade. By the second half of the 1960s, however, it appears to have become dormant or have passed away entirely. A new Parents' Association was established in March 1976 at a time when the college was experiencing severe pressures in numbers, facilities and staffing.[13] The new body was a sophisticated and energetic one for the next fifteen years at least. A Steering Committee, meeting monthly, monitored and supported the activities of six subsidiary groups with specific remits. These covered Adult Education, Building and Maintenance, Careers, Class Events, Games and Social Work. The Adult Education Committee organised courses of lectures for parents, focussing on matters of faith, practice and issues in contemporary society. Lectures dealing with faith and religious practice were delivered by various members of the Carmelite Communities of Terenure and Gort Muire. Others dealing with emerging issues of concern such as drugs — first mentioned in 1981 — or with areas of new knowledge such as computers and information technology, were addressed by specialist experts. The careers aspect of the association's work developed around the organisation of practice interviews and seminars. These grew into a very significant part of the association's work until the main burden was taken up by Fr Fennell at the start of the 1980s and his evolving careers department. The committee's work, with him, culminating in a major careers seminar day in September 1984, when over 30 careers specialists provided expert advice in separate sessions, finally established this dimension of pupil and parent concern as a permanent dimension of the college's work.

The group concerned with games developed a critical role in helping practically with the supervision of a huge range of recreational activities in the college at evenings and weekends and came to play an important role in sourcing parental support in coaching juniors across a range of college sports and in helping with increasingly complex logistics. As for the Social Work Committee, it became an important support to the development of an active social work volunteer spirit in the senior years. The Junior Conference of Terenure College St Vincent de Paul Society had been founded in January 1972, and although predating the new Parents' Association, the latter played an increasingly important practical role in helping fifth year boys in particular, to engage in charitable works of visitation of the elderly or infirm. Finally, during a critical period of college physical development, the Building and Maintenance Group within the Parent's Association provided professional oversight and advice during a critical phase of the college's expansion in the late 1970s and early 1980s.

Apart from sheer practicalities, the association was important in helping parents to appreciate the needs and to lighten the pressures experienced by pupils growing up in less innocent age. A typically fine example of that role, for example, was presented by outgoing chairman Brian Hogan in 1989, when he spoke on the theme of how best parents could 'be there' for their boys as they went through that crucial phase of their personal development.[14] Indeed, one of the rather special innovations that came courtesy of the Parents' Association at this time was the institution of a farewell reception for sixth years following upon the Sixth Year Farewell Mass. The Farewell Mass had been introduced in 1982 by Fr Billy Langan and Brendan McCauley, lay co-ordinator of religious education who later became second, transition and sixth years' form master.

Part of the crucial consulting role of the Parents' Association may have been refined or taken over by the formal institution of a Board of Advisors in 1994 — a small body of experts in finance, law and administration who would henceforth assist the Prior in his role as manager of the schools. It was a development, which occurred at a time when, with Mrs Joan Armstrong as chairperson of the Parents' Association, the authorities and Community issued the college mission statement. Five years later the Parents' Association, at an extraordinary general meeting in 26 April 1999, adopted a new and elaborate Constitution. It was drawn up by the college management and the Parents' Association Committee, during the Priorship of Fr Murray, 'to put parental representation within the school system on a more formal footing'.[15]

THE PAST PUPILS' UNION:

During all of these decades, a critical role in the life of the wider college was played by the Past Pupils' Union. Like any voluntary body subject to recurrent cycles of energy and *ennui*, the union over time could have its ups and downs: yet, what most marks its history over the course of the past 25 years has been a progressive extension of its activities, an increasing commitment to innovation and a steady growth in membership. In something of a slumber in the mid-1960s, by 2010 it was never more energetic or active in its undertakings.

In 1965, the union's annual dinner held in the rugby club pavilion had been poorly attended, its associated Drama Society had failed to stage a play 'due to scarcity of actors' and the committed but frustrated committee was given to remark of its union that 'it is a pity that so few take an active interest in it'.[16] In 1967, incoming president, Eamonn O'Nolan, was to suggest that, to energise it, the union needed an objective and one presented itself in the form of the College Building Fund. Activity quickened in the years that followed: not least through the energy and drive of Maurice O'Kelly – a wise advisor to the Carmelites, he would be associated with two major, successful fund-raising drives for college building funds in the years ahead and had four sons in the college who, like their father, distinguished themselves on the rugby pitch. When Maurice came into office as union president for the years 1970 and 1971, it was as though a whirlwind had struck. His committee, beginning their term in January 1970 with 330 past pupils on the union register, had increased this to over 1,000. Their dinner dance, now held jointly with the rugby club, enjoyed a record attendance of 465, up 40% on the previous highest attendance, while the union dinner itself, held in the college as well, also had a record subscription of 240. Not all its efforts were blessed with success: its cheese and wine reception in April 1972, to mark the opening of the new swimming pool, was cursed into darkness by an electricity strike and few, therefore, turned up. Nevertheless, out of the darkness — light — as a new venture started by Dermot Herbert, was a Past Pupils' Union *Bulletin*, something that would later become a permanent feature. By that stage the union was playing a major role in providing career guidance seminars and mock interviews, in supporting the traditional charity of the Boys' Club, had instituted a Past Pupil of the Year Award, which went to Donal McCann in 1970. It had also organised an annual golf outing and was donating finance to the College Building Fund. By the mid-1970s that energetic burst had led to a slight exhaustion and union business, for a time, ticked over rather than surged forward. The *Bulletin* did not reappear from 1974 until 1979, no published report appeared in the *Annual* in 1973, the annual dinner dance became 'informal' and was held in 'a well known Dun Laoire [*sic*] Club', with smaller attendances in 1974 and 1975. Still, no major activity ceased — the dinners, the golf outings and career guidance seminars continued, and, in 1977, a substantial £1,000 was presented to Raymond Cannon for the Boys' Club. Furthermore, innovation continued: from 1975 presidents of other college unions were invited as honoured guests to the annual PPU dinner and VIP guest speakers began to appear: John Hume in 1977, Tom Kiernan in 1979, Mike Murphy in 1985 and Derek Davis in 1987, the latter providing a 'virtuoso performance', for example. At the very end of the 1970s, a new dynamism was evident. In 1979, when John McClean was president, the union was 'revitalised', some 356 attending its dinner, its *Bulletin* re-appearing for the first time in five years, and a computer-based mailing list was being devised. By Paul McKay's presidency a year later, two bulletins were being produced, the mailing list reached 2,000, 300 of which were paying an annual subscription of £5; and in the person of Eugene McNamee the union secured formal representation on the Parents' Association. From 1985, in the union's sixtieth year, the annual dinner had reached new levels of professionalism and support, largely due to the organisational skill and commitment of Bernard Kenna. New effort was directed to targeting particular year groups, especially those from the classes of five, ten and twenty-five years before. Peter Blackbyrne and Kenna were now doing important work in the further computerisation of the union's data.

The generosity of the union had meanwhile continued unabated. In 1981, during the presidency of Michael Pender, the funding of the Joe Griffin Memorial Library became a special PPU project. A first donation of £2,500 was followed by a major one of £10,000 from the proceeds of a special dinner. In the following year, during Eugene McNamee's presidency an initial 50 past pupils had covenanted some £100 each to provide £2,000 a year for six years to the library project. Then in 1986, during Paddy Donaghy's time in office, another specific grant of £2,000 was made to provide the library with up-to-date audio visual equipment. All the while older objects of their benevolence — the Boys' Club — continued to receive substantial funding support and newer objects of their generosity emerged. In 1987, for example, during Bernard Kenna's presidency, support was instituted for the international African charity, ICROSS, an organisation in which Terenure past pupils, Kevin Niall and Michael Meegan, played a vital founding role.

By the end of the 1980s, there was no sign of energy waning. When Des Lamont was president in 1989 the annual bulletin had reached 36 pages and was now circulating to 3,500 past pupils. The annual union dinner that year achieved another record in attendance — so much so that, with 430 subscribing, the event had to be moved from concert hall to gymnasium. The annual golfing outing, organised by Jim Blake, was never stronger, with some 130 turning out each June for a memorable competitive get-together. Furthermore, a new development in the tradition of the union's giving emerged in that year with the institution of an Educational Bursary in European Languages: designed to award a fifth year pupil for excellence, improvement and attainment in a Continental language, the following year it became the Fr Hegarty Bursary.

By the start of the 1990s, the union executive was never busier. In Bobby Keogh's presidency in 1990, the executive had to meet on twelve occasions and he and his colleagues orchestrated a significant increase in union membership even as they doubled the annual fee to £10. The numbers turning up to golf outings and annual dinners continued to be at a maximum and new ideas continued to issue. One important innovation, devised during Joe Clancy's tenure in 1991, and coming to fruition during Jim Blake's in 1992, was the publication of the union diary, thanks to the work of Colm Hyland and Tony Kelly. The union was extending its influence in other ways too, notably with the institution of its London branch in which Jim Blake's son, Ian, of the class of 1980, played a seminal role. The moral strength of the union — that sense that it was at the heart of the college's life — was evident in small things and great: the making available of an office to the union by the college in 1993, the conferring of the

Past Pupil of the Year Award on the five-man Lake Restoration Committee in 1994. Then, in 1996 came the institution of the Past Pupils' Union Benevolent Fund with its board of six trustees and committee drawn from various representative elements in the life of the college, from the Carmelite Community to the Parents' Association and the rugby club. This was a substantial undertaking that required substantial pump-priming: among the major fundraising events helping to finance it was that memorable night in March 1997 when the college staged *The Play's the Thing*.[17]

By that stage the fee-paying membership of the union was close to 1,000 even though the fee had been increased to £20 to meet the increased outgoings and support funding commitments. Those commitments would expand as the union, from 2001, got behind the college's large development programme launched in 1998. There were new departures as well as new commitments: to mark the millennium, the union's annual dinner in 2000 was held outside the college for the first time in decades when, on a brilliantly successful night, organised by Fergus McCauley, some 320 attended at Jury's Hotel Ballsbridge. No stranger to change, Fergus had introduced a piper to play the school song at the 1998 PPU annual dinner, a practical as well as aesthetic innovation: it ensured a reasonable modicum of quiet for the speech of the president, Brendan McCauley, on the occasion. The new millennium witnessed ongoing innovation: during 2001 and 2002, in the presidencies of Paul Tuite and Paul Haycock, respectively, a new union website was developed and in 2002 a new junior committee was initiated to organise events and engage the interest of past pupils who had only left college within the previous five years. By the time of Joe Cleere's and Colin McKeon's terms of office in 2003 and 2004 the membership was as strong as ever, over 350 were still attending the annual dinners and the *Bulletins* or *Newsletters* were being mailed to some 4,000 former pupils. As if there was no end to the union's openness to innovation, during the presidency of Fr Micheál Ó Néill — the last of only four Carmelites to hold the office of PPU president — yet another new event was added to the busy calendar of the union when Jim Blake, Joe Cleere and Colin McKeon introduced the annual business lunch. As the union approached its own eighty-fifth birthday, it was never so strong nor so well-supported; nor, be it said, so committed in so many ways to supporting it's *Alma Mater*. By that stage the union's growth in extent and diversity mirrored that of the college itself.

503

The lake in the grounds of Terenure College following the restoration project, *c.* 1994.

Juniors at lunchtime, 1989.

Fr Hegarty looking after his charges, 1988.

CHAPTER 26

*What Future
for this Past?*

'The Way Ahead' by
Darragh McKeon, junior young
photographer of the year, 1988.

PATRICK O'BRIEN FROM RUTLAND HOUSE, THE MORAN BOYS FROM 'Garnavilla', the Lyons lads from 'Landore' — the first pupils; Thomas Bennett, Eugene Cullen, Simon Carr and Michael Gilligan — the founding fathers: if they could walk up the avenue 150 years later, what would they find? In externals, much change, such as these pages have retraced: the old avenue, yes, but no gate lodge; the old lake, renewed, but no farm or boarding school; remarkable extensions and wonderful facilities from pitches and playgrounds, through chapel and courts to gym and pool. And it is hard to believe, perhaps after tribulation and tough times, a ten-fold increase in pupils and a corresponding increase in staff on a campus with day-long, evening-long and year-round activities.

Founders and first pupils could hardly have anticipated this huge expansion with its accompanying growth in complexity of administration and in teaching professionalism. Teaching and administration have become more complex, and are infinitely more demanding in a culture of greater expectations, and in a world of significantly less stability and security. For teachers, there is the sheer range of subjects and the importunate demands of syllabus in a world where education has become a central concern of the state and where the pressure for 'results' could be an imperious one if not tempered by a longer perspective and wiser considerations.

The pioneers would certainly be impressed by the loyalty and professionalism of the long-serving administrative staff, from college secretary, Emer McElduff; school secretary, Margaret Cox; receptionist, Breda Moore; services manager, Shauna Pearse; matron, Elizabeth Brett; caretakers, Ray Mooney and Jim Doyle; and their long-serving predecessor, Tom Ennis; housekeeper, Anna Malone; and head gardener, Richard Hand; great people all, in a now long tradition. The founders of 1860 would surely have rejoiced in the obvious commitment of these administrators to support the Prior and his staff of 100, to promote the progress of their pupils and the mission of their teachers with a loyalty that speaks of vocation as much as profession.

What the pioneering generation would have not found new and strange, but old and familiar, would be the college's sense of community. Speaking as captain of his school, in 2004, Kevin Woulfe was to comment to his fellow-students:

> May you feel rewarded not because we have shown signs of brilliance or taken away academic prizes but because you feel that we are growing up to be young men of responsibility who have some idea of the meaning of life and the importance of relationships. This is largely due to the spirit, pride and commitment of the Carmelite Community at Terenure of which we are proudly a part ... It is an extended family and there is something for everyone here.[1]

Perhaps the only important difference between then and now is that this spirit is so much stronger in 2010. It is made stronger still by the continuity of ethos created by those past pupils who chose to become and remain devoted teachers there: notable among them still, Peter McDonagh (1973) in French, Seán Culligan (1991) in Irish,

Dan Parkinson (1997) in business studies and Michael Shanahan (2003) in biology; together with all their other teaching colleagues who have become *Terenuriores Terenuris ipsis.*

In a talk at prize giving in 2004, recalling times 30 years before, actor and alumnus, Philip O'Sullivan, in an almost stream-of consciousness address paid tribute to the Carmelites and was to capture that spirit in a very personal way:

> ... instinct, the greatest of all the actor's assets, leads me in one direction only. Always the same impulse. Back to here, this very space, this concert hall and this stage ... The fabric of a space is pro- saically just the bricks and mortar ... But the soul of a place is created by the spirits and energies that have inhabited it. The dreams, the laughter, the serious times, the high-jinks, the essence of a place that these energies have bequeathed to it ... Not a star pupil ... just a student with a dream ... You saw a flame and you protected it, you saw a light and you helped point its beam and you should be proud.[2]

The founding fathers could hardly have predicted the great future that is, today, Terenure College's great past. And so, for the college and its present generation of Carmelites, teachers, support staff and pupils, as they view that past, what future can they hope, for college? Fr Michael Troy voiced that wonder in his own prize-giving address to junior school six years before: 'Our children will go into a world we are not competent even to predict; a world that will pose problems and opportunities we cannot even envision. What can we give them for the journey?'[3]

One answer had been intimated eight years earlier by Fr Micheál Ó Néill: he offered a vision of the future, linked to Terenure's present and past, in an address appropri- ately entitled 'Building on What is Already There'. Central to the college's past, present and future is that Carmelite spirituality with its concern for three concepts: reverence for the word, awareness of the image of God, and the right and duty to participate in society. As to the first, in these times of clamour, there is the need to respect the words we say and the words we listen to and the centrality of the Carmelite tradition of silence as the safe bridge between them. As to the second, in these times of poverty and violence, there is the pressing need to be educated in the belief that we are created in the image and likeness of God. As to the third, if our future society is to find peace, our education has to ensure that we find a way so that 'every child of God may take part and contribute and, in turn, be honoured by the whole society'.[4]

Indeed, this evocation of that Carmelite tradition was echoed by Fr Troy when, in answer to the question he posed, 'What can we give them for their journey?', proposed:

> ... a passion for justice ... to create a world in which life is cherished and defended, a world where all people are treated with equality and dignity in God's own image. In this current time, with its emphasis on success, may we help each other appreciate that success in the eyes of God lies not so much in what we have as in what we are.[5]

For this observer, the dominant theme of Terenure College history has been that of a family sustained by that 'happy spirit so particularly its own'. One cannot predict but can well believe that this spirit will endure. From pupils and past pupils, parents and teachers, service personnel and priests, there is a palpable sense of community and of shared endeavour that constitutes a covenant for the future even as it celebrates this past: a promise to present and future generations of pupils that they may be privileged to experience as rich and rounded a formation as those who, for 150 years, have gone before: a privilege that owes so much to Terenure's Carmelites who with zeal have been zealous in the service of their boys — ever leading them not to the Elysian Fields but to the fields of St Elias.

END

512

ALIV

KIC

Leinster supporters' message to the opposition at Lansdowne Road, 1989.

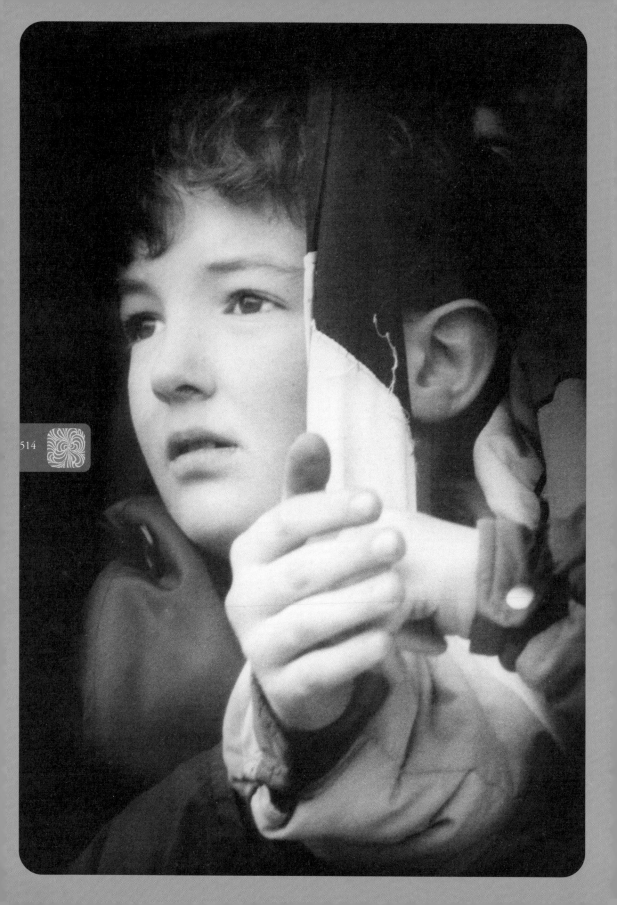

514

Left to right: Fr M. Ardiff, Fr J. McCouaig, Bishop D. Lamont; with Fr Des Clarke and Fr Des Kelly in lay clothes, *c.* 1993.
Left: Terenure College pupil, *c.* 1989.

Juniors pose for a photo, 1980s.

516

'A Study in Expressions'. Terenure v Blackrock, 13 March 1942.
© Independent Newspapers.

CHAPTER 1

[1] Dominick Street Academy was re-opening after the Christmas vacation.

[2] *Thom's Directory* (Dublin, 1872), p. 1,655.

[3] Peter Costello, *Clongowes Wood: A History of Clongowes Wood College, 1814–1989* (Dublin, 1989), pp. 20, 51–4.

[4] The provision of residential accommodation for university students may have been in the hope that some of these might join the Order as much as in the hope of generating revenue.

[5] Terenure College Papers in Carmelite Provincial Archives, Gort Muire, Dundrum, Dublin (TN), 01–4, *Register 1860*–1960, p. 1.

[6] *Thom's Directory*, p. 1,568.

[7] P. Dwyer, *The Irish Carmelites of the Ancient Observance* (Dublin, 1988), pp. 295–6, citing J.F. Byrne, *Silent Years* (New York, 1953). John Scanlan was born *c.* 1870 and was ordained in 1894.

[8] TN, 02/3, *Personal Accounts 1861–9*.

[9] S. Farragher and A. Wyer, *Blackrock College, 1860-1995* (Dublin, 1995), p. 8; J. Martin and D. Kerr (eds), *C.U.S. 1867-1967: A Centenary Record* (Dublin, 1967), 41.

[10] TN, 01/5, *School Roll-book 1862–9*.

[11] TN, 01/7, *Daily Roll of the School, 1869–85*.

[12] TN, 01/1, *Accounts 1860–4*.

[13] TN 01/7, *Daily Roll of the School 1869–85*.

[14] Farragher and Wyer, *Blackrock College,* p. 8; Costello, *Clongowes Wood,* p. 82. Clongowes actually reduced its fee from the 50 guineas charged to Daniel O'Connell for the education of his sons, a fee charged to all students from 1814 but which was reduced with falling enrolments after the days of the O'Connell boys.

[15] TN, 02/3, *Personal Accounts, 1862–9*.

[16] Dublin Diocesan Archives (DDA), Cullen Papers, 334/5/30, 1867.

[17] TN, 01/7, *Daily Roll of the School, 1869–85*.

[18] TN, 01/7, *Daily Roll of the School, 1869–85*.

[19] TN, 01/5, *Day Book, 1862-69*.

[20] *Whitefriars* 2:2 (May 1936), 4:3 (March 1938); Rose Willis, 'Christmas Carol Comes Home', *Roundup* 110 (March 2003).

CHAPTER 2

[1] *Terenure College Centenary Record 1860–1960* (*c.* 1960, Terenure College), p. 18. *Whitefriars* 22:3 (May–June 1960).

[2] *Whitefriars* 2:8 (August 1936).

[3] Gort Muire Provincial Archives (GMPA), Indenture 17 December 1858, [Doc. No. 8]; also, *Registry of Deeds* (Dublin, 1858), Book 38, No. 199, see Fallon and Others to Cullen and Others, 18 December 1858.

[4] *Irish Times*, 17 October 1874.

[5] Terenure College Archives (TCA), lease agreement, 5 September 1877.

[6] TCA, Lease 1881 for No. 2 Lakelands Park, Lease 1884 for No. 1 Lakelands Park, Lease 1885 for No. 3 Lakelands Park, Lease 1929 for No. 4 Lakelands Park.

[7] *Zelo* 1 (July 1948), p. 2; O'Dwyer, *Irish Carmelites*, p. 228.

[8] Valuation Office, Dublin, undated, untitled blue volume, described as 'Vol. C2 — Cancellation Book', p. 56c (177).

[9] TCA, *Memorandum of* agreement, 30 October 1909; *Counterpart lease of Lockerbie*, 10 April 1929.

[10] P. Kelly, *The Universal Cambist and Commercial Instructor* (London, 1835).

[11] *Freeman's Journal,* 21 September, 16 October, 30 November 1863; 3 May 1864.

12 W.W. Bentley, *Rental and Descriptive Particulars of the Mansion and Demesne of Terenure to be Sold by Auction on the 4th of August, 1859 by Messrs. Bentley & Son* ... (Dublin, 1859), p. 18.

13 *Registry of Deeds* (Dublin, 1859), Book 40, No. 46; see Alexander Hall to Cullen and others, 30 November 1859. This is the date of registration of the sale which occurred on 14 October 1859.

14 O'Dwyer, *Irish Carmelites,* pp. 203–04.

15 O'Dwyer, *Irish Carmelites,* p. 280.

16 Moore was Provincial from 1878 to 1881 and Prior of Terenure from 1878 to 1882.

17 O'Dwyer, *Irish Carmelites,* p. 205.

18 O'Dwyer, *Irish Carmelites,* p. 218.

19 O'Dwyer, *Irish Carmelites,* pp. 287–88, GMPA, *Catalogus Fratrum,* p. 3.

20 K. Condon, *The Missionary College of All Hallows, 1842-1981* (Dublin 1986), pp. 123, 213, 243–5, 275.

21 O'Dwyer, *Irish Carmelites,* p. 218.

22 O'Dwyer, *Irish Carmelites,* p. 205.

23 For Bennett in *The Lamp,* 310 (1897); Condon, *College of All Hallows,* pp. 123, 275, Dwyer, *Irish Carmelites,* 221–9, *Catalogus Fratrum,* p. 3.

24 DDA, Cullen Papers, 328/7/II/23, 1871.

25 O'Dwyer, *Irish Carmelites,* p. 280.

CHAPTER 3

1 O'Dwyer, *Irish Carmelites,* p. 140.

2 H. Fenning, *The Undoing of the Friars in Ireland* (Louvain, 1972), p. 44.

3 '150 Years of Ballygar Church', *Roscommon People,* 4 January 2008.

CHAPTER 4

1 E. Harrington and D. Brown (eds), *Memories of Terenure: A Terenure 2000 Millennium Project,* (Terenure, 2000), p. 15.

2 G.N. Wright, *Ireland Illustrated from original drawings by G. Petrie, W.H. Bartlett and T.M. Baynes, with descriptions* (London, 1829, 1st edn; London, 1831, 2nd edn), p. 27.

3 J. D'Alton, *History of the County of Dublin* (Dublin, 1838), pp.774–5.

4 B. Mac Giolla Phadraig, *History of Terenure* (Dublin, 1954), pp. 30–3.

5 Data from *House of Commons, Parliamentary Papers, Census of Ireland for the Year 1891,* C. 6,379.

6 Harrington and Brown, *Memories of Terenure,* p. 30.

7 J.C. O'Shea, 'Memories of Terenure College Fifty Years Ago', *Terenure College Annual* (1865), p. 8.

8 J. Kilroy, *Irish Trams* (Dublin, 1996), p. 19.

9 Mac Giolla Phadraig, *Terenure,* p. 38

10 *Irish Times,* 13 November 1915.

11 Information on Duncan and family is from the 1911 census; information on The Templeogue Inn is from an interview with Fr Jackie Madden, O. Carm., 25 June 2008.

12 O'Shea, 'Memories of Terenure', p. 8.

13 C.L. Sweeney, *The Rivers of Dublin* (Dublin, 1911), pp. 20–7, 29–30, 39–40, 53–60; C. Moriarty, *Down the Dodder* (Dublin, 1991), pp. 108–28; Mac Giolla Phadraig, *Terenure,* pp. 21–6.

14 Wright, *Ireland Illustrated,* p. 27.

15 S. Lewis, *A Topographical Dictionary of Ireland* (2 vols, London, 1837), vol. 2, p. 540.

16 D'Alton, *County of Dublin,* pp. 774–5.

17 K. Lamb and P. Bowe, *A History of Gardening in Ireland* (Dublin, 1995), pp. 56, 107–08; E. Malins and P. Bowe, *Irish Gardens and Demesnes from 1830* (London, 1980), pp. 21–2.

Chapter 5

[1] O'Dwyer, *Irish Carmelites*, p. 260.

[2] F.P. Carey, 'The Heroes of Hammer Hill', *Whitefriars* 3:2 (February 1941), pp. 43–5. The descriptions of Crotty and Behan are Carey's, that of Fr Tom Doyle is based on J.F. Byrne's account. Fr Doyle taught Byrne his Latin and Byrne was his altar-server at Whitefriar Street.

[3] O'Dwyer, *Irish Carmelites*, p. 272.

[4] *Irish Times*, 10 July 1874, 13 July 1877.

[5] See Chapter 1.

[6] TN01/7, *Daily Roll of the School, 1869–1885*, p. 2.

[7] *Irish Times*, 14 July 1875; O'Dwyer, *Irish Carmelites*, p. 274.

[8] *Terenure College Annual* (1960), p. 33–64; O'Dwyer, *Irish Carmelites*, pp. 266, 278.

[9] *Freeman's Journal*, 13 July 1877, *Irish Times*, 24 August 1877.

[10] 'How it Happened ', *Terenure College Annual* (1960), pp. 31–64.

[11] John Adye Curran, *Reminiscences of John Adye Curran, K.C,* (London, 1915), pp. 155–201; National Archives of Ireland (NAI), Ed, 2/3/48, *Pupil School Rolls, 1890-1915,* vol. 1, Roll 146, 1 November 1890.

[12] TN 01/2, *Personal Accounts, 1873–1883*, p. 18.

[13] TN 01/2, *Personal Accounts, 1873–1883*, p. 29.

[14] TN 01/2, *Personal Accounts, 1873–1883*, p. 9.

[15] TN 01/2, *Personal Accounts, 1873–1883*, p. 206.

[16] TN 01/2, *Personal Accounts, 1873–1883*, p. 338 & 48 respectively.

[17] TN 01/2, *Personal Accounts, 1873–1883*, p. 50, 25 & 30 respectively.

[18] TN 01/2, *Roll 1869–85,* 11 December 1880 & 18 December 1880.

[19] TN 01/2, *Personal Accounts, 1873–1883*, p. 79.

[20] TN 01/2, *Personal Accounts, 1873–1883*, p. 222, 223 & 306; *Whitefriars* 2:2 (March 1940), p. 55.

[21] TN 01/2, *Personal Accounts, 1873–1883*, p. 22. He is listed as living at 80 Great Britain Street in 1884.

[22] TCA, Miscellaneous uncatalogued papers, press1, boxfile 1.

[23] TN 01/2, *Personal Accounts, 1873–1883*, pp. 360, 323 & 359.

[24] TN 01/2, *Personal Accounts, 1873–1883*, p. 259 for James Healy and p. 265 for James Carey.

[25] *Irish Times*, 30 May 1871.

[26] TN01/7, *Daily Roll of the School, 1869–1885*.

[27] *Irish Times,* 10 July 1874.

[28] *Freeman's Journal*, 13 July 1877.

Chapter 6

[1] *The Catholic Directory* (Dublin, 1878), p. 73. Neither the list of Priors and presidents given in the *Terenure College Annual* (1960), p. 55, nor the *Catalogus Fratrum* entry on J.E. Bartley, in the Provincial Archives, mention that he was president of the college.

[2] O'Dwyer, *Irish Carmelites*, p. 285.

[3] G. Carter, 'Pioneers of the Purple Twilight: A Gawler Memory', *Nubecula* 32:1 (1981), pp. 17–23; J. Cogan, *The Advocate*, 8 May 1909, cited in O'Dwyer, 'Carmel in Australia', *Zelo* (Summer 1953), p. 3.

[4] O'Dwyer, *Irish Carmelites*, pp. 283: O'Dwyer says Carr was 78 in 1909 but the *Catalogus Fratrum* gives his year of birth as 1834, making him 75.

[5] O'Dwyer, *Irish Carmelites*, p. 306; *The Catholic Directory* (Dublin, 1900–03).

[6] *The Irish Catholic*, 26 August 1911.

[7] *Report of the Intermediate Education Board for Ireland* (Dublin, 1890), C.6001 and 1900, cd.172.

[8] *Irish Times,* 10 June 1880.

[9] House of Commons, Parliamentary Papers, *Reports of the Intermediate Education Board of Ireland for the years 1880–1884,* c. 2600, c. 2919, c. 3176, c. 3580 & c. 3990, respectively.

[10] A search for the years 1885, 1893–5 and 1898–1900 has yielded no names.

[11] *Irish Times,* 16 September 1905, 13 September 1906, 21 September 1908, 27 October 1909; *Irish Independent,* 13 September 1907.

[12] *Report of the Intermediate Education Board for Ireland for the years 1886 to 1909,* c. 5032, c. 5355, c. 5708, c. 6001, c. 6324, c. 6119, c. 7040, c. 7405, c. 7677, c. 8034, c. 8405, c. 8798, c. 9294, cd. 172, cd. 588, cd. 1092, cd. 1670, cd. 2113, cd. 2580, cd. 2944, cd. 3544, cd. 4047, cd. 4707 and cd. 5173.

[13] *Report of the Intermediate Education Board for Ireland, for the year 1908,* cd. 4707.

[14] TCA, *Results of Examinations, 1884-1942*: despite is title, the quality of the information is varied, with some years incomplete and with a large gap from 1891 to 1921.

CHAPTER 7

[1] O'Dwyer, *Irish Carmelites,* pp. 241, 280, 283, 297 and *Catalogus Fratrum,* p. 5.

[2] J.F. Byrne, *Silent Years,* p .5.

[3] *Irish Times,* 1 November 1902; *Carmelite Directory: Ireland and Zimbabwe* (Dublin, 2007), p. 38.

[4] F. Shortis, 'Going Forward in Hope: a look at our past one hundred years as a guide for the future', *Nubecula* 32:3 (1981), pp. 168–9.

[5] According to the *Catholic Directory* of 1924 he was Prior; however, the *Catalogus Fratrum* notes he was Vicar-Prior: given that Colfer only spent one of a normal three years as Terenure Prior in 1923 it is likely that Wade was Sub-Prior.

[6] So states the *Catalogus Fratrum* although the *Catholic Directory* for 1925 places him as a member of the Community in Moate.

[7] National University of Ireland (NUI) Archives, *Candidates for Matriculation, 1881*: he was one of eight Terenure students to matriculate there in that year, his later confreres, Fr Stephen Mulholland and Fr Joseph Cowley being among the others. His profession declaration is deposited in the TC Archives.

[8] Thomas J. Morrissey, *Towards a National University: William Delaney, S.J., 1835–1924* (Dublin, 1983), p.85; *Irish Times,* 30 July, 2 November 1889

[9] Farragher and Wyer, *Blackrock College,* pp. 34–5.

[10] D. McCartney, *UCD: A National Idea* (Dublin, 1999), p. 18. St Patrick's College Maynooth had acquired this status in 1876, and now, through Bartholomew Woodlock's initiative, Blackrock, Carlow, Clonliffe and St Kyran's Colleges (as did the Jesuit College in Temple Street) joined Terenure in becoming affiliated to the Catholic University.

[11] *Annual Record* (1881–2), pp. 27–8.

[12] The *Standard and River Plate News,* 28 and 29, 6 February, 27 March 1880. I am grateful to Laura Magnier, Gort Muire archivist, for this reference.

[13] *Annual Record* (1882–3), p. 15.

[14] TN 01/3, p. 59.

[15] NUI Archives, *Candidates for Matriculation, 1888.*

[16] *Irish Times,* 17 January 1936, Census 1911.

[17] TN 01/7, 12 November 1881; *Annual Record* (1881–2), p. 27; *Freeman's Journal,* 12 September 1882; *Irish Times;* 20 September 1884.

[18] *Irish Times,* 29 September 1880.

[19] TN 01/7, 9 October 1880.

[20] *Irish Times,* 4 October 1881.

[21] *Irish Times*, 2 June 1906.

[22] 'The late Rev. Brother Augustine Cosgrave', *Whitefriars* 2:3 (June 1936).

[23] *Annual Record* (1881–2), p. 23.

[24] *Annual Record* (1881–2), pp.23–5.

[25] *Annual Record (1882–3),*

[26] *Annual Record* (1882–3), pp. 23–5.

[27] *Irish Times*, 25 November, 17 December 1907.

[28] *Terenure College Annual* (1953), pp. 28–9; *Census 1911*, private information.

[29] N. Heaslip, 'Fr Elias O'Dwyer, Golden Jubilee', *Zelo* 10:2 (Summer 1958), pp. 54–9.

[30] Dublin County Board, *Official Brochure, 1934* (Dublin, 1934?), p. 26, cited in W. Nolan (ed.), *The GAA in Dublin, 1884-2000* (3 vols, Dublin, 2005), vol. I, p. 5.

[31] *Irish Times*, 29 April 1881.

[32] *Irish Times*, 7 February 1883.

[33] *Irish Times*, 21 December 1893.

CHAPTER 8

[1] O'Dwyer, *Irish Carmelites*, p. 301.

[2] W.E. Ellis (ed.), *Ellis's Irish Education Directory and Scholastic Guide* (4th edn, Dublin, 1885), p. lvi.
F.A. D'Arcy, 'Wages of skilled workers in the Dublin building industry, 1667–1918', in *Saothar* 15 (1990), pp. 31–3.

[3] T.J. McElligott, *Secondary Education in Ireland, 1870–1921* (Dublin, 1981), p. 8.

[4] Cited in J. Coolahan, *The ASTI and Post-Primary Education in Ireland, 1909–1984* (Dublin, 1984), p. 11.

[5] Cited in A. Hyland and K. Milne (eds), *Irish Educational Documents* (2 vols, Dublin, 1987), vol. 1, p. 230.

[6] *The Irish Catholic*, 15 May 1915; *Catalogus Fratrum*; O'Dwyer, *Irish Carmelites*, pp. 262, 288–9, 329.

[7] O'Dwyer, *Irish Carmelites*, pp. 306–11.

[8] Interview with Fr Joe Linus Ryan, O. Carm., 25 June 2008; Census of Ireland, 1911.

[9] *Complete Memoirs of Albert LeBrocquy, 1888–1976,* (typescript, 44 pp., courtesy of Ms Melanie LeBrocquy).

[10] P. Bradley *et al.*, *Knocklyon — Past and Present* (Dublin, 1992), p. 25.

[11] Interview with Dennis McGrane, 24 June 2008.

[12] *Terenure College Annual* (1959), p. 23; (1956), p. 28; (1958), p. 10.

[13] H.A. Lappin, 'Gerard Hopkins and his poetry', *Catholic World* (July 1919), pp. 501–12; see also *Cornell Alumni News*, 19 February 1925; Census of Ireland, 1911; *Terenure College Annual* (1946), p. 38. For his reception, profession and dispensation, see *Catalogus Fratrum* in the Provincial Archives, Gort Muire.

[14] J.F. Swaine, 'Terenure College fifty-nine years ago', *Terenure College Annual* (1950), pp. 30–3.

CHAPTER 9

[1] McCartney, *UCD: A National Idea,* pp. 47–8: Terenure had 13, Belvedere 16, Blackrock 19 and Castleknock 21 UCD enrolments in 1910.

[2] Mayer to Antonino, 14 November 1926, cited in O'Dwyer, *Irish Carmelites,* p. 364.

[3] O'Dwyer, *Irish Carmelites,* p. 282.

[4] Carr to Prior General, 13 May 1881, cited in O'Dwyer, *Irish Carmelites,* p. 284.

[5] O'Dwyer, *Irish Carmelites,* p. 283.

[6] L. Gallagher, 'Carmel in Australia', *Zelo* 6: 1 (Spring 1954), p. 7.

[7] O'Dwyer, *Irish Carmelites,* p. 291.

[8] O'Dwyer, *Irish Carmelites,* p. 298.

[9] O'Dwyer, *Irish Carmelites,* p. 316.

[10] J. Dominic McCouaig, 'Four decades of Carmel', *Zelo* 2: 2 (1949), p. 8.

[11] McCouaig, 'Four decades of Carmel', p. 9.

[12] GM, *Minutes of Definitors' Meetings, 28 May 1906 — 10 Sept 1969*, 18 November 1909, 1 December 1909.

[13] O'Dwyer, *Irish Carmelites*, p. 331, citing Southwell, 2 March 1910.

[14] O'Dwyer, *Irish Carmelites*, p. 290.

[15] H. Fitzpatrick, 'Carmel in Knocktopher', *Zelo* 9: 1 (Spring 1957), pp. 7–18.

[16] *Catalogus Fratrum*, p. 11.

[17] O'Dwyer, *Irish Carmelites*, p. 318.

[18] O'Dwyer, *Irish Carmelites*, p. 320.

[19] O'Dwyer, *Irish Carmelites*, p. 325.

CHAPTER 10

[1] *Irish Independent,* 20 October 1916.

[2] O'Dwyer, *Irish Carmelites,* p. 352.

[3] J.C. O'Shea, 'Memories of Terenure College Fifty Years Ago', *Terenure College Annual* (1965), p. 12.

[4] TCA, Souvenir and Programme 'Carmel Bazaar', *Terenure College Park, May 19th to May 28th 1917*, p. 19.

[5] O'Dwyer, *Irish Carmelites,* p. 350.

[6] NAI, ED 2/34/8, Boys School Rolls, 1906–07.

[7] *Catalogus Fratrum* gives Fr Gerhard's date of ordination as 6 June 1914; Frank Shortis, O. Carm., Brisbane, gives it as 6 July 1914.

[8] J. de M., 'Joseph Gerrard Bobbett 1905–1995', *Terenure College Annual* (1995), p.29.

[9] T.C. Murphy, in *Nubecula* 36 (1985), pp. 50–1.

[10] Communication from Fr Frank Shortis, 8 March 2009.

[11] P. O'Dwyer, *James Carmel O'Shea, 1899-1984* (Dublin, 1989), [Gort Muire], p. 2.

[12] *Irish World*, 1 July 1916, cited by O'Dwyer, p.381.

[13] O'Dwyer, *Irish Carmelites*, p. 349.

[14] A.J. Jordan, *W.T Cosgrave, 1880-1965: Founder of Modern Ireland* (Dublin, 2006), p. 29.

[15] Information supplied by Frank Shortis, O. Carm.

[16] Interview with Fr J. Linus Ryan, 16, 22 June 2008. There is also folklore that Dan Breen was sheltered by the Carmelites in Terenure College after he had been wounded in the Ashtown ambush on the viceroy, Lord French, on 19 December 1920. Neither Dan Breen, in his own memoir, nor Joseph Ambrose, in his account of Dan Breen and the Ashtown ambush mention Terenure as one of the hiding places. See Dan Breen, *My Fight for Irish Freedom* (Dublin, 1924); J. Ambrose, *The Dan Breen Story* (Dublin, 1981).

[17] Information based on documents in the War Office Papers in the British National Archives at Kew, kindly supplied by Brian J. Heffernan of the National University of Ireland, Maynooth.

[18] Frank Shortis communication.

[19] *Gaelic American*, 24 June 1916.

[20] *Irish Press* (Philadelphia), 2 March 1918, p. 3, cited in P. O'Dwyer, *A True Patriot* (Dublin, 1975), p. 15, unpublished typescript, Carmelite Provincial Archives.

[21] *Irish World*, 25 May 1918.

[22] D. Fitzpatrick, *Harry Boland's Irish Revolution* (Cork, 2003), p. 5; *Irish World*, 23 September 1922.

[23] *Catholic Bulletin* (1922), pp. 96–105.

[24] Except where otherwise indicated, all the material on Fr Magennis is to be attributed to P. O'Dwyer, *A True Patriot* (Dublin, 1975).

[25] P. O'Dwyer, 'Book Review', *Causa Nostra Laetitiae* 1:3 (July 1987), pp. 14–16.

[26] P. O'Dwyer, *The Carmelite Order in Post- Reformation Ireland* (Dublin, n.d.), p. 11.

[27] D. Keogh, *The Vatican, the bishops and Irish politics, 1919-39* (Cambridge, 1986), pp. 111–12; O'Dwyer, 'Book Review', pp. 14–16.

[28] Interview with David Kennedy, 7 April 2008.

[29] P. O'Leary, *Gaelic Prose in the Irish Free State, 1922-1939* (Dublin, 2004), p. 184.

[30] Interview with Tom Gunn, 4 October 2008.

CHAPTER 11

[1] *Irish Times*, 18 August 1923.

[2] *Irish Times*, 19 July 1930.

[3] *Irish Independent*, 9 December 1941; A. Corbett, 'Boarder at Terenure, 1931–32', *Terenure College Annual* (1992), p. 7. The quotation is Fr Corbett's description.

[4] D. Breathnach and M. Ní Mhurchú, *Beathathnéis, 1882–1982* (Dublin, 1990), pp. 138–40;S. Ó Neill and B. Ó Dubhthaigh, *Coláiste Uladh: Leabhar Cuimhne Inbhaile, Leith-chéad Bhlian, 1906-1956* (Donegal, 1956); S. Ó Ceallaigh, *Coláiste Uladh, 1906–2006* (Naas, 2006); P. O'Leary, *Gaelic Prose in the Irish Free State 1922-1939* (Dublin, 2004), pp. 113, 121; R.B. McDowell and D.A Webb, *Trinity College Dublin, 1592-1752: An Academic History* (Cambridge, 1982), p. 191; P. Ó Baoighill, *Ó Ghleann to Fanaid* (Dublin, 2000).

[5] *Freeman's Journal*, 31 August 1922.

[6] *Terenure College Annual* (1944) p. 5, (1946) p. 38; *Irish Independent*, 10 January 1946.

[7] P. O'Dwyer, *James Carmel O'Shea*, p. 6.

[8] Costello, *Clongowes Wood*, p. 203; Farragher and Wyer, *Blackrock College*, p. 173.

[9] E.D. O'Connor, 'In the "Come-Back"', *Terenure College Annual* (1976), p. 18.

[10] NAI, ED 2/34/8, *Pupil School Notes*, Box 4, vol. 1, 13 October 1904.

[11] O'Connor, '"Come-Back"', p. 18.

[12] NAI, Department of Education and Science, Miscellaneous Files 1920s and 1030s: ref 2006/120/1.

[13] S. Farren, *The Politics of Irish Education, 1920-1965* (Belfast, 1995), pp. 20–1.

[14] Farren, *Politics of Irish Education*, p. 52.

[15] A. Hyland and J.K. Milne, *Irish Educational Documents* (Dublin, 1987), Vol. 2, pp. 184–6; J. Coolahan, *The ASTI and Post-Primary Education in Ireland, 1919-1984* (Dublin, 1984), pp. 71–2; T.A. O'Donoghue, *The Catholic Church and the Secondary School Curriculum in Ireland, 1922-1962* (New York, 1999), pp. 22–3.

[16] To judge by the list in the *Irish Times*, 8 August 1929.

[17] *Irish Times*, 30 August 1930.

[18] *Whitefriars*, 2:9 (September 1936); *Irish Times*, 22 September 1937.

[19] National University of Ireland Archives, *Matriculation Examination Application Forms, 1925-1930*.

[20] Coolahan, *The ASTI*, p. 123.

[21] John Joy, S.J., 'Some points for a conference on secondary education', *Irish Monthly* (October 1930), cited in Coolahan, *The ASTI*, p. 123.

[22] Costello, *Clongowes Wood*, p. 203.

[23] *Irish Times*, 12 February 1926.

[24] *Irish Times*, 25 November 1927.

[25] *The Irish School Weekly*, 10 December 1927.

[26] In a letter of 14 November 1926 to Italian confrere, Antonino: see O'Dwyer, *Irish Carmelites*, p. 364.

[27] O'Dwyer, *Irish Carmelites*, p. 366.

[28] Farragher and Wyer, *Blackrock College*, p. 172.

[29] O'Shea, 'Memories of Terenure College Fifty Years Ago', pp. 8–13.

[30] *Freeman's Journal*, 10, 17 May 1920.

[31] *Freeman's Journal*, 24 May 1920.

[32] *Freeman's Journal*, 12 March 1921.

[33] *Freeman's Journal*, 28 May 1921.

[34] *Freeman's Journal*, 11 December 1922.

[35] *Freeman's Journal*, 19 February 1923.

[36] O'Dwyer, *James Carmel O'Shea,* p. 67.

[37] *Sport*, 13 March 1926.

[38] *Sport*, 19 March 1927.

[39] *Sport*, 14 January 1928.

[40] Farragher and Wyer, *Blackrock College*, pp. 172–3.

[41] Costello, *Clongowes Wood*, p. 203.

[42] O'Shea, 'Memories of Terenure College Fifty Years Ago', p. 13.

[43] *Irish Times*, 4 December 1924.

[44] *Irish Times*, 9 December 1958 — obituary: 'he died on 8 December 1958 survived by widow (Rose Warren) three sons and two daughters'. The quotation is from B. O'Donnell, *Irish Surgeons and Surgery in the Twentieth Century* (Dublin, 2008), pp. 271–2.

[45] *Irish Times*, 12 November 1952, obituary; O'Donnell, op.cit, pp. 200–01.

[46] *Irish Times*, 1 November 1948, 23 April 1936, 9 September 1938, 14 September 1939.

[47] *Irish Times*, 10 October 1924.

[48] Irish Architectural Archive, *Dictionary of Irish Architects* (see www.dia.ie, last accessed 4 October 2009).

[49] *Terenure College Annual* (1959), p. 25.

[50] *Irish Times*, 19 February 1909.

[51] *Irish Times*, 2 October 1961; *Terenure College Annual* (1962), p. 33.

[52] *Freeman's Journal*, 31 August 1896, 6 September 1897.

[53] L.J. Walsh, 'An Old Terenure Boy', in *Whitefriars* 4: 2 (March–April 1942), pp. 49–52.

[54] *Irish Independent*, 28 December 1942.

[55] *Irish Times*, 15 June 1925.

[56] O'Shea, 'Memories of Terenure College Fifty Years Ago', p. 12.

[57] *Terenure College Annual* (1995), p. 29.

[58] For Catholic Action in Ireland see M. Curtis, *The Splendid Cause: the Catholic Action Movement in Ireland in the Twentieth Century* (Dublin, 2008).

CHAPTER 12

[1] Claud Cockburn, *The Devil's Decade* (London, 1973).

[2] D. Keogh, *Twentieth Century Ireland: Nation and State* (Dublin, 1994), p. 80.

[3] Coolahan, *The ASTI*, p. 93.

[4] Keogh, *Nation and State*, p. 90.

[5] N.C. Fleming and A. O'Day, *The Longman Handbook of Modern Irish History since 1800* (Harlow, 2005), p. 407.

[6] Coolahan, *The ASTI*, p. 97.

[7] Coolahan, *The ASTI*, p. 107.

[8] 'A Diamond Jubilee: seventy five years of educational work', *Whitefriars* 2: 8 (August 1939).

[9] D. O'Connor, 'In the "Come-Back"', *Terenure College Annual* (1976), p. 18.

[10] Interview with Carmelite contemporary, 22 October 2008; interview with Joe Roche, 23 May 2008.

[11] *Sunday Independent*, 1 December 1935.

[12] *Irish Times*, 28 May 1936.

[13] TCA, *Results of Examinations, 1883-1942*.

[14] H.V. Woods, *Marketing at the Millennium* (Dublin, 2000).

[15] Interview with Terence Doyle, BA DPA, 26 May 2008.

[16] Interview with Seán Logue, 22 July 2008.

[17] *Irish Times*, 18 Oct 1982; interview with Charlie Roche, 6 February 2008.

[18] Interview with Joe Roche, 23 May 2008.

[19] O'Shea, 'Memories of Terenure College Fifty Years Ago', pp. 11–12.

[20] Interview with Tom Gunn, 4 October 2008.

[21] O'Connor, '"Come-Back"', p. 18.

[22] *Whitefriars* 5: 6 (August 1935), 5:6 (September 1936).

[23] *Whitefriars* 2: 2 (November–December 1940).

[24] *Whitefriars* 2: 6 (June 1936).

[25] O'Dwyer, *James Carmel O'Shea*, p. 7; *Whitefriars* 2: 9 (September 1936).

[26] *Irish Times*, 19 January 1937; *Whitefriars* 3: 2 (February 1937).

[27] *Irish Times, Irish Independent*, 2 December 1935.

[28] TCA, *Honours List* (from 1927–8 to 1948–9).

[29] TCA, *Honours List, 1927–1948; Terenure College Annual* (1995), p. 26.

[30] *Irish Times*, 10 January 1936.

[31] *Whitefriars* 2: 1 (April 1969).

[32] *Irish Times, Irish Independent*, 28 May 1936.

[33] *Irish Press*, 2 June 1934.

[34] *Irish Press*, 7 June 1939.

[35] *Irish Press*, 8 June 1939.

[36] O'Dwyer, *James Carmel O'Shea*, p. 18.

[37] Interview with Fr David Weakliam, 15 November 2007.

[38] *Irish Times*, 18 January 1939.

[39] *Irish Times*, 5 February 1941; editorial, 8 February 1941.

[40] Interview with Fr P.J. Cunningham, 3 September 2008.

CHAPTER 13

[1] O'Connor, '"Come-Back"', p. 18.

[2] J.V. Doyle, 'A Look Back in Time', *Terenure College Annual* (2002), p. 33.

[3] Interview with Terence Doyle, 26 May 2008.

[4] Interview with Richard Fleming, 1 April 2008.

[5] Interview with Tom Gunn, 4 October 2008.

[6] *Terenure College Annual* (1962), p. 12, (1987), p. 12; *Catalogus Fratrum*.

[7] Interview with Charlie Roche, 6 February 2008.

[8] Interview with Sé O'Connor, 5 February 2008.

[9] Interview with Paddy Ward, 4 September 2008; for an independent account of these events see the recent study, M. Kennedy, *Guarding Neutral Ireland* (Dublin, 2008), pp. 181, 193–6.

[10] *Irish Times*, 25 May 1940.

[11] *Irish Times*, 6 July 1940.

[12] P O Dwyer, 'Fr Timothy Enda Devane, 1916-1993', *Causa Nostra Laetitiae* 7: 3 (May 1994), p. 19.

[13] See Chapter 19.

[14] Interview with John McClean, 8 April 2008.

[15] Interview with Fr Chris O'Donnell, July 2008.

[16] *Terenure College Annual* (1993), p. 8, Fr E. Griffin's obituary of Fr Peter Egan.

[17] *Terenure College Annual* (1946), p. 381.

[18] *Irish Independent*, 25 March 1941.

[19] TCA, *Results of Examinations 1883–1942; Honours List 1927–1942.*

[20] P.A. Corbett, 'Fr Thomas Cyril Murphy, O. Carm., 1900–1990', *Terenure College Annual* (1990), pp. 15–16.

[21] *Terenure College Annual* (1946), p. 5.

[22] TCA, *Letters of Jim Timoney to Fr Bill [W.O. McGrath],* 18 September 1945 and n.d.; *Terenure College Annual* (1945), p. 25 and (1947), p. 29.

[23] *Terenure College Annual* (1945), p. 28.

[24] *Terenure College Annual* (1945), p. 29; TCA, *Register of Pupils, 1927-1962.*

[25] *Terenure College Annual* (1945), p. 28; TCA, *Register of Pupils, 1927-1962.*

[26] *Daily Telegraph*, 22 November 2001; I am grateful to Colin McKeon for providing this information.

[27] O'Connor, '"Come-Back"', p. 18.

[28] O'Dwyer, *Irish Carmelites*, p. 376.

[29] Interview with a Terenure College past pupil, 2008.

[30] *Whitefriars* 3: 5 (May 1937); TCA, *Results of Examinations, 1883–1942.*

[31] *Irish Times*, 23 January 1978.

[32] *The Leader*, I January 1944.

[33] *Whitefriars* 4: 2 (May 1938).

[34] *Irish Press*, 6 June 1940.

[35] *Irish Independent*, 1 February 1943.

[36] O'Connor, '"Come-Back"', p. 19.

[37] Interview with Paddy Ward, 4 September 2008 to whom I am grateful for the text of this cup song.

[38] *Evening Mail*, 13 June 1941.

[39] *Evening Herald*, 8 June 1942.

[40] *Irish Independent*, 3 June 1944.

[41] *Evening Herald,* 26 August 1944.

[42] *Irish Times*, 24 September 2001.

[43] Interview with Richard Fleming, 1 April 2008; D.C. Flanagan, 'The beginnings of the College *Annual*', *Terenure College Annual* (1981), p. 18.

[44] *Terenure College Annual* (1974), p. 10; an account by Hugh Gunn, in 'News of the Past'.

[45] President of the Opthalmic Institute in 1951 and President of the Union in 1944, 1945, 1957 and 1958.

[46] Interviews with Fr Des Kelly, 28 February 2008; Felim Corr, 11 February 2008; Frank Gildea, 27 June 2008.

[47] Interview with Felim Corr, 11 February 2008.

CHAPTER 14

[1] *Terenure College Annual* (1944 to 1950).

[2] *Terenure College Annual* (1944 to 1950).

[3] *Terenure College Annual* (1944 to 1950).

[4] SOKOL was a nineteenth-century gymnastic movement.

[5] *People's Weekly*, 4 May 1946.

[6] *Terenure College Annual* (1948), p. 110.

[7] *Terenure College Annual* (1959), pp .25–6.

[8] Interview with Fr P.J. Cunningham, 3 September 2008.

[9] D.R. Lamont, 'Mr Griffin', *Terenure College Annual* (1980), pp. 21–3.

[10] Interview with Charlie Weakliam, 15 February 2008.

[11] Interview with Fr Des Kelly, 28 February 2008.

[12] Interview with David Kennedy 8 April 2008.

[13] Interview with Dennis McGrane, 24 June; Eugene McNamee, 9 June; and John McClean, 8 April 2008.

[14] Interviews with David Kennedy, Charlie O'Sullivan and Frank Gildea, 27 June 2008.

[15] Interview with Fr Bob Kelly, 13 August 2008.

[16] *Terenure College Annual* (1981), p. 11.

[17] Interview with Fr P.J. Cunningham, 3 September 2008; *Terenure College Annual* (1989), p. 15.

[18] 'The Year', *Terenure College Annual* (1947), p. 44.

[19] *Irish Independent*, 29 April 1946.

[20] J.V. Doyle, 'A Look Back in Time', *Terenure College Annual* (2002), p. 34.

[21] *Terenure College Annual* (1944), pp. 16–17.

[22] M. Roche (ed.), *Terenure College Rugby Football Club, 1940-1990* (Dublin, 1990).

[23] *Terenure College Annual* (1948), p. 111.

[24] *Terenure College Annual* (1945), p. 18.

[25] *Irish Catholic*, 16 September 1948.

CHAPTER 15

[1] M. Hill, 'Team Spirit', M. Hender (ed.), *Celts Among the Shona* (Dublin, 2002), pp. 56–7.

[2] *Terenure College Annual* (1950), p. 22.

[3] The colonial names are used up to 1980: thereafter, the African names are used for the country and its dioceses, districts and towns.

[4] *Terenure College Annual* (1999), p. 29.

[5] O'Dwyer, *James Carmel O'Shea*, pp. 19–20, citing O'Shea to Gabriel Pausback, 5 February 1945.

[6] O'Dwyer, *James Carmel O'Shea*, p. 25.

[7] A. Corbett, 'The First Year – 1946', M. Hender (ed.), *Celts among the Shona*, pp. 7–12.

[8] Leo Gallagher (ed.), *The Catholic Church in Manicaland 1896–1996* (Harare, 1996), p. 18.

[9] M. Hender (ed.), *A Souvenir of the Golden Jubilee of the Irish Carmelites in Zimbabwe, 1946-1996* (Dublin, 1996), p. 12.

[10] *Irish Independent,* 14 October 1947.

[11] M. Hill, 'We too have lived in Arcadia', *Terenure College Annual* (1952), pp. 4–6.

[12] Interview with Fr Jarlath O'Hea, 13 November 2007.

[13] Interview with Fr Eoin Moore, 24 July 2008.

[14] J. O'Shea, 'St Benedicts Mission', in Hender, *Celts Among the Shona*, p. 61.

[15] M. Hill, 'Trusted Supporters', in Hender, *Celts Among the Shona*, p. 48.

[16] *Terenure College Annual* (1974), p. 11.

[17] *Causa Nostra Laetitiae* (Spring 2001), pp. 30–3, obituary by Jim Doyle.

[18] Gallagher, *Church in Manicaland*, p. 19.

[19] *Terenure College Annual* (1987), p. 9.

[20] Hender, *Irish Carmelites in Zimbabwe*, p. 12.

[21] *Terenure College Annual* (1960), p. 69.

[22] Interview with Fr Stan Hession, 22 October 2008.

[23] A fuller list is given in Hender, *50 years* as follows: From Ireland: Conleth Fitzgerald, Bonaventure Fitzgerald, Emmanuel McGrath, David Weakliam, Chris Crowley, Bob Kelly, Simon Grace, Patrick Burke, Chris O'Donnell, Eltin Griffin, Micheál Ó Néill, Aloysius Ryan, Jimmy Murphy, Billy Langan, Norbert Heaslip, Fintan Burke, Jim McCouaig, Paul Lennon, Des Flannagan, Peter O'Dwyer, Michael Morrissey, John Keating,

Charles Keogh, Martin Ryan, Chris Conroy, Gerry Hipwell, David Conaghan, J. O'Hea, T. Walsh, T. Higgins, P. Kehoe, Éanna Ó hÓbáin.

[24] B. McCauley, 'Terenure to Kriste Mambo', *Terenure College Annual* (1995), pp. 101–07.

CHAPTER 16

[1] The phrase is from J.A. O'Brien, *The Vanishing Irish: the enigma of the modern world* (New York, 1953).

[2] N.C. Fleming and A. O'Day, *The Longman Handbook of Modern Irish History since 1800*, (Harlow, 2005), p. 503.

[3] Fleming and O'Day, *The Longman Handbook*, p. 467.

[4] Fleming and O'Day, *The Longman Handbook*, pp. 405 – 410.

[5] Fleming and O'Day, *The Longman Handbook*, pp. 405 – 410.

[6] *Terenure College Annual* (1950–65).

[7] *Terenure College Annual* (1950–65).

[8] *Terenure College Annual* (1950–65).

[9] N. Heaslip, *Terenure College Annual* (1993), p. 10.

[10] *Terenure College Annual* (1953), p. 50.

[11] C. O'Donnell, 'Thomas Patrick Burke (1923-2008)', *Terenure College Annual* (2008), pp. 26–8.

[12] Interview with Fr Des Flanagan, 17 June 2008.

[13] According to the editorial in the *Terenure College Annual* (1948), p. 5, although the MS. volume, *Results of Examinations 1888-1942* makes no mention of him, nor does the MS. volume, *Register of Pupils, (1926–1962)* in the Terenure Archives.

[14] Fintan Burke, 'Patsy Keenan, O. Carm.', *Terenure College Annual* (2003), p. 25.

[15] Interview with Fr Joe Linus Ryan, 16 and 25 June 2008.

[16] Information supplied by Frs P J Cunningham and Des Kelly.

[17] V. Morris, 'Mr Patrick O'Brien', *Terenure College Annual* (1975), p. 20.

[18] Interview with Charlie O'Sullivan, 21 June 2008.

[19] *Terenure College Annual* (1986), p. 19.

[20] Interview with Joe Roche, 23 May 2008.

[21] Interview with Terence Doyle, 26 May 2008.

[22] E.D. O'Connor, 'Christopher B. Collins: An Appreciation', *Terenure College Annual* (1975), p. 12.

[23] Interview with Fr Bene O'Callaghan, 21 August 2008.

[24] Interview with Fr Des Flanagan, 17 June 2008.

[25] Interview with Professor David Kennedy and Dr Sé O'Connor 5 February 2008.

[26] Interviews with Fr Chris O'Donnell, I July 2008, and Tony Scott, 10 November 2008. A Kildare-man in origins, Christy apparently played to some effect with the county GAA footballers: according to Fr Jarlath O'Hea, Christy won a Minor All-Ireland medal with them. His obsequies were held in the Terenure College Chapel and he was brought home to Kildare to be laid to rest. Information from Fr O'Hea, courtesy of Brendan McCauley.

[27] *Terenure College Annual* (1952), p. 2.

[28] *Terenure College Annual* (1960), p. 58.

[29] *Irish Press*, 25 May 1956.

[30] DDA, McQuaid Papers, Folder 2 (1953–60), McQuaid to Carmelite Provincial Fitzgerald, 1 December 1953.

[31] Interview with Eugene McNamee, 27 May 2008.

[32] *Terenure College Annual* (1959), pp. 18–19.

Chapter 17

[1] M. Murphy, *Mike & Me: A Memoir by Mike Murphy* (Dublin, 1996), p. 21.

[2] Interviews with Dennis McGrane, 24 June 2008 and Bernard Kenna, 4 June 2008.

[3] Interview with Felim Corr, 11 February 2008.

[4] Interview with Fr Michael Hender, 11 August 2008.

[5] Interview with Fr Bob Kelly, 13 August 2008.

[6] Interviews with Fr Joe Linus Ryan, 16–25 June 2008 and Michael Grennell, 20 November 2008.

[7] *Terenure College Annual* (1955), p. 57.

[8] Interview with Ms Ita Clancy, 2 December 2008.

[9] Interview with Fr Jackie Madden, 18 and 25 June 2008.

[10] Editorial, *Terenure College Annual* (1960), pp. 2–3.

[11] Editorial, *Terenure College Annual*, p. 5.

[12] *Irish Independent*, 2 May 1960.

Chapter 18

[1] Interview with Fr P.J. Cunningham, 3 September 2008.

[2] TCA, *Register of Pupils 1927–1962*.

[3] Interview with Fr Des Kelly, 28 February 2008.

[4] Interview with Fr Billy Langan, 17 October 2008.

[5] Interview with Fr Bene O Callaghan, 28 July 2008.

[6] Interview with Fr Chris O'Donnell, 1 July 2008

[7] Interview with David Kennedy, 7 April 2008.

[8] *Terenure College Annual* (1959), p. 25, obituary.

[9] *Terenure College Annual* (1964), p. 19.

[10] *Terenure College Annual* (1962), p. 81.

[11] *Irish Times*, 25 October 1963.

[12] *Terenure College Annual* (1988), pp. 64–5; (1991), p. 76; (1996), pp. 2, 22–4.

Chapter 19

[1] *Sunday Press,* 1 December 1949.

[2] *Sunday Press,* 16 December 1951.

[3] *Times Pictorial*, 29 December 1951.

[4] B. Flynn, *Legends of Irish Boxing: stories seldom told* (Belfast, 2007).

[5] *Terenure College Annual* (1954), p. 27.

[6] John F. Larchet (1845–1967) was professor of music in UCD and at the Royal Irish Academy of Music from 1920 to 1955.

[7] *Terenure College Annual* (1962), p. 84.

[8] *Sunday Press,* 1 December 1949.

[9] TCA, *Register of Pupils, 1927–62*.

[10] *Terenure College Annual* (1965), p. 115.

[11] *Terenure College Annual* (1951), p. 91.

[12] *Terenure College Annual* (1952), p. 101.

[13] *Terenure College Annual* (1958), p. 13.

[14] See Chapter 25.

[15] *Sunday Independent*, 23 March 1952.

[16] *Terenure College Annual* (1952), pp. 84–6; *Sunday Independent*, 23 March 1952.

[17] Cited in *Terenure College Annual* (1958), p. 102.

[18] They became only the third college to secure the double since 1909 and remained the only one of four to do so to-date: Blackrock nineteen times, Castleknock once, in 1920, Terenure in 1958 and Belvedere in 2005.

[19] *Terenure College Annual* (1958), editorial, p. 3.

[20] B. Burke, 'Give Terenure Senior Status', *The People*, 2 December 1956.

[21] *Evening Press*, 2 June 1956.

[22] *Graphic*, 24 November 1957.

[23] *Irish Press*, 27 September 1959.

CHAPTER 20

[1] Coolahan, *ASTI*, pp. 272–3.

[2] Interview with Fr Bob Kelly, 13 August 2008.

[3] Interview with Fr Des Kelly, 28 February 2008.

[4] Interview with Fr Jackie Madden, 25 June 2008.

[5] Interview with John McClean, 8 April 2008.

[6] *Terenure College Annual* (1965–85).

[7] Interview with Fr J. Linus Ryan, 16 and 22 June 1968.

[8] Gort Muire Provincial Archives, *Catalogus Fratrum,* p. 29.

[9] Interview with Joe Cleere, 5 March 2008.

[10] Interview with Fr Des Kelly, 28 February 2008.

[11] Interview with Eugene McNamee, 9 June 2008.

[12] Interview with Terenure College past pupil, 25 November 2008.

[13] 'A Pillar of the College, 1949-'95', *Terenure College Annual* (1996), pp. 14–15.

[14] Coolahan, *ASTI*, pp. 267–316.

[15] Coolahan, *ASTI*, p. 283.

[16] Interview with Frank Gallan, 3 June 2008.

[17] Interview with Michael Grennell, 20 November 2008 and Paul Joyce, 3 November 2008.

[18] Interview with Fr Eoin Moore, 24 July 2008.

[19] Interview with Charlie O'Sullivan, 21 June 2008.

[20] *Terenure College Annual* (1989), p.12.

[21] 'Editorial', *Terenure College Annual* (1989), p. 5.

[22] Interviews with Frank Gildea, 27 June 2008, and Michael Grennell, 20 November 2008.

[23] Interview with Professor Ronan O'Connell 24 November 2008 and Fr Joe Mothersill, 13 October 2008.

[24] *Terenure College Annual* (1967), pp. 3, 80; (1976), p. 23.

[25] *Terenure College Annual* (1969), p. 74.

[26] *Terenure College Annual* (1974), p. 4.

[27] *Terenure College Annual* (1974), p. 25.

[28] Interview with Fr Bob Kelly, 13 August 2008.

CHAPTER 21

[1] Interview with Patrick O'Kane, 11 November 2008.

[2] Interview with John McClean, 16 April 2008.

[3] Interview with Joe McDonnell, 3 June 2008.

[4] Joe McDonnell, 'Seamus McCool, retired', *Terenure College Annual* (2003), p. 32.

[5] Interview with Bernard Kenna, 4 June 2008. The attribution of this story is contested by others who accept

the incident happened but not the name of the perpetrator of this particular mischief.

[6] Interviews with Charlie O'Sullivan, 21 June 2008, and Fr Billy Langan, 17 October 2008.

[7] Interview with Frank Gallen, 3 June 2008.

[8] Interview with Brendan McCauley, 15 April 2008.

[9] Interview with Billy Langan, 8 October 2008.

[10] F. Barron, *Swimming for a century* (Dublin, 1993), p. 142.

[11] Interview with Kevin Williamson, 8 September 2008.

[12] Interview with Paul Joyce, 3 November 2008.

[13] John McClean, 'James Hanley, Artist', Terenure *College Annual* (1995), p. 35.

[14] *Irish Times*, 19 June 1972.

[15] M. O'Kelly, 'Con A. Smith — An Appreciation', *Terenure College Annual* (1972), pp. 35–6; interview with Richard Fleming, 1 April 2008.

[16] J. Humphrey, 'Making a Little Go a Long Way', *Irish Times*, 21 June 2005.

[17] Interview with Declan Keane, 1 December 2008.

Chapter 22

[1] *Terenure College Annual* (1978), p. 119.

[2] This account by Rodney Bishop and John McClean is to be found at www.terenurecollegeafc.com/history-clubhistory.htm (26 July 2009).

[3] Interview with John McClean, 8 April 2008.

[4] Interview with Joe Cleere, 5 March 2008.

[5] Bishop and McClean, www.terenurecollegeafc.com/history-clubhistory.htm (26 July 2009).

[6] Interview with Frank Gallen, 3 June 2008.

Chapter 23

[1] R.J. Nolan 'The College Concert Hall — 50 Years' Celebrations', *The Play's the Thing* (Dublin, 1977), p. 3.

[2] *Irish Times,* 18 December 1985.

[3] *Irish Times*, 13 September 1972.

[4] *Terenure College Annual* (1949), p. 40.

[5] Murphy, *Mike and Me*, p. 24.

[6] P. Laffan and F. O'Grady (eds), *Donal McCann Remembered: A tribute* (Dublin, 2000), p. 165.

[7] Laffan and O'Grady, *Donal McCann*, p. 165.

[8] *Evening Press*, 14 December 1957.

[9] *Terenure College Annual* (1963), pp. 42–3.

[10] N. Grene and C. Morash (eds), *Shifting Scenes: Irish Theatre-Going, 1955-85* (Dublin, 2008), p. 62.

[11] *Sunday Tribune Magazine*, 17 August 2008.

[12] B. Sherry, 'McCann Finishes Strongly — Winner All Right', in Laffan and O'Grady, *Donal McCann Remembered: a tribute* (Dublin, 2000), pp. 153–7.

[13] *Terenure College Annual* (1966), p. 32.

[14] Grene and Morash, *Shifting Scenes*, p. 36.

[15] Interview with Michael Grennell, 20 November 2008.

[16] *Terenure College Annual* (1974), p. 69.

[17] *Terenure College Annual* (1976), p. 6.

[18] Interview with Joe McDonnell, 3 June 2008.

[19] *Terenure College Annual* (1988), p. 69.

[20] Interview with Joe McDonnell, 3 June 2008.

Chapter 24

[1] Hyland and Milne, *Irish Educational Documents*, p. 410.

[2] *Terenure College Annual* (2007), p. 21.

[3] Interview with Ita Clancy, 2 December 2008.

[4] *Terenure College Annual* (2002), pp. 11–15.

[5] *Terenure College Annual*, (1999), pp. 10–11; (2002), pp. 11–12.

[6] Interview with Fr Micheál Ó Néill, 22 October 2008.

[7] Gort Muire, Provincial Archives, *Diary of Fr Joseph Butler*. I am grateful to Ruth Long, Librarian, for this reference.

[8] *Irish Times*, 10 January 1895.

[9] *Terenure College Annual* (1972), p. 72.

[10] *Terenure College Annual* (1992), p. 58.

[11] Interview with Frank Gildea, 27 June 2008.

[12] Interview with Michael Jordan, 14 August 2008.

[13] This account of the project is based largely on the *Minutes and Correspondence of the Lake Restoration Committee*, (Dublin, 1991–4), except where otherwise indicated.

Chapter 25

[1] *Terenure College Annual* (2005), p. 123; (2004), pp. 26–7.

[2] For most of the information concerning badminton, I am indebted to Ms Margaret Cox and Fr Billy Langan.

[3] *Terenure College Annual* (1964), p. 128.

[4] *Terenure College Annual* (2007), p. 125.

[5] *Irish Times*, 6 June 1991.

[6] *Irish Times*, 29 March 1991.

[7] *Terenure College Annual* (1988), pp. 64–5.

[8] *Terenure College Annual* (1989), pp. 93–4.

[9] Interview with Ian Blake, 22 March 2008.

[10] *Terenure College Annual* (1992), p. 84.

[11] *Irish Times*, 18 March 1992.

[12] *Terenure College Annual* (1997), pp. 107–13.

[13] *Terenure College Annual* (1983), p. 10.

[14] *Terenure College Annual* (1989), p. 25.

[15] *Terenure College Annual* (1999), p. 24.

[16] *Terenure College Annual* (1965), p. 29.

[17] See Chapter 23.

Chapter 26

[1] K. Woulfe, 'Address' *Terenure College Annual* (2004), p. 75.

[2] Philip O'Sullivan, 'Telling the Story: Address by Philip O'Sullivan at Senior School Prize giving, 25th May 2004', in *Terenure College Annual* (2004), pp. 31–3.

[3] Fr M. Troy, 'Address to Junior School', 3 June 2004, *Terenure College Annual* (2004), pp. 152–4.

[4] Fr M. Ó Néill, 'Building on What is Already There', *Terenure College Annual* (1996), pp. 20–2.

[5] Fr M. Troy, 'Address to Junior School', 3 June 2004, *Terenure College Annual* (2004), pp. 152–4.

Appendices

Appendix One: Priors of Terenure, 1860–2010

1860–71	Michael Joseph Gilligan	1924–5	Charles Simon Gavin
1871–8	Andrew Elias Farrington	1925–31	Richard Brocard Taylor
1878–82	Michael Aloysius Moore	1931–7	James Carmel O'Shea
1882–3	Philip Paul McDonnell	1937–43	Andrew Eugene Wright
1883–5	Edward Patrick Southwell	1943–6	John Conleth Fitzgerald
1885–91	Thomas Stanislaus Bartley	1946–9	Joseph Augustine Kelly
1891–9	Michael Avertanus O'Reilly	1949–52	Dominic Fionan Reale
1899–1904	Richard James Colfer	1952–8	Eugene Dunstan O'Connor
1904–05	Michael Avertanus O'Reilly	1958–61	Thomas Patrick Burke
1905–06	Thomas Patrick Kelly	1961–7	Patrick Cornelius Keenan
1906–09	Richard James Colfer	1967–73	Patrick Simon Grace
1909	Peter Louis Nolan	1973–6	Adrian David Weakliam
1909–13	James John Cogan	1976–82	Robert Michael Kelly
1913–14	Denis Berchmans Devlin	1982–8	Patrick Eltin Griffin
1914–16	William Joachim Brennan	1988–94	James Dominic McCouaig
1916	Charles F.X. Ronayne	1994–7	Patrick William Staunton
1916	James John Cogan	1997–2003	James Murray
1916–22	Michael Louis Gerhard	2003–08	Micheál Ó Néill
1922–3	Richard James Colfer	2008–	Michael Troy
1923–4	Patrick Ambrose Wade		

Appendix Two: Carmelite Provincials of the Irish Province, 1852–2010

1852—63	Thomas Albertus Bennett	1925–9	Richard James Colfer
1863–71	John Francis Spratt	1929–34	Denis Berchmans Devllin
1871–5	John Simon Carr	1934–40	James John of the Cross Cogan
1875–8	John Elias Bartley	1940–6	James Carmel O'Shea
1878–81	Michael Aloysius Moore	1946–52	John Conleth Fitzgerald
1881–4	Andrew Elias Farrington	1952–8	Cyril Bonaventure Fitzgerald
1884–91	John Elias Bartley	1958–64	James Carmel O'Shea
1891–5	John Joseph Hall	1964–9	John Emmanuel McGrath
1895–9	Thomas Patrick Davis	1969–76	Joseph Linus Ryan
1899–1902	Andrew Elias Farrington	1976–82	Adrian David Weakliam
1902	Richard James Colfer	1982–8	Christopher Crowley
1903–06	Thomas Stanislaus Bartley	1988–94	Patrick William Staunton
1906–09	Michael Avertanus O'Reilly	1994–2000	Robert Michael Kelly
1909–13	Patrick Edward Southwell	2000–09	Fintan Burke
1913–25	James John of the Cross Cogan	2009–	Martin Kilmurray

1924	Leo Keegan	1953	Gerry Carr	1982	Eugene McNamee
1925	Leo Keegan	1954	Gerry Carr	1983	Hugh Cassidy
1926	Leo Keegan	1955	Gerry Carr	1984	Paddy Devlin
1927	Vincent P. Tighe	1956	J.P. Clarke	1985	Fr Billy Langan
1928	Fr P.A. Walsh	1957	P. McGivney Nolan	1986	Paddy Donaghy
1929	George P. Sheridan	1958	P. McGivney Nolan	1987	Bernard Kenna
1930	Seán Ó hÚadaigh	1959	Joe Milroy	1988	David Kennedy
1931	E.J. Mallins	1960	Joe Milroy	1989	Des Lamont
1932	Vincent P. Tighe	1961	Des McGarry	1990	Bobby Keogh
1933	Vincent P. Tighe	1962	Harry Woods	1991	Joe Clancy
1934	Michael Cole	1963	Frank Cole	1992	Jim Blake
1935	T.J. Malone	1964	Charlie Roche	1993	Fr Adrian Weakliam
1936	John J. Shiel	1965	Charlie Roche	1994	Sé O'Connor
1937	John J. Shiel	1966	Anthony Cole	1995	Paul Ryan
1938	Michael Cole	1967	Eamonn O'Nolan	1996	Colm Hyland
1939	J. Leonard	1968	Dick Fleming	1997	Ronan Nolan
1940	J. Leonard	1969	Gerry O'Connor	1998	Brendan McCauley
1941	R.G. Dunlop	1970	Terence Doyle	1999	Karl Ganter
1942	R.G. Dunlop	1971	Maurice O'Kelly	2000	Darren Phillips
1943	Maurice McGowan	1972	Maurice O'Kelly	2001	Paul Tuite
1944	P. McGivney Nolan	1973	Enda Ryder	2002	Paul Haycock
1945	P. McGivney Nolan	1974	Noel Searson	2003	Joe Cleere
1946	John J. Shiel	1975	James Doyle	2004	Colin McKeon
1947	P.P. Maguire	1976	Brendan Sherry	2005	Larry O'Driscoll
1948	P.P. Maguire	1977	Brendan Sherry	2006	Fr Micheál Ó Néill
1949	G.P. Stuart	1978	Martin Donnelly	2007	Peter Doyle
1950	G.P. Stuart	1979	John McClean	2008	Brendan Meehan
1951	P.P. Maguire	1980	Paul McKay	2009	Fras Cotter
1952	J.P. Clarke	1981	Michael Pender	2010	Tommy Keogh

The cloister, 1957.
Photo by Noel Doyle.

Primary Sources

1. Archives

Carmelite Order
      Archives and Library of the Irish Province, Gort Muire, Dundrum
      Archives of Terenure College
Dublin Diocesan Archives (DDA)
      Cardinal Cullen Papers
      Archbishop Walsh Papers
      Archbishop McQuaid Papers
Irish Architectural Archive
      Dictionary of Irish Architects
National Archives of Ireland (NAI)
      Census of Population, 1901 and 1911
      Department of Education Papers:
      NAI ED: *Minutes of Commissioners of Intermediate Education, 1878–1923*
      Pupil School Rolls, 1890–1915; Boys' School Rolls, 1906–07; School Rolls, 1907–09
National University of Ireland (NUI)
      Matriculation Papers:
      Candidates for Matriculation, 1879–1940
      Results of Examinations, 1888–1940
Registry of Deeds, Dublin
      Miscellaneous Deeds and Memorials, 1817–1909
University College Dublin Archives (UCDA)
      De Valera Papers (P150)
Valuation Office, Dublin
      Valuation Books for Dublin, 1859–72
      Cancellation Books

2. Official Publications

Census 1911
Parliamentary Papers
Reports of the Intermediate Education Board for Ireland, 1880 [C.2600] to 1900
Annual Report of the Commissioners of Education in Ireland, 1900 [Cd.164] to 1921 [Cmd.1398]
Landowners in Ireland: Return of Owners of Land of One Acre and Upwards in Counties, Cities and Towns in Ireland, 1876 [C.1492]

3. Newspapers, Periodicals & Directories

Terenure College Annual, 1944–2009
Annual Record (Terenure College, 1881–3)
Catholic Bulletin
Catholic Directory
Causa Nostra Laetitiae
Daily Telegraph
DCU Times
Ellis's Irish Education Directory and Scholastic Guide
Evening Herald
Evening Mail
Evening Press
Freeman's Journal
Gaelic American
Graphic
Irish Independent
Irish Monthly
Irish Press
Irish School Weekly
Irish Times
Irish World
Nubecula
People's Weekly
Roscommon People
Roundup (South Africa)
Sport
Sunday Independent
Sunday Tribune
The Irish Catholic
The Lamp
The Leader
The People
Thom's Dublin Directory
University View (Dublin City University)
Whitefriars
Zelo

4. Interviews:

Blake, Ian   28 March 2008
Blake, Jim   28 February 2008
Breen, P.J., Fr   24 July 2008

Cahill, Pat	25 November 2008
Clancy, Ita	02 December 2008
Cleere, Joe	05 March 2008
Corr, Felim	11 February 2008
Crown, John	08 September 2009
Cunningham, P.J., Fr	03 September 2009
Doyle, James	26 February 2008
Doyle, Terence	26 May 2008
Dunne, Richard	05 May 2008
Flanagan, Des, Fr	17 June 2008
Fleming, Richard	01 April 2008
Gallen, Frank	03 June 2008
Gildea, Frank	27 June 2008
Grennell, Michael	20 November 2008
Gunn, Tom	04 October 2008
Hender, Michael	11 March 2008
Hession, Stan, Fr	22 October 2008
Jordan, Michael	14 August 2008
Joyce, Paul	03 November 2008
Keane, Declan	01 December 2008
Kelly, Bob, Fr	13 August 2008
Kelly, Des, Fr	28 February 2008
Kenna, Bernard	04 June 2008
Kennedy, David	08 April 2008
Keogh, Tommy	19 May 2008
Kilmurray, Martin, Fr	01 September 2008
Langan, Billy, Fr	08 October 2008
Lewins, Martin	02 October 2008
Logue, Seán	18 August 2008
Madden, Jackie, Fr	18 June 2008
McCauley, Brendan	15 April 2008
McClean, John	08 April 2008
McDonnell, Joe	03 June 2008
McGrane, Dennis	24 June 2008
McKenna, Joseph T.	28 August 2009
McNamee, Eugene	27 May 2008
Moore, Eoin, Fr	24 July 2008
Mothersill, Joe, Fr	13 October 2008
O'Callaghan, Bene, Fr	28 July 2008
O'Connell, Ronan	25 November 2008
O'Connor, Sé	05 February 2008
O'Donnell, Chris, Fr	01 July 2008
O'Hea, Jarlath, Fr	13 November 2007

Ó hÓbáin, Éanna, Fr	19 November 2007
O'Kane, Patrick	11 November 2008
Ó Néill, Micheál, Fr	22 October 2008
O'Sullivan, Charlie	21 June 2008
Roche, Charlie	06 February 2008
Roche, Joe	23 May 2008
Ryan, Joe Linus, Fr	16 June 2008
Scannell, John	25 October 2008
Scott, Tony	10 November 2008
Sherry, Brendan	16 June 2008
Ward, Patrick	04 September 2008
Weakliam, Charlie	15 February 2008
Weakliam, David A., Fr	15 November 2007
Williamson, Kevin	08 September 2008
Woods, Harry	28 May 2008

SECONDARY SOURCES

5. BOOKS AND ARTICLES:

Ambrose, J., *The Dan Breen Story* (Dublin, 1981).

Barron, F., *Swimming for a Century* (Dublin, 1993).

Bentley, Mssrs., and Son, *Rental and Descriptive Particulars of the Mansion and Demesne of Terenure* (Dublin, 1859).

Breathnach, D. agus Ní Mhurchú, M., *'Beathathnéis, 1882–1982* (B.A.C., 1990).

Bradley, P. *et al.*, *Knocklyon — Past and Present* (Dublin, 1992).

Breen, D., *My Fight for Irish Freedom* (Dublin, 1924).

Burke, F., 'Patsy Keenan, O. Carm.', *Terenure College Annual* (2003), p. 25.

Byrne, J.F., *Silent Years* (New York, 1953).

Carey, F.P., 'The Heroes of Hammer Hill', *Whitefriars* 3: 2 (February 1941), pp. 43–5.

Carter, G., 'Pioneers of the Purple Twilight: A Gawler Memory', *Nubecula* 32:1 (1981), pp. 17–24.

Condon, K., *The Missionary College of All Hallows, 1842–1891* (Dublin, 1886).

Coolahan, J., *The ASTI and Post-Primary Education in Ireland, 1919-1984* (Dublin, 1984).

Corbett, A., 'Boarder at Terenure, 1931-32', *Terenure College Annual* (1992), p. 7.

Corbett, P.A., 'Fr Thomas Cyril Murphy, O. Carm., 1900-1990', *Terenure College Annual* (1990), pp.15–16.

Corbett, A., 'The First Year — 1946', in M. Hender (ed.), *Celts among the Shona* (Dublin, 1996), pp. 7–12.

Costello, P., *Clongowes Wood: A History of Clongowes Wood College, 1814-1989* (Dublin, 1989).

Curran, J.A., *Reminiscences of John Adye Curran, K.C.* (London, 1915).

Curtis, M., *Splendid Cause: The Catholic Action Movement in Ireland in the Twentieth Century* (Dublin, 2008).

D'Alton, J., *History of the County of Dublin* (Dublin, 1838).

D'Arcy, F.A., 'Wages of skilled workers in the Dublin building industry, 1667-1918', *Saothar* 15 (1990), pp. 31–3.

Doyle, J.V., 'A Look Back in Time', Terenure *College Annual* (2002), pp.33–4.

Farragher, S. and A. Wyer, *Blackrock College, 1860–1995* (Dublin, 1995).

Farren, S., *The Politics of Irish Education, 1920–1965* (Belfast, 1995).

Fenning, H., *The Undoing of the Friars in Ireland* (Louvain, 1972).

Fitzpatrick, D., *Harry Boland's Irish Revolution* (Cork, 2003).

Fitzpatrick, H., 'Carmel in Knocktopher', *Zelo* 9: 1 (Spring 1957), pp. 7–18.

Flanagan, D.C., 'The beginnings of the College *Annual*', *Terenure College Annual* (1981), p. 18.

Fleming, N.C. and O'Day, A., *The Longman Handbook of Modern Irish History since 1800* (Harlow, 2005).

Flynn, B., *Legends of Irish Boxing: Stories Seldom Told* (Belfast, 2007).

Gallagher, L., 'Carmel in Australia', *Zelo* 6: 1 (Spring 1954), pp. 1–15.

Gallagher, Leo. (ed.), *The Catholic Church in Manicaland 1896–1996* (Harare, 1996).

Grene, N. and Morash, C. (eds), *Shifting Scenes: Irish Theatre-Going, 1955-85* (Dublin, 2008).

Harrington, E. and Brown, D. (eds), *Memories of Terenure: A Terenure 2000 Millennium Project* (Dublin, 2000).

Heaslip, N., 'Fr Elias O'Dwyer, Golden Jubilee', *Zelo* 10: 2 (Summer 1958), pp. 54–9.

Hender, M. (ed.), *A Souvenir of the Golden Jubilee of the Irish Carmelites in Zimbabwe, 1946-1996* (Dublin, 1996).

Hender, M. (ed.), *Celts among the Shona* (Dublin, 2002).

Hill, M., 'Team Spirit', in Hender, *Celts among the Shona*, pp.54–9.

Hill, M., 'We too have lived in Arcadia', *Terenure College Annual* (1952), pp. 4–6.

Hill, M., 'Trusted Supporters', in Hender, *Celts among the Shona*, p. 48.

Humphrey, J., 'Making a Little Go a Long Way', *Irish Times*, 21 June 2005.

Hyland, A. and Milne, J.K., *Irish Educational Documents* (2 vols, Dublin, 1987).

Jordan, A.J., *W.T Cosgrave, 1880–1965: Founder of Modern Ireland* (Dublin, 2006).

Joy, J., S.J., 'Some points for a conference on secondary education', *Irish Monthly* (October 1930).

Kennedy, M., *Guarding Neutral Ireland* (Dublin, 2008).

Keogh, D., *The Vatican, the Bishops and Irish Politics, 1919–39* (Cambridge, 1986).

Kilmurray, M, 'Address given at the blessing and opening of the new College Development', *Terenure College Annual* (2000), pp. 11–14.

Kilroy, J., *Irish Trams* (Dublin, 1996).

Laffan, P. and O'Grady, F. (eds), *Donal McCann Remembered: A Tribute* (Dublin, 2000).

Lamb, K. and Bowe, P., *A History of Gardening in Ireland* (Dublin, 1995).

Lamont, D.R., 'Mr Griffin', *Terenure College Annual* (1980), pp. 21–3.

Lappin, H.A., 'Gerard Hopkins and his poetry', *Catholic World* (July 1919), pp. 501–12.

LeBrocquy, A, *Complete Memoirs of Albert LeBrocquy, 1888-1976*, (unpublished typescript, 44 pp., n.d., courtesy of Ms Melanie LeBrocquy).

Lewis, S., A *Topographical Dictionary of Ireland* (2 vols, London, 1837).

McCartney, D., *UCD: A National Idea* (Dublin, 1999).

MacGiolla Phadraig, B., *History of Terenure* (Dublin, 1954).

Malins, E. and Bowe, P., *Irish Gardens and Demesnes from 1830* (London, 1980).

Martin, J. and Kerr, D. (eds), *C.U.S. 1867-1967: A Centenary Record* (Dublin, 1967).

McCauley, B., 'Terenure to Kriste Mambo', *Terenure College Annual* (1995), pp. 101–07.

McClean, J., 'James Hanley, Artist', *Terenure College Annual* (1995), p. 35.

McCouaig, J.D., 'Four decades of Carmel', *Zelo* 2: 2 (1949), pp. 8–10.

McDonnell, J., 'Seamus McCool, retired', *Terenure College Annual* (2003), p. 32.

McDowell, R.B. and D.A Webb, *Trinity College Dublin, 1592-1752: An Academic History* (Cambridge, 1982).

McElligott, T.J., *Secondary Education in Ireland, 1870-1921* (Dublin, 1981).

Moriarty, C., *Down the Dodder* (Dublin, 1991).

Morris, V., 'Mr Patrick O Brien', *Terenure College Annual* (1975), p. 20.

Morrissey, T.J., *Towards a National University: William Delaney, SJ, 1835-1924* (Dublin, 1983).

Murphy, M., *Mike & Me: A Memoir by Mike Murphy* (Dublin, 1996).

Murphy, T.C., 'Fr Louis Michael Gerhard, O. Carm., a memoir (1889–1960)', *Nubecula* 36 (1985), pp. 45–54.

Nolan, R.J., 'The College Concert Hall — 50 Years Celebrations', in *The Play's the Thing* (Dublin, 1977), p. 3.

Nolan, W. (ed.), *The GAA in Dublin, 1884–2000* (3 vols, Dublin, 2005).

Ó Baoighill, P., *Ó Ghleann to Fanaid* (Dublin, 2000).

O'Brien, J.A., *The Vanishing Irish: The Enigma of the Modern World* (New York, 1953).

Ó Ceallaigh, S., *Coláiste Uladh, 1906-2006* (Naas, 2006).

O'Connor, E.D., 'In the "Come-Back"', *Terenure College Annual* (1976), pp. 18–20.

O'Donnell, B., *Irish Surgeons and Surgery in the Twentieth Century* (Dublin, 2008).

O'Donnell, C., 'Thomas Patrick Burke (1923-2008)', *Terenure College Annual* (2008), pp. 26–8.

O'Donoghue, T.A., *The Catholic Church and the Secondary School Curriculum in Ireland, 1922–1962* (New York, 1999).

Ó Dubhthaigh, B., *Coláiste Uladh: Leabhar Cuimhne Inbhaile, Leith-chéad Bhlian, 1906–1956* (Donegal, 1956).

O'Dwyer, P., *A True Patriot* (Dublin, 1975).

O'Dwyer, P., 'Book Review', *Causa Nostra Laetitiae* 1: 3 (July 1987), pp. 14–16.

O'Dwyer, P., 'Fr Timothy Enda Devane, 1916–1993', *Causa Nostra Laetitiae* 7: 3, (May 1994), p. 19.

O'Dwyer, P., *James Carmel O'Shea, 1899–1984* (Dublin, 1989 [Gort Muire, unpublished typescript]).

O'Dwyer, P., *The Carmelite Order in Post-Reformation Ireland* (Dublin, n.d.).

O'Dwyer, P., *The Irish Carmelites of the Ancient Observance* (Dublin, 1988).

O'Dwyer, P., 'Book Review', *Causa Nostra Laetitiae* 1:3 (1987), pp. 14–16.

O'Kelly, M., 'Con A. Smith — An Appreciation', *Terenure College Annual* (1972), pp. 35–6.

O'Leary, P., *Gaelic Prose in the Irish Free State, 1922-1939* (Dublin, 2004).

Ó Néill, Fr M., 'Building on What is Already there', *Terenure College Annual* (1996), pp. 20–2.

O'Neill, S. and Ó Dubhthaigh, B., *Coláiste Uladh: Leabhar Cuimhne Inbhaile, Leith-chéad Bhlian, 1906–1956* (Donegal, 1956).

O'Shea, J., 'Memories of Terenure College Fifty Years Ago', *Terenure College Annual* (1965), pp. 8–13.

O'Shea, J., 'St Benedict's Mission', in Hender, *Celts among the Shona*, p. 61.

O'Sullivan, P., 'Telling the Story: Address by Philip O'Sullivan at Senior School Prize Giving, 25th May 2004', *Terenure College Annual* (2004), pp. 31–3.

Roche, M. (ed.), *Terenure College Rugby Football Club, 1940-1990* (Dublin, 1990).

Shortis, F., 'Going Forward in Hope: A Look at Our Past One Hundred Years as a Guide for the Future', *Nubecula* 32: 3 (1981), pp. 168–9.

Swaine, J.F., 'Terenure College Fifty-Nine Years Ago', *Terenure College Annual* (1950), pp. 30–3.

Sweeney, C.L., *The Rivers of Dublin* (Dublin, 1911).

Terenure College Centenary Record 1860–1960 (c. 1960).

Troy, Fr M., 'Address to Junior School', *Terenure College Annual* (2004), pp. 152–4.

Van Esbeck, E., *The Story of Irish Rugby* (London, 1986).

Walsh, L.J., 'An Old Terenure Boy', *Whitefriars* 4: 2 (March–April 1942), pp. 49–52.

Woods, H.V., *Marketing at the Millennium* (Dublin, 2000).

Woulfe, K., 'Address', *Terenure College Annual* (2004), p. 75.

Wright, G.N. (with Bartlett, W.H., Petrie, G. and Baynes, T.M.), *Ireland Illustrated* (1st edn, Dublin, 1829; 2nd edn, Dublin, 1831).